TRANS-ATLANTIC DATA PRIVACY RELATIONS AS A CHALLENGE FOR DEMOCRACY

TRANS-ATLANTIC DATA PRIVACY RELATIONS AS A CHALLENGE FOR DEMOCRACY

Edited by
Dan Jerker B. Svantesson
Dariusz Kloza

intersentia
Cambridge – Antwerp – Portland

Intersentia Ltd
Sheraton House | Castle Park
Cambridge | CB3 0AX | United Kingdom
Tel.: +44 1223 370 170 | Fax: +44 1223 370 169
Email: mail@intersentia.co.uk
www.intersentia.com | www.intersentia.co.uk

Distribution for the UK and Ireland:
NBN International
Airport Business Centre, 10 Thornbury Road
Plymouth, PL6 7 PP
United Kingdom
Tel.: +44 1752 202 301 | Fax: +44 1752 202 331
Email: orders@nbninternational.com

Distribution for Europe and all other countries:
Intersentia Publishing nv
Groenstraat 31
2640 Mortsel
Belgium
Tel.: +32 3 680 15 50 | Fax: +32 3 658 71 21
Email: mail@intersentia.be

Distribution for the USA and Canada:
International Specialized Book Services
920 NE 58th Ave. Suite 300
Portland, OR 97213
USA
Tel.: +1 800 944 6190 (toll free) | Fax: +1 503 280 8832
Email: info@isbs.com

Trans-Atlantic Data Privacy Relations as a Challenge for Democracy

Front cover image: Pieter Bruegel the Elder, 'Landscape with the Fall of Icarus' (ca. 1560s). Photo © Musées royaux des Beaux-Arts de Belgique

Back cover image: Hanneke Beaumont, 'Stepping Forward' (2006) © Council of the European Union. Photo © Magdalena Witkowska 2016

ISBN 978-1-78068-434-5
D/2017/7849/17
NUR 828

GPRC
Guaranteed
Peer Reviewed
Content

British Library Cataloguing in Publication Data. A catalogue record for this book is available from the British Library.

FOREWORD

On the Path to Globally Interoperable Schemes of Data Protection Law

Wojciech Rafał Wiewiórowski*

The dawn of the second decade of the twenty-first century has forced lawyers to rethink some widely used yet basic concepts in order to extract the fundamental rights principles from the flood of European legislation generated since the European Union really begun its operation in 1993. At the same time, legislators have been bombarded with the question of legitimacy of some European legal concepts in the new century. For instance, while the whole concept of personal data seems to be solid enough to survive even strongest attacks, some particular elements of the legal heritage of Directive 95/46/EC of the European Parliament and of the Council of 24 October 1995 on the protection of individuals with regard to the processing of personal data and on the free movement of such data, are still being strongly questioned.

Among many trans-Atlantic data privacy aspects, this book examines the many questions concerning the classic concept of restrictions of personal data transfers beyond the area considered, from a European viewpoint, as safe. This concept is illustrative to the whole spectrum of trans-Atlantic relations and I would like to offer a few remarks on this matter. It is furthermore essential, on the road to global interoperable schemes of personal data protection, to answer questions of international transfers and their influence on international trade, big data processing and new roads to cybercrime.

Under the Lisbon Treaties, which have been in force since 2009, the European Union regards itself as a distinct political entity, not a federation of Member States, held together – as Luuk van Middelaar says – with a 'unique, invisible glue'. This connection is grounded with shared goals. One of them – expressed both in the Treaty on the Functioning of the European Union (Art. 16) and in the Charter of Fundamental Rights of the European Union (Arts. 7 and 8) – is a unique obligation to protect personal data. Stating that everyone has the right

* Assistant European Data Protection Supervisor; University of Gdansk. E-mail: wojciech.wiewiorowski@edps.europa.eu.

to the protection of personal data concerning them, the European Union feels obliged to observe how safe is the data both held in its territory and transferred outside thereof.

Having implemented this rule in Regulation 2016/679 of 27 April 2016 on the protection of natural persons with regard to the processing of personal data and on the free movement of such data (General Data Protection Regulation), the European legislator admits that rapid technological development and globalisation have brought new challenges for the protection of personal data. The legislator further recognises that the technology allows for both private companies and public authorities to make use of personal data on an unprecedented scale in order to pursue their activities and that this phenomenon has transformed both the economy and social life. But, bearing all this in mind, the Regulation – also by its very title – confirms that the European Union should further facilitate the free flow of personal data within its territory and the transfer thereof to third countries and international organisations, while ensuring a high level of the protection of personal data.

Recital 101 of the Regulation clearly states that flows of personal data to and from countries outside the European Union and international organisations are necessary for the expansion of free trade and international cooperation. The increase in such flows has raised new challenges and concerns with regard to the protection of personal data. Although the level of protection of natural persons ensured in the European Union should not be undermined when personal data are transferred to controllers, processors or other recipients in third countries, the possibility of transfer is obvious. Such transfers could take place only if the controller or processor complies with the conditions laid down in European law.

Nevertheless, many sceptics ask whether the notion of the whole concept of international transfer of personal data is still legitimate? Whether a national border is still significant in the time of big data?

Data is often regarded as a commodity, such as crude oil, which can be traded between two equally aware parties to the transaction. It is of course not a commodity and it is not an anonymous resource belonging to the entity that pays more. Moreover, in the age of big data, large-scale resources of data are significant not because they are 'large' but because it is easy to transfer them and merge with other accessible datasets. The transfer starts to be the driver itself. It causes additional problems with the purpose of processing since the purpose the personal data was collected for is not necessarily the one for which it is processed after the transfer. The sustainability of such processing vanishes and the transfer starts to be the goal in itself, as it multiplies the possibility to achieve new purposes.

The term 'transfer of personal data' has not been defined, neither in the Directive in 1995 nor in the Regulation in 2016. It can be assumed, as a starting point, that the term is used in its natural meaning, i.e. that data 'move' or are allowed to 'move' between different users. However, in reality, this issue is not always so straightforward. The European Data Protection Supervisor has called for a definition of this notion in the data protection reform, as it has proved to be a problematic issue in certain cases, which so far have been left for the Court of Justice of the European Union or for the legislator to resolve.

A group of leading scholars and practitioners examines in this book how transborder data flows regime – either having its roots in General Data Protection Regulation or driven by separate instruments such as EU–US Privacy Shield – influences the everyday basis of data processing on both sides of the Atlantic and how it limits the scope of operations on data. The impact of the judgment of the Court of Justice of the European Union in the so-called *Schrems* case on other transborder data flows regime instruments is taken into consideration to examine what are the internal and global implications of trans-Atlantic information exchange.

Additional importance is given to the studies on the scope of processing which may be excluded from general rules on the basis of public security, defence, national security or criminal law exceptions. Bearing in mind that the Article 29 Working Party has expressed its wish to keep the exchange regime compliant with four essential guarantees to be used whenever personal data are transferred from the European Union to a third country – not only the United States. According to these principles, any processing of such data should be subject to clear, precise and accessible rules known for data subjects. The necessity and proportionality with regard to legitimate objectives have to be pursued and the independent oversight mechanisms has to be put in place. A legal system has to contain effective remedies to be possible to use by data subject.

This creates a mechanism of transborder data flows which may be based on the decision on adequacy issued by the European Commission towards a third country system. It may equally be based on model contact clauses with no prior authorisation, which are drafted by data protection authorities, proposed to the European Commission and adopted by the Commission or, alternatively, drafted by the Commission itself. Binding corporate rules (BCR) – in the new European legal framework – will no longer need national validation after being passed by the European Data Protection Board. Finally, transfers can by authorised by data protection authorities on an *ad hoc* decision.

In its position paper on the transfer of personal data to third countries and international organisations by EU institutions and bodies from 2014, the European Data Protection Supervisor stated that the principle of adequate protection requires that the fundamental right to data protection is guaranteed even when personal data are transferred to a party outside the scope of the Directive. Although there is a growing consistency and convergence of data protection principles and practices around the world, we are far from full adequacy and full respect for EU fundamental rights cannot be assumed in all cases. It will often happen that the level of data protection offered by third countries or international organisations is much lower than that of the European Union, or – worse – does not exist at all. The checklist to be used by controllers before carrying out a transfer and set in Annex 2 to Supervisor's position paper is still valid. But because it needs some revision according not only to the text of the new General Data Protection Regulation but also according to the practice of international cooperation – where the EU–US Privacy Shield is the best example – I recognise this book to be a step towards explanation of new rules, but also a list of questions to be considered both by legislators, supervisors, regulators and controllers as well as by entities representing them.

Brussels, September 2016

PREFACE

Yet Another Book about Snowden and Safe Harbor?

Dan Jerker B. SVANTESSON* and Dariusz KLOZA**

I.

A series of events have led to the idea for this book and the first one is more than obvious: the Edward Snowden *affaire*.[1] On 6 June 2013 Glenn Greenwald published in *The Guardian* the first in a series of articles – and later co-authored a few other – on global mass surveillance practices led by the United States' National Security Agency (NSA).[2] On the first day, the worldwide public learned that the NSA has obtained a clandestine court order from a secretly operating court of law, called the Foreign Intelligence Surveillance Court (FISC), and on its basis the Agency has been collecting metadata on telephone calls of millions customers of a major private telecommunications provider, Verizon. This provider was forbidden from disclosing both the order itself and its compliance with it. On the second day (7 June), the worldwide public learned further that these practices had not been limited to a single provider and that the NSA was allegedly 'tapping directly into the central servers of nine

* Centre for Commercial Law, Faculty of Law, Bond University. E-mail: dan_svantesson@bond.edu.au.

** Research Group on Law, Science, Technology & Society, Vrije Universiteit Brussel; Peace Research Institute Oslo. E-mail: dariusz.kloza@vub.ac.be.

1 We understand 'Snowden *affaire*' broadly: it is both the disclosures Edward Snowden made to the journalists about global mass surveillance practices, as well as their ramifications. We have spent some time discussing how to name it in this book. It could have been e.g. 'NSA scandal' or 'PRISM-gate', but ultimately we have named it after the person who stands behind the disclosures. We chose the French word '*affaire*' since it can signify both a case in a court of law as well as a political scandal, as contributions in this book are concerned with legal and political analysis of trans-Atlantic data privacy relations. Cf. *Le trésor de la langue française*, <http://atilf.atilf.fr>.

2 GLENN GREENWALD, 'NSA collecting phone records of millions of Verizon customers daily', *The Guardian*, 6 June 2013, <https://www.theguardian.com/world/2013/jun/06/nsa-phone-records-verizon-court-order>.

leading U.S. Internet companies': Microsoft, Yahoo, Google, Facebook, PalTalk, AOL, Skype, YouTube, and Apple.[3] The worldwide public also learned that the NSA has been 'listening' to anything about anybody whose data merely flew through servers located on US soil, even when sent from one overseas location to another. Finally, the NSA has shared these data with its fellow agencies in the US, such as with the Federal Bureau of Investigation (FBI). These practices were variously codenamed – labels of surveillance programmes such as PRISM, Xkeyscore, Upstream, Quantuminsert, Bullrun or Dishfir have since entered the public debate[4] – and their aim was to procure national security with the help of surveillance. (These practises were not a novelty for the NSA has operated domestic surveillance programmes since the Agency's establishment in 1952.[5] It is also true that surveillance practices are as old as humanity and over time have became an integral part of modernity,[6] but these have intensified in the aftermath of the 11 September 2001 terrorist attacks.)[7]

These revelations were built on a series of leaks from a former NSA contractor to a number of major media outlets worldwide such as *The Guardian*, *The Washington Post* and *Der Spiegel*. He revealed his identity on the fourth day (9 June).[8] The disclosures Edward Snowden brought to the public eye have sparked a continuous, and sometimes rather heated, debate about the pursuit of national security through the use of mass surveillance practices and individual rights and freedoms – not least in the trans-Atlantic setting.[9]

Initially, the whole *affaire* had a predominantly vertical dimension, focusing on the relations between an individual and the state. However, this changed when it was revealed that the NSA, in its global mass surveillance practices, had been cooperating with its counterparts in the Anglo-Saxon world. This included, *inter alia*, the United Kingdom's Government Communications Headquarters

---

3 Barton Gellman and Laura Poitras, 'U.S., British intelligence mining data from nine U.S. Internet companies in broad secret program', *The Washington Post*, 7 June 2013, <https://www.washingtonpost.com/investigations/us-intelligence-mining-data-from-nine-us-internet-companies-in-broad-secret-program/2013/06/06/3a0c0da8-cebf-11e2-8845-d970ccb04497_story.html>.

4 Zygmunt Bauman et al., 'After Snowden: Rethinking the Impact of Surveillance' (2014) 8(2) *International Political Sociology* 122.

5 George F. Howe, 'The Early History of NSA' (1974) 4(2) *Cryptologic Spectrum* 11, <http://www.senderling.net/6988th.org/Docs/The_Early_History_of_the_NSA.pdf>.

6 David Lyon, *Surveillance Studies: An Overview*, Wiley, 2007, p. 12.

7 On this matter, cf. esp. David Lyon, *Surveillance After September 11*, Wiley, 2003.

8 Glenn Greenwald, Ewen MacAskill and Laura Poitras, 'Edward Snowden: the whistleblower behind the NSA surveillance revelations', *The Guardian*, 9 June 2013, <https://www.theguardian.com/world/2013/jun/09/edward-snowden-nsa-whistleblower-surveillance>.

9 Francesca Musiani, 'Edward Snowden, L'«homme-Controverse» de La Vie Privée Sur Les Réseaux' (2015) 3(73) *Hermès, La Revue* 209, <www.cairn.info/revue-hermes-la-revue-2015-3-page-209.htm>.

(GCHQ) and Australian Signals Directorate (ASD),[10] both members of the 'Five Eyes' alliance. The worldwide public's attention was drawn to the GCHQ who had used the PRISM programme to directly obtain data without 'the formal legal process required to seek personal material ... from an internet company based outside the UK' (7 June).[11]

Next, on 29 June 2013 *Der Spiegel* published a finding in the Snowden leaks that European leaders had also been spied on.[12] The bugged mobile phone of the German Chancellor Angela Merkel became iconic. (There was even a cartoon that went viral on social media in which the US President Barack Obama on a phone says to Merkel: 'I will tell you how I am because I already know how you are doing'.)[13] This created political turmoil in Europe and many of the political leaders, bugged or not, criticised the excessive surveillance practices and began to question the *status quo* of the Euro-American relations. In November 2013 the then European Union Commissioner for Justice Viviane Reding even threatened taking steps to suspend the (now defunct) Safe Harbor arrangement.[14] Thus, the Snowden *affaire* took on another, international dimension (horizontal) in which relations between states have been put at stake.

II.

The second source of our inspiration is perhaps a little more surprising. John Oliver, a British comedian and a host of popular US TV programme *The Daily Show*, devoted an episode (10 June 2013) to the then-breaking Snowden *affaire*.[15] He quoted President Obama's San José, California speech (7 June), in which the latter had stated 'there are a whole range of safeguards involved' against the surveillance practices of the NSA, thus implying they are OK. Oliver concluded with a comment: 'I think you are misunderstanding the perceived problem here,

---

10 Philip Dorling, 'Australia gets "deluge" of US secret data, prompting a new data facility', *The Sydney Morning Herald*, 13 June 2013, <http://www.smh.com.au/it-pro/security-it/australia-gets-deluge-of-us-secret-data-prompting-a-new-data-facility-20130612-2o4kf>.

11 Nick Hopkins, 'UK gathering secret intelligence via covert NSA operation', *The Guardian*, 7 June 2013, <https://www.theguardian.com/technology/2013/jun/07/uk-gathering-secret-intelligence-nsa-prism>.

12 Laura Poitras, Marcel Rosenbach, Fidelius Schmid and Holger Stark, 'NSA horcht EU-Vertretungen mit Wanzen aus', *Der Spiegel*, 29 June 2013, <http://www.spiegel.de/netzwelt/netzpolitik/nsa-hat-wanzen-in-eu-gebaeuden-installiert-a-908515.html>.

13 Quoting from memory.

14 Ian Traynor, 'NSA surveillance: Europe threatens to freeze US data-sharing arrangements', *The Guardian*, 26 November 2013, <https://www.theguardian.com/world/2013/nov/26/nsa-surveillance-europe-threatens-freeze-us-data-sharing>.

15 Victor Luckerson, 'How the 'John Oliver Effect' Is Having a Real-Life Impact', *Time*, 10 July 2015, <http://time.com/3674807/john-oliver-net-neutrality-civil-forfeiture-miss-america>.

Mr President. No one is saying that you broke any laws. We are just saying it is a little bit weird that you did not have to'.[16]

John Oliver formulated in this context the very question about the *limits*, about the *use* and *abuse*, of the law and of the state's power when it comes to global mass surveillance practices. Where does lie the 'thin red line' between the two legitimate yet seemingly competing interests: national security and privacy? This question touches upon all the 'stars' in a classical 'constellation of ideals that dominate our political morality',[17] i.e. democracy, the rule of law and/or the legal state (*Rechtsstaat*), and fundamental rights. Two aspects triggered our particular attention: the conformity of these practices with the rule of law and/or the *Rechtsstaat* doctrines, and the extent of the permissible interference with the fundamental rights affected, such as the right to (data) privacy and the freedom of expression.

First, both the rule of law and the *Rechtsstaat* concepts serve multiple purposes in society and one of them is to channel the exercise of 'public power through law'.[18] They achieve their goals in two different manners, yet these manners share a few characteristics.[19] For the sake of our argument, it shall suffice to acknowledge that they occur in two understandings. In the narrow, rather formal one ('thin'), both concepts comprise the requirement of some form of 'legality', such as the enactment of a legal statute in accordance with a given procedure, and certain safeguards, such as access to a court of law.[20] The comprehensive, substantive understanding ('thick') of the rule of law (*Rechtsstaat*) 'encompass[es] procedural elements, and, additionally, focus[es] on the realization of values and concern[s] the content of law'.[21]

---

16 John Oliver, 'Good News! You're not paranoid – NSA Oversight', *Comedy Central*, 10 June 2013, <http://www.cc.com/video-clips/cthyr1/the-daily-show-with-jon-stewart-good-news--you-re-not-paranoid---nsa-oversight>.

17 Jeremy Waldron, 'The Rule of Law and the Importance of Procedure,' in James Fleming (ed.), *Getting to the Rule of Law*, New York University Press, 2011, p. 3, <http://lsr.nellco.org/cgi/viewcontent.cgi?article=1235&context=nyu_plltwp>.

18 Geranne Lautenbach, *The Concept of the Rule of Law and the European Court of Human Rights*, Oxford University Press, 2013, p. 18.

19 We are aware that there exist essential differences between the rule of law and the *Rechtsstaat* doctrines. We are further aware of a never-ending debate both as to the delineation between these two and as to their building blocks. Both doctrines overlap in many aspects, yet their origins are different, each of them having slightly different contents and *modus operandi*. Each of them can be found applied differently in different jurisdictions; the former concept dominates in the Anglo-Saxon world, the latter on continental Europe. The analysis of all these aspects lies beyond the scope of this contribution. Cf. e.g. James R. Silkenat, Jr., James E. Hickey and Peter D. Barenboim (eds.), *The Legal Doctrines of the Rule of Law and the Legal State (Rechtsstaat)*, Springer, 2014; Tom Bingham, *The Rule of Law*, Allen Lane, 2010; Brian Z. Tamanaha, *On the Rule of Law: History, Politics, Theory*, Cambridge University Press, 2004.

20 Geranne Lautenbach, *The Concept of the Rule of Law and the European Court of Human Rights*, Oxford University Press, 2013, p. 18.

21 Ibid., pp. 18–21.

The Snowden *affaire* demonstrated that the contents of legal provisions matter too. If we look at the rule of law and the *Rechtsstaat* doctrines in their narrow understanding, then – simplifying – when a legal provision fulfils only formal criteria, it is all ok. There are indeed commentators who prefer this 'thin' understanding as it is simply 'easier to identify' its meaning; it is a fair, theoretical argument. There are too sometimes businesses and authoritarian governments who prefer the 'thin' understanding as formal criteria are 'easier to satisfy'. They create an illusion in diplomatic and international trade circles that their actions are (to be) judged ok. 'Legality' or the mere access to a court of law are important but they are not enough. Consequently, many commentators 'find thin conceptions quite inadequate':[22] it is of lesser importance that a legal statute validly exists; it is of much greater importance what this statute actually does.

Second, fundamental rights – short of a few – are not absolute. Their enjoyment can be limited in some circumstances. For example, in the European context, an interference with a fundamental right is permissible when it is made 'in accordance with the law and is necessary in a democratic society' and serves some public interest, e.g. national security or public safety.[23] In this sense – and again, simplifying – a legal norm is judged to be in conformity with fundamental rights when it does not exceed what is necessary and proportionate to a legitimate aim pursued and such a norm was enacted legally. Some parallels can be drawn here with the rule of law and the *Rechtsstaat* doctrines: there exist both formal (i.e. legality) and substantive limitation criteria of fundamental rights (i.e. proportionality, necessity and legitimacy). Again, the latter are of much greater importance. Some commentators even heralded that 'to speak of human rights is to speak about proportionality'.[24] The Snowden *affaire* demonstrated disproportionality of global mass surveillance practices to the main legitimate aim these practices pursued: security. As Lyon asks, '[i]s mass surveillance the right way to achieve it?'[25]

The sequence of events sketched above has inspired the main idea for this book with John Oliver formulating its central research question: to explore trans-Atlantic relations challenging the doctrines of democracy, rule of law (*Rechtsstaat*) and fundamental rights. The perspective is that of data privacy.

---

22 Martin Krygier, 'Rule of Law (*and Rechtsstaat*)', in James R. Silkenat, Jr., James E. Hickey and Peter D. Barenboim (eds.), *The Legal Doctrines of the Rule of Law and the Legal State (Rechtsstaat)* Springer, 2014, p. 46, pp. 51–52.

23 European Convention on Human Rights, Rome, 4 November 1950, ETS 5. Cf. Arts. 8–11.

24 Grant Huscroft, Bradley W. Miller and Grégoire C.N. Webber (eds.), *Proportionality and the Rule of Law: Rights, Justification, Reasoning*, Cambridge University Press, 2014, p. 1.

25 David Lyon, *Surveillance After Snowden*, Polity Press, 2015, p. 13.

III.

Subsequent events led the idea for this book to grow and mature. These took place predominantly on the European side of the Atlantic.[26] On 8 April 2014 the Court of Justice of the European Union (CJEU; Luxembourg Court) delivered a landmark judgment in *Digital Rights Ireland*.[27] In essence, the Court not only declared the 2006 Data Retention Directive[28] invalid but also held under what conditions personal data retention practices can be considered proportionate to the national security goals pursued.

In parallel, the European Union (EU) has been reforming its data privacy legal framework, which on 27 April 2016 eventually took the form of General Data Protection Regulation (GDPR),[29] and of Police and Criminal Justice Data Protection Directive.[30] The works on the 'update' of Regulation 2001/45[31] and e-Privacy Directive continue.[32] The Council of Europe is nearing the conclusion of the five-year process of modernisation of its data privacy convention (the so-called 'Convention 108'),[33] at the same time aiming to make it a global instrument. It was the need to keep up with technological developments, on the one hand, as well as political, economic and societal changes, on the other, that created a need to update both legal frameworks.

---

26 We have been closely observing the European response to the Snowden *affaire*, account of which is given e.g. in David Wright and Reinhard Kreissl, 'European Responses to the Snowden Revelations' in id., *Surveillance in Europe*, Routledge, 2014, pp. 6–49. Cf. also Lindsay, Ch. 3, Sec. 4, in this volume. Here we only give account of some of our further inspirations.

27 Joined Cases C-293/12 and C-594/12, *Digital Rights Ireland Ltd v. Minister for Communications, Marine and Natural Resources and Others and Kärntner Landesregierung and Others*.

28 Directive 2006/24/EC of the European Parliament and of the Council of 15 March 2006 on the retention of data generated or processed in connection with the provision of publicly available electronic communications services or of public communications networks and amending Directive 2002/58/EC, [2006] OJ L 105/54–63.

29 Regulation (EU) 2016/679 of the European Parliament and of the Council of 27 April 2016 on the protection of natural persons with regard to the processing of personal data and on the free movement of such data, and repealing Directive 95/46/EC (General Data Protection Regulation), [2016] OJ L 119/1–88.

30 Directive (EU) 2016/680 of the European Parliament and of the Council of 27 April 2016 on the protection of natural persons with regard to the processing of personal data by competent authorities for the purposes of the prevention, investigation, detection or prosecution of criminal offences or the execution of criminal penalties, and on the free movement of such data, and repealing Council Framework Decision 2008/977/JHA, [2016] OJ L 119/89–131.

31 Regulation (EC) No 45/2001 of the European Parliament and of the Council of 18 December 2000 on the protection of individuals with regard to the processing of personal data by the Community institutions and bodies and on the free movement of such data, [2001] OJ L 8/1–22.

32 Directive 2002/58/EC of the European Parliament and of the Council of 12 July 2002 concerning the processing of personal data and the protection of privacy in the electronic communications sector (Directive on privacy and electronic communications), [2002] OJ L 201/37–47.

33 Convention for the Protection of Individuals with regard to Automatic Processing of Personal Data, ETS 108, 28 January 1981, Strasbourg <http://conventions.coe.int/Treaty/en/Treaties/Html/108.htm>. Cf. also Council of Europe, *Modernisation of Convention 108*, Strasbourg, 29 November 2012, T-PD(2012)4Rev3_en.

Simultaneously, the EU has been negotiating comprehensive free trade agreements with numerous countries.[34] Agreements with the US and Canada are particularly high on the political agenda. Even though free trade *prima facie* does not concern data privacy, all parties keep in mind the failure on such grounds of the multilateral Anti-Counterfeit Trade Agreement (ACTA) in February 2012. Among other provisions, its Art. 27 provided for a possibility of requesting an order from a competent authority aiming at the disclosure of information to identify the subscriber whose account allegedly been used for intellectual property rights (IPR) infringement, upon which right holders might take action. Many commentators considered this and many similar solutions in the text of ACTA as disproportionate, thus not living up to the democratic standards.[35] At the same time, the Luxembourg Court held that the monitoring of Internet traffic in order to prevent infringements of IPR, seek violators and/or police them constitutes a disproportionate interference with fundamental rights (cf. *Scarlet v. Sabam* (24 November 2011)[36] and *Sabam v. Netlog* (16 February 2012)).[37]

In the time since work on this book commenced, the Luxembourg Court rendered another milestone judgment in *Schrems* (6 October 2015),[38] invalidating the Safe Harbor arrangement.[39] For 15 years it allowed American data controllers, who had self-certified to the US Department of Commerce their adherence to the principles of this arrangement, to freely transfer personal data from Europe. Building to a large extent on its *Digital Rights Ireland* judgment, the Court declared invalid the so-called adequacy decision that laid behind the arrangement. The judges in Luxembourg held that bulk collection of personal data compromises 'the essence of the fundamental right to respect for private life'.[40] Nine months later the Safe Harbor was replaced by a very similar Privacy Shield arrangement (12 July 2016).[41] Its compatibility with fundamental rights in the EU remains questionable.

---

34 Cf. <http://ec.europa.eu/trade/policy/countries-and-regions/agreements>.

35 Irina Baraliuc, Sari Depreeuw and Serge Gutwirth, 'Copyright Enforcement in the Digital Age: A Post-ACTA View on the Balancing of Fundamental Rights' (2013) 21(1) *International Journal of Law and Information Technology* 93–100.

36 Case C-70/10, *Scarlet Extended SA v. Société belge des auteurs, compositeurs et éditeurs SCRL (SABAM)*.

37 Case C-360/10, *Belgische Vereniging van Auteurs, Componisten en Uitgevers CVBA (SABAM) v. Netlog NV*.

38 Case C-362/14, *Maximillian Schrems v. Data Protection Commissioner*.

39 Commission Decision of 26 July 2000 pursuant to Directive 95/46/EC of the European Parliament and of the Council on the adequacy of the protection provided by the safe harbour privacy principles and related frequently asked questions issued by the US Department of Commerce, 2000/520/EC, [2000] OJ L 215/7–47.

40 Case C-362/14, *Maximillian Schrems v. Data Protection Commissioner*, §94.

41 Commission Implementing Decision (EU) 2016/1250 of 12 July 2016 pursuant to Directive 95/46/EC of the European Parliament and of the Council on the adequacy of the protection provided by the EU–U.S. Privacy Shield, C/2016/4176, [2016] OJ L 207/1–112.

As the gestation of this book was coming to an end (September 2016), the Luxembourg Court was seized, *inter alia*, with the questions who controls the handling of personal data on a 'fan page' on a major social network site, therefore determining responsibilities for violations of data privacy laws,[42] and whether the use of such a social network site for purposes both private and professional still qualifies its user as a consumer, therefore allowing her to benefit from protective rules on jurisdiction.[43] The Court has also to decide two joined cases on data retention: in *Watson et al.*, whether the requirements laid down in *Digital Rights Ireland*[44] are mandatory, and in *Tele2 Sverige*, whether the post-*Digital Rights Ireland* retention of personal data is compatible with EU fundamental rights.[45]

On the other side of the Atlantic – among 'two dozen significant reforms to surveillance law and practice since 2013'[46] – President Obama signed into law the USA Freedom Act of 2015, which, *inter alia*, increases transparency of the work of the Foreign Intelligence Surveillance Court (FISC)[47] as well as the Judicial Redress Act of 2015, extending 'Privacy Act [of 1974][48] remedies to citizens of certified states'.[49]

These legislative developments and judicial decisions (as well as those in the future) have significant implications for trans-Atlantic data privacy relations. Not only because they either involve a private organisation or an authority originating from one or another side of the Atlantic or because they concern conditions for handling personal data within global mass surveillance practices, but rather because they set step-by-step standards for data privacy protection.

IV.

There has been one more inspiration for this book. Outside the *Consilium* building on rue de la Loi/Wetstraat in Brussels, hosting both the European Council and the Council of Ministers of the European Union, stands the bronze statue depicted on the back cover of this book. 'Stepping Forward' was created by Dutch-born sculptor Hanneke Beaumont, and erected where it stands today in 2007. We think this statue – and the multiple ways that it can be viewed – is

42 Case C-210/16, *Wirtschaftsakademie Schleswig-Holstein GmbH v. Unabhängiges Landeszentrum für Datenschutz Schleswig-Holstein.*

43 Case C-498/16, *Maximilian Schrems v. Facebook Ireland Limited.*

44 Above n. 27.

45 Joined Cases C-203/15 and C-698/15, *Tele2 Sverige AB v. Post-och telestyrelsen* and *Watson et al.*

46 Swire, Ch. 4 in this volume.

47 Uniting and Strengthening America by Fulfilling Rights and Ensuring Effective Discipline Over Monitoring Act of 2015 [USA Freedom Act of 2015], Public Law 114-23, 50 USC 1801, §601 ff.

48 Privacy Act of 1974, Public Law 93-579, 5 USC 552a.

49 Judicial Redress Act of 2015, Public Law 114-126, 5 USC §552a.

an interesting symbol for data privacy regulation. One way to look at the statue is to focus on how this proud androgynous person, representing humanity (or at least the people of Europe), clad in only a thin gown, bravely takes a necessary leap of faith into the unknown. This is no doubt a suitable representation of how some people view (European) efforts aimed at data privacy regulation.

However, the statue also lends itself to quite a different – less flattering – interpretation. One can perhaps see the statue as a malnourished, clearly confused, possibly deranged, frail man in a lady's night gown, engaging in a foolish endeavour bound to end in a nasty, indeed catastrophic, fall. Those sceptical of data privacy regulation, at least it its current forms, may see some parallels between this interpretation and the current European approach to data privacy.

This is indeed how different are the perspectives people may have on data privacy regulation. And while the difference in perspectives is too complex to be mapped geographically, it may be fair to say that more people in Europe would prefer the first interpretation of the parallels between Beaumont's statue and data privacy regulation, while more people in the US are likely to see the parallel as we described second; in any case, the trans-Atlantic divide remains palpable.

V.

For our ideas to bear fruit, we chose the *European Integration and Democracy* series, edited at the Centre for Direct Democracy Studies (CDDS) at the University of Białystok, Poland and published by Belgian-based Intersentia, a suitable outlet for our book. Both institutions welcomed our proposal. Since the Series was launched in 2011, each volume therein is meant to look at a particular aspect of European integration as matter of – broadly understood – democracy, rule of law (*Rechtsstaat*) and fundamental rights. Therefore the title of each volume finishes with '… as a challenge for democracy'.[50]

The present book is a response to a call for papers. It was issued in June 2015 and we have been overwhelmed with the answer thereto: we have accepted 18 submissions from around the world. All of them underwent a double blind peer-review process in accordance with the Guaranteed Peer-Review Contents (GPRC) scheme, a standard used by Intersentia.[51] In parallel, a number of

50 The previous volumes are: Elżbieta Kużelewska and Dariusz Kloza (eds.), *The Challenges of Modern Democracy and European Integration*, Aspra-JR, 2012; Elżbieta Kużelewska and Dariusz Kloza (eds.), *Elections to the European Parliament as a Challenge for Democracy*, Aspra-JR, 2013; Elżbieta Kużelewska, Dariusz Kloza, Izabela Kraśnicka and Franciszek Strzyczkowski (eds.), *European Judicial Systems as a Challenge for Democracy*, Intersentia, 2015.

51 Cf. <http://www.gprc.be/en/content/what-gprc>.

informal conversations during the gestation of the book led to eight invited contributions by distinguished experts in the field.

On 29 January 2016, we hosted a dedicated authors' panel at the 9th Computers, Privacy and Data Protection (CPDP) in Brussels, Belgium, a world-leading annual event in the field.[52] Four authors accepted our invitation – in the order of appearance – Peter Swire, Els De Busser, Michał Czerniawski and Trisha Meyer; Gemma Galdon Clavell moderated the debate. We thank them for their participation. With the then-upcoming European football championships in France (10 June–10 July 2016), the panellists at the very end were asked – in an imaginary 'data privacy game' – in which team they would play – European or American, in what role and why. The vast majority chose the European team.

The result we present to the reader might seem merely another book about the Snowden *affaire* and the fall of Safe Harbor, but these two have been (only) an inspiration. Our object of interest is the protection of data privacy[53] in relations between Europe and Americas as a challenge for democracy, the rule of law (*Rechtsstaat*) and fundamental rights. Both geographical notions are understood *sensu largo*.[54] (A careful reader would notice we have not necessarily been consistent and we have included also contributions treating Austral-Asian data privacy matters, as we found that they add value to the book.) As the regulation of data privacy is in the competences of the EU, our object of interest has gained relevance for European integration.[55] Therefore, this book looks into the *status quo* of such relations. In parallel, Hanneke Beaumont's sculpture – a step into the unknown – inspired us to conclude this book with some postulates as to their future shape.

We have split this book into three main parts. The first part deals with five pertaining problems the concept of data privacy protection faces in trans-Atlantic relations. The opening problem is that of transborder flows of personal data. The scene is set in the first chapter in which *Weber* analyses the place of the protection of data privacy in the EU Digital Single Market Strategy.[56] Two

---

52 Cf. <http://www.cpdpconferences.org>.

53 We deliberately chose 'data privacy' as a term to encompass both the European understanding of 'data protection' and the Anglo-Saxon one of 'informational privacy'. Cf. Christopher Kuner et al., 'Taking Stock after Four Years' (2014) 4(2) *International Data Privacy Law* 87–88.

54 By 'Europe *sensu largo*' we mean the patchwork of supranational and regional arrangements of political and economic nature occurring at the European continent. In particular, our understanding comprises, but is not limited to, the European Union and the Council of Europe. By 'Americas *sensu largo*' we deploy its geographical meaning, but the reader will notice that the focus is predominantly on the United States of America.

55 Cf. Art. 16(2) of the Treaty on the Functioning of the European Union, [2012] OJ C 326/47–390.

56 European Commission, *A Digital Single Market Strategy for Europe*, COM(2015) 192 final, Brussels, 6 May 2015.

subsequent chapters analyse the principles for the trans-Atlantic data flows: *Schweighofer* gives a broad picture, while *Lindsay* focuses on the principle of proportionality. Next, *Swire* analyses the reforms 'US surveillance law' underwent since the Snowden *affaire* broke out and *Vermeulen* argues the Privacy Shield arrangement does not meet the necessity and proportionality criteria set forth in the EU fundamental rights law. Finally, *Doneda* offers an insight on international data transfers from Brazil, a jurisdiction without a comprehensive data privacy legal framework.

The second problem discussed in this part deals with the regulation of international trade. *Meyer & Vetulani-Cęgiel* write about public participation in a decision making process concerning a free trade agreement (FTA); their observations are equally applicable to the data privacy universe. *Greenleaf* surveys the variety of ways in which FTAs have affected the protection of data privacy. *Schaake* concludes with her suggestions for regulating trade and technology. The third problem deals with territorial application of the data privacy laws. *Czerniawski* asks whether 'the use of equipment' is – in a contemporary digitalised and globalised world – an adequate determinant for such laws to apply. *Bentzen* and *Svantesson* give a comprehensive overview of applicable laws when personal data containing DNA information are being processed. The fourth problem confronted is that of data privacy and crime. *Kovič Dine* attempts to understand the peacetime economic cyber-espionage among states under international law with a special reference to the theft of personal and otherwise privileged data. *Gerry* takes a critical look at existing legal arrangements to better understand how cyber law deals with combating terrorism and paedophilia on the Internet. *Amicelle* gives three hypotheses to understand the failure of the US Terrorist Finance Tracking Program after 15 years of its operation. The fifth and final problem deals with data privacy and the passage of time. *Szekely* comparatively analyses the regulation of the post-mortem privacy in the EU and the US. *Miyashita* compares the legal *status quo* of the 'right to be forgotten' in the EU and Japan.

The second part discusses the constitutive elements of the notion of data privacy. The four contributions published here discuss the understanding of a piece of 'information linked to an individual' in jurisdictions ranging from Europe to US to Australia (*Míšek; Maurushat & Vaile*), the distinction between 'privacy' and 'security' (*Wilson*) and the ethicality of personal data markets (*Spiekermann*).

The final, third part suggests a few alternative approaches to the protection of data privacy. It subconsciously builds on a premise that contemporary, existing approaches do not necessarily live up to the expectations vested therein and thus more is needed. This part looks at possible lessons to be learned from US environmental law – about community right-to-know, impact assessments and 'mineral rights' in property (*Emanuel*) as well as from criminal law – to replace the European criterion of 'adequacy' in transborder data flows by the criterion of a flagrant denial of data protection (*De Busser*). A subsequent contribution recognises a new category of data privacy protections – i.e. behavioural – that is to supplement existing regulatory, technological and organisational protections (*Kloza*). *Goldenfein* explores ideas around automated privacy enforcement and the articulation of individual protections from profiling into the telecommunications infrastructure. Subsequently, *De Hert & Papakonstantinou* plea for more data privacy at the political agenda of the United Nations (UN). This is to be achieved by establishing a dedicated data privacy agency, similar to the World Intellectual Property Organisation (WIPO). Finally, *Kwasny* discusses the prospects of the (modernised) 'Convention 108' of the Council of Europe as an international standard for data privacy protection. A few of our observations as to the *status quo* and the future of trans-Atlantic data privacy relations conclude this book.

The present book is very clearly an anthology – it is a compilation of diverse contributions, from different perspectives, within a broad topic. Our aim with this volume is to highlight a selection of particularly 'hot' questions within the topic of trans-Atlantic data privacy relations as they look at the end of 2016. In a sense, what we have aimed to create could be seen as a snapshot, giving a picture of what is on the agenda for scholars concerned with data privacy at this particular point in time, which just happens to be a particularly important, indeed formative, moment within this area.

We have been exceptionally careful to allow the authors to express their ideas as they wish to do so, with only minimal editorial intervention. The advantage of this approach is obvious given our stated aim of reflecting the great diversity of thinking that exists on the matters addressed. However, we hasten to acknowledge that this approach comes at the cost of a lower level of consistency and coherence within the volume. Put simply, we have not aimed at any, and the reader is unlikely to find any, *fil rouge* apart from the above-mentioned broad terms. However, that is not to say that the contributions to this volume – as a collective – do not lend themselves to conclusions. In the final chapter, we too draw out and highlight those themes we see emerging within the body of this work. We eventually attempt to suggest a few lessons *de lege ferenda*.

This book is predominantly addressed to policy-makers and fellow academics on both sides of the Atlantic, and indeed, around the world. It is our hope that this volume will be an interesting read from front to back as well as serve as a reference work.

VI.

This book is a fruit of 'nomadic writing operations'[57] and these operations have at least two aspects. First, throughout the gestation of the book we have met with

[57] Mireille Hildebrandt coined this term.

the majority of authors at various occasions around the world. The exchange of ideas has been inestimable. Second, the book has been practically edited *en route*, naturally contributing to the said exchange of ideas, yet to a slight detriment to the regularity of the writing process. A good deal of work was done in Australia. Dan is based in Gold Coast, Queensland where he is a Professor of Law at the Faculty of Law, Bond University and a Co-Director of the Centre for Commercial Law. Dariusz, who on a daily basis is a researcher at the Vrije Universiteit Brussel (VUB), was a visiting scholar at Bond University from March to May 2016. (Dariusz Kloza gratefully acknowledges the financial support he received for that purpose from the Fonds Wetenschappelijk Onderzoek – Vlaanderen in Belgium.) The book was finalised in Scandinavia. Dan has spent the summer of 2016 at Stockholm University and Dariusz – at his other academic home, the Peace Research Institute Oslo (PRIO).

In producing this volume, we have racked up numerous debts which it is a pleasure to record. We both thank and congratulate the authors for their excellent work. We thank Wojciech R. Wiewiórowski, Assistant European Data Protection Supervisor (EDPS), for providing this book with an insightful foreword. Furthermore, the series editors, the anonymous reviewers and the peer-reviewers helped us ensuring academic quality of this volume. We received further help and support from (in alpha order) Rocco Bellanova, Katja Biedenkopf, Michał Czerniawski, Barry Guihen, Władysław Jóźwicki, Catherine Karcher, Christopher Kuner, Elżbieta Kużelewska and Lucas Melgaço. We have been fortunate to work again with Intersentia and our editor Tom Scheirs. Magdalena Witkowska took the picture printed on the back cover of this book. We extend our gratitude to all of them. Finally, we gratefully acknowledge the financial support of the Research Group on Law, Science, Technology and Society (LSTS) at VUB.

Stockholm/Oslo, September 2016

CONTENTS

INVITED COMMENT

SECTION V
PRIVACY AND TIME

INVITED COMMENTS

PART II
THEORY OF PRIVACY

LIST OF ABBREVIATIONS

AANZFTA	ASEAN–Australia–New Zealand Free Trade Area
ACTA	Anti-Counterfeiting Trade Agreement
AEPD	Agencia Española de Protección de Datos
APEC	Asia-Pacific Economic Cooperation
API	Advance Passenger Information
APP	Australian Privacy Principle
ASD	Australian Signals Directorate
ASEAN	Association of South East Asian Nations
BCR	Binding Corporate Rules
BD	big data
CETA	Comprehensive Economic and Trade Agreement
CFR	Charter of Fundamental Rights of the European Union
CISA	Convention Implementing the Schengen Agreement
CJEU	Court of Justice of the European Union
CMPPA	Computer Matching and Privacy Protection Act [US]
CoE	Council of Europe
COPPA	Children's Online Privacy Protection Act [US]
CPDP	Computers, Privacy and Data Protection conference
CPO	chief privacy officer
Cth	Commonwealth [Australia]
DG	Directorate-General (of the European Commission)
DNA	deoxyribonucleic acid
DPD	Data Protection Directive
DPIA	data protection impact assessment
DPO	data protection officer
DRM	Digital Rights Management
DSM	Digital Single Market
DTC	direct-to-consumer
EC	European Commission
ECHR	European Convention on Human Rights
ECJ	European Court of Justice (former name of CJEU)
ECtHR	European Court of Human Rights
EDPB	European Data Protection Board
EDPS	European Data Protection Supervisor
EEA	European Economic Area

EFTA	European Free Trade Agreement
EIS	environmental impact statement
EP	European Parliament
EPAL	Enterprise Privacy Authorisation Language
ETS	European Treaty Series
EU	European Union
FBI	Federal Bureau of Investigation
FCC	Federal Communications Commission
FISA	Foreign Intelligence Surveillance Act
FISC	Foreign Intelligence Surveillance Court
FoI	Freedom of Information
FONSI	finding of no significant impact
FTA	free trade agreement
FTC	Federal Trade Commission [US]
GAO	Government Accountability Office [US]
GATS	General Agreement on Trade in Services
GCHQ	Government Communications Headquarters
GDPR	General Data Protection Regulation
GPS	Global Positioning System
HIPPA	Health Insurance Portability and Accountability Act [US]
HTML	HyperText Markup Language
IaaS	Infrastructure as Service
IANA	Internet Assigned Numbers Authority
IATA	International Civil Aviation Organization
ICANN	Internet Corporation for Assigned Names and Numbers
ICC	International Criminal Court
ICCPR	International Covenant on Civil and Political Rights
ICDPPC	International Conference of Data Protection and Privacy Commissioners
ICRC	International Committee of the Red Cross
ICT	information and communications technologies
IDPC	Irish Data Protection Commissioner
ILO	International Labor Organization
IMAP	Internet Mail Access Protocol
IP	intellectual property
IP	Internet Protocol
IPR	intellectual property rights
ISDS	investor-state dispute settlement
IT	information technology
JHA	Justice and Home Affairs
LEA	law enforcement agency
MEP	Member of European Parliament

NAFTA	North American Free Trade Agreement
NEPA	National Environmental Policy Act
NGO	non-governmental organisation
NIS	Network and Information Security
NIST	National Institute of Standards and Technology [US]
NSA	National Security Agency
NSL	National Security Letter
OAIC	Office of Australian Information Commissioner
ODNI	Office of the Director of National Intelligence
OECD	Organization of Economic Cooperation and Development
OJ	Official Journal
OMB	Office of Management and Budget [US]
PaaS	Platform as Service
PACER	Pacific Agreement on Closer Economic Relations
PbD	Privacy by Design
PCLOB	Privacy and Civil Liberties Oversight Board
PD	personal data
PET	Privacy Enhancing Technologies
PGP	Pretty Good Privacy
PI	personal information
PIA	privacy impact assessment
PII	personally identifiable information
PNR	passenger name record
POP3	Post Office Protocol 3
PPD	Presidential Policy Directive
RCEP	Regional Comprehensive Economic Partnership
RFID	radio-frequency identification
RTBF	right to be forgotten
SAARC	South Asia Area of Regional Cooperation
SaaS	Software as Service
SIGINT	signal intelligence
SWIFT	Society for Worldwide Interbank Financial Telecommunication
TAMI	Transparent Accountable Data Mining Initiative
TFEU	Treaty on the Functioning of the European Union
TFTP	Terrorist Finance Tracking Programme
TISA, TiSA	Trade in Services Agreement
TPP	Trans-Pacific Partnership
TRIMS	Trade Related Investment Measures
TRIPS	Agreement on Trade-Related Aspects of Intellectual Property Rights
TTIP	Transatlantic Trade and Investment Partnership
UDHR	Universal Declaration of Human Rights

UK	United Kingdom
UKSC	United Kingdom Supreme Court
UN	United Nations
URL	uniform resource locator
US	United States of America
VIS	Visa Information System
VPN	virtual private network
WIPO	World Intellectual Property Organization
WP29	Article 29 Working Party
WTO	World Trade Organisation
XACML	eXtensible Access Control Markup Language

PART I

PRIVACY AND …

SECTION I

PRIVACY AND TRANSBORDER FLOWS OF PERSONAL DATA

1. TRANSNATIONAL DATA PRIVACY IN THE EU DIGITAL SINGLE MARKET STRATEGY

Rolf H. Weber*

1. INTRODUCTION

The creation of a Digital Single Market is an important objective of the European Union (EU); a basic concretisation of this objective can be seen in the Commission's proposition for a 'Digital Single Market Strategy for Europe', presented on 6 May 2015.[1] This Communication is based on the acknowledgement that the EU needs liberalised digital facilities encompassing better online-access for consumers and businesses and addressing cross-border e-commerce rules that are trustworthy. Apart from specific topics, the Commission proposes to create the right conditions and a level playing field for advanced digital networks and innovative services.[2] In addition, trust and security in the handling of personal data are to be improved.[3]

However, the main objective of the Digital Single Market Strategy of the Commission consists in strengthening the digital ecosystem and overcoming market fragmentation.[4] In this context, two elements are of major importance, namely (i) building a data economy (big data, cloud services, Internet of Things) that is likely to increase the competitiveness of the EU industry, and (ii) boosting wealth maximisation through interoperability and standardisation based on innovative technologies.[5] Obviously, a stable and foreseeable legal framework for digital services is a desirable cornerstone of the single market concept, but

* Faculty of Law, University of Zurich. E-mail: rolf.weber@rwi.uzh.ch.

1 See European Commission, Communication of 6 May 2015, 'A Digital Single Market Strategy for Europe' [2015] OJ L 192, final.

2 Ibid., pp. 9–11.

3 Ibid., pp. 11–13.

4 Rolf H. Weber, 'Competitiveness and Innovation in the Digital Single Market' (2016) 2 *European Cybersecurity Journal* 72, 73.

5 European Commission, above n. 1, p. 14.

a parallel framework for cross-border data flow should also be implemented in order to equally satisfy data privacy requests.

The new General Data Protection Regulation (GDPR) is a cornerstone of the European data protection effort. Data protection should no longer be viewed by enterprises as a negative factor but as 'an essential competitive advantage'[6] in the Digital Single Market, which aims at adding up to €415 billion per year to Europe's economy. Correspondingly, data protection principles need to be embedded into the Digital Single Market Strategy.

Public consultations are currently ongoing in respect of a wide range of issues relating to the Digital Single Market. Their aim is to ascertain the concerns that citizens as well as enterprises might have, and to adjust the Strategy and the corresponding legal instruments accordingly. The implementation is to be expected in 2017.

The subsequent contribution presents the key pillars of the Digital Single Market Strategy and of the applicable data protection framework in the EU, particularly by discussing the tensions between free data flow and data privacy. Thereby, the current developments in the EU as well as in the US, being the main markets for business transactions, are exposed in detail. Thereafter, the article pleads for the inclusion of more actors in data protection rule-making. The described tensions can only be solved if commercial entities and civil society are more deeply engaged in the development of the respective normative principles. The most recent approach mainly developed in the Internet governance context is the multi-stakeholderism concept. The implementation of this concept in the data privacy field brings the opportunity to overcome the existing fragmentation of different national (sovereign) regimes and to improve the legal interoperability between these regimes. New participation models can also increase the quality of rule-making. The contribution concludes that the challenges created by evolving technologies require an interdisciplinary approach to the issues of the free flow of data and data privacy.

2. TENSIONS BETWEEN FREE DATA FLOW AND DATA PRIVACY

2.1. FREE DATA FLOW AND DATA PRIVACY AS PARALLEL EU OBJECTIVES

In the Digital Single Market (DSM) Strategy, the Commission proposes putting more emphasis on a 'free flow of data' approach; such a concept should remove

6 European Commission press release, 'Agreement on Commission's EU data protection reform will boost Digital Single Market', 15 December 2015 <http://europa.eu/rapid/press-release_IP-15-6321_en.htm>.

all restrictions related to the free flow of data for reasons other than the protection of personal data.[7] However, the details of the tensions between the free movement of data and the protection of personal data are not addressed by the Commission. Furthermore, the legal frameworks as to consumer rights and contract law differ substantially within the EU.

As a consequence of the DSM Strategy, the Commission also launched a European Cloud Initiative that encompasses topics such as services certification, contracts, switching of providers and open research facilities; this initiative aims at bringing the public and private sector together in order to create an EU-wide cloud market.[8] The two parallel activities show that the free flow of data cannot be perceived only as an expression of fundamental rights, but must also be understood as a 'network' of legal relations that are influencing and channelling information distribution.[9]

Currently, the uncertainties surrounding data protection and mainly the cross-border transfer of data in the cloud environment mean that there is a lack of trust in these services on the part of both the consumer as well as business. In particular, the lack of security and compliance with fundamental rights is an often-cited issue which requires a stronger focus on the security of the infrastructure by regulators. The EU has insofar become active by implementing a new Network and Information Security Directive.[10] Operators of critical infrastructures will be required to take appropriate action to prevent security risks, as well as to inform potentially affected parties in instances where security is breached. In this regard the fast exchange between private sector actors and public agencies is necessary in order to identify potential threats or risks and to implement appropriate counter-measures. However, companies are resisting these requirements.

Transparency is another core issue that has been raised in various contexts over the last couple of years. While public access rules have been expanded and procedures developed for sharing information in the hands of public agencies, the private sector which impacts private life in a very serious manner through the control of electronic communication has largely remained untouched, although the General Data Protection Regulation will require a minimum level of disclosure to the data subjects if there has been a breach of data security and the affected individual's data was disclosed. Furthermore, the way in which data

---

7 European Commission, above n. 1, p. 15.

8 Ibid.

9 Weber, above n. 4, p. 75.

10 Directive (EU) 2016/1148 of the European Parliament and of the Council of 6 July 2016 concerning measures for a high common level of security of network and information systems across the Union, [2016] OJ L 194/1–30.

transfer is restricted should be made public, in order to increase competitiveness and limit adverse effects.

The European Cloud Partnership Steering Board (composed of high-level representatives of the IT and telecom industry, and decision-makers from governmental IT policy-making institutions) highlighted the need for an EU-wide cloud procurement strategy by public services which will lead to common sectorial requirements and thus bolster the EU cloud service provisioning in areas such as eHealth, eGovernment and social care.[11] The barrier-free transfer of data under such a uniform cloud system will further add to the protection of personal data within the EU Digital Single Market.

2.2. DATA PRIVACY AS POLICY AND REGULATORY TOPIC

2.2.1. Tensions between fundamental rights and regulatory frameworks

Data privacy on the international level is mostly driven by two different legal sources: on the one hand, most multilateral agreements as well as most national constitutions contain the privacy principle as a fundamental right (protection of an individual's personal sphere); privacy as a fundamental right is particularly enshrined in Art. 8 ECHR and Art. 8 EU Charter. On the other hand, international legal instruments (regulations, laws, etc.) encompass data protection provisions restricting the processing of personal data.

The two bodies of law are not fully coherent: the fundamental right of privacy stands in certain tensions with other fundamental rights such as the freedom of expression or the freedom of information; the specific data protection provisions are to be implemented in the given international and/or constitutional framework, and need to be brought in line with international trade rules. The respective tensions can be exemplified through an analysis of the current developments in the EU and in the US.

2.2.2. Current developments in the EU

During the last decade, a movement towards more detailed data protection provisions has become apparent; the best example is the repeal of the EU Data Protection Directive (DPD) 95/46 by the General Data Protection Regulation (GDPR) which will come into force in late May 2018. The new Regulation contains more than double the amount of provisions as compared to the

[11] Cf. <https://ec.europa.eu/digital-agenda/en/european-cloud-partnership>.

Directive. Supposedly this quantitative increase is due to the need for specific protective measures based on the acknowledgement that without legislative action, the infringement of personal data is going to grow exponentially through new emerging technology such as big data or the Internet of Things.

The GDPR places a strong focus on industry action by allowing for certifications as a compliance tool and advocating for industry standards which bring industry practice in line with the EU data protection requirements. On the EU level, the European Data Protection Board (EDPB) can issue guidelines on certification requirements which will enable enterprises to better understand the technical measures that the data protection authorities will refer to when assessing compliance with the Regulation. This will in particular be the case when the EDPB approves the criteria of a certification resulting in an EU-wide European Data Protection Seal (Art. 42(5) GDPR).

Based on the changes caused by the GDPR to the EU data protection framework, the ePrivacy Directive (EPD),[12] which regulates the processing of personal data in the communications sector, is also undergoing revision, being close to finalisation. The proposed changes aim at resolving issues surrounding the scope of the ePrivacy Directive in light of the new market and technological reality, enhancing security and confidentiality of communications as well as addressing inconsistent enforcement and fragmentation at national levels. Commercial reality has shown that the use of consent requirements under Art. 5 EPD present a challenge, as most vendors apply a take-it-or-leave-it approach, essentially asking the customer to either click the appropriate consent button or be blocked from using a site. The cookie notification is a good example of the intent of the EU legislator relating to the regulation of data tracking and to the monitoring of browsing behaviour, which in its practical application has not achieved a balanced result. The focus of the revision process should therefore be on ensuring that the actual tracking is limited, and understandable terms are used when informing a customer of an underlying processing operation rather than requiring consent, which based on the information provided to an average user can by no means be described as informed.

In parallel, the fundamental right to privacy has also gained importance and has been the centre of attention during the last three years because of a lack of action on the part of the data protection authorities: in two landmark decisions the EU Court of Justice has acknowledged a specific right to be forgotten (*Google/Spain*)[13] as a new fundamental right, and has also invalidated the Safe Harbour Agreement (namely the Commission's adequacy decision 520/2000/EC)

---

12 Directive 2002/58/EC of the European Parliament and of the Council of 12 July 2002 concerning the processing of personal data and the protection of privacy in the electronic communications sector (Directive on privacy and electronic communications), [2002] OJ L 201/37–47.

13 Case C-131/12 *Google Spain SL, Google Inc. v. Agencia Española de Protección de Datos, Mario Costeja González.*

between the EU and the US (*Schrems/Ireland*)[14] for various reasons, not least the nonconformity of some US surveillance measures with European constitutional privacy rights. This increased importance of the EU fundamental rights approach complements the data protection framework. However, it conflicts with foreign laws and regulations and thus will pose a great challenge for businesses conducting transborder data transfers. The finally successful negotiations, having replaced the Safe Harbor Agreement with the new Privacy Shield, have shown the issues arising from both private as well as public data access rights in the EU and US.[15] In the long run, concepts should be explored creating solutions how the differing data protection laws can interact and grow together.

The European Convention of Human Rights as well as the EU Charter include a fundamental human right to privacy which presents a further frame of reference with respect of the limits of data protection infringements. EU Member States must adhere to the basic principles of individual privacy included in these agreements. However, the boundaries of the general principles are not clear, as they will be determined on a case-by-case basis requiring a balancing of the right to privacy against the interests of the State. In essence, the GDPR includes more general concepts of privacy contained in the human rights treaties and presents practical and targeted rules as to their execution in the European context.

The EU has had a leadership role in respect of human rights and privacy in the international sphere. Many countries have followed and also implemented data and privacy protection laws mirroring some of the EU provisions. Recently, for example, Indonesia has passed its first data protection law in the country's history. Australia also has a long-standing tradition of data protection principles, which for example recommends a serious data breach to be disclosed to the Office of the Australian Information Commissioner, as well as notification of the affected individual.[16] Despite this international progress on data protection, China has passed a new counterterrorism law which requires Internet Service Providers to supply their encryption keys, allowing government access to communications.

2.2.3. Current developments in the US

The increased international regulations have led to higher compliance costs as well as to a major complexity in international data transfers. Companies are

[14] Case C-362/14 *Maximillian Schrems v. Data Protection Commissioner Ireland.*

[15] See European Commission, *EU–US Privacy Shield*, factsheet, 2016.

[16] Office of the Australian Information Commissioner, 'Data breach notification – A guide to handling personal information security breaches', Sydney 2014, <https://www.oaic.gov.au/agencies-and-organisations/guides/data-breach-notification-a-guide-to-handling-personal-information-security-breaches>.

increasingly facing requirements they currently are unable to meet because of the way in which their data collection is set up.[17] Thus, becoming compliant with all the various data protection laws requires a step-by-step approach, taking into account the areas in which the risk is highest and addressing them first.

In the US, regulatory supervision of cybersecurity and data protection issues are governed by states as well as federal agencies. For example, the Federal Trade Commission (FTC) administers the aspects that relate to interstate trade and commerce as well as any matter concerning the new Privacy Shield with the EU. The FTC further possesses the power to regulate cybersecurity practices through its 'unfairness' authority under section 5 FTC Act,[18] and has expressed its willingness to apply this power more frequently with regard to new technologies. Other regulators such as in the financial sector are also stepping up their cybersecurity supervision by imposing more frequent audits and conducting regular inspections. This trend is expanding from finance into other areas, and includes oversight bodies from the state as well as at the federal level.

For companies, the US state laws create a great amount of uncertainty and compliance costs, as for example data breach notifications vary heavily from state to state; depending on which state an incident has occurred in, the requirements to notify various parties differ. For example, California has recently revised its data breach laws, which now force companies with operations in California to consider these new notification requirements as well as their compatibility with the requirements in other states they operate in.[19] As a consequence, the notification requirements must be checked for each state in which a company operates, as some states restrict the amount of information that can be provided to the data subject.[20]

Slowly the scope of privacy regulation is expanding into all sectors. For example the Federal Communications Commission (FCC) has reclassified Internet Service Providers in 2016 so as to allow for their regulation under new privacy rules.[21] These rules aim at addressing data sharing, breach notification and data protection issues as they pertain to ISP operations.

---

17 These issues in particular arise in the context of data protection laws and the combination of big data, resulting in a higher degree of identifiability of a person. The initial collection of the data may not have required consent; however, based on the nature of the processing conducted at a later time and the result of such processing, the person's consent as an identifiable data subject is required.

18 Federal Trade Commission Act, 15 USC §§41–58.

19 California Civil Code, ss. 1798.29 and 1798.82.

20 This is for example the case in Massachusetts, where the law prohibits a notification from including information on the nature of the breach, or how many people have been affected (see M.G.L. c. 93H, s. 3(c)).

21 Rebecca R. Ruiz and Steve Lohr, 'F.C.C. Approves Net Neutrality Rules, Classifying Broadband Internet Service as a Utility', *New York Times*, 26 February 2015 <http://www.nytimes.com/2015/02/27/technology/net-neutrality-fcc-vote-internet-utility.html?_r=0>.

The US has seen an increase in class actions for data breaches and a higher willingness by affected individual's to claim damages. However, issues remain in respect of class certification[22] as most class members usually suffer varying types and extents of damages, which generally require a more individualised proceeding. Nevertheless, the likelihood of being subjected to a class action for a data security breach has grown significantly over the last two years.

EU customers as well as businesses are also being impacted by the US discovery rules, which require US-based companies to disclose information which is governed by EU data protection rules to a US-based counterparty. This fact creates an immensely difficult situation for companies, as they are required to uphold the laws of both jurisdictions, which are contrary to each other – one requiring disclosure, the other prohibiting it. This problem has increased due to the new Cybersecurity Information Sharing Act of 2015,[23] which allows the sharing of information by companies with the government, undermining the EU Safe Harbour Agreement that allowed personal data transfers from the EU to the US. The Court of Justice of the European Union (CJEU) has already highlighted that it will not accept vast public access rights to European personal data by US authorities, as this would violate EU law and could not be considered to offer an adequate protection or sufficient safety.

On the international level, the US as the world's largest data recipient is a strong proponent of abolishing data transfer restrictions. Over recent decades it has been largely successful in preventing such restrictions, or limiting their effectiveness by offering trade advantages in international treaty negotiations in return for reduced transfer restrictions. In particular, the data protection measures hindering free flow of data and their conformity with the GATS have so far not been fully explored.[24] However, the prevailing opinion is that the EU's 'adequacy' requirement could not successfully be challenged.[25] Until the CJEU recently invalidated the Safe Harbour Agreement, even the EU law had a workaround which enabled US companies to transfer data freely from the EU without any real oversight.[26]

The draft of the new Trans-Pacific Partnership Agreement (which now appears unlikely to be ratified by the US) is a recent example of the US position

---

22 A judge must first certify the class of affected individuals, which means that all parties that have been damaged are included in this class and they have consented to the class action or have elected to opt out.

23 Cybersecurity Information Sharing Act of 2015 <https://www.congress.gov/bill/114th-congress/senate-bill/754>.

24 For a detailed discussion of this issue see Rolf H. Weber, 'Regulatory Autonomy and Privacy Standards under the GATS' (2012) 7 *AJWH* 32.

25 Gregory Shaffer, 'Globalization and social protection: The impact of EU and international rules in the ratcheting up of US privacy standards' (2000) 25 *Yale Journal of International Law* 1–88.

26 Greenleaf, Ch. 8, in this volume.

on data flow, encompassing a wide scope in relation to electronic services. Furthermore, exceptions limiting the export of personal data must be justified under Art. 14.11.3 by fulfilling four requirements. These requirements include a showing of (i) a legitimate public policy objective, (ii) no arbitrary or unjustified discrimination, (iii) no disguised restriction on trade and (iv) no greater restrictions than necessary to achieve the objective of the law. In contrast to other international treaties this agreement would place the onus to prove the elements on the state implementing the law. Based on the unpredictability of the interpretation of these requirements, it is unlikely that an exception would ever be granted. Thus, the international law-making efforts can have severe repercussions for the local data protection laws and must be considered carefully, i.e. often fundamental rights are (partly) bargained away for the promise of economic benefit.

3. INCLUSION OF MORE ACTORS IN DATA PROTECTION RULE-MAKING

3.1. CONCEPT OF MULTI-STAKEHOLDERISM

Multi-stakeholderism has become a buzzword in many international discussions about regulatory structures, without gaining a coherent institutional form.[27] Originally applied by the International Labour Organization (ILO) in 1919 and later taken up during the sustainability/climate change debates, mainly at the Earth Summit (Rio de Janeiro) in 1992 and in subsequent corresponding conferences, the term was particularly current in the Internet Governance context. The acknowledgment of the need to have more actors involved in rule-making processes has led to a working definition referring to the 'development and application by governments, the private sector, and civil society, in their respective role, of shared principles, norms, rules, decision-making procedures, and programs that shape the evolution and use of the Internet'.[28] Thereby, the interests of the actors involved should not be defined by any specific group but through participatory mechanisms reflecting the whole of society's views.[29]

More and more, not only in the Internet context, it is accepted that the involvement of civil society in rule-making procedure can have a legitimising effect and allow for greater credibility of actions taken by the governing bodies; the participation of the general public in the decision-making efforts,

---

27 See Mark Raymond and Laura DeNardis, 'Multistakeholderism: anatomy of an inchoate global institution' (2015) 7 *International Theory* 572, 575.

28 Report of the Working Group on Internet Governance (WGIG) of June 2005 <http://www.wgig.org/docs/WGIGREPORT.pdf>, 4.

29 Rolf H. Weber, 'Future Design of Cyberspace Law' (2012) 5 *Journal of Politics* 1, 8.

based on adequate transparency mechanisms, strengthens confidence in and accountability of the competent institutions.[30] The inclusion of new issues, interests, and concerns communicated by civil society can also encourage the governing bodies to look at a specific substantive question from different angles.[31]

Practical considerations in the multi-stakeholder context lead to the following questions:[32]

1. How can greater transparency and dialogue between different civil society groups and experts be achieved?
2. How can it be ensured that the benefits of rapid standard- or rule-making are maintained even with additional scrutiny due to increasing multi-stakeholder arrangements?

In answering these questions, participatory models must be founded on the prevailing interests, capacities, and needs; thereby, appropriate legitimacy strategies are to be developed which should take the following factors into consideration:[33]

1. Identification of the most adequate set of participating stakeholders, definition of criteria and mechanisms for representatives' selection, avoidance of capture of multi-stakeholder processes by influential public or private powers.
2. Establishment of technologies supporting the liaison with constituencies.
3. Creation of a technological framework facilitating dialogue between the participants.
4. Implementation of models supporting consensus-building and decision-making as well as accelerating the respective processes in a multi-stakeholder environment.

The multi-stakeholder discussions are quite intensive in the Internet governance context, but they have not yet spread over to the data privacy field. This fact

---

30 Rolf H. Weber, 'Shift of legislative powers and multi-stakeholder governance' (2011) 1/1 *International Journal of Public Law and Policy* 4, 6.

31 Ibid., p. 7.

32 Ian Brown and Christopher T. Marsden, *Regulating Code: Good Governance and Better Regulation in the Information Age*, MIT Press, 2013, p. 200.

33 Rolf H. Weber, *Realizing a New Global Cyberspace Framework: Normative Foundations and Guiding Principles*, Springer, 2014, p. 129; see also Joe Waz and Phil Weiser, 'Internet Governance: The Role of Multistakeholder Organizations' (2013) 10 *Journal of Telecommunications and High Technology Law* 331, 342/43; to the strategies in particular Kristina Tamm Hallström and Magnus Boström, *Transnational Multi-stakeholder Standardization: Organizing Fragile Non-state Authority*, Edward Elgar Publishing, 2010, p. 141.

constitutes a weakness of the rule-making processes attempting to achieve an adequate data protection framework. Business, civil society and academia (technological, economic, social, legal knowledge) could contribute to an improved regulatory regime for data privacy.

3.2. IMPLEMENTATION IN THE DATA PRIVACY FIELD

As a consequence of the outlined developments towards a more active inclusion of different stakeholders into the rule-making processes, many issues such as the models of data privacy governance, their convergence, the need for globalised data protection standards and the regulation of transborder data flows need to be reflected on anew.

The respective refinement and adaption of privacy rules can be carried out through the improvement and the practical implementation of privacy management programmes that enable enterprises to satisfy the regulators and supervisors of their compliance with privacy standards. Such programmes also have the potential to act as a strong marketing instrument, since they send a signal that businesses care about the privacy of their customers and stakeholders by attempting to reduce the risk of a privacy breach. The content and structure of such programmes can be quite flexible, enabling the necessary adaptation to the given circumstances. Nevertheless, a stronger coordination on the international level as to privacy standards seems warranted in light of the great differences in protection levels. In particular, cooperation among data protection authorities from different states must be enhanced in order to prevent violations.[34]

In view of the described features of privacy as a fundamental right and the application of data protection laws, businesses must develop a strategy for complying with the applicable legal requirements from manifold sources:

1. Organisational rules have to describe the functions of responsible persons and segregate the duties amongst the persons.
2. The data protection policy must describe the security levels and the measures applied to achieve such levels.
3. A project management needs to be implemented and conditions for user participation should be established.
4. A data classification scheme must be developed in order to control access rights.
5. Adequate responsibility measures and surveillance requirements for review processes must be introduced.

---

[34] Antonella Galetta and Dariusz Kloza, 'Cooperation Among Data Privacy Supervisory Authorities: Lessons from Parallel European Mechanisms' (2016) *Jusletter IT* 25, n. 1.

Private initiatives such as the implementation of privacy management systems are particularly important, since it appears unlikely that the two major regulatory approaches for data protection regimes will be overcome in the near future. On the one hand, some countries (for example the Member States of the European Union, Switzerland and Hong Kong) know a comprehensive data protection model containing core principles such as provisions on data processing and on international data transfers as well as specific rules related to e-privacy measures, on the other hand, some countries have implemented sectoral or self-regulatory/co-regulatory models (for example the US, Australia). The different approaches will most likely remain in place for the next decade, creating challenges for cross-border data flows due to the incoherent levels of protection.

Certifications according to the new GDPR also present a step in unifying data protection compliance, by having an independent third party evaluate a processing operation. These certifications are accompanied by an industry-approved code of conduct which enables standards to be created that match the requirement of a subset of processor and are tailored to their needs. Furthermore, the European Data Protection Board, consisting of the heads of the EU Member State data protection authorities, is empowered to issue guidelines for certain processing operations or general matters which aim at ensuring a uniform application of the GDPR across all Member States.

4. TRANSBOUNDARY IMPACTS OF THE DATA PRIVACY FRAMEWORK

4.1. SOVEREIGNTY AND LEGAL INTEROPERABILITY

4.1.1. Traditional notion

The traditional concept of sovereignty leading to the territoriality principle of nation state jurisdiction necessarily comes into a conflict with the global information and communications networks.

The concept of state sovereignty goes back to the Westphalian Peace Treaty of 1648 incorporating the four basic elements of (i) exclusive state powers, (ii) the equality of nations principle, (iii) the immunity principle, and (iv) the right against interference by any foreign power into domestic affairs.[35]

---

[35] For a detailed discussion see: Rolf H. Weber, 'New Sovereignty Concepts in the Age of Internet?' (2010) *Journal of Internet Law* 12–20; Rolf H. Weber, above n. 33.

4.1.2. Challenges of a global cyberspace

The focus of these principles has shifted significantly over the last 20 years with the realisation of a need for international cooperation in a globalised world. With the creation of international and supranational organisations such as the EU, states transfer governmental functions to either the transnational level or the non-state actors. Furthermore, national laws can have extraterritorial effects, such as the EU General Data Protection Regulation creating legally binding rules without attempting to get sufficient democratic legitimisation in other countries.

However, despite these shifts, state sovereignty remains a central concept which cannot be easily replaced. Nevertheless, this assessment does not mean that a 'cybered Westphalian age'[36] should remediate the threats in the Internet, since such an approach would lead to a 'fenced cyberspace'[37] which ultimately produces unwanted results. A strict territorial approach will not function in cyberspace which by its very own nature is meant to work without being hindered by borders. This is particularly important in light of the fact that social changes are questioning the perception of states and the growing understanding of global public commons.

Attention should also be paid to the concept of so-called 'walled gardens', which are giant platforms with a monopolistic business model and their counterpart of an open and transparent Internet.[38] Cooperation has been a cornerstone of the Internet since the beginning. Nevertheless, as the design of the Internet changes over time, more regulation becomes necessary to address issues that have been created at choke-points such as Internet Service Providers (ISPs). Today, the main issues surround the collection of user data, that stands in tension with the right to self-determination being the core of data privacy.

Experience has shown that national legislators are ill-equipped to regulate the challenges created by global cyberspace. In order to design an appropriate framework for the regulation of cyberspace, superior technical knowledge is essential. Additionally, the external effects of such laws must be closely considered in order to avoid technology battles or a shift into another jurisdiction and a loss of business. As the Internet is viewed as a public good providing general

---

36 Chris C. Demchak and Peter Dombrowski, 'Rise of a Cybered Westphalian Age' (2011) *Strategic Studies Quarterly* 36–39.

37 Rolf H. Weber, above n. 35, p. 9.

38 Francesca Musiani, 'Walled Gardens or a Global Network?: Tensions, (De)centralization, and Pluralities of the Internet Model' in J. Kulesza and R. Balleste (eds.), *Cybersecurity and Human Rights in the Age of Cyberveillance*, Rowman & Littlefield Publishers, 2016, p. 130.

benefits independent from a normative framework, its governance should also be global.[39]

Thus, sovereignty in this context must be understood as an approach containing cooperative elements and entailing an understanding of meaningful coordination of different levels of governance (local to global). Sovereign thinking will hinder a transnational approach to cyberspace regulation and will not be able to address pressing problems which need to be resolved by all involved actors in a joint coordinated effort.[40]

4.1.3. *Interoperability of legal frameworks*

Legal interoperability is the key concept in achieving cooperation of legal rules across jurisdictions and preventing fragmentation.[41] However, a certain degree of individuality must be maintained in order to account for social and cultural differences whilst facilitating a global standard. Such legal interoperability can be implemented by a bottom-up or top-down approach. The first approach is bound to be more successful, as it is carried out by all parties involved, but is harder to achieve than the top-down approach applied by already established or new international organisations. If an international treaty is not a feasible solution, policies should still aim at achieving general principles.[42]

The costs of a reduced interoperability in a highly networked world are substantial and will cause dominant states to enlarge the geographical scope of their laws through extraterritorial application. With a low level of interoperability also comes a low level of connectedness, which limits innovation as censorship or privacy controls increase the burden on the individual or business.

Interoperability functions can be identified with reference to four layers. These include (i) technology, (ii) data, (iii) human elements and (iv) institutional aspects. The layers must support non-restricted interoperability through measures such as transparent and undistorted procedures, pro-competitive goals, objective and relevant criteria for technology selection, and renunciation of over-standardisation.[43] In order to achieve an optimum level of interoperability, various targeted laws are necessary which conform to the developed architecture

---

39 See e.g. the US position on netneutrality: Tim Fernholz, 'Barack Obama says the internet is a public good, and that's why the US needs net neutrality', *Quartz*, 10 October 2014 <http://qz.com/293904/barack-obama-says-the-internet-is-a-public-good-and-thats-why-the-us-needs-net-neutrality/>.

40 Rolf H. Weber, 'Regulatory Competition and Coordination as Policy Instruments' 30(11) *Journal of International Banking Law and Regulations* 607.

41 Rolf H. Weber, 'Legal Interoperability as a Tool for Combatting Fragmentation', Global Commission on Internet Governance Paper Series no. 4 (2014), p. 5.

42 Weber, above n. 33, p. 115.

43 Brown and Marsden, above n. 32, p. 200.

and take account of all the important underlying factors. However, the measures taken to reach this goal can either be instituted by the government or led by the private sector. Often the private sector pushes ahead when governments fail to take action by, for example, setting their own open standards or entering into technical collaboration.

In order to achieve legal interoperability the main question is whether to adjust existing laws or implement new ones. This will depend strongly on the circumstances and the complexity of the matter. If the basics of the existing laws are already substantially in line with the goals, then adjustments will suffice. However, if the law is outdated and does not reflect today's approach regarding the topic to be regulated, it makes more sense to pass a new law based on the issues that present themselves today. By implementing such interoperable rules, a level playing field is created for the next generation of technologies and cultural exchange.[44] Nevertheless, based on the high degree of involvement of various actors in the legislative process, often the most interoperable solution is not passed but rather a compromise is reached.

4.1.4. *Achieving legal interoperability*

Various approaches are available to achieve legal interoperability which aim at finding the right balance between full harmonisation and complete fragmentation. A good starting point for an analysis of the interoperability of various laws across jurisdictions is the existing conflict of law rules. However, these rules only provide guidance related to the applicable norms but do not overcome the differences in the legal systems, and thus only have an indirect influence.

This fact is evidenced by the importance of venue selection by the parties. As national laws are a result of state sovereignty, they are legitimately applied within the scope of sovereignty. Thus, data protection laws can generally only be enforced within the state to which they apply, as they are of an administrative nature. Potential risk-shifting is part of the private law sphere and thus venue selection as well as a choice of the applicable law is contractually possible to the extent a state has not enacted special limitations for the protection of consumers.

An increase in legal interoperability between various data protection laws reduces the costs of international trade significantly and benefits the local economies. In addition to the economic factors, the legal interoperability facilitates the balancing of fundamental rights such as the freedom of expression and results in more effective laws. Fundamental issues are mostly addressed by international organisations such as the United Nations, based on their universal

---

44 Weber, above n. 33, p. 183.

membership. These have taken up the issue of data protection and privacy by appointing a Special Rapporteur who is tasked with assessing international data protection laws and reporting to the UN Human Rights Commissioner.[45] Ultimately the coordination and research by the Commissioner will lead to more interoperable data protection laws worldwide. Based on the complexity of the matter and the various legal areas affected, this remains a long-term goal.

International organisations are a good example of the top-down approach which in practice creates large bureaucracies.[46] However, often consensus is hard to achieve at such a level thus the development of new laws or standards is slow. In contrast, a bottom-up approach is more likely to be approved and followed, as all concerned entities and persons are involved from the beginning in a step-by-step process.[47] Nevertheless, this coordination process is also very time-consuming. Minimal regulatory harmonisation such as the EU Data Protection Directive can be a solution, as it sets basic standards but does not prescribe a specific wording of the national Member State law. But on the international level, such an approach carries the risk of a regulatory race to the bottom if harmonisation takes place on a low level and in a generalised manner.[48]

Another approach in order to combat the fragmentation of laws is standardisation, which is driven by various actors including states, organisations or industries. These standardisation efforts are grouped into technical, economic and legal challenges that are present on an international level. Often these standards are designed as soft law, thus they are an informal agreement between entities to conduct themselves in a certain manner without strict legal enforceability. Sometimes the argument is raised that international standard setting institutions lack legitimacy as they are for most part private organisations. Based on the vast number of such organisations and the rigorous competition between them, those lacking legitimacy are unlikely to succeed in the market.

State rules will be recognised when they are satisfactory for a different state regulatory environment. This situation is present within the EU, which uses a so-called 'single passport' system that allows for privileged cross-border market access. On the global level, the World Trade Organization's (WTO) General Agreement on Trade in Services (GATS) ensures that the mutual recognition principle is enforced by all member countries. Nevertheless, this is only a second-best solution after harmonisation or standardisation.[49]

---

45 For the first three-year term Prof. Joseph Cannataci was appointed as Special Rapporteur on the right to privacy <http://www.ohchr.org/EN/Issues/Privacy/SR/Pages/SRPrivacyIndex.aspx>.

46 John Palfrey and Urs Gasser, *Interop: The Promise and Perils of Highly Interconnected Systems*, Basics Books, 2012, p. 182.

47 Ibid., p. 185.

48 Rolf H. Weber, 'Mapping and Structuring International Financial Regulation – A Theoretical Approach' (2009) 20(5) *European Banking Law Review* p. 659.

49 Weber, above n. 41, p. 9.

Reciprocity has been used to achieve balanced outcomes between countries. However, in the context of international agreements, for example the WTO's most favoured nation principle, such an approach is no longer feasible. Today, the involved regulators are focusing more on cooperation in order to define clear mandates, and to apply and enforce different regulatory measures.[50] These measures are highly efficient in individual cases, but do not present a solution for the general interoperability of laws.

Nevertheless, certain reservations based on social and cultural perceptions create problems, as for example in the context of the fundamental right of freedom of expression. The US has a very wide scope of protection of such a right, whereas the scope is quite limited in China. Even in instances where the right to freedom of expression is similarly constituted, such as in the context of the US and the EU, substantial differences in its application exist. In France an anti-Semitism organisation initiated legal proceedings against Yahoo, based on a sale of Nazi memorabilia in California. The French court found itself to be competent and applied French law restricting the freedom of expression to the offering of these goods to French citizens.[51] In the *Google Spain* decision[52] the CJEU highlighted that in this case, the individual right to data protection outweighs the right to freedom of expression (being in particular the US constitutional argument).

In terms of Internet regulation which requires trust, the ideal solution appears to be standardisation based on a self-regulatory regime. On the technical level, selective interoperability which takes into account fine differences in jurisdictions, such as the varying data protection levels, must be designed and implemented in order to facilitate the cross-border provisioning of services.[53] The EU's Binding Corporate Rules as a corporate law solution may also be a valid substitute for laws or international treaties, being more efficient in establishing privacy than a potentially ineffective multilateral treaty.

4.1.5. Increased legal interoperability in the data privacy field

The EU's approach to the subject matter of transnational data transfer has sent a strong signal to other countries around the world, which have started to mirror

---

50 Rolf H. Weber, above n. 48, p. 664.

51 *Yahoo!, Inc. v. La Ligue Contre le Racisme et L'Antisemitisme* 169 F. Supp. 2d 1181, 1186 (N.D. Cal. 2001).

52 Case C-131/12, above n. 13.

53 Rolf H. Weber, 'Transborder Data Transfers: Concepts, Regulatory Approaches and New Legislative Initiatives' (2013) *International Data Privacy Law* 5.

the EU provisions. For example the Asia-Pacific Economic Cooperation (APEC) Member States have agreed on similar rules to the EU Binding Corporate Rules (BCR) based on the EU Data Protection Directive. BCR aim at ensuring the application of data protection standards within a corporate structure or undertaking. In the context of APEC they allow for international data transfers within the framework of the APEC Member States whilst allowing for their own data protection laws. Only a minimum standard is set to which they must adhere in order to receive and process data from other APEC Member States.[54]

Furthermore, the US, although reluctantly and due to strong pressure, has agreed to the EU–US Privacy Shield under which the US agrees to limit its access to European data for national security reasons subject to judicial redress.[55] The Federal Trade Commission is required to carry out intensive compliance measures. In essence, the EU data protection authorities and the US counterparts must now work more closely together, and enterprises having transferred data are bound by certain procedural safeguards. These measures include that the enterprises process complaints within a certain timeframe, as well as that an aggrieved party is granted with free alternative dispute resolution procedures. This international coordination and stronger involvement of important stakeholders increase the legal interoperability of the EU as well as the US data protection framework, and create the basis for ongoing improvements of the transnational data flow laws and procedures.

If the needs of all concerned stakeholders are taken into account in the development of data protection regimes and systems, and if the concerned stakeholders are able to participate in such a scheme, democratic elements are not only realised in connection with the preparation of the legal framework, but also in the implementation of the applicable regulations.

4.2. NEW PARTICIPATION MODELS FOR DATA PRIVACY RULE-MAKING

In the future, a democratically legitimised framework needs to be implemented to integrate the scattered legal provisions. Participation of as many stakeholders as possible is key to achieving a functioning and accepted framework for transnational data transfers. Initially this will involve complex public

---

54 APEC, Privacy Framework <http://www.apec.org/Groups/Committee-on-Trade-and-Investment/~/media/Files/Groups/ECSG/05_ecsg_privacyframewk.ashx>.

55 Larry Downs, 'The Business Implications of the EU–U.S. "Privacy Shield"', *Harvard Business Review*, 10 February 2016 <https://hbr.org/2016/02/the-business-implications-of-the-eu-u-s-privacy-shield>.

consultations such as the ones currently carried out in light of the Digital Single Market Strategy. However, with the information as to the technical, organisational as well as other concerns, a holistic approach must be implemented by the European legislator through negotiations with various international parties, and in particular the US, that represent most of the EU's international data transfer volume.

Any new approach to regulating the technological advancements of the last decade must be based on multi-stakeholder involvement, taking into account the various concerns that arise in the context of data protection, data collection and flows as well as security and privacy in the online world. Industry standards as well as other self-regulatory measures must be assessed before taking action by way of binding legal frameworks. Furthermore, interest groups and consumer organisations which are tasked with highlighting issues and proposing solutions must be heard to determine the most efficient solution to the presented challenges.

By providing information on decision-making processes and encouraging public participation in the respective procedures, the creation of ineffective rules can be reduced. As the right to privacy and data protection concerns all Internet users, a process similar to the Aarhus Convention could be utilised in order to present a more meaningful and holistic approach to these issues. As the Internet is partly self-regulated through non-governmental actors, a stronger interaction between governmental regulation at national and international levels (via treaties) as well as between the parties involved in the design of the self-regulatory framework is warranted.[56]

One of the greatest challenges for transnational data flow is the wide interpretation of the European, and particularly the human rights, law in relation to privacy. Without clear legal boundaries, enterprises transferring data abroad will be left in a legal grey zone from which they are unable to flee.[57] This uncertainty as to how to act on a transnational basis leads to a loss of investment and efficiency gains which otherwise would have been realised through new technologies.[58] Thus, it is in the interests of all stakeholders to agree on workable

---

56 Rolf H. Weber, *Shaping Internet Governance: Regulatory Challenges*, ZIK 46, 2009, pp. 88 et seq.

57 The Financial Markets Law Committee, 'Discussion of legal uncertainties arising in the area of EU Data Protection Reforms', October 2014 <http://www.fmlc.org/uploads/2/6/5/8/26584807/fmlc_paper_discussing_issues_of_legal_uncertainty_arising_in_the_context_of_european_data_protection_reform_proposals.pdf>.

58 To the involvement of private actors in the development of cross-border data privacy standards see Friederike Voskamp, *Transnationaler Datenschutz. Globale Datenschutzstandards durch Selbstregulierung*, Nomos, 2015, p. 68 et seq.

solutions benefiting the individual through protection of his or her privacy rights as well as the economy through efficient and practicable laws.

4.2.1. Increased quality of rule-making

An interconnected approach taking into account the various data protection rules in the international context leads to better and more efficiently applicable laws. However, in order to achieve a balanced outcome the legislators must not only take account of the laws in other countries, but in light of the electronic nature of data protection a strong focus must be set on the way in which technology shapes privacy. This focus is currently missing, although many non-governmental actors try to supplement the legislative process with information on the applicability of the privacy laws.

In order to overcome the gap between business reality and the interpretation of the law, stronger cooperation between states on the international level as well as with the IT industry is necessary. More attention must be paid to the needs of the digital market, how business is conducted in today's online world and what future technology will look like. Thus, the quality of data protection will depend strongly on whether an international basic data protection level can be agreed upon which incentivises higher rather than lower standards.

Public acceptance of laws is also a qualitative measure of rule-making and should take into account the needs of the populace. Opinion on data protection and in particular the privacy versus security argument differs widely throughout the world.[59] Some communities are more willing to give up personal privacy and data protection in order to increase public security. However, the practical benefit of such a view is hard to measure. Achieving a transnational data privacy framework will thus first have to address the data protection and privacy issues present in a common market such as the EU before integrating a more globalised approach.

Throughout the process of creating a transnational data privacy framework within the EU, transparency and public consultation are key factors to achieving legitimacy and acceptance. Agency rule-making as a subsidiary form of law should also follow these principles, as the precise implementation of data protection and privacy laws is often highly discretionary. With the increase in legitimacy through such measures the level of compliance can be raised, and the overall quality of the law improved.

---

[59] Rolf H. Weber and Dominic N. Staiger, 'Privacy versus Security: Identifying the Challenges in a Global Information Society' in J. Kulesza and R. Balleste (eds.), *Cybersecurity and Human Rights in the Age of Cyberveillance*, Rowman & Littlefield Publishers, 2016, p. 63 et seq.

5. OUTLOOK

Due to the challenging and shifting landscape in the electronic world, the experiences gained through multi-stakeholder involvement in the design of international frameworks must also be applied to finding a solution to the data protection privacy and security issues posed by the interconnected online world. The Digital Single Market Strategy is a first step in the right direction, unifying the legal framework in relation to these issues within the EU. In doing so a public consultation is carried out and concerns as well as ideas can be submitted. Once this single market is fully established, the transfer of data within the EU will be uninhibited by national data protection laws. However, many other barriers still remain and must be addressed in the course of the Digital Single Market Strategy. These risks include contractual as well as consumer protection limitations. As a second step the EU can explore possible solutions to these issues that have been resolved by the Digital Single Market on an international level.

The EU's Digital Single Market has so far been viewed internationally, and in particular by the US, as erecting protectionist trade barriers, rather than solving Europe's innovation deficit. In this context the increased antitrust actions against leading US Internet companies also remains a controversial topic. However, on the international level the US is also targeting local data protection and privacy laws through preventing the inclusion of exceptions for such matters in international trade agreements. This shows that ultimately the protection of personal data is influenced by the bargaining power of the states involved. The EU, due to its strong human rights protection regime and the complicated power structure, has been able to avert the advances by the US limiting such protection in international treaties. However, as the Trans-Pacific Partnership Agreement proves, other states are much more susceptible to the offers made by the US representatives, which could lead to devastating effects for privacy protection in these areas.

Furthermore, the EU must seriously rethink its approach to privacy protection, as it seems that there is a strong disparity between customers' willingness to give up personal information in return for a service, versus the manner in which protection is to be provided. For example, cookies must be accepted by the EU user before a site can track an individual. However, in reality most people consent to such cookies, as they want to use the site, thus the 'protection measure of informed consent' is seen more as an annoyance than a protection. Thus, the EU data protection framework must take stronger account of the technologies used, as for example there are other more intrusive measures employed of which the user is not aware and which are currently not regulated by EU data protection laws.

Taking account of the legal interoperability questions that arise on the global level, the challenges created by evolving technologies as well as the application (social sciences) of the law require an interdisciplinary approach to the issues of data protection and privacy. Unfortunately such interdisciplinarity is so far mostly used in the academic research community and not fully reflected in the wider legislative process. Although public consultations are carried out, the law that subsequently follows is negotiated by politicians, thus it can only be hoped that the EU Digital Single Market will take account of the needs of the digital services sector and the EU citizens.

2. PRINCIPLES FOR US-EU DATA FLOW ARRANGEMENTS

Erich SCHWEIGHOFER*

1. INTRODUCTION

We are living in a knowledge and network society.[1] Exchanges of goods and services cannot take place without intensive data transfer. The term 'digital economy' properly describes this change. Data, information and knowledge are major elements of production; figuratively, they are the 'new oil' of the economy. Knowledge is more and more organised in networks,[2] organising trade flows and improving its efficiency, in particular concerning marketing and distribution. In some areas, data, information and knowledge are the hard core of the business.[3]

Much has been written about the transnational exchange of data.[4] The main challenge, however, still remains: data protection is an area of dissent in cyberspace governance. Principles of international law, human rights and state sovereignty govern this area, with often very different regulatory aims: protection of private data and privacy, protection of trade secrets, protection of national security, protection of free speech, etc. It is a challenge to find some *modus vivendi* for this important question. Not all countries have data protection laws; few comply with the EU standards of data protection. The EU has the ambition to establish its data protection law as a de facto standard worldwide.

---

* Arbeitsgruppe Rechtsinformatik, Universität Wien. E-mail: erich.schweighofer@univie.ac.at.

1 A. SAARENPÄÄ, 'The Digital Lawyer. What skills are required of the lawyer in the network society?' in E. SCHWEIGHOFER, F. KUMMER and W. HÖTZENDORFER (eds.), *Co-operation, Proceedings of the 18th International Legal Informatics Symposiom IRIS2015*, OCG Publishers, Wien 2015, p. 73.

2 Cf. proceedings of IRIS2016 on networks: E. SCHWEIGHOFER ET AL., *Networks, Proceedings of the 19th International Conference on Legal Informatics 2016*, OCG Publishers, Wien, 2016; E. SCHWEIGHOFER, 'Von der Wissensrepräsentation zum Wissensmanagement im e-Government' in E. SCHWEIGHOFER ET AL. (eds.), *IT in Recht und Staat, Aktuelle Fragen der Rechtsinformatik 2002*, Verlag Österreich, Wien 2002, pp. 85–94.

3 Cf. *The Economist*, 17 June 2016.

4 F. BOEHM, *Information Sharing and Data Protection in the Area of Freedom, Security and Justice: Towards Harmonised Data Protection Principles for Information Exchange at EU-level*, Springer, 2013; M. ARENAS, P. BARCELÓ, L. LIBKIN and F. MURLAK, *Foundations of Data Exchange*, Cambridge University Press, Cambridge 2014.

Unfortunately, the Union lacks the flexibility required to develop international standards gradually.[5]

Data, information and knowledge are interchangeable terms describing (subjectively) justified true beliefs in different forms and situations. Data protection law typically uses its own abstraction, focusing on data containers and purpose limitation. It has to be emphasised that data as such is a raw material, it constitutes only characters on paper or in electronic media. Data has to be put in a container, e.g. a document, a file, or a data stream, that can be used for a certain purpose. For legal purposes, data can be classified in several – often overlapping – categories and is then subject to different rules: personal data, commercial data, open (or free) data, law enforcement data and intelligence data. Detailed definitions are found in the respective instruments on data protection. These types are dynamic, depending on regulatory goals restricting the use of the otherwise public good knowledge. There is no need to explain the restriction for personal data here. Commercial data refers to the restrictions of IP law for intellectual property (copyright, patents, design models, business secrets, etc.). Law enforcement data is a very broad concept, covering all data needed for crime prevention, criminal justice or risk prevention. Intelligence data is the broadest concept, including all data considered as relevant for national security. For a working legal environment, these data types require precise definitions and use purposes; this is not sufficiently the case at the moment, creating many problems, including in US–EU data transfer.

The framework of international data exchange is based on global commons, territorial sovereignty and human rights. There are no universal treaties, but some soft law instruments. The regulatory dilemma between the goals of free flow of data, information and knowledge, freedom of expression, privacy and data protection, territorial sovereignty with law enforcement and national security has not yet been solved and each dispute reflects this challenge. Data transfer between the US and the EU is just another example of this regulatory dilemma, but by far the most prominent and important one. Besides the public view of an agreement, the instruments – Safe Harbour and now Privacy Shield – are in effect unilateral acts of an EU organ, the European Commission, based on a negotiation process. Thus, the whole process is characterised by two economic superpowers, strong legal systems and very powerful courts trying to maintain the purity of its legal system and not very open to international law.[6] The US

---

5 Cf. C. Kuner, 'The European Union and the Search for an International Data Protection Framework' (2014) 2 *Groningen Journal of International Law* 55–71. For a long time, international lawyers have complained about the EU approach. Refering to the *Kadi* decision of the ECJ, J. Weiler described it as 'withdrawing into one's own constitutional cocoon, isolating the international context and deciding the case exclusively by reference to internal constitutional precepts'. J. Weiler, Editorial (2009) 19(5) *EJIL Talk* <ejiltalk.org/letters-to-the-editorrespond-to-ejil-editorials-vol-195/> accessed 20.08.2016.

6 Cf. Kuner, above n. 5.

and the EU share regulatory goals concerning commercial data, but strongly disagree on data protection and intelligence data. Therefore, any arrangement concerning US–EU data flow is an attempt to fulfil as well as possible different regulatory goals, a nearly impossible task.

This chapter is structured as follows: section 2 analyses the challenge of balancing between sovereignty and international data transfer; section 3 deals with the requirement of essentially equivalent level of data protection requirement; section 4 focuses on data exchange regimes between the US and the EU, in particular treaties, unilateral decisions and estoppel, Safe Harbour and Privacy Shield; section 5 describes the option of a bilateral data transfer treaty; section 6 recommends additional safeguards; conclusions, in section 7, complete this analysis.

2. STATE SOVEREIGNTY AND THE LEGAL FRAMEWORK FOR INTERNATIONAL DATA TRANSFER

Data, information and knowledge belong to everybody and are thus part of global commons.[7] This principle is strongly restricted by territorial jurisdiction and related human rights, in particular concerning data protection, protection of intellectual property, freedom of expression etc. However, it is a recognised principle under international law that a sovereign State has access to all data under its jurisdiction for its regulatory goals, in particular for the purposes of crime prevention, risk prevention and national security. States will use all data accessible under their respective jurisdictions, e.g. processed and stored in its territories or by its nationals. Extraterritorial jurisdiction is restricted to specific areas (mostly US or EU competition policy) but is also often practised extensively (e.g. US Trading with the Enemy Act).[8] Kuner has rightly mentioned that according to new case law of the ECJ, 'any distinction between territorial sovereignty has become meaningless in the context of regulation of international data transfers.'[9] Therefore, a disputed principle of jurisdiction – extraterritorial application of laws – is confronted with the undisputed jurisdictional principle

7 Cf. E. Ostrom, *Governing the Commons: The Evolution of Institutions for Collective Action*, Cambridge University Press, Cambridge 1990; cf. the overview in Wikipedia <https://en.wikipedia.org/wiki/Global_commons> accessed 15.06.2016.

8 The Trading with the Enemy Act of 1917 (40 Stat. 411, enacted 06.09.1917, codified at 12 U.S.C. §§ 95a–95b and 50 U.S.C. App. §§ 1–44), is a United States federal law to restrict trade with countries hostile to the United States.

9 Cf. C. Kuner, 'Reality and Illusion in EU Data Transfer Regulation Post Schrems', Paper No. 14/2016, University of Cambridge, Legal Studies Research Paper Series, March 2016.

of territorial sovereignty, with now over 350 years of practice. Conflicts are inevitable and have to be solved by means of international law.

It is nothing new that subjects and objects of a jurisdiction are continuously changing. Persons also come, stay and leave; goods are imported, processed, sold and exported, the territory is changed by nature and human beings, etc. Data, now mostly digital, is a relatively new focus of regulation (formerly mostly considered as questions of freedom of expression and IP law). Data is transferred in huge quantities at high speed across borders, making control difficult and costly. Borders in cyberspace, with its data highways, are virtual and cannot be established at the frontier. Unlike goods, data transfers rush in nanoseconds to other countries without any border stops. Except for some countries, jurisdiction in cyberspace lies at both ends of the communication. Sometimes, communication lines also are under surveillance, in particular obliging Internet intermediaries.

This change of control from physical sites, e.g. borders to virtual or abstract entities, e.g. relations of subjects, is happening in many cases. International legal theory speaks of the gradual replacement of the territorial system – the so-called Westphalian system – by the liberal system. In this system, the State remains the most powerful regulation-provider for adjudication and enforcement, but the State must share this power with other regulation-providers. The framework for this new system of regulation is set by internationally recognised principles and human rights law. Cyberspace with its Internet governance is the best example of this development. States have to take into account growing regulatory roles of international governmental organisations, international organisations *sui generis* (e.g. ICANN), multi-stakeholder regimes, extraterritorial jurisdiction, international associations, transnational corporations, and, last but not least, the international civil community.[10] Thus, these regulation-providers must cooperate in order to achieve a strong, robust, fair and just regulatory framework for businesses and civil society. In the technical regulation of the Internet, this system works quite efficiently.[11]

International data transfer, like many other regulatory topics in cyberspace, is characterised by a slightly chaotic transitory phase. The territorial approach is still at the centre of regulation. Data should only be transferred to other states if there exists an adequate level of data protection. This rule works well between

---

10 E. Schweighofer, 'A Review of ICANN's Uniform Dispute Resolution Policy' (2001) 6 *Austrian Review of International and European Law* 91–122; E. Schweighofer, 'Accountability in internationalen und europäischen Entscheidungsprozessen', *Jusletter IT*, May 2016.

11 The transition process of the Internet Assigned Numbers Authority (IANA) stewardship function from the US Department of Commerce to the ICANN, which was completed by 30 September 2016, proves the efficiency of this multi-stakeholder model. Cf. <https://www.icann.org/news/announcement-2016-10-01-en> accessed 30.12.2016.

states with similarly high levels of data protection and not much personal data is transferred to other countries not complying with these standards. In cyberspace, these conditions cannot be fulfilled, as data exchange is worldwide. Therefore, flexible solutions are required in this dissent area of international regulation in order to avoid a 'muddling through approach' concerning the applicable but contradictory principles of international law: territorial sovereignty, freedom of speech, freedom of communications, regardless of frontiers, privacy and net neutrality.[12]

A closer look at international instruments supports this view. In recent years, the number of soft law instruments on privacy and data protection has been growing: Privacy Resolution of the UN General Assembly in 2013, UN Human Rights Council, Council of Europe and also growing calls from business and civil society.[13] All these instruments lack precise language on proportionality between territorial sovereignty, crime prevention and criminal justice, national security and privacy. Principles are reaffirmed and – the positive element – privacy is also included. For legal practice, these principles provide guidance but do not change the traditional rules of international law not taking privacy into account.

Data is a global common, but restricted by territorial sovereignty under Art. 2 para. 1 of the Charter of the United Nations. This principle is endorsed in all instruments, supplemented by open textured and broad exception clauses for national security interests. International human rights instruments reflect this position. Data, information and knowledge are protected by human rights regimes (United Nations Covenant on Civil and Political Rights (ICCPR)[14] or the European Convention on Human Rights,[15] etc.), in particular by the right to privacy, freedom of expression, freedom of communication, freedom of

---

12 Art. 3 of EU Regulation 2015/2120 laying down measures concerning open Internet access and amending Directive 2002/22/EC on universal service and users' rights relating to electronic communications networks and services and Regulation (EU) No. 531/2012 on roaming on public mobile communications networks within the Union, [2015] OJ L 310/1. Details are regulated by the Guidelines of BEREC <http://berec.europa.eu/eng/document_register/subject_matter/berec/regulatory_best_practices/guidelines/6160-berec-guidelines-on-the-implementation-by-national-regulators-of-european-net-neutrality-rules> accessed 30.12.2016.

13 Cf. Kuner, above n. 5, with further references. General Assembly Resolution 68/167 (68th session) A/RES/68/167, The right to privacy in the digital age, 18 December 2013 <https://www.un.org/en/ga/68/resolutions.shtml>; United Nations, Office of the High Commissioner of Human Rights, 'The Right to Privacy in the Digital Age' <http://ohchr.org/EN/Issues/DigitalAge/Pages/DigitalAgeIndex.aspx>; cf. Council of Europe, 'Human Rights and Rule of Law' <http://www.coe.int/t/dghl/standardsetting/dataprotection/Default_en.asp> accessed 30.08.2016.

14 M. Nowak, 'U.N. Covenant on Civil and Political Rights: CCPR Commentary', 1993; cf. for an overview and ratification status Wikipedia <https://en.wikipedia.org/wiki/International_Covenant_on_Civil_and_Political_Rights> accessed 15.06.2016.

15 C. Grabenwarter and K. Pabel, *Europäische Menschenrechtskonvention*, 6th ed, C.H. Beck, München 2016.

thought, conscience and religion, etc.[16] The derogation clauses are evidence of the unsolved question of balancing. Article 19 para. 3 of the ICCPR reads: '(a) For respect of the rights or reputations of others; (b) For the protection of national security or of public order *(ordre public)*, or of public health or morals.' In addition to that, derogations are possible in time of public emergency (Art. 4 ICCPR). More detailed is the derogation clause of Art. 8 para. 2 of the ECHR:

> There shall be no interference by a public authority with the exercise of this right except such as is in accordance with the law and is necessary in a democratic society in the interests of national security, public safety or the economic well-being of the country, for the prevention of disorder or crime, for the protection of health or morals, or for the protection of the rights and freedoms of others.[17]

Therefore, in general, international human rights regimes leave this question to the territorial state, subject to more detailed human rights case law that exists only within the EU and the ECHR and will be discussed below.

International trade law supports this statement. Freedom of communication and data exchange, subject to law enforcement and national security, is also protected, in particular the Agreement Establishing the WTO, the Multilateral Agreements on Trade in Goods including the GATT 1994 and the Trade Related Investment Measures (TRIMS), the General Agreement on Trade in Services (GATS) and the Agreement on Trade-Related Aspects of Intellectual Property Rights (TRIPS)[18] and the Constitution and Convention of the International Telecommunications Union (ITU).[19] In WTO law, Art. XX of the GATT contains a list of 'General Exceptions'. Data transfer is not specially mentioned, but it may be included in compliance measures (Art. XX(e)). The communication freedoms of the ITU law are subject to broad exception clauses. The rights of freedom of transborder communication (Art. 33 ITU Convention) and privacy of telecommunications (Art. 37 ITU Convention) are established, but subject to the enforcement of national laws (Art. 35 ITU Convention). Further, it is up to the State to create or close communication lines (Arts. 35 and 36 ITU Convention).

International courts – acting as human rights courts – have gone deeper into this proportionality assessment and tried to end this blockage in favour of effective data protection. Two recent judgments – the ECJ *Schrems* judgment

---

16 Cf. for a more detailed analysis Nowak, above n. 14.

17 In similar wording, the phrase is found in many other instruments.

18 P. Van den Bossche and D. Prévost, *Essential of WTO Law*, Cambridge University Press, Cambridge 2016; A.F. Lowenfeld, *International Economic Law*, Oxford University Press, Oxford 2008.

19 The Constitution and Convention of the ITU are available at <http://www.itu.int/en/history/Pages/ConstitutionAndConvention.aspx> accessed 20.07.2016.

in October 2015[20] and the ECtHR *Szabo* judgment in January 2016[21] – have dealt with this question of balancing between sovereignty, e.g. data collection for purposes of law enforcement and national security and human rights. The ECJ in the *Schrems* case has prohibited bulk access to data without reasons. In para. 94, the Court held that 'legislation permitting the public authorities to have access on a generalised basis to the content of electronic communications must be regarded as compromising the essence of the fundamental right to respect for private life, as guaranteed by Article 7 of the Charter'. Further, in para. 95, the ECJ held that the lack of legal remedies concerning data protection rights violates the 'essence of the fundamental right to effective judicial protection, as enshrined in Article 47 of the Charter'.[22] The position of the ECtHR in the recent *Szabo* judgment is similar:

> (86) Moreover, the Court has held that the question of subsequent notification of surveillance measures is inextricably linked to the effectiveness of remedies and hence to the existence of effective safeguards against the abuse of monitoring powers, since there is in principle little scope for any recourse by the individual concerned unless the latter is advised of the measures taken without his or her knowledge and thus able to challenge their justification retrospectively. As soon as notification can be carried out without jeopardising the purpose of the restriction after the termination of the surveillance measure, information should be provided to the persons concerned ....[23]

3. REQUIREMENT OF ESSENTIALLY EQUIVALENT LEVEL OF DATA PROTECTION

Both the ECJ and the ECtHR refer to territorial jurisdiction for international data transfer. Based on the Charter on Fundamental Rights, the ECJ asked for an essentially equivalent level of data protection. A high level of data protection must be ensured if personal data is transferred to a third country (para. 72).

> The word 'adequate' in Article 25(6) of Directive 95/46 admittedly signifies that a third country cannot be required to ensure a level of protection identical to that guaranteed in the EU legal order. However, as the Advocate General has observed in

---

20 ECJ Case C-362/14, 6 October 2015, EU:C:2015:650.

21 *Szabó and Vissy v. Hungary*, App. no. 37138/14 (ECtHR, 12.01.2016); request for referral to the Grand Chamber pending.

22 Further relevant judgments, also cited by the ECJ, are: *Digital Rights Ireland and Others*, C-293/12 and C-594/12, EU:C:2014:238, para. 39; *Les Verts v. Parliament*, 294/83, EU:C:1986:166, para. 23; *Johnston*, 222/84, EU:C:1986:206, paras. 18 and 19; *Heylens and Others*, 222/86, EU:C:1987:442, para. 14; and *UGT-Rioja and Others*, C-428/06 to C-434/06, EU:C:2008:488, para. 80.

23 *Szabó*, above n. 21. The ECtHR refers to the former judgments in *Weber and Saravia*, App. no. 54934/00, §135; *Roman Zakharov*, App. no. 47143/06, §287.

> point 141 of his Opinion, the term 'adequate level of protection' must be understood as requiring the third country in fact to ensure, by reason of its domestic law or its international commitments, a level of protection of fundamental rights and freedoms that is essentially equivalent to that guaranteed within the European Union by virtue of Directive 95/46 read in the light of the Charter. (para. 73).

Thus, EU Member States and Contracting Parties of the ECHR are bound to respect a high level of data protection in their relations with third countries. Kuner rightly mentioned that EU data protection law has to extend globally.[24] Considering the strong disagreement on data protection worldwide, this ruling of the ECJ establishes a very high threshold on international data transfer that cannot easily be achieved in practice, in particular with a superpower like the US.

If there is not a data transfer between intelligence agencies – not covered by EU law – or a data transfer between law enforcement agencies, the general regime of international data exchange applies. This regime is also applicable for access of intelligence agencies to such data in third countries or transferred from them, giving the EU law a strong extraterritorial effect.

To assess the adequacy of data protection, the level of data protection in respective countries, e.g. principles, rights and duties and redress procedures, must be compared and assessed. According to the ECJ, the level of protection must be essentially equivalent to the standards of the EU Fundamental Rights Charter and its implementing instruments,[25] now the Directive 95/46[26] and from 2018 onwards, the new General Data Protection Regulation.[27] Article 25 of the Data Protection Directive, in particular para. 6, defines the adequacy requirement as follows:

> The Commission may find, in accordance with the procedure referred to in Article 31(2), that a third country ensures an adequate level of protection within the meaning of paragraph 2 of this Article, by reason of its domestic law or of the international commitments it has entered into, particularly upon conclusion of the negotiations referred to in paragraph 5, for the protection of the private lives and basic freedoms and rights of individuals.

This provision was clarified by the ECJ in the *Schrems* decision as requiring an essentially equivalent level of protection.[28]

---

24 Kuner, above n. 9, p. 5.

25 *Schrems*, above n. 20, para. 73.

26 Directive 95/46/EC of the European Parliament and of the Council of 24 October 1995 on the protection of individuals with regard to the processing of personal data and on the free movement of such data, [1995] OJ L 281/31.

27 Regulation (EU) 2016/679 of the European Parliament and of the Council of 27 April 2016 on the protection of natural persons with regard to the processing of personal data and on the free movement of such data, and repealing Directive 95/46/EC (General Data Protection Regulation), [2016] OJ L 119/1.

28 *Schrems*, above n. 20, recital 73.

4. US–EU DATA TRANSFER REGIMES

Both unions are based on the rule of law and respect for human rights. The problems lie in their different regulatory goals on data protection. The US approach is characterised by territorial privacy and specific rules.[29] As described above, the EU is obliged to apply its data protection law worldwide. This goal is nearly impossible to achieve, given the very different standards on data protection worldwide. Thus, instruments with the highest flexibility of regulation have to be used to achieve a workable standard. The main instrument for balancing different regulatory aims is still the international treaty.[30] Human rights instruments permit interference in fundamental rights, but it must be in the form of a law. International treaties comply with this requirement. The treaty offers also the advantage of parliamentary approval and thus highly authoritative interpretation of fundamental rights that can later be accepted by human rights courts. Regulatory fine-tuning of principles and rules is best placed with parliaments rather than courts.

The situation is further complicated as international data transfer between the US and the EU distinguishes three different data categories: law enforcement data (now Directive 2016/680),[31] intelligence data (not covered by EU law) and the non-specified personal data (former Safe Harbour, now Privacy Shield). It is evident that these data categories overlap, but they establish different and legitimate purposes for data exchange. The access of police authorities or intelligence agencies to such data was a major point in the negotiations. Data transferred to other countries is then subject to territorial sovereignty and states have access to this data for law enforcement and national security. As the ECJ required a respect of data protection also for these purposes, the Privacy Shield has to address this question, too.

The Convention for the Protection of Individuals with regard to Automatic Processing of Personal Data[32] remains mostly restricted to the contracting parties of the Council of Europe.[33] Neither the US nor the EU are parties to

---

29 Article 29 Group, Working Paper 15, 26.01.1999 (5092/97/EN/final).

30 Cf. I. Brownlie, *Principles of Public International Law*, 7th ed., Oxford University Press, Oxford 2008.

31 Directive (EU) 2016/680 of the European Parliament and of the Council of 27 April 2016 on the protection of natural persons with regard to the processing of personal data by competent authorities for the purposes of the prevention, investigation, detection or prosecution of criminal offences or the execution of criminal penalties, and on the free movement of such data, and repealing Council Framework Decision 2008/977/JHA, [2016] OJ L 119/89.

32 European Treaty Series No. 108. Signed in Strasbourg, 28.01.1981, with additional protocol. The Recommendation No. R (87) 15 of the Committee of Ministers to Member States regulating the use of personal data in the police sector is a non-binding but influential instrument in law enforcement.

33 Status of ratifications and accessions: <http://www.coe.int/de/web/conventions/full-list/-/conventions/treaty/108/signatures?p_auth=IfpDjAbU> accessed 15.06.2016.

this convention. Therefore, not even a regional treaty framework is possible at the moment. For a bilateral solution, the European Commission would need a special mandate not even discussed so far due to the lack of interest on the part of the US for a general data treaty. The option of international treaties for solving the different perception on data protection was chosen only for law enforcement. The principle of self-regulation is considered as very important in US trade law and also applied to data protection. Thus, a treaty was out of scope in the negotiations for both Safe Harbour as well as Privacy Shield. This increases the compliance level for an arrangement, as it not only complies with EU fundamental rights but also with the much more detailed EU data protection law.

Thus, the European Commission decision on the adequacy of data protection in third countries was the remaining option for general data. With the *Schrems* judgment, the ECJ has set a strong corset for such an arrangement. The principle of essentially equivalent levels of data protection has to be respected, requiring a long and detailed analysis of the legal situation in a third country. After checking the facts, the Commission can adopt a unilateral decision of adequacy. It is evident that some negotiation process is required for getting sufficient details for assessing adequacy. As discussed below, a negotiation process does not give the same flexibility and has only some international protection under the principle of estoppel.

The difficulty of the adequacy instrument is highlighted by looking at the list of countries. The only non-European countries are Argentina, Canada (commercial sector only), Israel, New Zealand and Uruguay.[34] Normally, only countries with a similar data protection law are eligible for an adequacy decision. As this is not the case in the US, special frameworks were required: first the Safe Harbour Agreement of 26 July 2000[35] and now the new framework for trans-Atlantic data transfers, the EU–US Privacy Shield Agreement of 12 July 2016.[36] The Agreement is in fact the result of a negotiation process, but formally only a unilateral decision of the European Commission.

4.1. INTELLIGENCE DATA

The situation in the intelligence sector was highly unsatisfactory due to non-compliance with data protection law. Intelligence data was covered by the exception of national security and considered 'beyond restriction of data

---

34 Cf. status of adequacy decisions: <http://ec.europa.eu/justice/data-protection/international-transfers/adequacy/index_en.htm> accessed 15.06.2016.

35 Commission Decision 2000/520, [2000] OJ L 215/7.

36 Commission Implementing Decision (EU) 2016/1250 of 12 July 2016 pursuant to Directive 95/46/EC of the European Parliament and of the Council on the adequacy of the protection provided by the EU–US Privacy Shield (notified under document C(2016) 4176), [2016] OJ L 207/1.

protection'. Bulk access to personal data without proper legal safeguards and effective judicial protection were and are still common. International cooperation agreements exist, but only at the administrative level and not published in official journals.[37] Since the Snowden revelations, strong suspicions exist concerning intelligence services collecting and analysing all data available without much respect for human rights.[38] The *Schrems* judgment has defined the conditions of data processing also for intelligence agencies. A recent study of the EU Fundamental Rights Agency[39] on surveillance confirms the sovereign right of states but recalls that human rights standards have to be properly respected. Thus, a legislative framework with a strong legal determination and proper oversight and redress procedures is required. The access of intelligence services to data does not easily comply with these standards, as applicable rules are often vague and oversight mechanisms do not work properly. In international data transfer, the EU has to insist that third countries comply with this requirement. Concerning Member States, intelligence is part of national security that is in general out of scope for the EU (Arts. 346 and 347 TFEU). It is a strange fact and argumentative weakness that the European Commission has to insist that this principle is respected by third countries, yet can only recommend better compliance by the Member States.

4.2. LAW ENFORCEMENT DATA

Interestingly, the exchange of law enforcement data has followed the treaty approach for a long time. Crime prevention, risk prevention and criminal justice are legitimate reasons for data exchange and data processing. However, the purpose of data use and appropriate procedures must be established as acceptable to both parties. In law enforcement, a mix of multi- and bilateral treaties establishes this framework. The INTERPOL Convention is the basic instrument, supplemented by many regional and bilateral agreements.[40] After 30 years of functioning without a solid legal document as its foundation, and following a series of less uniform statutes since 1923, the constitution of the organisation was adopted in 1956.[41] In Europe, Europol, Schengen and Prüm, and the new Police Data Protection

37 Cf. as a main example for this practice J. Foschepoth, *Überwachtes Deutschland. Post- und Telefonüberwachung in der alten Bundesrepublik*, Vandenhoeck & Ruprecht, Göttingen 2013.

38 Cf. D. Lyon, *Surveillance after Snowden*, Polity Press, Malden, MA 2015; for an overview, cf. Wikipedia: <https://en.wikipedia.org/wiki/Edward_Snowden> accessed 15.06.2016.

39 European Union Agency for Fundamental Rights, *Surveillance by intelligence services: fundamental rights safeguards and remedies in the EU, Mapping Member States' legal frameworks*, Office for Publications, Luxembourg 2015.

40 E. Schweighofer and A. Wiebe (eds.), *International rules on data exchange between police/security authorities*, OCG Publishers, Vienna 2016.

41 Cf. INTERPOL's official website: <https://www.interpol.int/Public/ICPO/LegalMaterials/constitution/Default.asp> accessed 20.06.2016.

Directive 2016/680, are the main instruments. The European Police Office (Europol) is the EU law enforcement agency that was originally established by the Europol Convention 1998 and is now based on Regulation (EU) 2016/794.[42] It has no executive powers in the Member States but supports national law enforcement authorities, mainly by exchanging information including personal data. In 1985, five EU Member States signed the Schengen Agreement in an act of enhanced cooperation that was transformed into the Convention Implementing the Schengen Agreement of 14 June 1985 (CISA).[43] The Prüm Convention enables Member States to access other Member States' databases directly, including DNA, fingerprint and vehicle registration data.[44] The Visa Information System (VIS) is a system for the exchange of data concerning visas between the Schengen states.[45] EURODAC is a central database for the storage and processing of fingerprint data of certain third-country nationals.[46] There are two notable regional instruments concerning the Nordic countries including PTN (Politi Toll Norden), providing for cooperation between the police and customs authorities, formalised in 1984, and the Police Cooperation Convention for South East Europe of 2006. Supporting the increasing cooperation between police authorities on multilateral, European and bilateral levels, bilateral agreements, also covering data exchange, have been concluded. The main importance of such treaties lies on the one hand in the data exchange with third countries (e.g. the US) and on the other hand in matters not within the scope of data exchange, e.g. joint operations, cross-border hot pursuit, etc.

Several bilateral law enforcement treaties exist for data exchange between the US and the EU authorities, in particular the Umbrella Agreement, the PNR Agreement and the SWIFT Agreement. In addition, the Agreement between the US and the European Police Office of 6 December 2001,[47] the Agreement on extradition between the EU and the US of 25 June 2003,[48] the Agreement

---

42 Regulation (EU) 2016/794 of the European Parliament and of the Council of 11 May 2016 on the European Union Agency for Law Enforcement Cooperation (Europol) and replacing and repealing Council Decisions 2009/371/JHA, 2009/934/JHA, 2009/935/JHA, 2009/936/JHA and 2009/968/JHA, [2016] OJ L 135/53.

43 Established by Regulation (EC) No. 1987/2006 of the European Parliament and of the Council of 20 December 2006 on the establishment, operation and use of the second generation Schengen Information System (SIS II), [2006] OJ L 381/4.

44 The Prüm Convention was transformed into a European Council Decision (2008/615/JHA). Cf. P. Schaar, 'Datenaustausch und Datenschutz im Vertrag von Prüm' (2000) 30(11) *DuD* 691–693.

45 Council Decision 2004/512/EC of 8 June 2004 establishing the Visa Information System (VIS), [2004] OJ L 213/5.

46 Council Regulation (EC) No. 2725/2000 of 11 December 2000 concerning the establishment of 'Eurodac' for the comparison of fingerprints for the effective application of the Dublin Convention, [2000] OJ L 316/1.

47 The Agreement is available at <https://www.europol.europa.eu/sites/default/files/flags/united_states_of_america.pdf> accessed 20.07.2016.

48 [2003] OJ L 181/27.

between the European Community and the US on intensifying and broadening the Agreement on customs cooperation and mutual assistance in customs matters to include cooperation on container security and related matters of 24 April 2004,[49] and the Agreement on mutual legal assistance between the EU and the US of 25 June 2003[50] are all relevant to data exchange.

In September 2015, the finalisation of the Agreement between the US and the EU on the Protection of Personal Information relating to the Prevention, Investigation, Detection, and Prosecution of Criminal Offences (the so-called 'Umbrella Agreement') was announced, putting in place a comprehensive high-level data protection framework for EU–US law enforcement cooperation,[51] e.g. all personal data exchanged between the EU and the US for the purpose of prevention, detection, investigation and prosecution of criminal offences, including terrorism. It is not sufficient space here to go into the details of this Umbrella Agreement. It regulates purpose and use limitations, onward transfer, quality and integrity of information, information security, data breach notification, records, retention period, special categories of personal information, accountability, automated decisions, access and rectification, administrative redress, judicial redress, effective oversight, cooperation between oversight authorities and joint review. The 'Umbrella Agreement' does not cover the access of law enforcement authorities to data transmitted to the US to private parties.[52] The required modification of the Judicial Redress Act became public law on 24 February 2016.[53] The European Commission submitted a proposal for signing on 29 April 2016.[54] Both the European Parliament and the European Data Protection Supervisor have asked for improvements of the draft agreement.[55]

---

49 [2004] OJ L 304/34.

50 [2003] OJ L 181/34.

51 European Commission Fact Sheet, 'Questions and Answers on the EU–US data protection "Umbrella agreement"', Brussels, 08.09.2015, <http://europa.eu/rapid/press-release_MEMO-15-5612_de.htm> accessed 15.06.2016.

52 However, it could have been easily extended in this direction if US Congress had been willing to do so. That, unfortunately, was not the case. It seems to fulfil the legal remedies requirements of the *Schrems* case. The judicial review and the enforceability of rights would provide sufficient safeguards for the data protection principles.

53 Legislative process in the US 114th Congress <https://www.congress.gov/bill/114th-congress/house-bill/1428/all-actions> accessed 15.06.2016.

54 Proposal for a Council Decision on the signing, on behalf of the European Union, of an Agreement between the United States of America and the European Union on the protection of personal information relating to the prevention, investigation, detection, and prosecution of criminal offenses, COM(2016) 238 final.

55 European Data Protection Supervisor, Opinion 1/2016, Preliminary Opinion on the agreement between the United States of America and the European Union on the protection of personal information relating to the prevention, investigation, detection and prosecution of criminal offences, 12 February 2016, <https://secure.edps.europa.eu/EDPSWEB/webdav/site/mySite/shared/Documents/Consultation/Opinions/2016/16-02-12_EU-US_Umbrella_Agreement_EN.pdf> accessed 30.08.2016. The Legal Service of the European Parliament issued a critical opinion on 14.01.2016 (SJ-0784/15).

The Agreement between the US and the EU on the use and transfer of passenger name records to the United States Department of Homeland Security (PNR Agreement) of 14 December 2011[56] establishes the legal framework for PNR transfers to the US. It places limits on the amount of data to be transferred (no sensitive data) and restricts its use to terrorism and crimes that are or may be linked to terrorism. Data can be retained for five years in the active system. Data can be stored inactive and depersonalised for a further 10 years.

The Agreement between the EU and the US on the transfer of financial messaging data of 27 July 2010[57] ('SWIFT Agreement') allows the US Treasury Department access to the data of the Society for Worldwide Interbank Financial Telecommunication (SWIFT) in connection with its Terrorist Financing Tracking Program (TFTP).

Without question, international data transfer for law enforcement purposes is of the highest interest for governments, but it must also comply with human rights. Treaties are the obvious solution. The US and the EU have taken great efforts to establish a comprehensive and working legal environment. This is not the place to discuss issues of compliance and improvement.[58] These treaty regimes have been checked repeatedly in courts, leading to subsequent improvements. Therefore, this solution seems to be much more appropriate than the cumbersome and inflexible adequacy arrangement.

4.3. US–EU ADEQUACY ARRANGEMENTS: FROM SAFE HARBOUR TO PRIVACY SHIELD

The Safe Harbour Agreement 2000 was the first attempt to find a compromise. A set of fine principles was adopted that had to be implemented in practice, mostly based on the goodwill of parties and improving oversight of data protection authorities. The Safe Harbour Agreement was reviewed several times, in particular in 2004[59] and in 2008.[60] It became evident that, while the principles could work, they did not work in practice, as Safe Harbour was not

56 [2012] OJ L 215/5.

57 [2010] OJ L 195/5.

58 Cf. Schweighofer and Wiebe, above n. 40. Observation of the purpose limitation principle and effective judicial protection remain open challenges.

59 J. Dhont, M.V.P. Asinari and Y. Poullet, 'Safe Harbour Decision Implementation Study, at the request of the European Commission', Internal Market DG, Namur 2004, <http://ec.europa.eu/justice/policies/privacy/docs/studies/safe-harbour-2004_en.pdf> accessed 15.06.2016.

60 Ch. Connolly, *The US Safe Harbor – Fact or Fiction?* Galexia, Pyrmont 2008, <http://www.galexia.com/public/research/assets/safe_harbor_fact_or_fiction_2008/safe_harbor_fact_or_fiction.pdf> accessed 15.06.2016; Ch. Connolly, 'EU/US Safe Harbor – Effectiveness of the Framework in relation to National Security Surveillance', Speaking Notes, 07.10.2013, <http://www.europarl.europa.eu/document/activities/cont/201310/20131008ATT72504/20131008ATT72504EN.pdf> accessed 15.06.2016.

taken sufficiently serious, either by the American firms or by the European data protection authorities, who were not using their powers. Thus, Safe Harbour was a non-working arrangement that merely served to buy time for some 16 years.

The invalid Safe Harbor Agreement did not contain limitations on access to data by law enforcement agencies, and mostly excluded the applicability of EU data protection law. Access could be granted to the 'extent necessary to meet national security, public interest, or law enforcement requirements' and 'by statute, government regulation, or case-law that create conflicting obligations or explicit authorisations'. This provision was far too broad and ineffective.

Considering this difficulty and also later assessments, as described in two Communications of the Commission,[61] the ECJ was easily able to establish non-compliance with EU human rights law and declare the Safe Harbour Arrangement to be invalid. The difficult international legal framework was not considered in the *Schrems* case. Thus, extraterritorial application of EU law for data transfer between the US and the EU remains to be achieved. US legislation allowing public authorities, e.g. police authorities and intelligence services, access to the content of electronic communities has to respect the essence of the right to privacy under Art. 7 of the EU Fundamental Rights Charter.

The new decision on the Privacy Shield was agreed between the US and the EU on 12 July 2016. It is a complex document with only six articles, but 155 recitals and seven annexes: ANNEX I: Letter from US Secretary of Commerce Penny Pritzker; *Annex 1: Letter from Under Secretary for International Trade Stefan Selig;* ANNEX II: EU–US Privacy Shield Principles, *Annex I: Arbitral Model;* ANNEX III: Letter from US Secretary of State John Kerry, *Annex A: EU–US Privacy Shield Ombudsperson Mechanism;* ANNEX IV: Letter from Federal Trade Commission Chairwoman Edith Ramirez; ANNEX V: Letter from US Secretary of Transportation Anthony Foxx; ANNEX VI: Letter from General Counsel Robert Litt, Office of the Director of National Intelligence; ANNEX VII: Letter from Deputy Assistant Attorney General Bruce Swartz, US Department of Justice. In its fact sheets, the European Commission considers as main improvements the stronger obligations on companies and robust enforcement, clear conditions, limitations and oversight of access of public authorities to personal data transferred under the new arrangement, a redress possibility in the area of national intelligence through an ombudsman mechanism and effective protection with several redress options (complaints, alternative dispute resolution, complaints via the data protection authorities to the US Department of Commerce and the Federal Trade Commission and, as a last resort, an enforceable arbitration

---

61 Communication from the Commission to the European Parliament and the Council, Rebuilding Trust in EU–US Data Flows, COM(2013) 846 fin and Communication from the Commission to the European Parliament and the Council on the Functioning of the Safe Harbour from the Perspective of EU Citizens and Companies established in the EU, COM(2013) 847 fin.

mechanism). The arrangement is to be reviewed annually.[62] Comparing the final version with its draft of 29 February 2016, the Commission has worked very hard to improve the draft version, taking into account the criticism from the Article 29 Committee and the European Parliament.

The Privacy Shield Agreement better respects the purpose limitation principle, e.g. defining a list of crime prevention, risk prevention and national security tasks allowing access by law enforcement agencies to this data. As mentioned above, a right to access and rectification should be included. All these rules require scope for judicial review. Considering present multilateral and bilateral treaty practice concerning data exchange between law enforcement agencies, it will be challenging to respect the purpose limitation principle. Only if the ombudsman and the data protection authorities develop a strong practice will the ECJ consider this practice sufficient. Much depends on the US reducing its use of bulk collection of data.

The draft document was immediately the subject of many comments and much criticism, in particular Opinion 01/2006 of the Article 29 Working Party of 13 April 2016[63] and the European Data Protection Supervisor in its Opinion 4/2016 of 30 May 2016.[64] Both recognised the improvement in the US regulation regarding the access of police and security agencies and intelligence and secret services to data. The draft Privacy Shield did not include all the essential procedural guarantees (necessity, proportionality, independent legal authority, etc.). Further, the self-regulatory principle is questioned and a US law is called for in the medium term for 'substantial equivalence'. A more practical problem concerns the entry into force of the new General Data Protection Regulation in May 2018, as some provisions have to be modified.

The European Commission had to respect the 'new comitology rules' for adopting this decision pursuant to Art. 291 TFEU and Regulation No. 182/2011.[65] The Commission was assisted by the Article 31 Committee under the examination procedure. A qualified majority was required in favour of the Commission's proposed measure that was established in its decision of 8 July 2016.

The Privacy Shield decision entered into force on 12 July 2016. Pending another annulment decision of the ECJ, this decision provides a basis for data

---

62 European Commission Fact Sheet, 'EU–U.S. Privacy Shield: Frequently Asked Questions', MEMO 16-2462, Brussels, 12.07.2016, MEMO-16-434, Brussels, 29.02.2016.

63 Cf. Opinions and recommendations of the Article 29 Working Party <http://ec.europa.eu/justice/data-protection/article-29/documentation/opinion-recommendation/index_en.htm> accessed 15.06.2016.

64 Cf. homepage of the European Data Protection Supervisor <https://secure.edps.europa.eu/EDPSWEB/edps/site/mySite/OpinionsC> accessed: 15.06.2016.

65 Regulation (EU) No. 182/2011 of the European Parliament and of the Council of 16 February 2011 laying down the rules and general principles concerning mechanisms for control by Member States of the Commission's exercise of implementing powers, [2011] OJ L 55/13.

exchange between the US and the EU. However, the adequacy decision option cannot deliver the required flexibility of data exchange between the US and the EU. The rule of data sovereignty as contained in EU human rights law has to be respected in case of an adequacy decision. The criticisms of the Article 29 Working Party are evident: lack of essential procedural guarantees (necessity, proportionality, independent legal authority etc.) and still possible extensive bulk collection and data retention. Thus, the Privacy Shield decision will be challenged in court very soon and may also be annulled. The Commission has arrogated a regulatory flexibility (very likely due to US demands) in order to achieve a solution that cannot be justified by the authorisations of the Data Protection Directive or the new General Data Protection Regulation.

4.4. PROTECTION OF THE NEGOTIATION PROCESS BY THE ESTOPPEL PRINCIPLE

Concerning the exchange of data between commercial and private entities, a negotiation process with a unilateral decision has been chosen, first for the Safe Harbour decision and now for the Privacy Shield.[66] This process as such is protected by the principle of estoppel, in particular considering the correspondence, as it is has happened in advance of the Safe Harbour Decision between 1998 and 2000, between the Commission and the US Department of Commerce, and now the Privacy Shield negotiations between 2013 and 2016. The principle of estoppel protects legitimate expectations of a state establishing behaviour in trusting in good faith on the conduct of another state or supranational organisation.[67] In the negotiation process it was clear that no unilateral decision but a bilateral solution was sought. The EU has established practice, on which the United States can rely in good faith. The Privacy Shield contains seven annexes that are mostly an exchange of letters between US authorities and the European Commission. It should be checked in more detail if the European Commission has established a practice that is now part of international law and thus has to be taken into account also by the other Community organs. In the *Schrems* case, neither the parties,

---

66 A. Genz, *Datenschutz in Europa und den USA: Eine rechtsvergleichende Untersuchung unter besonderer Berücksichtigung der Safe-Harbor-Lösung*, Deutscher Universitäts-Verlag, Wiesbaden 2004, p. 158; W. Hötzendorfer and E. Schweighofer, 'Safe Harbor in der „Post-Snowden-Ära"', in D. Lück-Schneider, T. Gordon, S. Kaiser, J. von Lucke, E. Schweighofer, M.A. Wimmer and M.G. Löhe (eds.), *Gemeinsam Electronic Government ziel(gruppen)gerecht gestalten und organisieren, Gemeinsame Fachtagung Verwaltungsinforamtik (FTVI) und Fachtagung Rechtsinformatik (FTRI) 2014, 20.-21. März 2014 in Berlin*, GI-Edition Lecture Notes in Informatics, 2014, pp. 125–136.

67 T. Cottier and J.P. Müller, 'Estoppel', in R. Wolfrum (ed.), *Max Planck Encyclopedia of Public International Law*, Oxford University Press, Oxford 2007.

the Advocate General nor the Court has raised this issue as access of intelligence agencies to data was expressly excluded from the Safe Harbour Agreement. In a very likely case on the Privacy Shield, this question cannot be ignored as the legal relevance of the complex negotiation process has to be checked in order to comply with international law. The Privacy Shield is an attempt to solve the dilemma of different sovereign perceptions in finding a compromise respecting both views. The new Privacy Shield covers extensively the access of intelligence agencies to data. Contrary to widely held perceptions, the legal framework of the US Government on intelligence services is more developed than its European counterparts, but also confirms the difficulties of effective oversight. Therefore, the negotiation process should be a major topic of judicial review if the Privacy Shield meets the requirements of the ECJ's *Schrems* decision.

5. AN INTERNATIONAL TREATY AS A BETTER SOLUTION FOR THIS DILEMMA?

A much better solution would seem to be an agreement between the US and the EU allowing much more flexibility between different regulatory approaches, as parliaments have much more authority for interference in human rights. The US Government is not willing to change its laws but offers only administrative guarantees. The EU cannot be flexible but has to assess if the US privacy situation is adequate. This dilemma can be solved with a treaty.

The ECJ stated in the *Schrems* judgment that effectiveness of data protection must be demonstrated if the legal framework can be considered as essentially equivalent. The still broad options of extensive bulk collection and data retention are under stronger legal scrutiny with the USA Freedom Act.[68] The Commission has assessed the oversight and redress procedures concerning the US intelligence community (recitals 92–110).

However, it remains to be seen whether the ECJ will accept this solution, considering its strict position on extensive bulk collection of data without proper authorisation and essential procedural guarantees. The adequacy decision describes in detail the judicial and administrative oversight and redress procedures: PPD-28, compliance staff, privacy officers, Inspector Generals, the Office of the Director of National Intelligence (ODNI) Civil Liberties and Privacy Office, the Privacy and Civil Liberties Oversight Board (PCLOB), the President's Intelligence Oversight Board, the House and Senate Intelligence and Judiciary Committees with oversight responsibilities regarding all US foreign intelligence

---

68 *U*niting and *S*trengthening *A*merica by *F*ulfilling *R*ights and *E*nding *E*avesdropping, *D*ragnet-collection and *O*nline *M*onitoring Act of 2 June 2016 <https://www.congress.gov/114/bills/hr2048/BILLS-114hr2048enr.pdf> accessed 20.07.2016.

activities, including US signals intelligence, the Foreign Intelligence Surveillance Court (FISC) and the Foreign Intelligence Surveillance Court of Review (FISCR) authorising surveillance programmes such as PRISM and UPSTREAM. The various and complex redress procedures are supported and facilitated with the establishment of an ombudsman on the US site and stronger control rights of the data protection authorities of the Member States. In comparison to Safe Harbour, the Privacy Shield provides extensive (mostly) administrative authorisation and redress procedures. Two weaknesses have to be observed. First, the procedures are established by administrative order and can be easily changed by the next administration. Secondly, the efficiency of the procedures must be checked with scrutiny after sufficient practice for assessment is available. Certainly, the Privacy Shield does not offer a quick 'rubber stamp' solution for data exchange between the US and the EU. However, the same can be said of the Safe Harbour Agreement. A final assessment depends on a working compliance infrastructure that will be checked by EU data protection authorities and the ECJ: it is evident the ECJ cannot accept this solution as long as extensive practice does not prove efficient compliance with EU law. The lack of sufficient guarantees for a lasting system, e.g. a law or an international agreement, can be overcome only by strong practice. Contrary to other statements,[69] in our opinion it is too early to decide about this oversight and redress system unless its ineffectiveness has been proven.

An international agreement can solve most of these questions: acceptance of different regulatory principles, data protection rules, procedural guarantees and access of US intelligence services to data. EU data protection law and US privacy rules and its different implementation (data protection authority versus self-regulation) will be recognised at the same level. Further, the procedural guarantees can be placed at a much higher level: from administrative law to US federal treaty law and thus having a binding nature. As such, they comply with the requirements of the ECJ and the Article 29 Working Party. Conceptual differences can also be handled (e.g. on the different notions of data). As access on a generalised basis to the content of electronic communications compromises the essence of the fundamental right to respect for private life, sufficient constraints and safeguards must be given by the US authorities. The US model of oversight of intelligence agencies can be complemented by an ombudsman solution on the part of non-US data subjects if the role is based on a treaty and not an administrative decision.

However, the chances for such an international agreement seem minimal, as the US Government is unwilling to change its position on data protection regulation. The principle of estoppel and extensive practice of effective compliance

69 For many, see the homepage of Max Schrems: <http://www.europe-v-facebook.org/DE/de.html> accessed 20.07.2016.

can solve this problem, establishing some form of customary law. However, this was also the goal of Safe Harbour, and that did not work out properly. It remains to be seen if the hopes of the EU and US negotiators will be fulfilled.

6. USE OF DEROGATIONS AS ADDITIONAL SAFEGUARDS FOR DATA EXCHANGE DUE TO THE INSUFFICIENTLY SOLVED DATA EXCHANGE QUESTION

In its statement on 6 October 2015, the European Commission explicitly referred to the derogations of Art. 26 of Directive 95/46. It is up to the data protection authorities to check the legal framework of data transfer. The derogations in Art. 26 of the Data Protection Directive also reflect that data are first of all data of persons and then governed by the principle of territorial sovereignty. Thus, in general, data subjects can consent to any form of data transfer. However, states may restrict data transfer for reasons of national security but also for safeguarding principles of good faith. According to the opinion of Thilo Weichert, the former Data Protection Commissioner of Schleswig-Holstein, consent to bulk investigation by US intelligence agencies violates the principle of good faith of section 138 of the German Civil Code.[70]

Article 26 of the Data Protection Directive allows data transfer, if

> (a) the data subject has given his consent unambiguously to the proposed transfer; or (b) the transfer is necessary for the performance of a contract between the data subject and the controller or the implementation of precontractual measures taken in response to the data subject's request; or (c) the transfer is necessary for the conclusion or performance of a contract concluded in the interest of the data subject between the controller and a third party; or (d) the transfer is necessary or legally required on important public interest grounds, or for the establishment, exercise or defence of legal claims; or (e) the transfer is necessary in order to protect the vital interests of the data subject; or (f) the transfer is made from a register which according to laws or regulations is intended to provide information to the public and which is open to consultation either by the public in general or by any person who can demonstrate legitimate interest, to the extent that the conditions laid down in law for consultation are fulfilled in the particular case.

Considering the inadequately resolved issue of access of intelligence services to EU data, stronger commitments on the part of US data importers to respect EU data protection principles are wise. Standard contractual clauses, binding

---

[70] *Netzwerk Datenschutzepertise* <http://www.netzwerk-datenschutzexpertise.de/dokument/folgen-der-safe-harbor-entscheidung-des-eugh-privacy-shield> accessed 15.06.2016.

corporate rules, contract, consent, important public interests and vital interests of the data subject are presenting legitimate grounds for data exchange. Regulation and enforcement are established at the data importer–data exporter level. Both have to agree on such rules, taking into account the EU data protection principles. Thus, it seems to be a good solution in encouraging new special contractual clauses or binding corporate rules that should regulate data protection relations. Such rules should contain the EU data protection principles, rules on liability and redress procedures. This solution is also feasible if an appropriate standard contract is available that has to be added to each contractual relationship with a longer duration and extended data transfer between the US and the EU. A major principle is that the data transfer is governed by the rules of the data exporter.

The main problem remains the access of US authorities to private data. The data importer has to give an assurance that no local laws exist that will have a substantial adverse effect on the provided guarantees. At present, such guarantees cannot be given in good faith, as extensive access of US law enforcement bodies still seem to exist. It is disputable whether the new Privacy Shield Agreement solves this question. Thus, even standard contractual clauses or binding corporate rules contain an element of insecurity. However, the data exporter has done everything at his disposal in limiting possible damage to the data subject. These facts have to be taken into account in questions of enforcement and possible fines.

7. CONCLUSIONS

The importance of the data flows between the US and the EU, two major economic blocs, requires a working data protection regime. Due to different data protection standards and the invalidation of the Safe Harbour Agreement, a new solution with the Privacy Shield has been established. As this arrangement is subject to strong criticism and cannot comply with all the regulatory requirements of the ECJ concerning data protection, a treaty is proposed that can solve this regulatory issue on privacy, e.g. reasons of data transfer, limited access of US authorities to such data and sufficient legal remedies. However, chances are minimal for achieving this goal. Until then, it is recommended to have additional safeguards for data transfer, in particular consent, standard contractual clauses and binding corporate rules. The problem as such is not solved, but the liability of the data exporter is minimised, as he has done everything possible to respect EU data protection law.

3. THE ROLE OF PROPORTIONALITY IN ASSESSING TRANS-ATLANTIC FLOWS OF PERSONAL DATA

David LINDSAY*

1. INTRODUCTION

Security and law enforcement agencies have become reliant on the mass collection and analysis of data, especially personal data or potentially personal data, as an investigative tool, and often as a tool of first recourse.[1] The mass collection and processing of data is, moreover, notionally independent of the geographical or legal jurisdiction in which the data originates. These evolving practices give rise to considerable difficulties in determining the appropriate balance between national security and law enforcement objectives, on the one hand, and the protection of fundamental rights, on the other. Under the law of the European Union (the EU), the principle of proportionality is the single most important legal concept in establishing the balance between public interests, especially the interest in national security, and the fundamental rights to privacy and data privacy.[2] There are, nevertheless, significant complexities – both conceptual and practical – and unresolved issues, in satisfactorily applying this contested principle to rapidly changing social and technological circumstances, such as surveillance practices. These difficulties are exacerbated where surveillance

---

* Associate Professor, Monash University, Australia. E-mail: david.lindsay@monash.edu. This chapter was improved significantly by very helpful comments from Professor Annalisa Ciampi, University of Verona, Professor Ian Brown, Oxford Internet Institute, and two anonymous referees. All errors and oversights remain my responsibility. So far as possible, the chapter is accurate to end of June 2016.

1 See, for example, PRIVACY and CIVIL LIBERTIES OVERSIGHT BOARD (PCLOB), *Report on the Surveillance Program Operated Pursuant to Section 702 of the Foreign Intelligence Surveillance Act*, 2 July 2014; D. LYON, *Surveillance After Snowden*, Polity Press, Cambridge 2015.

2 As Tranberg has observed: 'The key to deciding the extent of a person's right to protection in connection with the processing of personal data has proved to lie largely in the ECJ's application of the basic principle of proportionality': C.B. TRANBERG, 'Proportionality and Data Protection in the Case Law of the European Court of Justice' (2011) 1(4) *International Data Privacy Law* 239.

practices cut across legal borders, including where data is transferred from one legal territory to another, such as occurs with trans-Atlantic flows of personal data.

In *Maximillian Schrems v. Data Protection Commissioner ('Schrems')*,[3] the Court of Justice of the European Union (CJEU) ruled that the Commission decision on the Safe Harbour Agreement,[4] which effectively authorised flows of personal data from the EU to the US, was invalid. The Court invalidated the decision on the basis that, contrary to Art. 25(1) of the 1995 Data Protection Directive (DPD),[5] the agreement failed to provide an adequate level of protection for personal data. Underpinning this conclusion, however, were concerns with the disproportionate mass and indiscriminate collection and access to personal data (including data originating in the EU) by US intelligence agencies, as revealed by the whistle-blower, Edward Snowden. While these US practices complied with the Safe Harbour Agreement, the Court, in effect, held that such widespread, unconstrained surveillance would breach the fundamental rights to privacy and data privacy guaranteed by EU law which, under CJEU jurisprudence, must be protected to a 'high level'.

This chapter explains the *Schrems* ruling, and the legal background to the ruling, from the particular perspective of the role of the principle of proportionality, as developed under EU law, in leading the Court to invalidate the Safe Harbour decision. In doing so, the chapter identifies legal difficulties and uncertainties in the application of proportionality analysis to cases involving interference with the rights to privacy and data privacy. While a cursory reading might suggest that the ruling is based almost entirely on the interpretation and application of the 'adequacy' test in Art. 25(1), this chapter contends that the ruling is better seen as an application of the CJEU's jurisprudence on fundamental rights and proportionality to the context of unconstrained state access to cross-border flows of personal data. Beyond this, the chapter addresses two fundamental conceptual issues arising from the *Schrems* ruling. First, the chapter explains and analyses the relationship between privacy and democracy in the context of contemporary surveillance practices, and the importance of an appropriately rigorous proportionality principle in reigning in apparently inexorable tendencies to unconstrained surveillance. Second, the chapter examines issues relating to the protection of rights against unconstrained

3 Case C-362/14, *Maximillian Schrems v. Data Protection Commissioner*, 6 October 2015.

4 See Commission Decision of 26 July 2000 pursuant to Directive 95/46/EC of the European Parliament and of the Council on the adequacy of the protection provided by the Safe Harbour privacy principles and related frequently asked questions issued by the US Department of Commerce, 2000/520/EC, [2000] OJ L 215 ('Safe Harbour decision').

5 Directive 95/46/EC of the European Parliament and of the Council of 24 October 1995 on the protection of individuals with regard to the processing of personal data and on the free movement of such data, [1995] OJ L 281 (DPD).

extra-territorial state surveillance, contending that the controversy surrounding trans-Atlantic data flows should be seen in the broader context of the obligations of territorially based states in relation to the rights of those outside of their territories.

In essence, the main argument made in the chapter is that while the proportionality principle is the proper legal framework for analysing the balance between security and rights, the principle, as a matter of both EU law and international human rights law, needs to be more rigorously defined and applied so as to establish a satisfactory balance between the protection of fundamental rights, on the one hand, and appropriate deference to institutions responsible for public policy, on the other. The importance of the proportionality principle, and the relevance of the argument presented in this chapter, are further illustrated by debates concerning the adequacy of the political agreement reached between the US and the EU, proposed to replace the Safe Harbour Agreement, known as the Privacy Shield. The chapter therefore concludes with an explanation and analysis of the Privacy Shield, especially from the perspective of whether or not it allows for disproportionate interferences with the rights of EU persons.

2. PROPORTIONALITY UNDER EU LAW

While as a principle for balancing government objectives and the protection of individual rights, proportionality is compelling, as a matter of implementation it presents considerable difficulties. At the most general level, the principle of proportionality, in the context of the protection of rights, is simply that any interference with rights must be justifiable in accordance with a legitimate objective and, in addition, the means for pursuing the objective must not involve a disproportionate interference with rights. As Barak puts it:

> There are two main justificatory conditions: an appropriate goal and proportionate means. … Proportionality therefore fulfills a dual function: On the one hand, it allows the limitation of human rights by law, and on the other hand, it subjects these limitations to certain conditions; namely – those stemming from proportionality.[6]

The implementation of the principle of proportionality in positive legal regimes is, however, both complex and contestable; such that, in the European context, it is more accurate to speak of principles of proportionality, and quite misleading to assume that, except at the most general level, there exists a single uniform notion of proportionality.

---

6 A. Barak, 'Proportionality and Principled Balancing' (2010) 4(1) *Law & Ethics of Human Rights* 2, 6.

The origins of the principle of proportionality in Europe can be traced to eighteenth and nineteenth century Prussian law, where it emerged as a principle for limiting the power of the administrative state.[7] Following the Second World War, it was accepted as a fundamental principle of German law, known as *Verhältnismassigkeit*, which still underpins the German rights-based constitution, or Basic Law.[8] Reflecting the mutual interdependence between the protection of individual rights and public interest limitations on rights, both the protection of fundamental rights[9] and the principle of proportionality[10] were later recognised as general principles of EU law in the jurisprudence of the CJEU. Article 52 of the EU Charter[11] now specifically provides that:

> Any limitation on the exercise of the rights and freedoms recognised by this Charter must be provided for by law and respect the essence of those rights and freedoms. Subject to the principle of proportionality, limitations may be made only if they are necessary and genuinely meet objectives of general interest recognised by the Union or the need to protect the rights and freedoms of others.

While the CJEU jurisprudence on fundamental rights (and, accordingly, on proportionality) draws inspiration from the constitutional traditions common to the Member States and from the European Convention on Human Rights (ECHR), the principle of proportionality under EU law differs from both the principle under the national laws of the Member States and the principle applied by the Strasbourg Court under the ECHR.[12] As formulated by the United Kingdom Supreme Court (UKSC) in *Bank Mellat v. Her Majesty's Treasury (No. 2)*,[13] the Strasbourg Court applied the following four-stage analysis in determining whether an administrative measure is proportionate:

1. whether its objective is sufficiently important to justify the limitation of a fundamental right;

---

7 M. Cohen-Eliya and I. Porat, 'American Balancing and German Proportionality: The Historical Origins' (2010) 8(2) *I•CON (International Journal of Constitutional Law)* 263; N. Emiliou, *The Principle of Proportionality in European Law: A Comparative Study*, Kluwer, The Hague 1996.

8 T. Tridimas, *The General Principles of EU Law*, 2nd ed., Oxford University Press, Oxford 2006, p. 136; The Rt. Hon. Lady Justice Arden, 'Proportionality: The Way Ahead?' [2013] *Public Law* 498, 499.

9 Case C-11/70, *International Handelsgesellschaft v. Einfurh-und Vorratsstelle Getreide* [1970] ECR 125.

10 Case C-331/88, *R. v. Ministry of Agriculture, Fisheries and Food ex p. Federation Europeene de la Sante Animale (FEDESA)* [1990] ECR I-4023.

11 Charter of Fundamental Rights of the European Union [2000] OJ C 364/1.

12 Arden, above n. 8; W. Sauter, 'Proportionality in EU Law: A Balancing Act?', TILEC Discussion Paper, DP 2013-003, 25.01.2013, <http://ssrn.com/abstract=2208467>.

13 *Bank Mellat v. Her Majesty's Treasury (No. 2)* [2013] UKSC 39, at [20].

2. whether it is rationally connected to the objective;
3. whether a less intrusive measure could have been used; and
4. whether, having regard to these matters and to the severity of the consequences, a fair balance has been struck between the rights of the individual and the interests of the community.

The clearest statement of the proportionality principle under EU law, on the other hand, was set out by the Luxembourg Court in the landmark *FEDESA* case, in the following terms:

> the lawfulness of the prohibition of an economic activity is subject to the condition that the prohibitory measures are appropriate and necessary in order to achieve the objectives legitimately pursued by the legislation in question; when there is a choice between several appropriate measures recourse must be had to the least onerous, and the disadvantages caused must not be disproportionate to the aims pursued.[14]

The precise elements of the proportionality test under EU law are not expressed consistently, and have been formulated in different terms by commentators and courts alike. On any formulation, however, it involves three components which, drawing on Tridimas, are as follows:[15]

1. Suitability – whether the measure is suitable to achieve a legitimate aim.
2. Necessity – whether the measure is necessary to achieve that aim, namely, whether there are other less restrictive means capable of producing the same result.
3. Proportionality *stricto sensu* – even if there are no less restrictive means, it must be established that the measure does not have an excessive effect on the applicant's interests.[16]

As the UKSC has explained in *R. (on the application of Lumsdon and others) v. Legal Services Board ('Lumsdon')*,[17] the third question (proportionality *stricto sensu)*, while sometimes addressed separately, is often omitted and incorporated into the necessity test.[18]

---

14 Case C-331/88, *R. v. Ministry of Agriculture, Fisheries and Food ex p. Federation Europeene de la Sante Animale (FEDESA)* [1990] ECR I-4023, at [13].

15 Tridimas, above n. 8, p. 139. For a slightly different, four-stage, formulation see: W. Sauter, 'Proportionality in EU Competition Law' (2014) 35(7) *European Competition Law Review* 327.

16 As Tranberg points out, the three-part test at the EU level is analogous to the three components of the principle of proportionality under German law: Tranberg, above n. 2, p. 240, citing *Kreutzberg-Urteil*, PrOVG [1882] E 9, at 353.

17 *R. (on the application of Lumsdon and others) v. Legal Services Board* [2015] UKSC 41, at [33].

18 See also Tridimas, above n. 8, p. 139.

In its important judgment in *Lumsdon*, the UKSC provided a helpful summary of the Luxembourg jurisprudence,[19] including an explanation of the different levels of scrutiny applied by the CJEU in assessing measures adopted by EU institutions, on the one hand, and national measures implementing EU law, on the other.[20] In short, in assessing EU-level measures, the Court applies a 'manifestly inappropriate' test (as opposed to a 'least restrictive means' test), whereas in evaluating national measures that may derogate from fundamental rights and freedoms the Court applies the stricter 'less restrictive alternative' test. The main explanation for the different standards is that, where national implementation of an EU measure is concerned, the CJEU is 'concerned first and foremost with the question whether a member state can justify an interference with a freedom guaranteed in the interests of promoting the integration of the internal market, and the related social values, which lie at the heart of the EU project'.[21]

Within these broad parameters, it is important to appreciate that, under EU law, there is considerable flexibility in the application of the principle of proportionality to particular disputes.[22] As the UKSC observed in *Lumsdon:*

> any attempt to identify general principles risks conveying the impression that the court's approach is less nuanced and fact-sensitive than is actually the case. As in the case of other principles of public law, the way in which the principle of proportionality is applied in EU law depends to a significant extent upon the context.[23]

Given this background, we can now examine how the principle of proportionality has been applied in EU data privacy law.

3. PROPORTIONALITY AND EU DATA PRIVACY LAW

The significance of the legal context to the application of the principle of proportionality is nowhere better illustrated than in how the CJEU has applied the principle to cases involving the extent to which measures, whether at the EU or national levels, may interfere with the fundamental right to data privacy. The relevant legal context involves, first of all, the terms of the DPD, which under Recital 10 is aimed at ensuring a 'high level' of protection of data privacy and,

---

19 The CJEU is, however, the only authoritative source on the meaning of proportionality under EU law.

20 [2015] UKSC 41, at [40]–[82]. See also Sauter, above n. 12.

21 [2015] UKSC 41, at [37].

22 Thus, proportionality has been referred to as a 'flexi-principle': *R. (ProLife Alliance) v. British Broadcasting Corporation* [2004] 1 AC 185, at [138] per Walker LJ.

23 [2015] UKSC 41, at [23].

under Art. 1, has the express objective of protecting the rights and freedoms of natural persons and, in particular, their right to privacy. This high level of protection is reinforced by the EU Charter, which must be taken into account in the interpretation of the DPD and which, in Art. 8, recognises a distinct right to data privacy, such that it is an independent right and not subsidiary to the more general right to privacy (recognised in Art. 7).

In a series of rulings, the CJEU has adopted a strict approach to the application of the necessity component of the proportionality principle in the context of determining permissible limits on the right to data privacy. The best starting point for understanding the Court's approach is the ruling in *Satamedia*.[24] That case concerned the publication of extracts of public data, including names and income brackets, by a Finnish regional newspaper. The key issue addressed by the Court concerned the balance to be struck between the rights to privacy and personal data, on the one hand, and the right to freedom of expression, on the other. Article 9 of the DPD establishes a balance by allowing exemptions or derogations for the processing of personal data 'carried out solely for journalistic purposes ... only if they are necessary to reconcile the right to privacy with the rules governing freedom of expression'. In interpreting the legislative balance in the light of the importance of the right to privacy, the CJEU stated that:

> in order to achieve a balance between the two fundamental rights, the protection of the fundamental right to privacy requires that the derogations and limitations in relation to the protection of data provided for in ... [the DPD] ... must apply only in so far as is strictly necessary.[25]

While the Court in *Satamedia* adopted an expansive interpretation of 'journalistic purposes', for the first time it interpreted the test for confining legitimate exceptions and derogations as requiring 'strict necessity', a concept that was expanded upon in subsequent cases.[26]

The *Satamedia* approach was further elaborated by the Court in a case involving the Common Agricultural Policy, *Schecke*.[27] In that case, the German state of Hesse had published the names of recipients of funding, their postal codes and the amounts received on a publicly accessible, searchable website. Finding that the requirement for publication of personal data under relevant EU regulations was an interference with the rights to privacy and data privacy guaranteed by the Charter, the Court turned to a consideration of whether the limitation was proportionate. Applying the 'strict necessity' test from *Satamedia*,

---

24 Case C-73/07, *Satakunnan Markkinapörssi and Satamedia* [2008] ECR I-9831.
25 Ibid., at [56].
26 Tranberg, above n. 2, p. 245.
27 Joined Cases C-92 and C-93/09, *Volker and Marcus Schecke Eifert*, 9 November 2010.

the CJEU held that the regulations imposed a disproportionate interference with privacy rights as 'it is possible to envisage measures which affect less adversely the fundamental right of natural persons and which still contribute effectively to the objectives of the European Union rules in question'.[28] Accordingly, the Court ruled that, in introducing the regulations, the EU institutions had not established a proportionate balance between the transparency-related objectives of public disclosure, on the one hand, and the protection of the Art. 7 and 8 rights, on the other.

In *Digital Rights Ireland*,[29] the CJEU ruled that the 2006 Data Retention Directive,[30] which imposed mandatary metadata retention requirements for a period of up to two years on private telecommunications service providers, was invalid as a disproportionate interference with fundamental Charter rights. Turning first to the question of whether the directive interfered with the relevant rights, the Court held that both the retention requirements and the access arrangements in the directive amounted to interferences, to both the Art. 7 and 8 rights, that were 'wide-ranging' and 'particularly serious'.[31] In addition, the Court found that the mass retention and use of metadata without the data subjects being informed was likely to create a generalised feeling of constant surveillance.[32]

Although the Court held that the data retention law did not affect the 'essence' of the Charter right to privacy, as it did not concern retention of or access to communications content, and that the prevention of terrorism and crime were legitimate objectives of general interest, the case turned on an assessment of whether the interferences were proportionate. Where EU legislation is subject to judicial review on the basis of interference with fundamental rights, the Court's case law embodies a degree of flexibility in the application of the principle, depending on the area concerned, the nature of the right, the nature and seriousness of the interference and the object pursued by the interference.[33] In the circumstances of this case, the Court held that:

> in view of the important role played by the protection of personal data in the light of the fundamental right to respect for private life and the extent and seriousness of the

---

28 Ibid., at [86].

29 Joined Cases C-293/12 and C-594/12, *Digital Rights Ireland Ltd v. Minister for Communications, Marine and Natural Resources* [2013] ECR I-847.

30 Directive 2006/24 on the retention of data generated or processed in connection with the provision of publicly available electronic communications services or of public communications networks and amending Directive 2002/58/EC, [2006] OJ L 105/54.

31 Joined Cases C-293/12 and C-594/12, *Digital Rights Ireland Ltd v. Minister for Communications, Marine and Natural Resources* [2013] ECR I-847, at [37].

32 Ibid.

33 Ibid., at [47].

> interference with the right caused by Directive 2006/24, the EU legislature's discretion is reduced, with the result that review of that discretion should be strict.[34]

Moreover, in relation to the crucial component of necessity, the Court applied the established case law on the rights to privacy and data privacy which, as explained above, permits derogations and limitations to the extent only that they are strictly necessary.[35]

As the data retention obligations under the directive applied indiscriminately to all electronic communications, and to all persons using electronic communications, even where there was no evidence of a link, however indirect, with serious crime or a threat to national security, the directive constituted an interference that was not strictly necessary.[36] Additionally, the absence of substantive and procedural safeguards in relation to access to the retained metadata rendered the interference more than strictly necessary. Taking into account the over-broad scope of the directive, and the lack of adequate safeguards, the CJEU ultimately concluded that the Data Retention Directive entailed 'a wide-ranging and particularly serious interference with those fundamental rights in the legal order of the EU, without such interference being limited to what is strictly necessary'.[37]

As these cases illustrate, the jurisprudence of the CJEU, in the context of cases alleging infringements of the fundamental rights to privacy and data privacy, has displayed an increasingly rigorous or 'rights protective' approach in the application of the proportionality principle and, in particular, its necessity component (which, as explained above, in practice often incorporates, or substitutes for, an assessment of proportionality *stricto sensu*). Concomitantly, this increased level of scrutiny has entailed progressively less deference to EU-level laws.[38]

Nevertheless, the flexibility in the application of the level of scrutiny applied by the Court gives rise to some uncertainty in the application of the principle.[39] First, there are questions about whether or not the strict scrutiny applied to infringements of rights applies to all Charter rights, or applies to some rights and not to others. To date, the strict level of scrutiny evident in cases such as those dealt with above appears to be confined to rights to non-discrimination, due process, property, and privacy and data privacy.[40] Although the CJEU

34 Ibid., at [48].

35 Ibid., at [52].

36 Ibid., at [59].

37 Ibid., at [65].

38 M-P. Granger and K. Irion, 'The Court of Justice and the Data Retention Directive in Digital Rights Ireland: telling off the EU legislator and teaching a lesson in privacy and data protection' (2014) 39(6) *European Law Review* 835, 845.

39 Ibid., p. 846.

40 Ibid., p. 846.

eschews the creation of a hierarchy of rights, it seems clear, especially from recent jurisprudence, that some rights, including the rights to privacy and data privacy, have been accorded particular protection. Second, there are questions about the relationship between the nature of the interference with the relevant rights and the level of intensity of the proportionality analysis. While the Court's jurisprudence clearly establishes that the more serious an interference with rights the more likely the interference will be disproportionate, the precise relationship between the seriousness of an interference and the level of scrutiny remains uncertain. In *Digital Rights Ireland*, however, the Court clearly took the seriousness of the interference into account in applying a strict level of review. In addition, there is little guidance on the circumstances that may lead the Court to conclude that an interference is 'wide-ranging' or 'particularly serious', such as to justify strict review. Third, while the Court in *Digital Rights Ireland* emphasised the flexibility in the application of the principle of proportionality, taking into account a variety of circumstances, there is a lack of precision as to what strict review of an EU measure actually entails. As explained above, the CJEU has applied a 'manifestly inappropriate' test when assessing the proportionality of EU-level measures, giving a degree of deference to EU policy-making institutions. While it is clear that where strict review is applied the deference given to EU institutions is reduced, precisely how this might affect the 'manifestly inappropriate' analysis is not clear. A number of considerations are relevant here. As the UKSC pointed out in *Lumsdon*, the CJEU 'has not explained how it determines whether the inappropriateness of a measure is or is not manifest'.[41] Furthermore, at least in some cases, the Court has applied a 'least restrictive means' test to an EU-level measure in preference to the 'manifestly inappropriate' test, meaning that a measure will be regarded as disproportionate unless it is the least restrictive means of achieving a legitimate public interest objective.[42] It is therefore unclear whether the strict standard of review referred to in the cases culminating in *Digital Rights Ireland* is simply more likely to find a measure to be 'manifestly inappropriate', whether it entails applying a 'least restrictive means' test, or whether the standard is somewhere between the 'manifestly inappropriate' and 'least restrictive means' tests. To be clear, I am not suggesting that the Court adopt an overly rigid approach in assessing the proportionality of an interference with fundamental rights; merely that the legal tests for scrutinising EU-level laws should be more clearly and precisely explained. The need for greater analytical precision is clearly illustrated by the substantial legal uncertainty, following the CJEU decision in *Digital Rights*

---

41 [2015] UKSC 41, at [42].

42 See Sauter, above n. 12, p. 13, citing Case C-210/03, *Swedish Match UK Ltd* [2004] ECR I-11893.

Ireland, concerning whether bulk data collection by intelligence agencies can ever be proportionate.

Bearing these observations on the application of the proportionality principle in the context of the right to data privacy in mind, we can turn to an analysis of the *Schrems* decision. Before doing so, however, it is necessary to explain some recent practices of US government security agencies in collecting and accessing personal data originating from outside the US, as revealed by Edward Snowden in 2013.

4. THE SNOWDEN REVELATIONS AND THE PRISM PROGRAMME

Starting in June 2013, the Snowden revelations altered the public understanding of the extent to which US security agencies have accessed and processed data originating from outside the US, including data sourced from the EU.[43] On 6 June 2013, one day after the publication of the first reports that the US National Security Agency (NSA) was collecting telecommunications log records from Verizon, *The Guardian* and *The Washington Post* published details of a programme, popularly known as PRISM, under which the NSA collected a range of data from large Internet companies, including Google, Microsoft and Facebook.[44] The reports, based on 41 PowerPoint slides leaked by Edward Snowden, revealed the mass collection of Internet data, including both content and metadata, under the authority of the US Foreign Intelligence Surveillance Court (the FISA Court).[45]

To date, the most comprehensive explanation of the operation of the PRISM programme is contained in a July 2014 report by the US Privacy and Civil Liberties Oversight Board (PCLOB) on surveillance programmes authorised pursuant to section 702 of the US Foreign Intelligence Surveillance Act 1978.[46]

---

43 Although, as Hogan J. in the Irish High Court observed, 'only the naïve or the credulous could really have been surprised' by the Snowden revelations, the factual details revealed by Edward Snowden confirmed suspicions and exposed disingenuous denials: *Schrems v. Data Protection Commissioner* [2014] IEHC at [4].

44 B. Gellman and L. Poitras, 'US Intelligence Mining Data from Nine U.S. Internet Companies in Broad Secret Program', *The Washington Post*, 6 June 2013, <https://www.washingtonpost.com/investigations/us-intelligence-mining-data-from-nine-us-internet-companies-in-broad-secret-program/2013/06/06/3a0c0da8-cebf-11e2-8845-d970ccb04497_story.html>; G. Greenwald and E. MacAskill, 'NSA Taps in to Internet Giants' Systems to Mine User Data, Secret Files Reveal', *The Guardian*, 6 June 2013, <http://www.theguardian.com/world/2013/jun/06/us-tech-giants-nsa-data>.

45 For the slides see: PRISM/US-984XN Overview, April 2013, <https://www.aclu.org/files/natsec/nsa/20130816/PRISM%20Overview%20Powerpoiny%20Slides.pdf>.

46 PCLOB, above n. 1.

Section 702 establishes a regime under which the US Attorney General and the Director of National Intelligence may jointly authorise surveillance of non-US persons, who are reasonably believed to be located outside of the US, in order to acquire foreign intelligence information.[47] The government authorisations must be approved by the FISA Court, which operates in secret. Once approval has been given, written directives are sent to the Internet companies requiring them to assist in the collection of data.

The data collected is based on certain 'selectors', such as telephone numbers or e-mail addresses, associated with targeted persons. Once the government sends a selector to an Internet company, the company is compelled to pass on all communications sent to or from that selector. The NSA receives all of the data generated by the PRISM programme, while the CIA and FBI receive portions of the data.[48] Each of the relevant intelligence agencies has certain minimisation procedures, approved by the FISA Court, that restrict the use, retention and disclosure of the collected data.

The collection of data under the PRISM programme has been extensive. As the PCLOB report explained: 'Compared with the "traditional" FISA process ..., Section 702 imposes significantly fewer limits on the government when it targets foreigners located abroad, permitting greater flexibility and a dramatic increase in the number of people who can realistically be targeted.'[49] Furthermore, according to the report, about 91 per cent of Internet communications obtained by the NSA each year are acquired from the PRISM programme,[50] with an estimated 89,138 persons being targeted in 2013.[51] While the programme is targeted at non-US persons, there is considerable incidental collection of data relating to US citizens. At the time of writing, US Senate Judiciary Committee hearings had commenced on the re-authorisation of section 702, which is currently scheduled to expire in December 2017.[52] In the context of this chapter, it is important to note that, although there has been considerable focus on the PRISM programme, it is but one of a range of US intelligence agency programmes which may involve the collection of personal data of Europeans. In particular, a range of data collection activities, the precise scope of which remain unclear, are authorised by Executive Order 12333 (EO-12333).

47 50 U.S.C. sec. 1881a, introduced by the FISA Amendment Act 2008. For a comprehensive explanation of the history of s. 702 see: L.K. Donohue, 'Section 702 and the Collection of International Telephone and Internet Content' (2015) 38 *Harvard Journal of Law & Public Policy* 117.

48 The collection is undertaken by the Data Intercept Technology Unit (DITU) of the FBI, acting on behalf of the NSA: PCLOB, above n. 1, p. 33.

49 PCLOB, above n. 1, pp. 9–10.

50 Ibid., pp. 33–34.

51 Ibid., p. 33.

52 'Senate Judiciary Committee holds first public review of Section 702 surveillance programs', 12 May 2016 <http://www.openthegovernment.org/node/5209>.

5. THE *SCHREMS* DECISION

5.1. BACKGROUND

The Snowden revelations, and especially those concerning the PRISM programme, form the background to a complaint made by the Austrian privacy activist, Maximillian Schrems, to the Irish Data Protection Commissioner (the IDPC) in June 2013. The complaint concerned the mass transfer of personal data from Facebook Ireland to its US parent, Facebook Inc. Within Europe, Facebook users are required to enter into agreements with Facebook Ireland, which stores the data on servers in Ireland and transmits the data to servers in the US. As Facebook Inc. is a company subject to authorisations under the section 702 programme, personal data transmitted by Facebook to the US may be collected and stored by the NSA. As a Facebook user, Schrems complained that Facebook Ireland was facilitating over-broad access to his personal data by US intelligence agencies and, accordingly, that the IDPC should direct Facebook Ireland to cease transferring personal data to the US.

The IDPC rejected the Schrems complaint, principally on the basis that as the transfers were authorised by the Safe Harbour Agreement between the EU and the US,[53] the Commissioner was prevented from investigating the complaint. The Safe Harbour Agreement was adopted by a decision of the Commission in July 2000, pursuant to Art. 25(6) of the DPD. While Art. 25(1) of the DPD sets out the principle that EU Member States must provide that transfer of personal data to a third country may take place only if that country ensures an adequate level of protection, Art. 25(6) establishes a mechanism for the Commission to determine that a third country ensures an adequate level of protection.

The Safe Harbour Agreement, which was negotiated between the EU and the US to ensure the viability of the trans-Atlantic transfer of personal data, consisted of a set of privacy principles, implemented in accordance with guidance provided by frequently asked questions (FAQs), both issued by the US Department of Commerce on 21 July 2000. The privacy principles included broad obligations relating to: providing notice of collection and processing of personal data; disclosure of personal data to third parties; data security and data integrity; and access to, and correction of, personal data. The scheme, intended for use by US private sector organisations receiving personal data from Europe, operated entirely by means of self-certification. As explained in the FAQs, the main mechanism for enforcing the self-regulatory scheme was by the US Federal

---

53 Safe Harbour decision, above n. 4. The Safe Harbour principles appear as Annex I to the Commission decision.

Trade Commission (FTC) taking action on the basis of deceptive representations of compliance with the privacy principles.

The fourth paragraph to Annex I of the Commission decision adopting the Safe Harbour Agreement established significant derogations limiting the application of the principles. In particular, the decision allowed for derogations 'to the extent necessary to meet national security, public interest, or law enforcement requirements' and 'by statute, government regulation, or case-law that create conflicting obligations or explicit authorisations, provided that, in exercising any such authorisation, an organisation can demonstrate that its non-compliance ... is limited to the extent necessary to meet the overriding legitimate interests furthered by such authorisation'. Moreover, Part B of Annex IV of the Commission decision provided that, in the event of conflicting obligations imposed by US law, organisations were required to comply with the US law.

Following the rejection of his complaint, Schrems applied to the Irish High Court for judicial review of the IDPC decision. The main issue before the Court was whether the Commission decision finding that the Safe Harbour Agreement provided an adequate level of protection conclusively prevented complaints about data transfers from Facebook Ireland to its US parent falling within the scope of the agreement. Hogan J., making limited distinctions between the various NSA programmes, simply concluded that, once in the US, the Facebook data was subject to 'mass and indiscriminate surveillance' by the NSA.[54] If the question were to be determined in accordance with Irish national law, the national court held that this level of mass and undifferentiated surveillance would create a serious issue as to whether it was a disproportionate interference with the fundamental rights to dignity, autonomy and privacy protected by the Irish constitution.[55]

However, as the case concerned a Commission decision made pursuant to an EU level directive and, accordingly, the implementation of EU law by a Member State, review of the IDPC decision fell to be determined by EU law, and especially by reference to the rights guaranteed by the EU Charter. Given the express protection of data privacy by Art. 8 of the Charter, mass and undifferentiated surveillance with weak judicial oversight, and with no appeal rights for EU data subjects, would likely breach the Charter. That said, the Irish data protection law, on its face, prevented the IDPC from second-guessing a Commission decision on adequacy. The key questions in the case were therefore whether the IDPC was bound by the Commission's Safe Harbour decision, which necessarily raised the issue of whether the Safe Harbour Agreement complied with EU law. In this respect, the High Court of Ireland observed that, as the Charter entered into

54 *Maximillian Schrems v. Data Protection Commissioner* [2014] IEHC 310 (18 June 2014), at [13].

55 Ibid., at [52].

effect after the Safe Harbour Agreement, it was essential to determine whether the agreement should be re-evaluated in the light of the Charter. The national court therefore referred the issue of whether the IDPC was bound by the Safe Harbour Agreement or whether, taking into account developments since the agreement, it could conduct an independent investigation, to the CJEU for a ruling.

5.2. THE CJEU RULING

On 6 October 2015, the CJEU handed down its ruling finding that, first, the Commission's Safe Harbour decision did not prevent a national supervisory authority, such as the IDPC, from examining whether or not a third country ensures an adequate level of protection and, second, that the Safe Harbour decision was, as a matter of EU law, invalid.[56]

In evaluating the powers of EU data protection regulators, the Court placed considerable emphasis on the legal requirements for national supervisory authorities to act independently, as derived both from the Charter and the DPD. In relation to the Charter while, as explained above, Art. 8 relevantly establishes an express right to data privacy, significantly, Art. 8(3) specifically requires rules protecting data privacy to be subject to control by an independent authority. Furthermore, Art. 28(1) of the DPD, which must be interpreted in light of the Charter, expressly requires national supervisory authorities to 'act with complete independence'. Consequently, although the Safe Harbour Agreement, while in force, was binding on EU Member States and their organs, the Court held that this could not prevent national regulators from independently examining, pursuant to Art. 28, claims that the transfer of personal data to third countries was in breach of the rights and freedoms conferred by the Charter. In this respect, the Court emphasised that 'the European Union is a union based on the rule of law in which all acts of its institutions are subject to review of their compatibility with, in particular, the Treaties, general principles of law and fundamental rights'.[57] Consequently, although only the CJEU has the competence to declare invalid an EU-level act, such as the Safe Harbour decision, the Court held that, if a supervisory authority were to find a breach of the Charter rights, national legislation must provide for recourse to national courts which, in turn, can make a reference to the CJEU.[58] In other words, while national supervisory authorities could not rule on the validity of the Safe Harbour Agreement, this did not prevent them from independently examining claims that the processing of personal data by third countries was in breach of Charter rights.

---

56 Ibid.

57 Ibid., at [60].

58 Ibid., at [65].

Given that the transfer of personal data by Facebook to the US complied with the Safe Harbour Agreement, the fundamental underlying question raised by the case concerned the validity of the Commission decision on adequacy, interpreting the DPD adequacy requirement in the light of the Charter. As explained above, the combination of the Art. 8 right and the express text of the DPD result in a high level of legal protection of data privacy in the EU. On this basis, the CJEU held that to comply with the adequacy test, a third country must ensure a level of protection which, while not identical, was 'essentially equivalent' to that conferred by EU Member States.[59] Furthermore, the importance given to the right to data privacy under the EU legal regime led the Court to conclude that, first, in reviewing the Safe Harbour decision, account must be taken of circumstances arising subsequent to the decision and, second, that the Commission decision should be subject to strict scrutiny.

In applying the 'manifestly inappropriate' test to EU measures, the CJEU traditionally held that the assessment must be made at the time of the adoption of the measure, as future effects of rules cannot be predicted with accuracy. In *Jippes*, for example, the Court stated that:

> Where the Community legislature is obliged to assess the future effects of rules to be adopted and those effects cannot be accurately foreseen, its assessment is open to criticism only if it appears manifestly incorrect in the light of the information available to it at the time of the adoption of the rule in question.[60]

In *Gaz de France – Berliner Investissements*,[61] however, the Court appeared to open the door to consideration of factors arising after the adoption of a measure in certain limited circumstances. Given that the Snowden revelations concerning widespread collection and access to data by US government authorities occurred long after the Safe Harbour decision, the extent to which subsequent developments can be taken into account in assessing the validity of the decision was especially important. The legal issues were dealt with in some detail in the advisory opinion of Advocate General Bot.[62]

Taking advantage of the limited qualification to the rule against retrospective assessment allowed in *Gaz de France*, the Advocate General emphasised the particular characteristics of a Commission decision on adequacy which favour its assessment by reference to circumstances in existence at the time of the ruling rather than the time of the adoption of the measure. In sum, the Advocate General concluded that as a decision on adequacy is intended to have an ongoing effect,

---

59 Ibid., at [74].

60 Case C-189/01, *Jippes and Others* [2001] ECR I-5689, at [84].

61 Case C-247/08, *Gaz de France – Berliner Investissements* [2009] ECR I-9255.

62 Case C-362/14, *Maximillian Schrems v. Data Protection Commissioner*, Opinion of Advocate General Bot, 23 September 2015.

whether or not the legal protection provided by a third country is adequate must 'evolve according to the factual and legal context prevailing in the third country'.[63] Therefore, even though the continuation in force of a Commission decision amounts to an implied confirmation of the original assessment, where a reference has been made to the Court to determine the validity of a Commission decision, taking into account the ongoing effect of the decision the Court can appropriately examine circumstances that have arisen since the decision was adopted, which may cast doubt on the continued validity of the decision.[64] In its ruling, the CJEU essentially confirmed the approach adopted by the Advocate General, such that an adequacy decision must be reviewed in the light of legal and factual circumstances that may have arisen since the decision was adopted.[65] In effect, the Court is not merely reviewing the original adequacy decision, but the Commission's ongoing obligation to review the adequacy of third country protection, taking into account changing circumstances.

Referring by analogy to the ruling in *Digital Rights Ireland*, the Court held that, in view of the importance of the protection of personal data in the context of the fundamental right to privacy, review of the Commission's adequacy decision should be strict.[66] Applying this standard, the CJEU identified a number of inadequacies with the Safe Harbour arrangements, especially in relation to the processing of data pursuant to the NSA programmes. For example, self-certification under the arrangements is available only to US 'organisations', which means that the principles do not apply to US public authorities.[67] More importantly, the national security, public interest and law enforcement derogations under Annex I, referred to above, effectively meant that these interests could prevail over the fundamental rights of EU data subjects. As the Court put it, the derogations meant that the Safe Harbour decision:

> enables interference, founded on national security and public interest requirements or on domestic legislation of the United States, with the fundamental rights of the persons whose personal data is or could be transferred from the European Union to the United States.[68]

Moreover, as far as procedural safeguards were concerned, the Safe Harbour arrangements provided for enforcement only in relation to commercial disputes, with no safeguards whatsoever against state interference with fundamental rights.

63 Ibid., at [134].
64 Ibid., at [136].
65 Ibid., at [76].
66 Ibid., at [78].
67 Ibid., at [82].
68 Ibid., at [87].

Accordingly, the combination of the broad derogations for public security and law enforcement, with a lack of legal remedies for access by state authorities, led the Court to conclude that the Safe Harbour Agreement failed to provide adequate protection under Art. 25 of the DPD, when read in the light of the Charter. In particular, the broad derogations were not limited to what was strictly necessary for the legitimate objectives of national security and law enforcement, as they enabled generalised, undifferentiated storage of, and access to, personal data, without any limiting criteria. As the Court put it, citing *Digital Rights Ireland:*

> Legislation is not limited to what is strictly necessary where it authorises, on a generalised basis, storage of all the personal data of all the persons whose data has been transferred from the European Union to the United States without any differentiation, limitation or exception being made in light of the objective pursued and without an objective criterion being laid down by which to determine the limits of the access of the public authorities to the data, and of its subsequent use, for purposes which are specific, strictly restricted and capable of justifying the interference which both access to that data and its use entail…[69]

From this, the CJEU concluded that the generalised access enabled by the Safe Harbour Agreement compromised the essence of the fundamental right to privacy guaranteed by Art. 7 of the Charter.[70] Moreover, the lack of legal recourse for state intrusions, such as the NSA surveillance, compromised the essence of the fundamental right to effective judicial protection, guaranteed by Art. 47 of the Charter.[71] Finally, Art. 3 of the Safe Harbour decision, which effectively limited the circumstances in which national supervisory authorities may suspend data flows to self-certifying organisations, impermissibly denied the power of supervisory authorities to independently examine complaints that a third country does not ensure an adequate level of protection.[72] In short, on a number of bases, but especially on the grounds that the Safe Harbour Agreement did not provide satisfactory protection against surveillance by US government authorities, the CJEU ruled that the Commission decision on adequacy was invalid.

While, on a superficial reading, it might appear that the CJEU ruling is based entirely on an interpretation of the adequacy requirement in Art. 25(1) of the DPD, a closer reading indicates that it is a ruling on the proportionality of extra-territorial state data surveillance, in which the Court builds upon previous rulings determining whether or not an infringement of the Art. 7 and 8 rights

---

69 Ibid., at [93].
70 Ibid., at [94].
71 Ibid., at [95].
72 Ibid., at [102].

is proportionate to emphasise the need for any derogations or limitations on the protection of personal data to be confined to what is strictly necessary. This interpretation follows from the following reasoning: the high level of protection of data privacy means that 'adequate' protection must be interpreted as 'essentially equivalent' protection; therefore the proportionality analysis applied to an EU law, such as the Data Retention Directive, must be applied *ipso facto* in an 'essentially equivalent' manner to the laws of a third country in assessing whether or not that jurisdiction provides adequate protection.

That said, it must be acknowledged that the Court's explicit statements on the application of the proportionality principle are limited; one must to an extent read between the lines, taking into account the above implicit reasoning and the following three main points made by the Advocate General. First, analogous to the reasoning and language used in *Digital Rights Ireland*, the Advocate General held that the almost unfettered access to personal data enjoyed by US intelligence agencies meant that the interference with Charter rights was 'wide-ranging' and 'particularly serious'.[73] Second, distinguishing the reasoning in *Digital Rights Ireland*, the Advocate General held that, as the PRISM programme enabled access to content, the interference was such as to compromise the 'essence' of the fundamental right to privacy.[74] Third, the Advocate General applied the approach taken to the 'strict necessity' test in *Digital Rights Ireland* to effectively hold that the infringement was disproportionate as it allowed untargeted and indiscriminate access to all data, including content, of EU data subjects, without any relevant link to the general interest objective of national security.[75]

Apart from the disproportionality flowing from the undifferentiated mass access to personal data, the Court's decision on validity was, on my reading, influenced by the absence of any effective procedural safeguards, in the form of enforceable rights, available to EU data subjects. According to the jurisprudence of the CJEU, the proportionality analysis may be affected by the existence of procedural safeguards, such as where an otherwise problematic interference with rights may be found to be proportionate due to procedural guarantees.[76] In relation to the Safe Harbour decision, however, the limitation of enforcement proceedings before the FTC to commercial disputes meant that EU data subjects had no administrative or judicial means of redress against access by US government authorities. As the Court itself explained, the Commission's Safe Harbour decision completely failed to refer to 'the existence of effective

---

73 Ibid., at [171].

74 Ibid., at [177].

75 Ibid., at [198].

76 See Sauter, above n. 12, p. 14, citing Joined Cases C-154/04 and C-155/04, *The Queen, on the application of Alliance for Natural Health and Others v. Secretary of State for Health and National Assembly for Wales (Food supplements)* [2005] ECR I-6451.

legal protection' against interferences with fundamental rights resulting from measures originating from the US State.[77]

6. LEGAL EVALUATION OF THE *SCHREMS* DECISION

The EU is a legal entity based upon the rule of law which, applying the EU Charter, incorporates the protection of fundamental rights and freedoms as significant grounds for judicial review. Historically, review of EU-level measures by the CJEU, including in applying the principle of proportionality, has accorded a significant degree of deference to EU institutions. The main reason for this level of deference has been a reluctance for the Court to second-guess policy decisions which involve complex political, economic and social choices.[78] As explained above, however, since the introduction of the Charter, the Court has adopted an increasingly strict approach to rights-based review of EU measures, especially in cases involving infringements of particular rights, such as the Charter rights to privacy and data privacy. Particularly in the context of data privacy, the combination of the express Art. 8 Charter right, which may well go beyond the right to privacy protected under Art. 8 of the ECHR,[79] and the objectives of the DPD have led the Court to apply a high level of protection to data subjects. To date, this can be regarded as culminating, in *Digital Rights Ireland*, with the application of strict review to cases involving serious infringements to the rights to privacy and data privacy.

In most respects, the CJEU's ruling in *Schrems* amounts to little more than an application of the Court's approach to proportionality, especially as formulated in *Digital Rights Ireland*, to the context of the Commission's Safe Harbour adequacy decision. Applying this approach, the unconstrained derogations for national security and law enforcement in Annex I of the agreement clearly failed the strict necessity test. Moreover, the absence of any procedural safeguards against widespread access and use of personal data by US government agencies was a significant distinct consideration reinforcing the conclusion that the Safe Harbour decision was invalid as it allowed a disproportionate interference with rights. As distinct from *Digital Rights Ireland*, however, the Court held that the interference allowed by the Safe Harbour Agreement compromised the 'essence' of the relevant rights as it facilitated generalised access to communications content, as opposed to metadata.

---

[77] Case C-362/14, *Maximillian Schrems v. Data Protection Commissioner*, 6 October 2015, at [89].

[78] See, e.g., Case C-491/01 *R v. Secretary of State for Health, ex p. British American Tobacco (Investments) Ltd and Imperial Tobacco Ltd* [2002] ECR I-11453.

[79] See, e.g., the reasoning of the English High Court in *The Queen v. The Secretary of State for the Home Department* [2015] EWHC 2092.

Of potentially more long-term legal significance, however, may be the conclusion of the Court that the Commission decision on adequacy can be assessed taking into account factual and legal circumstances arising after the adoption of the decision. But, on this, the Court was careful to emphasise the distinctive characteristics of a decision on adequacy, which is intended to ensure a continuing and ongoing high level of protection in relation to transfers of personal data to third countries. As such, a failure of the Commission to appropriately review a decision in the light of important changes in circumstances, such as the Snowden revelations, may be as damaging to the protection of rights as a failure to adequately take into account known circumstances at the time of an original decision.

That said, the *Schrems* ruling neither adds much to, nor advances the law, in relation to significant unresolved legal issues concerning the application of the proportionality principle to contexts involving infringements to privacy and data privacy identified earlier in this chapter. In particular, it does not resolve especially difficult issues relating to whether or not the bulk, indiscriminate collection of personal data by intelligence agencies can ever be justifiable, which have been left unclear by the Court's ruling in *Digital Rights Ireland*. At the time of writing, it was hoped that these issues would be more explicitly addressed, and potentially resolved, by the CJEU in its forthcoming ruling in the joined cases of *Tele2 Sverige AB v. Post-och telestyrelsen* and *Secretary of State for the Home Department v. Davis and others*;[80] and the forthcoming advice on the validity of the draft PNR (Passenger Name Records) Canada agreement.[81] On the other hand, as explained in this chapter, the *Schrems* case does provide an important opportunity for examining these legal issues in a broader factual and legal context, especially involving the protection of rights across territorial borders, which are taken up in the sections of this chapter immediately following.

7. PROPORTIONALITY, PRIVACY RIGHTS AND DEMOCRACY

CJEU jurisprudence concerning the application of the principle of proportionately to interferences with the fundamental rights to privacy and data privacy has progressively increased the intensity of scrutiny applied to infringements and,

80 Joined Cases C-203/15 and C-698/15. On 19 July 2016, Advocate-General Henrik Saugmandsgaard Øe issued an advisory opinion which, in part, concluded that a general data retention obligation may be compatible with EU law: ECLI:EU:C:2016:572.

81 Case A-1/15. On 8 September 2016, Advocate-General Paolo Mengozzi issued an Advisory Opinion finding that certain provisions of the draft PNR agreement were incompatible with the EU Charter as not being sufficiently 'targeted': Opinion 1/15, ECLI:EU:C:2016:656.

concomitantly, decreased deference to EU-level policy-making. Rights-based judicial review of legislation and policy-making, based on a relatively 'thick' concept of the rule of law,[82] such as that embodied in an expansive application of the principle of proportionality incorporating strict review, is controversial. The main objections to the effective substitution of a court's decision to that of a policy-making institution, such as a legislature, relate to the relative lack of competency of the courts to take into account the complex considerations relevant to proper policy-making, and their lack of democratic accountability.[83] This chapter is not the place to canvass these arguments; let alone to provide a satisfactory rebuttal to the claims of rights sceptics. In this section of the chapter, however, it is possible to provide some limited reflections on the protection of privacy rights by the Court, and the relationship between privacy rights and democracy, in the context of the application of the principle of proportionality to trans-Atlantic data flows.

At base, liberal democracies depend upon some degree of mutual trust between citizens and State, which appears to be increasingly precarious, especially in Western democracies.[84] The asymmetric relationship between State and citizen necessarily engenders a degree of mutual suspicion. While the liberal State has a monopoly on legitimate power, intelligence-gathering and analysis are effectively delegated to specialised security agencies (and outsourced to sub-contractors), which have a relatively independent sphere of operation. The imperatives facing security agencies invariably tend to over-reach, with an almost gravitational attraction to total information surveillance. In periods of heightened and generalised security risk, elected officials face incentives to publicly support expert security agencies, inexorably tending to capture. Once over-reach is revealed, however, trust is further eroded in what, effectively, may become a vicious cycle.

The extent to which democracies – in the loosest sense of government by representatives accountable to the people – depend upon a degree of trust draws attention to the pre-conditions for democratic government. Insufficient or ineffective limits on government intrusions on individual rights erodes the capacities of people to effectively participate in, and sustain, a democratic

---

82 See J. Goldsworthy, 'Legislative Sovereignty' in T. Campbell, K.D. Ewing and A. Tomkins (eds.), *Sceptical Essays on Human Rights*, Oxford University Press, Oxford 2001, pp. 61–78.

83 The literature, of course, is extensive. For some of the most sophisticated 'rights-sceptic' arguments see: J. Waldron, *The Dignity of Legislation*, Cambridge University Press, Cambridge 1999; M. Tushnet, *Taking the Constitution Away from the Courts*, Princeton University Press, Princeton 1999.

84 This chapter was written before the 23 June 2016 referendum resulting in a majority vote in favour of the United Kingdom withdrawing from the European Union; that vote, being contrary to the position advocated by both major parties in the UK, seems to have been, in part, attributable to the trust deficit.

polity. Although few would frame the issues in such unsophisticated terms, rights and democracy are not a zero-sum game but, in senses that count, are mutually reinforcing. In the context of mass government surveillance, if people perceive that their activities, and especially their online interactions, are being perpetually monitored, this undermines the very concepts of an engaged citizenry, democratic pluralism and free political debate. As Richards has put it:

> When the government is keenly interested in what people are saying to confidants in private, the content of that private activity is necessarily affected and skewed towards the ordinary, the inoffensive, and the boring, even if the subject of surveillance is not a terrorist. If the government is watching what we say and who we talk to, so too will we make our choices accordingly. The ability of the government to monitor our communications is a powerful one, and one that cuts to the very core of our cognitive and expressive civil liberties.[85]

To claim that rights to privacy and data privacy are essential to democracy does not, of course, entail that an expansive protection of these rights must be guaranteed by the courts. While governments have a tendency to be captured by national security agendas, as Waldron has cautioned, in times of national emergency courts have been reluctant to impose limits on government actions.[86] Nevertheless, in the absence of effective internal limits, the courts are the main candidate for imposing limits on state power. The key questions then resolve to the extent of the courts' discretion in exercising rights-based review and the bases on which such discretion is exercised. But just as the principle of proportionality arose in eighteenth- and nineteenth-century Prussia as a limit on the nascent growth of the administrative state in the absence of democratically imposed constraints, so the manifest failure of democratic processes to effectively curtail the excesses of state surveillance programmes, as revealed by Edward Snowden, suggests that the legal principle of proportionality has an important role to play in filling this gap in contemporary circumstances.

While the principle of proportionality may be an appropriate lens through which to analyse the balance between security and rights, it must be acknowledged that the application of the principle, and especially the necessity test and proportionality *stricto sensu*, entails the Court substituting, at least to an extent, its own assessment of the merits of a law or policy for that of the promulgating institution.[87] The problem then becomes how effectively to limit the Court's

---

85 N.M. Richards, 'Intellectual Privacy' (2008) 87 *Texas Law Review* 387, 433. See also Lyon, above n. 1, pp. 107–113.

86 J. Waldron, 'Security and Liberty: The Image of Balance' (2003) 11 *Journal of Political Philosophy* 191, 191.

87 Tridimas, above n. 8, p. 140.

discretion, as unconstrained decision-making can easily veer to the arbitrary. The answer is that the limits must come from internal constraints imposed by the Court on itself in the form of its reasoning process, or what Stone Sweet and Mathews have described as 'an argumentation framework', meaning simply a system of reasoning that gives coherence by means of stable decision-making procedures.[88] While some, principally Alexy, claim that the proportionality balancing exercise can be conducted with almost mathematical precision,[89] it remains essential for any analysis to incorporate sufficient flexibility for the courts to remain sensitive to both significant factors that may influence the analysis and the facts of instant cases. As explained in this chapter, however, the CJEU jurisprudence applying the principle of proportionality, especially in the context of infringements of the rights to privacy and data privacy, has so far produced a degree of legal uncertainty including, importantly, in relation to the precise level of scrutiny to be applied to limitations on the rights, and whether the bulk collection of data can ever be proportionate. That said, the continued and growing importance of privacy rights to a democratic constitution, in contemporary circumstances, suggests that the Court has been correct in according less deference to EU institutions when these rights are implicated. Nevertheless, a greater degree of precision and discipline in identifying and explaining the legal constraints on the proportionality analysis would help significantly to dissipate concerns about potential judicial over-reach, as well as to add much-needed certainty.

8. PROPORTIONALITY, TRANS-ATLANTIC AND TRANSBORDER DATA FLOWS

On any approach taken to the balancing of rights and security, the mass, indiscriminate data surveillance by US government agencies, with no effective procedural safeguards, as revealed by Snowden, would be disproportionate.[90] In the online environment, however, interferences with rights, such as disproportionate surveillance by state agencies, may occur at a distance.[91] The

88 A. Stone Sweet and J. Mathews, 'Proportionality Balancing and Global Constitutionalism' (2008) 47 *Columbia Journal of Transnational Law* 73, 89–90.

89 R. Alexy, *A Theory of Constitutional Rights*, trans. J. Rivers, Oxford University Press, Oxford 2002; see also M. Klatt and M. Meister, *The Constitutional Structure of Proportionality*, Oxford University Press, Oxford 2012.

90 In Europe, these practices would be in breach of the distinct proportionality principles in national laws, as well as the principles applied by the Strasbourg and Luxembourg courts.

91 As Brown and Korff put it: 'the global infrastructure of the Internet and electronic communications has made surveillance of ... extraterritorial communications easier': I. Brown and D. Korff, 'Foreign Surveillance: Law and Practice in a Global Digital Environment' (2014) 3 *European Human Rights Law Review* 243, 245.

border-transgressing features of online communications raise conspicuous problems of transborder protection of rights. As territorial legal jurisdictions commonly provide less protection to foreigners than is accorded domestic citizens and residents,[92] transborder infringements of rights commonly escape judicial rights-based review. The DPD's requirement that transfers of personal data to third countries should be permissible only where that jurisdiction provides an adequate level of protection implements the EU's obligation to protect the rights of EU data subjects irrespective of territorial borders. The mechanism whereby the Commission determines the adequacy of a legal regime of a third country, however, raises the spectre of one legal jurisdiction imposing its standards on other jurisdictions in order to ensure the flow of transborder data, which has become essential to global commerce. The Commission's decision, back in July 2000, approving the Safe Harbour Agreement was clearly a pragmatic political compromise, which accorded some protection to data subject to trans-Atlantic transfers, while ensuring the continuation of the vital transborder trade. However, as explained in this chapter, the CJEU's ruling in *Schrems* confirms that any political agreement regarding adequacy must comply with the high level of protection of the rights to privacy and data privacy guaranteed by EU law.

In an era of mass transborder data flows, questions relating to the obligations of territorially based states to protect the rights of people physically located outside of their territory have become increasingly pressing. The lacuna in legal protection clearly opens the door to mass, unconstrained interference with rights across borders. The prevalence of these practices, as revealed by Snowden, exposes a significant gap in international human rights protection. This gap is too important to leave to essentially political negotiations between state parties even where, as is the case with data flows from the EU, such agreements are subject to rights-based judicial review. While some, including the UN Human Rights Committee, interpret existing international human rights law as imposing rights-based obligations on states where their actions have extra-territorial effects,[93] the legal position is far from clear. More importantly, significant state actors, and especially the US, continue to refuse to accept that their international human rights obligations extend to actions and persons outside their territorial borders.[94]

The CJEU ruling in *Schrems* invalidating the Safe Harbour decision, and the negotiations between the EU and US concerning a replacement agreement,

92 For example, in *Verdugo-Urquidez*, the US Supreme Court held that the Fourth Amendment does not apply to the search and seizure by US agents of property owned by a non-resident alien and located in a foreign country: *United States v. Verdugo-Urquidez*, 494 U.S. 259 (1990).

93 United Nations Human Rights Committee, *Concluding observations on the fourth periodic report of the United States of America*, CCPR/C/USA/CO/4, p. 2.

94 I. Brown and D. Korff, above n. 91, p. 248.

should not be seen in isolation from international human rights law. Just as the principle of proportionality is applied by the Court in relation to personal data originating from the EU, transborder rights obligations should ideally apply to all transfers of personal data, of whatever origin. Applying a broad proportionality principle would ensure that the transborder surveillance practices of state actors are both appropriately targeted and incorporate sufficient procedural safeguards. Nevertheless, just as this chapter has argued for greater clarity and rigour in the development and exposition of the proportionality principle under EU law, so there is a pressing need for clarification of the position under international human rights law, and ideally for the development of an appropriate transborder framework for the application of a proportionality principle. In this, the developing jurisprudence of the CJEU may serve as a test-bed; but there clearly remains work to be done at both the EU and international levels. In this respect, it is hoped that the opportunities presented by the impending CJEU decisions involving bulk data collection will give rise to significant developments, including in appropriately refining the proportionality principle.

9. THE 'PRIVACY SHIELD' AND PROPORTIONALITY

Following the Snowden revelations, the European Commission adopted two communications identifying weaknesses with the Safe Harbour Agreement in the light of the revelations and setting out a plan for restoring trust in trans-Atlantic data flows.[95] Thereafter, in 2014, negotiations between the US and the EU commenced with a view to revising the Safe Harbour Agreement to take into account the Commission's concerns, but failed to advance due mainly to difficulties experienced in negotiating a separate agreement, known as the 'Umbrella Agreement', that was designed to deal with trans-Atlantic cooperation, including data-sharing, relating to criminal and terrorism investigations.[96]

---

95 European Commission, Communication to the European Parliament and the Council on Rebuilding Trust in EU–US Data Flows, COM(2013) 846 final, 27 November 2013; European Commission, Communication to the European Parliament and the Council on the Functioning of the Safe Harbour from the Perspective of EU Citizens and Companies Established in the EU, COM(2013) 847 final, 27 November 2013.

96 R. Massey and H.E. Sussman, 'The US–EU safe harbor framework is invalid: now what?' (2016) 22(1) *Computer and Telecommunications Law Review* 1. On 2 June 2016, representatives of the US and EU announced the signing of the 'Umbrella' agreement: European Commission, 'Joint EU–U.S. press statement following the EU–U.S. Justice and Home Affairs Ministerial Meeting', Amsterdam, 2 June 2016. The agreement was approved by the European Parliament on 1 December 2016, but implementation in the US may be complicated by the approach of the incoming Trump administration: D. Bender, 'European Parliament Approves EU–U.S. Umbrella Agreement', *Inside Privacy*, 2 December 2016, <https://www.insideprivacy.com/international/european-union/european-parliament-approves-eu-u-s-umbrella-agreement/>.

The *Schrems* ruling, however, made it imperative for a new agreement to be reached; and the Article 29 Working Party, which consists of data protection regulators of Member States, set the end of January 2016 as the deadline for the European Commission and the US to reach agreement before enforcement actions, arising from the invalidation of the Safe Harbour Agreement, would be taken. This section of the chapter explains and analyses the proposed replacement agreement, with a focus on the role of proportionality in assessing the adequacy of the proposed agreement.[97]

Eventually, on 2 February 2016, the European Commission and the US Department of Commerce announced that they had reached a political agreement, known as the Privacy Shield, designed to replace the Safe Harbour Agreement.[98] Nevertheless, the details of the agreement were not published until 29 February 2016, when the Commission released a communication,[99] a draft adequacy determination[100] and the annexed text of the Privacy Shield. The agreement was aimed at ensuring an adequate ('essentially equivalent') level of protection by satisfactorily addressing the problems identified by the CJEU with the Safe Harbour Agreement while, as might be expected from an international agreement, embodying a series of political compromises. Significantly, enforcement of the Privacy Shield on US organisations remains based on self-certification of compliance with privacy principles, subject to overview by the FTC.

The main features of the Privacy Shield Framework are as follows:

- A revised and strengthened set of privacy principles, including a notice principle that requires a link to the Privacy Shield List (a list of self-certifying organisations maintained by the US Department of Commerce and including organisations removed from the list) and reference to the individual right of

97 Since this chapter was written, on 12 July 2016 the European Commission adopted the final version of the Privacy Shield which came into effect on the same day: European Commission, *Commission Implementing Decision of 12.7.2016 pursuant to Directive 95/46/EC of the European Parliament and of the Council on the adequacy of the protection provided by the EU-U.S. Privacy Shield*, C(2016) 4176 final, 12 July 2016. On 27 October 2016, Digital Rights Ireland lodged a challenge to the Privacy Shield before the CJEU: J. Fioretti and D. Volz, 'Privacy group launches legal challenge against EU-U.S. data pact', *reuters.com*, 27 October 2016, <http://www.reuters.com/article/us-eu-dataprotection-usa-idUSKCN12Q2JK>.

98 European Commission, 'EU Commission and United States agree on new framework for trans-Atlantic data flows: EU-US Privacy Shield', Press Release, 2 February 2016, <http://europa.eu/rapid/press-release_IP-16-216_en.htm?locale=en>.

99 European Commission, Communication to the European Parliament and the Council, Transatlantic Data Flows: Restoring Trust through Strong Safeguards, COM(2016) 117 final, 20 February 2016.

100 European Commission, Draft Commission Implementing Decision pursuant to Directive 95/46/EC of the European Parliament and of the Council on the adequacy of the protection provided by the EU-U.S. Privacy Shield, 29 February 2016.

access to personal data, and an onward transfer principle that places some limits on transfers of personal data to third parties.

- Revised enforcement and liability mechanisms, conferring greater rights on EU data subjects. The new redress mechanisms include: an obligation on self-certifying organisations to designate an independent dispute settlement body to address complaints; a commitment by the Department of Commerce to receive and undertake best efforts to resolve complaints, including receiving complaints from EU member data protection authorities; a commitment by the FTC to give priority consideration to referrals of non-compliance with the privacy principles and to receive complaints directly from individuals; and an obligation on self-certifying organisations to cooperate with EU Member State data protection authorities.
- As a 'last resort' recourse mechanism, after the exhaustion of all other avenues, binding arbitration is to be available from a Privacy Shield Panel, consisting of at least 20 arbitrators selected jointly by the US Department of Commerce and the European Commission, and which can award non-monetary equitable relief.
- Increased transparency, and overview mechanisms, of access to personal data of EU data subjects by US public authorities, including intelligence agencies. As explained in the Commission's draft adequacy decision, a range of internal and political oversight and transparency mechanisms apply to US intelligence agencies. Nevertheless, as the draft decision acknowledged, available recourse mechanisms for EU data subjects against US public authorities are limited and, in some cases, such as activities authorised under EO-12333, non-existent. To address this, in a letter from the US Secretary of State set out in Annex III of the draft decision, the US government undertook to create a Privacy Shield Ombudsperson to receive and respond to complaints about US public authorities. The proposed scheme requires individual complaints to be directed to the EU Member State bodies responsible for oversight of security services, then sent to a centralised EU complaint handling body (if created), before being referred to the Ombudsperson to investigate whether US laws have been complied with.
- Limitations and derogations from privacy principles for US public authorities for national security, public interest and law enforcement purposes. Annex II, Section I.5 to the Privacy Shield draft adequacy decision specifically provides that adherence to the privacy principles is 'limited to the extent necessary to meet national security, public interest or law enforcement requirements'.[101] Accordingly, in making a determination on adequacy, the Commission was required to assess limitations under US law relating to national security, public interest or law enforcement purposes. In particular, the Commission's draft

[101] Ibid., Recital 52.

adequacy decision refers to limitations on the activities of US intelligence agencies that have been imposed since the Snowden revelations and, especially, limitations imposed by Presidential Policy Directive 28 (PPD-28), a binding Presidential directive which applies to 'signals intelligence' activities, issued on 17 January 2014. According to PPD-28, signals intelligence may be collected only where there is a foreign intelligence or counterintelligence purpose and collection of personal data must always be 'as tailored as feasible'. Elaborating on this, the draft adequacy decision refers to representations of the US Office of the Director of National Intelligence (ODNI), in a letter set out in Annex VI to the draft decision, which explain that, while bulk collection of signals intelligence is sometimes necessary, there is a general rule preferring targeted collection.[102] In addition, the US government assured the Commission that it does not engage in 'indiscriminate surveillance' and that any bulk collection of Internet data, including via access to trans-Atlantic cables, applies only to a 'small proportion of the Internet'.[103]
- An annual joint review of the Privacy Shield framework, involving the European Commission, the US Department of Commerce and the FTC, and being open to all EU data protection authorities, resulting in a public report prepared by the Commission and submitted to the European Parliament and the Council.

Since its release, the Privacy Shield agreement has been subject to considerable analysis, and criticism, including by relevant EU-level institutions. On 13 April 2016, the Article 29 Working Party published its opinion on the Privacy Shield draft adequacy decision.[104] While welcoming the improvements made by the Privacy Shield when compared with the Safe Harbour Agreement, the Working Party identified a number of important shortcomings which, in its view, need to be resolved or clarified in order for the agreement to confer the high level of protection required for an adequacy decision. Given its focus, it is beyond the scope of this chapter to engage in a detailed critical analysis of all aspects of the complex Privacy Shield agreement. Instead, this section of the chapter concentrates on the main problems identified by the Working Party and its assessment of the extent to which the agreement satisfies the requirements of necessity and proportionality.[105]

---

102 Ibid., Recital 59.

103 Ibid., Recital 69.

104 Article 29 Data Protection Working Party, *Opinion 01/2016 on the EU–U.S. Privacy Shield draft adequacy decision*, 16/EN WP 238, adopted on 13 April 2016.

105 On 24 May 2016, the European Parliament agreed to a joint resolution on the Privacy Shield which, amongst other things, called on the European Commission to implement the recommendations made by the Article 29 Working Party in its Privacy Shield opinion: European Parliament, Joint Motion for a Resolution pursuant to Rule 123(2) and (4) of

Overall, the Working Party considered that the format adopted by the Privacy Shield, with the relevant principles and guarantees being set out in both the adequacy decision and annexes to the decision, resulted in a lack of clarity and, at times, inconsistency.[106] Consequently, the Working Party called for further clarification and consistency in the draft decision, including the preparation of a glossary of terms. In relation to transfers of personal data by commercial organisations, the Working Party pointed to significant omissions in the privacy principles when compared with EU data privacy law, including the lack of a data retention limitation principle, requiring organisations to delete data if they are no longer necessary, and a lack of legal guarantees for individuals subject to automated decisions which produce legal effects or otherwise significantly affect an individual.[107] On the key issue of limitations and derogations from the privacy principles for US public authorities, the Working Party engaged in an analysis of the relevant US legal framework, including PPD-28, EO-12333 and the ODNI letter set out in Annex VI to the Commission's draft decision. While acknowledging the significant steps taken by the US to increase transparency of the practices of security agencies since the Snowden revelations, the Working Party concluded that, in important respects, the draft adequacy decision lacked clarity on the limitations and the extent of safeguards under US law. In particular, the Working Party was concerned that US law (and practice) did not exclude the possibility of mass, indiscriminate data collection; and that the role of the proposed Privacy Shield Ombudsperson was not spelt out in sufficient detail.[108] In particular, the Working Party considered that the powers and position of the Ombudsperson needed to be clarified to demonstrate that the role was truly independent and capable of offering effective remedies. Given that these issues are central to any assessment of the extent to which the Privacy Shield complies with the CJEU's ruling in *Schrems*, including the analysis of proportionality, this section of the Working Party's analysis is expanded upon immediately below. Finally, the Working Party welcomed the ongoing annual joint review process for the Privacy Shield, but recommended clarification and agreement on the elements to be included in the joint reviews.[109]

---

the Rules of Procedure, 24 May 2016. Subsequently, on 30 May 2016, the European Data Protection Supervisor released an opinion on the Privacy Shield draft adequacy decision which expressed very similar concerns to those set out in the Working Party's opinion: European Data Protection Supervisor, *Opinion on the EU-U.S. Privacy Shield draft adequacy decision*, Opinion 4/2016, 30 May 2016.

106 Article 29 Data Protection Working Party, *Opinion 01/2016 on the EU-U.S. Privacy Shield draft adequacy decision*, 16/EN WP 238, adopted on 13 April 2016, pp. 12–14.

107 Ibid., pp. 17–18.

108 Ibid., pp. 51–52.

109 Ibid., p. 58.

As explained above, on the analysis presented in this chapter, in *Schrems* the CJEU found that the Safe Harbour Agreement was invalid mainly on the basis that the broad derogation for national security, public interest and law enforcement requirements in Annex I to the Commission decision, which allowed for bulk collection and access to personal data by US public authorities, was disproportionate to the legitimate objectives of national security and law enforcement. This conclusion was reinforced by a lack of enforceable remedies, and absence of procedural safeguards, for EU data subjects in relation to the actions of US public authorities. It is therefore unsurprising that the most significant weaknesses with the Privacy Shield draft decision identified by the Working Party concern the extent to which the derogations for US public authorities in Annex II to the draft decision fail to comply with EU jurisprudence relating to the protection of fundamental rights.

In undertaking this analysis, the Working Party adopted a framework, which it set out in a working document, on the justification of interferences with the rights to privacy and data privacy through surveillance measures, especially in the context of data transfers to the US, which it published contemporaneously with its Privacy Shield opinion.[110] Given the policy orientation of the Working Party's analysis, its approach to justifications for interferences with privacy rights is unsurprisingly more structured and complete than that applied by the CJEU in invalidating the Safe Harbour Agreement in *Schrems*. Drawing on the human rights jurisprudence of both the Strasbourg and Luxembourg courts, the working document formulated the following four European Essential Guarantees, which must be in place if interferences to fundamental rights are to be justifiable:

A. Processing should be in accordance with the law and based on clear, precise an accessible rules.
B. Necessity and proportionality with regard to the legitimate objectives pursued need to be demonstrated.
C. An independent oversight mechanism should exist, which is both effective and impartial.
D. Effective remedies need to be available to the individual.[111]

Regarding Guarantee A, which essentially relates to the foreseeability of lawful interferences as a means of protection against arbitrariness, the Working Party

[110] Article 29 Data Protection Working Party, *Working Document 01/2016 on the justification of interferences with the fundamental rights to privacy and data protection through surveillance measures when transferring data (European Essential Guarantees)*, 16/EN WP 237, adopted on 13 April 2016.

[111] Article 29 Data Protection Working Party, *Opinion 01/2016 on the EU–U.S. Privacy Shield draft adequacy decision*, 16/EN WP 238, adopted on 13 April 2016, pp. 11–12.

noted the significant improvements in the transparency of US public intelligence activities since the Snowden revelations, including information published in relevant PCLOB reports and limitations introduced by PPD-28. Nevertheless, especially in light of remaining uncertainties concerning the operation of EO-112333, the Working Party concluded that, without further clarification, it was impossible to determine whether the US regime was sufficiently foreseeable.[112]

On the analysis presented in this chapter, the availability of procedural safeguards, including effective remedies, is relevant to the proportionality assessment; it is therefore appropriate to consider Guarantees B to D together. One possible reading of the *Schrems* ruling is that, building on *Digital Rights Ireland*, the CJEU effectively concluded that bulk collection of personal data by US intelligence agencies can never be proportionate. Nevertheless, as pointed out by the Working Party in its working document on justifications, to date neither the Strasbourg nor the Luxembourg courts appear to have adopted a final position on whether or not bulk collection can ever be justifiable, with some clarification on this issue expected from the forthcoming CJEU decisions referred to earlier in this chapter.[113] That said, and while noting that the application of proportionality to this area may be qualified or revised by the CJEU in the impending decisions, the Working Party reiterated its consistent conclusion that 'massive and indiscriminate collection of data (non-targeted bulk collection) in any case cannot be considered proportionate'.[114] This means that the extent to which collection of data by intelligence agencies is targeted so as to be related to legitimate national security objectives must be absolutely central to the proportionality analysis, especially where communications content is collected.

As explained above, since the Snowden revelations, the US government has taken steps to ensure that intelligence gathering is less indiscriminate, including the injunction in PPD-28 that collection of personal data must always be 'as tailored as feasible'. Nevertheless, as made clear in the ODNI letter annexed to the Commission's draft adequacy decision, the US continues to reserve the right to engage in bulk collection of signals intelligence where necessary. As, according to publicly available information, US intelligence agencies continue to engage in bulk, indiscriminate collection, or at least refuse to exclude doing so, the Working Party reached the inevitable conclusion that the Privacy Shield,

112 Ibid., p. 37.

113 Article 29 Data Protection Working Party, *Working Document 01/2016 on the justification of interferences with the fundamental rights to privacy and data protection through surveillance measures when transferring data (European Essential Guarantees)*, 16/EN WP 237, adopted on 13 April 2016, p. 8.

114 Ibid., p. 12.

by not ruling this out, allowed a disproportionate interference with rights.[115] Above and beyond this, the Working Party expressed concerns that the broad assurance that data collection would be 'as tailored as feasible' could still allow for massive data collection, which might also fail the proportionality test.[116] Accordingly, the Working Party, at a minimum, required further information on mass collection practices by US intelligence agencies before a final conclusion on adequacy could be reached.

Regarding the need for effective and independent oversight, the Working Party noted the substantial internal oversight mechanisms in place in the US, but pointed out that effective oversight depends on an independent, external body. As there is no oversight whatsoever of surveillance programmes undertaken pursuant to EO-12333, Guarantee C could hardly be satisfied in relation to these programmes. Moreover, the regime administered by the FISA Court provides no effective oversight for non-US persons.[117]

As explained earlier in this chapter, in the *Schrems* ruling, the CJEU identified the absence of any effective legal remedies against US public authorities as an important weakness in the Safe Harbour Agreement, and also found that the lack of legal recourse against state intrusions compromised Art. 47 of the Charter. Significant elements of the Privacy Shield are aimed at improving the legal recourse mechanisms available to EU persons. In relation to the activities of US public authorities, the main new recourse avenue is the proposal to create a Privacy Shield Ombudsperson, to receive and respond to individual complaints. While welcoming the introduction of this new recourse mechanism, the Working Party concluded that the Privacy Shield failed to specify the powers and position of the Ombudsperson with sufficient detail, leaving doubts regarding its independence from government, the extent of its investigatory powers, its remedial powers, and the absence of an appeals process.[118] As explained above, according to the Working Party, the two major factors compromising the adequacy of the Commission's draft decision are the failure of the Privacy Shield to exclude untargeted mass collection of data by US security agencies and the lack of clarity regarding the role and powers of the Ombudsperson. Both of these shortcomings arise from the disproportionality of the US legal and administrative regimes that apply to the collection and analysis of data by security agencies, and especially the regime that applies to the data of non-US persons.

---

115 Article 29 Data Protection Working Party, *Opinion 01/2016 on the EU–U.S. Privacy Shield draft adequacy decision*, 16/EN WP 238, adopted on 13 April 2016, p. 40.

116 Ibid., p. 40.

117 Ibid., pp. 42–43.

118 Ibid., pp. 49–51.

The Privacy Shield, as a negotiated international agreement, necessarily embodied compromises between the parties. It is clear that both parties to the negotiation, the US Department of Commerce and the European Commission, share interests in ensuring the continued viability of trans-Atlantic data transfers while insulating the agreement against the potential for an adverse CJEU ruling. The negotiations took place in the shadow of considerable uncertainties in the CJEU's application of the proportionality principle to mass data collection, including uncertainties arising from the rulings in *Digital Rights Ireland* and *Schrems*, and including whether or not bulk collection by security agencies can ever be proportionate. These uncertainties enabled the negotiators to conclude that a regime in which some form of bulk collection by security agencies is restricted, but not ruled out could, nevertheless, be adequate. The Commission also concluded that the Privacy Shield Ombudsperson mechanism provided sufficient safeguards for EU data subjects, including by receiving individual complaints and investigating compliance with US law. Nevertheless, the agreement and the Commission's draft decision cannot disguise the hallmarks of haste. On the basis of the CJEU's ruling in *Schrems*, the Working Party's conclusions that more information on US mass data collection practices and on the details of the ombudsperson mechanism is needed before an adequacy decision can be made must surely be correct. But, that said, as argued in this chapter, gaps and ambiguities in the CJEU's proportionality analysis mean that precisely what changes might be required for the agreement to be adequate, including whether the US must undertake to engage only in targeted data collection, is necessarily uncertain, and may require further rulings by the CJEU, some of which are forthcoming, to be clarified.

10. CONCLUSION

In Europe, proportionality has emerged as a meta-principle which, among other things, is the key legal standard for establishing the balance between the protection of rights, on the one hand, and public policies, on the other. Thus, it is unsurprising that the principle, as applied by the CJEU, has played the central role in establishing the balance between state surveillance and the rights to privacy and data privacy in cases such as *Digital Rights Ireland*, but also, as argued in this chapter, underpins the *Schrems* ruling. As illustrated by these cases, under the influence of the EU Charter, the Court has taken an increasingly expansive approach to the protection of privacy and data privacy, according less deference to EU policy-making institutions. This is clearly reflected in the level of scrutiny applied to interferences with these rights, which under proportionality analysis now requires a form of strict review. While a degree of flexibility and sensitivity to the facts of instant cases must be retained by courts applying the proportionality principle this should not, however, be at the expense of properly constrained judicial decision-making. Applying a rigorous approach to the application of the proportionality principle is essential if courts are to escape charges of arbitrarily substituting their judgments for those of policy-making institutions, and for the promotion of greater certainty and predictability. Yet, as this chapter has explained, the jurisprudence of the CJEU, culminating in the *Digital Rights Ireland* and *Schrems* rulings, has given rise to significant legal uncertainties, including in relation to the standard and intensity of review of measures that may interfere with the rights to privacy and data privacy and, from a policy-making perspective, creating much uncertainty about whether bulk data collection is ever permissible.

Despite weaknesses with the CJEU's approach to proportionality, this chapter contends that the principle is the correct legal framework for evaluating infringements of fundamental rights, including the rights to privacy and data privacy. This is because, applying a rights-based perspective, the principle ensures that the courts ask the right questions. While rights sceptics contend that rights-based judicial review, such as that undertaken in jurisdictions with a 'thick' concept of the rule of law, is somehow antithetical to democracy, the appropriate protection of rights is a pre-condition to sustainable democratic polities. This is especially the case where democratic processes are incapable of effectively limiting state-based intrusions, which appears to be the case with the apparently inexorable drive to broader and more intensive surveillance practices by state intelligence agencies. In this context, an appropriately defined proportionality principle may well be the main legal bulwark against privacy and democracy-corrosive practices.

While mass indiscriminate surveillance, with no adequate procedural safeguards, would fall foul of any rights-based review, extra-territorial surveillance by state-based agencies may escape review in jurisdictions where rights are not extended to foreigners. Under EU law, the requirement that transborder transfers of personal data should be permissible only where a third country provides adequate protection is a mechanism for ensuring transborder protection of the rights of EU data subjects. Nevertheless, the need for a single jurisdiction, such as the EU, to establish such a mechanism, reflects a significant limitation of the international human rights framework. In an era of ubiquitous transborder transfers of personal data, where rights can be readily invaded at a distance, the proper protection of rights must entail limitations on extra-territorial interferences by state parties. The proportionality principle, appropriately defined and rigorously applied, is an eminently suitable legal rubric for evaluating the extra-territorial surveillance practices of state agencies.

The current process of revising the data transfer arrangements between the EU and the US, in the shadow of the *Schrems* ruling, therefore represents a highly significant test of the principles that should apply to transborder data surveillance practices. As explained in this chapter, however, uncertainties in the EU rights-based framework, and especially in the content and application of the proportionality principle, have complicated the process for finalising a US–EU framework to replace the invalidated Safe Harbour Agreement. The uncertain jurisprudence has, in particular, created wriggle room for the European Commission to conclude, in its February 2016 draft decision on the Privacy Shield, that a US regime that fails to sufficiently exclude the possibility of bulk data collection, and includes scant details on the key ombudsperson recourse mechanism, nevertheless confers the required high level of protection of the rights to privacy and data privacy of EU data subjects. Yet, the Article 29 Working Party was surely correct to express serious concerns that, at a minimum, without further details concerning US bulk collection practices and the ombudsperson mechanism, it would be imprudent to conclude that the Privacy Shield agreement confers adequate protection. At the time of writing this chapter, the position was further complicated by the prospect of two impending, and likely highly relevant, CJEU rulings on the critical issue of bulk data collection. These two related pending developments – the process for adjusting the Privacy Shield agreement so that it is able to comply with EU law and the forthcoming CJEU rulings – seem likely to set the framework establishing the permissible limits on state based surveillance, especially in the trans-Atlantic context, for some time to come. As this chapter argues, the development of a clearer, more rigorously elaborated proportionality principle by the CJEU would serve both to better protect the rights of EU data subjects and add much-needed commercial and political certainty.

4. US SURVEILLANCE LAW, SAFE HARBOUR AND REFORMS SINCE 2013

Peter SWIRE*

1. INTRODUCTION

This chapter is based on a submission to the Belgian Privacy Authority for its December 2015 Forum on 'The Consequences of the Judgment in the *Schrems* Case.'[1] The Forum discussed the decision of the European Court of Justice in *Schrems v. Data Protection Commissioner*[2] that the EU/US Safe Harbour Agreement was unlawful under the EU Data Protection Directive, particularly due to concerns about US surveillance law.

For the Forum, I was asked to comment on two issues:

1. Is US surveillance law fundamentally compatible with EU data protection law?
2. What actions and reforms has the US taken since the Snowden revelations began in June 2013?

The chapter draws on my background as a scholar of both EU data protection law and US surveillance law. The following three sections address serious

---

* Huang Professor of Law and Ethics, Georgia Tech Scheller College of Business; Senior Fellow, Future of Privacy Forum; Senior Counsel, Alston & Bird, LLP; nothing in this chapter should be attributed to any client of the firm. E-mail: peter.swire@scheller.gatech.edu.

Swire thanks DeBrae Kennedy-Mayo, Research Associate at the Georgia Tech Scheller College of Business, for her work on this chapter. This chapter is updated through January 2016 and does not address subsequent developments, such as the promulgation of the EU/US Privacy Shield. As an exception, the chapter does provide citation to final passage of the Judicial Redress Act.

1 <https://www.privacycommission.be/en/events/forum-consequences-judgment-schrems-case>. The Belgian Privacy Commission studied these issues for the broader group of European privacy regulators in the Article 29 Working Party. The level of EU scepticism of US surveillance law practices is reflected in the title of my panel: 'Law in the EU and the US: impossible coexistence?'

2 Case C-362/14, *Maximillian Schrems v. Data Protection Commissioner* (6 October 2015).

misunderstandings of US national security law, reflected in official statements made in the *Schrems* case and elsewhere.

Section 2: The fundamental equivalence of the United States and EU Member States as constitutional democracies under the rule of law. In the *Schrems* decision, the US was criticised for failing to ensure 'a level of protection of fundamental rights essentially equivalent to that guaranteed in the EU legal order.' This chapter critiques that finding, instead showing that the United States has strict rule of law, separation of powers, and judicial oversight of law enforcement and national security surveillance, which together make the US legal order 'essentially equivalent' to the EU legal order.

Section 3: The section 702 PRISM and Upstream programmes are reasonable and lawful responses to changing technology. The Advocate General's opinion in the *Schrems* case said that the PRISM programme gave the NSA 'unrestricted access to mass data' stored in the US, and that section 702 enabled NSA access 'in a generalised manner' for 'all persons and all means of electronic communications.' This chapter refutes those claims, which appear to be based in part on incorrect stories in the press. Instead, the section 702 programmes operate with judicial supervision and subject to numerous safeguards and limitations. They examine the communications only of targeted individuals, and only for listed foreign intelligence purposes. The total number of individuals targeted under section 702 in 2013 was 92,707, a tiny fraction of Internet users in the EU or globally.

Section 4: The US Congress and executive branch have instituted two dozen significant reforms to surveillance law and practice since 2013. The *Schrems* decision said that US privacy protections must be evaluated in the 'current factual and legal context,' but did not address the numerous changes put in place since 2013. This chapter provides a readable explanation of each of these actions, which together constitute the biggest set of pro-privacy actions in US surveillance law since the passing of the Foreign Intelligence Surveillance Act in 1978.

2. THE FUNDAMENTAL EQUIVALENCE OF THE UNITED STATES AND EU MEMBER STATES AS CONSTITUTIONAL DEMOCRACIES UNDER THE RULE OF LAW

This section addresses the most basic requirement of the European Court of Justice (ECJ) in the *Schrems* decision, that the United States must ensure 'a level of protection of fundamental rights essentially equivalent to that guaranteed in the EU legal order.'[3] In the wake of the *Schrems* decision, there are now serious

[3] Ibid., paras. 96, 98, and 107.

debates in the EU about whether any transfer of personal data to the US can be considered 'adequate' under the requirements of the Data Protection Directive.[4] If the European legal regime makes a firm finding that the United States lacks the necessary legal order, then transfers of personal data may be essentially blocked, affecting large portions of trans-Atlantic commerce and communication.

This section seeks to explain the US system of law and surveillance to a European audience. It stresses *the fundamental equivalence of the United States and EU Member States as constitutional democracies under the rule of law.* The United States has its Constitution, continually in effect since 1790. The US has deeply established rule of law, separation of powers, and judicial oversight of both law enforcement and national security surveillance. For Europe to decide that the US 'legal order' is unacceptable and deficient – requiring the blocking of most or all data transfers – would be a consequential judgment, and one not supported by the facts. Among the many problems with such a decision, Europe would have to determine what other countries in the world have a constitutional law and practice that is the same as, or less protective than, the United States – such countries would logically also be ineligible to receive data transfers from the EU.

The discussion here of 'fundamental equivalence' is different from a country-by-country comparison of the details of US surveillance law compared to the surveillance law of the 28 EU Member States. Others undoubtedly will present reports about whether the details of US law are 'essentially equivalent' to the details of surveillance in the Member States. The discussion here of 'fundamental equivalence' gives a deeper meaning to the ECJ's discussion of 'essential equivalence' – in its 'essence', does the US legal system provide protection for fundamental rights that is essentially equivalent to the EU Member States? At the basic, fundamental, and constitutive level, does the US legal system meet the minimum standard for protection of rights under the legal systems of any of the EU Member States?

As a law professor who has long studied both US and EU law,[5] my answer is a clear yes. To explain the fundamental equivalence of the US legal system, this

---

4 For instance, along with doubts about the validity of the Safe Harbour Agreement, German data protection authorities have questioned the legality of transfers of personal data to the US under model contracts or Binding Corporate Rules. The German DPA position paper is available, in German, at <https://www.datenschutzzentrum.de/artikel/967-Positionspapier-des-ULD-zum-Safe-Harbor-Urteil-des-Gerichtshofs-der-Europaeischen-Union-vom-6.-Oktober-2015,-C-36214.html>. A summary of the position paper is located at <http://www.dataprivacymonitor.com/enforcement/german-data-protection-authorities-limit-use-of-alternative-data-transfer-mechanisms-in-light-of-safe-harbor-decision/>.

5 For instance, I was a student at L'Institut d'Études Européennes in Brussels in 1980–81. I was the lead author of a book on EU data protection law in 1998: Peter Swire and Robert Litan, *None of Your Business: World Data Flows, E-Commerce, and the European Privacy Directive* (Brookings Institution, 1998). See also Peter Swire, 'Of Elephants, Mice, and Privacy: International Choice of Law and the Internet' (1998) 32 *The International Lawyer*

section provides a brief introduction to the US as a constitutional democracy under the rule of law. It next explains the way that the Fourth Amendment to the US Constitution, governing searches and seizures, has been applied to wiretaps and changing technology over time in law enforcement cases. Then, the discussion turns to the related regime for foreign intelligence and national security wiretaps and surveillance. For both law enforcement and national security surveillance, independent judges with life tenure have thoroughly reviewed government surveillance programs, and have assured that legal protections are updated to match changing communications technology.

Some readers who are more familiar with the US legal system and its surveillance laws may decide to skip ahead to section 3 of this chapter, concerning the section 702 PRISM and Upstream programmes, and section 4, listing 24 US actions and legal changes in the surveillance sphere since the Snowden stories began in June 2013. This chapter provides some basic information on US constitutional and surveillance law, however, because the idea and the fact of fundamental equivalence has not been prominent to date in discussions related to the *Schrems* Safe Harbour decision.

2.1. THE UNITED STATES IS A CONSTITUTIONAL DEMOCRACY UNDER THE RULE OF LAW

Readers of this chapter will generally agree, I hope, that the United Sates is a constitutional democracy under the rule of law. The United States' Constitution, which was ratified in 1790, creates three branches of government. The separation of the legislative, executive, and judicial branches matches the views of Montesquieu in his 1748 treatise on 'The Spirit of the Laws' – divided power among the three branches protects 'liberty' and guards against 'tyrannical' uses of power.[6] Under the US Constitution, Congress is elected by the people; the

991 (analysing choice of law issues under the EU Data Protection Directive) <http://ssrn.com/abstract=121277>; 'Peter Hustinx and Three Clichés About E.U.-US Data Privacy' in Hielke Hijmans and Herke Kranenborg (eds.), *Data Protection Anno 2014: How to Restore Trust?* (Intersentia, 2014) <http://ssrn.com/abstract=2404258>.

6 'When legislative power is united with executive power in a single person or in a single body of the magistracy, there is no liberty, because one can fear that the same monarch or senate that makes tyrannical laws will execute them tyrannically. Nor is there liberty if the power of judging is not separate from legislative power and from executive power. If it were joined to legislative power, the power over the life and liberty of the citizens would be arbitrary, for the judge would be the legislator. If it were joined to executive power, the judge could have the force of an oppressor. All would be lost if the same man or the same body of principal men, either of nobles, or of the people, exercised these three powers: that of making the laws, that of executing the laws, that of executing public resolutions, and that of judging the crimes or the disputes of individuals.' Montesquieu, Book 11 ch 6 – 'On the Constitution of England' <http://oll.libertyfund.org/titles/837>.

President is elected to no more than two four-year terms; and federal judges are nominated by the executive, confirmed by the legislature, and appointed for life to ensure their independence.

The Bill of Rights to the United States Constitution specifically enumerates provisions to protect freedoms and privacy of individuals. Most important for surveillance issues, the Fourth Amendment limits the Government's ability to conduct searches and seizures, and warrants can issue only with independent review by a judge. The Fourth Amendment governs more than simply a person's home or body; its protections apply specifically to communications, covering a person's 'papers and effects'.[7] Other fundamental rights and safeguards included under the Bill of Rights include: the First Amendment's protection of freedom of speech and freedom of association;[8] the Third Amendment's protection of the privacy of the home, prohibiting the quartering of soldiers within a person's home;[9] and the Fifth Amendment's protection of the privacy of a person's thoughts, specifically by prohibiting the Government from making persons testify about their own thoughts to incriminate themselves.[10]

2.2. FUNDAMENTAL PROTECTIONS RELATED TO LAW ENFORCEMENT SURVEILLANCE

To address changing technology, judges with life tenure have developed detailed case law concerning the Fourth Amendment, with somewhat different rules for law enforcement uses (crimes) and national security (foreign intelligence).

7 The Fourth Amendment to the United States Constitution reads: 'The right of the people to be secure in their persons, houses, papers, and effects, against unreasonable searches and seizures, shall not be violated, and no warrants shall issue, but upon probable cause, supported by oath or affirmation, and particularly describing the place to be searched, and the persons or things to be seized.' <https://www.law.cornell.edu/constitution/fourth_amendment> (text); see <http://www.uscourts.gov/about-federal-courts/educational-resources/about-educational-outreach/activity-resources/what-does-0> (explanation).

8 The First Amendment to the United States Constitution reads: 'Congress shall make no law respecting an establishment of religion, or prohibiting the free exercise thereof; or abridging the freedom of speech, or of the press; or the right of the people peaceably to assemble, and to petition the Government for a redress of grievances.' <https://www.law.cornell.edu/constitution/first_amendment> (text).

9 The Third Amendment to the United States Constitution reads: 'No soldier shall, in time of peace be quartered in any house, without the consent of the owner, nor in time of war, but in a manner to be prescribed by law.' <https://www.law.cornell.edu/constitution/third_amendment> (text).

10 The Fifth Amendment to the United States Constitution reads, 'No person … shall be compelled in any criminal case to be a witness against himself.' <https://www.law.cornell.edu/constitution/fifth_amendment> (text).

As many have described, the Supreme Court has announced strict rules under the Fourth Amendment for wiretaps.[11] Initially, a closely divided Supreme Court in 1928 held that the Fourth Amendment did not apply, because the wiretap was done 'in public' at the telephone pole[12] Soon after, the Congress passed a law regulating wiretaps.[13] In the 1960s, the Supreme Court reversed that decision in the famous *Katz* and *Berger* cases, and set forth detailed requirements for law enforcement wiretaps.[14] Congress enacted those protections in 1968 in Title III of that year's crime bill, including strict minimisation requirements and the requirement that wiretaps be used only when other investigative methods would not succeed.[15]

As an important part of the overall enforcement of the Fourth Amendment, the Supreme Court developed the 'exclusionary rule', so evidence from an illegal search could not be used in court.[16] In addition, the Court barred evidence that was 'the fruit of a poisonous tree' – additional evidence similarly could not be used in court if it was derived from an illegal search.[17]

In recent years, three Supreme Court cases have illustrated the continuing judicial scrutiny of surveillance practices in light of changing technology:

1. *Riley v. California* (cell phones).[18] The longstanding rule has been that police can search a person 'incident to arrest' – they can go through the person's pockets to spot possible weapons or evidence. The government took the position that this rule applied to cell phones. In 2014, the Supreme Court unanimously disagreed, holding that a judicial warrant was needed before police could search the contents of the cell phone. The Court said: 'a cell phone search would typically expose to the government far more than the most exhaustive search of a house.' In short, the Court updated fundamental rights protections to adapt to the changing technology of the cell phone.
2. *United States v. Jones* (search conducted in public).[19] The longstanding rule has been that police can 'tail' a suspect in public – they can observe where a suspect goes. Police had also placed tracking devices on objects – the

---

11 One discussion of the history of law enforcement and national security wiretaps is in Peter Swire, 'The System of Foreign Intelligence Surveillance Law' (2004) 72 *Geo. Wash. L. Rev.* 1306 <http://ssrn.com/abstract=586616>.

12 *Olmstead v. United States*, 277 US 438 (1928). Justice Brandeis wrote a famous dissent, which was essentially adopted by the Supreme Court in the 1968 *Katz* case.

13 Communications Act of 1934, Pub. L. No. 97–259 (codified at 47 USC §307).

14 *Katz v. United States*, 389 US 347 (1967); *Berger v. New York*, 388 US 41 (1967).

15 Omnibus Crime Control and Safe Streets Act of 1969, Pub. L. No. 90-351, 82 Stat. 197 (1968) (codified at 18 USC §§2510–21).

16 *Mapp v. Ohio*, 367 US 643 (1961).

17 *Wong Sun v. US*, 371 US 471 (1963).

18 *Riley v. California*, 573 US __ (2014).

19 *United States v. Jones*, 132 S. Ct. 945, 565 US __ (2012).

Supreme Court had previously ruled that the tracking device couldn't enter the home without a warrant, but had never prohibited tracking a suspect in public. In 2012, the Court unanimously held that a warrant was required for a tracking device put on a suspect's car for 30 days. One problem was that the police were 'trespassing' on the suspect's car when they attached a device. Justices wrote at length, however, about the constitutional protections that were needed to prevent long-term and widespread surveillance in public, in light of changing technology.

3. *Kyllo v. United States* (search of house conducted from the street).[20] Longstanding doctrine has permitted the police to gather evidence that is in 'plain view.' In this 2001 case, the police used a thermal imaging device to detect a high level of electricity usage in a house where marijuana was being grown. The Court stated: 'Where, as here, the Government uses a device that is not in general use, to explore details of the home that would previously have been unknowable without physical intrusion, the surveillance is a "search" and is presumptively unreasonable without a warrant.' This holding constrained police surveillance even when the evidence was gathered from the street rather than entering the home.

In conclusion on the rules on law enforcement surveillance, the independent judiciary in the US has a long practice, as well as prominent recent examples, of constraining surveillance conducted by new technologies.

2.3. FUNDAMENTAL PROTECTIONS RELATED TO NATIONAL SECURITY SURVEILLANCE

The US rules applying to national security surveillance are different in certain ways from the law enforcement rules, but multiple, significant constitutional and statutory protections apply even in the national security setting.

The Supreme Court's discussion of national security wiretaps notably began in the 1967 *Katz* case, where the Court announced Fourth Amendment requirements for law enforcement wiretaps. With regard to national security, the Court stated: 'Whether safeguards other than prior authorisation by a magistrate would satisfy the Fourth Amendment in a situation involving the national security is a question not presented in this case.'

The Supreme Court addressed the lawfulness of national security wiretaps in 1972 in *United States v. United States District Court*, generally known as the 'Keith' case, after the name of the district court judge in the case. The defendant was charged with the dynamite bombing of an office of the Central Intelligence

20 *Kyllo v. United States*, 533 US 27 (2001).

Agency. In what the New York Times referred to as a 'stunning' victory for separation of powers, the Supreme Court concluded that 'Fourth Amendment freedoms cannot be properly guaranteed if domestic security surveillance may be conducted solely within the discretion of the Executive Branch.'[21] The Court held that, for wiretaps or other electronic surveillance of domestic threats to national security, the Government must first receive a judicial warrant. The Court expressly withheld judgment 'on the scope of the President's surveillance power with respect to the activities of foreign powers, within or without this country.'[22]

The modern rules for national security surveillance were shaped by Watergate. The break-in to the office in the Watergate building was an example of a classic threat from unchecked executive power – an intrusion into the office of the opposing political party. Following the resignation of President Nixon in 1974, Congress passed the Privacy Act of 1974, creating new protection against misuse of personal information by federal agencies. In 1978, Congress passed the Foreign Intelligence Surveillance Act (FISA), a path-breaking legal structure to address the problem of secret surveillance in an open society.

I have previously written in detail about the numerous legal provisions in FISA.[23] A key point, for present purposes, is that the law created the Foreign Intelligence Surveillance Court (FISC), staffed by independent federal judges with lifetime tenure. Wiretaps and electronic surveillance for foreign intelligence purposes, conducted within the US, could only be done with approval by a FISC judge, regardless of whether the target was a US person or a non-US person. Except for short-term emergency orders, the President, the Attorney General, and the FBI could no longer conduct national security wiretaps on their own – the judges served as a crucial check on the executive branch. Safeguards for FISA orders include:

- requirement for high-level approval within the Department of Justice for any FISA order;
- minimisation procedures to reduce the effects on persons other than the targets of surveillance;
- provision for electronic surveillance for a limited time, with the opportunity to extend the surveillance; and

---

21 Trevor Morrison, 'The Story of the *United States v. United States District Court (Keith)*: The Surveillance Power', p. 2 (Columbia Policy Law & Legal Theory Working Papers, 2008) <http://lsr.nellco.org/cgi/viewcontent.cgi?article=1047&context=columbia pllt>.

22 The Court specifically invited Congress to pass legislation creating a different standard for probable cause and designating a special court to hear the wiretap applications. Congress accepted this invitation in FISA.

23 Peter Swire, 'The System of Foreign Intelligence Surveillance Law' (2004) 72 *Geo. Wash. L. Rev.* 1306 <http://ssrn.com/abstract=586616>.

- requirement for details to the judge concerning the targets of the surveillance and the nature and location of the facilities placed under surveillance.

Congress created institutional checks on the issuance of the secret FISA wiretaps. For instance, Congress created the Senate and House Intelligence Committees, which receive classified briefings about intelligence surveillance. The Attorney General must report to these committees every six months about FISA electronic surveillance, including a description of each criminal case in which FISA information has been used for law enforcement purposes. The Attorney General also must make an annual report to Congress and the public about the total number of applications made for orders and extensions of orders, as well as the total number that were granted, modified, or denied.

Section 3 of this chapter discusses the judicial oversight and safeguards under the section 702 PRISM and Upstream programmes. Section 4 discusses numerous actions and reforms undertaken since 2013 to promote oversight, transparency, and democratic accountability for national security surveillance.

2.4. CONCLUSION

Under the Data Protection Directive, transfers of personal data can be made to third countries if there is 'adequate' protection, which the ECJ has stated means 'essentially equivalent' protection. One aspect of this essential equivalence determination for Safe Harbour 2.0 will concern specific provisions of law, such as data subject access rights or right to have investigation by an independent data protection authority in the data subject's country. I leave that sort of essential equivalence analysis to other authors.

The discussion here has instead focused on the *Schrems* discussion of essential equivalence to the protections guaranteed in the 'EU legal order'. That comparison requires understanding of the 'US legal order'. As discussed in this section, both the US and EU Member States are constitutional democracies under the rule of law. The US has a long tradition of, and recent examples of, independent judges updating fundamental rights protections to adapt to changing technology. The system for governing national security surveillance features the vital principles of oversight, transparency, and democratic accountability. The latter was illustrated in 2015 with the passage of the USA Freedom Act limiting national security surveillance.

Fundamental rights advocates in the EU and the US often propose ways that particular rights can be better protected. There is no claim here that the legal order in either the EU or US protects human rights in the best possible way. The key point instead is that both legal orders are essentially equivalent in their method of democratic governance with constitutional protections. Dismissing the US legal order as fundamentally flawed would be contrary to the facts and would cause major disruptions to commerce and communications between allied nations.

3. THE SECTION 702 PRISM AND UPSTREAM PROGRAMMES ARE REASONABLE AND LAWFUL RESPONSES TO CHANGING TECHNOLOGY

This section explains and analyses the PRISM and Upstream programmes under section 702 FISA. Although there are specific issues where I believe current law should be improved, section 702 overall is a reasonable and lawful response to technological changes.

This section of the chapter explains the legal structure of section 702 before providing more detail about the PRISM and Upstream programmes. Section 702 applies to collections that take place within the US, and only authorises access to the communications of targeted individuals, for listed foreign intelligence purposes. The independent Privacy and Civil Liberties Oversight Board, after receiving classified briefings on section 702, came to this conclusion as part of its 196-page report:

> Overall, the Board has found that the information the programme collects has been valuable and effective in protecting the nation's security and producing useful foreign intelligence. The programme has operated under a statute that was publicly debated, and the text of the statute outlines the basic structure of the programme. Operation of the Section 702 programme has been subject to judicial oversight and extensive internal supervision, and the Board has found no evidence of intentional abuse'.[24]

The section 702 programmes received stern criticism from European officials in the *Schrems* case. Notably, the Advocate General's Opinion included the following statements (with emphasis added):

> According to the Snowden revelations, the NSA established a programme called 'PRISM' under which it obtained *unrestricted access to mass data* stored on servers in the United States owned or controlled by a range of companies active in the Internet and technology field, such as Facebook USA.[25]

Later, the Opinion states as fact: 'Indeed, the access of the United States intelligence services to the data transferred covers, *in a comprehensive manner*, all persons using electronic communications services, without any

24 PCLOB Section 702 report (2014), p. 2.
25 Case C-362/14, above n. 2, Opinion of AG Bot, § 26.

requirement that the persons concerned represent a threat to national security.' The Opinion says the access covers '*in a generalised manner, all persons and all means of electronic communication* and all the data transferred, including the content of the communications, without any differentiation, limitation or exception according to the objective of general interest pursued.' It adds that, for information transferred by a company such as Facebook to the US, there is '*mass, indiscriminate surveillance*.'

I quote the Advocate General's Opinion in detail because of the large gap between these statements and how section 702 actually operates. One difficulty, described in detail here, is that the original *Washington Post* story about PRISM was inaccurate and subsequently corrected. Observers, including the Fundamental Rights Agency of the European Union, have now recognised the factual mistakes. Based on the corrected facts, the Fundamental Rights Agency[26] and the US Privacy and Civil Liberties Oversight Board have found that PRISM is not a bulk collection programme, but instead is based on the use of targeted selectors such as e-mails.

The Upstream programme similarly acquires only targeted communications. From a recently declassified opinion of the Foreign Intelligence Surveillance Court, we now know that the number of electronic communications acquired through Upstream in 2011 was only about 10 percent of the number acquired by PRISM. We also know, based on the same opinion, that the FISC has carefully reviewed NSA's implementation of section 702 and has required the Government to modify aspects of its procedures to address compliance incidents reported by the Government to the Court. In my view, this and other declassified opinions show the willingness and ability of independent judges to hold US intelligence agencies accountable if they stray from the law.

People of good will and intelligence can disagree on what constitutes a reasonable approach to changing technology. Section 4 of this chapter discusses section 702 reforms that have been put in place since 2013. President Obama's Review Group on Intelligence and Communications Technology, on which I served, made recommendations about section 702 that have not been made to date, some of which can only be made by Congress, which will review the law when it sunsets in 2017.[27] I am not saying section 702 is perfect, but it is perfectly clear that the rule of law applies under statutory, executive, and judicial oversight, and section 702 is not 'unrestrained.'

---

26 European Union Agency for Fundamental Rights, 'Surveillance by Intelligence Services: Fundamental Rights Safeguards and Remedies in the EU' (2015), p. 17 <http://fra.europa.eu/sites/default/files/fra_uploads/fra-2015-surveillance-intelligence-services_en.pdf>.

27 Review Group Report, Recommendation 12, at 145–150.

3.1. THE LEGAL STRUCTURE OF SECTION 702

The rationale for what is commonly referred to as section 702 of FISA[28] evolved from the changing nature of international communications. Prior to the Internet, surveillance of communications between two people outside of the US took place outside of the US. For instance, a phone call between someone in France and someone in Pakistan could be collected either in France or Pakistan (or perhaps somewhere in between). Under US law, the Fourth Amendment of the US Constitution clearly applies to wiretaps that are made within the US. By contrast, these constitutional protections do not apply to communications between a French person in France and a Pakistani in Pakistan – they are not part of the community that has agreed to live under the governance of the US Constitution. Accordingly, collection of this type of information historically was outside of FISA's jurisdiction. As discussed further in section 4 below, EU and other democracies have similarly given themselves greater freedom to conduct surveillance outside of their borders than within.

With the rise of the Internet, the facts changed. Now, the same communication between France and Pakistan quite possibly did pass through the United States – much of the Internet backbone has been built in the US, and many communications thus route through the US. One legal question answered by section 702 was how to govern foreign–foreign communications[29] when the intercept occurred within the US.[30] A related factual change concerned the growing use of US-based providers for webmail, social networks, and other services. This change meant that communications between two non-US persons more often would be stored within the US. In light of these factual changes, as well as technological issues affecting the previous statutory text,[31] in 2008 Congress passed section 702 of FISA.

The basic structure of section 702 is that the Foreign Intelligence Surveillance Court must annually approve certifications by the Director of National Intelligence and the Attorney General setting the terms for section 702 surveillance.[32] To target the communications of any person, the Government

[28] 'Section 702' refers to a provision in the Foreign Intelligence Surveillance Act Amendments Act of 2008, which revised the Foreign Intelligence Surveillance Act of 1978 <https://www.govtrack.us/congress/bills/110/hr6304/text>.

[29] This type of communication was historically handled under EO-12333 <http://www.archives.gov/federal-register/codification/executive-order/12333.html>.

[30] This type of communication was historically governed by the stricter standards of FISA <https://it.ojp.gov/PrivacyLiberty/authorities/statutes/1286>.

[31] Laura K. Donohue, 'Section 702 and the Collection of International Telephone and Internet Content' (2015) 38 *Harv. J. L. & Pub. Policy* 117, 142 (discussing technical issues with FISA's definition of 'electronic surveillance').

[32] For discussion of the numerous specific requirements in section 702, see Donohue, above n. 31; see also NSA Director of Civil Liberties and Privacy Office Report,

must have a foreign intelligence purpose to conduct the collection and a reasonable belief that the person is a non-US citizen located outside of the US.[33] Section 702 can provide access to the full contents of communications, and not just to/from information. The Court annually reviews and must approve targeting criteria, documenting how targeting of a particular person will lead to the acquisition of foreign intelligence information. As discussed in section 4 below, the administration has agreed to strengthen the targeting rules.[34] The Court annually also approves minimisation procedures, to cover the acquisition, retention, use, and dissemination of non-publicly available information about US persons.[35]

The Review Group discussed the following set of safeguards that accompany NSA access to information under section 702. These safeguards show the enormous difference between 'unrestricted access to mass data' and actual US law and practice:

1. Targeting must be for a valid foreign intelligence purpose in response to National Intelligence Priorities.
2. Targeting must be under a Foreign Intelligence Surveillance Court (FISC) approved section 702 certification and targeted at a person overseas.
3. All targeting is governed by FISC-approved targeting procedures.
4. Specific communications identifiers (such as a phone number or e-mail address) are used to limit collections only to communications to, from, or about a valid foreign intelligence target.
5. Queries into collected data must be designed to return valid foreign intelligence (or, in the case of the FBI, foreign intelligence information or evidence of a crime), and overly broad queries are prohibited and supervised by the FISC.
6. Disseminations to external entities, included select foreign partners (such as EU Member States) are made for valid foreign intelligence purposes.
7. Raw data is destroyed after two years or five years, depending on the collection source.[36]

'NSA's Implementation of Foreign Intelligence Surveillance Act Section 702' (April 2014) <https://www.nsa.gov/civil_liberties/_files/nsa_report_on_section_702_programme.pdf>.

33 Review Group Report, Appendix A.

34 The changes include: (1) revision of the NSA's targeting procedures to specify criteria for determining the expected foreign intelligence value of a particular target; (2) further revision to require a detailed written explanation of the basis for the determination; (3) FISC review of the revised targeting procedures and requirements of documentation of the foreign intelligence finding; (4) other measures to ensure that the 'foreign intelligence purpose' requirement in section 702 is carefully met; (5) submission of the draft targeting procedures for review by the PCLOB (an independent agency with privacy responsibilities); and (6) compliance, training, and audit.

35 <https://www.nsa.gov/civil_liberties/_files/nsa_report_on_section_702_programme.pdf>.

36 Review Group Report, Appendix B.

The PCLOB's report on section 702 provides step-by-step examples about how these safeguards apply in practice.[37]

To give perspective on section 702, enacted in 2008, it provides more detailed legal restrictions than applied previously to foreign–foreign communications. Previously, if the US conducted surveillance overseas, to target foreign communications, the US Constitution and other laws did not restrict US government activities.[38] Now, when the same two non-US persons communicate, and the communication is accessed within the US, any access to the contents must be done under a federal court order and the multiple safeguards of the section 702 regime.

3.2. THE PRISM PROGRAMME IS NOT A BULK COLLECTION PROGRAMME

The PRISM programme became famous when it was publicly named in one of the first stories based on the Snowden documents. The initial story was incorrect in important respects, but those inaccuracies have been widely repeated. As found by independent European and US reviews, the PRISM programme is not even a bulk collection programme, much less a basis for 'mass and indiscriminate surveillance' when data is transferred from the EU to the US.

The actual operation of PRISM is similar to data requests made in other settings to service providers. In PRISM collection, acting under a section 702 court order, the Government sends a directive requiring collection of certain 'selectors', such as an e-mail address. The directive goes to a United States-based service provider. The company lawyers have the opportunity to challenge the Government request. If there is no appeal to the court, the provider is compelled to give the communications sent to or from that selector to the Government.[39]

Widespread misunderstanding of PRISM can be traced to a *Washington Post* story that led with this statement:

> The National Security Agency and the FBI are tapping *directly* into the *central* servers of nine leading U.S. Internet companies, extracting audio, video, photographs, e-mails, documents, and connection logs that enable analysts to track a person's movements and contacts over time.[40]

---

37 PCLOB Section 702 report, p. 46.

38 Access to those communications, acquired overseas, would typically be governed by EO-12333, which is less strict than section 702.

39 PCLOB Section 702 report, p. 7.

40 Barton Gellman, 'US intelligence mining data from nine US Internet companies in broad secret programme', *Washington Post*, 6 June 2013 (emphasis added) <https://fg3qua.

We now know that the Government does not have direct access under the PRISM programme, but instead serves legal process on the providers similar to other stored records requests.

The inaccuracies in the news story led to immediate responses. Technology companies named in the article[41] issued statements denying that the Government had direct access to their servers to collect user data.[42] Within 24 hours, the *Washington Post* itself heavily edited the original story, but left the lead sentence intact.[43] In reviewing the events, prominent media sources soon reported the *Washington Post* account was inaccurate, because each company had only responded to government requests for information after receiving a directive requiring them to do so.[44]

As can easily happen with press stories, the corrections never caught up with the original mistake. The mistake about direct access to servers was quoted in the High Court of Ireland's decision in *Schrems v. Data Protection Commissioner*:[45]

> According to a report in *The Washington Post* published on 6th June 2013, the NSA and the Federal Bureau of Investigation ('FBI'): 'are tapping directly into the central servers of nine leading US internet companies, extracting audio and video chats, photographs, e-mails, documents and connection logs that enable analysts to track foreign targets….' According to the *Washington Post* the programme is code-named PRISM and it apparently enables the NSA to collect personal data such as e-mails, photographs and videos from major internet providers such Microsoft, Google and Facebook.[46]

---

dm2302.livefilestore.com/y3mKC7oGF-GpV3F7dq9wjirtfXMk8TIfCYCDL59yJI0k24j_SqPf2jTlZTcEq1ZtVFSOaCKrPOuYarNeNJ3Ykt_NSBD_ut-_9oMMOXLdcMb6Np6Bx78sjfzftnHDswYoKzQUeeC81zjcldDgZSy3rCY7g/WaPo%20NSA%20report%20-%20heavy%20editing.pdf?psid=1>. When the original version of the article was withdrawn from the *Washington Post's* website on 7 June 2013 and replaced with a revised version, the headline of the article was also changed, explanation at <https://pjmedia.com/blog/wapo-quietly-changes-key-details-in-nsa-story>. The new headline read, 'US, *British* intelligence mining data from nine US Internet companies in broad secret programme' (emphasis added), <https://www.washingtonpost.com/investigations/us-intelligence-mining-data-from-nine-us-internet-companies-in-broad-secret-programme/2013/06/06/3a0c0da8-cebf-11e2-8845-d970ccb04497_story.html>. Gellman further asserted that, '[f]rom inside a company's data stream the NSA is capable of pulling out anything it likes.'

41 The nine companies named were AOL, Apple, Facebook, Google, Microsoft, PalTalk, Skype, Yahoo, and YouTube.

42 <http://www.cbsnews.com/news/apple-google-facebook-yahoo-microsoft-paltalk-aol-issue-statements-of-denial-in-nsa-data-mining/>.

43 <https://www.washingtonpost.com/investigations/us-intelligence-mining-data-from-nine-us-internet-companies-in-broad-secret-programme/2013/06/06/3a0c0da8-cebf-11e2-8845-d970ccb04497_story.html>.

44 <http://www.engadget.com/2013/06/06/washington-post-nsa-fbi-tapping-directly-into-servers-of-9-lea/>; <http://www.cnet.com/news/no-evidence-of-nsas-direct-access-to-tech-companies/>; <http://www.businessinsider.com/washington-post-updates-spying-story-2013-6>.

45 *Schrems v. Data Protection Commissioner* [2014] IEHC 310 <http://fra.europa.eu/en/caselaw-reference/ireland-high-court-ireland-2014-iehc-310>.

46 Ibid.

The Advocate General to the European Court of Justice did not directly cite the *Washington Post* story, but relied on the mistaken view of the facts in saying:

> According to those revelations, the NSA established a programme called 'PRISM' under which it obtained *unrestricted access to mass data* stored on servers in the United States owned or controlled by a range of companies active in the Internet and technology field, such as Facebook USA.[47]

The Opinion added that, for information transferred by a company such as Facebook to the US, there is 'mass, indiscriminate surveillance'.[48]

These sensational but incorrect factual assertions are a close fit with the crucial statement by the European Court of Justice that the United States lacks 'a level of protection of fundamental rights essentially equivalent to that guaranteed in the EU legal order'.[49]

The correction has already been understood by leading European and US institutions. The European Union Agency for Fundamental Rights recently released a major report about surveillance by intelligence services, at the request of the European Parliament.[50] This report adopted the corrected view of PRISM. It cites an article by M. Cayford and others that stated:

> The interpretation by *The Washington Post* and *The Guardian*[51] was that this meant these companies were collaborating with the NSA to give it a direct connection to their servers, to 'unilaterally seize' all manner of communications from them. This proved, however, to be incorrect.[52]

---

47 Para. 26 of the Advocate General's Opinion in Case C-362/14, *Maximillian Schrems v. Data Protection Commissioner*, September 2015 (emphasis added) <http://curia.europa.eu/juris/document/document_print.jsf?doclang=EN&docid=168421>.

48 Ibid., para. 200.

49 Ibid., para. 96.

50 <http://fra.europa.eu/sites/default/files/fra_uploads/fra-2015-surveillance-intelligence-services_en.pdf>.

51 The *Guardian* article revealing the PRISM programme also reported that this programme gave the NSA direct access to the servers of major Internet providers such as Google, Apple, Skype and Yahoo. The slide speaks of PRISM 'collection directly from the servers' of nine US Internet Service Providers. The article is entitled, 'NSA Prism programme taps in to user data of Apple, Google, and others' <http://www.theguardian.com/world/2013/jun/06/us-tech-giants-nsa-data>.

52 M. Cayford et al., 'All Swept Up: An Initial Classification of NSA Surveillance Technology', <http://www.crcnetbase.com/doi/abs/10.1201/b17399-9>, pp. 645–646. The European Union Agency for Fundamental Rights report reviewed the PRISM programme in light of the Cayford article, which found that '[t]he "direct access" described ... is access to a particular foreign account through a court order for that particular account, not a wholesale sucking up of all the information on the company's users.' European Union Agency for Fundamental Rights, 'Surveillance by Intelligence Services: Fundamental Rights Safeguards and Remedies in the EU' (2015) <http://fra.europa.eu/sites/default/files/fra_uploads/fra-2015-surveillance-intelligence-services_en.pdf>, p. 17.

The Agency for Fundamental Rights report agreed with the Cayford article statement that PRISM is 'a targeted technology used to access court ordered foreign Internet accounts', and not mass surveillance.[53] The US Privacy and Civil Liberties Oversight Board, an independent agency that received classified information about the PRISM programme, similarly concluded: 'the Section 702 programme is not based on the indiscriminate collection of information in bulk. Instead the programme consists entirely of targeting specific [non-U.S.] persons about whom an individualised determination has been made.'[54]

The public also now has access to official statistics about the number of individuals targeted under section 702. The US intelligence community now releases an annual Statistical Transparency Report,[55] with the statistics subject to oversight from Congress, Inspector Generals, the FISC, the PCLOB, and others.[56] For 2014, there were 92,707 'targets' under the section 702 programme, many of whom were targeted due to evidence linking them to terrorism.[57] That is a tiny fraction of US, European, or global Internet users. It demonstrates the low likelihood of the communications of ordinary citizens being acquired.[58]

3.3. THE UPSTREAM PROGRAMME ACCESSES FEWER ELECTRONIC COMMUNICATIONS THAN PRISM

The Upstream programme gains e-mails and other electronic communications from the Internet backbone, and thus the European Union Agency for Fundamental Rights noted that the same Cayford article that found PRISM not to

---

53 European Union Agency for Fundamental Rights, above n. 52, p. 17.

54 Privacy and Civil Liberties Oversight Board, 'Report on the Surveillance Programme Operated Pursuant to Section 702 of the Foreign Intelligence Surveillance Act' (July 2014) <https://www.pclob.gov/library/702-Report.pdf>, p. 111.

55 The first two have been released: Calendar Year 2014 Transparency Report; Statistical Transparency Report Regarding Use of National Security Authorities – Annual Statistics for Calendar Year 2014 (22 April 2015) <http://icontherecord.tumblr.com/transparency/odni_transparencyreport_cy2014>; 2013 Transparency Report; Statistical Transparency Report Regarding Use of National Security Authorities – Annual Statistics for Calendar Year 2013 (26 June 2014) <http://icontherecord.tumblr.com/transparency/odni_transparencyreport_cy2013>.

56 For a listing of the multiple oversight entities, see Review Group Report, Appendix C.

57 The statistical reports define 'target' in detail, and the number of individuals targeted is lower than the reported number, to avoid any possible understatement of the number of targets.

58 The 2014 Statistical Transparency Report reiterates the targeted nature of the surveillance: 'Given the restrictions of Section 702, only selectors used by non-US persons reasonably believed to be located outside the United States and who possess, or who are likely to communicate or receive, foreign intelligence information that is covered by an approved certification may be tasked.'

be 'mass surveillance' has called the Upstream programme 'mass surveillance'.[59] Upon examination, I believe a better view is that the legal rules that authorise Upstream mean that it is a targeted programme as well. Indeed, the targeting and minimisation procedures for Upstream collection are the same as or stronger than those that are applied to PRISM collection. A declassified FISC opinion found that over 90 per cent of the Internet communications obtained by the NSA in 2011 under section 702 actually resulted from PRISM, with less than 10 per cent coming from Upstream.[60] Upstream collection takes place with the same targeted selector process that is used for PRISM. In short, given the positive findings from European experts about the PRISM programme, there is a strong basis for rejecting the conclusion that Upstream is 'mass surveillance', given its much smaller scale.

3.3.1. How the Upstream technology works

The Upstream programme is clearly explained in the PCLOB's report on section 702.[61] The NSA may target non-US persons by tasking specific selectors, such as e-mail addresses or telephone numbers, and may not use key words or the names of targeted individuals.[62]

As discussed at the start of this section, the Upstream programme is a response to changing technology. As the Internet developed, a large portion of the Internet backbone passed through the United States, meaning that many foreign–foreign communications could be accessed by surveillance done inside the US. Previously, foreign–foreign communications would have been accessed outside of the US, where the US Constitution and various laws are less strict than for access inside the US. The Upstream programme, like the PRISM programme, was authorised by the FISC under section 702 as a way to apply the statute's safeguards to communications accessed in the US.

The PCLOB report explained the key role of a filter under section 702, including for the Upstream programme: 'To identify and acquire Internet transactions associated with the Section 702-tasked selectors on the Internet

---

59 European Union Agency for Fundamental Rights, above n. 52, p. 17.

60 The analysis of Judge Bates' opinion is in the PCLOB Section 702 report, pp. 33–34. I am not aware of a similar quantitative comparison of PRISM and the Upstream programme for telephone communications, but the discussion here of filtering and acquisition of targeted communications applies in the same way to both telephone and electronic communications.

61 PCLOB Section 702 report, pp. 36–39.

62 The PCLOB writes: 'The NSA may only target non-US persons by tasking specific selectors to upstream Internet transaction collection. And, like other forms of section 702 collection, selectors tasked for upstream Internet transaction collection must be specific selectors (such as an e-mail address), and may not be key words or the names of targeted individuals.' PCLOB Section 702 report, p. 36.

backbone, Internet transactions are first filtered to eliminate potential domestic transactions, and then are screened to capture only transactions containing a tasked selector.'[63] Under section 702, the filter selects only the communications that match the approved selectors, such as e-mails. Those e-mails make it through the filters, and are stored for access by the NSA. The information that doesn't make it through the filters is never accessed by the NSA or anyone else.[64]

Figure 1 is taken from a US National Research Council report on 'Bulk Signals Analysis: Technical Options'. The diagram can be used to illustrate the role of the filter in the Upstream programme. At the left side of the diagram, signals go through the Internet backbone. The signal is split ('extract') and then goes through the filter. The filter only allows authorised messages to pass through, based on 'discriminants' or 'selectors' such as e-mail addresses. Authorised messages go into storage. At this point, for the first time, the messages can be queried. That is, under Upstream, only NSA employees can make queries, and they only have the ability to make queries on messages that have reached storage after filtering. Put another way, the NSA accesses only targeted communications, based on approved selectors.

Figure 1. Conceptual model of signals intelligence

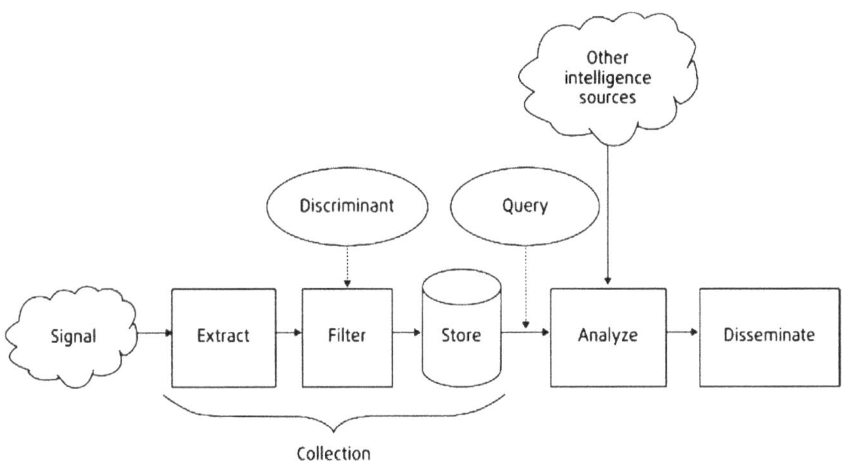

Source: United States, National Research Council (2015), p. 28.

63 PCLOB Section 702 report, p. 37.

64 Some readers may not believe the NSA follows the rules and gains access only to approved communications that have made it through the filters. My own view is that the NSA has built a large and generally effective compliance programme in recent years. As documented by the Review Group, multiple layers of oversight exist over these NSA actions, including oversight by judges, Congress, and the NSA Inspector General. Review Group Report, Appendices B and C. Systematic violation of the section 702 rules would thus be highly risky for the NSA to undertake.

Based on these technological realities, the National Research Council report noted that there are two differing conceptions of privacy for when data is acquired. One view (taken for instance by Cayford)[65] posits that violation of privacy occurs when the electronic signal is first captured, regardless of what happens to the signal after that point. The second view, which I share, is that processing the signal only for filtering purposes does not constitute mass surveillance. Access only to the filtered results, under rules such as those in section 702, means that the communications of an individual are only retained if there is a match with a selector such as an e-mail address.

The ultimate question is whether this sort of filtering, under law, should be permitted as a way to access communications flowing through the Internet. If the US (or an ally) has the technical ability to perform the filtering and find high-value intelligence communications, society must decide whether to do so. Changing technology means that potentially vital national security information may be available, under a court order, as data flows through the system.

The PCLOB has written lengthy reports, based on classified information, on section 215 telephone meta-data and on the section 702 programme, including Upstream. The PCLOB found the former to be unlawful, bad policy, and not vital for national security. By contrast, the PCLOB unanimously came to a different verdict on the section 702 programme: (1) section 702 'is not based on the indiscriminate collection of information in bulk';[66] (2) section 702 meets the standard for reasonableness under the Fourth Amendment to the US Constitution;[67] and (3) section 702 has been effective at addressing international terrorism.[68]

---

65 M. Cayford et al., above n. 52, pp. 644–645.

66 The PCLOB found: 'Unlike the telephone records program conducted by the NSA under Section 215 of the USA PATRIOT Act, the Section 702 program is not based on the indiscriminate collection of information in bulk. Instead, the program consists entirely of targeting specific persons about whom an individualized determination has been made. Once the government concludes that a specific non-U.S. person located outside the United States is likely to communicate certain types of foreign intelligence information — and that this person uses a particular communications "selector," such as an e-mail address or telephone number — the government acquires only those communications involving that particular selector.' PCLOB Section 702 report, p. 111.

67 The PCLOB concluded that 'the core of the Section 702 programme – acquiring the communications of specifically targeted foreign persons who are located outside the United States, upon a belief that those persons are likely to communicate foreign intelligence, using specific communications identifiers, subject to FISA court-approved targeting rules and multiple layers of oversight – fits within the "totality of the circumstances" standard for reasonableness under the Fourth Amendment, as that standard has been defined by the courts to date.' PCLOB Section 702 report, p. 9.

68 'Presently, over a quarter of the NSA's reports concerning international terrorism include information based in whole or in part on Section 702 collection, and this percentage has increased every year since the statute was enacted. Monitoring terrorist networks under Section 702 has enabled the government to learn how they operate, and to understand their priorities, strategies, and tactics. In addition, the program has led the government to identify previously unknown individuals who are involved in international terrorism, and it has

3.3.2. *Judge Bates' declassified opinion about section 702 illustrates judicial oversight of NSA surveillance*

One persistent question about US surveillance law has been whether there is independent judicial oversight of NSA practices. Based on recently declassified opinions of the Foreign Intelligence Surveillance Court, the general public can now see the FISC holding NSA practices unlawful, and refusing to continue a surveillance programme without modifications. As someone who has studied FISA for more than a decade, the declassified opinions match my prior view that the FISC has often provided stricter oversight of surveillance practices than most on the outside have realised.[69] It has always been clear that judges on the FISC were independent, in the sense that they have life tenure and cannot be removed from office except for good cause. Instead of the 'indiscriminate surveillance' alleged by the Advocate General in *Schrems*, the declassified opinions show the FISC to be independent in the broader sense of applying judicial oversight to practices the judges find unlawful.

A 2011 opinion by Judge Bates of the FISC found that NSA's minimisation procedures were not adequate to deal with one portion of Upstream collection, and therefore required that those procedures be amended before he would authorise continuation of the programme.[70] The controversy concerned NSA access to certain kinds of e-mails.[71] Judge Bates found that the Upstream programme at that time did not satisfy the requirements of either FISA or the Fourth Amendment. He therefore refused to approve NSA's continuing acquisition of this category of e-mails.[72] Thereafter, the Government substantially revised its procedures for handling the e-mails, and in November 2011 Judge Bates approved the future acquisition of those e-mails subject to the new minimisation standards.[73] In addition, NSA took the additional step of deleting all previously acquired Upstream communications.[74]

---

played a key role in discovering and disrupting specific terrorist plots aimed at the United States and other countries.' PCLOB Section 702 report, p. 10.

69 As with any court, reasonable people can differ on particular cases. I am critical of some of the declassified opinions, especially those upholding the lawfulness of the telephone metadata programme under section 215.

70 *In re DNI/AG 702(g)*, Docket Number 702(i)-11-01 (FISC, 30 November 2011) (redacted version) <http://www.dni.gov/files/documents/1118/CLEANEDPRTT%202.pdf>.

71 The problem arose where multiple e-mails were included in threads. For these 'multi-communications transactions', the minimisation procedures were not being applied in the way the judge believed was necessary. Essentially, the judge found that information was visible in the string of e-mails included within one e-mail, in ways contrary to the minimisation requirements.

72 The Court's opinion is discussed in detail in Review Group Report, p. 142.

73 Report and Recommendation of the President's Review Group on Intelligence and Communications Technologies, 'Liberty and Security in a Changing World' <https://www.whitehouse.gov/sites/default/files/docs/2013-12-12_rg_final_report.pdf>, p. 142.

74 Ibid., p. 142.

In my view, this and other declassified FISC decisions show vigorous and critical scrutiny by independent judges of the details of NSA surveillance.

3.4. CONCLUSION

The legal structure and implementation of PRISM and Upstream under section 702 have been far more targeted and subject to oversight than the initial press reports claimed. With declassification of court orders, as well as documents such as the PCLOB report on section 702, the general public and experts in Europe and the United States have a far stronger factual basis than prior to 2013 to debate what reforms may be appropriate when the law sunsets in 2017.

A key point of this chapter is that NSA acquisition of people's e-mails and other communications under section 702 is not 'pervasive', as has often been claimed. The Fundamental Rights Agency of the European Union has agreed with the PCLOB and others that the PRISM programme is targeted, rather than bulk collection. We know from declassified FISC documents that Upstream acquired less than 10 per cent as many electronic communications in 2011 as PRISM, and so it is not pervasively acquiring electronic communications. Taken together, the total number of individuals targeted under section 702 in 2013 was 92,707, a tiny fraction of total EU or global Internet users.

4. THE US HAS TAKEN MULTIPLE AND SIGNIFICANT ACTIONS TO REFORM SURVEILLANCE LAWS AND PROGRAMMES SINCE 2013

Since the Snowden disclosures in 2013, the US has undertaken at least two dozen significant actions to reform surveillance laws and programmes. To explain these changes, this section of the chapter looks at the many (and detailed) reforms that have been put in place. These reforms exemplify the democratic response of the US Government to concerns raised about surveillance practices, and show a legal system responding to changes in technology.

4.1. INDEPENDENT REVIEWS OF SURVEILLANCE ACTIVITIES

Issue: It is difficult to get informed and independent counsel about how to reform intelligence agencies. Many agency actions and programmes are necessarily kept classified, to avoid revealing sources and methods for achieving their missions. To create one source of independent review, Congress established the Senate and House Intelligence Committees in the 1970s, in the wake of Watergate. Within the executive branch,[75] the most expert individuals generally have worked within the agencies that are being reviewed. That experience provides the expertise, but can also establish loyalties that are not easily set aside for purposes of critique and review.

Action: Beginning soon after June 2013, President Obama worked with two independent review efforts, staffed by knowledgeable people and able to get briefings at the TS/SCI level (Top Secret/Sensitive Compartmented Information), the highest level of security clearance. Reports have since been published, with detailed recommendations, from both the Review Group on Intelligence and Communications Technology (Review Group) and the Privacy and Civil Liberties Oversight Board (PCLOB).

4.1.1. Review Group on Intelligence and Communications Technology

The Review Group was announced in August 2013, published its final report in December, and met with the President to receive its mission and discuss its recommendations.[76] The five members have diverse expertise: (1) Richard Clarke, former counter-terrorism and cybersecurity senior advisor to both President Clinton and George W. Bush; (2) Michael Morrell, former Deputy Director of the CIA, with 30 years of experience in the Intelligence Community; (3) Geoffrey Stone, eminent legal scholar on constitutional issues in time of crisis; (4) Cass Sunstein, the most-cited American legal scholar, and former Director of the Office of Information and Regulatory Affairs in the Office of Management and Budget; and (5) myself, with experience in areas including cybersecurity, foreign intelligence law, and privacy.

The Review Group's report was over 300 pages, made 46 recommendations, and has been reprinted as a book by the Princeton University Press. When

---

75 Both houses of the US Congress, the Senate and the House of Representatives, have intelligence oversight committees. The mandate of these committees is to make continuing studies of the intelligence activities and to provide legislative oversight over the intelligence activities of the US to ensure that these activities are in conformity with the US Constitution and laws. Members of these committees have access to classified intelligence assessments, access to intelligence sources and methods, programmes and budgets. For details on the US Senate Select Committee on Intelligence, see <http://www.intelligence.senate.gov/about>. Information on US House of Representatives Permanent Select Committee on Intelligence can be found at <http://intelligence.house.gov/>.

76 'Liberty and Security in a Changing World: Report and Recommendations of the President's Review Group on Intelligence and Communications Technology' <https://www.whitehouse.gov/sites/default/files/docs/2013-12-12_rg_final_report.pdf>. The Review Group's task from the President was to find an approach 'that optimally protects our national security and advances our foreign policy while respecting our commitment to privacy and civil liberties, recognizing our need to maintain the public trust, and reducing the risk of unauthorized disclosure.' Ibid. The Report has been republished by the Princeton University Press <http://press.princeton.edu/titles/10296.html>.

President Obama made his major speech on surveillance reform in January 2014, the Review Group was told that 70 per cent of its recommendations were being adopted in letter or spirit, and others have been adopted since. The Review Group's report received widespread attention in the press, especially this finding: 'Our review suggests that the information contributed to terrorist investigations by the use of Section 215 telephony meta-data was not essential to preventing attacks and could readily have been obtained in a timely manner using conventional Section 215 orders.'

4.1.2. Privacy and Civil Liberties Oversight Board

By coincidence, the chair of the Privacy and Civil Liberties Oversight Board (PCLOB) started work the week the first Snowden story broke.[77] The PCLOB is the sort of independent oversight agency that has often been recommended by European data protection experts, with the same independent structure as the Federal Trade Commission. There are five members (no more than three from any political party), who serve a term of six years. Members of the PCLOB and their staff receive TS/SCI security clearances and investigate and report on the counterterrorism activities of the US intelligence community.[78]

The PCLOB has distinguished members with relevant expertise: (1) David Medine, the Chair, was a senior FTC privacy official who helped negotiated the Safe Harbour Agreement; (2) Rachel Brand has been the Assistant Attorney General for Legal Policy, serving as chief policy advisor to the US Attorney General; (3) Beth Collins has also served as Assistant General for Legal Policy at the US Department of Justice; (4) Jim Dempsey is a leading surveillance expert in US civil society, working for many years at the Center for Democracy and Technology; and (5) Patricia Wald was a judge on the Court of Appeals for the DC Circuit for twenty years, and has also served as a judge on the International Criminal Tribunal for the Former Yugoslavia.

Since 2013, the PCLOB has released detailed reports on the section 215[79] and section 702[80] surveillance programmes, making numerous recommendations. Its central recommendations on the section 215 telephone meta-data programme were enacted in the USA Freedom Act, discussed below. Overall, PCLOB made 22 recommendations in its sections 215 and 702 reports, virtually all of which have been accepted and are either implemented or in the process of being implemented.

---

77 I have sympathy for David Medine, the Chair, for trying to get his office furniture in place at the same time that the biggest intelligence story in decades hit the headlines.

78 <https://it.ojp.gov/PrivacyLiberty/authorities/statutes/1283>.

79 <https://www.pclob.gov/library/215-Report_on_the_Telephone_Records_Program.pdf>.

80 <https://www.pclob.gov/library/702-Report.pdf>.

In summary on the Review Group and the PCLOB, the overall reforms of the US intelligence system since Snowden have been informed by detailed reports, based on top-secret briefings. These reports have been written by independent groups who presented them to the President.

4.2. LEGISLATIVE ACTIONS

4.2.1. *Increased funding for the PCLOB*

Issue: At the time of the Snowden revelations, the PCLOB was a new agency whose Chair had just been sworn into office. The annual budget was too low to hire many staff members.

Action: In 2014 Congress increased the PCLOB funding substantially, to $7.5 million, and in 2015 to $10 million, bringing total staff to 32 plus five board members.[81] This funding increase enables the PCLOB, going forward, to hire enough staff to continue to carry out its mandates and write detailed reports about intelligence community activities.

4.2.2. *Greater judicial role in section 215 orders*

Issue: Under the section 215 statute, as enacted in 2001, Foreign Intelligence Surveillance Court judges issued a general order to authorise the bulk collection of telephone meta-data. The decision to look at the information, however, was made by NSA employees, subject to oversight by the Department of Justice, based on a standard of 'reasonable, articulable suspicion' that a telephone number was associated with terrorism.

Action: President Obama announced in 2014 that judicial approval would also be required for an NSA employee to look at the information. This approach was codified in the USA Freedom Act, passed in 2015, which also prohibited the bulk collection of telephone meta-data and required the queries to be submitted with court approval to the providers.[82]

As a separate amendment, the statute also required that judges will review the minimisation procedures under section 215 orders, to ensure that information, once accessed, is minimised to exclude records that are not foreign intelligence information, which previously were approved only by the Attorney General.[83]

81 The statistics are based on an interview with the PCLOB.

82 USA Freedom Act, s. 104 <https://www.congress.gov/bill/114th-congress/house-bill/2048>.

83 Ibid., s. 104.

4.2.3. *Prohibition on bulk collection under section 215 and other laws*

Issue: Congress reacted, in the USA Freedom Act, to its concern that there could be bulk collection under a number of foreign intelligence authorities.

Action: The law prohibited bulk collection under three distinct authorities: (1) section 215, for collection of 'tangible things' (including phone records);[84] (2) FISA pen register and trap and trace authorities (to/from information about communications);[85] and (3) National Security Letters (phone, financial, and credit history records).[86] The law went beyond section 215 orders to prevent the agencies from using alternative statutory authorities for bulk collection. These clear statements in law from the Congress plainly state the limits on appropriate use of section 215 and other authorities.[87]

4.2.4. *Addressing the problem of secret law – declassification of FISC decisions, orders and opinions*

Issue: A long-standing problem in the foreign intelligence area is how to avoid the development of secret law. Secret law is contrary to the basic theory of democracy, that citizens should govern themselves, and thus should know the laws that apply to themselves. The Foreign Intelligence Surveillance Court (FISC) was created in 1978 as a compromise, that generalist federal judges would oversee issuance of foreign intelligence orders but keep the orders secret to protect national security.

The risk of secret law became more acute after 2001, as the FISC faced the question of whether entire programmes, such as section 215 telephone meta-data, PRISM, and Upstream, were being carried out in compliance with statutory provisions. In calling for greater transparency, PCLOB's section 215 report urged that, to the maximum extent consistent with national security, the Government create and release with minimal redactions declassified versions of new decisions, orders and opinions by the FISC in cases involving novel interpretations of FISA or other significant questions of law, technology or compliance.

Action: Although significant opinions of the FISC had always been provided to congressional oversight committees, the Obama administration began systematic declassification of FISC opinions, for the first time, in 2013. The stated goal was to carefully review each opinion, and disclose the actions of the FISC to the extent possible. By February 2015, the intelligence community had posted

---

84 Ibid., s. 103.

85 Ibid., s. 201.

86 Ibid., s. 501.

87 The programme ended in November 2015.

more than 250 declassified documents comprising more than 4,500 pages. Many of these documents related to proceedings of the FISC.[88]

The USA Freedom Act codified this effort.[89] From now on, the Government will review each decision, order, and opinion of the FISC or the court that reviews it that includes 'a significant construction or interpretation of any provision of this Act'. After the review, the full or redacted opinion shall be made publicly available 'to the greatest extent practicable'. If a court action cannot be made public due to national security, the Government must summarise 'the significant construction or interpretation' of the legal provision.[90]

4.2.5. Appointment of experts to brief the FISC on privacy and civil liberties

Issue: When the FISC was created in 1978, its principal task was to decide whether a phone wiretap for one individual met the statutory standard. This task is essentially the same as a judge deciding to issue a warrant or other court order for a traditional law enforcement case. Under US law, such orders are issued *ex parte*, that is, the Government presents its evidence and the court makes its decision, without representation from the criminal defendant.

After 2001, along with these individual orders, the FISC was faced with the decision whether to issue court orders for entire surveillance programmes, such as section 215 phone meta-data, section 702 PRISM, and section 702 Upstream. In my view, the FISC was acting somewhat similarly to a regulatory agency – is this overall programme operating under the correct procedures and safeguards? Under US law, regulatory decisions of this magnitude generally occur only after a judge has received briefing from one or more non-government viewpoints. Both the Review Group and the PCLOB recommended that a panel of advocates be appointed so that the FISC would hear independent views on novel and significant matters.

Action: The USA Freedom Act authorised the creation of a group of independent experts, called *amicus curiae* ('friend of the court'), to brief the FISC on important cases.[91] The law instructs the FISC to appoint an *amicus curiae* for a matter that, in the opinion of the court, 'presents a novel or significant interpretation of the law'. The court retains some discretion on when to appoint an *amicus curiae*, but the clear intent of the statute is that independent lawyers with security clearances shall participate before the FISC in important cases.

---

88 <http://icontherecord.tumblr.com/ppd-28/2015/enhancing-transparency>; <www.icontherecord.tumblr.com>.

89 The newly re-issued Intelligence Community Directive on the National Intelligence Priorities Framework, ICD 204, codifies some of these issues <http://fas.org/irp/dni/icd/icd-204.pdf>.

90 USA Freedom Act, s. 602.

91 Ibid., s. 401.

This reform provides the opportunity for independent views to be heard by the FISC for important cases, so that the assertions of government officials can be carefully tested before the judge. The statute does not precisely state what role the amicus curiae should play, but the first criterion for selection is 'expertise in privacy and civil liberties.' The FISC has named five expert lawyers, including Professor of Law Laura Donohue of Georgetown University, who has written extensively on civil liberties and foreign intelligence law, as well as lawyers who have been involved in these matters either in prior government service or in private practice.[92]

4.2.6. *Transparency reports by companies subject to court orders*

Issue: As discussed in section 1, transparency is a central component of governing secret intelligence agencies in an open democracy. Historically, the companies who receive national security-related requests have been under strict limits about what they could disclose. For instance, companies could not even confirm or deny whether they had ever received a National Security Letter. In the absence of information about the scope of requests, sceptical people outside of the intelligence agencies feared 'mass and indiscriminate surveillance'. Both the Review Group and the PCLOB recommended that the Government work with Internet service providers and other companies that regularly receive FISC orders to develop rules permitting the companies to voluntarily disclose more detailed statistical information concerning those orders.

Action: In 2014, the US Department of Justice reached agreement with major service providers (e.g. webmail and social network providers) that they could disclose considerably more detailed and extensive information about national security requests. Going forward, these service providers could publish these details in the annual or semi-annual Transparency Reports that a growing range of companies have released in recent years.

Consistent with the 2014 agreement, the USA Freedom Act guaranteed the right of those subject to national security orders to publish detailed statistics.[93] The companies can report statistics in a number of categories, such as content, non-content, and National Security Letters. Notably, the companies can report 'the total number of all national security process received,' including National Security Letters and orders under FISA. They can also report 'the total number of customer selectors targeted under all national security process received.'

---

92 <http://www.fisc.uscourts.gov>. For a recent report on how one such *amicus curiae* case has worked in practice, see <https://www.techdirt.com/articles/20151210/08175733048/fisa-courts-appointed-advocate-not-allowing-governments-national-security-assertions-to-go-unchallenged.shtml>.

93 USA Freedom Act, s. 604.

In my view, these statistics provide important evidence about the actual scope of national security investigations in the United States. The percentage of users whose records are accessed in the most recent six-month period is vanishingly small. I have examined the most recent transparency reports of Facebook and Google, because European privacy regulators have focused particular attention on them in recent years. These statistics show what accounts have been accessed in the United States – the precise European concern about how individual data is handled once it leaves Europe and goes to the US. The statistics show far more targeted activity than the speculation in the popular press.[94]

Of the six categories reported, the highest percentage of users affected is for content requests to Google, a maximum of .0014 per cent, or about 1 in 100,000. In total, the number of customer accounts accessed by the US Government for national security in the most recent time period is approximately 10,000[95] for Facebook, out of approximately 1.55 billion[96] active users per month. The number of customer accounts accessed is approximately 17,000[97] for Google, out of approximately 1.17 billion[98] active users per month.

Facebook	No. of users accessed in 6 months	Percentage based on users per month
Non-Content Requests	0–999	.00006 %
Content Requests	7,000–7,999	.00052%
National Security Letters	0–999	.00006%

94 My understanding is that the company transparency reports clearly cover the PRISM programme, where specific selectors are made available to service providers such as Facebook and Google under the law. I do not know whether the statistics also include any government access under the Upstream programme, where the Government may gain access to an e-mail, for example, without directly requesting that information from the e-mail service provider. In terms of overall volume, however, it is relevant to consider Chapter 2, which discussed the declassified FISC opinion in 2011 that over 90 per cent of the electronic communications acquired under section 702 came from the PRISM programme rather than the Upstream programme. Even if Upstream statistics are not included in the transparency reports, that would shift one of the statistics here from roughly 1 in 1 million subscribers to 1 in 900,000 subscribers. The main point would remain the same – a vanishingly small fraction of users' communications are actually acquired by the NSA.

95 For the most recent reporting period, companies were permitted to report aggregate numbers of requests received, during a six-month time period, from the Government for intelligence purposes; the number of requests are reported in increments of 1,000. For the time period from July to December 2014, Facebook received the following: 0–999 non-content requests; 7,000–7,999 content requests; and 0–999 national security letters <https://govtrequests.facebook.com/country/United%20States/2014-H2/>.

96 <http://www.statista.com/statistics/264810/number-of-monthly-active-facebook-users-worldwide/>.

97 For the time period from January to June 2014, Google received the following: 0–999 non-content requests; 15,000–15,999 content requests; and 0–999 national security letters <https://www.google.com/transparencyreport/userdatarequests/US/>.

98 <http://expandedramblings.com/index.php/by-the-numbers-a-gigantic-list-of-google-stats-and-facts>.

Google	No. of users accessed in 6 months	Percentage based on users per month
Non-Content Requests	0–999	.00009%
Content Requests	15,000–15,999	.00137%
National Security Letters	0–999	.00009%

These statistics put into perspective concerns that US intelligence agencies are massively accessing the information held by US service providers when data is transferred to the US. Both Facebook and Google are widely used in the EU. Based on the public reports, a maximum of 1 in 100,000 users has his or her content accessed in a six-month period, with other categories of request considerably lower. For the less-used categories, such as non-content requests to Facebook, that figure is approximately 1 in 1 million users.

4.2.7. Transparency reports by the US government

Issue: The Government has access to the classified information about national security investigations, and so is in the best position to report accurately to Congress and the public. FISA in 1978 established some reporting to the public, particularly the number of orders issued and the number denied. Congress, through the Senate and House Intelligence Committees, received more detailed reports and conducted classified oversight investigations into intelligence community activities. The required transparency reports, however, had not been updated after 2001 to reflect the broader set of intelligence and national security activities.

Action: The USA Freedom Act overhauled the annual reporting by the US Government about its national security investigations.[99] Going forward, the Government each year will report statistics publicly for each category of investigation. For instance, for section 702, the Government will report the total number of orders as well as the estimated number of targets affected by such orders. The plain language of the statute thus provides that the US Government will report annually on how many total targets have been affected by the PRISM and upstream collection programmes. This level of transparency is remarkable for the actions of secret intelligence agencies. As with the transparency reports by companies, European officials and the general public can thus know the magnitude of these surveillance programmes and changes in size over tune, in my view rebutting the claim of 'mass and unrestrained surveillance'.

[99] USA Freedom Act, s. 603.

4.2.8. Passage of the Judicial Redress Act

Issue: The Privacy Act of 1974 provides a number of data protection measures that apply to 'US persons' – US citizens and permanent residents. For a number of years, European data protection authorities and other officials have made reform of the Privacy Act a priority in trans-Atlantic privacy discussions. For instance, the issue was highlighted by the European Commission and members of the European Parliament when they briefed the Review Group in 2013. The basic request has been to provide the same protections to EU citizens as applied to US persons.

Action: The US Government took steps before 2013 to provide Privacy Act protections in important respects. For instance, in 2007 the Department of Homeland Security applied the Privacy Act to 'mixed' systems of records (databases that include both US and non-US persons) to the extent permitted by law.[100] The Privacy Act, however, had not enabled an agency to provide an appeal from an agency action to a judge, and this was a concern of European officials.

The Judicial Redress Act was passed by Congress in February 2016 to address this topic.[101] In EU/US negotiations related to privacy, passage of the Judicial Redress Act had become important both for discussions of a revised Safe Harbour Agreement and for the 'Umbrella Agreement' concerning law enforcement information to go into full effect.[102]

4.3. EXECUTIVE BRANCH ACTIONS

As discussed in the section on legislation, the executive branch was the first to take a number of actions that were subsequently codified into law by Congressional action. This part of the chapter focuses on the numerous other executive branch actions since June 2013. Many of these actions are summarised in 'Signals Intelligence Reform: 2015 Anniversary Report',[103] which was published near the one-year anniversary of President Obama's major speech on intelligence reform.[104] A similar report was published in January 2016.[105]

---

100 Department of Homeland Security: Privacy Policy Guidance Memorandum No. 2007-1 (7 January 2007) (amended 19 January 2007).

101 <https://www.congress.gov/bill/114th-congress/house-bill/1428>.

102 <http://europa.eu/rapid/press-release_MEMO-15-5612_en.htm>.

103 <http://icontherecord.tumblr.com/ppd-28/2015/factsheet>.

104 <https://www.whitehouse.gov/blog/2014/01/17/president-obama-discusses-us-intelligence-programs-department-justice>.

105 <https://icontherecord.tumblr.com/ppd-28/2016>.

The discussion here begins with broad conceptual reforms to US signals intelligence (SIGINT) that President Obama announced in 2014, and then examines the multiple other actions since 2013.

Issue: Historical practice, for the US and other nations, has been to provide greater latitude for surveillance outside of the country than within the country. Simply put, nations have spied on each other since Sun Tzu's classic *The Art of War* in ancient China, and well before that.[106] That is consistent with the Intelligence Community's mission to conduct foreign intelligence activities. Spying on hostile actors is especially understandable during time of war or when there is reason to believe hostile actors may attack.

The United States and the Member States of the European Union have a shared legal tradition and strong alliances. Many in the EU have objected strongly to the scope of US surveillance reported since 2013. One way to understand the objections is that Europeans believe that EU citizens deserve similar treatment to US citizens when it comes to US surveillance activities. The longstanding international practice of greater latitude to spy on non-citizens outside of one's own country is, as applied to Europeans, contrary to the views of many in Europe about what is proper today for an ally such as the US.

Action: In 2014 President Obama issued Presidential Policy Directive-28 (PPD-28),[107] which I consider a historic document. Binding on all US intelligence agencies for their signals intelligence activities, the directive 'articulates principles to guide why, whether, when, and how the United States conducts signals intelligence activities for authorized foreign intelligence and counterintelligence purposes.' PPD-28 sets forth a number of new and distinct policies, with key items featured here.[108] In short, PPD-28 makes protecting the privacy and civil liberties rights of persons outside the US an integral part of US surveillance policy, and a direct order from the President, who is also Commander-in-Chief.[109]

---

106 For a translation of the chapter on spies in *The Art of War*, see <http://suntzusaid.com/book/13>.

107 <https://www.whitehouse.gov/sites/default/files/docs/2014sigint_mem_ppd_rel.pdf>.

108 An Interim Progress Report on Implementing PPD-28 was released in October 2014 <http://icontherecord.tumblr.com/post/100240011473/interim-progress-report-on-implementing-ppd-28>. Additional information is included in the 2015 Anniversary Report <http://icontherecord.tumblr.com/post/100240011473/interim-progress-report-on-implementing-ppd-28>.

109 As with any other US Executive Order or Presidential Policy Directive, the President's announcement cannot create a right of action enforceable in court. Based on my experience in the US Government, however, agencies go to great lengths to comply with directives from the President of the United States. The PPD is binding upon executive branch agencies as an instruction from the head of the executive branch, even if it cannot be enforced by outsiders.

4.3.1. *New surveillance principle to protect privacy rights outside of the US*

Issue: Longstanding law and practice in the US (and all other nations of which I am aware that follow the rule of law) is that greater legal protections are provided within a nation's borders than for surveillance conducted outside the borders.

Action: PPD-28 announced a new principle that applies to all intelligence agencies in the US when conducting signals intelligence: 'Our signals intelligence activities must take into account that all persons should be treated with dignity and respect, regardless of their nationality or wherever they might reside, and that all persons have legitimate privacy interests in the handling of their personal information.' It adds: 'Privacy and civil liberties shall be integral considerations in the planning of US signals intelligence activities.' I am not aware of any other country having announced and adopted principles of this sort in their intelligence activities.

4.3.2. *Protection of civil liberties in addition to privacy*

Issue: The EU treats privacy as a fundamental right, among other fundamental rights such as freedom of expression.

Action: PPD-28 protects civil liberties as well as privacy: 'The United States shall not collect signals intelligence for the purpose of suppressing or burdening criticism or dissent, or for disadvantaging persons based on their ethnicity, race, gender, sexual orientation, or religion.' PPD-28 clearly states that signals intelligence must be based on a legitimate purpose: 'Signals intelligence shall be collected exclusively where there is a foreign intelligence or counterintelligence purpose to support national and departmental missions and not for any other purposes.'

4.3.3. *Safeguards for the personal information of all individuals, regardless of nationality*

Issue: In order for the general principle of protecting privacy rights to matter in practice, it must be built into the operations of the agencies.

Action: Section 4 of PPD-28 sets forth detailed safeguards for handling personal information. It instructs each agency to establish policies and procedures, and to publish them to extent consistent with classification requirements. By 2015, all intelligence agencies had completed new policies or revised existing policies to meet the President's mandates.[110] The policies and

[110] The NSA policies and procedures to protect personal information collected through SIGINT can be found at: <https://www.nsa.gov/public_info/_files/nsacss_policies/PPD-28.pdf>.

procedures address topics including: data security and access; data quality; and oversight, and 'to the maximum extent feasible consistent with the national security, these policies and procedures are to be applied equally to the personal information of all persons, regardless of nationality.'

One of the over-arching principles of PPD-28 is minimisation, an important issue often mentioned by EU data protection experts. The new safeguards in PPD-28 include:

> Signals intelligence activities shall be as tailored as feasible. In determining whether to collect signals intelligence, the United States shall consider the availability of other information, including from diplomatic and public sources. Such appropriate and feasible alternatives to signals intelligence should be prioritized.

This quotation does not mention words from EU data protection law such as 'necessary' and 'proportionate', but being 'as tailored as feasible' and prioritising alternatives to signals intelligence are two of many examples in US law where specific safeguards address those concerns.

4.3.4. *Retention and dissemination limits for non-US persons similar to US persons*

Issue: A frequent concern expressed by European data protection officials is that stricter rules apply to US persons than to non-US persons, such as for the retention and dissemination of personal data.

Action: The agency procedures put in place pursuant to section 4 of PPD-28 have created new limits that address this concern.[111] The new retention requirements and dissemination limitations are consistent across agencies and similar to those for US persons.[112] For retention, different intelligence agencies previously had different rules for how long information about non-US persons could be retained. Under the new procedures, agencies generally must delete non-US personal information collected through signals intelligence five years

Links to the policies and procedures for the ODNI, the CIA, the FBI, and other agencies can be found at: <http://icontherecord.tumblr.com/ppd-28/2015/privacy-civil-liberties>.

Additional policies on the site include: National Reconnaissance Office, Department of Homeland Security, Drug Enforcement Administration, State Department, Treasury Department, Department of Energy, US Coast Guard, and other IC elements in the Department of Defense.

111 The US Government will not consider the activities of foreign persons to be foreign intelligence just because they are foreign persons; there must be some other valid foreign intelligence purpose.

112 The agency procedures create new limits on dissemination of information about non-US persons, and require training in these requirements.

after collection.[113] For dissemination, there is an important provision applying to non-US personal information collected outside of the US: 'personal information shall be disseminated only if the dissemination of comparable information concerning U.S. persons would be permitted.'

The agency procedures make other changes for protection of non-US persons, including new oversight, training, and compliance requirements: 'The oversight programme includes a new requirement to report any significant compliance incident involving personal information, regardless of the person's nationality, to the Director of National Intelligence.'[114]

4.3.5. Limits on bulk collection of signals intelligence

Issue: In the wake of the Snowden revelations, there has been particular concern about bulk collection by US intelligence agencies.

Action: Section 2 of PPD-28 creates new limitations on the use of signals intelligence collected in bulk, where 'bulk' is defined as 'authorized collection of large quantities of signals intelligence data which, due to technical or operational considerations, is acquired without the use of discriminants' such as the e-mail or other selectors discussed in section 3.[115]

PPD-28 announces purpose limitations – when the US collects non-publicly available information in bulk, it shall use that data only for purposes of detecting and countering:

1. espionage and other threats and activities directed by foreign powers or their intelligence services against the United States and its interests;
2. threats to the United States and its interests from terrorism;
3. threats to the United States and its interests from the development, possession, proliferation, or use of weapons of mass destruction;
4. cybersecurity threats;
5. threats to US or allied Armed Forces or other US or allied personnel;
6. transnational criminal threats, including illicit finance and sanctions evasion related to the other purposes named in this section.

---

113 There are exceptions to the five-year limit, but they can only apply after the Director of National Intelligence considers the views of Office of the Director of National Intelligence Civil Liberties Protection officer and agency privacy and civil liberties officials <http://icontherecord.tumblr.com/ppd-28/2015/privacy-civil-liberties>.

114 <http://icontherecord.tumblr.com/ppd-28/2015/privacy-civil-liberties#ppd-28>.

115 Consistent with the discussion if filtering in section 2, PPD-28 says: 'The limitations contained in this section do not apply to signals intelligence data that is temporarily acquired to facilitate targeted collection.' The detailed rules governing targeted collection under section 702 are discussed in section 2 of this chapter.

If this is updated, it will be 'made publicly available to the maximum extent feasible'.

4.3.6. *Limits on surveillance to gain trade secrets for commercial advantage*

Issue: European and other nations have long expressed concern that US surveillance capabilities would be used for the advantage of US commercial interests. These concerns, if true, would provide an economic reason to object to US signals intelligence, in addition to privacy and civil liberties concerns.

Action: The Review Group was briefed on this issue, and we reported that US practice has *not* been to gain trade secrets for commercial advantage. There is a subtlety here that is sometimes overlooked. PPD-28 states that the 'collection of foreign private commercial information or trade secrets is authorized', but only 'to protect the national security of the United States or its partners and allies'. For instance, the national security of the US and its EU allies justifies surveillance of companies in some circumstances, such as evading sanctions and shipping nuclear materials to Iran, or money laundering to support international terrorism.

The distinction in PPD-28 is that '[i]t is not an authorized foreign intelligence or counterintelligence purpose to collect such information to afford a competitive advantage to U.S. companies and U.S. business sectors commercially.' In the above examples, it would not be justified to collect information for the purpose of assisting a US nuclear equipment manufacturer or US banks.

4.3.7. *New White House oversight of sensitive intelligence collection, including of foreign leaders*

Issue: In the aftermath of the attacks of 11 September 2001, the view of intelligence agencies was that they tended to conduct surveillance activities to collect foreign intelligence information against a wide range of targets, without necessarily taking into account non-intelligence consequences of that targeting.

Action: To review sensitive intelligence collection more closely, there is now a stricter procedure to assess sensitive intelligence collection, as part of the National Intelligence Priorities Framework.[116] The procedures have been revised to require more senior policymaker participation in collection decisions. In the first year, the new procedures applied to nearly one hundred countries and organisations, resulting in new collection restrictions.[117] In addition, the NSA

---

116 <http://icontherecord.tumblr.com/ppd-28/2015/limiting-sigint-collection>.
117 Ibid.

'has enhanced its processes to ensure that targets are regularly reviewed, and those targets that are no longer providing valuable intelligence information in support of these senior policy-maker approved priorities are removed.'[118]

The new oversight process responds in part to the new principles of respecting privacy and civil liberties abroad.The rationale for careful oversight is bolstered by heightened awareness that 'US intelligence collection activities present the potential for national security damage if improperly disclosed.'[119] Potential damage cited in PPD-28 includes compromise of intelligence sources and methods, as well as harm to diplomatic relationships and other interests.

This process includes review of collection efforts targeted at foreign leaders. For many observers, it is reasonable for the US or another country to seek to monitor the communications of foreign leaders in time of war or in the case of clearly hostile nations. By contrast, the US was widely criticised for reported efforts to monitor the communications of German Chancellor Angela Merkel and the leaders of other allied countries. Collection targeted at foreign leaders is now reviewed as part of the overall White House oversight of sensitive intelligence collection. President Obama stated in 2014: 'I have made clear to the intelligence community that unless there is a compelling national security purpose, we will not monitor the communications of heads of state and government of our close friends and allies.'[120]

4.3.8. New White House process to help fix software flaws rather than use them for surveillance

Issue: The Review Group recommended a new process to evaluate what to do with so-called 'Zero Day' attacks, where software developers and system owners have zero days to address and patch a vulnerability.[121] The Review Group recommended that the Government should generally move to ensure that Zero Days are quickly blocked, so that the underlying vulnerabilities are quickly patched on government and private networks.

Action: Previously, the decision was made in the NSA about how to balance the equities between the usefulness of a Zero Day for offence (to penetrate someone else's network for surveillance) versus for defence (to patch our own networks). In 2014 the White House announced what it called a 'disciplined, rigorous and high-level decision-making process for vulnerability disclosure'.[122] In my

118 Ibid.
119 PPD-28, s. 3.
120 <https://www.whitehouse.gov/the-press-office/2014/01/17/remarks-president-review-signals-intelligence>.
121 Review Group Report, p. 219.
122 <https://www.whitehouse.gov/blog/2014/04/28/heartbleed-understanding-when-we-disclose-cyber-vulnerabilities>.

view, this new inter-agency process, chaired by the President's Cybersecurity Coordinator, improves on the old system by bringing in perspectives from more stakeholders who emphasise the importance of defending networks. In other words, the new process creates a new and useful check on any intelligence agency temptation to emphasise surveillance capabilities at the expense of good cybersecurity and protection of the personal data in computer systems.

4.3.9. *Greater transparency by the executive branch about surveillance activities*

Issue: Section 4.2.7 above discussed new government transparency reports required in the USA Freedom Act.

Action: Since 2013, the executive branch has gone well beyond these legislative requirements in its transparency activities. In its January 2015 report on Signals Intelligence Reform, the Government reported eight categories of greater transparency that it had undertaken to that point, and additional items were listed in the 2016 report.[123] Compared to the secrecy that historically had applied to signals intelligence, the shift toward greater transparency is remarkable, such as:

- The already-mentioned declassification of numerous FISC decisions.
- A new website devoted to public access to intelligence community information.[124]
- The first 'Principles of Intelligence Transparency for the Intelligence Community'.[125]
- The first two Intelligence Community Statistical Transparency Reports.[126]
- Unclassified reports on NSA's implementation of section 702[127] and its 'Civil Liberties and Privacy Protections for Targeted SIGINT Activities'.[128]
- Numerous speeches and appearances by intelligence community leadership to explain government activities, in contrast to the historical practice of very little public discussion of these issues.[129]

---

123 <http://icontherecord.tumblr.com/ppd-28/2015/enhancing-transparency>; <https://icontherecord.tumblr.com/ppd-28/2016>.

124 <http://icontherecord.tumblr.com>.

125 <http://www.dni.gov/files/documents/ppd-28/FINAL%20Transparency_poster%20v1.pdf>; <http://www.dni.gov/files/documents/Newsroom/Reports%20and%20Pubs/Principles%20of%20Intelligence%20Transparency%20Implementation%20Plan.pdf>.

126 <http://icontherecord.tumblr.com/transparency/odni_transparencyreport_cy2014>.

127 <https://www.nsa.gov/civil_liberties/_files/nsa_report_on_section_702_program.pdf>.

128 <https://www.nsa.gov/civil_liberties/_files/nsa_clpo_report_targeted_EO12333.pdf>.

129 <http://icontherecord.tumblr.com/transparency/odni_transparencyreport_cy2014>.

4.3.10. *Creation of the first NSA civil liberties and privacy office*

Issue: In a 2013 talk, President Obama said: 'Just because we can do something, doesn't mean we should do it.'[130] The NSA staffed up its already significant compliance efforts after FISC criticism of its implementation of programmes under FISA, including hiring a Director of Compliance, and now has over 300 compliance employees.[131] Simply complying with the law, however, does not mean that there is sufficient attention to how privacy should be treated within an intelligence agency.

Action: NSA appointed a Civil Liberties and Privacy Officer for the first time,[132] and other agencies have similar positions. That office becomes a point of expertise within the agency, and a point of contact for those outside of the agency who have privacy concerns.[133]

4.3.11. *Multiple changes under section 215*

Issue: In his 2014 speech, President Obama ordered multiple changes to the bulk telephony meta-data programme conducted under section 215.[134]

Action: In response, the executive branch changed its practices under section 215 in numerous ways.[135] Congress faced a 'sunset' of the section 215 authority in 2015 – if Congress did not act, then the legal authority as it currently existed would have expired. The existence of this sunset created a powerful incentive for Congress to consider the USA Freedom Act, which extended section 215 with the numerous pro-privacy changes described earlier in this chapter.

---

130 <http://www.politico.com/story/2013/10/obama-surveillance-message-lost-in-translation-099003#ixzz3uLEoiGaW>.

131 <https://www.nsa.gov/civil_liberties/_files/nsa_clpo_report_targeted_EO12333.pdf>.

132 President Obama issued PPD-28 on 17 January 2014 <http://icontherecord.tumblr.com/ppd-28/2015/privacy-civil-liberties#section-215>. The US Government announced NSA's first CLPO on 29 January 2014 <http://icontherecord.tumblr.com/tagged/becky+richards>.

133 The Office of Director of National Intelligence similarly has a Civil Liberties Protection Officer <www.dni.gov/clpo>. Other relevant agency positions include: Department of Homeland Security Privacy Officer <http://www.dhs.gov/privacy-office>; Department of Homeland Security Office for Civil Rights and Civil Liberties <http://www.dhs.gov/office-civil-rights-and-civil-liberties>; Department of Justice Office of Privacy and Civil Liberties <http://www.justice.gov/opcl>; Department of Defense Oversight and Compliance Directorate <http://dcmo.defense.gov/About/Organization/OCD.aspx>, which includes the Defense Privacy and Civil Liberties Office <http://dpcld.defense.gov/> and Department of Defense Intelligence Oversight <http://dodsioo.defense.gov/Home.aspx>.

134 <https://www.whitehouse.gov/the-press-office/2014/01/17/remarks-president-review-signals-intelligence>.

135 'New privacy protections for bulk telephony meta-data collected under Section 215' <http://icontherecord.tumblr.com/ppd-28/2015/privacy-civil-liberties#section-215>.

4.3.12. *Stricter documentation of the foreign intelligence basis for targeting under section 702*

Issue: A prominent criticism of US surveillance law has been that it constitutes 'indiscriminate' surveillance, including under the PRISM and Upstream programs of section 702. Under the OECD Privacy Guidelines[136] and EU data protection law, there should be a clear purpose specification for the processing of personal data. While collection under section 702 has always been targeted rather than indiscriminate, the executive branch has instituted measures to ensure that the targeting is appropriately documented.

Action: In its detailed report on section 702 in 2014, the first recommendation by the PCLOB was to 'Revise NSA Procedures to Better Document the Foreign Intelligence Reason for Targeting Decisions'.[137] In 2015, the PCLOB reported: 'The Administration has agreed to implement this recommendation.'[138]

The PCLOB's 2015 assessment provides details about the change, including:

- Revision of the NSA's targeting procedures to specify criteria for determining the expected foreign intelligence value of a particular target.
- Further revision to require a detailed written explanation of the basis for the determination.
- FISC review of the revised targeting procedures and requirements of documentation of the foreign intelligence-finding.
- Other measures to ensure that the 'foreign intelligence purpose' requirement in section 702 is carefully met.
- Submission of the draft targeting procedures for review by the PCLOB (an independent agency with privacy responsibilities).
- Compliance, training, and audit.[139]

4.3.13. *Other changes under section 702*

Issue: Section 2 of this testimony discussed in detail section 702's PRISM and Upstream programmes. Section 702 sunsets in 2017, so Congress will face a similar debate to the one in 2015 for section 215.

Action: The PCLOB issued a lengthy report on section 702 in 2014, which included recommendations for reform by the executive branch.[140] In 2015, the

---

136 <http://www.oecd.org/internet/ieconomy/oecdguidelinesontheprotectionofprivacyandtransborderflowsofpersonaldata.htm>.

137 <https://www.pclob.gov/library/702-Report.pdf>.

138 <https://www.pclob.gov/library/Recommendations_Assessment-Report.pdf>.

139 PPD-28's s. 2 also provides guidance for clearer purpose specification in connection with bulk collection.

140 Above n. 54.

PCLOB assessed the Government's response: 'The Administration has accepted virtually all of the recommendations in the Board's Section 702 report and has begun implementing many of them.'[141] A number of the recommendations apply to US persons and thus are not the focus here.

In addition to the new requirements for purpose specifications, the detailed assessment by the PCLOB included the following:[142]

- Provide the FISC random samples of selectors used for targeting under the section 702 programme, to enhance the court's review of the overall programme. As of the time of the report, this was being implemented.
- Provide the FISC with consolidated documentation about section 702. According to the PCLOB, the programme had become so complex that this documentation was necessary. As of the time of the report, this was being implemented.
- Periodically assess Upstream collection technology to ensure that only authorised communications are acquired. The administration has accepted this recommendation.
- Examine the technical feasibility of limiting particular forms of 'about' information. 'About' information was discussed in section 2 of this testimony. The NSA has been assessing how to achieve greater minimisation of 'about' information.
- Publicly release the current section 702 minimisation procedures for the CIA, FBI, and NSA. This has been done.

4.3.14. *Reduced secrecy about national security letters*

Issue: As enacted in 2001, recipients of a National Security Letter were 'gagged' – they were not allowed to tell anyone that they had received the NSL.[143] In law enforcement investigations, recipients of a wiretap order are similarly prohibited from telling the target about the wiretap, for obvious reasons – targets will not say incriminating things if they know the police are listening. Within weeks or at most months of the end of the investigation, however, targets are informed about the wiretap. For NSLs, however, the prohibition on disclosure continued indefinitely.[144]

---

141 <https://www.pclob.gov/library/Recommendations_Assessment-Report.pdf>.

142 A number of the recommendations apply to US persons and thus are not the focus here.

143 I first wrote about problems with this gag rule in 2004. Peter Swire, 'The System of Foreign Intelligence Surveillance Law' (2004) 72 *Geo. Wash. L. Rev.* 1306 <http://ssrn.com/abstract=586616>.

144 The statistical number of NSLs received can be reported in increments of 1,000 by providers, as discussed above concerning government transparency reports.

Action: In his 2014 speech, President Obama announced the indefinite secrecy would change. As of 2015, the FBI will now presumptively terminate NSL secrecy for an individual order when an investigation closes, or no more than three years after the opening of a full investigation. Exceptions are permitted only if a senior official determines that national security requires otherwise in the particular case and explains the basis in writing.[145]

4.4. CONCLUSION

Since the first press disclosures from Snowden approximately 30 months ago, the US Government has taken the two dozen actions discussed in this chapter. As this chapter has shown, these reforms emerged from a transparent and extensive process, including extensive debate in the US Congress and hundreds of pages of expert reports and declassified intelligence documents.

These reforms were not mentioned in the European Court of Justice decision in *Schrems*, or in the Opinion of the Advocate General, despite the latter's statement that assessment of US practices must be done 'by reference to the current factual and legal context.'

The reforms show the nature of the US 'legal order' relating to surveillance activities. They show a constitutional democracy under the rule of law, with independent judicial oversight, transparency, and democratic accountability. As discussed in section 1, they show the essential and fundamental equivalence of the US and EU Member States with respect to surveillance activities.

145 <http://icontherecord.tumblr.com/ppd-28/2015/privacy-civil-liberties>.

INVITED COMMENT

5. THE PAPER SHIELD

On the Degree of Protection of the EU–US Privacy Shield against Unnecessary or Disproportionate Data Collection by the US Intelligence and Law Enforcement Services

Gert VERMEULEN*

1. BACKGROUND: INADEQUACY OF THE US DATA PROTECTION REGIME: CLEAR TO EVERYONE AFTER SNOWDEN

The Europol–US agreement of 20 December 2002[1] and the EU–US mutual assistance treaty in criminal matters of 25 June 2003,[2] both concluded in the immediate aftermath of 9/11, soon set the tone, in that US non-compliance with key EU data protection standards was set aside in favour of enabling EU–US data flows after all. Neither in terms of police or judicial cooperation could the adequacy of US data protection be established, something required by both the (then) Europol Agreement and Directive 95/46.[3] Purpose limitation (specialty)[4]

---

* Institute for International Research on Criminal Policy, Ghent University; Commission for the protection of privacy (Belgium). E-mail: gert.vermeulen@ugent.be.

1 Supplemental agreement between the Europol Police Office and the United States of America on the exchange of personal data and related information, 20.12.2002, <https://www.europol.europa.eu/content/supplemental-agreement-between-europol-police-office-and-united-states-america>.

2 Agreement on mutual legal assistance between the European Union and the United States of America, [2003] OJ L 181/34.

3 Directive 95/46/EC of the European Parliament and of the Council of 24 October 1995 on the protection of individuals with regard to the processing of personal data and on the free movement of such data, [1995] OJ L 281.

4 E. DE BUSSER, 'Purpose limitation in EU–US data exchange in criminal matters: the remains of the day' in M. COOLS, S. DE KIMPE, B. DE RUYVER, M. EASTON, L. PAUWELS, P. PONSAERS,

in the use of data provided by Europol or EU Member States proved an almost nugatory concept, where the US was allowed to freely make use of information that was procured in criminal cases for purely administrative or intelligence purposes.[5]

Later, in 2006, it was revealed that the US Treasury had procured access to worldwide scriptural bank transactions by means of administrative subpoenas *vis-à-vis* the US hub of the (Belgium-based) Society for Worldwide Interbank Financial Telecommunication (SWIFT) in the context of combating the financing of terrorism, but surely alluding to other (including economic) goals as well.[6] Moreover, SWIFT itself defected herein, as its US hub did not endorse the so-called Safe Harbour principles.[7] These had been developed in 2000 by the European Commission[8] to ensure that, given that the US data protection regime in itself could not be qualified as adequate, commercial EU–US data transfers would nonetheless be enabled.[9] Companies that indicated (and self-certified) their compliance with the principles laid down in the Commission's Safe Harbour Decision, were to be considered as – from a data protection perspective – 'safe harbours' within US territory, to which EU companies were allowed to transfer data. This, however, was not the case for the SWIFT hub in the US, so the Belgian company should have refrained from localising (backup) data in it.

The EU response to this scandal was far from convincing. While intra-European payment transactions were admittedly no longer sent to the US hub (albeit that in the meantime SWIFT had registered it as a 'safe harbour'),

---

G. Vande Walle et al. (eds.), *Readings on Criminal Justice, Criminal Law and Policing* (Vol. 2), Maklu, Apeldoorn 2009, pp. 163–201.

5 S. Peers, 'The exchange of personal data between Europol and the USA' (2003) *Statewatch Analysis* 1–3, <www.statewatch.org>; G. Vermeulen, 'Transatlantisch monsterverbond of verstandshuwelijk? Over het verschil tussen oorlog en juridische strijd tegen terreur en de versterkte politie- en justitiesamenwerking tussen EU en VS' (2004) 25(1) *Panopticon* 90–107; P. De Hert and B. De Schutter, 'International Transfers of Data in the Field of JHA: The Lessons of Europol, PNR and Swift' in B. Martenczuk and S. Van Thiel (eds.), *Justice, Liberty, Security: New Challenges for EU External Relations*, VUB Press, Brussels 2008, pp. 326–327 and 329–333.

6 See the Privacy Commission's Opinion on the Transfer of Personal Data by the CSLR SWIFT by Virtue of UST (OFAC), 37/2006, <https://www.privacycommission.be/sites/privacycommission/files/documents/advies_37_2006_1.pdf>; furthermore see: P.M. Connorton, 'Tracking Terrorist Financing through SWIFT: When U.S. subpoenas and foreign privacy law collide' (2007) 76(1) *Fordham Law Review* 283–322.

7 G. Gonzalez Fuster, P. De Hert and S. Gutwirth, 'SWIFT and the vulnerability of transatlantic data transfers' (2008) 22(1–2) *International Review of Law Computers & Technology* 191–202.

8 Commission Decision of 26 July 2000 pursuant to Directive 95/46/EC of the European Parliament and of the Council on the adequacy of the protection provided by the safe harbour privacy principles and related frequently asked questions issued by the US Department of Commerce, 2000/520/EC, [2000] OJ L 215.

9 See, e.g. W.J. Long and M.P. Quek 'Personal data privacy protection in an age of globalization: the US–EU safe harbor compromise' (2002) 9(3) *Journal of European Public Policy* 325–344.

the Commission negotiated on behalf of the EU an agreement with the US, allowing the latter, via a Europol 'filter' (which painfully lacks proper filtering capacity) to obtain *bulk* access on a case-by-case basis to these intra-European payment transactions. This 2010 agreement, the Terrorist Financing Tracking Programme (TFTP),[10] furthermore contains an article in which the US Treasury is axiomatically deemed adequate in terms of data protection.[11] Notwithstanding this, and given the known practice of wide data-sharing between US government administrations and bodies, contrary to the European purpose-limitation principle, the *in*adequacy of the US data protection regime was at the time beyond doubt. That the Foreign Intelligence Surveillance Act (FISA),[12] amended in the aftermath of 9/11 with the Patriot Act[13] and further expanded in 2008,[14] allowed the US to monitor – either with or without a court order – electronic communication in a way that was disproportionate, worldwide and in bulk, was clear as well.[15]

This and more was confirmed in the summer of 2013 with the revelations of whistleblower Edward Snowden.[16] These revelations were particularly shocking because of the revealed extent of the interception practices of the National Security Agency (NSA) – *inter alia* through the PRISM programme – and

10 Agreement between the European Union and the United States of America on the processing and transfer of Financial Messaging Data from the European Union to the United States for purposes of the Terrorist Finance Tracking Program, [2010] OJ L 8.

11 Art. 6 of the TFTP Agreement (above n. 10) reads: 'the U.S. Treasury Department is deemed to ensure an adequate level of data protection for the processing of financial payment messaging and related data transferred from the European Union to the United States for purposes of this Agreement'.

12 The Foreign Intelligence Surveillance Act of 1978, 50 USC §§1801–11, 1821–29, 1841–46, 1861–62, 1871, <https://www.law.cornell.edu/uscode/text/50/chapter-36/subchapter-I>.

13 Uniting and Strengthening America by Providing Appropriate Tools Required to Intercept and Obstruct Terrorism Act of 2001 (USA Patriot Act), Pub. L. 107–56; 10/26/01, <https://www.gpo.gov/fdsys/pkg/PLAW-107publ56/pdf/PLAW-107publ56.pdf>; see also: P.T. Jaeger, J.C. Bertot and C.R. McClure, 'The impact of the USA Patriot Act on collection and analysis of personal information under the Foreign Intelligence Surveillance Act' (2003) 20 *Government Information Quarterly* 295–314.

14 Foreign Intelligence Surveillance Act of 1978 Amendments Act of 2008, Pub. L.110–261; 7/10/2008, <https://www.gpo.gov/fdsys/pkg/PLAW-110publ261/pdf/PLAW-110publ261.pdf>.

15 E. De Busser, 'Purpose limitation in EU–US data exchange in criminal matters: the remains of the day' in M. Cools, S. De Kimpe, B. De Ruyver, M. Easton, L. Pauwels, P. Ponsaers, G. Vande Walle et al. (eds.), *Readings on Criminal Justice, Criminal Law and Policing*, (Vol. 2), Maklu, Apeldoorn 2009, pp. 163–201; E. De Busser, *Data Protection in EU and US Criminal Cooperation*, Maklu, Antwerp–Apeldoorn–Portland 2009.

16 The outrage broke in June 2013, when the *Guardian* first reported that the US National Security Agency (NSA) was collecting the telephone records of tens of millions of Americans, see: G. Greenwald 'NSA collecting phone records of millions of Verizon customers daily', *The Guardian*, 06.06.2013, <http://www.theguardian.com/world/2013/jun/06/nsa-phone-records-verizon-court-order>; see also: M-R. Papandrea, 'Leaker Traitor Whistleblower Spy: National Security Leaks and the First Amendment' (2014) 94(2) *Boston University Law Review* 449–544.

the British intelligence service Government Communications Headquarters (GCHQ),[17] which for years had spied on Belgacom International Carrier Service (BICS). As a subsidiary of Belgium-based (tele)communications provider Proximus, BICS provides worldwide hardware through which telecom companies and government agencies run their electronic communication (Internet, telephony, mobile and text traffic). Intense mutual cooperation between the NSA and GCHQ, and within the so-called Five Eyes Community (comprising also the intelligence services of Canada, Australia and New Zealand) was confirmed by the revelations, although many were well aware that these five, within the context of Echelon, had been monitoring worldwide satellite communications for decades, including for commercial purposes. In 2000 the European Parliament had already instigated an investigative commission against these practices.[18] From the US side, the publication of NSA newsletters in the summer of 2015 as a result of the Snowden revelations plainly confirmed these allegations.[19]

2. SAFE HARBOUR UNSAFE

Using the leverage handed to her under the Lisbon Treaty,[20] the then Commissioner of Justice Viviane Reding launched an ambitious legislative data protection package at the outset of 2012.[21] A proposed Regulation was initiated

---

17 The involvement of the British GCHQ was revealed by the *Guardian*, 21.06.2013. See: E. MacAskill, J. Borger, N. Hopkins, N. Davies and J. Ball, 'GCHQ taps fibre-optic cables for secret access to world's communications', *The Guardian*, 21.06.2013, <http://www.theguardian.com/uk/2013/jun/21/gchq-cables-secret-world-communications-nsa>.

18 See European Parliament decision setting up a temporary committee on the ECHELON interception system, <http://www.europarl.europa.eu/sides/getDoc.do?type=MOTION&reference=B5-2000-0593&language=EN> and the final report that was published in 2001: Report on the existence of a global system for the interception of private and commercial communications (ECHELON interception system) (2001/2098(INI)), FINAL A5-0264/2001 PAR1, 11.07.2001. See also: F. Piodi and I. Mombelli, *The ECHELON Affair. The European Parliament and the Global Interception System 1998–2002*, European Parliament History Series, European Parliamentary Research Service (EPRS), Luxembourg 2014, <http://www.europarl.europa.eu/EPRS/EPRS_STUDY_538877_AffaireEchelon-EN.pdf>.

19 See e.g. H. Farrell and A. Newman, 'Transatlantic Data War. Europe fights back against the NSA' (2016) 95(1) *Foreign Affairs* 124–133.

20 Treaty of Lisbon Amending the Treaty on European Union and the Treaty establishing the European Community [2007] OJ C 306.

21 V. Reding, 'The European data protection framework for the twenty-first century' (2012) 2(3) *International Data Privacy Law* 119–129; Communication from the Commission to the European Parliament, the Council, the Economic and Social Committee and the Committee of the Regions, 'Safeguarding Privacy in a Connected World – A European Data Protection Framework for the 21st Century', COM(2012) 9 final.

to replace Directive 95/46,[22] and aimed *inter alia* to bind (American) service providers on the EU territory by European rules on data protection. In parallel, a proposed Directive had to upgrade the 2008 Framework Decision on data protection in the sphere of police and judicial cooperation in criminal matters.[23] In December 2015, after a great deal of to-ing and fro-ing – and almost four years and a European Commission later – political agreement was reached on the new Regulation and the Directive.[24] Both were formally adopted in April 2016[25] and EU Member States are due to apply them from, respectively, 25 May and 6 May 2018 onwards.

The adequacy requirement for data transfers to third states moreover remains intact. Reding also took up the defence for EU citizens for what concerns US access to their personal data.[26] Just a few months after the Snowden revelations, she came up with two parallel communications at the end of November 2013: 'Rebuilding Trust in EU–US Data Flows'[27] and 'Communication on the functioning of the Safe Harbour from the perspective of EU citizens and companies established in the EU'.[28]

---

22 C.J. Bennet and C.D. Raab, 'The Adequacy of Privacy: the European Union Data Protection Directive and the North American Response' (1997) 13 *The Information Society* 252.

23 Council Framework Decision 2008/977/JHA of 27 November 2008 on the protection of personal data processed in the framework of police and judicial cooperation in criminal matters, [2008] OJ L 350; see also: E. De Busser and G. Vermeulen, 'Towards a coherent EU policy on outgoing data transfers for use in criminal matters? The adequacy requirement and the framework decision on data protection in criminal matters. A transatlantic exercise in adequacy' in M. Cools, B. De Ruyver, M. Easton, L. Pauwels, P. Ponsaers, G. Vande Walle, T. Vander Beken et al. (eds.), *EU and International Crime Control* (Vol. 4), Maklu, Antwerpen–Apeldoorn–Portland 2010, pp. 95–122.

24 For an overview of the route leading up to these instruments, see the (then) European Data Protection Supervisor's 2004–14 overview: P. Hustinx, 'EU Data Protection Law: The Review of Directive 95/46/EC and the Proposed General Data Protection Regulation', <https://secure.edps.europa.eu/EDPSWEB/webdav/site/mySite/shared/Documents/EDPS/Publications/Speeches/2014/14-09-15_Article_EUI_EN.pdf>.

25 Regulation (EU) 2016/679 of the European Parliament and of the Council of 27 April 2016 on the protection of natural persons with regard to the processing of personal data and on the free movement of such data, and repealing Directive 95/46/EC (General Data Protection Regulation), [2016] OJ L 119; Directive (EU) 2016/680 of the European Parliament and of the Council of 27 April 2016 on the protection of natural persons with regard to the processing of personal data by competent authorities for the purposes of the prevention, investigation, detection or prosecution of criminal offences or the execution of criminal penalties, and on the free movement of such data, and repealing Council Framework Decision 2008/977/JHA, [2016] OJ L 119.

26 See, e.g. E. De Busser, 'Privatization of Information and the Data Protection Reform' in S. Gutwirth et al. (eds.), *Reloading Data Protection*. Springer, Dordrecht 2014, pp. 129–149.

27 European Commission, Communication from the Commission to the European Parliament and the Council, 'Rebuilding Trust in EU–US Data Flows', COM(2013) 846 final.

28 European Commission, Communication from the Commission to the European Parliament and the Council on the Functioning of the Safe Harbour from the Perspective of EU Citizens and Companies Established in the EU, COM(2013) 847 final (hereafter: Safe Harbour Communication).

The first communication was accompanied by a report containing the 'findings on the *ad-hoc* workgroup data protection of the EU and the US',[29] which, among others, stipulated that the improvements in the Safe Harbour Decision should address the 'structural deficiencies in relation to the transparency and enforcement, the material safe harbour principles and the functioning of the *exception for national security*' (emphasis added). After all, the Safe Harbour Decision explicitly determined that the demands of 'national security, public interest and law enforcement' of the US supersede the Safe Harbour principles.[30] As it turned out, these exceptions rendered the safe harbours unsafe.

In its 2013 Safe Harbour Communication the Commission established that 'all companies involved in the PRISM programme, and which grant access to US authorities to data stored and processed in the US, appear to be Safe Harbour certified'. As such, '[t]his has made the Safe Harbour scheme one of the conduits through which access is given to US intelligence authorities to collecting personal data initially processed in the EU'.[31] This was indeed the case – Microsoft, Google, Facebook, Apple, Yahoo, Skype, YouTube, etc. – all of them were self-certified under Safe Harbour and simultaneously involved in the PRISM programme. The Commission concluded that

> The large scale nature of these programmes may [have] result[ed] in [*more*] data transferred under Safe Harbour being accessed and further processed by US authorities *beyond what is strictly necessary and proportionate to the protection of national security* as foreseen under the exception provided in the Safe Harbour Decision.[32]

3. SAFE HARBOUR IS DEAD

Real urgency in the negotiations with the US only (re)surfaced following the ruling of the Court of Justice on 6 October 2015 in response to the appeal of *Max Schrems* against the Irish Data Protection Commissioner (in proceedings against Facebook,[33] which has its European headquarters in Dublin) before the Irish High Court.[34] The latter had requested a preliminary ruling by the Court in Luxembourg, namely as to whether the Irish Data Protection Commissioner

---

29 Report on the Findings of the EU Co-Chairs of the Ad Hoc EU–US Working Group on Data Protection, 27.11.2013, <http://ec.europa.eu/justice/data-protection/files/report-findings-of-the-ad-hoc-eu-US-working-group-on-data-protection.pdf>.

30 Annex I, para. 4.

31 Point 7.

32 Safe Harbour Communication, above n. 27, point 7.1 (emphasis added).

33 See e.g. N. Simmons, 'Facebook and the Privacy Frontier' (2012) 33(3) *Business Law Review* 58–62.

34 Case C-362/14, *Maximillian Schrems v. Data Protection Commissioner* (CJEU, 6 October 2015).

(as it had itself upheld) was bound by the Safe Harbour Decision to the extent that it could no longer be questioned whether the US data protection regime was adequate, as such leading the Irish Data Protection Commissioner to conclude that it could not investigate the complaint filed by Schrems. The latter had argued the contrary, based on the post-Snowden ascertainment that Facebook was active in the PRISM programme, regardless of its self-certification under the Safe Harbour principles.[35]

The Court concluded *inter alia* that

> The right to respect for private life, guaranteed by Article 7 of the Charter and by the core values common to the traditions of the Member States, would be rendered meaningless if the State authorities were authorised to access electronic communications on a casual and generalised basis without any objective justification based on *considerations of national security or the prevention of crime that are specific to the individual concerned and without those practices being accompanied by appropriate and verifiable safeguards.*[36]

The Court furthermore recalled, with explicit reference to its Data Retention judgment of 8 April 2014[37] (in which the Court had declared the Data Retention Directive invalid) and several earlier judgments, its consistent case law that

> EU legislation involving interference with the fundamental rights guaranteed by Articles 7 and 8 of the Charter [regarding the respect for private and family life and the protection of personal data respectively] must, according to the Court's settled case-law, lay down *clear and precise* rules governing the scope and application of a measure.[38]

---

35 A. Kirchner, 'Reflections on privacy in the age of global electronic data processing with a focus on data processing practices of Facebook' (2012) 6(1) *Masaryk University Journal of Law and Technology* 73–86; M. Hildebrandt, 'The rule of law in cyberspace?', Inaugural Lecture, Chair of Smart Environments, Data Protection and the Rule of Law, Institute of Computing and Information Sciences (iCIS), Nijmegen, Radboud University, <http://works.bepress.com/mireille_hildebrandt/48/>; B.J. Koops, 'The trouble with European data protection law' (2014) *International Data Privacy Law*; F. Coudert, 'Schrems vs. Data Protection Commissioner: a slap on the wrist for the Commission and new powers for data protection authorities', European Law Blog, 15.10.2015, <https://lirias.kuleuven.be/bitstream/123456789/511500/1/FannyCoudert_Post+CJEU+Schrems_final.pdf>; R. Day, 'Let the magistrates revolt: A review of search warrant applications for electronic information possessed by online services' (2015) 64(2) *University of Kansas Law Review* 491–526; S. Darcy, 'Battling for the Rights to Privacy and Data Protection in the Irish Courts' (2015) 31(80) *Utrecht Journal of International and European Law* 131–136; D. Flint, 'Computers and internet: Sunk without a trace – the demise of safe harbor' (2015) 36(6) *Business Law Review* 236–237, <http://www.kluwerlawonline.com/document.php?id=BULA2015031>; H. Crowther, 'Invalidity of the US Safe Harbor framework: what does it mean?' (2016) 11(2) *Journal of Intellectual Property Law & Practice* 88–90; N. Ni Loideain, 'The End of Safe Harbor: Implications for EU Digital Privacy and Data Protection Law' (2016) 19(8) *Journal of Internet Law*.

36 §34 (emphasis added).

37 Cases C-293/12 and C-594/12, *Digital Rights Ireland* (CJEU, 8 April 2014).

38 §91 (emphasis added).

Still with reference to the Data Retention judgment (and the case law cited under point 52 thereof), the Court stated that

> furthermore and above all, protection of the fundamental right to respect for private life at EU level requires derogations and limitations in relation to the protection of personal data to apply *only in so far as is strictly necessary*,[39]

whereby of course

> Legislation *is not limited to what is strictly necessary* where it authorises, on a generalised basis, *storage* of all the personal data of all the persons whose data has been transferred from the European Union to the United States without any differentiation, limitation or exception being made in the light of the objective pursued and without an objective criterion being laid down by which to determine the limits of the access of the public authorities to the data, and of its subsequent use, *for purposes which are specific, strictly restricted* and capable of justifying the interference which both *access to* that data and its *use* entail.[40]

In other words: collection (storage), access and use for reasons of national security, public interest or law enforcement require *specific and precise* criteria and are but allowed when *strictly necessary for specific purposes that are strictly restricted*. Given the fact that the Commission had omitted to implement such an assessment in its Safe Harbour Decision, the Court decided on the invalidity of the latter. Hence, with the *Schrems* case, the Court firmly put the finger on the following issue: engagements by US companies through self-certification (under the Safe Harbour principles) do not provide (adequate) protection as long as it remains unclear whether, despite large-scale interception programmes like PRISM, the US privacy regime may be considered adequate.

With the sudden invalidity of the Safe Harbour Decision, a replacement instrument became an urgent necessity. The new European Commission – since November 2014 the Juncker Commission, with Věra Jourová as the Commissioner for Justice, Consumers and Gender Equality, competent *inter alia* for data protection, under custody of Super-Commissioner (Vice-President of the Commission) Frans Timmermans – was quick to temper emotions. In a Communication on the very day of the Court's decision, Timmermans recognised the Court's confirmation of the necessity 'of having robust data protection safeguards in place before transferring citizens' data'. He furthermore added that, following its 2013 Safe Harbour Communication, the Commission was working with the US authorities 'to make data transfers *safer* for European citizens' (emphasis added) and that, in light of the *Schrems* judgment, it would

39 §92 (emphasis added).

40 §93 (emphasis added).

continue to work 'towards a renewed and safe framework for the transfer of personal data across the Atlantic'.[41]

4. LONG LIVE THE PRIVACY SHIELD!

On 29 February 2016 the Commission presented its eagerly awaited 'solution'. It launched a new Communication, 'Transatlantic Data Flows: Restoring Trust through Strong Safeguards',[42] and immediately attached hereto – in replacement of the invalidated Safe Harbour Decision – its draft adequacy decision of the US data protection regime (with seven annexes) for data transfers under the protection of the so-called 'EU–US Privacy Shield'. On the Justice and Home Affairs (JHA) Council the day after, Jourovà hooted '[w]ritten assurances regarding the limitations on access to data by U.S. public authorities on national security grounds'.[43] Following a negative initial opinion about the initial draft decision, issued by the Article 29 Data Protection Working Party on 13 April 2016,[44] the Commission had no viable choice but to initiate summary renegotiations with the US, leading to just marginal adjustments of the Privacy Shield. The Article 29 Working Party (having nothing but mere advisory power in the first place) gave in,[45] as did the Article 31 Committee[46] (which had veto power over the draft decision). The revised version of the Privacy Shield adequacy decision was adopted by the European Commission on 12 July 2016.

Unsurprisingly, the Privacy Shield is already facing legal challenges before the General Court of the EU, following an action for annulment filed by Digital Rights Ireland on 16 September 2016 in a case against the Commission.[47] At best,

---

41 Communication from the Commission to the European Parliament and the Council on the transfer of personal data from the EU to the United States of America under Directive 95/46/EC following the Judgment by the Court of Justice in Case C-362/14 (*Schrems*), COM(2015) 566 final, 6 November 2015.

42 Communication from the Commission to the European Parliament and the Council, 'Transatlantic Data Flows: Restoring Trust through Strong Safeguards', COM(2016) 117 final, 29 February 2016.

43 Ibid.

44 WP29 Press release 13 April 2016, <http://ec.europa.eu/justice/data-protection/article-29/press-material/pressrelease/art29_press_material/2016/press_release_shield_en.pdf>; WP29 Opinion on the draft EU–U.S. Privacy Shield adequacy decision, <http://ec.europa.eu/justice/data-protection/article-.29/documentation/opinionrecommendation/files/2016/wp238_en.pdf>.

45 WP29 Press release, 1 July 2016, <http://ec.europa.eu/justice/data-protection/article-29/pressmaterial/press-.release/art29_press_material/2016/20160701_wp29_press_release_eu_us_privacy_shield_en.pdf>.

46 On 8 July 2016, following its non-decision of 19 May on the initial version of the Privacy Shield.

47 Case T-670/16, *Digital Rights Ireland v. Commission.*

the Court may consider the case by the autumn of 2017. If it does, it remains to be seen whether discussions about *locus standi* of Digital Rights Ireland will not prevent the Court from judging on the substance. In any event, the future of the Privacy Shield, even if 1,500 companies[48] have already self-certified themselves under the new scheme, remains uncertain.

Especially since the Court of Justice has issued yet another judgment on 21 December 2016, following a request for a preliminary ruling in the case *Tele2 Sverige AB*[49] on data retention under the ePrivacy Directive. As will be explained in the analysis below, the findings of the Court at least indirectly place a bomb under the Privacy Shield as well, where it holds that 'general and indiscriminate retention of traffic data and location data' is inacceptable, leaving Member States the possibility for only 'targeted'[50] retention of traffic and location data, meaning that such retention must then be defined also in terms of the 'public …that may potentially be affected'[51] and on the basis of 'objective evidence which makes it possible to identify a public whose data is likely to reveal a link, at least an indirect one, with serious criminal offences, and to contribute in one way or another to fighting serious crime or to preventing a serious risk to public security'.[52] Indiscriminate data collection, irrespective of later access or use restrictions, has been formally invalidated by the Court, in an even clearer fashion than in its 2014 Data Retention judgment. Interestingly, the Court has moreover explicitly ruled that data concerned must be retained within the European Union, which indirectly raises fresh doubts about the legitimacy of transferring (electronic communications) data under the Privacy Shield, and even under the Umbrella Agreement or the TFTP.

Before we can evaluate the Privacy Shield on its merits, it pays to bear in mind that, conceptually, it bears a very strong resemblance to the Safe Harbour regime. The Safe Harbour principles have been renamed as *privacy* principles, which should serve as the new basis for data transfers coming from the EU to organisations – essentially corporations – in the US, who endorse these principles through the act of self-certification. Mirroring the Safe Harbour Decision, there is furthermore a general exception hereto should national security, public interest or law enforcement require. Hence, the central question is whether the 'limitations' and 'safeguards' that are presented by the Privacy Shield – the Safe Harbour regime did not foresee any of these – are convincing enough. The way in which the European Commission desperately tried to convince everyone, through the means of its Communication and the attached (draft) adequacy decision, of the satisfactory nature of the new regime, and that the US will

48 <https://www.privacyshield.gov/list>.
49 Case C-203/15, joined with Case C-698/15.
50 §108.
51 §110–111.
52 §111.

effectively display an adequate data protection level under the Privacy Shield, was painful to witness. The heydays of former European Justice Commissioner Reding seem long gone.

Apparently, demanding a genuine commitment of the US to refrain from collecting bulk personal data of EU citizens coming from the EU, and to only intercept communications and other personal data when strictly necessary and proportionate, was a political bridge too far. It seems that Commissioner Jourová (and Super-Commissioner Timmermans) have succumbed to the dominant importance of maintaining benevolent trans-Atlantic trade relations. Allowing trans-Atlantic transfers of personal data from companies or their subsidiaries in the EU to companies based in the US is after all the primordial goal of the Privacy Shield. As it turns out, tough negotiating was apparently not considered an option, not even in the renegotiation stage. Nonetheless, one fails to see why such a commercial transfer of personal data *without* the option to do so in bulk, or without resorting to a capturing of such data that is disproportionate for intelligence or law enforcement purposes, would have been too high a stake during negotiations. Companies – including the major US players like Google, Apple, Facebook and Microsoft – will in the long run not benefit from the fact that they will not be able to protect the data of their European or other users against government access. It is regrettable that they themselves seem insufficiently aware of this, leaving aside scarce counter-examples like the Apple–FBI clash.[53] In the meantime, the very minimum is to burst the bubble of the European Commission's discourse in the Privacy Shield Communication and its (draft) adequacy decision. The 'limitations' and 'safeguards' that the Shield – according to the Commission – offers against US data collection in the interest of national security (by the intelligence services), public interest or law enforcement (by the police) are by absolutely no means sufficient. A simple focused reading and concise analysis hereof suffice to show this.

5. LIMITATIONS AND SAFEGUARDS REGARDING DATA COLLECTION IN THE INTEREST OF NATIONAL SECURITY

5.1. COLLECTION AND ACCESS VERSUS ACCESS AND USE: ONE BIG AMALGAMATION

The Commission's analysis is misleading because it repeatedly posits that the 'limitations' to which the US will commit and that are applicable on the parts

[53] See, e.g. The Economist, 'Taking a bite at the Apple. The FBI's legal battle with the maker of iPhones is an escalation of a long-simmering conflict about encryption and security', 27.02.2016, <http://www.economist.com/news/science-and-technology/21693564-fbis-legal-battle-maker-iphones-escalation>.

concerning 'access' and 'use' (see paragraph 67 of the revised adequacy decision) for the purpose of national security, public interest or law enforcement, will be sufficient in light of EU law to amount to an adequate level of data protection. According to EU law, however, processing of personal data takes place as soon as 'collection' takes place, regardless of any future 'access' to this data or the 'use' thereof. By systematically wielding the term 'access' instead of 'collection', or by posing as if the limitations regarding 'access' will – with the proverbial single stroke of a brush – also include sufficient limitations in terms of 'collection', the Commission is wilfully pulling one's leg.

To the extent still necessary, it suffices to recall the previously mentioned 2014 Data Retention judgment of the Court of Justice. In the latter, the Court abundantly made clear that limitations are necessary both in the phase of the 'collection' of personal data (*in casu* retention or conservation by suppliers of electronic communication services of traffic data in fixed and mobile telephony, Internet access, Internet e-mail and Internet telephony) as in the phases of 'accessing' this data or its later 'use' (*in casu* by the competent police and judicial authorities). As such, the Commission skips a step, or at least tries to maintain the illusion that the Privacy Shield's limitations in terms of 'access' and 'use' will suffice to speak of an adequate data protection. This, however, is flagrantly false rhetoric. Just the same, the part that concerns the initial 'collection' of personal data by the competent authorities (*in casu* the US intelligence or law enforcement services) is also bound by strict requirements. After all, one of the reasons why the Court dismissed the Data Retention Directive as invalid was because

> in particular, it is not restricted to a retention in relation (i) to data pertaining to a particular time period and/or a particular geographical zone and/or to a circle of particular persons likely to be involved, in one way or another, in a serious crime, or (ii) to persons who could, for other reasons, contribute, by the retention of their data, to the prevention, detection or prosecution of serious offences.[54]

It is important to bear in mind that back then, the debate was only on the conservation (and as such 'collection') by service providers of electronic communications, and not even on the direct 'collection' by intelligence and law enforcement services themselves, as is currently the case with the Privacy Shield.

With the Court's judgment in *Tele2 Sverige AB* of December 2016, there is no doubt that any preventative data retention must be 'limited … to what is strictly necessary', 'with respect to the categories of data to be retained, the means of communication affected, *the persons concerned* and the retention period

---

[54] §59.

adopted',[55] these limitation criteria being explicitly cumulative, whilst the initial Data Retention judgment of 2014 (by the use of 'and/or') left the door open for data retention which would not be targeted in terms of also the 'persons concerned' or the 'public affected'.

Apart from this, the Court argued that in the Data Retention Directive there is

> not only … a general absence of limits [but that it] also fails to lay down any objective criterion by which to determine the limits of the *access* of the competent national authorities to the data and their subsequent *use* for the purposes of prevention, detection or criminal prosecutions concerning offences that, in view of the extent and seriousness of the interference with the fundamental rights enshrined in Articles 7 and 8 of the Charter, may be considered to be sufficiently serious to justify such an interference.[56]

The Court continued:

> [The] Directive does not contain substantive and procedural conditions relating to the *access* of the competent national authorities to the data and to their subsequent *use*. Article 4 of the directive, which governs the *access* of those authorities to the data retained, does not expressly provide that that *access* and the subsequent *use* of the data in question must be *strictly restricted* to the purpose of preventing and detecting *precisely defined* serious offences or of conducting criminal prosecutions relating thereto; it merely provides that each Member State is to define the procedures to be followed and the conditions to be fulfilled in order to gain access to the retained data in accordance with necessity and proportionality requirements.[57]

Ultimately, and still with reference to 'access' and 'use', the Court lamented that the Directive 'does not lay down any objective criterion by which the number of persons authorised to *access* and *subsequently use* the data retained is limited to what is strictly necessary in the light of the objective pursued', and that

> Above all, the access by the competent national authorities to the data retained is not made dependent on a prior review carried out by a court or by an independent administrative body whose decision seeks to limit *access* to the data and their *use* to what is strictly necessary for the purpose of attaining the objective pursued and which intervenes following a reasoned request of those authorities submitted within the framework of procedures of prevention, detection or criminal prosecutions. Nor does it lay down a specific obligation on Member States designed to establish such limits.[58]

---

55 §108 (emphasis added).
56 §60.
57 §61 (emphasis added).
58 §62 (emphasis added).

Mutatis mutandis[59] both the necessity and proportionality requirements can be firmly derived from the Data Retention judgment, and this with regard to the 'collection' of data on the one hand, and the 'access' to and 'use' of this data on the other. It was (as a minimum) to be expected from the Commission's Privacy Shield Communication that it would, for the discerned phases of 'collection' and 'access and use' respectively, carefully and systematically inquire into the US-proposed 'limitations' to the EU privacy requirements such as those employed by the Court in its 2014 Data Retention judgment. Unfortunately, the Privacy Shield Communication does not do so. From a substantive perspective, it is moreover the case that the guarantees in terms of 'collection' are clearly insufficient, since for example bulk collection of data remains perfectly possible under certain scenarios. Not only – and contrary to how it is presented by the Commission – will the Privacy Shield fail to solve this with the limitations it contains in terms of 'access and use', these limitations are inherently flawed as well, as they do not comply with nor mirror the (EU) requirements of strict necessity and proportionality.

5.2. BULK COLLECTION REMAINS POSSIBLE

In itself (paragraph 70 of the revised adequacy decision) it is gratifying that under PPD-28 (Presidential Policy Directive 28 of 17 January 2014)[60] intelligence operations concerning SIGINT (signals intelligence, the interception of electronic communication) will from now on only be allowed for purposes of foreign or counter-intelligence in support of government missions, and no longer with a view to benefit US companies' commercial interests. SIGINT for industrial espionage, or to allow US companies to poach orders from European counterparts – which, as it turned out, happened *inter alia* with Echelon – has now been prohibited.

As far as diversions go, this is a big one. Following the *Schrems* judgment, this is evidently no longer the issue. The real question is whether the limitations on data collection for government purposes in the fields of national security, public interest (other than for economic motives or to gain a competitive advantage) or law enforcement are convincing enough. The reality is they are not, regardless of the Commission's attempts to mask this. Yet, on the other hand, what we do

---

59 In the context of the Privacy Shield it is not just about the collection of, access to and use of personal data by police and judicial authorities in the framework of serious criminal offences, but also by intelligence and law enforcement services in the context of national security, public interest and law enforcement.

60 PPD-28, Signals Intelligence Activities, 17.01.2014, <https://www.whitehouse.gov/the-press-office/2014/01/17/presidential-policy-directive-signals-intelligence-activities>.

get is an abundance of vague engagements on behalf of the US. The following is an anthology:

Data collection under PPD-28 shall always be 'as tailored as feasible',[61] and members of the intelligence community '*should* require that, *wherever practicable*, collection *should* be focused on specific foreign intelligence targets or topics *through the use of discriminants* (e.g. specific facilities, selection terms and identifiers'.[62] There is a little too much of 'should' in this sentence for it to be genuinely convincing. Also, 'wherever practicable' is both very conditional and open-ended, and the mere use of 'discriminants' evidently does not guarantee compliance with strict necessity and proportionality requirements. At the very most, they imply that bulk collection will not take place without at least some form of selection. Furthermore, the US engagements coming from the Office of the Director of National Intelligence (ODNI) recognise without much ado that bulk SIGINT under 'certain' circumstances (that are not very 'certain' to begin with, 'for instance in order to identify and assess new or emerging threats')[63] will still take place. The Commission on its part apparently considers it sufficiently reassuring that this may only take place when targeted collection through the use of discriminants is not deemed feasible 'due to technical or operational reasons'.

The recognition by the Commission (dextrously stashed away in footnote 71) that the feasibility report, which was supposed to be presented to President Obama by the Director of National Intelligence with reference to the possibility of developing software that would make it easier for the intelligence community to '*rather* conduct targeted instead of bulk-collection' (emphasis added), concluded that there is *no* software-based alternative to replace bulk collection entirely, apparently does not contradict this reasoning. On the contrary, the Commission smoothly falls in with the ODNI's own estimation that bulk collection will not be the rule (rather than the exception)[64] – as if that would be sufficient in light of the EU requirements in terms of collection. Similarly comforting to the Commission is that the assessment of when a more targeted collection would be deemed technically or operationally 'not feasible', is not left to the individual discretion of individual staff of the intelligence community.[65] Now that really would have been quite wrong.

In addition, the Commission sees an extra 'safeguard' in the fact that the potential 'discriminants' shall be determined by high-level policy makers, and that they will be (re-)evaluated on a regular basis.[66] Ultimately, the Commission seems fully convinced when the ODNI engagements make it clear that bulk SIGINT use will – in any case – remain 'limited' to a list of six 'specific' national

[61] §71 revised decision.
[62] §70 revised decision (emphasis added).
[63] §72 revised decision.
[64] §71 revised decision.
[65] §60 draft decision; more broadly phrased in §70 revised decision.
[66] §70 revised decision.

security purposes (cf. below, section 5.3). Limitations to the phase of 'use' do not, however, imply safeguards to the phase of 'collection'. This is rather basic in EU privacy law.

To sum up, in the Commission's own view, the conclusion is that 'although not phrased in those legal terms', there is compliance with the EU requirements of necessity and proportionality:[67] bulk collection needs to remain the exception rather than the rule, and should it nevertheless take place, the six 'strict' limitations for use are applicable. Rephrased in non-misleading terms: bulk collection remains possible, and such collection is by no means compliant with the tight restrictions of EU privacy law in terms of data collection.

5.3. ACCESS AND USE DO NOT COMPLY WITH STRICT NECESSITY AND PROPORTIONALITY REQUIREMENTS

The six 'specific' national security purposes to which the bulk SIGINT use will be 'limited' according to the ODNI engagements are the following: 'detecting and countering certain activities of foreign powers, counterterrorism, counter-proliferation, cybersecurity, detecting and countering threats to U.S. or allied armed forces, and combating transnational criminal threats, including sanctions evasion'.[68] Downright optimistic is he who can discern the specificity hereof. Moreover, it remains an arduous task to assess these purposes *überhaupt* in the sense of 'restrictions', let alone that they would be convincing in light of the EU requirements in this field as operationalised in the Court's Data Retention judgment. Nevertheless, the Commission appears to see such considerations as nitpicking. In its adequacy decision, the Commission even attempts to embellish all of this[69] by *not* mentioning the six vague purposes by name, but by adducing their potential to detect and counter threats stemming from espionage, terrorism, weapons of mass destruction, threats to cybersecurity, to the armed forces or military personnel, or in the context of transnational criminal threats to any of the other purposes. Such a misrepresentation is without honour. What we should be able to expect from the European Commission is that it protects the privacy of the European citizen and that it will inform the latter (via its communication and (draft) adequacy decision) in a clear and correct way, not that the Commission contemptuously approaches EU citizens with hollow and US-friendly rhetoric whilst continuing to give away their privacy via bulk collection in order to facilitate almost any US-intelligence purpose.

As if all of this weren't enough already, the above-mentioned use 'limitations' will also be applicable to the collection of personal data that runs through

67 §76 revised decision.

68 Annex VI, p. 4, third paragraph, of the original letter, annexed to the initial decision; see paragraph 4 on page 93 of [2016] OJ L 207 as regards Annex VI to the revised decision.

69 §74 revised decision.

trans-Atlantic submarine cables located outside of US territory and this – at least according to the Commission – is the icing on the cake in terms of reassurance.[70] Just for completion, for this specific type of data, collection is not liable for a request conformant to FISA legislation or through a so-called National Security Letter of the FBI. Such a request – accentuated by the Commission – will be mandatory when the intelligence community wishes to retrieve information from companies on US territory that are 'self-certified' under the new Privacy Shield.[71]

This type of 'access' – and for that matter, a relief that for once this term is utilised in its proper, genuine meaning – would continuously need to be specific and limited, as it would require specific terms of selection or criteria. The fact that this would (even) be applicable to the PRISM programme is considered a real windfall, at least by the Commission: this information is after all selected on the basis of individual selection criteria such as e-mail addresses and telephone numbers, and not through keywords or names of individuals (sic!).[72]

As the Commission itself cannot resist emphasising, according to the Privacy and Civil Liberties Oversight Board this would mean that in the US, when necessary, it would exclusively concern 'targeting specific [non-US] persons about whom an individualised determination has been made'. Footnote 87 clarifies that the continuation of unleashing PRISM on US companies under the Privacy Shield will therefore *not* entail the undirected (unspecific) collection of data on a large scale. PRISM apparently is *not* a programme for the collection of data on a large scale, or it is (at least) sufficiently selective to pass the test of European privacy law.

It seems the Commission itself was mistaken when, at the end of November 2013, it claimed in its Safe Harbour Communication that

> the large scale character of these programmes ... [could] have as a consequence that, of all the data that was transferred in the framework of the safe harbour, more than was strictly necessary for, or proportionate to, the protection of national security, was consulted and further processed by the American authorities, as was determined by the exception foreseen in the Safe Harbour decision.

Moreover, as the Commission is so eager to allege, there is empirical evidence that the number of targets affected through PRISM on a yearly basis is 'relatively small compared to the overall flow of data on the internet'.[73] The source for this statement is the 2014 annual report of the ODSI itself, hence it indeed appears that the PRISM authorisation under FISA was applicable 'only' to 93,000 targets.

70 §75 revised decision.
71 §78 revised decision.
72 §81 revised decision.
73 §82 revised decision.

Thus, nothing too large-scale for the Commission. Add to this the ODSI warranty (in annex VI to the adequacy decision) that the bulk collection only takes place on a 'small proportion of the internet', this including the capturing of data on the trans-Atlantic cables,[74] and finally, everyone is convinced.

Finally, what is added are a number of nugatory additional guarantees in the following paragraphs (83–87) such as, for instance, that it is insufficient that SIGINT was collected over the course of the 'routine activities of a foreign person' to spread it or to retain it permanently without there being other intelligence-based reasons for this.[75] EU citizens may rest assured: electronic communication regarding their day-to-day routines will not be retained permanently when there are no well-founded reasons to do so. All of this leads the Commission to conclude that, in the US, there are ample rules in place specifically designed to ensure that 'any interference for purposes of national security with the fundamental rights of the persons whose personal data are transferred … under the E.U.–U.S. Privacy Shield [is limited] to what is *strictly necessary* to achieve the legitimate objective in question' (emphasis added).[76] And with this alone the European citizen will have to make do. Those who thought that, following the *Schrems* judgment, there would be a real *issue* with the commercial transfers of personal data to the US simply because the companies on its territory had to run this data through the PRISM filter were sorely mistaken. The Court based the invalidity of the Safe Harbour decision of the Commission on the techno-legal establishment that the latter had omitted to include in its decision that

> it must find, duly stating reasons, that the third country concerned in fact ensures, by reason of its domestic law or its international commitments, a level of protection of fundamental rights essentially equivalent to that guaranteed in the EU legal order, a level that is apparent in particular from the preceding paragraphs of the present judgment.[77]

In essence, the Court herewith refers to the substantive criteria of the Data Retention judgment. The European Commission's failure to mention 'that the United States in fact "ensures" an adequate level of protection by reason of its domestic law or its international commitments'[78] was enough for the Court to decide on a techno-legal breakpoint, 'without there being any need to examine the content of the safe harbour principles'.[79] Unfortunately, this (and only this) seems to be precisely what the European Commission remembers from the *Schrems* judgment, and is the (sole) reason why the Commission seems

[74] §82 revised decision.
[75] §87 revised decision.
[76] §88 revised decision.
[77] §96.
[78] §97.
[79] §98.

convinced that its reasoned ascertainment of the adequate safeguards in the US privacy regime will suffice. While the *reasoning* aspect of this ascertainment is not open to question, the adequacy hereof is very equivocal – yet this was surely one of the *Schrems* judgment's demands.

In brief, the presented argumentation is selective, often misleading, sometimes plain bogus. And last but not least, any effort to introduce a profound scrutiny based on the criteria established in the Data Retention judgment was omitted by the Commission, contrary to the Court's *Schrems* judgment that specifically referred thereto.

5.4. OMBUDSPERSON

Elaborating on the ultimate 'safeguard' that was introduced via the creation of a Privacy Shield ombudsperson is largely irrelevant. The Commission's adequacy decision emphasises the independence of the mechanism, devoid of any instruction from the US intelligence community.[80] This notwithstanding, it suffices to say that it revolves around a vice-secretary of the US State Department, an arrangement not without scope for partiality (to put it mildly) in terms of national security. Moreover, there is absolutely no direct EU involvement in the ombudsperson mechanism.

Putting two and two together, it becomes apparent that the Commission's viewpoint is rather gratuitous. Be that as it may, the only real engagement of the ombudsperson is to evaluate potential complaints and to confirm that US legislation, including the aforementioned 'limitations' (which are, by repetition, insufficient in light of EU law) have been observed, and should that not be the case (which in such an event shall *not* be informed towards to plaintiff, nor whether he or she was the subject of a surveillance measure) whether this situation is resolved.[81]

Last but not least, the curtain is pulled on potential complaints featuring – with good reason – arguments that the Privacy Shield in itself is not conformant with EU data protection requirements. The ODNI letter to this point simply, and laconically, states that the ombudsperson mechanism shall in any such case refrain from being applicable.[82] In any interpretation, this renders the ombudsperson nothing more than a subterfuge measure.

---

80 §121 revised decision.

81 §121 revised decision; Annex III, point 4.e.

82 Annex III, point 4.g.

6. LIMITATIONS AND SAFEGUARDS REGARDING DATA COLLECTION IN THE INTEREST OF LAW ENFORCEMENT OR PUBLIC INTEREST

In its adequacy decision, the Commission also evaluates the data protection relevant limitations and safeguards afforded by US law within the law enforcement sphere. At the risk of sounding redundant, very much like all of the foregoing, the Commission's conclusion, unsurprisingly, is that the US data protection level is to be considered adequate.[83]

Search and seizure by law enforcement authorities principally requires, according to the Fourth Amendment, a prior court order based on 'probable cause'. In certain circumstances, however, the Fourth Amendment is not applicable because for some forms of electronic communication there are no legitimate privacy expectations. In such an event, a court order is not mandatory, and law enforcement may revert to a 'reasonability test'. The latter simply implies that a consideration is made between the level of infringement of an investigative measure with respect to an individual's privacy and the extent to which that measure is deemed necessary in function of legitimate government purposes like law enforcement (or another public interest). For the European Commission, this suffices to conclude that this 'captures the idea' of necessity and proportionality under EU law.[84] The cold fact that the Fourth Amendment is quite simply not applicable to non-US citizens outside of US territory does not change the Commission's viewpoint. The reasoning is that EU citizens would receive and enjoy the indirect protection that US companies – where their data is being stored – enjoy. The establishment that such a protection can be bypassed fairly easily via a simple reasonability test, and that the privacy of a company is not automatically at stake when law enforcement are after the private data of a user (only), conveniently is not addressed.

According to the Commission, there are furthermore additional protective mechanisms, such as directives of the Ministry of Justice that allow law enforcement access to private data only on grounds that are labelled by the Commission as 'equivalent' to the necessity and proportionality requirement: these directives after all stipulate that the FBI must take recourse to the 'least intrusive measure'.[85] That such a principle only addresses the *subsidiarity* of applying certain investigative measures, instead of dealing with their *necessity* or *proportionality* will probably be considered as nitpicking again.

Finally, the Commission deals with the practice of administrative subpoenas (as issued at the time against the SWIFT US hub). These are, as it can be read,

83 §125 revised decision.

84 §126 revised decision.

85 §127 revised decision.

allowed only in particular circumstances and are subject to an independent judicial appraisal. What remains underemphasised – perhaps not to spoil the fun – is that the latter is only a possibility when a company refuses to spontaneously give effect to an administrative subpoena, thus forcing the government to have recourse to a judge for effecting said subpoena.

Likewise, when administrative subpoenas are issued in the public interest, similar limitations (so we learn in paragraph 129) are applicable. After all, administrations are only allowed to order access to data that is deemed relevant for matters under their competence – who would have thought any different? – and of course need to pass through the aforementioned reasonability test. All the more reason for the Commission, without wasting any more words on the matter – to promptly come to a conclusion similar to the one on the collection of data in view of national security.[86] As it is seemingly evidently stated, the US has rules in place that are specifically designed so that

> any interference for law enforcement or other public interest purposes with the fundamental rights of the persons whose personal data are transferred [will be limited] to what is *strictly necessary* to achieve the legitimate purpose in question ... and that ensure effective legal protection against such interference.[87]

7. CONCLUSION

The European Commission's adequacy decision is all the added value of a scrap of paper, nothing more: insufficient, lacking credibility, misleading. The Commission has nevertheless gone through the lengths to extensively set forth why all of us *should* believe that the 'limitations' and 'safeguards' available under US law are in line with the EU requirements of strict necessity and proportionality. The *Schrems* case, apparently, has not changed anything. The Privacy Shield is nothing but a new jackstraw for the previous Safe Harbour approach. As it is, we are simply presented with the same old thing in a new coat of paint, without any intrinsic change in the situation in the US. None of the US harbours have become safer, PRISM and the like remain on track. But was anyone naïve enough to think differently? The only novel thing is that the European Commission has gone above and beyond to a build a Trojan horse – that is all the Privacy Shield really is – and then pushed it in front of the EU gates. Unfortunately for EU citizens and their privacy, the EU has knowingly taken it inside.

---

86 §135 revised decision.

87 §135 revised decision (emphasis added).

May this contribution, reinforced by the Court's decision in *Tele2 Sverige AB*, serve as ammunition for civil society and EU data protection authorities to make sure that EU data protection standards are respected at last, in the trans-Atlantic relations as well as in the EU relations with key trading partners in East and South-East Asia and with countries in Latin America and the European neighbourhood, with which the Commission in early 2017 has declared it intends to negotiate similar 'shields'.[88]

[88] Communication from the Commission to the European Parliament and the Council, 'Exchanging and Protecting Personal Data in a Globalised World', COM(2017) 7 final, 10 January 2017, p. 8.

INVITED COMMENT

6. INTERNATIONAL DATA TRANSFERS IN BRAZIL

Danilo Doneda*

1. INTRODUCTION

International data transfers are currently regulated by frameworks that vary considerably among countries.[1] The lack of harmonisation, even between countries that have very considerable exchanges of personal data, has been the cause of intense debate. In this matter, however, Brazil emerges as a jurisdiction which has approached the issue of regulating international data transfers in a mostly empirical frame, and references to some resources and instruments found, for example, in European data protection legislation, have been introduced in the country's debates only recently.

2. THE SITUATION IN BRAZIL AND LATIN AMERICA

International data transfers are not directly addressed in Brazilian legislation. In fact, despite some vivid debate that has taken place in Brazil in recent years regarding similar subjects, such as jurisdiction over personal data and data localisation, the first proposition which aimed to focus the discussion in the general terms of international data transfer has been the Data Protection Bill[2] drafted by the Federal Government and submitted to the National Congress in May 2016.

Brazil does not have a general data protection law as yet, although a rough legal framework for privacy and data protection has developed over recent

* Rio de Janeiro State University. E-mail: danilo@doneda.net.

1 Take, for instance, the different perspectives currently encountered in the European Union, United States and Canada, to name a few.

2 Congress Bill 5276 of 2016, <http://www.camara.gov.br/proposicoesWeb/fichadetramitacao?idProposicao=2084378>.

decades, from constitutional to specific legal measures, based on constitutional grounds, the Consumer Protection Code and other sources, none of them having any particular international transfer provisions.[3] The Brazilian Constitution identifies privacy as a fundamental right but does not extend this attribute to data, so it can be said that, besides not having enacted a data protection framework, Brazilian law does not consider data protection a fundamental right. However, more recent legislation such as the Internet Civil Rights Framework (*Marco Civil da Internet*) identifies data protection, along with privacy protection, as two of the core principles of Internet usage.[4]

The international data transfers rules found today in Europe as well as in other countries developed at a time when global data-sharing was noticeably less intense than today. Concepts such as cloud computing basically did not exist back then, and furthermore personal data has become more and more an essential component in international commerce.

These international data transfer rules incorporate some of the most rigid sets of rules in the field of data protection legislation. It is not common to find in other forms of data treatment a combination of tools such as prior approval from a public body as a condition to treatment, or even the mandatory inclusion of a strict set of contractual clauses.

These symptoms of rigidity in the general framework of international data transfers rules have their roots in the fear that data protection laws could become irrelevant if foreign countries with no data protection framework enacted, or with faulty ones, attracted data treatment services based on the seduction of low costs and an unregulated jurisdiction.[5] Today, not much remains of this original issue, as a very consistent proportion of countries (109, by a 2015 estimate)[6] have their own data protection legal framework, and even if it is an issue, they tend not to be as good an option for transferring data treatment services due to several other factors, such as legal, security or safety risks.

Interestingly, the very existence and rigidity of international data transfers rules may have contributed to changing the landscape of data protection regulation into a more coherent and interchangeable one.

---

3 D. Doneda and L. Schertel Mendes, 'Data Protection in Brazil: New Developments and Current Challenges' in S. Gutwirth, R. Leenes and P. De Hert (eds.), *Reloading Data Protection. Multidisciplinary Insights and Contemporary Challenges*, Springer, Dordrecht 2014, pp. 3–20.

4 Art. 3, II and III of Law 12.965 of 2014, <http://www.planalto.gov.br/ccivil_03/_ato2011-2014/2014/lei/l12965.htm>. An unofficial English translation is available at: <http://itsrio.org/wp-content/uploads/2015/11/Understanding-Brazils-Internet-Bill-of-Rights.pdf>.

5 R. Barceló and M.V. Pérez Asinari, 'Transferencia internacional de datos personales' in R. Martinez Martinez (eds.), *Protección de Datos: Comentarios a la LOPD y su Reglamento de Desarrollo*, Tirant lo Blanch, Valencia 2009, pp. 141–142.

6 G. Greenleaf, 'Global Data Privacy Laws 2015: Data Privacy Authorities and Their Organisations' (2015) 134 *Privacy Laws & Business International Report* 16–19, <http://papers.ssrn.com/sol3/papers.cfm?abstract_id=2641772>.

This is due to international data transfer rules such as those of the European Union (EU) having a role in disseminating standards to other data protection regulations around the world. Using an expression taken from the works of Colin Bennett and Charles Raab,[7] the phenomenon of convergence among different data protection laws has its roots in the incentive many countries have in sharing standards in data protection law. In a similar way, Stefano Rodotà noted that the spread of similar standards in data protection laws, even without a treaty or any central coordination, was an interesting example of 'globalisation through rights': that is, of law acting as a catalyst for social change that globally improved respect for human rights.[8]

To illustrate this statement, we can take a quick look at how data protection laws first spread through Latin America. The first general data protection law in the sub-continent was enacted in Argentina in 2000,[9] in the middle of a major economic crisis, which led the country to search for innovative ways of making its own economy more competitive, to attract capital. Three years after enacting the legislation, Argentina's data protection legal framework was recognised as adequate by the European Commission (EC),[10] making it easier for the country to host the outsourcing of IT services from European countries, which included treatment of personal data.

The pursuit of EU adequacy also played a relevant role in the approval of Uruguay's data protection law of 2008 (Uruguay also happened to have its legal framework recognised as adequate by the EC in 2012),[11] and in Colombia the outsourcing of call centres by Spanish companies was one of the factors that drove the country to adopt a general data protections legislation in 2012. Even if Argentina and Uruguay are currently the only Latin American countries to have 'adequacy' status, harmonisation with European Union standards has been one of the driving forces of the debate regarding the adoption of a general data protection framework throughout Latin America.[12]

Regardless of a rational need for standardisation and a harmonised set of rules for international data transfers, the international scenario today is not

---

7 C. Bennett and C. Raab, *Regulating Privacy, Data Protection and Public Policy in Europe and the United States*, Cornell University Press, Ithaca 1992, pp. 116–152.

8 S. Rodotà. 'Per la globalizzazione dei diritti' (2001) 2 *MicroMega* 156–165.

9 Law 25326 of 2000, <http://www.jus.gob.ar/media/33481/ley_25326.pdf>.

10 2003/490/EC: Commission Decision of 30 June 2003 pursuant to Directive 95/46/EC of the European Parliament and of the Council on the adequate protection of personal data in Argentina, [2003] OJ L 168/19–22.

11 2012/484/EU: Commission Implementing Decision of 21 August 2012 pursuant to Directive 95/46/EC of the European Parliament and of the Council on the adequate protection of personal data by the Eastern Republic of Uruguay with regard to automated processing of personal data, [2012] OJ L 227/11–14.

12 Organisations such as the *Red Iberoamericana de Protección de Datos Personales*, for example, have been a key inductor for the legislative process concerning the adoption of data protection legislation in Latin America <http://www.redipd.org/index-iden-idphp.php>.

exactly moving in the direction of any treaty or international document about international data transfers. This is largely due to the difficulty in finding recognised international leadership in the matter, partly because models of international data transfer are facing the imminence of being reformed, together with the reform of the whole data protection legal framework with the advent, for instance, of the European General Data Protection Regulation (GDPR).

For now, considering these situations and considering that valid efforts towards international harmonisation in this field (take, for instance, the Madrid Resolution issued in the International Conference of Data Protection and Privacy Commissioners in 2009)[13] are not yet ready for use as a basis for actual international standardisation, an international framework for transnational data transfers can be only inferred by the consolidation of several national and regional standards – which is, in fact, a puzzle.

3. ELEMENTS OF REGULATION OF INTERNATIONAL DATA TRANSFERS IN BRAZIL

In Brazil, the lack of a general data protection framework implies that specific rules on international data transfer are also missing. In fact, international data transfers are basically an unregulated matter in Brazil. Brazil was one of the founding members of the Intergovernamental Bureau for Informatics (IBI) along with other countries (a total of around 45 members, mostly developing countries). This group's mission was to foster the use of computers in developing countries, and one of the subjects it debated was the need for regulating international data flows (FDT, or *Fluxo Transfronteiriço de Dados*).[14] However, after some countries left, IBI was discontinued.

The next occasion that international data transfers were mentioned in official documents was when the Information Technology Law of 1984 created the National Council for Informatics and Automation (*Conselho Nacional de Informática e Automação*, CONIN), which was formed by members of government and from the private sector, with the mission of debating public policy issues related to information technology. Its original aim was to 'establish rules to control transborder data flows and to grant permissions to build channels and data transfer utilities to international interchange of data'.[15] Even if this particular proposition was vetted by the Federal Government, regulating international flow of data was recognised as one of the missions of the Council.

13 See <http://privacyconference2011.org/htmls/adoptedResolutions/2009_Madrid/2009_M1.pdf>.

14 M. Carvalho, 'A trajetória da Internet no Brasil: do surgimento de redes de computadores à instituição dos mecanismos de governança', Master's thesis, COPPE-UFRJ, 2006, p. 59.

15 Art. 7°, X of Law 7.232/84 (free translation).

However, the necessary regulation was never delivered by the CONIN (which was dissolved). Since then, international flow of data is being implemented in Brazil as something that can be addressed by a sectorial perspective, as frameworks of international data interchange such as the SWIFT (Society for Worldwide Interbank Financial Telecommunication, in the financial sector) or SITA (*Société Internationale de Télécommunications Aéronautique*, in the aviation sector) were adopted.

Afterwards, the discussion about regulation of international transfer of data in Brazil lost some of its political and strategic tone, becoming more of a technical topic. Later, by the time networking experiments which pre-dated the Internet were being implemented in Brazil, this facilitated their authorisation by a technical government office such as the Special Secretariat for Informatics (*Secretaria Especial de Informática,* SEI), even without specific legislation concerning the subject, as Art. 7°, X of Information Technology Law was never regulated or enforced.

The sectorial approach to international data transfer is a work in constant progress in Brazil. For example, in the aviation sector, the issue of passenger name records, which has been subject to intense debate between the European Union and the United States, was implemented in Brazil by the civil aviation regulator without any specific provisions regarding passenger privacy.

This framework was enacted with the creation of two systems: the Passenger Name Record (PNR) and the Advance Passenger Information (API). Introduced by the Brazilian National Civil Aviation Agency (ANAC) in 2012 through its Resolution 255,[16] these systems work in parallel by requiring airlines[17] to store and transmit a wide range of data on each and every international flight, its passengers and crew members entering or leaving or simply with a stopover in Brazilian territory. The information collected must be electronically transmitted to the Federal Police Department (DPF) before each flight – so passengers' personal data is collected before the flight arrives in Brazil. Officially, the system aims to 'prevent and suppress illegal actions' – including, for example, tax evasion on imported goods, or flight of wanted felons – as well as facilitating entry processes at multiple bureaucratic levels. There are also plans to broaden the security framework to which these systems belong, for example, with the adoption of biometric facial recognition technology in airports, capable of matching passengers' faces with a database of 'high risk' individuals.[18] Moreover, PNR systems have also been implemented or proposed in both the US[19] and

---

16 See ANAC Resolution 255/12 <http://www2.anac.gov.br/transparencia/audiencia/aud22_2012/3%20-%20Resolucao%20-%20API%20e%20PNR%20(versao%20final).pdf>.

17 Except for services such as private jets or helicopters – in Portuguese, *táxi aéreo* ('air taxi') services.

18 See 'Receita Federal lança declaração eletrônica de bens de viajantes', <http://www.receita.fazenda.gov.br/AutomaticoSRFsinot/2013/08/16/2013_08_16_13_09_50_734484890.html>.

19 See <http://www.cbp.gov/document/forms/passenger-name-record-pnr-privacy-policy>.

the EU[20] and over 50 other countries, and are recommended by the International Civil Aviation Organization (IATA).[21]

In spite of the lack of a general data protection law, issues regarding the international flow of personal data, of course, affect the country, as they have implications over several fields, not the least being foreign trade. Also, since 2013, state sovereignty emerged as a factor which would foster the internal debate about data protection in Brazil, as the Snowden revelations had a great impact, drawing attention to several effects of the misuse of personal data. This issue, generally not regarded as a priority in the governmental agenda, became an urgent one. It also happened that concerns about digital privacy, generally confined to a rather small part of the population, attracted public interest.

The way the issue was conducted on the internal front and also on the international level, however, has not led to the adherence to international standards for international data transfers – in fact, it was not even treated as a problem that had to do with data protection but rather with the concept of digital sovereignty. The issue – interception of communications – was mostly considered from the point of view of the potential loss of sovereignty it could cause, than as a problem that could affect individual freedoms and civil rights. In this sense, the very fact that Brazil, Germany and other countries proposed and in 2013 approved a UN Declaration, 'Right to Privacy in the Digital Age',[22] still has not led to any significant domestic impact on the formulation of public policies towards the adoption of standard rules regarding international data transfers in Brazil.

In fact, the approach taken to conduct the question was, basically, profiting from the fact that the legislation known as the Internet Civil Rights Framework (*Marco Civil da Internet*)[23] had not yet been enacted, to implement instruments that could in theory protect the Internet traffic in the country from surveillance by foreign actors.

In trying to achieve this goal, basically two propositions were considered: (i) mandatory localisation of databases, meaning that every database connected to the Internet that treated personal information of Brazilian citizens should be localised in Brazil, and (ii) routing of Internet communications, meaning that all communications in the Internet that had sender and destination located

---

20 See <https://euobserver.com/justice/130430>.

21 See 'ANAC determina regras sobre repasse de dados de passageiros à Polícia Federal', <http://economia.uol.com.br/ultimas-noticias/infomoney/2012/11/19/anac-determina-regras-sobre-repasse-de-dados-de-passageiros-a-policia-federal.jhtm>.

22 Resolution 68/167 ('The right to privacy in the digital age'), adopted by United Nations General Assembly on 18 December 2013, <http://www.un.org/ga/search/view_doc.asp?symbol=A/RES/68/167>.

23 Above n. 4.

inside Brazil must necessarily be routed exclusively inside the country. This second proposition was not supported for long, however, most probably due to engineering and also financial problems that its implementation could lead to. The localisation proposal, however, remained on the table until the last moments before approval of the legislation by Brazilian Parliament.

4. CONCLUSION

While no decision has been taken in regard to a data protection legal framework in Brazil, specific and sectorial regulation with regard to international data transfers is being considered and, as mentioned, sometimes enacted. This, however, can lead to future problems, such as the lack of harmonisation and interoperability among different sectors, adding to legal uncertainty in analogue or in-between situations. This adds to the case of the adoption of a general data protection law with measures concerning international transfer of data.

The debate in Brazil is currently focusing on two data protection bills which are being examined by the Brazilian National Congress: Bill 5276 of 2016, which was drafted by the federal government, and Bill PLS 330 of 2013.[24] Both include dispositions about international transfer of data, and in the case of Bill 5276, instruments such as binding corporate rules or general contractual clauses are present as a means to allow international data transfer. The outcome of Brazil's regulatory approach on international data transfer depends, however, on the appreciation that Congress has of the propositions.

---

24 Senate Bill 330 of 2012, <http://www25.senado.leg.br/web/atividade/materias/-/materia/107228>.

SECTION II

PRIVACY AND INTERNATIONAL TRADE

7. FROM ACTA TO TTIP

Lessons Learned on Democratic Process and Balancing of Rights

Trisha MEYER* and Agnieszka VETULANI-CĘGIEL**

1. INTRODUCTION

The Anti-Counterfeiting Trade Agreement (ACTA) marked the rise of a new lobbying power. Although traditionally, international trade negotiations have been state-centric forums, public opinion can no longer be ignored when negotiating agreements that include intellectual property rights as a topic of discussion. In the aftermath of the ACTA negotiations, civil society actors were lauded for their successful citizen mobilisation and online advocacy. Indicative were street protests of thousands during the Polish winter.[1] ACTA was heavily criticised for its lack of transparency and fundamental rights safeguards, especially in relation to data privacy. Similar concerns have arisen in ongoing discussions on Transatlantic Trade and Investment Partnership (TTIP) between the United States and the European Union. Is it possible to include a diverse stakeholder group in a negotiation process without suffering significant delays in its progress?

ACTA is also illustrative of an ongoing political economy struggle over knowledge creation and information control. The arguments brought forward

* Institute for European Studies, Vrije Universiteit Brussel and Vesalius College. E-mail: Trisha.Meyer@vub.be. Research for this chapter was financed by a grant from the Academy of Finland for the 'eCoherence – Reconciling Economic and Non-Economic Values in a Multi-Polar Society' project.

** Faculty of Political Science and Journalism, Adam Mickiewicz University in Poznań. E-mail: a.vetulani-cegiel@amu.edu.pl. Research for this chapter was financed, in part, by a grant from the National Science Centre in Poland for the postdoctoral research of Agnieszka Vetulani-Cęgiel (Decision No. DEC-2014/12/S/HS5/00006).

1 M. HORTEN, *A Copyright Masquerade: How Corporate Lobbying Threatens Online Freedoms*, Zed Books, London 2013, pp. 110–112; B. FARRAND, *Networks of Power in Digital Copyright Law and Policy: Political Salience, Expertise and the Legislative Process*, Routledge, London 2014, pp. 184–185; D. MATTHEWS and P. ŽIKOVSKÁ, 'The Rise and Fall of the Anti-Counterfeiting Trade Agreement (ACTA): Lessons for the European Union' (2013) 44(6) *International Review of Intellectual Property and Competition Law* 630, 652.

by stakeholders in the ACTA debate were not new: the devastating harm of intellectual property rights (IPR) infringement, the necessity of IPR enforcement for economic growth, the value of the Internet for democratic and societal participation, and the importance of fundamental rights. Underlying these arguments are conflicting views on the role of copyright and the Internet to foster innovation and creativity.[2] Opponents of ACTA feared that the multilateral agreement would be used to circumvent existing international and domestic legislation that balances IPR against other rights and exceptions. Can we find a middle ground between protecting rights and providing access to knowledge and culture in trade negotiations?

This chapter contributes to improving the societal acceptability of trade negotiations on the one hand, and intellectual property rights on the other. It is important to note at the beginning of this chapter that the topic is approached from a Eurocentric point of view. The core of the chapter elaborates on democratic governance and political economy of intellectual property literature, and analyses the views of interested stakeholders on democratic process and balancing of rights in ACTA. It also includes a preliminary analysis of stakeholder views on these topics in the context of the ongoing TTIP discussions (sections 2 and 3). The chapter concludes with lessons learned on improving popular legitimacy in international trade negotiations including intellectual property rights (section 4). First however, the chapter provides a brief overview of the ACTA and TTIP negotiations (section 1).

1.1. ANTI-COUNTERFEITING TRADE AGREEMENT

The Anti-Counterfeiting Trade Agreement (ACTA) is a trade agreement aimed at enhanced international cooperation and more effective international enforcement of intellectual property rights. Formal negotiations on the Anti-Counterfeiting Trade Agreement[3] started in June 2008 and ended in November 2010. The final text on ACTA was published in May 2011. Throughout the negotiations, the European Union was represented by DG Trade and the EU Member States.[4] Other negotiating parties were Australia, Canada, Japan,

---

2 G. Murdock, 'Political Economies as Moral Economies: Commodities, Gifts, and Public Goods' in J. Wasko, G. Murdock and H. Sousa (eds.), *The Handbook of Political Economy of Communications*, Wiley-Blackwell, Chichester 2011, pp. 13–40; D. Winseck, 'The Political Economies of Media and the Transformation of the Global Media Industries' in D. Winseck and D.Y. Jin (eds.), *The Political Economies of Media. The Transformation of the Global Media Industries*, Bloomsbury Academic, London and New York 2011, pp. 3–48.

3 Australia, Canada, the European Union and its Member States, Japan, the Kingdom of Morocco, New Zealand, et al., Anti-Counterfeiting Trade Agreement, 2011, accession ongoing.

4 The EU's Member States negotiated section 4 of ACTA on criminal enforcement.

Republic of Korea, Mexico, Morocco, New Zealand, Singapore, Switzerland and the United States.

The European Parliament published three resolutions on ACTA, requesting public access to documents and raising concerns on transparency and the state of play.[5] In December 2011 the Council of the European Union adopted the convention unanimously. Shortly thereafter, in January 2012, the European Commission and 22 Member States[6] signed ACTA. However, on the same day, MEP Kader Arif (S&D) resigned as ACTA rapporteur 'to denounce in the strongest manner the process that led to the signing of this agreement: no association of civil society [and] lack of transparency from the beginning'.[7]

In the weeks before and after the signature of ACTA, citizens in Europe took to the streets to protest against the trade agreement. As a consequence, in February 2012, the European Commissioner for Trade Karel De Gucht requested an opinion from the Court of Justice of the European Union on ACTA's compatibility with the European Treaties, in particular with the Charter of Fundamental Rights of the European Union. Nonetheless, citizen and civil society mobilisation continued, notably through use of social media and e-mail campaigns.

In July 2012, the European Parliament rejected ACTA, denying its consent and prohibiting ratification of the agreement by the European Union. Trade agreements do not follow the ordinary legislative procedure in the European Union. Although its role remains limited, the Lisbon Treaty's entry into force in 2009 (midway through the formal negotiations on ACTA) did provide the Parliament with some more say. The Parliament saw its consultative powers increased and importantly now votes to consent to or deny the ratification of the final text of trade agreements. Thus it could not amend ACTA, but its consent was necessary for ratification of the treaty by the EU and its Member States.[8]

---

5 European Parliament, European Parliament Resolution of 11 March 2009 regarding Public Access to European Parliament, Council and Commission Documents (COM(2008)0229 – C6-0184/2008 – 2008/0090(COD)), Strasbourg 2009; European Parliament, European Parliament Resolution of 10 March 2010 on the Transparency and State of Play of the ACTA Negotiations (2010/2572(RSP)), Strasbourg 2010; European Parliament, European Parliament Resolution of 24 November 2010 on the Anti-Counterfeiting Trade Agreement (ACTA) (2010/2935(RSP)), Strasbourg 2010.

6 Cyprus, Estonia, Germany, the Netherlands and Slovakia did not sign ACTA. Croatia was not yet a member of the EU when ACTA was signed (it joined the EU on 1 July 2013).

7 C. Arthur, 'Acta Goes Too Far, Says MEP', *The Guardian*, 1 February 2012 <http://www.theguardian.com/technology/2012/feb/01/acta-goes-too-far-kader-arif>.

8 European Parliament, 'Consent', 2016 <http://www.europarl.europa.eu/aboutparliament/en/0087a559c8/Consent.html>; European Parliament and Council, Consolidated Version of the Treaty on the Functioning of the European Union (TFEU), 2010, Art. 289(2).

Figure 1. ACTA timeline

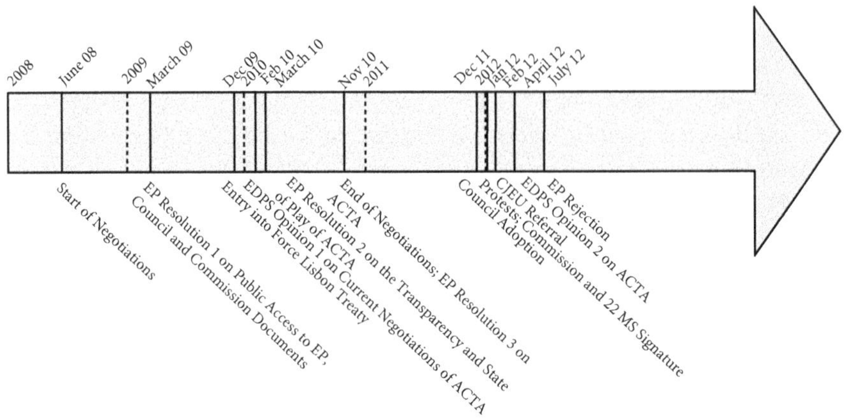

1.2. TRANSATLANTIC TRADE AND INVESTMENT PARTNERSHIP

Turning to the second trade agreement in this chapter, the United States and the European Union are currently striving for economic rapprochement through Transatlantic Trade and Investment Partnership (TTIP). Formal negotiations on TTIP started in June 2013 and have focused on providing access to each other's markets, cutting red tape through regulatory cooperation, and agreeing on new rules to facilitate exports, imports and investments.[9] As of June 2016, 13 negotiation rounds had taken place, with both parties aiming to conclude the agreement before the end of the Obama administration in January 2017. DG Trade represents the EU's interests in the negotiations.

The European Parliament published a first resolution on trans-Atlantic relations prior to the start of the negotiations in May 2013.[10] After the new Parliament took office, it passed a second resolution on a more reserved note in July 2015.[11] Substantively, major concerns of European citizens and

---

9 European Commission, 'In Focus: Transatlantic Trade and Investment Partnership (TTIP)', 2016 <http://ec.europa.eu/trade/policy/in-focus/ttip/>.

10 European Parliament, European Parliament Resolution of 23 May 2013 on EU Trade and Investment Negotiations with the United States of America (2013/2558(RSP)), Strasbourg 2013.

11 European Parliament, European Parliament Resolution of 8 July 2015 containing the European Parliament's Recommendations to the European Commission on the Negotiations for the Transatlantic Trade and Investment Partnership (TTIP) (2014/2228(INI)), Strasbourg 2015.

stakeholders have related to the proposed investor-state dispute settlement (ISDS) mechanism,[12] environmental, consumer safety and data protection standards. At the core is a desire to protect hard-won rights and procedures.[13] The EU Ombudsman also opened own-initiative inquiries into and held a public consultation on TTIP in July 2014. Here, concerns were raised primarily on procedural aspects of the negotiations, in particular the transparency of the negotiations and the equality of access to negotiating documents.[14]

DG Trade's outreach to its partner institutions, civil society and other interest groups is extensive.[15] A dedicated section on DG Trade's website explains the negotiation process and is a repository for European Commission positions and factsheets on negotiating topics.[16] The directorate-general has held four public consultations and six civil society dialogues to provide updates and exchange views on the trans-Atlantic partnership.[17] The public consultation on the investor-state dispute settlement mechanism received nearly 150,000 responses and the European Commission has set up an advisory group (this has been much criticised due to the very limited number of members, 16).[18] Formal and informal exchanges take place with the European Council and Parliament. Importantly, under pressure of the EU Ombudsman, European Parliament and citizens, all MEPs have access to confidential documents (including consolidated texts with the US position) in secure reading rooms.[19]

---

12 ISDS mechanisms have already been negotiated in previous EU trade agreements, such as the EU-Canada Comprehensive Economic and Trade Agreement (CETA).

13 M. Armanovica and R. Bendini, *In-Depth Analysis: Civil Society's Concerns about the Transatlantic Trade and Investment Partnership (DG EXPO/B/PolDep/Note/2014_118)*, European Parliament, Directorate-General for External Policies of the Union, Brussels 2014.

14 European Ombudsman, 'Transparency and Public Participation in relation to the Transatlantic Trade and Investment Partnership ('TTIP') Negotiations' (Case: OI/11/2014/RA), 2016 <http://www.ombudsman.europa.eu/en/cases/caseopened.faces/en/54631/html.bookmark>.

15 European Commission, *Towards an EU-US Trade Deal. Making Trade Work for You*, Brussels 2014.

16 European Commission, 'In Focus: Transatlantic Trade and Investment Partnership (TTIP)', 2016.

17 European Commission, 'Meetings: Update on the Transatlantic Trade and Investment Partnership (TTIP) – 11th Negotiation Round', 2015 <http://trade.ec.europa.eu/civilsoc/meetdetails.cfm?meet=11461>.

18 European Commission, 'Register of Commission Expert Groups and Other Similar Entities. Transatlantic Trade and Investment Partnership Stakeholder Advisory Group' (E02988), 2015 <http://ec.europa.eu/transparency/regexpert/index.cfm?do=groupDetail.groupDetail&groupID=2988&NewSearch=1&NewSearch=1>.

19 European Parliament, 'Access to TTIP-Related Documents – Comprehensive Agreement on Operational Arrangements between the INTA Committee and DG TRADE' (Ref. Ares(2015)5740097-10/12/2015), 2015 <https://polcms.secure.europarl.europa.eu/cmsdata/upload/9eb1ebb4-3205-4cb1-9b57-72a87a298048/Access%20to%20TTIP-related%20docs.pdf>.

Figure 2. TTIP timeline

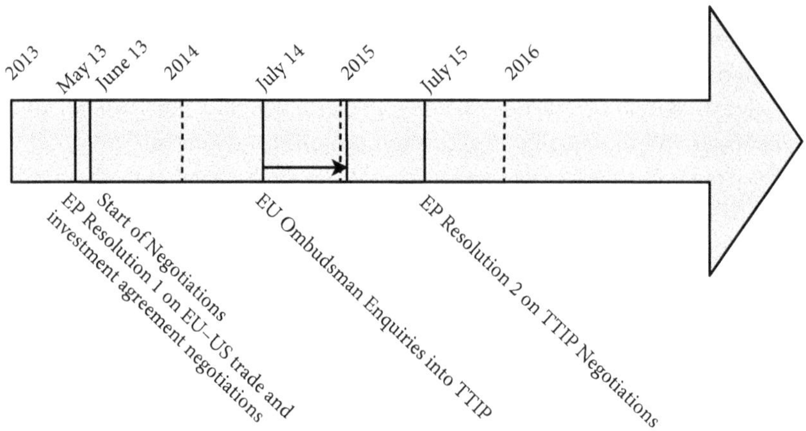

2. PARTICIPATORY TURN

2.1. PROBLEM DEFINITION

Public disenchantment with politics and the complex nature of policy issues call for the involvement of non-traditional stakeholders in the formulation and implementation of policy. At a European level, the European Commission's White Paper on European Governance[20] heralded the start of experimental policy-making that aims at being less hierarchical, more inclusive, and therefore more legitimate and effective. Over the years, these initiatives to engage stakeholders have been extensively scrutinised and theorised.[21] This section reflects on democratic governance in the context of international trade negotiations. In particular it applies the European Commission's five good governance principles – openness, participation, accountability, coherence, and effectiveness – to ACTA and TTIP.

By nature, transnational policy-making does not happen within boundaries of state, and is further removed from citizens. It cannot therefore rely as easily

[20] European Commission, 'European Governance: A White Paper' (COM(2001) 428 final), Brussels 2001.

[21] See for instance, A. Héritier and M. Rhodes (eds.), *New Modes of Governance in Europe. Governing in the Shadow of Hierarchy*, Palgrave Macmillan, Basingstoke 2010; B. Jobert and B. Kohler-Koch (eds), *Changing Images of Civil Society*, Routledge, London 2008; B.G. Peters, 'Forms of Informality: Identifying Informal Governance in the European Union' (2006) (7) 1 *Perspectives on European Politics and Society* 25–40.

on traditional forms of legitimacy available to the state, such as representation through elected officials. In 'The Legitimacy of International Governance: A Coming Challenge for International Environmental Law?', Daniel Bodansky differentiates between normative and popular legitimacy:

> Whether an institution or regime is normatively legitimate – whether it is worthy of support – is an important question in and of itself. In contrast, a regime's popular legitimacy is instrumentally important, since legitimacy represents a potentially important basis of effectiveness, in addition to power and self-interest.[22]

Bodansky here indicates that although an institutional structure may be normatively legitimate (in the author's words, 'justified in some objective sense'),[23] perceptions matter. The European Union continues to struggle with a poor public image, especially in times of crisis when the benefits of cooperation are less visible. ACTA demonstrates that the EU's democratic deficit has become a matter of debate in its international trade relations as well. On the one hand, the legal basis for the European Commission's mandate to represent the EU in trade policy is well established in the EU treaties (Art. 207 TFEU). Speaking with one voice on trade provides bargaining power and fits squarely in the economic aims of the European Union. On the other hand, despite the European Commission's normative legitimacy, its popular legitimacy is amiss. Its trade negotiations are mostly held behind closed doors, with limited access to documents, and few obligations in terms of stakeholder engagement. The impact of trade agreements on citizens is high, yet the main body representing European citizens only has the right to sign off on the agreements.

2.2. EUROPEAN COMMISSION PRINCIPLES OF GOOD GOVERNANCE

In its European Governance White Paper, the European Commission acknowledges that its external relations need to be subject to principles of good governance. At the same time, the selected focus in the White Paper is primarily on 'reform[ing] governance successfully at home in order to enhance the case for change at an international level'.[24] This might work in most cases, but as ACTA

---

22 D. Bodansky, 'The Legitimacy of International Governance: A Coming Challenge for International Environmental Law?' (1999) (93) 3 *The American Journal of International Law* 602–603.

23 Ibid., p. 601.

24 European Commission, 'European Governance: A White Paper' (COM(2001) 428 final), 2001, p. 26.

illustrates, not all. Table 1 summarises the European Commission's interpretation of its principles of good governance – openness, participation, accountability, coherence, and effectiveness. Through the application of these principles, the European Commission seeks to communicate and increase the (normative and popular) legitimacy of European policy action. In the paragraphs below, we analyse stakeholder views on ACTA and TTIP to the European Commission's good governance principles. It is important to note that, as negotiations are ongoing, our analysis of the Transatlantic Trade and Investment Partnership is preliminary.

Table 1. European Commission's Good Governance Principles (2001)[25]

Principle	Description
Openness	EU institutions and member states *actively communicate* on the EU's role and decisions, using language that is *accessible* and *understandable* for the general public.
Participation	EU institutions and member states *include stakeholders* in policymaking from the conception of policy problems to the implementation of policy solutions.
Accountability	EU institutions, member states and all stakeholders involved *clarify and take responsibility* for their policy actions.
Effectiveness	Policies are *proportionate* to the problem at hand, based on *clear objectives and impact assessments*. Decisions are taken and implemented at the *most appropriate* level and in a *timely* manner.
Coherence	Policies are *consistent* across policy areas and levels of governance.

2.2.1. Anti-Counterfeiting Trade Agreement

Regarding the European Commission's good governance principles of *openness and participation*, DG Trade took a defensive stance when communicating on and involving stakeholders in ACTA. During the trade negotiations, the European Parliament adopted two resolutions, raising concerns about transparency and public access to documents.[26] DG Trade emphasised that Member States were present and had first-hand information on ACTA. It also held debriefing meetings with the European Parliament and stakeholders during the negotiations and responded to MEPs' numerous oral and written questions. At the request of

---

25 This table draws on European Commission, 'European Governance: A White Paper' (COM(2001) 428 final), 2001.

26 European Parliament, European Parliament Resolution of 11 March 2009 regarding Public Access to European Parliament, Council and Commission Documents (COM(2008)0229 – C6-0184/2008 – 2008/0090(COD)), 2009; European Parliament, European Parliament Resolution of 10 March 2010 on the Transparency and State of Play of the ACTA Negotiations (2010/2572(RSP)), 2010.

the European Parliament, the Commission pushed for the release of the draft texts on ACTA.[27] However, this reactive approach proved to be too little, too late. Due to the limited release of documents, drafts of negotiating texts (often early and outdated versions) were leaked throughout the process. The most significant form of stakeholder participation took place in the form of protests, after the negotiations on ACTA had ended.

Regarding *accountability*, ACTA was criticised for its reach, venue and the establishment of an ACTA committee. Opponents of ACTA, such as the European Parliament ALDE group, indicated that they had 'doubts about the overall effectiveness of a 'catch-all' agreement that does not include the countries that are the main source of counterfeit goods.'[28] Further, as we explain below, stakeholders took issue with the choice to negotiate ACTA outside of the World Trade Organisation and the World Intellectual Property Organisation.[29] Stakeholders also protested the establishment of an ACTA committee (Art. 36 ACTA) tasked with reviewing the implementation and considering amendments to the Agreement, viewing it as another opaque regulatory body.[30] The choice to negotiate a broad agreement on intellectual property rights while excluding key players in the policy field indeed seems to point to the avoidance of established international forums and accountability mechanisms to ease the adoption of higher standards among like-minded countries. This point is further explored in section 3 on balancing of rights.

Regarding *effectiveness and coherence*, ACTA's appropriateness and proportionality, as well as its compatibility with international and EU law, were questioned. Opponents objected to ACTA's double, yet exclusive focus on counterfeiting and piracy.[31] It proved premature to negotiate a trade agreement on a topic so heavily disputed within the European Union. At the same time, the European Commission did not issue an impact assessment of ACTA, arguing

---

27 European Commission, 'Transparency of ACTA Negotiations', Brussels 2012.

28 Alliance of Liberals and Democrats for Europe (ALDE), 'Parliament Must Listen Carefully to Citizens Concerns over ACTA', 2012 <http://www.alde.eu/press/press-and-release-news/press-release/article/parliament-must-carefully-listen-to-citizens-concerns-over-acta-37926/>. See also the European Parliament Committee on Civil Liberties, Justice and Home Affairs (LIBE), European Digital Rights (EDRi) and La Quadrature du Net (LQDN).

29 Article 19, European Consumers' Organisation (BEUC), EDRi, European Economic and Social Committee (EESC), European United Left/Nordic Green (GUE/NGL), LQDN, Member of Parliament GUE/NGL (Helmut Scholz), Open Rights Group (ORG).

30 EDRi, Foundation for a Free Information Infrastructure (FFII), Internet Society (ISOC), Joint Internet Companies, LQDN, ORG.

31 ALDE, EESC, European Parliament Committee on Industry, Research and Energy (ITRE), Greens/European Free Alliance (Green/EFA), LQDN, Member of European Parliament Progressive Alliance of Socialists and Democrats (S&D) (Kader Arif – Former ACTA Rapporteur), ORG, Oxfam, S&D.

that an impact assessment of the trade agreement was not necessary, as it did not exceed the EU *'acquis communautaire'*.[32] However, every external opinion and study on ACTA discouraged unconditional consent to the trade agreement.[33] Despite reassurances that ACTA complies with international and EU law, stakeholders criticised its imprecise wording and lack of specific safeguards.[34] For instance, on the subject of fundamental rights, the European Data Protection Supervisor stated that

> the Agreement does not contain sufficient limitations and safeguards in respect of the implementation of measures that entail the monitoring of electronic communications networks on a large-scale. In particular, it does not lay out safeguards such as the respect of the rights to privacy and data protection, effective judicial protection, due process, and the respect of the principle of the presumption of innocence.[35]

2.2.2. *Transatlantic Trade and Investment Partnership*

Regarding the European Commission's good governance principles of *openness and participation*, DG Trade has adopted a responsive stance when communicating on and involving stakeholders in TTIP. The dedicated TTIP webpage contains a myriad of information, ranging from fact sheets and position papers on negotiating topics to advisory group meeting minutes. MEPs and government officials in member states have been granted access to negotiating texts in secure reading rooms. Further European Commission's engagement techniques on TTIP include public consultations, civil society dialogues, inter-institutional and stakeholder meetings. However this has not stopped stakeholders from raising concerns on procedural aspects of the

---

32 European Commission and Parliament, *Anti-Counterfeiting Trade Agreement (ACTA). List of Answers by the European Commission to Written Questions by the European Parliament (Filed Between 1 January 2010 and 31 January 2012)*, Brussels 2012.

33 European Data Protection Supervisor (EDPS), EESC, Joint European Academics, Organisation for Security and Co-operation in Europe (OSCE) Representative on Freedom of the Media, Opinion for the Green/EFA group (Korff & Brown), Study for the EP INTA committee (Institute for Globalisation and International Regulation et al.).

34 ALDE, EDPS, EDRi, FFII, Green/EFA, GUE/NGL, ISOC, ITRE, LIBE, LQDN, Member of European Parliament S&D (David Martin, ACTA Rapporteur), ORG, S&D.

35 European Data Protection Supervisor, Opinion of the European Data Protection Supervisor on the proposal for a Council Decision on the Conclusion of the Anti-Counterfeiting Trade Agreement between the European Union and its member states, Australia, Canada, Japan, the Republic of Korea, the United Mexican States, the Kingdom of Morocco, the Republic of Singapore, the Swiss Confederation and the United States of America, Brussels 2012, p. 16.

negotiations.[36] The EU Ombudsman has been vocal, taking particular issue with the incomplete and unequal access to information and documents.[37] As an example, the European Commission has not fully disclosed its meetings with stakeholders. The exclusivity of the European Commission's advisory group is another thorn in the critics' side. Indeed it seems unlikely that the small number of experts selected can represent the economic and societal concerns on TTIP.

Regarding *accountability*, concerns in TTIP are similar to those in ACTA. On the one hand, stakeholders question the impact that the agreement might have on global trade relations in the future. Academics Clara Weinhardt and Fabian Bohnenberger deem that 'the initiative incentivises the formation of economic blocs, rather than the much vaunted shaping of globalization'.[38] On the other hand, strong stakeholder protests on the Investor State Dispute Settlement (ISDS) mechanism has resulted in a return to the drawing board on the part of the European Commission.[39]

Regarding *effectiveness and coherence*, it can be noted that DG Trade issued an impact assessment on TTIP. Although negotiating texts have not been completed or officially shared, it is clear that the agreement will change EU law. Naturally this raises concerns with stakeholders. For instance, the European Parliament made it clear in its 2015 Resolution on the Negotiations for the Transatlantic Trade and Investment Partnership that 'the safety of the food we eat, the protection of Europeans' personal data and its services of general interest are non-negotiable unless the aim is to achieve a higher level of protection'.[40]

---

36 M. Armanovica and R. Bendini, *In-Depth Analysis: Civil Society's Concerns about the Transatlantic Trade and Investment Partnership (DG EXPO/B/PolDep/Note/2014_118)*, 2014; European Ombudsman, 'Transparency and Public Participation in relation to the Transatlantic Trade and Investment Partnership ("TTIP") Negotiations' (Case: OI/11/2014/RA), 2016.

37 European Ombudsman, 'Transparency and Public Participation in relation to the Transatlantic Trade and Investment Partnership ("TTIP") Negotiations' (Case: OI/11/2014/RA), 2016. To the European Commission's credit, the European Ombudsman has also remarked that while more could be done, she is pleased with the progress made on transparency measures; European Ombudsman, 'Ombudsman's analysis of the Commission's Follow-Up Reply in OI/10/2014/RA on Transparency and Public Participation in the TTIP Negotiations' (Case: OI/10/2014/RA), 2016 <http://www.ombudsman.europa.eu/en/cases/correspondence.faces/en/59898/html.bookmark>.

38 C. Weinhardt and F. Bohnenberger, 'TTIP vs. WTO: Who sets global standards?', *EurActiv.com*, 13 January 2016 <http://www.euractiv.com/section/sustainable-dev/opinion/ttip-vs-wto-who-sets-global-standards/>.

39 M. Armanovica and R. Bendini, *In-Depth Analysis: Civil Society's Concerns about the Transatlantic Trade and Investment Partnership (DG EXPO/B/PolDep/Note/2014_118)*, 2014; European Commission, 'News: Commission Proposes New Investment Court System for TTIP and Other EU Trade and Investment Negotiations', 2015 <http://trade.ec.europa.eu/doclib/press/index.cfm?id=1364>.

40 European Parliament, European Parliament Resolution of 8 July 2015 containing the European Parliament's Recommendations to the European Commission on the Negotiations for the Transatlantic Trade and Investment Partnership (TTIP) (2014/2228(INI)), 2015.

The European Commission has sought to reassure stakeholders that TTIP will not result in a lowering of environmental, consumer safety and data protection standards, nor will areas excluded from the negotiating mandate, such as audio visual services, be affected.[41]

As our analysis reveals, ACTA does not measure up well against the European Commission's good governance principles. At the same time, while there is always room for improvement, the increase in transparency, openness and participation from ACTA to TTIP is striking. These points will be discussed in further detail in the conclusion.

3. BALANCING OF RIGHTS

3.1. PROBLEM DEFINITION

Intellectual property (IP) provisions in trade agreements are sensitive, as they touch upon the problem of balancing of rights. The variety of rationales for IP protection (natural law, economic incentive and social requirements) and the complexity of interests of parties touched by IP provisions (various kinds of stakeholders: right holders, intermediaries, users) lead to tensions. On the one hand, protecting IP is important to foster innovation and creativity, as well as economic growth. On the other hand, these provisions may interfere with fundamental freedoms of citizens (as users of the protected content) or other stakeholders, especially in view of the extremely complicated legal regime of IP provisions and its application to the digital environment. A good illustration of the problem constitutes the issues of the data privacy of users or of the liability of Internet service providers, as raised by the ACTA provisions (see further below).

Moreover, the rapid development of new technologies and the challenges of exploiting immaterial goods, mean it is the voice of the various creative industries (such as entertainment industries in the music and film sectors) that is particularly audible. Traditionally international intellectual property regulations have been set in conventions and treaties governed by the World Intellectual Property Organisation (WIPO) and the World Trade Organisation (WTO, such as[42] the Trade-Related Aspects of Intellectual Property Rights (TRIPS) Agreement). Recently, however, we have been observing a strong tendency to regulate IP provisions outside of WIPO and WTO by introducing them in international trade agreements (regional or bilateral).[43] In such cases,

41 European Commission, *The Top 10 Myths About TTIP. Separating Fact from Fiction*, Brussels 2014.

42 H. Grosse Ruse-Khan, J. Drexl, R.M. Hilty et al., 'Principles for Intellectual Property Provisions in Bilateral and Regional Agreements' (2013) (44) 8 *International Review of Intellectual Property and Competition Law* 878–883.

43 P.K. Yu, 'The Non-Multilateral Approach to International Intellectual Property Normsetting' in D. Gervais (ed.), *International Intellectual Property*, Edward Elgar, Cheltenham 2015, pp. 83–120.

intellectual property rights are often used as a 'bargaining chip' or trade-off in the negotiation processes.[44] Such a form of policy-making constitutes an easy means for powerful stakeholders to exert pressure to strengthen IP protection at a global level.

This section highlights the current global contention on intellectual property rights. We analyse stakeholder views on the balancing of rights in ACTA and TTIP, using the Max Planck Principles for Intellectual Property Provisions in Bilateral and Regional Agreements as our framework of reference. Both ACTA and TTIP touch upon intellectual property issues. However, the substance and nature of these agreements differ significantly. While the Anti-Counterfeiting Trade Agreement is an IP-tailored instrument aimed at regulating IP enforcement issues and is of a multilateral (but not regional) character, the Transatlantic Trade and Investment Partnership is a bilateral agreement between the United States and the European Union, where IP issues form only a part of all the provisions in the agreement.

3.2. MAX PLANCK PRINCIPLES FOR INTELLECTUAL PROPERTY PROVISIONS IN BILATERAL AND REGIONAL AGREEMENTS

In 2013 the Max Planck Institute for Intellectual Property and Competition Law issued Principles for Intellectual Property Provisions in Bilateral and Regional Agreements.[45] The Max Planck Principles apply to international trade agreements that include provisions on the protection and enforcement of intellectual property rights. The document contains two parts: (1) observations and considerations and (2) recommendations. The observations and considerations concern: (a) IP as a trade-off in bilateral and regional agreements, (b) the relevance of multilateral framework, (c) the eroding multilateral policy space, and (d) transparency, inclusiveness and equal participation in the negotiation process. In turn, the recommendations relate to: (a) the negotiation mandate and strategy, (b) the negotiation process, (c) the negotiation outcome, and (d) the interpretation and implementation of bilateral and regional agreements. Bearing in mind objections to ACTA, concerns related to TTIP, as well as relying on the analysis of ACTA in the context of the Max Planck Principles, we address what should be done in order to make TTIP conform to standards on international intellectual property policy-making. In particular, we focus on the Max Planck considerations and recommendations on substantive and institutional issues of IP provisions as well as on procedural aspects of trade negotiations. The key

---

44 Grosse Ruse-Khan, Drexl, Hilty et al., above n. 42, p. 878.

45 Ibid., pp. 878–883.

points here are, respectively, the multilateral policy balance (especially the flexibilities and ceilings for IP domestic implementation) as to the substantive issues, the existing framework for multilateral IP policy-making as to the institutional problems, and the transparency, inclusiveness and participation of trade negotiations as to the procedural aspects.

3.2.1. Anti-Counterfeiting Trade Agreement

An argument common to all stakeholders in the ACTA debate was the need to balance rights and interests for innovation, creativity and economic growth. There was no agreement, however, on whether ACTA found this balance. According to Jeremy de Beer, ACTA represents almost all substantive, institutional and procedural problems addressed in the Max Planck Principles,[46] even though ACTA is a multilateral agreement (not bilateral or regional), dedicated only to intellectual property issues.

Regarding what concerns the balancing of rights in *substance*, de Beer points, among others, to the lack of respect for multilateral policy balance, especially the TRIPS Agreement and the Berne and Paris Conventions, in the context of 'flexibilities' (i.e. norms providing for policy space in domestic implementation) and 'ceilings' (i.e. obligations that place limits on intellectual property protection).[47] He quotes, then, the European Parliament report on the Agreement, where the EP concludes that ACTA is 'significantly more stringent and right holder friendly than the TRIPS Agreement' and adds that 'substantive concerns are justified'.[48]

ACTA's 'Internet chapter' raised many concerns related to fundamental rights, such as the right to property, to freedom of expression and information, to privacy and data protection or to a remedy and a fair trial.[49] In this context, one of the most controversial provisions was ACTA Art. 27(4):

> A Party may provide, in accordance with its laws and regulations, its competent authorities with the authority to order an online service provider to disclose expeditiously to a right holder information sufficient to identify a subscriber whose account was allegedly used for infringement, where that right holder has filed a legally sufficient claim of trademark

46 J. de Beer, 'Applying Best Practice Principles to International Intellectual Property Lawmaking' (2013) (44) 8 *International Review of Intellectual Property and Competition Law* 887–890.

47 Ibid., p. 888.

48 Ibid., p. 889.

49 D. Korff and I. Brown, Opinion on the Compatibility of the Anti-Counterfeiting Trade Agreement (ACTA) with the European Convention on Human Rights & the EU Charter of Fundamental Rights, European Parliament, Brussels 2011.

or copyright or related rights infringement, and where such information is being sought for the purpose of protecting or enforcing those rights ...

Controversies concerned both the statement about the subscriber ('whose account was allegedly used for infringement') and the order to disclose such information to a right holder, and not to the court. Opponents argued that such a provision constituted a risk of infringement of rights to privacy and data protection. In addition, academics pointed to the incompatibility of ACTA's 'disclosure of subscribers' data' clause in Art. 27(4) with TRIPS, as ACTA poses a duty to disclose subscribers' data on non-infringing intermediaries.[50] Another controversial issue was the liability of Internet service providers who would have to monitor the content and the users' activities. In view of this, ACTA critics believed there was a risk of violation of the freedom of expression, for instance in cases where, due to the rights holders' pressure, Internet service providers would be forced to block legal and valuable content.

A second package of doubts concerned the enforcement of IPRs. ACTA critics were afraid of restrictions to the use of protected content on the Internet. In particular, people were anxious about introducing strict penalties for IP infringement on the Internet (such as denying Internet access, censorship, or criminal sanctions for so-called 'camming').[51] In general, public opinion was against further strengthening the rights and protection of IP holders. Civil society organisations pointed to the risk of decreasing the competitiveness of European companies (especially start-ups) who would be afraid of being sued for IP infringements and of the necessity to bear high costs of damages.

As a final example of concerns on the balancing of rights, stakeholders emphasised that the agreement would introduce stronger protection of technological measures than the protection established by international treaties.[52] This would be incompatible with international law and would enable introducing further restrictions related to the lawful use of the protected content (on the basis of limitations and exceptions to copyright). Academics commented that

---

50 R. D'Erme, C. Geiger, H. Grosse Ruse-Khan, C. Heinze, T. Jaeger, R. Matulionuyte et al., 'Opinion of European Academics on Anti-Counterfeiting Trade Agreement' (2011) (2)1 *Journal of Intellectual Property, Information Technology and E-Commerce Law* 69.

51 J. Sobczak, 'ACTA a globalizacja' (in Polish only, English title: 'ACTA and globalisation') in J.W. Adamowski and A. Jaskiernia (eds.), *Komunikowanie masowe i polityka medialna w epoce globalizacji i cyfryzacji – aspekty międzynarodowe* (in Polish only, English title: *Mass communication and media policy in era of globalisation and digitisation – international aspects*), Instytut Dziennikarstwa Uniwersytetu Warszawskiego, Oficyna Wydawnicza ASPRA-JR, Warszawa 2013, p. 124.

52 D'Erme, Geiger, Grosse Ruse-Khan, Heinze, Jaeger, Matulionuyte et al., above n. 50, p. 69.

'from a European perspective, the obligation to implement criminal sanctions against the circumvention of DRM [Digital Rights Management] systems would go beyond the obligations under the Information Society Directive'.[53] In turn, proponents of ACTA took a defensive stance, arguing that the Agreement would not change international or EU law. They advocated ACTA as a solution to the growing problem of IPR infringement and argued that ACTA targeted large-scale crime rather than individual Internet users.

In terms of *institutional* issues, academics criticised the multilateral setting of the agreement. In particular, they pointed out that ACTA was a '"country club" approach to international norm-setting'[54] and that it was 'neither negotiated under the auspices of WIPO nor in the framework of WTO but as a free-standing instrument among the parties involved'.[55] They argued that the 'country club' model was likely to exacerbate existing geopolitical power imbalances in international IP policy-making. Moreover, ACTA foresees a new governing body, which in practice means a move away from the institutional use of WIPO and WTO.[56] Reference was also made to one of the main Principles' observations, namely the use of IP provisions as a bargaining chip in international trade negotiations. Although ACTA itself was an IP-only instrument, it is 'obvious that countries like Jordan, Mexico and Morocco are only included in ACTA on account of their economic and political relationship with the United States', and that 'the concession offered by such countries are rooted in other instruments' (such as bilateral and multilateral agreements).[57] In response, the European Commission indicated that they would have preferred to negotiate ACTA within conventional international forums.

Finally as to *procedural* issues, concerns were raised in relation to the secrecy and (lack of) transparency of the ACTA negotiations.[58] Critics emphasised the exclusion of consumer groups and other civil society organisations from the formal negotiating process and the ineffectiveness and illegitimacy of international IP agreements negotiated in secret (see more in section 2 above). According to de Beer, lack of transparency, inclusiveness, and equal participation constitute ACTA's most egregious violations of the Max Planck Principles.[59]

---

53 A. Metzger, 'A Primer on ACTA. What Europeans Should Fear about the Anti-Counterfeiting Trade Agreement' (2010) (1) 2 *Journal of Intellectual Property, Information Technology and E-Commerce* 115.

54 P.K. Yu, 'Six Secret (and Now Open) Fears of ACTA' (2011) *SMU Law Review* 1077.

55 Metzger, above n. 53, p. 110.

56 De Beer, above n. 46, p. 889.

57 Ibid., 890.

58 D. Matthews 'Negotiating the IP Chapter of an EU–US Transatlantic Trade and Investment Partnership. Let's Not Repeat Past Mistakes' (2013) (44) 5 *IIC* 492.

59 De Beer, above n. 46, p. 889.

3.2.2. *Transatlantic Trade and Investment Partnership*

Bearing in mind the above-mentioned case, we could ask whether it is possible to avoid similar problems in TTIP, and how to make TTIP conform to the Max Planck Principles.

As to the balancing of rights, there has not been much critique on the *substance* of TTIP in relation to IP and data protection related issues. This is due to the fact that the scope of the agreement remains undisclosed. Nevertheless, we can already hear some preliminary concerns about the scope of the intellectual property rights provisions in TTIP.[60] In particular, they relate to encompassing software by patents, introducing further restrictions on limitations and exceptions to copyright, and extending the term of copyright protection. The European Commission underlines in its position paper on intellectual property rights,[61] that TTIP will not touch on the controversial issues raised previously in ACTA, such as criminal enforcement and the liability of Internet Service Providers. It also emphasises the need for a section on the compliance of TTIP with international IP treaties. According to the Commission, the IP chapter of TTIP should cover industrial property, geographical indications (GIs), and copyright and related rights. As to the first issue, the Commission foresees 'high standard agreed principles' that would cover: anti-bad-faith registration of trade marks, customs enforcement (including counterfeit goods in small consignments) and patent procedures and patentability criteria. With reference to geographical indications (GIs), the EU seeks rules guaranteeing an appropriate level of protection for EU GIs, as the US system differs in this subject matter. With regard to copyright and related rights, the key issues are: remuneration rights for broadcasting and communication to the public (public performance) for performers and producers in phonograms, right of communication to public (public performance) for authors in bars, restaurants and shops, and a resale right for creators of original works of art.

At this stage, it is not possible to estimate the compliance of IP provisions to the Max Planck Principles. It is worth mentioning, however, that to some extent the European Parliament refers to these issues in its 2015 Resolution. Namely, regarding the rules, it recommends:

- to ensure that TTIP includes an ambitious, balanced and modern chapter on and precisely defined areas of intellectual property rights, including recognition and

---

60 A. Rymsza, 'TTIP przyniesie patenty i surowe prawo autorskie? Nie wiemy, bo jest tajne', *Dobreprogramy.pl*, 14 March 2015 <http://www.dobreprogramy.pl/TTIP-przyniesie-patenty-i-surowe-prawo-autorskie-Nie-wiemy-bo-jest-tajne,News,61274.html>.

61 European Commission, *EU Position Paper: Intellectual Property*, Brussels 2015. So far no position paper covering issues related to privacy and data protection has been published.

enhanced protection of geographical indications and reflects a fair and efficient level of protection, without impeding the EU's need to reform its copyright system and while ensuring a fair balance of IPRs and the public interest, in particular the need to preserve access to affordable medicines by continuing to support the TRIPS flexibilities (point (2)(d)(xvi)),

- to ensure that the IPR chapter does not include provisions on the liability of internet intermediaries or on criminal sanctions as a tool for enforcement, as having been previously rejected by Parliament including the proposed ACTA treaty (point (2)(d)(xviii)),
- to consider it to be of great importance that the EU and the US remain committed and engaged in global multilateral patent harmonisation discussions through existing international bodies and thus cautions against attempting to introduce provisions on substantive patent law, in particular with regard to issues relating to patentability and grace periods, into the TTIP (point (2)(d)(xvii)).[62]

Undoubtedly, in order for provisions to conform to the Max Planck Principles, they should respect the multilateral policy balance. In particular, they should conform to the provisions of the international treaties on IP (especially in relation to flexibilities and ceilings) and to the EU *'acquis communautaire'* (especially regarding liability of Internet Service Providers, criminal enforcement and privacy/data protection provisions). More generally, according to the principles, they should respect all international obligations, such as public health, environment, biological diversity and human rights.[63] Next, in relation to protection and enforcement of IP, the rules should encompass exceptions, limitations and other rules that balance the interests of right holders against those of users, competitors and the general public.[64]

With regard to *institutional* issues, TTIP foresees the creation of a new governing body, namely the Investor-State Dispute Settlement (ISDS) system. Comparable to ACTA, introducing such a body would be incompatible with the Max Planck Principles, as it would constitute a way to bypass the existing forums (such as WIPO and WTO).[65] The European Parliament recommends, however, in its 2015 Resolution on TTIP Negotiations,

> to replace the ISDS system with a new system for resolving disputes between investors and states which is subject to democratic principles and scrutiny, where potential cases are treated in a transparent manner by publicly appointed, independent professional

[62] European Parliament, European Parliament Resolution of 8 July 2015 containing the European Parliament's Recommendations to the European Commission on the Negotiations for the Transatlantic Trade and Investment Partnership (TTIP) (2014/2228(INI)), Strasbourg 2015.

[63] Grosse Ruse-Khan, Drexl, Hilty et al., above n. 42, points 20, 23.

[64] Ibid., point 25.

[65] De Beer, above n. 46, p. 889.

> judges in public hearings and which includes an appellate mechanism, where consistency of judicial decisions is ensured, the jurisdiction of courts of the EU and of the Member States is respected, and where private interests cannot undermine public policy objectives (point (2)(d)(xv)).[66]

Moreover, similar to ACTA (or perhaps because of the large debate and rejection of ACTA), the lion's share of TTIP critique concerns *procedural* issues, especially the legitimacy of the legislative process. People are against secret negotiations and lack of public debate/consultations with civil society organisations (see more in section 2 above). In order to fulfil the Principles for IP Provisions, the negotiations should be carried out in an open and transparent manner and allow for participation by all stakeholders in the negotiating countries. Right holder and industry groups should not enjoy preferential treatment over other stakeholders.[67]

4. CONCLUSION

Building on previous sections, a number of questions arise on how to improve societal acceptability of international trade negotiations including intellectual property rights.

The Anti-Counterfeiting Trade Agreement scored poorly on all European principles of good governance. The adoption of the Lisbon Treaty granted the European Parliament increased insight and power in trade negotiations. This procedural change can perhaps explain (although not excuse) the European Commission's dramatic failure on its good governance principles pertaining to policy input and process. The ACTA negotiations certainly could not be described as open and participatory. Further, while the European Commission's limited inclusion of stakeholders during the negotiations simplified whom to hold accountable for the policy outcome, even the initial choice to negotiate the agreement in its multilateral format was subject to criticism. Within the European Union, ACTA was not perceived as an effective or coherent policy solution to the global problem of intellectual property rights enforcement. The good news is that the European Commission has shown marked improvement on the application of its good governance principles in the context of the Transatlantic Trade and Investment Partnership. As much of the substance of the agreement remains to be determined, the main question at this point is whether

---

66 European Parliament, European Parliament Resolution of 8 July 2015 containing the European Parliament's Recommendations to the European Commission on the Negotiations for the Transatlantic Trade and Investment Partnership (TTIP) (2014/2228(INI)), Strasbourg 2015.

67 Grosse Ruse-Khan, Drexl, Hilty et al, above n. 42, point 14.

the approach taken towards openness and participation suffices. DG Trade has gone beyond its legal obligations, seeking to increase popular legitimacy in this subject area. However, restricted public access to negotiating texts raises (perhaps unnecessary) concerns about the policy process and outcome. Importantly, the continued use of a select number of special advisers is questionable. The premise of the European Commission's Governance White Paper is that participatory policymaking results in more legitimate and effective policy outcomes. Structural involvement of a wider base of non-governmental stakeholders may be a necessary next step.

The analysis of the Anti-Counterfeiting Trade Agreement against the Max Planck Principles illustrated that ACTA provides for stricter rules compared to current international standards. At the same time, the analysis showed that intellectual property rights are increasingly viewed as being in opposition to citizens' fundamental rights, especially in relation to the Internet (rights to privacy and data protection, freedom of expression, limited liability of Internet Service Providers). There is also an expectation of full compatibility of new/proposed provisions with the EU '*acquis communautaire*' as well as with international intellectual property treaties. IP provisions included in international trade agreements have to respect the multilateral framework, in particular the TRIPS Agreement and the Berne and Paris Conventions. Importantly, there is no acceptance for a new international agreement beyond WIPO and WTO. Having in mind the tendency to introduce IP rules in international trade agreements (that are stricter compared to current international – WIPO/WTO TRIPS – standards) and that such a form of policy-making constitutes an easy means to strengthen IP protection at a global level, it would be valuable to ask whether general trade negotiations should include IP rights at all. The answer to this question would certainly require more in-depth analysis. However, we can imagine it could depend, at least, on the objective of introducing IP regulations to international trade agreements. If their aim were to circumvent well-established international IP and/or fundamental rights standards, the answer would certainly be 'no'. On the contrary, if their goal were to make IP provisions (between signatories' legislations) conform with each other, without somehow overruling other international rules, the answer would probably be 'yes'.

Coming back to the main question on how to improve the societal acceptability in international trade negotiations including intellectual property rights, the example of ACTA shows that we cannot underestimate public disagreement concerning closed negotiations and IP protection. Citizens and other stakeholders are not indifferent to the weaknesses of international policy-making processes. In this chapter we highlighted issues related to the choice of venue, secret nature of negotiations and strengthening of IP protection in particular. Introducing transparency, participatory elements, and explicit balancing of rights into the international legislative process is necessary in order to address the popular legitimacy of international trade agreements. There is a need to permit interested stakeholders to provide meaningful input during predetermined moments of the negotiation process to ensure acceptability of output, and to include detailed reference to fundamental rights, as well as limitations and exceptions in intellectual property, to ensure acceptability of IP provisions. These recommendations leave the institutional dilemma as highlighted by the Max Planck Principles unresolved. If the aim of the EU–US preferential agreement is to create new standards of protection, for intellectual property in particular and beyond what is established in WTO and WIPO, strong criticism is likely to persist.

8. FREE TRADE AGREEMENTS AND DATA PRIVACY

Future Perils of Faustian Bargains

Graham Greenleaf*

1. INTRODUCTION – BARGAINING WITH PRIVACY RIGHTS

Free Trade Agreements (FTAs) are unlikely to be sources of privacy rights, yet may act as limitations on the operation of data protection/data privacy[1] laws. Countries negotiating new bilateral or multilateral trade agreements, particularly but not exclusively the USA, are likely to attempt to include requirements that the parties do not include any significant data export restrictions or 'data localisation' provisions in their laws. This chapter surveys the variety of ways in which FTAs have affected data privacy by considering a range of examples, without being comprehensive. Examples include FTAs in which the USA is involved in both Europe and the Asia-Pacific, and a number in which the USA is not involved. The extent to which the effects of FTAs on data privacy may be changing is assessed. One theme of this chapter is the extent to which it is appropriate to include what are essentially human rights or civil liberties in FTAs, where they are traded against economic benefits.

An essentially chronological structure is adopted: the effect of FTAs on data privacy prior to 2016's Trans-Pacific Partnership (TPP) agreement is first considered, then the TPP's effect is analysed in some detail, followed by

* Professor of Law & Information Systems, University of New South Wales. E-mail: g.greenleaf@unsw.edu.au. Valuable comments have been received from Prof Leon Trakman, Chris Connolly, Bob Gellman, Prof Lee Bygrave, Sanya Reid Smith, Blair Stewart, Prof Nohyoung Park and two anonymous reviewers. All content remains the responsibility of the author.

1 Distinctions between privacy and data protection are not important for the purposes of this chapter. The term 'data privacy' is preferred, but it will sometimes be convenient to refer to 'privacy' as an underlying interest, and 'data protection' as a term used in FTAs and other instruments.

consideration of possible future FTAs which are still at the negotiation stage. The TPP is the first multilateral trade agreement with detailed provisions relating to privacy protection. Because of this, and because other potentially relevant FTAs are still at the negotiating stage and there is no final treaty text available at the time of writing, the TPP is given more extended consideration.

1.1. THE USA'S FORUM-SHIFTING ON PERSONAL DATA EXPORTS

The main effect of FTAs on data privacy concerns data exports, and the key to understanding the changing importance of FTAs in this field may lie in understanding the changing options available to the USA to achieve its goals to maximise the free flow of personal data and minimise personal data export restrictions. The USA is masterful at forum-shifting to attain its diplomatic goals:[2] at one time it will focus on bilateral relationships, then shift to regional agreements, next global multilateral fora – and back and forth as the need requires. Other countries do similarly, but none with the stamina of the USA. Since the first national data privacy laws in the 1970s, the USA (through both trade diplomats and local US chambers of commerce and the like) has steadfastly opposed all impediments to the transfer of personal data from other countries to US companies, and to the US government. This often involves opposition to countries enacting strong data privacy laws at all, but that has proved to be a losing battle, with 111 jurisdictions having now adopted such laws, most of them including data export restrictions of some type.[3] Revisions of existing data privacy laws have also often added or strengthened data export restrictions.[4] With multilateral agreements the USA has had significant success in keeping both the 2013 revisions to the OECD Privacy Guidelines, and the APEC (Asia-Pacific Economic Cooperation) Privacy Framework, weak and unenforceable and with no data export restrictions of concern. For nearly two decades it seemed as though it had tamed the toughest regional data export restrictions, those in the EU Data Protection Directive, by obtaining a 'Safe Harbour' for its companies from the EU. That stratagem failed with the *Schrems* decision finding

---

2 For a sustained discussion of its successes in the field of intellectual property, see P. Drahos with J. Braithwaite, *Information Feudalism: Who Owns the Knowledge Economy?*, Earthscan 2002, particularly chs. 6 and 7.

3 G. Greenleaf, 'Global data privacy laws 2015: 109 countries, with European laws now in a minority' (2015) 133 *Privacy Laws & Business International Report* 14–17 <http://ssrn.com/abstract=2603529>. To that 109 can now be added Turkey and Sao Tome & Principe.

4 During this decade, these include (considering only the Asia-Pacific region) revisions to laws in Australia, Japan, New Zealand and Taiwan.

that it was illegal for the European Commission to bargain with privacy rights instead of following the Directive's requirements. The proposed replacement, the 'EU–US Privacy Shield' agreement negotiated by the EU Commission, is at the time of writing still facing considerable opposition from numerous EU institutions (Article 29 Working Party, EDPS and European Parliament) and its future is uncertain. Attempts to convince the EU that there was some type of 'interoperability' with the APEC Cross-Border Privacy Rules system (APEC-CBPRs), that should be accorded a willing suspension of disbelief by the EU, have also been politely dismissed.[5]

This chapter concerns yet another US stratagem to prevent personal data export restrictions, and another complex set of fora in which this game is played out: free trade agreements (bilateral, regional and global), and the shadowy world of FTA negotiations. It is very similar territory to the world of TRIPS and trade agreements in which the USA has succeeded with intellectual property (IP).[6]

Throughout this chapter, as in the preceding paragraphs, I refer to the USA, and the interests of US companies and its government, as the principal driver of the use of FTAs to restrict data privacy laws. The position of the USA is the most explicit on these issues, and its interests the most obvious, but in many negotiations other countries, for example Japan or Australia, may advocate what I refer to as 'the US position' just as strongly. This chapter is not an analysis of the political economy of neo-liberalism in the context of FTAs.

1.2. DATA PRIVACY AGREEMENTS: NOT BANANAS

International treaties are bargains between countries. There have been a number of international agreements concerning privacy rights, but they have been of a very different nature from free trade agreements. Council of Europe Data Protection Convention 108 (1981), the EU Data Protection Directive (1995) and the EU Data Protection Regulation (GDPR, 2016) all involved guarantees of free flow of personal data (in part, an aspect of freedom of speech, although mainly commercial or government speech) in return for guarantees of minimum standards of privacy protection by other treaty parties, so as to help ensure that free flow of personal data would not endanger the privacy of their citizens. Although they are not binding international agreements, the OECD Privacy Guidelines (1980) and the APEC Privacy Framework (2004) involve similar balancing of privacy-related interests. The main other international agreements

---

5 For a summary, see G. Greenleaf, *Asian Data Privacy Laws: Trade and Human Rights Perspectives*, OUP, Oxford 2014, ch. 18, section 2.

6 Drahos and Braithwaite, above n. 2.

involving rights of privacy, namely the International Covenant on Civil and Political Rights (1967), the European Convention on Human Rights (1950) and other regional equivalents in Africa and Latin America, each involve the parties making commitments to protect numerous human rights, subject to certain conditions, in return for other countries doing likewise. These agreements all involve some trade-offs in relation to privacy protection, because (for example) the right of free expression necessarily places limits on the right of privacy. Similarly, freedom of religion, or of other beliefs, would be meaningless unless there was some protection of privacy. So these agreements can be described as bargains that only concern human rights, and necessarily must consider more than one human right (including related commercial/governmental freedom of speech).

Free trade agreements require countries to do something quite different. They must determine the extent to which stronger protection of their citizens' privacy should be traded for greater access to foreign markets in rice, cars or textiles. Should freedom of speech, freedom of religion, the right to criticise foreign governments, or to legislate for marriage equality, or against racial discrimination, be traded in FTAs for reduced tariffs on car tyres or wheat or liberalisation of insurance service markets? If not, then why should the privacy rights of a country's citizens be bargaining chips? As Spiros Simitis, 'Europe's de facto privacy doyen', said when discussing EU/US tensions over the 1995 EU Privacy Directive, 'This is not bananas we are talking about.'[7]

Taking this approach, the only role that privacy rights should play in free trade agreements is a negative one: as explicit exceptions confirming that other FTA provisions have nothing to do with limiting the protection of privacy (or other human rights). Perhaps it is reasonable that there should also be limitation on such privacy protections where they are shams, merely disguising limitations on trade but with no justifiable role in privacy protection. However, as this chapter's discussion will show, it is very difficult to include any such provisions in FTAs without genuine privacy protections also being sacrificed, bargained away for bananas.

We therefore proceed to examine the history and likely future of privacy-related provisions in FTAs, while taking a sceptical view of the relationship between FTAs and human rights such as the protection of privacy.[8]

---

7 As described and cited by L. Bygrave, 'International agreements to protect personal data' in J. Rule and G. Greenleaf (eds.), *Global Privacy Protection: The First Generation*, Edward Elgar, Cheltenham 2008, p. 15.

8 For a detailed discussion of human rights considerations in relation to the TPP and other FTAs, see S. Reid Smith, 'Potential Human Rights Impacts of the TPP', section 'Some TPP issues common to multiple human rights', Third World Network, 2015 <http://www.twn.my/title2/FTAs/General/TPPHumanRights.pdf>.

2. FTAs AND DATA PRIVACY PRIOR TO 2016 – A QUIESCENT PAST

Until 2016 the most significant multilateral FTAs referring to privacy or data protection had been the global General Agreement on Trade in Services (GATS), and a few post-GATS regional multilateral agreements. There are however a large number of completed regional multilateral FTAs, with one incomplete list including 21 such agreements,[9] and it is not feasible to consider all of them. Some examples are discussed here, particularly from the Asia-Pacific region.

Bilateral FTAs, of which there are a vast number,[10] also sometimes refer to data protection, but often only in very general terms, with specific provisions unknown. They are not discussed here.

2.1. GATS EXCEPTION AND UNPREDICTABLE WTO JURISPRUDENCE

The issue of privacy laws being used as trade barriers could potentially be raised at the World Trade Organization (WTO). Article XIV(c)(ii) of the GATS (General Agreement on Trade in Services, 1995) provides that:

> Subject to the requirement that such measures are not applied in a manner which would constitute a means of arbitrary or unjustifiable discrimination between countries where like conditions prevail, or a disguised restriction on trade in services, nothing in this Agreement shall be construed to prevent the adoption or enforcement by any Member of measures: ... (c) necessary to secure compliance with laws or regulations which are not inconsistent with the provisions of this Agreement including those relating to: ... (ii) the protection of the privacy of individuals in relation to the processing and dissemination of personal data and the protection of confidentiality of individual records and accounts.

---

9 Wikipedia, List of multilateral free trade agreements – Operating agreements <https://en.wikipedia.org/wiki/List_of_multilateral_free_trade_agreements>: ASEAN Free Trade Area (AFTA), 1992; ASEAN–China Free Trade Area (ACFTA), 2010; ASEAN–India Free Trade Area (AIFTA), 2010; Asia-Pacific Trade Agreement (APTA), 1975; Central American Integration System (SICA), 1993; Central European Free Trade Agreement (CEFTA), 1992; Commonwealth of Independent States Free Trade Area (CISFTA), 2011; Common Market for Eastern and Southern Africa (COMESA), 1994; G-3 Free Trade Agreement (G-3), 1995; Greater Arab Free Trade Area (GAFTA), 1997; Dominican Republic–Central America Free Trade Agreement (DR-CAFTA), 2004; European Economic Area (EEA; European Union–Norway–Iceland–Lichtenstein), 1994; European Free Trade Association (EFTA), 1960; Gulf Cooperation Council (GCC), 1981; North American Free Trade Agreement (NAFTA), 1994; Pacific Alliance, 2012; South Asia Free Trade Agreement (SAFTA), 2004; Southern African Development Community (SADC), 1980; Southern Common Market (MERCOSUR), 1991; Trans-Pacific Strategic Economic Partnership (TPP), 2005.

10 See, for an incomplete list, Wikipedia, List of bilateral free trade agreements <https://en.wikipedia.org/wiki/List_of_bilateral_free_trade_agreements>.

The article's carve-out of data privacy protections therefore includes four potentially significant limits. The chapeau[11] refers to application of measures which constitute 'arbitrary or unjustifiable discrimination', which are also 'between countries where like conditions prevail', or which are 'disguised' trade restrictions. The article also requires that the enforcement measures are 'necessary' to secure compliance with the data privacy laws enacted.

There has been little extensive discussion of the implications of this or other GATS provisions[12] for data privacy restrictions. The New Zealand Law Commission[13] in 2008 found it 'difficult to predict' and merely agreed with Bennett and Raab that it is possible 'that at some point, and in some context, international data protection will be tested within the WTO',[14] noting Shaffer's conclusion[15] that it was unlikely that the EU's 'adequacy' requirements[16] could be successfully challenged at the WTO.[17] Bygrave, however, considered that 'a fairly cogent argument can be made that the EU has breached the chapeau criteria by entering into the Safe Harbor agreement with the USA but without, it would seem, offering third countries (for example, Australia) the same opportunity to negotiate such an agreement'.[18] Reyes is of a similar view. Safe Harbour has been declared illegal in *Schrems*, but the EU might run a similar risk with the newly completed Privacy Shield agreement with the USA, unless it offers other countries similar opportunities, at least those that have applied for an 'adequacy assessment'.

---

11 'Chapeau' in international law refers to introductory text in a treaty provision, often stating the general objective of the provision.

12 GATS further requires in Art. VI(1) that '[i]n sectors where specific commitments are undertaken, each Member shall ensure that all measures of general application affecting trade in services are administered in a reasonable, objective and impartial manner'. There is also a need to comply with Art. II(1) of GATS, requiring that '[w]ith respect to any measure covered by this Agreement, each Member shall accord immediately and unconditionally to services and service suppliers of any other Member treatment no less favourable than that it accords to like services and service suppliers of any other country'.

13 New Zealand Law Commission (NZLC), *Privacy Concepts and Issues: Review of the Law of Privacy, Stage One*, Wellington 2008, para. 7.69.

14 C. Bennett and C. Raab, *The Governance of Privacy: Policy Instruments in Global Perspective*, MIT Press, Boston MA 2006, p. 111.

15 G. Shaffer, 'Globalization and social protection: The impact of EU and international rules in the ratcheting up of US privacy standards' (2000) 25 *Yale Journal of International Law* 1–88.

16 In brief, Art. 25 of the EU's Data Protection Directive (1995) prevents EU Member States allowing exports of personal data to a non-EU country unless the data protection provided by that country has been found to be 'adequate' by the European Commission. Other exceptions are also provided.

17 Bennett and Raab, above n. 14, p. 111.

18 L. Bygrave, *Data Privacy Law: An International Perspective*, OUP, Oxford 2014, p. 198. The Safe Harbour Agreement is no longer functioning, following the *Schrems* decision, but the point is still valid.

In a detailed assessment of the position of the EU Privacy Directive in light of GATS, Reyes[19] concludes that, despite the apparent clarity of the GATS exception for privacy protection, 'the possibility that any given measure will withstand GATS exceptions analysis is unpredictable'. 'Unfortunately, the latitude given to the WTO DSB [Dispute Settlement Bodies] in interpreting the general exceptions may allow a challenge to the Privacy Directive to overcome the EU's reliance on GATS art XIV(c)(ii).' The *US-Gambling* decision[20] by the WTO Appellate Body in 2005 is the only one to yet consider Art. XIV(c) (although not the privacy exception), and it imposed a more stringent (and unpredictable) analysis of 'necessity' than scholars had expected. Reyes concludes that, in relation to any proposed measure, an 'in-depth analysis of necessity and the chapeau must be undertaken', and that an initially compliant measure can also 'mutate into a WTO-inconsistent measure if the implementing agency fails to consider the effects of their chosen method of application'. Bygrave[21] and Weber[22] conclude similarly, that there is a degree of unpredictability of WTO jurisprudence, and thus of whether a challenge at the WTO against EU or national data export restrictions would succeed.

Despite statements by US officials that the EU's requirements in the EU Privacy Directive are contrary to WTO commitments, neither the USA nor any other country has yet challenged them in that forum. This may be because there have not yet been any instances of the EU Directive (or other data export restriction) posing a sufficient threat to US (or another country's) interests to justify the risks of a potentially unsuccessful WTO challenge. If the Privacy Shield negotiations failed, the USA might take a different view. After two decades of GATS, perhaps a practical conclusion is that GATS is not a threat to all data export or data localisation restrictions, but that it could be used to challenge some ill-considered or over-broad restrictions, in light of the arguments raised by scholars.

2.2. REGIONAL TRADE AGREEMENTS – EXAMPLES

Regional FTAs are not known to have had any significant effect on data privacy prior to 2016. Early agreements pre-dating GATS, such as the North American Free Trade Agreement (NAFTA, 1994),[23] had no relevant clauses. Some regional

19 C. Reyes, 'WTO-Compliant Protection of Fundamental Rights: Lessons from the EU Privacy Directive' (2011) 12(1) *Melbourne Journal of International Law* 141 <http://www.austlii.edu.au/au/journals/MelbJIL/2011/5.html>.

20 WTO Appellate Body Report, *US – Gambling*, WTO Doc WT/DS285/AB/R, [338]–[369].

21 Bygrave, above n. 18, p. 198.

22 R. Weber, 'Regulatory Autonomy and Privacy Standards Under the GATS' (2012) 7(1) *Asian Journal of WTO & International Health Law and Policy* 25–48.

23 NAFTA Secretariat <https://www.nafta-sec-alena.org/Home/Welcome>.

Asia-Pacific agreements (one area of focus of this chapter), discussed in the following, do include privacy-related clauses, but they do not go beyond the GATS provisions.

2.2.1. SAARC trade agreements

The only reference to privacy protection in the SAARC (South Asia Area of Regional Cooperation) agreements and conventions is in the SAARC Agreement on Trade in Services,[24] made in 2010. That agreement allows for exceptions to be made in the domestic laws of SAARC countries for measures for the protection of data privacy which might otherwise be contrary to their free trade requirements. Clause 23 is in all relevant respects the same as Art. XIV(c)(2) of the GATS, except that it only applies as between the SAARC countries. While this is essentially a negative measure, it is an important one, allowing SAARC Member States to impose restrictions on data exports, and on outsourced data processing to other SAARC Member States, in order to protect data privacy.

2.2.2. ASEAN trade agreements (ASEANFAS and AANZFTA)

The ASEAN (Association of South East Asian Nations) Framework Agreement on Services (1995) provides in effect[25] that the exemption for laws protecting data privacy in Art. XIV(c)(2) of the GATS also applies under the ASEAN Framework, in default of specific provisions, and that there is, therefore, no impediment to data export restrictions resulting from ASEAN agreements. The position is therefore essentially the same as in the SAARC region.

The Agreement establishing the ASEAN-Australia-New Zealand Free Trade Area (AANZFTA),[26] signed in 2009, was Australia's first multi-country FTA. It is now in force for all parties.[27] In the chapter on electronic commerce,

---

24 See discussion on SAARC website <http://www.saarc-sec.org/areaofcooperation/detail.php?activity_id=46>.

25 ASEAN Framework Agreement on Services Art. XIV(1) provides that: 'The terms and definitions and other provisions of the [General Agreement on Trade in Services] GATS shall be referred to and applied to matters arising under this Framework Agreement for which no specific provision has been made under it' and Art. IX(1) provides that: 'This Framework Agreement or any action taken under it shall not affect the rights and obligations of the Member States under any existing agreements to which they are parties'.

26 DFAT Australia, AANZFTA page <http://dfat.gov.au/trade/agreements/aanzfta/Pages/asean-australia-new-zealand-free-trade-agreement.aspx>.

27 DFAT, AANZFTA Resources <http://dfat.gov.au/trade/agreements/aanzfta/resources/Pages/resources.aspx>.

Art. 7[28] includes a very general obligation to 'protect the personal data of the users of electronic commerce' (but without any obligation until it enacts laws to do so), and in doing so to 'consider the international standards and criteria of relevant international organisations'. No provision deals explicitly with data export restrictions. AANZFTA includes an investor-state dispute resolution mechanism, but it does not apply to the e-commerce chapter.[29] AANZFTA therefore has little effect on data privacy laws.

2.2.3. Latin America – the Pacific Alliance agreement

Latin America provides an example on the edge of the Asia-Pacific, the region which is the main focus of this chapter. One of the main features of current FTA developments is the attempt to merge the effects of existing FTAs into larger regional agreements. In Latin America, progress on regional FTAs (aside from the TPP) is occurring at the sub-regional level. Plans for comprehensive FTAs in the Americas as a whole have stalled.[30] Mercosur has as full members Argentina, Brazil, Paraguay, Uruguay and Venezuela, plus associate members and observers.[31] It is attempting to negotiate FTAs with other trade blocs such as the EU and the Pacific Alliance.

The Pacific Alliance is an agreement[32] which commenced development in 2011 as a regional integration initiative comprised of Chile, Colombia, Mexico and Peru, within the framework of the Latin American Pacific Basin Initiative; Panama and Costa Rica have also expressed their interest in forming part of the bloc. Its 2012 Framework Agreement entered into force on 20 July 2015. It has followed that up with an Additional Protocol defining the terms of free trade within the bloc in 2015,[33] and most of national implementation procedures are underway. In Chapter 13 on Electronic Commerce, the agreement only states that the parties will adopt or maintain laws or other measures to protect the personal information of those involved in electronic commerce, taking into

28 AANZFTA, Ch. 10, Art. 7, 'Online Data Protection' provides: '1. Subject to Paragraph 2, each Party shall, in a manner it considers appropriate, protect the personal data of the users of electronic commerce. 2. A Party shall not be obliged to apply Paragraph 1 before the date on which that Party enacts domestic laws or regulations to protect the personal data of electronic commerce users. 3. In the development of data protection standards, each Party shall consider the international standards and criteria of relevant international organisations.'

29 AANZFTA, Ch. 10, Art. 10.

30 See for example Wikipedia, Free Trade Area of the Americas <https://en.wikipedia.org/wiki/Free_Trade_Area_of_the_Americas>.

31 <https://en.wikipedia.org/wiki/Mercosur>.

32 <http://www.sice.oas.org/Trade/PAC_ALL/Index_PDF_s.asp>.

33 'Pacific Alliance Trade Pact Enters into Force', DataMyne Blog, 20 July 2015 <http://www.datamyne.com/blog/markets/pacific-alliance-trade-pact-enters-into-force/>.

account international standards, and will exchange information and experiences regarding this.[34]

2.3. THE IMPACT OF MULTILATERAL FTAs ON PRIVACY PRIOR TO 2016

Regional FTAs, or bilateral FTAs, completed prior to 2016, have rarely included significant restrictions on the enactment of data privacy laws by countries which are parties to them. However, this matters less than it might, because most countries are parties to GATS.[35] Where FTAs did have explicit privacy clauses, the examples known did not go beyond the GATS provisions. Although the interpretation of the privacy-related provisions in GATS, particularly Art. XIV(c)(ii), is still uncertain (despite being unchallenged for 20 years), we can say that GATS imposes on most countries a minimum level of restriction on enactment of data privacy laws, irrespective of other multilateral or bilateral agreements.

This position has potentially changed in late 2015 and early 2016 with the completion and signing of the Trans-Pacific Partnership (TPP) Agreement, which (if it comes into effect) will impose what appear to be a higher level of restrictions on countries which are parties to it. Will it set a pattern for a higher level of restrictions than GATS in other FTAs still being negotiated? The TPP will now be discussed.

3. THE TRANS-PACIFIC PARTNERSHIP (TPP) AGREEMENT (2016) – PRESENT DANGER

Twelve Pacific-rim nations accounting for 40 per cent of the global economy, including most significant APEC economies other than China, have reached agreement on a historic free-trade agreement, or are queuing up to join. The Trans-Pacific Partnership Agreement (TPP)[36] was agreed to in Atlanta, Georgia on 5 October 2015 at the conclusion of eight years of negotiation, and signed in

---

34 'ARTÍCULO 13.8: *Protección de la Información Personal* 1. Las Partes deberán adoptar o mantener leyes, regulaciones o medidas administrativas para la protección de la información personal de los usuarios que participen en el comercio electrónico. Las Partes tomaran en consideración los estándares in ternacionales que existen en esta materia. 2. Las Partes deberán intercambiar información y experiencias en cuanto a su legislación de protección de la información personal.'

35 All members of the WTO are signatories to the GATS, and the WTO had 162 members as of December 2015 <https://www.wto.org/english/thewto_e/whatis_e/tif_e/org6_e.htm>.

36 New Zealand Foreign Affairs & Trade, 'Text of the TPP Agreement' <http://tpp.mfat.govt.nz/text>.

Auckland, New Zealand on 4 February 2016.[37] The TPP is primarily an agreement 'to establish a free trade area',[38] an agreement which 'will strip thousands of trade tariffs in the region and set common labour, environmental and legal standards among signatories.'[39] But it is also the first legally binding agreement affecting data privacy that has been entered into by APEC members, although it is not formally an APEC (Asia-Pacific Economic Cooperation) instrument. The APEC Privacy Framework (2004), like all other APEC 'agreements', is not legally binding on its parties. In contrast, the TPP is a real international agreement, with enforcement provisions.

The TPP only imposes the most limited positive requirements for privacy protection, but imposes stronger and more precise limits on the extent of privacy protection that TPP parties can legally provide. The principal aim of this section is to explain these provisions and their overall effect on privacy protection.[40]

3.1. THE PARTIES, NOW AND FUTURE: NEARLY ALL OF APEC, PERHAPS BEYOND

All 12 initial parties to the TPP are APEC Member States: Australia, Brunei Darussalam, Canada, Chile, Japan, Malaysia, Mexico, New Zealand, Peru, Singapore, the United States and Vietnam. Five more APEC member countries have stated that they wish to join the TPP: Indonesia, the second most populous country in APEC;[41] South Korea, the third-largest economy in East Asia;[42] as well as Taiwan,[43] Thailand,[44] the Philippines[45] and Papua New

---

37 C. Reilly, 'Pacific Grim: How the controversial TPP signed away your digital rights' C|Net, 4 February 2016 <http://www.cnet.com/au/news/pacific-grim-how-the-controversial-tpp-signed-away-your-digital-rights/>.

38 TPP, Art. 1.1.

39 N. O'Malley, 'The Trans-Pacific Partnership: Pacific countries agree to historic trade pact', *The Sydney Morning Herald*, 6 October 2015 <http://www.smh.com.au/business/the-economy/tpp-deal-pacific-countries-agree-to-historic-trade-pact-20151005-gk1vq2#ixzz3ruWzAAic>.

40 A shorter version of this section, 'The TPP Agreement: An anti-privacy treaty for most of APEC' is in (2015) 138 *Privacy Laws & Business International Report.*

41 'Indonesia will join Trans-Pacific Partnership, Jokowi tells Obama', *The Guardian*, 27 October 2015.

42 J.J. Lee, 'The Truth About South Korea's TPP Shift', *The Diplomat*, 23 October 2015 <http://thediplomat.com/2015/10/the-truth-about-south-koreas-tpp-shift/>.

43 Executive Yuan, 'Taiwan determined to join TPP', 27 October 2015.

44 K. Takenaka, 'Thailand "highly likely" to decide to join TPP: deputy prime minister', *bilaterals.org*, 27 November 2015 <http://www.bilaterals.org/?thailand-highly-likely-to-decide>.

45 Reuters, 'Philippines' Aquino wants to join Trans-Pacific Partnership', 14 October 2015 <http://uk.reuters.com/article/2015/10/14/uk-philippines-trade-tpp-idUKKCN0S80WJ20151014>; see also Prashanth Parameswaran, 'Confirmed: Philippines Wants to Join TPP', *The Diplomat*, 25 June 2015 <http://thediplomat.com/2015/06/confirmed-philippines-wants-to-join-tpp/>.

Guinea.[46] That leaves just five of the 21 APEC Member States not involved at present. Neither China nor the Hong Kong SAR, both APEC members, are parties to the TPP,[47] although significant opinion-makers in China are open to joining the TPP.[48] The other 'missing' APEC member economy is Russia. In effect, almost all of APEC wants to join the TPP, except China and Russia.

It is still speculative whether, and when, the TPP will come into force, but it now seems unlikely. President-Elect Trump has not yet been sworn in, but he has stated that his policy is that the USA should not go ahead with TPP membership.[49] Every other party will also need to go through any domestic processes required for ratification, possibly including enacting legislation. There are two methods by which the TPP may come into force. It can come into effect 60 days after the 12th ratification by the original signatories. Alternatively, if, after two years (i.e. about December 2017), all 12 signatories have not ratified the TPP, it may still come into force if at least six original signatories have ratified it, and between them they represent 85 per cent of the total GDP of the 12 original signatories. Assessments indicate that this requires ratification by both the USA and Japan.[50] Many politicians on both sides of US politics have expressed opposition to the TPP, and there is still some opposition in Japan. A report by World Bank staff estimates that the TPP will only boost the Australian economy by 0.7 per cent by 2030,[51] making it difficult to regard the Australian government's fervent support as anything more than ideological.

Provided they are willing to comply with its requirements, the TPP is open to accession by (a) any state or separate customs territory that is a member of APEC, and (b) such other state or separate customs territory as the parties may agree (Art. 30.4). TPP therefore has ambitions to be a global agreement, and at least an APEC-wide agreement.

---

46 S. Laob, 'Papua New Guinea Leader Confident Country Able to Join TPP Deal', *Sputnik News*, 17 November 2015 <http://sputniknews.com/politics/20151117/1030233189/papua-new-guinea-leader-tpp-deal.html#ixzz3xZPzEEWd>.

47 Macau SAR, the other Chinese territory which has a data privacy law, is not an APEC member economy.

48 Reuters, 'China communist party paper says country should join U.S.-led trade pact', 24 October 2015 <http://www.reuters.com/article/2015/10/25/us-china-trade-tpp-idUSKCN0SJ01X20151025#2GF0PVwz1pTAh15m.99>.

49 M. Doran, 'Donald Trump Vows To Withdraw From Trans-Pacific Partnership Trade Deal', *ABC News*, 22 November 2016 <http://www.abc.net.au/news/2016-11-22/trump-vows-to-withdraw-from-tpp-trade-deal/8045236>.

50 A. Panda, 'Here's What Needs to Happen in Order for the Trans-Pacific Partnership to Become Binding', *The Diplomat*, 8 October 2015 <http://thediplomat.com/2015/10/heres-what-needs-to-happen-in-order-for-the-trans-pacific-partnership-to-become-binding/>.

51 P. Martin, 'Trans-Pacific Partnership will barely benefit Australia, says World Bank report', *Sydney Morning Herald*, 12 January 2016 <http://www.smh.com.au/federal-politics/-gm3g9w.html>.

3.2. SCOPE INCLUDES ANY MEASURES AFFECTING TRADE

Chapter 14 ('Electronic Commerce') applies to 'measures adopted or maintained by a Party that *affect* trade by electronic means' (Art. 14.2.2, emphasis added), so the scope may be much broader than measures that govern or 'apply to' trade, and broader than the normal meaning of 'electronic commerce' (the Chapter title). The key terms 'trade by electronic means', and 'affecting' remain undefined, as does the less important 'e-commerce'.[52] The wide scope of the TPP in relation to electronic services is confirmed by Art. 14.2.4: 'measures affecting the supply of a service delivered or performed electronically are subject to the obligations contained in the relevant provisions of Chapter 9 (Investment), Chapter 10 (Cross-Border Trade in Services) and Chapter 11 (Financial Services)'.

However, Chapter 14 does not apply to '(a) government procurement; or (b) information held or processed by or on behalf of a Party, or measures related to such information, including measures related to its collection' (Art. 14.2.3). Although government-owned or controlled enterprises may be subject to the TPP,[53] this provision creates exclusions. It will for most purposes exclude the collection or processing of information by or on behalf of governments, reinforcing that the provisions only apply to 'trade by electronic means' and not all processing of information by electronic means. This means, for example, that legislation requiring local storage and processing of government information (e.g. health data held by governments) is exempt from the TPP. In such cases, there is no need to consider the restrictions in Arts. 14.11 and 14.13 (discussed below). Areas of uncertainty include whether state-owned enterprises (SEOs), regional and local governments etc. are included as 'Parties'.[54] The scope of any privacy protection required is further limited to only some private sector activities by Art. 14.8, discussed below.

3.3. VAGUE AND UNENFORCEABLE REQUIREMENTS FOR PERSONAL INFORMATION PROTECTION

Article 14.8 ('Personal Information Protection') is the only TPP provision requiring some positive protection of personal information, other than the

---

52 B. Kilic and T. Israel, 'The Highlights of the Trans-Pacific Partnership E-commerce Chapter', Public Citizen/CIPPIC, 5 November 2015 <http://www.citizen.org/documents/tpp-ecommerce-chapter-analysis.pdf>.

53 TPP Art. 1.3, definition of 'enterprise': 'enterprise means any entity constituted or organized under applicable law, whether or not for profit, and whether privately or governmentally owned or controlled, including any corporation, trust, partnership, sole proprietorship, joint venture, association, or similar organization.'

54 Thanks to Sanya Reid Smith for pointing out these issues.

direct marketing provision. For the purpose of 'enhancing consumer confidence in electronic commerce',[55] (but without any mention of protecting human rights) Art. 14.8.2 requires that 'each Party shall adopt or maintain a legal framework that provides for the protection of the personal information of the users of electronic commerce'. This legal framework need only apply to 'users of electronic commerce'. It need not apply to all private sector activities (even if commercial), nor to categories of private sector personal data such as employee information. Public sector personal data need not be included unless it comes within 'electronic commerce', and even then might fall outside Art. 14.2.2 discussed above. Because this article is so weak and unimportant (as explained below), the lack of definition of 'electronic commerce' does not matter much.

As to what type of 'legal framework' will suffice, a note to Art. 14.8.2 specifies that

> For greater certainty, a Party may comply with the obligation in this paragraph by adopting or maintaining measures such as a comprehensive privacy, personal information or personal data protection laws, sector-specific laws covering privacy, or laws that provide for the enforcement of voluntary undertakings by enterprises relating to privacy.

This last clause seems to be written with the USA's Federal Trade Commission in mind. Given that a 'legal framework' is required, mere self-regulation would not appear to be sufficient, which is an advance on the APEC Privacy Framework,[56] albeit a small one. However, since a 'measure' is defined to include 'any ... practice' (Art. 1.3), as well as laws, even this is not completely free from doubt.

Article 14.8.2 also requires that 'in the development of its legal framework for the protection of personal information, each Party should take into account principles and guidelines of relevant international bodies'. However, no specific international instruments are mentioned, and there is no list of principles included in the TPP. Nor are any specific enforcement measures mentioned. These absences make the 'legal framework' required by the article completely nebulous. These content provisions are even weaker than the APEC Privacy Framework,[57] which is ridiculous given that TPP parties are also APEC member economies, and that the APEC Framework standards are very low.

---

55 TPP Art. 14.8.1: 'The Parties recognise the economic and social benefits of protecting the personal information of users of electronic commerce and the contribution that this makes to enhancing consumer confidence in electronic commerce'.

56 G Greenleaf, *Asian Data Privacy Laws: Trade and Human Rights Perspectives*, OUP, Oxford 2014, p. 36.

57 G. Greenleaf, 'Five Years of the APEC Privacy Framework: Failure or Promise?' (2009) 25 *Computer Law & Security Report* 28–43.

Article 14.8.5 provides that

> Recognising that the Parties may take different legal approaches to protecting personal information, each Party should encourage the development of mechanisms to promote compatibility between these different regimes. These mechanisms may include the recognition of regulatory outcomes, whether accorded autonomously or by mutual arrangement, or broader international frameworks.

The APEC Cross-Border Privacy Rules Scheme (CBPRS) purports to be such a mechanism, but the 'autonomous' recognition of EU 'adequacy' status, or recognition under other 'white-list' approaches could also constitute such 'recognition of regulatory outcomes'. No standards for such 'interoperability' are provided, and this is likely to be, in effect, an anti-privacy provision which supports 'lowest common denominator' downward compatibility.

Article 14.8.3 requires that '[e]ach Party shall endeavour to adopt non-discriminatory practices in protecting users of electronic commerce from personal information protection violations occurring within its jurisdiction'. 'Non-discriminatory practices' are not defined, but would presumably include a requirement that data privacy laws should not limit their protection only to the citizens or residents of the country concerned, as was once the case with privacy laws in countries such as Australia, and is still proposed in India. In any event, the inclusion of 'shall endeavour' removes any force from this provision, as does 'shall encourage' in Art. 14.8.5.

The article also encourages countries to publicise how their legal frameworks operate.[58] Although increased transparency is valuable, this is probably another useless provision given that similar attempts via the APEC Privacy Framework have been largely ignored.[59]

All but two of the current parties to the TPP already have a 'legal framework' in force. Article 14.8 notes that 'Brunei Darussalam and Viet Nam are not required to apply this Article before the date on which that Party implements its legal framework that provides for the protection of personal data of the users of electronic commerce'. There is no such exemption from immediate application of the two restrictions discussed below. Brunei does not at present have a data

[58] Art. 14.8.4: 'Each Party should publish information on the personal information protections it provides to users of electronic commerce, including how: (a) individuals can pursue remedies; and (b) business can comply with any legal requirements.' The note to the Article also says that 'the Parties shall endeavour to exchange information on any such [compatibility] mechanisms applied in their jurisdictions and explore ways to extend these or other suitable arrangements to promote compatibility between them.'

[59] APEC, 'Data Privacy Individual Action Plan' <http://www.apec.org/Groups/Committee-on-Trade-and-Investment/Electronic-Commerce-Steering-Group/Data-Privacy-Individual-Action-Plan.aspx>. Only 14 of 21 APEC economies have lodged such plans, of which only three (Singapore, Hong Kong and Mexico) have been updated since 2011.

privacy law, only a self-regulatory scheme,[60] so it appears they intend to legislate. Vietnam already has extensive e-commerce legislation,[61] but this implies it intends to legislate further.

3.4. DIRECT MARKETING LIMITATIONS

Parties are required to take measures (which need not be laws) regarding unsolicited commercial electronic messages, to facilitate recipients preventing their ongoing receipt (opt-out), or requiring consent to receipt (opt-in), or otherwise providing for their minimisation. They must provide 'recourse' (which is not required for general privacy protection) against non-compliant suppliers, and shall endeavour to cooperate with other parties (Art. 14.14: Unsolicited Commercial Electronic Messages). Brunei has been given time to comply.

3.5. RESTRICTIONS ON DATA EXPORT LIMITATIONS

'Cross-Border Transfer of Information by Electronic Means' is addressed in Art. 14.11. This first recognises 'that each Party may have its own regulatory requirements concerning the transfer of information by electronic means' (Art. 14.11.1). It then requires that cross-border transfers of personal information be allowed when this activity is for the conduct of the business of a service supplier from one of the TPP parties.[62] It has been argued that 'it is likely this provision would be interpreted broadly by a dispute resolution body so as to include any and all elements of a service', and not restricted to outsourcing of internal services.[63]

Any exceptions from this obligation to allow personal data exports must be justified under Art. 14.11.3, which allows such a restrictive measure only if it satisfies four requirements: (i) it is 'to achieve a legitimate public policy objective'; (ii) it 'is not applied in a manner which would constitute a means of arbitrary or unjustifiable discrimination'; (iii) it is not applied so as to be 'a disguised restriction on trade'; and (iv) it 'does not impose restrictions on

60 G. Greenleaf, 'ASEAN data privacy developments 2014–15' (2015) 134 *Privacy Laws & Business International Report* 9–12.

61 Greenleaf, above n. 56, Ch. 13 'Vietnam and Indonesia: ASEAN's Sectoral Laws'; see also Greenleaf, above n. 60, for subsequent developments.

62 TPP, Art. 14.11.2: 'Each Party shall allow the cross-border transfer of information by electronic means, including personal information, when this activity is for the conduct of the business of a covered person'. See also Art. 14.1, definition of 'covered person'.

63 Kilic and Israel, above n. 52.

transfers of information greater than are required to achieve the objective.'[64] Kilic and Israel argue that, while these requirements all have some lineage in other FTAs, they are presented here in a much stronger form.[65] They point out that what are stated here as conditions (ii) and (iii) that the party imposing a restriction has the onus to prove, are in GATS only found in the chapeau (introductory text), without such an onus arising. The requirements to prove that the restriction is 'to achieve a legitimate public policy objective', and is being achieved in the least burdensome way, can each be interpreted in different and unpredictable ways, imposing a difficult burden to discharge. For example, the aim of obtaining a positive 'adequacy' assessment by the European Union could be argued to be a 'legitimate policy objective'. However, it is of concern that these requirements might create a 'regulatory chill',[66] particularly when coupled with ISDS provisions (as discussed below).

Alleged failure to meet any one of these requirements in this 'four-step test' could result in a country's data export restrictions facing dispute settlement proceedings. Aspects of this four-step test are typical of conditions to allow exceptions in trade agreements, and do not at first sight appear to be extreme restrictions on data exports or localisation (at least not compared with what might have been included). However, the TPP versions are even more difficult tests than their WTO predecessors, and start from the assumption that any such restrictions are illegitimate. The weaker WTO versions have been shown to have been successfully satisfied (for all steps) in only one of 44 challenges, and attempts to satisfy the 'least burdensome way' test (described as a necessity test by the WTO Secretariat) fail in 75 per cent of attempts.[67]

3.6. PROHIBITIONS ON DATA LOCALISATION

Post-Snowden, everyone knows, and the European Court of Justice has confirmed,[68] that personal data cannot be protected against US agencies

64 TPP Art. 14.11.3: 'Nothing in this Article shall prevent a Party from adopting or maintaining measures inconsistent with paragraph 2 to achieve a legitimate public policy objective, provided that the measure: (a) is not applied in a manner which would constitute a means of arbitrary or unjustifiable discrimination or a disguised restriction on trade; and (b) does not impose restrictions on transfers of information greater than are required to achieve the objective.'

65 Kilic and Israel, above n. 52.

66 L. Nottage and L. Trakman, 'As Asia embraces the Trans-Pacific Partnership, ISDS opposition fluctuates' *The Conversation* (Australia), 20 November 2015 <https://theconversation.com/as-asia-embraces-the-trans-pacific-partnership-isds-opposition-fluctuates-50979>.

67 Public Citizen, 'Only One of 44 Attempts to Use the GATT Article XX/GATS Article XIV "General Exception" Has Ever Succeeded: Replicating the WTO Exception Construct Will Not Provide for an Effective TPP General Exception', August 2015 <http://www.citizen.org/documents/general-exception.pdf>.

68 Case C-362/14, *Schrems v. Data Protection Commissioner* (CJEU, 6 October 2015).

once it is located on US servers. One response is for a country to require that some categories of data be stored and processed only on local servers ('data localisation').

The TPP deals with data localisation in much the same way as data export restrictions: a prima facie ban, subject to tough tests to overcome the ban. Its anti-data-localisation provisions are in Art. 14.13 ('Location of Computing Facilities'), which follows a similar approach to the data export provisions. First, formal acknowledgment is given to each Party's right to have its own 'regulatory requirements regarding the use of computing facilities, including requirements that seek to ensure the security and confidentiality of communications' (Art. 14.13.1). 'Computing facilities',[69] for this article, only include those 'for commercial use', but whether that means exclusively or only primarily for such use is unclear.

A TPP party is then prohibited from requiring a service supplier from one of the TPP parties (a 'covered person') 'to use or locate computing facilities in that Party's territory as a condition for conducting business in that territory' (Art. 14.13.2). In other words, data localisation is prima facie banned. Then, the same 'four-step test' of justification for any exceptions is applied as was the case for data export limitations.[70] It will similarly be very difficult to satisfy.

Data localisation requirements in the laws of various Asian countries will have to meet this four-step test, or breach TPP. These include the laws of Vietnam and (if they wish to join TPP) Indonesia and China.[71] Russia's sweeping data localisation requirements would have little chance of passing these tests, if it became a TPP party. While even some large US companies are offering services which purport to be 'local clouds' (but this might be ineffective in the face of US law), such market practices are not directly relevant here: legal localisation requirements by state parties are the target.

3.7. DISPUTE SETTLEMENT

State parties to the TPP can use the dispute settlement provisions of Chapter 28 to resolve disputes concerning interpretation or application of the TPP, and whenever they consider that another party's 'actual or proposed

69 TPP Art. 14.1 definition: '*computing facilities* means computer servers and storage devices for processing or storing information for commercial use.'

70 TPP Art. 14.13.3: 'Nothing in this Article shall prevent a Party from adopting or maintaining measures inconsistent with paragraph 2 to achieve a legitimate public policy objective, provided that the measure: (a) is not applied in a manner which would constitute a means of arbitrary or unjustifiable discrimination or a disguised restriction on trade; and (b) does not impose restrictions on the use or location of computing facilities greater than are required to achieve the objective.'

71 In its draft Cyber-security Law and health data guidelines.

measure' does not comply with its TPP obligations. If such disputes cannot be resolved by consultations between the parties, the complaining party can request establishment of a panel of three members to arbitrate the dispute (Arts. 28.7–28.9). Other state parties can request to attend and make submissions (Art. 28.13). The panel is to determine in a draft report whether the party's measures are inconsistent with the TPP, make recommendations, and give reasons (Art. 28.16). After the parties have time to comment, it makes a final report (Art. 28.17). If a party found to be in breach does not 'eliminate the non-conformity' in an agreed reasonable period of time, the other party may require negotiations for 'mutually acceptable compensation', failing which it may 'suspend benefits' under the TPP (i.e. institute trade counter-measures, such as raising tariffs) (Art. 28.19). Complex procedures follow, beyond the scope of this article, but they can result in a panel awarding monetary assessments against a party, in lieu of the suspension of TPP benefits. These Chapter 28 procedures between states will apply to any disputes concerning the Electronic Commerce provisions of Chapter 14.

3.8. THE SPECTRE OF ISDS

Potentially of greater importance are the procedures in relation to investment disputes under Chapter 9 ('Investment'), and the possibility of investor-state dispute settlement (ISDS) provisions being used. ISDS potentially applies whenever an investor from state party A makes an investment in the territory of state party B (Art. 9.1 definition: 'investor of a Party'). The essence of Chapter 9 is that a party must give investors from other parties 'National Treatment' (i.e. treatment no less favourable than it accords its own investors) and 'Most-Favoured-Nation Treatment' (i.e. treatment no less favourable than it accords investors of any other state). In addition, it must accord such investments 'fair and equitable treatment and full protection and security' (Art. 9.6.1). These provisions do not appear to pose problems for privacy protection.

The most significant investment protection relevant to data privacy is the prohibition of direct or indirect expropriation of investments,[72] except for a public purpose and for payment of fair and prompt compensation (Art. 9.7.1). Failure to compensate will lead to the threat of ISDS procedures.

There are some superficially appealing limits on the scope of Chapter 9. 'A determination that there has been a breach of another provision of this Agreement, or of a separate international agreement, does not establish that there has been a breach of this Article' (Art. 9.6.3). Therefore, a breach by a party of

72 TPP Art. 9.7.1: 'No Party shall expropriate or nationalise a covered investment either directly or indirectly through measures equivalent to expropriation or nationalisation (expropriation) …'.

the data export limitation or data localisation provisions will not automatically trigger entitlement to ISDS provisions by affected companies in, say, the USA.

However, what if the main benefit to a company in the USA in setting up e-commerce facilities in another country A was the transfer of personal data to the USA where data privacy laws posed far less interference in what could be done with the data than under the laws of country A? Could breaches of the data export limitation or data localisation provisions then constitute an indirect expropriation of the investment (allowing reliance on Art. 9.7.1)? The ISDS possibilities should frighten every country that has a data privacy law but has a smaller litigation budget than Google or Facebook.

This may not cause countries that already have data export restrictions to rush to water them down, but any party that is considering enacting new or stronger data privacy laws (including any data localisation) will have to give some very serious thought to the possibilities of actions, particularly ISDS actions. They may also need to draw breath before embarking on any strong enforcement of existing laws, for fear of an ISDS reaction.

Some scholars argue that concerns about ISDS are exaggerated, and that 'regulatory chill' is not borne out in at least one study,[73] but this is disputed in numerous studies recognising such effects.[74] Also, privacy protection usually has few friends in government, and regulatory chill can easily turn to pneumonia.

3.9. THE TPP AS AN ANTI-PRIVACY PRECEDENT

These TPP requirements seem to embody the type of binding international privacy treaty that the USA (in particular) wishes to achieve: (a) no substantive or meaningful requirements to protect privacy; (b) coupled with prohibitions on data export limitations or data localisation requirements that can only be overcome by a complex 'four-step test' of justification; and (c) backed up by the risk of enforcement proceedings between states or under ISDS provisions, both involving uncertain outcomes from dubious tribunals[75] and potentially very large damages claims. This approach is consistent with the 2013 revisions to the OECD Privacy Guidelines,[76] but with much sharper teeth.

For the USA, it would be a great bargain: no need to worry about how strong local privacy laws in other countries may be (that battle is largely lost anyway,

---

73 See Nottage and Trakman, above n. 66, for discussion.

74 See numerous studies cited by Reid Smith, above n. 8, section 'Chilling Effects; J. Hill, 'ISDS: The devil in the trade deal', *Background Briefing* (transcript), ABC Radio National, 14 September 2014 <http://www.abc.net.au/radionational/programs/backgroundbriefing/isds-the-devil-in-the-trade-deal/5734490>.

75 Hill, above n. 74.

76 Greenleaf, above n. 56, Ch. 19, section 3.1 'Revised OECD privacy Guidelines 2013'.

with 111 countries already having data privacy laws), because it will now be more difficult to prevent most personal data from being exported to the USA, where such laws do not significantly impede commercial use, and where state surveillance also has wide reign. Perhaps there are TPP signatories other than the USA aiming to be net personal data importers, or who explicitly do not care about which overseas countries their own citizens' personal data is exported to, but they are difficult to identify.

For all the other states whose personal data will be 'hoovered up' and transferred to the USA, it is more likely to be a Faustian bargain: put at risk the protection of the privacy of your citizens (except at home)[77] in return for the golden chalice of trade liberalisation.

Treaties are always bargains. International privacy agreements since the 1980 OECD Guidelines and the 1981 Council of Europe Convention 108 have always sought free flow of personal data (with trade benefits) in return for a required international minimum standard of privacy protection, either as non-binding commitments, or as obligations under international law. In comparison, TPP may mean no enforceable requirements of privacy protection, but enforceable free flow of personal data (with potentially substantial penalties), and a one-way flow at that. For privacy, it is a poor bargain. The main problem with the TPP is that human rights such as privacy protection should not be bargaining chips in trade agreements, where their inclusion requires that states decide what their protection is worth compared with greater access to trade in bananas.

The strength of this argument depends on the extent to which the two four-step tests (satisfaction of which will now be required to justify data export restrictions or data localisation requirements), coupled with the prospect of ISDS actions, will have the consequences of regulatory chill and regulatory roll-back that I predict and fear. There can be reasonable arguments that they will not, and some privacy experts are not overly concerned. But should this risk be taken?

The TPP is the first multilateral trade agreement with detailed provisions relating to privacy protection that go beyond the GATS provisions. If the TPP is defeated in the US Congress (or abandoned by a new President), this will be a net gain for privacy protection, whatever one thinks about the other potential economic advantages of the TPP. The TPP's privacy-related provisions reflect US interests to a considerable extent (and those of some other countries, as noted in the introduction). It remains to be seen whether future multilateral trade agreements will contain similar provisions. We will now turn to examine how much we know about the likely treatment of privacy in future FTAs.

77 It does not matter (to the USA) if a country has strong data privacy protection within its borders (i.e. 'at home'), if the personal data in question can be exported to countries with lesser protection.

4. FTAs IN PROGRESS: THE VEIL OF SECRECY, LIFTED IN PART

It may be years before we know whether the TPP will 'fall over' and never come into effect – or perhaps it will be known soon after the US Presidential election. Irrespective, free trade agreements are proliferating, and overlapping in confusing ways. Although details of their content are only known intermittently, because of the secrecy in which negotiations are usually cloaked, there are a few exceptions due to both leaks and a rare policy of openness. Speculation is possible on whether they might follow or go further than the TPP in their treatment of privacy issues, or might allow privacy to be treated as a right to be protected. Where the USA is a party, we can assume that its negotiating position will be at least as strong as the TPP result, and there is no reason to assume this will change with the election of a new US President. FTA negotiations are most likely to produce a result concerning privacy different from that obtained in the TPP if they involve other parties with sufficient economic strength (and negotiating ability) to withstand US demands. This might be provided by the European Union, or perhaps by some combinations of China, India and Russia.

There are a very large number and variety of multilateral FTAs concerning services (and therefore relevant to data privacy) which are currently being negotiated, mainly at the regional level, but effectively global in the case of TISA. One admittedly incomplete list has 24 proposed multilateral agreements.[78] Since the possible texts of almost all of these agreements are unknown, it would be pointless to attempt to discuss most of them here. The FTAs discussed here are: (i) the broadest agreement (TISA), known partly through leaks; (ii) two FTAs concerning the EU, for which the EU's negotiating position is known; (iii) an alternative or perhaps complement to the TPP (RCEP), important for that

[78] Wikipedia, List of multilateral free trade agreements – Proposed agreements <https://en.wikipedia.org/wiki/List_of_multilateral_free_trade_agreements>: Commonwealth of Independent States Free Trade Agreement (CISFTA); Union of South American Nations (USAN); 2021 Pacific Island Countries Trade Agreement (PICTA); African Free Trade Zone (AFTZ) between SADC, EAC and COMESA; Arab Maghreb Union (UMA); Asia-Pacific Economic Cooperation (APEC); Association of Caribbean States (ACS); Bolivarian Alternative for the Americas (ALBA); Bay of Bengal Initiative for MultiSectoral Technical and Economic Cooperation (BIMSTEC); Community of Sahel-Saharan States (CEN-SAD); Economic Community of West African States (ECOWAS); Euro-Mediterranean free trade area (EU-MEFTA); Economic Community of Central African States (ECCAS); Free Trade Area of the Americas (FTAA); Free Trade Area of the Asia Pacific (FTAAP); GUAM Organization for Democracy and Economic Development (GUAM); Intergovernmental Authority on Development (IGAD); Pacific Agreement on Closer Economic Relations (PACER and PACER Plus); People's Trade Treaty of Bolivarian Alternative for the Americas (ALBA); Regional Comprehensive Economic Partnership (RCEP) (ASEAN plus 6); Shanghai Cooperation Organisation (SCO); Transatlantic Free Trade Area (TAFTA); Tripartite Free Trade Area (T-FTA); China–Japan–South Korea Free Trade Agreement.

reason; and (iv) an Australasia-Pacific agreement with uncertain implications. It is beyond the scope of this chapter to consider the wider range of potential agreements in Latin America, Africa and elsewhere.

4.1. TRADE IN SERVICES AGREEMENT (TISA) – POTENTIALLY THE BROADEST FTA

One-third of WTO members (50 countries, accounting for 68.2 per cent of world trade in services) are now involved in the Trade in Services Agreement (TISA) negotiations, which could not be included in the Doha round. The main proponents are the USA and the EU, but Australia is among the leading countries. Negotiations started in 2013.

A draft of the Financial Services Annex of TISA dated 14 April 2014 was released by Wikileaks in June 2014,[79] stating that TISA 'would allow uninhibited exchange of personal and financial data'. Another tranche of leaked TISA documents was released by Wikileaks in May 2016.[80] The only clause included in the 2014 leaked documents which had significant implications for privacy was Art. X.11, for which the US proposal was:

> Each Party shall allow a financial service supplier of another Party to transfer information in electronic or other form, into and out of its territory, for data processing where such processing is required in the financial service supplier's ordinary course of business.

This blunt 'shall allow' (anything required in the ordinary course of business), with no exceptions stated, would prevent any party from restricting any flows of personal data that could possibly be of value in commerce – in other words, all personal data. The *Sydney Morning Herald* stated: 'The changes could see Australians' bank accounts and financial data freely transferred overseas.'

The EU proposal, however, stated:

> No Party shall take measures that prevent transfers of information or the processing of financial information, including transfers of data by electronic means, into and out of its territory, for data processing or that, subject to importation rules consistent with international agreements, prevent transfers of equipment, where such transfers of information, processing of financial information or transfers of equipment are necessary for the conduct of the ordinary business of a financial service supplier. *Nothing in this*

---

79 (Draft) Trade in Services Agreement (TISA) Financial Services Annex, 14 April 2014 <https://wikileaks.org/tisa-financial/>.

80 Wikileaks, 'Trade in Services Agreement – Press release', 25 May 2016 <https://wikileaks.org/tisa/press.html>.

> *paragraph restricts the right of a Party to protect personal data, personal privacy and the confidentiality of individual records and accounts so long as such right is not used to circumvent the provisions of this Agreement.*[81]

The final sentence (italicised) is diametrically opposed to the US position. The reference to non-circumvention probably keeps the EU position consistent with GATS.

The 2016 leaked draft of 'Annex [X]: Financial Services'[82] is dated 25 September 2015. In it, the EU (supported by other countries) maintains the above position. The USA's position is modified to include recognition that parties have the right to maintain measures to protect personal data, 'provided that such measures are not used as a means of avoiding a Party's obligations under the provisions of this Article'. The possible differences between 'circumvent' and 'this Agreement' (EU position) and 'avoid' and 'this Article' (US position) makes it difficult to determine whether the US shifted its position between 2014 and 2015. The 2016 leaked TISA 'Annex on Electronic Commerce'[83] is of a 2013 documents and shows numerous countries seeking to protect regulation of cross-border personal information flows, but is perhaps now too old to be very informative.

Kelsey and Kulic also obtained and analysed the US Government's proposal put forward in the April 2014 negotiations.[84] It was even more anti-privacy than the draft text emerging from April 2014. They interpret the US position as including (i) banning any restrictions on data transfers (X.4), including those allowed by GATS (as is the case in the leaked draft); (ii) banning any 'local presence' requirements (X.1); and (iii) banning all data localisation requirements (X.4). The exceptions provisions (X.7) do not include exceptions for privacy protection.

The leaked TISA draft from April 2014 includes only item (i) of these three aims, whereas the TPP agreement includes both (i) and (iii), but both with exceptions provisions (albeit ones very difficult to satisfy). The TPP therefore seems to be the high water mark of US negotiating success concerning privacy as yet, but not the limit of its negotiating ambitions. However, the USA is not a party to every multilateral FTA being negotiated at present.

---

81 From the Wikileaks leaked 2014 draft.

82 Wikileaks leaked draft of TISA 'Annex [X]: Financial Services', 25 September 2015 <https://wikileaks.org/tisa/document/20150925_Annex-on-Financial-Services/20150925_Annex-on-Financial-Services.pdf>.

83 Wikileaks, TISA, 'Annex on Electronic Commerce', September 2013 <https://wikileaks.org/tisa/document/20151001_Annex-on-Electronic-Commerce/20151001_Annex-on-Electronic-Commerce.pdf>.

84 Prof Jane Kelsey (University of Auckland) and Dr Burcu Kilic (Public Citizen, Washington), 'Briefing on US TISA Proposal on E-Commerce, Technology Transfer, Cross-border Data Flows and Net Neutrality', 17 December 2014 <http://www.world-psi.org/en/briefing-us-tisa-proposal-e-commerce-technology-transfer-cross-border-data-flows-and-net-neutrality>.

4.2. FTAs INVOLVING THE EU – UNUSUAL OPENNESS AND PRIVACY CONSTRAINTS

There are two unusual aspects to the future negotiating position of the EU concerning data protection in any of the many FTAs negotiations in which the EU may be involved.[85]

First, the EU has a policy which requires an unusual amount of openness in its FTA negotiations, at many different points in the negotiating process.[86] Although the Commission's position is that '[t]he negotiations and their texts are not themselves public', in some cases at least the 'negotiating position' of the EU, based on the 'negotiating mandate' given to the Commission by the Council, is made public. Following disquiet with previously secret negotiations, particularly those concerning the failed Anti-Counterfeiting Trade Agreement (ACTA), complaints were made to the EU Ombudsman in relation to secrecy concerning the EU negotiating position in the Transatlantic Trade and Investment Partnership (TTIP) negotiations, eventually resulting in an adverse decision by the Ombudsman.[87] Meanwhile, the European Commission decided, from January 2015, to publish the texts of its negotiating position in the TTIP negotiations, the first time it had done so.[88] The history of how this reform arose is told in detail elsewhere.[89]

The second unusual aspect of the EU's position, in relation to FTA clauses affecting data protection, is that the EU's negotiating scope is constrained. Although the final decisions on treaties are made by the Member States of the EU and the European Parliament, the European Commission can negotiate potential terms. However, it can only do so within the parameters of, and according to the procedures of, Art. 25 of the EU Data Protection Directive, as interpreted by the European Court of Justice in *Schrems*. The Council of the EU confirmed in

---

85 See the European Commission 'Trade' page <http://ec.europa.eu/trade/policy/countries-and-regions/agreements/>, and the map 'The State of EU Trade' at <http://trade.ec.europa.eu/doclib/docs/2012/june/tradoc_149622.png>.

86 European Commission, *Factsheet – Transparency in EU Trade Negotiations*, undated <http://trade.ec.europa.eu/doclib/docs/2013/june/tradoc_151381.pdf>; see also 'Ensuring transparency in TTIP negotiations' <http://ec.europa.eu/trade/policy/in-focus/ttip/documents-and-events/index_en.htm#transparency>.

87 Decision of the European Ombudsman closing the inquiry into complaint 119/2015/PHP on the European Commission's handling of a request for public access to documents related to TTIP <http://www.ombudsman.europa.eu/en/cases/decision.faces/en/61261/html.bookmark>.

88 J. Crisp, 'TTIP papers published as EU Ombudsman demands more transparency', *Euractiv*, 8 January 2015 <http://www.euractiv.com/section/trade-society/news/ttip-papers-published-as-eu-ombudsman-demands-more-transparency/>.

89 See the preceding chapter in this volume, 'From ACTA to TTIP: Lessons Learned on Democratic Process and Balancing of Rights'.

December 2015 that the Commission cannot negotiate away privacy rights in trade agreements:

> The Council stresses the need to create a global level playing field in the area of digital trade and strongly supports the Commission's intention to pursue this goal *in full compliance with and without prejudice to the EU's data protection and data privacy rules, which are not negotiated in or affected by trade agreements.*[90]

4.2.1. *Transatlantic Trade and Investment Partnership (TTIP) – the EU/USA FTA*

The EU is negotiating what it describes as 'a trade and investment deal with the US', the Transatlantic Trade and Investment Partnership (TTIP).[91] Unlike most other FTAs, the EU's position in the negotiations is disclosed publicly,[92] as discussed above. The EU's negotiation position in relation to Trade in Services, Investment and E-commerce, published in July 2015[93] includes in Chapter V ('Regulatory Framework'), Art. 33 'Data processing', which is limited in its scope to the supply of financial services. These provisions are of little assistance to privacy protection. Article 33(2) requires 'appropriate safeguards for the protection of privacy … in particular with regard to the transfer of personal data', but does not even require legislation to protect privacy, let alone set any standard.[94] Article 33(1), on the other hand, is an unrestricted requirement to allow transfer of personal data necessary for financial services supply,[95] and any privacy protections must come from the exceptions provisions.

The significant provision for protection of data privacy laws is Art. 7-1 'General exceptions',[96] which attempts to exempt measures for 'the protection

---

90 Council of the European Union, 3430th Council meeting Outcome of the Council Meeting Brussels, 27 November 2015 <http://www.consilium.europa.eu/en/meetings/fac/2015/11/st14688_en15_pdf/> (emphasis added).

91 European Commission's TTIP pages <http://ec.europa.eu/trade/policy/in-focus/ttip/documents-and-events/index_en.htm>.

92 See <http://ec.europa.eu/trade/policy/in-focus/ttip/documents-and-events/index_en.htm#eu-position>.

93 The European Union's proposal for services, investment and e-commerce text, tabled 31 July 2015 <http://trade.ec.europa.eu/doclib/docs/2015/july/tradoc_153669.pdf>.

94 '2. Each Party shall adopt appropriate safeguards for the protection of privacy and fundamental rights, and freedom of individuals, in particular with regard to the transfer of personal data.'

95 '1. Each Party shall permit a financial service supplier of the other Party to transfer information in electronic or other form, into and out of its territory, for data processing where such processing is necessary in the ordinary course of business of such financial service supplier.'

96 Article 7-1 provides: '1. Subject to the requirement that such measures are not applied in a manner which would constitute a means of arbitrary or unjustifiable discrimination

of the privacy of individuals in relation to the processing and dissemination of personal data and the protection of confidentiality of individual records and accounts'. This exception is subject to three similar qualifications to those found in GATS, namely that the measures must be 'necessary to secure compliance' with the legislated privacy protections, and two requirements in the chapeau to Art. 7-1, that they must not constitute 'arbitrary or unjustifiable discrimination between countries where like conditions prevail' and must not be 'a disguised restriction on establishment of enterprises, the operation of investments or cross-border supply of services'.

Of course, this is only the EU negotiating position (apparently unaltered as at April 2016),[97] not the final result. However, the EU already has some track record in refusing to negotiate away privacy rights in FTAs, having declined in 2013 to grant what India called 'data secure status' (i.e. recognition of completely inadequate laws as being adequate) as part of a proposed EU–India FTA.[98] That FTA has not yet been completed.[99]

Depending on what the EU negotiates, this may have even more direct benefits for some other countries because of 'side letters' to the TPP. For example, such a 'side letter' between Australia and the USA provides that 'Should the Government of the United States of America undertake any relevant additional commitments to those in the TPP Agreement with respect to the treatment of personal information of foreign nationals in another free trade agreement, it shall extend any such commitments to Australia.'[100] According to Michael Geist, Canada did not obtain such a TPP concession from the USA.[101] The TPP and other multilateral FTAs do not create 'level playing fields' for trade: they are

between countries where like conditions prevail, or a disguised restriction on establishment of enterprises, the operation of investments or cross-border supply of services, nothing in Chapter II Section 1, Chapter III, Chapter IV, Chapter V and Chapter VI shall be construed to prevent the adoption or enforcement by any Party of measures:

(a) necessary to protect public security or public morals or to maintain public order;
(b) necessary to protect human, animal or plant life or health;
...
(e) necessary to secure compliance with laws or regulations which are not inconsistent with the provisions of this Title including those relating to:
 ...
 (ii) the protection of the privacy of individuals in relation to the processing and dissemination of personal data and the protection of confidentiality of individual records and accounts.'

97 European Commission, *The Transatlantic Trade and Investment Partnership (TTIP) - State of Play*, 27 April 2016 <http://trade.ec.europa.eu/doclib/docs/2016/april/tradoc_154477.pdf>; the report does not mention any changes in relation to personal information.

98 Greenleaf, above n. 56, pp. 432–433.

99 EU–India <http://ec.europa.eu/trade/policy/countries-and-regions/countries/india/>.

100 US–Australia side letter, undated <https://ustr.gov/sites/default/files/TPP-Final-Text-US-AU-Letter-Exchange-on-Privacy.pdf>.

101 Michael Geist, 'The Trouble with the TPP, Day 14: No U.S. Assurances for Canada on Privacy', michaelgeist.ca Blog, 21 January 2016 <http://www.michaelgeist.ca/2016/01/the-trouble-with-the-tpp-day-14-no-u-s-assurances-for-canada-on-privacy/>.

more like minefields, depending on a country's 'on the side' bargaining position with other countries.

4.2.2. EU–Canada Comprehensive Economic and Trade Agreement (CETA)

Not all EU FTAs explicitly include GATS-like provisions concerning personal data. CETA[102] is one of the most recently completed EU FTAs, for which the negotiations were completed in 2014, but the agreement still needs to be approved by the EU Council and the European Parliament. The trade negotiating mandate was made public in December 2015,[103] rather belatedly, but indicating that transparency is now becoming EU practice. Canada's data protection laws have received a positive 'adequacy assessment' under Art. 25 of the EU data protection Directive, thus allowing (but not requiring) personal data exports from EU countries to Canada. CETA only mentions obligations concerning personal data in two places. First, Chapter 16 on Electronic Commerce includes a very generally phrased obligation to maintain laws or administrative measures 'for the protection of personal information of users engaged in electronic commerce', taking into account the data protection standards of international organisations 'of which both Parties are a member'.[104] That would seem to refer to the UN, the OECD and the WTO (including the GATS provisions), and might refer to Council of Europe Convention 108 if Canada decided to accede to it. Provisions in Chapter 13 'Financial Services' similarly requires each party to 'adequate safeguards to protect privacy' and states that transfers of personal information must be in accordance with the legislation of the country where the transfer originates, so transfers originating from Canada must comply with Canadian law,[105] and those from EU countries with EU law. The EU therefore seems to be negotiating two quite different approaches to privacy in FTAs with two adjoining countries.

---

102 EU's CETA webpage <http://ec.europa.eu/trade/policy/in-focus/ceta/>; CETA text at <http://trade.ec.europa.eu/doclib/docs/2014/september/tradoc_152806.pdf>.

103 EU Commission, 'EU-Canada trade negotiating mandate made public', 15 December 2015 <http://www.consilium.europa.eu/en/press/press-releases/2015/12/15-eu-canada-trade-negotiating-mandate-made-public/>.

104 CETA Art. 16.4, Trust and confidence in electronic commerce: 'Each Party should adopt or maintain laws, regulations or administrative measures for the protection of personal information of users engaged in electronic commerce and, when doing so, shall take into due consideration international standards of data protection of relevant international organisations of which both Parties are a member.'

105 CETA Art. 13.15, Transfer and processing of information: 'Each Party shall maintain adequate safeguards to protect privacy, in particular with regard to the transfer of personal information. If the transfer of financial information involves personal information, such transfers should be in accordance with the legislation governing the protection of personal information of the territory of the Party where the transfer has originated.'

4.3. REGIONAL COMPREHENSIVE ECONOMIC PARTNERSHIP (RCEP) – A TPP ALTERNATIVE OR COMPLEMENT

If the TPP falls over, China is advocating an alternative, the Regional Comprehensive Economic Partnership (RCEP). It can also be regarded as complementary to TPP, if it survives.[106] RCEP is an ASEAN-centred FTA, intended to comprise the ten countries of ASEAN (Association of Southeast Asian Nations) plus the six others with which ASEAN already has FTAs (China, India, Japan, South Korea, Australia and New Zealand) – but not the USA, Canada, nor any of the Latin American countries in the TPP. Negotiations started in 2012, on the overall structure ('modality'), but in 2015 becoming more concrete about market access in particular 'disciplines'. The leaders of the countries concerned had agreed on an end-2015 deadline, but this was too ambitious.[107]

Will ASEAN, China and India offer a better trade deal than the TTP, so far as privacy is concerned? No one knows, because it is still the subject of secret negotiations. No content details are yet known, either officially or via leaks. The 'Guiding Principles and Objectives for Negotiating' RCEP state that 'RCEP will be consistent with the WTO', but do not explicitly refer to personal information or to GATS Art. XIV(c)(ii).

4.4. PACIFIC AGREEMENT ON CLOSER ECONOMIC RELATIONS (PACER) PLUS – A PRIVACY OPPORTUNITY?

PACER Plus includes most Pacific Island countries and Papua New Guinea plus New Zealand and Australia. It originated in the Pacific Islands Forum in 2011, with negotiations starting in 2012. Australia states that its objective is to foster greater regional integration, stability and economic growth and to assist Australian business interests, and it expects trade-in-services benefits, and investment benefits. However, it does not have an emphasis on e-commerce or financial services, so the data protection implications may be limited. Services account for 65 per cent of all economic activity in Pacific Island countries.[108] No drafts are available, and whether it covers data protection issues is unknown.

No Pacific Island countries (nor Papua New Guinea) have data privacy legislation,[109] but Australia and New Zealand do have such laws. Although this is

---

106 A. Morimoto, 'Should America Fear China's Alternative to the TPP?' *The Diplomat*, 17 March 2016 <http://thediplomat.com/2016/03/should-america-fear-chinas-alternative-to-the-tpp/>.

107 Notes – Australia Department of Foreign Affairs and Trade, *Trade in Services Negotiations briefing* 11 March 2015, Sydney.

108 Ibid.

109 Vanuatu has provision for rules to be made in its e-commerce law.

speculative, if there are provisions in PACER Plus concerning e-commerce and financial services, these could include provisions encouraging the development of personal information protection (where there is none at present), offset against what can be expected to be prohibitions on data export limitations or data localisation. Whether such prohibitions are excessive or reasonable, some version of them would be unsurprising.

5. CONCLUSIONS: FUTURE FTAs, THE FOG OF TRADE AND NATIONAL PRIVACY LAWS – FAUSTIAN BARGAINS?

Free trade agreements have not yet had a major effect on the development or implementation of national data privacy laws, and have to a large extent been ignored by privacy and data protection scholars. Reasons for this include that the GATS provisions remain untested and unused for over 20 years, and that the likely content of privacy-related provisions in the myriad of FTAs currently under negotiation is usually shrouded in secrecy – the 'fog of trade'. The uncertainty surrounding the TPP's future make its provisions of hypothetical significance, although now known. All in all, there has not been much to write about. From the admittedly incomplete survey of a selection of the post-TPP FTAs currently in progress, what can be learned is unfortunately limited, because only those FTAs involving the EU have some degree of transparency.

One of the main purposes of this chapter is to demonstrate, despite these multiple uncertainties, that the significance of FTA provisions in the international data protection landscape could change rapidly, and data protection scholars need to pay them much more attention. The untested Art. XIV(c)(ii) of the GATS is, and is likely to remain, the global base-line for the relationship between free trade and data privacy, because of the number of countries that are parties to it, but its meaning is uncertain. A challenge to a data protection law in the WTO could quickly give it more substance. If agreements such as the TPP, which impose even stronger limits on data privacy laws than GATS, start coming into force, that will also change the global base-line.

The best-case scenario for data privacy is that the EU holds to the GATS position in the TTIP negotiations (and in its other FTA negotiations), that the TPP falls over, and that data privacy laws are not successfully challenged at the WTO (continuing the position of the last 20 years). Other agreements such as RCEP may than take the same approach, and either explicitly stick to the GATS position, or say nothing and do so by implication.

The worst-case scenario for data privacy is that the TPP comes into force quickly, that other TPAs (possibly including RCEP) emulate it since so many of their parties are also TPP parties, and that challenges to privacy laws start to emerge from the WTO or under these stronger agreements.

One way or another, FTAs are likely to be one of the defining factors in the future evolution of data privacy laws, both at the national level, and in the development of international agreements such as Council of Europe Convention 108, or even the EU's General Data Protection Regulation (GDPR), which cannot simply be assumed to be immune to GATS.

However, despite the immovable reality of GATS Art. XIV(c)(ii), for anyone interested in advancing data privacy as a value, and as a human right, the broader question that should still be asked – as discussed earlier in this chapter – is whether data privacy provisions have any proper place in any future FTAs. Dr Faust agreed with Mephistopheles to sell his soul for both earthly pleasures and unlimited knowledge. In most versions, eternal damnation awaits. In the context of FTA negotiations, countries faced with both the worldly temptations of trade liberalisation and the more ethereal promises that they too will benefit from the unlimited free flow of personal information, can easily be led to conclude that the benefits outweigh the hypothetical risks to their citizens privacy. If countries should not barter human rights for bananas, and should not be tempted to do so, then what is already in GATS would seem to be a sufficient disincentive against potential trade barrier abuses of data protection laws. NGOs and other parties with interests in data privacy and human rights should aim to keep such provisions out of future FTAs.

INVITED COMMENT

9. NINE TAKEAWAYS ON TRADE AND TECHNOLOGY

Marietje SCHAAKE*

Cross-border trade, (digital) rights and the use and regulation of new technologies increasingly overlap, but discussions about these topics remain fragmented. Trade negotiators, civil society organisations, legislators and tech experts try to address the opportunities of the digital economy, Internet governance, the protection of digital rights in various fora – without necessarily having a clear overview of who is doing what.

Some actors have raised concerns about the potential dangers of trade agreements, such as the cementing of outdated copyright rules or the circumvention of privacy standards. Others have focused on opportunities to safeguard and strengthen the open Internet, for instance by banning unjustified forced data-localisation or prohibiting online censorship.

Below are my initial takeaways on trade and technology. I invite you to share your input about what can work and what does not work, where trade rules can help advance the open Internet, and where we should be careful not to overregulate.

1. NO OLD-SCHOOL TRADE – VIEWS TO ADDRESS THE DIGITAL ECONOMY OF THE FUTURE

The Internet has fundamentally changed the way companies do business and reach consumers globally. Some business models are purely data-driven, or focus only on the provision of digital goods and services. Other companies – in

* Member of the European Parliament, Alliance of Liberals and Democrats for Europe (ALDE). E-mail: marietje.schaake@europarl.europa.eu. This contribution was originally published on my blog at <https://marietjeschaake.eu/nine-takeaways-on-trade-and-technology> accessed 23.05.2016.

sectors ranging from design to legal services – have digitised their services, and used the Internet to profoundly change their business models or value chains. Small and medium-sized enterprises are now able to easier find and reach new customers and markets. The potential of digitisation processes is clear and goes far beyond only a digital economy.

For the European Union (EU), this increasing digitisation of more traditional aspects of our services economy provides great opportunities. Services make up around 70 per cent of the EU's GDP, and they are more often being delivered digitally. Close to a third of the growth of the overall industrial output in Europe is now a result of the uptake of digital technologies. The expectation is that the importance of the digital economy will continue to grow, as more of the world's population gains access to the Internet, and new technologies such as the Internet of Things become more widespread.

These changes to how companies do business are having a profound impact on the global trading system, and raise new questions. Many of the global trading rules were not made for the digital twenty-first century, but for trade in goods, focusing on tariffs and manufacturing standards for example. The question of how we shape the rules for digital trade is becoming ever more relevant as technological advance continues.

Trade agreements can play a crucial role in constructing a global, rules-based framework for digital trade. However, we must avoid using an old-school vision that focuses only on 'removing trade barriers', if we are to solve challenges posed by this new economic reality. In this new reality, consumer protection and digital rights such as free speech and access to information, as well as questions of cyber security, cryptography and copyright, play an equally important role. The current process of creating a Digital Single Market for Europe (DSM) will address many of these principles. Furthermore, the Digital Single Market seeks to end the fragmentation between 28 different legal systems. While some have too easily dismissed European proposals as protectionist, they should instead make rules- and principles-based trade in the digital economy run smoothly.

2. TRADE NEGOTIATIONS CAN LEARN FROM INTERNET GOVERNANCE

Precisely because trade and online rights are so intertwined, it is important to discuss digital trade measures with all relevant stakeholders. The future of the open Internet cannot be decided behind closed doors. At the same time it is clear that we cannot have television cameras rolling inside trade negotiation rooms. Trade negotiators need to have some space to be able to make proposals and counterproposals and to be able to set out a strategy. However, demystification of negotiations would go a long way towards taking away suspicion and perceived threats.

Some elements of the 'multi-stakeholder' model can serve as a source of inspiration. Trade negotiators should brief all relevant stakeholders, including digital rights groups, before and after negotiation rounds. Their views on proposed texts and drafts of trade agreements will be helpful for trade negotiators and beneficial for EU citizens.

Under pressure from the European Parliament, liberal Trade Commissioner Malmström began a transparency initiative for the Transatlantic Trade and Investment Partnership (TTIP) negotiations, putting more texts than ever before online. This initiative should be broadened to other agreements under negotiation, and the EU should try to convince its negotiating partners to do the same. The public should be able to see both EU proposals and counter proposals. The alternative is growing suspicion of the process of negotiations.

3. DON'T PANIC! PROPOSALS IN NEGOTIATIONS ARE NOT FINAL TEXTS

There have been a number of leaks of proposals in negotiations which have caused turmoil, such as the leaking of the American proposal on e-commerce in the Trade in Services Agreement (TiSA). While this proposal from the US was clearly not in line with what the EU would be aiming for in such an agreement, there is no reason to panic just yet. Proposals are in no way final texts or final agreements. And it cannot be a surprise that a country tables an aggressive proposal which contains its goals.

By looking at finalised texts, such as that of the Trans-Pacific Partnership (TPP), we can see negotiated outcomes. Even so, the TPP will not necessarily provide the answer to what TTIP or TiSA (or any other agreement) would look like. Each agreement should be assessed on its own.

4. DATA FLOWS HAVE A LEGITIMATE PLACE IN 21ST-CENTURY TRADE AGREEMENTS, BUT THIS DOES NOT MEAN OUR PRIVACY WILL BE DESTROYED

Some see trade agreements in general as a threat to human rights, labour rights, the environment and the social system of the EU. Some digital rights organisations in particular are concerned about the inclusion of data flows in trade agreements, and the negative impact this may have on the right to privacy and data protection.

Data-driven economies require the free flow of data, but this does not mean the EU will use trade negotiations to lower data protection standards. It is clear that the European Commission has no mandate to negotiate about data protection within TTIP, nor has it any intention to do so. The Americans know this too. Trade negotiations are not the arena to negotiate about fundamental EU law.

European data protection law protects the personal data of European citizens, even when they are transferred to a third country. If your business model requires you to process European personal data, than you have to make sure data is protected in the same way as they would be protected in Europe. This is not a protectionist measure but a fundamental rights issue.

That being said, it is clear that there is a legitimate place for data flows in a twenty-first century agreement. Some types of forced data localisation only serve a protectionist agenda, and trade agreements can be useful to break down these unnecessary barriers. Similarly, as the digital economy continues to grow, the percentage of non-personal data that is generated will continue to grow with it. Open data, research data, anonymous data and other non-personal data that are generated as a by-product by machines/sensors must be able to be freely processed, transferred and aggregated to develop a truly data-driven economy.

5. TRADE AGREEMENTS CAN IMPROVE DIGITAL RIGHTS

It must be clear that trade agreements are not a zero-sum game between economic interests on one side and digital rights on the other. As the EU, we need to use trade agreements to try to improve and strengthen digital rights elsewhere, just as we do with other values such as respect for the environment, labour rights, animal welfare and human rights. Removing forced data localisation requirements can be beneficial for freedom of speech. Clear provisions that specify which traffic management practices are always prohibited could enforce net neutrality and the open Internet. Trade agreements can also improve privacy and security by allowing the unrestricted import, use and sale in commercial markets of products with cryptographic capabilities.

6. STRENGTHENING DIGITAL TRADE IS NOT JUST A QUESTION OF DATA FLOWS

When we talk about digital trade, many people automatically think of Google, Facebook and Amazon and the flow of (personal) data. However, there is much more to it. Digital trade and the digital economy are dependent on the physical trade in high-tech products that give consumers access to the Internet and digital services. The expansion of the Information Technology Agreement under the World Trade Organization (WTO), which was signed earlier this year, removes tariffs on over 200 high-tech products, from GPS devices to medical products and gaming consoles. This is good for trade in those products and should make them more widely available.

Most trade agreements also contain a telecoms chapter, which regulates the access that foreign providers actually have to the telecoms market and network in another country. Access is crucial in order to be able to do business.

7. THE POSSIBILITY OF SETTING INFORMATION AND COMMUNICATIONS TECHNOLOGIES STANDARDS IN TRADE AGREEMENTS SHOULD BE EXPLORED

As the Internet of Things increasingly becomes a reality, it will be crucial to ensure interoperability, security and to avoid fragmentation or the creation of separate architectures. To make sure that products are user-friendly and to reap the full economic benefits, we must avoid a scenario like the format wars of the 1970s and 1980s, where VHS and Betamax formats battled for market dominance. Setting common standards within the European Digital Single Market and furthering them through international trade agreements must be explored to avoid this kind of scenario.

With the exponential growth of the Internet of Things, clarity on data protection as well as security will be key. Before the market will be filled with unsafe, communicating machines, minimum standards must be agreed. In a globally connected ecosystem online, these should be global standards.

8. DISCUSSIONS AT BILATERAL AND MULTILATERAL LEVELS ARE MOVING, MORE SHOULD BE DONE AT THE WTO

In February 2016, the Trans-Pacific Partnership was signed. Although not yet ratified, it has already created a new mould for the way that digital chapters of trade agreements can be modelled. The negotiations on the Trade in Services Agreement and Transatlantic Trade and Investment Partnership are also progressing and the outcome of these talks will also provide updates for future e-commerce chapters.

However, while these bilateral and plurilateral agreements are progressing, there is hardly any movement at the World Trade Organisation level, even though there is a working group on e-commerce. In the end, the goal must be to strengthen the multilateral trading system and reach agreements at the WTO. In the post-Nairobi framework, the EU should make a push to move towards more concrete discussions on digital trade at the WTO. The work that the EU is doing at the bilateral and plurilateral level should provide a model for that.

9. LESSONS FROM ACTA ARE STILL RELEVANT

In the past, attempts to strictly enforce intellectual property rights through a trade agreement failed. The European Parliament voted down the proposed Anti-Counterfeiting Trade Agreement (ACTA) out of concern for the impact on digital rights and access to medicines.

Copyright and patent reforms should not be hindered as a result of trade agreements. The difference in purchasing power of consumers in developing economies must be considered, and a better balance between public and commercial interests must be found. Particularly in the digital economy, copyright protection risks stifling innovation, and enforcement can endanger people's freedoms.

SECTION III

PRIVACY AND TERRITORIAL APPLICATION OF THE LAW

10. EXTRATERRITORIALITY IN THE AGE OF THE EQUIPMENT-BASED SOCIETY

Do We Need the 'Use of Equipment' as a Factor for the Territorial Applicability of the EU Data Protection Regime?

Michał CZERNIAWSKI*

1. INTRODUCTION

There is a constant flow of information, including personal data, between the European Union and its largest trading partner – the United States.[1] The EU–US cooperation, including in the digital trade area, may soon be further strengthened if the Transatlantic Trade and Investment Partnership (TTIP) negotiations are successfully concluded.[2] As American privacy standards – and in general the American way of thinking about privacy and personal data protection[3] – differ from the approach adopted by the EU, it is crucial for US companies to be able to assess whether particular processing operations they conduct fall within the scope of the EU data protection legal regime. The territorial scope of the EU

* Vrije Universiteit Brussel (VUB) – Research Group on Law, Science, Technology & Society (LSTS), Brussels, Belgium. E-mail: michal.czerniawski@vub.ac.be.

1 EUROPEAN COMMISSION, DG TRADE, 'Client and Supplier Countries of the EU28 in Merchandise Trade', <http://trade.ec.europa.eu/doclib/docs/2006/september/tradoc_122530.pdf>, accessed 20.05.2016.

2 However, one should bear in mind that the issues of 'data flows' and 'data protection' are currently not included in TTIP. See the Sustainability Impact Assessment prepared by Ecorys for the European Commission in May 2016: 'Trade SIA on the Transatlantic Trade and Investment Partnership (TTIP) between the EU and the USA', Draft Interim Technical Report, p. 167, <http://www.trade-sia.com/ttip/wp-content/uploads/sites/6/2014/02/TSIA-TTIP-draft-Interim-Technical-Report.pdf>, accessed 20.05.2016.

3 In the US there is no law which would set a general privacy protection standard. However, some American sectoral regulations provide for stricter data protection rules than the EU data protection regime. A good example here might be the Health Insurance Portability and Accountability Act of 1996 (HIPAA; Pub.L. 104–191, 110 Stat. 1936, enacted 21 August 1996), which regulates processing of personal data for health insurance in the US.

data protection law, together with rules on transfers of personal data, constitute one of the most important elements of the EU data protection regime from the trans-Atlantic perspective.

EU–US exchange of information should be seen in the context of a bigger picture, which is the development of the information society and a global digital market. General access to the Internet, breakthroughs in processing, storage and transmission of information technologies as well as the constant fall in costs of IT equipment – all these have allowed the application of technology in almost all areas of our day-to-day life.[4] Advocate General Jääskinen is right when he compares the development of the Web to the invention of printing in the fifteenth century.[5] Both printing and the Internet irretrievably changed the way information is shared. Both allowed for processing of information on a scale never seen before. In the information society, processing of data constitutes an inseparable part of our life. Connected devices such as smartphones, connected cars, wearables and smart TVs are being used on day-to-day basis as means to not only provide certain services but also to obtain information about their users.

However, globalisation of technology has not been followed by globalisation of legal standards. For example, the European data protection standards, set – in particular – in legal acts such as the Council of Europe's Convention 108[6] and the EU Directive 95/46/EC[7] (the Directive, Data Protection Directive) date from the 1980s and 1990s, the age of telefaxes and land-line phone services.[8] They were drafted in times that can today be considered as technological prehistory. The information society, which introduced solutions that were unknown 20 or 30 years ago, makes it more and more difficult to apply current European data protection laws, both by data protection authorities and courts of law. Therefore,

---

4 When referring to the Data Protection Directive, Advocate General Jääskinen stressed that '[i]n 1995, generalised access to the internet was a new phenomenon. Today, after almost two decades, the amount of digitalised content available online has exploded. It can be easily accessed, consulted and disseminated through social media, as well as downloaded to various devices, such as tablet computers, smartphones and laptop computers. However, it is clear that the development of the internet into a comprehensive global stock of information which is universally accessible and searchable was not foreseen by the Community legislator', Opinion of Advocate General Jääskinen delivered on 25 June 2013, Case C-131/12, *Google Spain SL, Google Inc. v. Agencia Española de Protección de Datos (AEPD), Mario Costeja González*, 27.

5 Ibid., 28.

6 Council of Europe's Convention 108 for the Protection of Individuals with regard to Automatic Processing of Personal Data, 28 January 1981.

7 Directive (EC) 95/46 of the European Parliament and of the Council of 24 October 1995 on the protection of individuals with regard to the processing of personal data and on the free movement of such data [1995] OJ L 281/31–50.

8 There are also other relevant documents, such as OECD Guidelines Governing the Protection of Privacy and Transborder Flows of Personal Data, adopted on 23 September 1980.

it is no surprise that in recent years the number of data protection cases before the Court of Justice of the European Union (CJEU) is constantly increasing.

The General Data Protection Regulation[9] (General Regulation, GDPR) may address some of the data protection related problems created by the development of technology. As of 25 May 2018 the General Regulation will be directly applicable in all the EU Member States, providing for a higher level of harmonisation of EU Member States law. It will also allow EU Members States to deal at least with some of the challenges to the personal data protection created with the development of technology. One of the most important is the changes made by the EU co-legislators with respect to the territorial scope of the EU data protection regime, which go in the direction of so-called destination approach[10] (explained below). Their aim is to ensure the protection of EU data subjects' rights when their data is processed by controllers and processors whose establishment is not within EU territory. Simultaneously, by creation of the one-stop-shop mechanism and the European Data Protection Board (EDPB),[11] the General Regulation is expected to put an end to jurisdictional disputes between European national data protection authorities.[12]

The EU data protection regime is the most influential and one of the strictest data privacy laws in the world.[13] Therefore, expanding of its territorial scope may have far reaching consequences, as it *de facto* entails imposing additional

---

9 Regulation (EU) 2016/679 of the European Parliament and of the Council of 27 April 2016 on the protection of natural persons with regard to the processing of personal data and on the free movement of such data, and repealing Directive 95/46/EC (General Data Protection Regulation) [2016] OJ L 119/1–88.

10 U. Kohl, 'Jurisidiction in Cyberspace' in N. Tsagourias and R. Buchan (eds), *Research Handbook on International Law and Cyberspace*, Edward Elgar Publishing, Cheltenham 2015, pp. 35ff.

11 A body established under GDPR, able to issue opinions binding for national data protection authorities, which will replace the Article 29 Working Party.

12 National data protection authorities seems to have more and more problems with harmonised application of the EU data protection law. Cases such as C-230/14 *Weltimmo* and C-210/16 *Wirtschaftsakademie Schleswig-Holstein* show that EU data protection authorities do not necessarily have the same approach towards data protection issues. In particular, the latter case confirms existence of such dissonance: the Data Protection Authority of Schleswig-Holstein wishing to take investigative and enforcement actions in factual circumstances where it is the Irish authority that has jurisdiction over a data controller. One of the most recent examples illustrating this problem is a Belgian case regarding Facebook tracking Internet users who do not use this social network. The case was dismissed by the Brussels Court of Appeal on 29 June 2016. The Court of Appeal concluded that Belgian courts do not have jurisdiction over Facebook Ireland, which is the controller for Belgian users of Facebook, and Facebook Inc., the US-based parent company.

13 See among others, D.J.B. Svantesson, *Extraterritoriality in Data Privacy Law*, Ex Tuto Publishing, Copenhagen 2013, pp. 21 and 89; L.A. Bygrave, 'Privacy and Data Protection in an International Perspective' (2010) 56 *Scandinavian Studies in Law* 183; M. Taylor, 'The EU's human rights obligations in relation to its data protection laws with extraterritorial effect' (2015) 5 *International Data Privacy Law* 246.

obligations on foreign companies, including American ones. In fact, the EU co-legislators had no other choice – in the age of globalisation of data processing operations only extraterritoriality can ensure effective protection of data subjects' rights. In the GDPR, the co-legislators decided to modify the current basis for extraterritorial application of the EU data protection law. The aim of this chapter is to compare Art. 4(1)(c) of the Directive with the relevant provision of the General Data Protection Regulation – i.e. Art. 3(2). Any provision expanding territorial scope of law beyond any given territory should provide clarity as to the scope and should be based on a real connection between processing operations and the applicable law. In this chapter I argue that the information society is at the same time an 'equipment-based' society, which may result in almost universal application of Art. 4(1)(c) of the Data Protection Directive. In this light, its successor – Art. 3(2) of the General Regulation – seems to be a moderate solution, providing for more legal certainty than Art. 4(1)(c) currently does and raising less concerns as regards possible enforcement. However, its practical application needs to be carefully monitored and all relevant stakeholders, in particular the EDPB, should provide clear guidance on how this provision should be interpreted and where its boundaries lie.

2. TERRITORIAL SCOPE OF THE DATA PROTECTION DIRECTIVE

In the age of general access to the Internet and the existence of a global digital market the territorial scope of law is a very complex issue.[14] This however was not the case in the 1990s, when the Data Protection Directive was drafted. Kuner[15] and Moerel[16] both point out that the aim of Art. 4 of the Data Protection Directive was in principle to regulate data flows within the EU and

14 E.g. conflicts of jurisdiction, issues of legitimacy or enforcement are inseparably linked with extraterritoriality. See, among others: N. Thorhauer, 'Conflicts of Jurisdiction in Crossborder Criminal Cases in the Area of Freedom, Security, and Justice. Risks and Opportunities from an Individual Rights-Oriented Perspective' (2015) 6 *New Journal of European Criminal Law* 78–101; P. de Hert and M. Czerniawski, 'Expanding the European data protection scope beyond territory: Art. 3 of the General Data Protection Regulation in its wider context' (2016) 6 *International Data Privacy Law* 230–243.

15 '[T]he intent of the drafters was not to provide a comprehensive jurisdictional and choice of law framework for data processing anywhere in the world, but first to ensure that data flows function properly within the EU, and second to prevent the possibility of evading EU rules through the relocation of data processing to third countries': Ch. Kuner, *European Data Protection Law: Corporate Compliance and Regulation*, Oxford University Press, Oxford 2007, p. 111.

16 L. Moerel, 'The Long Arm of EU Data Protection Law: Does the Data Protection Directive Apply to Processing of Personal Data of EU Citizens by Websites Worldwide?' (2011) 1 *International Data Privacy Law* 33.

to prevent the possibility of EU rules being evaded through the relocation of data processing outside of the Union. It seems justified to say that the drafters of the Directive worked in a different technological reality and perhaps lacked the broader, global perspective on the territorial scope of law which we have today. They did introduce in the Data Protection Directive provisions allowing for its extraterritorial application. However, its Art. 4 is considered 'arguably the most controversial, misunderstood and mysterious of the Directive's provisions'.[17] The processing of personal data carried out in the context of the activities of an establishment of the data controller on the territory of a Member State (Art. 4(1)(a) of the Directive) is considered the primary and most commonly applied factor giving rise to the territorial applicability of the EU Member State's national data protection legislation, adopted pursuant to the Directive.

Further, the Directive based its territorial scope also on another important, often omitted, ground that is the 'use of equipment' in the EU. According to Art. 4(1)(c) of the Directive, each Member State shall apply the national provisions it adopts pursuant to the Directive to the processing of personal data where 'the controller is not established on Community territory and, for purposes of processing personal data makes use of equipment, automated or otherwise, situated on the territory of the said Member State, unless such equipment is used only for purposes of transit through the territory of the Community'.[18]

There is finally a third factor – Art. 4(1)(b), which allows for the Directive to be applied to the processing of personal data by a controller not established in the Member State's territory, but in a place where its national law applies by virtue of international public law, e.g. to ships, airplanes or embassies and other diplomatic missions.[19] This basis, due to the very limited scope, has a relatively small significance in practice.

---

17 L.A. Bygrave, *Data Privacy Law: An International Perspective*, Oxford University Press, Oxford 2014, p. 199.

18 Art. 4(1) states that:
'1. Each Member State shall apply the national provisions it adopts pursuant to this Directive to the processing of personal data where:
(a) the processing is carried out in the context of the activities of an establishment of the controller on the territory of the Member State; when the same controller is established on the territory of several Member States, he must take the necessary measures to ensure that each of these establishments complies with the obligations laid down by the national law applicable;
(b) the controller is not established on the Member State's territory, but in a place where its national law applies by virtue of international public law;
(c) the controller is not established on Community territory and, for purposes of processing personal data makes use of equipment, automated or otherwise, situated on the territory of the said Member State, unless such equipment is used only for purposes of transit through the territory of the Community.'

19 D.J.B. Svantesson, above n. 13, pp. 98–99.

The 'establishment' criterion, laid down in Art. 4(1)(a), is assessed on the basis of a two-step test:[20] does the controller have an establishment in an EU Member State (first step), and does a particular processing operation take place in the context of such an establishment's activities (second step). According to Recital 19 of the Data Protection Directive, which provides an additional explanation for the interpretation of this provision, 'establishment on the territory of a Member State implies the effective and real exercise of activity through stable arrangements and that the legal form of such an establishment, whether simply branch or a subsidiary with a legal personality, is not the determining factor in this respect'.

However, the 'establishment' criterion in the EU data protection law is not defined and thus subjected to multiple analysis, rendering some controversies. Several papers have been published dealing with the territorial scope of the Data Protection Directive and the notion of 'establishment', the most recent being written in the aftermath of the CJEU verdict in Case C-131/12 *Google Spain*.[21] For the purposes of this analysis it is enough to point out that Art. 4(1)(a), interpreted in the light of C-131/12 *Google Spain*, allows for application of the Directive even when there is a very loose nexus between a particular processing operation and the EU territory. The broad interpretation of the term 'establishment' was subsequently supported by the CJEU in Case C-230/14 *Weltimmo*: 'the concept of "establishment", within the meaning of Directive 95/46, extends to any real and effective activity – even a minimal one – exercised through stable arrangements'.[22] It was further confirmed in Case C-191/15 *Verein für Konsumenteninformation*: 'the fact that the undertaking responsible for the data processing does not have a branch or subsidiary in a Member State does not preclude it from having an establishment there within the meaning of

---

20 Opinion of Advocate General Pedro Cruz Villalón delivered on 25 June 2015 in Case C-230/14, *Weltimmo s.r.o. v. Nemzeti Adatvédelmi és Információszabadság Hatóság*, 26.

21 See among others H. Hijmans, 'Right to have Links Removed: Evidence of Effective Data Protection' (2014) 21 *Maastricht Journal of European and Comparative Law* 555–561; H. Kranenborg, 'Google and the Right to be Forgotten' (2015) 1 *European Data Protection Law Review* 70–79; B. Van Alsenoy and M. Koekkoek, 'The Territorial Reach of the EU's "Right To Be Forgotten": Think Locally, but Act Globally?', <http://www.ejiltalk.org/the-territorialreach-of-the-eus-right-to-be-forgotten-think-locally-but-act-globally/>, accessed 20.05.2016; B. Van Alsenoy and M. Koekkoek, 'Internet and Jurisdiction after Google Spain: the Extraterritorial Reach of the Right to be Delisted' (2015) 5 *International Data Privacy Law* 105–120. There is at least one important issue the Court could have addressed but did not in the *Google Spain* ruling – whether EU data protection law might be applied globally, or just within the European Union's territory. The latter could create parallel digital realities for EU and non-EU countries, see: D.J.B. Svantesson, *The Google Spain case: Part of a harmful trend of jurisdictional overreach*, EUI Working Papers, RSCAS 2015/45 Robert Schuman Centre for Advanced Studies, Florence School of Regulation, European University Institute 2015, p. 7.

22 Case C-230/14, *Weltimmo*, 31.

Article 4(1)(a) of Directive 95/46'.[23] As the General Regulation, in general, repeats the jurisdiction nexus known from Art. 4(1)(a) of the Directive,[24] the understanding of the term 'establishment' as presented by the three above-mentioned cases will remain valid also after the General Regulation becomes effective.

During the past 20 years, Art. 4(1)(c) received much less attention than the concept of 'establishment'. It is based on the somewhat ambiguous 'use of equipment' criterion. The first part of this criterion is not problematic – 'making use' consists of two elements: activity of the controller and the clear intention to process personal data.[25] However, the 'equipment' part is much more complex. Recital 20 of the Directive includes a direct reference to the term 'means'[26] instead of 'equipment', thereby creating confusion within the text of the Directive. The Cambridge Dictionary defines 'equipment' as 'the set of necessary tools, clothing, etc. for a particular purpose'.[27] The Merriam-Webster dictionary explains this term as 'the set of articles or physical resources serving to equip a person or thing'.[28] Therefore, it seems reasonable to conclude that the term 'equipment' should be understood as describing physical objects. Simultaneously, it seems that the technologically neutral term 'equipment', which was introduced to the EU data protection law before expansion of the Internet, was initially aimed to cover a relatively narrow number of physical objects, such as computer servers, terminals or questionnaires.[29] Moerel, when speaking about Art. 4(1)(c) of the Directive, seems to be right when stating: '[i]t is clear that the drafters of the Directive had the physical location of physical objects on EU territory in mind.'[30] This view is also supported by the Directive's Explanatory Memorandum.[31] Such a restrictive interpretation of the term

23 Case C-191/15, *Verein für Konsumenteninformation v. Amazon EU Sàrl*, 76.

24 Art. 3(1) GDPR states that '[t]his Regulation applies to the processing of personal data in the context of the activities of an establishment of a controller or a processor in the Union, regardless of whether the processing takes place in the Union or not'.

25 Article 29 Working Party, Opinion 8/2010 on applicable law, adopted on 16 December 2010, WP 179, p. 29.

26 According to Recital 20 of Data Protection Directive: 'the fact that the processing of data is carried out by a person established in a third country must not stand in the way of the protection of individuals provided for in this Directive ... in these cases, the processing should be governed by the law of the Member State in which the means used are located, and there should be guarantees to ensure that the rights and obligations provided for in this Directive are respected in practice'.

27 Cambridge Dictionaries Online, <http://dictionary.cambridge.org/dictionary/english/equipment>, accessed 20.05.2016.

28 Merriam-Webster, <http://www.merriam-webster.com/dictionary/equipment>, accessed 20.05.2016.

29 Ch. Kuner, 'Data Protection Law and International Jurisdiction on the Internet (Part 2)' (2010) 3 *International Journal of Law and Information Technology* 229.

30 L. Moerel, above n. 16, p. 36.

31 Explanatory Memorandum to the Amended Proposal of the Commission (COM)(92)0422, p. 14 (after: L. Moerel, above n. 16, p. 36).

'equipment' was, however, not shared by the Article 29 Working Party. Several years ago the Working Party supported the reading of 'equipment' as 'means'. One of the arguments in favour of such an interpretation is the fact that the word 'equipment' is used only in the English, Italian, and Swedish language versions of the Directive. The remaining language versions use the term 'means'.[32] However, in national laws implementing the Directive, the use of the term 'equipment' is much more common, as it was applied among others by Danish, Greek, Maltese, Portuguese and Finnish legislators.[33] Thus, in some cases, although certain language versions of the Directive use the term 'means', its national implementation includes a reference to 'equipment'. One of the most interesting is the case of Poland. The Polish Act on the Protection of Personal Data, in a provision implementing Art. 4(1)(c), refers to 'processing of personal data by technical *means* located in the territory of the Republic of Poland'.[34] It includes a direct referral to 'technical means', which is definitely not in line with the broad understanding of the term 'equipment' as adopted by the Working Party. The lack of consistency not only in translation, but also in the implementation of the Directive, intensifies the confusion around Art. 4(1)(c).

According to the Cambridge Dictionary, 'means' shall be understood as 'a method or way of doing something'.[35] Oxford dictionaries define 'means' as '[a]n action or system by which a result is achieved; a method'.[36] Merriam-Webster provides a definition similar in its spirit: 'something that helps a person to get what he or she wants'.[37] Therefore, it should be clearly apparent that there is a significant difference between the meanings of the term 'means' and the term 'equipment'. Beyond any doubt, the term 'means', not being limited to physical objects, has a broader scope than the word 'equipment'.

---

32 Swire noticed that: 'rather than mentioning "makes use of equipment," the French text would apply national law wherever the controller has recourse "à des moyens" ("to any means") situated on the territory of the member state. The German and Italian versions may be more similar to the French than the English version' (footnotes omitted); see: P. Swire, 'Of Elephants, Mice, and Privacy: International Choice of Law and the Internet' (1998) 32 (4) *The International Lawyer* 1009. See also L. Moerel, above n. 16, p. 33.

33 See European Commission, DG JUST, Status of implementation of Directive 95/46 on the Protection of Individuals with regard to the Processing of Personal Data, <http://ec.europa.eu/justice/data-protection/law/status-implementation/index_en.htm>, accessed 20.05.2016.

34 Art. 3 para. 2 point 2 of the Act of 29 August 1997 on the Protection of Personal Data (emphasis added) (original text – *Journal of Laws* of 1997, No. 133, item 883) (unified text – *Journal of Laws* of 2015, item 2135, with amendments). English translation issued by the Polish Inspector General for Personal Data Protection, <http://www.giodo.gov.pl/144/id_art/171/j/en/>, accessed 20.05.2016.

35 Cambridge Dictionaries Online, <http://dictionary.cambridge.org/dictionary/english/means>, accessed 20.05.2016.

36 Oxford Dictionaries, <http://www.oxforddictionaries.com/definition/english/means>, accessed 20.05.2016.

37 Merriam-Webster, <http://www.merriam-webster.com/dictionary/means>, accessed 20.05.2016.

Besides the opinion of the Working Party, there is however a lack of further guidance on the meaning of Art. 4(1)(c). To a certain extent the lack of guidance may be justified by the supplementary character of this provision,[38] in particular in the context of the broad understanding of the term 'establishment' as adopted by the CJEU. As possible examples of 'equipment', the Working Party indicated not only physical objects, but also tools ranging from cookies, JavaScript banners, to cloud computing.[39] A broad understanding of the term 'equipment', as supported by the Article 29 Working Party, significantly extends the territorial scope of the EU data protection law, therefore claiming its helpfulness for the protection of the EU data subjects' rights in the digital world.[40] The Working Party is correct in stating that

> This provision is especially relevant in the light of the development of new technologies and in particular of the internet, which facilitate the collection and processing of personal data at a distance and irrespective of any physical presence of the controller in EU/EEA territory.[41]

It is also true that

> The objective of this provision in Article 4 paragraph 1 lit. c) of Directive 95/46/EC is that an individual should not be without protection as regards processing taking place within his country, solely because the controller is not established on Community territory.[42]

However, some of the claims made by the Working Party, such as qualifying human beings as 'equipment' can be seen as controversial.[43] Only the CJEU could

---

38 See Article 29 Working Party, Opinion 8/2010 on applicable law, adopted on 16 December 2010, WP 179, p. 20: 'Working Party considers that Article 4(1)c should apply in those cases where there is no establishment in the EU/EEA which would trigger the application of Article 4(1)a or where the processing is not carried out in the context of the activities of such an establishment' and Ch. Kuner, 'The European Union and the Search for an International Data Protection Framework' (2014) 2(1) *Groningen Journal of International Law* 64. This view was also confirmed by the CJEU in Case C-131/12 *Google Spain*, 61.

39 Article 29 Working Party, Opinion 8/2010 on applicable law (WP 179, 16 December 2010, pp. 21–22.

40 The Court of Justice noted that 'it is clear in particular from Recitals 18 to 20 in the preamble to Directive 95/46 and Article 4 thereof that the European Union legislature sought to prevent individuals from being deprived of the protection guaranteed by the directive and that protection from being circumvented, by prescribing a particularly broad territorial scope'. See: Case C-131/12, *Google Spain*, 54.

41 Article 29 Data Protection Working Party, Opinion 8/2010 on applicable law, adopted on 16 December 2010, WP 179, p. 19.

42 Article 29 Data Protection Working Party, Working document on determining the international application of EU data protection law to personal data processing on the Internet by non-EU based web sites, adopted on 30 May 2002, WP 56, p. 7.

43 Article 29 Data Protection Working Party: 'the Working Party understands the word "equipment" as "means". It also notes that according to the Directive this could be "automated

conduct the 'verification' of the Working Party's position. In the past, national courts asked the CJEU about 'use of equipment' only twice. The most recent (and the most interesting – as it concerned a human intermediary) request for a preliminary ruling by a national court that dealt with this issue was made in Case C-192/15, *Rease et Wullems*,[44] which was subsequently withdrawn by the referring court and removed from the Court's register in 2015.[45]

The second request regarding 'use of equipment' was made in Case C-131/12 *Google Spain*, where the Audiencia Nacional, the referring court, asked the CJEU the following questions:

> Must Article 4(1)(c) of Directive 95/46 be interpreted as meaning that there is 'use of equipment ... situated on the territory of the said Member State':
> - when a search engine uses crawlers or robots to locate and index information contained in web pages located on servers in that Member State, or
> - when it uses a domain name pertaining to a Member State and arranges for searches and the results thereof to be based on the language of that Member State?[46]

and

> Is it possible to regard as a use of equipment, in the terms of Article 4(1)(c) of Directive 95/46, the temporary storage of the information indexed by internet search engines? If the answer to that question is affirmative, can it be considered that that connecting factor is present when the undertaking refuses to disclose the place where it stores those indexes, invoking reasons of competition?'[47]

Both questions remained unanswered, as the CJEU found that Google Inc. has an establishment on the EU territory and this fact makes the applicability of 'use of equipment' condition as laid down in Art. 4(1)(c) of the Directive irrelevant.[48] Both questions however provide good examples of how broadly the term 'equipment' could be understood. The Spanish court in its request for a preliminary ruling explicitly mentioned crawlers, robots, domain

or otherwise". This leads to a broad interpretation of the criterion, which thus includes human and/or technical intermediaries, such as in surveys or inquiries' See Article 29 Working Party, Opinion 1/2008 on data protection issues related to search engines', adopted on 4 April 2010, WP 148, p. 11.

44 Request for a preliminary ruling from the Raad van Staat (Netherlands) lodged on 24 April 2015 – *T.D. Rease, P. Wullems; other party: College bescherming persoonsgegevens* (Case C-192/15). The referring court was asking whether a detective agency based in the EU receiving commission from a data controller from outside the EU can be considered as an equipment for the processing of personal data on the territory of a Member State and fall within the scope of makes 'use of equipment' for the purposes of Art. 4(1)(c) of the Directive.

45 Ordonnance du President de la Cour, 9 décembre 2015, ECLI:EU:C:2015:861.

46 Case C-131/12, *Google Spain SL, Google Inc. v. Agencia Española de Protección de Datos (AEPD), Mario Costeja González*, 20.

47 Ibid., 20.

48 Ibid., 61.

name, temporary storage of the information,[49] thus means that are used on a day-to-day basis by basically any company operating online, no matter whether located in the EU or in a third country.

As the General Data Protection Regulation does not include any reference to 'use of equipment' criterion and – as of the time of writing – there is no pending case dealing with this issue before the Court, there are no chances that such an analysis would ever be performed by the CJEU.

Of course it is true that currently the notion of 'equipment' goes beyond computer servers, terminals or questionnaires. Today we can add to this list various kinds of electronic devices, such as smartphones, connected cars, wearables, smart TVs or mobile applications. For example, in Poland, the Supreme Administrative Court has thus far issued only one verdict dealing with the issue of 'equipment' (understood as 'technical means' – see above), confirming that cars with cameras used in Poland by Google Inc. for the purposes of the Google Street View project[50] shall be considered as 'equipment'. It further decided that Google Inc., a US-based company, when processing data collected by the cars should be considered as a data controller and fall within the scope of the Polish data protection law.[51] However, this was a rather straightforward case, as it dealt with physical objects. The qualification of digital tools – such as cookies or JavaScript – and, in particular, human intermediaries as 'equipment', seems to be more problematic.

3. ROLE OF 'EQUIPMENT' CRITERION IN PRACTICE

It is justified to say that the information society and the digital market rely on various kinds of equipment, used for processing of information. Therefore, the information society can be seen also as the 'equipment-based' society. Many manufacturers and providers of the most popular electronic devices and mobile applications, including *inter alia* American, Japanese or Indian companies, do not have an establishment in the EU. At the same time, they are processing

---

[49] I believe that by 'temporal storage of information' the Spanish court thought about caching as defined in Art. 13 of the Directive 2000/31/EC of the European Parliament and of the Council of 8 June 2000 on certain legal aspects of information society services, in particular electronic commerce, in the Internal Market ('Directive on electronic commerce'), [2000] OJ L 178/1–16.

[50] As described by the Electronic Frontier Foundation, 'Google's Street View feature allows users to see photographs of specific addresses on a Google map. To generate these pictures, Google deployed a fleet of cars with cameras mounted on top of their roofs to drive across the world and take pictures of everything it could', <https://www.eff.org/deeplinks/2013/09/what-google-street-view-decision-means-researchers-and-cops>, accessed 20.05.2016.

[51] Verdict of the Supreme Administrative Court no I OSK 2445/12. This one seems to be the only ruling in Poland regarding the notion of 'equipment' during almost 20 years of the Polish data protection law being in force.

millions of records regarding EU data subjects, including their sensitive personal data. Leaving them outside of the territorial scope of the EU data protection law could negatively affect EU data subjects' rights. Thus, one may think that in the twenty-first century the role of the 'use of equipment' criterion as a nexus used to establish the EU jurisdiction over data protection operations conducted by a third country's data controllers is constantly increasing. This is however not the case.

The main basis for the EU jurisdiction – the 'establishment' criterion – was subject to an analysis by the CJEU, which provided useful clarifications as to how it should be applied. Although the Directive has been in force for almost 20 years, this did not take place in the case of Art. 4(1)(c). Of course, one may assume that since the Court supported a broad understanding of the term 'establishment', it would apply a similar rationale when analysing the 'use of equipment' basis. However, such a conclusion would be premature, as in the case of Art. 4(1)(c) 'the EU had cast its net too wide'[52] and in my opinion some limitations with respect to its scope would be justified.

In the world of interconnected devices we live in, where 'use of equipment' within the meaning of Art. 4(1)(c) is essential for almost all data processing operations, Art. 4(1)(c) if interpreted in a broad manner, could be considered as a picklock allowing for application of the EU data protection rules to virtually anyone operating online. For example, for the 'use of equipment' criterion to be applicable, it is sufficient if an EU data subject installs software offered by a data controller on his/her mobile phone or visits a data controller's website.[53] Theoretically, it allows European data protection authorities to initiate proceedings against any non-EU data controller who provides devices used for processing of personal data (such as wearables, smart phones, PCs, laptops) as well as software installed on the devices to EU data subjects or uses cookies or JavaScript banners on websites visited by Europeans. The Working Party underlined that 'it is not necessary for the controller to exercise ownership or full control over such equipment for the processing to fall within the scope of the Directive'.[54] Article 4(1)(c) of the Directive, if applied in all such factual circumstances, would result in a jurisdiction which lacks a solid nexus with the European Union. Specifically, it would lack links between particular data processing operations and the EU territory. If, for example, an EU data subject visits a Chinese website when surfing online and gets its cookies (considered by the Working Party as 'equipment') stored on his personal computer, how strong is the link between this processing operation and the European Union? I would argue it is rather weak. To use another example, if a JavaScript banner, which is

52 J. Scott, 'The New EU "extraterritoriality"' (2014) 51 *Common Market Law Review* 1350.

53 Which results in storage of a cookie file on his/her computer.

54 Article 29 Working Party, Opinion 8/2010 on applicable law, adopted on 16 December 2010, WP 179, p. 20.

a technology commonly used on websites all around the world, is displayed on a EU data subject PC's monitor, what is such a link? In the twenty-first century, the 'use of equipment', both physical and digital, as understood by the Article 29 Working Party, covers common and routine activities of organisations and individuals in the Internet. Therefore, such an approach brings the risk of jurisdictional overreach. What is interesting, the Article 29 Working Party, is aware of this problem:

> a broad interpretation of the notion of 'equipment' – justified by its expression by 'means' in other EU languages – may in some cases result in European data protection law being applicable where the processing in question has no real connection with the EU/EEA.[55]

However it seems that the Working Party accepts such a risk, considering it a necessary side-effect of having a high level of data protection online. Although the goal pursued by the Working Party is fair, some questions arise. Broad extraterritoriality, which lacks real connection with the EU, may constitute an example for other countries to follow. This may result in conflicts of jurisdiction and new obligations on data controllers and processors arising from different legal regimes. Also, there remains an open question whether national data protection authorities in Europe can handle the scale of processing of personal data online on the basis of 'use of equipment' that involves information about Europeans.

In particular, such a broad territorial scope may lead to situations where Art. 4(1)(c), if applied by any of the European national data protection authorities, would be impossible to enforce. As pointed out by Kuner, 'jurisdiction under EU law against a data controller without assets in the EU but that was using cookies on its website to process the data of Europeans should be of little concern to the controller, since there is no realistic chance of enforcement against it'.[56] Definitely, low chances of enforcement do not encourage foreign data controllers to obey EU data protection law. The issue of probable unenforceability brings into question the whole idea lying at the foundation of the broad understanding of the 'use of equipment' criterion.

Article 4 of the Directive is one of the provisions very significantly affected by technological progress.[57] However, this cannot be seen as justification of its weaknesses. Any provision allowing for extraterritorial application of law must

55 Ibid., p. 29.

56 Ch. Kuner, above n. 29, p. 235.

57 For example Svantesson identified seven important characteristics of ICT which cause significant changes to the handling of personal information: (i) large data collections; (ii) interconnectivity between networks; (iii) the border-disregarding nature; (iv) the ease of data distribution; (v) the difficulty of data deletion; (vi) the ease of data searches; and (vii) the security difficulties. See: D.J.B. Svantesson, above n. 13, p. 46.

be formulated in a reasonable way and provide a high level of legal certainty. Of course, the problem described in this chapter was not foreseen by the drafters of the Data Protection Directive. Nevertheless, technological progress in this case led to the situation in which the 'use of equipment' basis can be potentially applied in a much broader way than initially intended. In this context, it is difficult not to agree with Advocate General Jääskinen:

> The potential scope of application of the Directive in the modern world has become ... surprisingly wide ... In fact, anyone today reading a newspaper on a tablet computer or following social media on a smartphone appears to be engaged in processing of personal data with automatic means, and could potentially fall within the scope of application of the Directive to the extent this takes place outside his purely private capacity.[58]

This problems seems to be the reason why Art. 4(1)(c) is very seldom used as a basis for application of the EU data protection law by European data protection authorities. Except for a few cases, the broad understanding of the 'use of equipment' criterion was never implemented in practice by the authorities.

4. ARTICLE 3(2) OF THE GENERAL DATA PROTECTION REGULATION

4.1. GENERAL DESCRIPTION

On 24 May 2016, the General Regulation came into force and will apply from 25 May 2018. Among things that set it apart from its predecessor, the Directive, is the fact that territorial scope was considered from the very beginning as one of the key elements of the new law. The General Regulation essentially repeats the first of the jurisdictional basis of the Data Protection Directive, which is the 'establishment' criterion.[59] At the same time, the EU co-legislators decided not to repeat the 'use of equipment' basis. Article 3(2) of the General Regulation states that

> This Regulation applies to the processing of personal data of data subjects who are in the Union by a controller or processor not established in the Union, where the processing activities are related to: (a) the offering of goods or services, irrespective of whether a

---

58 Opinion of Advocate General Jääskinen delivered on 25 June 2013 in Case C-131/12, *Google Spain SL, Google Inc. v. Agencia Española de Protección de Datos (AEPD), Mario Costeja González*, 29.

59 The main change made by the EU co-legislators in this provision is introduction of a direct reference to processor, which expands its scope in comparison to Art. 4(1)a of the Data Protection Directive. The EU co-legislator also decided to explicitly underline that the fact of whether the processing takes place in the Union or not is irrelevant.

payment of the data subject is required, to such data subjects in the Union; or (b) the monitoring of their behaviour as far as their behaviour takes place within the Union.

Definitely the character of new nexus is different from the previous one, as in case of Art. 3(2) GDPR we deal with targeting, i.e. market access trigger,[60] which was unknown to the Directive. Art. 3(2) GDPR introduces what shall be seen as a moderate version of the so-called destination approach.[61] Kohl defines it as follows: 'according to the moderate version not every State where [an online] site can be accessed has the right to regulate it but only those States that are specifically targeted by it.'[62] Such a jurisdictional approach should be considered as a reasonable one in the age of the Internet, where the territoriality principle exhibits significant shortcomings. In particular, in the legal area of personal data protection, bearing in mind the lack of global standards, jurisdiction based on territoriality, due to its limitations, cannot guarantee effective protection of data subjects' rights. Territorial scope based on targeting of data subjects is therefore clearly a solution that should be considered.

It is not my aim to conduct an in-depth analysis of Art. 3(2) GDPR. The point I would like to make is that – in comparison to Art. 4(1)(c) of the Data Protection Directive – Art. 3(2) GDPR seems to be reasonable and provides a higher level of legal certainty. The new territorial scope is not absolute and Art. 3(2) sets relatively clear limits to the extraterritorial scope of the GDPR. Data controllers and processors are able to assess whom they target with their activities. Both Art. 3(2)(a) and Art. 3(2)(b) are based on a 'you might be targeted by the EU law only if you target EU data subjects'[63] rule and are explained in recitals. Recital 24 is an important clarification with respects to Art. 3(2)(b), specifying that *de facto* this provision is applicable only to tracking of online activities of data subjects in the EU.[64] This clarification very well specifies intentions of the EU co-legislators. At the same time, Recital 23, although based on negative selection (i.e. indicating what is insufficient to ascertain that data controller or processor intention is to offer goods or services to data subjects within the EU), and

60 For more information on the market access trigger see J. Scott, above n. 56, p. 1348.

61 See U. Kohl, above n. 10, p. 35; P. de Hert and M. Czerniawski, above n. 14.

62 U. Kohl, above n. 10, p. 45.

63 For an in-depth analysis of this approach see P. de Hert and M. Czerniawski, above n. 14.

64 According to Recital 24, '[t]he processing of personal data of data subjects who are in the Union by a controller or processor not established in the Union should also be subject to this Regulation when it is related to the monitoring of the behaviour of such data subjects in so far as their behaviour takes place within the Union. In order to determine whether a processing activity can be considered to monitor the behaviour of data subjects, it should be ascertained whether natural persons are tracked on the internet including potential subsequent use of personal data processing techniques which consist of profiling a natural person, particularly in order to take decisions concerning her or him or for analysing or predicting her or his personal preferences, behaviours and attitudes'.

therefore being not as clear and precise as Recital 24, also provides guidance with respect to the scope of Art. 3(2)a.[65]

Svantesson points out that the regulation 'bites off more than it can chew' and believes that it would be enforced only against big non-EU companies, which have a substantial impact on the European market, leaving smaller players without control.[66] Beyond any doubt the new territorial scope of the EU law might be, at least at the beginning, challenging in particular for data controllers and processors from third countries, including US. However, if considered as a replacement of Art. 4(1)(c) of the Data Protection Directive and the 'use of equipment' criterion, Art. 3(2) should be seen as a move in the right direction, for the reasons mentioned above, providing for more legal certainty than its predecessor. Keeping a moderate degree of extraterritoriality is in line with developments in other areas of EU law.[67] At the same time, there is a need to see how Art. 3(2) GDPR will work in practice.

4.2. POSSIBLE IMPACT ON THE EU–US DATA PRIVACY RELATIONSHIPS

As regards the impact of the GDPR territorial scope on trans-Atlantic data privacy relationships in commercial matters,[68] it is justified to expect that Art. 3 will contribute to strengthening them.

First of all, in order to be effective, the new law requires a certain level of cooperation between the relevant EU and US authorities. The Commission

---

65 According to Recital 24, 'the mere accessibility of the controller's, processor's or an intermediary's website in the Union, of an e-mail address or of other contact details, or the use of a language generally used in the third country where the controller is established are insufficient to ascertain that data controller or processor intention is to offer goods or services to data subjects within the EU'.

66 D.J.B. Svantesson, 'Extraterritoriality and Targeting in EU Data Privacy Law: the Weak Spot Undermining the Regulation' (2015) 5 *International Data Privacy Law* 232.

67 J. Scott points out that this is in line with changes in other fields of the EU law: 'The range, use and potential use of legislation that imposes over the border obligations is growing and EU legislators, regulators and arbiters of jurisdictional disputes need to equip themselves with a broad knowledge of this rapid cycle of change'. See J. Scott, above n. 56, p. 1346. Advocate General Jääskinen confirms that the direction in which the EU co-legislators went is correct: 'In the Commission Proposal for a General Data Protection Regulation (2012) the offering of goods or services to data subjects residing in the European Union would be a factor making EU data protection law applicable to third country controllers. Such an approach, attaching the territorial applicability of EU legislation to the targeted public, is consistent with the Court's case-law on the applicability of the ecommerce Directive 2000/31, Regulation No. 44/2001, and Directive 2001/29 to cross-border situations.' Jääskinen, at 56.

68 With respect to criminal matters, such cooperation is already in place, with at least seven agreements covering this area: (i) Agreement between the US and EU on the protection of personal information relating to the prevention, investigation, detection, and prosecution of criminal offences ('Umbrella Agreement') of 2016; (ii) Agreement between the US and EU on

and supervisory authorities are obliged to establish such cooperation under Art. 50 GDPR. Experience that will be gained thanks to cooperation mechanisms established in the recently negotiated Privacy Shield scheme,[69] which involves European data protection authorities and the Federal Trade Commission, might be of use here. However, effective application of all the GDPR provisions to third country data controllers and processors is a much more complex issue than the relatively narrow matter of EU–US data transfers, and will have an impact on an incomparably bigger scale than roughly 5,000 American organisations, i.e. the number of American companies previously certified within the Safe Harbour scheme.[70]

Second, the new regime, with a broad catalogue of data subjects' rights and related obligations of data controllers and processors, requires raising awareness among US businesses.[71] In particular, relevant information shall be given to companies operating online. Such information shall, *inter alia*, include a description of factors triggering application of the EU data protection rules. Comprehensive information with this respect to be provided to American organisations is in the interest of all stakeholders – EU data subjects, data protection authorities and businesses. Any campaign directed at raising awareness would require a close cooperation between European data protection authorities, the US Department of Commerce and the Federal Trade Commission.

Third – the new data protection regime requires European national data protection authorities not only to respond to any complaint about a third country data controller or processor submitted to them, but also to monitor data processing operations taking place outside of the EU, including in the US, on their own. European authorities need to be capable of enforcing the new law

the use and transfer of passenger name records to the US Department of Homeland Security ('PNR Agreement') of 2012; (iii) Agreement between the EU and the US on the processing and transfer of Financial Messaging Data from the European Union to the United States for purposes of the Terrorist Finance Tracking Programme of 2010; (iv) Agreement between the US and the European Police Office of 2001; (v) Supplemental Agreement between the US and the European Police Office on the Exchange of Personal Data and Related Information of 2002; (vi) Agreement on Mutual Legal Assistance between the EU and US of 2003; and (vii) Agreement between Eurojust and the US of 2006.

69 See Commission Implementing Decision of 12 July 2016 pursuant to Directive 95/46/EC of the European Parliament and of the Council on the adequacy of the protection provided by the EU–US Privacy Shield (C(2016) 4176 final).

70 See Commission Decision of 26 July 2000 pursuant to Directive 95/46/EC of the European Parliament and of the Council on the adequacy of the protection provided by the Safe Harbour privacy principles and related frequently asked questions issued by the US Department of Commerce (notified under document number C(2000) 2441), [2000] OJ L 215/7–47.

71 Researches such as that described by TRUSTe show that there is still much to be done: '50% Of American Businesses Aren't Aware Or Preparing For The Most Significant Data Privacy Change In 20 Years', <https://www.truste.com/about-truste/press-room/businesses-data-privacy-change/>, accessed 20.05.2016. At the same time, it is important to point out that among third country companies, probably the American ones have the highest level of awareness with respect to the recent developments in the EU data protection field.

against US companies infringing it. If they would try to avoid taking investigative and enforcement actions against third country data controllers and processors, or initiate such actions only on a very limited scale, the perception of the GDPR outside of the EU might be that it is nothing more than a whim of Europeans, which basically, as not enforceable, may be ignored. Some kind of cooperation, in particular involvement of American authorities in investigative actions, would be very beneficial from the EU perspective. At the same time, the open question is whether the Department of Commerce and the Federal Trade Commission, having their own task and limited resources, would be ready for such cooperation. One should bear in mind that the EU co-legislators when introducing Art. 3(2) GDPR had in mind in particular large online organisations such as Facebook Inc. or Google Inc., which process millions of records regarding EU citizens. But Art. 3(2) and its market access trigger will be also applicable to micro, small and medium companies all around the world. Ensuring effective protection of data subjects' rights in the EU will require also pursuing this kind of organisations. A selective approach, where European national data protection authorities only pursue actions against large, US-based companies, might undermine trust in the rule of law and question effectiveness of the new EU data protection framework.

On the margin of this analysis, taking into consideration that the EU–US Privacy Shield Framework was the most important recent development in the area of personal data protection, it is important to mention that adherence to the Privacy Shield scheme does not exempt American organisations whose activities fall within the scope of Art. 3 GDPR, from abiding by obligations arising from the provisions of the GDPR. The Privacy Shield scheme, although based on the concept of 'adequacy', included both in the Data Protection Directive and the GDPR, is a separate instrument, aimed only at addressing the issue of data transfers. Thus, a number of US companies will be obliged to fulfil obligations arising from both the GDPR and – currently – the Privacy Shield Framework.

Finally, the increasing complexity of EU–US data privacy relations in commercial matters may concern US business and result in a temptation on the American side to regulate this matter on the international agreement level, for example in TTIP.[72] Should this prove to be the case, one should bear in mind that the possible TTIP data privacy provisions included in an international trade agreement, would have priority over the GDPR. This is because a regulation,

---

[72] This would be however against the intentions of both the European Commission and the Council of the European Union, and the negotiation mandate for the EU Commission. R. Bendrath points out that the EU data protection standards may be undermined through the concept of "interoperability" of European and US data processing rules; see: R. Bendrath, 'TTIP and TiSA: big pressure to trade away privacy', September 2014, <https://netzpolitik.org/2014/ttip-and-tisa-big-pressure-to-trade-away-privacy>, accessed 20.05.2016. However, already back in 2013 V. Reding stated that: 'a discussion on standards of data protection should be kept separate from the give and take of a trade negotiation. I am grateful to my colleague Karel de Gucht for saying that data protection is outside the scope of Transatlantic

as one of the types of EU legislative acts, constitutes a secondary source of EU law, and potentially could allow circumvention of the high EU data protection standards introduced in the General Regulation.

5. CONCLUSION

The information society is at the same time the 'equipment-based' society. The term 'equipment', introduced in the Data Protection Directive before the expansion of the Internet, covers a much broader spectrum of tools today, than just terminals or questionnaires – i.e. examples indicated by the drafters of the Data Protection Directive. However, the Directive lacks clear criteria as regards its scope. An effective global legal framework for data protection requires a high level of protection of data subjects' rights combined with an equally high level of clarity about rules of jurisdictional scope, applicable law[73] and enforcement. Art. 4(1)(c) of the Directive and the 'use of equipment' basis, confusing and problematic from the moment it was published, does not provide such clarity. In particular, if interpreted in a broad manner, this provision allows for application of the Data Protection Directive in situations where there is no real connection between processing operations and the European Union, and thus leads to jurisdictional overreach. The lack of sufficient nexus, questionable legitimacy and problems with enforcement are the reasons why 'use of equipment' criterion is practically not applied by data protection authorities in Europe.

The complexity of technology and of data processing operations will continue to increase. In these circumstances, the EU jurisdiction in the area of data protection needs to be based on a solid nexus with the EU and clear criteria that allow data controllers and processors to identify potential links between processing operations and EU law. Thus, the EU co-legislators made the right choice by not reintroducing the reference to 'use of equipment' in the General Data Protection Regulation. However, at the same time, a moderate degree of extraterritoriality is necessary in order to efficiently protect EU data subjects rights in the digital world. It is also needed for the sake of establishing a level playing field for European and non-European, in particular American, data

---

Trade and Investment Partnership (TTIP)'. See EC Press release, 'Data protection reform: restoring trust and building the digital single market', <http://europa.eu/rapid/press-release_SPEECH-13-720_en.htm>, accessed 20.05.2016. As regards the Council, on 27 November 2015, it concluded that '[t]he Council stresses the need to create a global level playing field in the area of digital trade and strongly supports the Commission's intention to pursue this goal in full compliance with and without prejudice to the EU's data protection and data privacy rules, which are not negotiated in or affected by trade agreements.' See document 14688/15: Outcome of the 3430th Council meeting, p. 9.

73 Ch. Kuner, above n. 39, p. 64.

controllers and processors, as they should be obliged to follow the same rules when operating in the EU and accessing the European Single Market.

Do we indeed need the 'use of equipment' as a factor for the territorial applicability of the EU data protection regime? It is my opinion that, in the light of the above analysis, the answer to this question should be negative. Art. 4(1)(c) is creating interpretation problems from the moment it was published. At the same time, it is obvious that the whole concept of 'use of equipment' is not future-proof and would require thorough re-thinking as time passes by. National data protection authorities in Europe support broad understanding of the term 'equipment' and at the same time, aware of potential problems, are not keen to apply this provision, which potentially allows them to investigate a great number of organisations without an establishment in the EU, in practice. The lack of practical application and relevant administrative decisions results in lack of cases before national courts and no guidance from the CJEU.

Article 4(1)(c) provides a good example on how technology may influence law and affect it in a way which was not foreseen by the legislator at the time the law was drafted. It also proves that in the age of the equipment-based society and constant technological progress, just a couple of years may be sufficient for such a situation to occur.

The jurisdictional scope of Art. 3(2) GDPR, based on targeting and gaining access to the EU market seems to be more reasonable for the territorial applicability of the EU data protection regime than 'use of equipment' criterion. Nevertheless, practical application of the new provision should be carefully monitored with the aim of providing high level of protection of personal data online, without creating a risk of jurisdictional overreach. All relevant stakeholders, in particular the European Data Protection Board, bearing in mind controversies arose around Art. 4(1)(c) of the Data Protection Directive, should provide clear guidance on how it should be interpreted, how it should be applicable in practice and where its boundaries lie.

11. JURISDICTIONAL CHALLENGES RELATED TO DNA DATA PROCESSING IN TRANSNATIONAL CLOUDS

Heidi Beate BENTZEN* and Dan Jerker B. SVANTESSON**

1. INTRODUCTION

Genetic research has the potential to change how we diagnose, prevent and treat medical conditions, by making the diagnosis more precise and the prevention and treatment more personalised. However, such research cannot be carried out without the collection, use and disclosure of sensitive data – our DNA. Furthermore, to be effective, such research currently depends on DNA data being shared across borders and processed in cloud computing arrangements. Thus, genetic research is global, but it is not regulated similarly across the world.

In this chapter, we examine the jurisdictional issues that arise in both private, and public, international law, where DNA data is stored or processed in transnational cloud computing arrangements. Further, the broad contours of a potential approach to dealing with those issues will be canvassed. First, to set the scene for that discussion, we will commence with a brief discussion of what types of data we are dealing with here, what they are used for and the role cloud computing plays in the processing.

* Centre for Medical Ethics, Faculty of Medicine; Norwegian Research Centre for Computers and Law, Faculty of Law, both at the University of Oslo. Bentzen collaborates with the Norwegian Cancer Genomics Consortium. E-mail: h.b.bentzen@medisin.uio.no. Her research is financed by the Research Council of Norway through the project Legal Regulation of Information Processing relating to Personalised Cancer Medicine (BIOTEK2021/238999).

** Co-Director, Centre for Commercial Law, Faculty of Law, Bond University (Australia); Visiting Professor, Faculty of Law, Masaryk University (Czech Republic); Researcher, Swedish Law & Informatics Research Institute, Stockholm University (Sweden). E-mail: Dan_Svantesson@bond.edu.au. Professor Svantesson is the recipient of an Australian Research Council Future Fellowship (project number FT120100583). The views expressed herein are those of the author and are not necessarily those of the Australian Research Council.

The authors wish to thank the two anonymous reviewers for their useful feedback on this chapter. In addition, the authors would like to thank Professor Dag Wiese Schartum and PhD candidate Isabelle Budin-Ljøsne for their helpful comments.

Our aim is modest. We do not aim to be exhaustive on any one topic. Rather, by providing a brief introduction to both DNA data processing and to the legal issues, we aim to make the presentation accessible to a diverse audience, hopefully making this chapter a suitable starting point for anyone considering researching in detail the cross-section of transnational DNA databases and international law.

2. DNA IN THE CLOUDS – THE BASICS

2.1. HOW AND WHY DNA DATA IS USED

The human genome refers to an individual human being's complete set of DNA. In the current European Data Protection Directive 95/46/EC, genetic data is commonly considered health data, which is characterised as sensitive personal data. In the upcoming European Union General Data Protection Regulation (EU) 2016/679, genetic data is explicitly regulated as a special category of data alongside, *inter alia*, health data. We will return to the legal regulation in section 4 below.

Genomic data is a unique identifier. Furthermore, an individual can be identified even by very little DNA data. Anonymous processing is therefore rarely an option, so the processing must be in compliance with the applicable personal data legislation. Some also take the view that the characteristics of genomic data sets it apart from other kinds of sensitive personal data, and that the processing requires even more consideration than for other types of sensitive personal data.[1]

DNA testing can be used for various purposes, ranging from personalised medicine and parentage identification, to ancestry research and sport talent identification.[2] There has also been a proliferation of direct-to-consumer (DTC) genetic tests, which has created concerns, not least due to the fact that the laboratories carrying out the DTC tests often are located in a different country to where the consumer is located. And immediately, we see the type of (cross-border) data privacy concerns that arise in the field that we focus on in this chapter. For example, Australia's National Health and Medical Research Council has pointed out that: 'Some DTC companies also sell information about you and your genetic results to pharmaceutical and other companies. It is important

1 According to the UNESCO Declaration on Human Genetic Data, Art. 4 genetic data have a 'special status'.

2 NHMRC, 'Use of genetic infromation in sport', 2013, <https://www.nhmrc.gov.au/_files_nhmrc/publications/attachments/g003_genetic_sequencing_in_sport_150622.pdf> accessed 08.07.2016.

to understand that DTC genetic testing companies may ask if your sample and results can be used for other purposes, such as research.'[3]

At any rate, a particularly important area of DNA use is linked to so-called 'personalised medicine'. Personalised medicine is the tailoring of prevention, diagnosis and treatment to each individual's DNA. The aim is to be able to identify the most effective treatment, decrease the time it takes for patients to be given that effective treatment, and minimise side-effects.

Of the various types of DNA test, the one that is usually considered most relevant to personalised medicine is genome sequencing. Genome sequencing maps an individual's entire DNA, including all the genes and all the non-coding regions. That means that all of the about 3.2 billion base pairs that constitute the genome are mapped. The genes themselves only make up a small portion of the DNA, about 1.22 per cent.[4] The non-coding regions are by far the biggest part of the DNA. These are interesting because they play a part in gene regulation. Other available DNA tests are exome sequencing, that maps all the genes but not the non-coding regions, gene tests that only map select genes, and DNA tests usually used for identification purposes that only map small parts of the non-coding regions.[5]

The opportunity to tailor medical care to the individual in the manner done in personalised medicine is new. It has been made possible by advances in medical research and technology. In 2000, a rough draft sequence of the human genome was finished, and the achievement was announced jointly by US President Bill Clinton and UK Prime Minister Tony Blair, before it was published in 2001.[6] In 2004, the first complete human genome sequence was published.[7] These are considered to be among the main medical research achievements in history. Simultaneously, technological advances have rapidly made genome sequencing affordable. It cost about $3 billion to sequence the first human genome. In October 2015, the cost had fallen to $1,245.[8]

---

3 NHMRC, 'Understanding Direct-to-Consumer (DTC) Genetic DNA Testing: An information resource for consumers', 2014, <https://www.nhmrc.gov.au/_files_nhmrc/publications/attachments/g8_understanding_direct_to_consumer_genetic_testing_consumers_141208.pdf> accessed 08.07.2016.

4 The Encode Project Consortium, 'An integrated encyclopedia of DNA elements in the human genome' (2012) 489 *Nature* 57–74.

5 H.B. Bentzen, 'Persontilpasset medisin – Utvalgte rettslige problemstillinger i tilknytning til klinisk bruk av genomsekvensering og behandling av genetiske opplysninger', forthcoming in *CompLex*.

6 J.C. Venter et al., 'The Sequence of the Human Genome' (2001) 291 (5507) *Science* 1304–1351; International Human Genome Sequencing Consortium, 'Initial sequencing and analysis of the human genome' (2001) 409 *Nature* 860–921.

7 International Human Genome Sequencing Consortium, 'Finishing the euchromatic sequence of the human genome' (2004) *Nature* 431 pp. 931–945.

8 K.A. Wetterstrand, 'DNA Sequencing Costs: Data from the NHGRI Genome Sequencing Program (GSP)' <https://www.genome.gov/sequencingcostsdata/> accessed 08.07.2016.

In 2014, UK Prime Minister David Cameron announced a £300 million research investment, aimed to map 100,000 human genomes in the UK by 2017, and in time implement personalised medicine as part of routine care in the British health care system.[9] In 2015, US President Barack Obama announced The Precision Medicine Initiative, a research effort on personalised medicine in the US, which was granted $215 million in the President's 2016 budget.[10] Several other countries have also launched or are considering similar initiatives. These initiatives require massive DNA data processing.

2.2. WHY CLOUD?

Relatively recent developments in research have sparked a move to genomics. Gibbons et al. explain:

> Recent genetic research has focused on mapping similarities and differences at the level of the whole genome (that is, all of a person's genes taken collectively). These investigations often use genetic markers called single nucleotide polymorphisms (SNPs) or haplotypes (groups of SNPs that are commonly inherited together). Using these genetic markers makes it possible to screen very large numbers – often many millions – of genetic variations across whole genomes. Scientists, including epidemiologists, thus have begun to investigate correlations (associations) between SNPs or haplotypes and the occurrence of common diseases. Such research investigations study the complexities in the functioning of cells, or the genome, rather than focusing simply on genes. They demonstrate the change from genetic to genomic research. This kind of research, however, requires extremely large biosample collections and associated databases of medical and family history data and environmental and lifestyle information.[11]

In other words, this change in research direction has created an even more pronounced need for DNA data being stored and processed in cloud arrangements. However, there are many reasons why our DNA may end up 'in the clouds'.

International collaborations are necessary and useful in order to achieve progress in the genomic field. Such collaborations can involve the use of human

---

9 GOV.UK, 'Human Genome: UK to become world number 1 in DNA testing', 01.08.2014 <https://www.gov.uk/government/news/human-genome-uk-to-become-world-number-1-in-dna-testing> accessed 08.07.2016.

10 The White House Office of the Press Secretary, 'Fact Sheet: President Obama's Precision Medicine Initiative', 30.01.2015 <https://www.whitehouse.gov/the-press-office/2015/01/30/fact-sheet-president-obama-s-precision-medicine-initiative> accessed 08.07.2016.

11 S.M.C. Gibbons, J. Kaye, A. Smart, C. Heeney and M. Parker, 'Governing Genetic Databases: Challenges Facing Research Regulation and Practice' (2007) 34 *Journal of Law and Society* 163–189, 166 (internal footnote omitted).

genetic databases. In the absence of a universally agreed definition of genetic databases, we will provide some typical examples.

One example relates to analytical validity. Medical tests are usually evaluated according to the ACCE criteria: *a*nalytical validity, *c*linical validity, *c*linical utility and *e*thical aspects. Analytical validity relates to a test's sensitivity and specificity. A challenge related to genome sequencing is that one can find genetic variants that have not been classified, so it is not possible to determine if the genetic variant is disease causing or harmless. If a harmless variant is classified as disease-causing, this decreases the test's specificity. It is therefore beneficial to establish a database of genetic variants in order to better be able to determine if the variant is normal and harmless or disease causing. Such databases need large numbers, meaning that they ought to be international; in addition, they also need a good representation from the local area of the patient being tested.[12]

Further, researchers and clinicians in the genomics field tend to collaborate internationally, often in large consortia. By centralising data management in the cloud, data and methods can easily be shared by scientists around the world. It is plausible that this is the single strongest reason why DNA data is put in the cloud.

Uploading research data, including research participants' DNA data, into joint databases where other researchers can be granted access is increasingly required by research funders and publishers.[13]

Genomic data requires so much storage space that the most convenient manner for researchers and clinicians to collaborate is through cloud-based processing of the genomic data. It has been calculated that by 2025, human genomes will require 2–40 exabytes of storage capacity.[14] In comparison, YouTube's projected annual storage need is 1–2 exabytes of video by 2025.[15] Shipping hard copies of genome data is not a practical option due to the data size, thus cloud computing is considered the most suitable option for handling such data.

Genomic cloud computing can consequently be defined as Dove et al. do as 'a scalable service where genetic sequence information is stored and processed virtually (in other words, in the "cloud") usually via networked, large-scaled data centres accessible remotely through various clients and platforms over the Internet.'[16] Cloud computing activities are usually divided into three

12 H.B. Bentzen, above n. 5.

13 D.B. Taichman et al., 'Sharing clinical trial data — a proposal from the International Committee of Medical Journal Editors' (2016) 374 *New England Journal of Medicine* 384–386.

14 Z.D. Stephens, S.Y. Lee, F. Faghri, R.H. Campbell, C. Zhai, M.J. Efron, R. Iyer, M.C. Schatz, S. Sinha and G.E. Robinson, 'Big Data: Astronomical or Genomical?' (2015) 13(7) *PLoS Biology*: e1002195 <http://journals.plos.org/plosbiology/article?id=10.1371/journal.pbio.1002195> accessed 08.07.2016.

15 Ibid.

16 E.S. Dove, Y. Joly and B.M. Knoppers, 'International genomic cloud computing: "mining" the terms of service' in A.S.Y. Cheung and R.H. Weber (eds.), *Privacy and Legal Issues in Cloud Computing*, Edward Elgar Publishing, Cheltenham 2015, pp. 237–259, 240.

categories: Infrastructure as Service (IaaS) which are raw computing resources such as processing power ('compute') and storage, Platform as Service (PaaS) that provide platforms for developing and deploying software applications, or Software as Service (SaaS) which are end-user applications.[17] PaaS genomic cloud computing includes Galaxy, Bionimbus and DNAnexus, and IaaS genomic cloud computing include the Genome Analysis Toolkit.[18] The platforms usually run on clouds provided by cloud service providers such as Amazon.[19]

3. WHY IT IS SO IMPORTANT TO FIND LEGAL SOLUTIONS IN THIS FIELD

Given the obvious benefits society can gain from effective DNA-based research, it may seem somewhat gratuitous to include a section on why we need to find legal solutions that properly regulates the type of situations discussed above. However, it is worthwhile to stop and reflect on the various interest involved. Here we will approach those interest structured around the various relevant actors, including: the researchers who are using DNA databases, the operators of the databases, the individuals whose DNA information is included in the databases, the data subjects' relatives whose information may be revealed, the ethics committees that seek to regulate these databases, as well as a range of third-party users such as law enforcement bodies wishing to access the data in these databases,

The researchers who are using the cloud-based transnational DNA databases have a strong and obvious interest in the legal framework that govern their conduct. As noted by Gibbons et al.: 'If legal standards are unclear and inaccessible, this could ... place researchers at risk of criminal or civil liability, and inhibit the progress of research.'[20] Thus, clarity and certainty are two key requirements for the research community, aside from the obvious requirement that the legal framework actually allows for the type of processing the researchers need in order to carry out their research. This same need for clarity and certainty is a key requirement for the database operators.

For individuals, DNA information is one of the most sensitive types of information; as Gibbons et al. remind us:

> It is also worth recalling why research involving human genetics is sometimes considered to be problematic – and, thus, why many believe that genetic databases do

[17] W.K. Hon and C. Millard, 'Cloud Technologies and Services' in C. Millard (ed.), *Cloud Computing Law*, Oxford University Press, Oxford 2013, pp. 3–17, 4.

[18] E.S. Dove, above n. 17, pp. 240–241.

[19] Ibid., pp. 240–243.

[20] S.M.C. Gibbons, above n. 12, p. 164.

> warrant special, categorical treatment. It is often claimed that human genetic material is 'special' when compared to other healthrelated materials. The claimed 'special' qualities include that it can be predictive, it is immutable, it is personally identifiable, and it may have implications for others (including family and social groups). These qualities mean that genetic data may have implications for personal life choices, insurance, and employment; raise the spectre of discrimination against individuals or population groups; have significant ramifications for relatives that can shift the balance of rights and interests away from just the individual; contain information which only becomes significant some time after collection; and have cultural significance for certain persons or groups.[21]

In light of this, genetic data can pose a threat to privacy. In this context, it is worth emphasising what can be seen as a definitional mismatch. While data privacy laws typically are aimed at protecting the personal data of identifiable living individuals, DNA information – given the familial nature of genetic information – typically includes information about more than one individual. Data regarding a deceased person in one country may well reveal sensitive information about a relative living in another country.

A special mention must be made of the great potential for secondary use, or misuse, of DNA databases. Even where the data subject is perfectly satisfied with how the research community is handling her DNA data, the database operators may willingly, or unwillingly, share the data for secondary purposes not (specifically or consciously) intended or foreseen at the time of data collection. O'Doherty et al. discuss six such secondary uses:

1. forensic investigations;
2. civil lawsuits;
3. identification of victims of mass casualty events;
4. denial of entry for border security and immigration;
5. making health resource rationing decisions;
6. facilitating human rights abuses and eugenics in autocratic regimes.[22]

While we may perhaps feel comfortable with DNA databases being used for the identification of victims of mass casualty events – such as occurred after the Christmas Day Tsunami of 2004[23] – other secondary uses, for instance civil lawsuits, are more controversial. The noted familial nature of genetic information also makes for complex grey zones in which questions such as whether person A's DNA data also is person B's personal data will arise.

---

[21] Ibid., p. 175 (internal footnote omitted).

[22] K.C. O'Doherty, E. Christofides, J. Yen, H.B. Bentzen, W. Burke, N. Hallowell, B.A. Koenig and D.J. Willison, 'If you build it they will come: Unintended future uses of organised health data collections', *BMC Medical Ethics*, 2016, 17:54.

[23] H.B. Bentzen, above n. 5.

The use of DNA databases by law enforcement agencies (LEAs) and for border control can also be controversial. On the one hand, where a person is aware that the genetic data she provides to a database may be accessed by LEAs, she may be reluctant to provide the sample in the first place which may negatively impact both research and the health of the individual in question. When several people opt not to contribute their samples and data, this can create biases in the research material. On the other hand, LEA access to information held in DNA databases can help solve crime, which is of a general value to society, and a specific value to victims and those wrongly accused. In this context, we can draw parallels to how LEAs have approached data stored by Internet intermediaries such as search engines, cloud storage and social media. We will return to the jurisdictional issues involved below; here it suffices to note that LEAs are displaying an increasing appetite for accessing such data, and that there is a perceivable trend that this appetite is being satisfied by courts approving LEA access to user data held by Internet intermediaries also where the intermediaries are based in other countries and hold that data in other countries.[24]

Further on this, there are secondary uses for which we would never want to see DNA databases being used. Yet we cannot close our eyes to the risk of such databases being misused for discrimination or even ethnic cleansing and genocide. We should always keep in mind the devastating impact the Netherlands population registration system had in the hands of Nazi occupiers in the 1940s. As noted by O'Doherty et al.:

> The death rate among Dutch Jews (73%) was dramatically higher than that among Jews in France (25%) and Belgium (40%), as well as Jewish refugees living in the Netherlands during the Nazi occupation. Seltzer and Anderson argue that this was largely due to the fact that the registration system in the Netherlands facilitated the apprehension of Dutch Jews.[25]

Apart from the research community and the data subjects, we must take account also of the interests of the data subject's relatives and indigenous peoples.[26]

Furthermore, as discussed extensively by Reichel, the role of ethics committees must be considered:

> The main question seems to be how decisions from research ethics committees of different kind may be enacted in composite administrative procedures and allowed

24 See eg: *Yahoo! v. Belgium*, Belgium Supreme Court decision, Cass. P.13.2082.N., 01.12.2015 and Danish Supreme Court Order delivered 10.05.2012 (Case 129/2011), discussed and analysed by L.B. Langsted and H.L. Guðmundsdóttir, 'Case Translation' (2013) 10 *Digital Evidence and Electronic Signature Law Review* 162–165 <http://journals.sas.ac.uk/deeslr/article/view/2038/1975> accessed 08.07.2016.

25 K.C. O'Doherty et al., above n. 22.

26 K.S. Bull, 'Genetiske undersøkelser – Er dagens regulering god nok?' in H. Stenstadvold (ed.), *Georgs bok*, Pax, Oslo 2010, pp. 209–215.

> to have extraterritorial effects. The difficulty lies in the traditional understanding of administrative law of being a legal discipline closely connected to the nation state, with its constitutionally based task to implement the politics of the democratically elected parliaments. Globalisation has challenged this idea and within many areas of administrative law, authorities and public bodies today act beyond the state. The importance of the nation-based democracy as a cradle for legitimate rule making has decreased. ... When it comes to administration of ethical approval for medical research, the nation state still seems to remain strong. ... [S]everal different administrative jurisdictions, national and European, are involved in one and the same cross-border research project, creating a web of ethical approvals for researchers to adhere to.[27]

As Reichel also points out, Kaye has accurately 'referred to the conceptual underpinnings of current research governance structures as based on the "one researcher, one project, one jurisdiction" model'[28] – a poor fit indeed with the reality of modern cloud-based DNA research.

Finally, one cannot assess the risks associated with the discussed databases without acknowledging the potential for so-called 'function creep'; that is, as correctly stressed by O'Doherty et al., 'shifting social priorities and interests might lead to repurposing of health data collections'.[29] In other words, we can never be sure what the collected data may be used for in the future – a most unsettling thought.

Having noted some of the various key interests involved, we hasten to acknowledge the herculean nature of the task ahead. After all, there are numerous areas of law that impact these databases:

> To get a sense of the sheer range of legal challenges that emerge around genetic databases, it is worth summarizing the principal matters covered by these various governance instruments and common law doctrines. These illustrate the matters which different bodies have seen as requiring attention from regulators. While not exhaustive, in broad terms the following issues feature most prominently: consent; capacity; privacy; confidentiality; the collection, handling, storage, use, and disposal of human tissue and biosamples; data processing, sharing, and preservation; access to data and records by individuals and third parties, including researchers; the use and disclosure of health data and genetic data, including transborder flows; data security and information technology standards; good research practice; healthcare professionals' duties; sharing of genetic information; research governance; ethical scrutiny and ethical approval of research; patenting and other intellectual property rights; ownership, property,

---

27 J. Reichel, 'Transparency in EU Research Governance? A Case Study on Cross-border Biobanking' in A.S. Lind, J. Reichel and I. Österdahl (eds.), *Information and Law in Transition – Freedom of Speech, the Internet, Privacy and Democracy in the 21st Century*, Liber, Stockholm 2015, pp. 351–382, 376.

28 Ibid., p. 353. See further: J. Kaye, 'From Single Biobanks to International Networks: Developing e-Governance' (2012) 130 *Human Genetics* 377–392, 377.

29 K.C. O'Doherty et al., above n. 22.

> and commercial dealings; human rights; benefit-sharing; licensing and inspection of biobanking activities; and the establishment of regulatory authorities, their remits and powers.[30]

If this was not daunting enough, each country will typically have its own laws on these matters with variations between the different countries. And given the cross-border nature of the databases discussed, the operators of such databases, and indeed the users of the databases, are likely to expose themselves to the laws of several countries. Thus, in the cloud arena, the legal issues outlined in the quote above can be multiplied by the (typically large) number of legal systems to which the databases are exposed.

4. ENTERING THE INTERNATIONAL ARENA – PUBLIC, AND PRIVATE, INTERNATIONAL LAW

As already mentioned, the processing of genomic data is regulated differently across the world. To use the European Union as an example; in the EU, data processing, the right to respect for physical and mental integrity, the right to respect for private life, and the prohibition against genetic discrimination, are all considered fundamental rights according to the EU Charter of Fundamental Rights.

One of the changes in the upcoming EU General Data Protection Regulation (EU) 2016/679 (GDPR) as compared to the EU Data Protection Directive 95/46/EC (DPD), is that genetic data is specifically regulated as a special category of data alongside, *inter alia*, health data. Under the DPD, it has been common to consider genetic data health data, which is considered sensitive personal data. The point of departure in Art. 9 GDPR is that processing of genetic data is prohibited. There are exemptions to this, *inter alia*, for scientific research purposes. Nevertheless, there is no doubt that the European Union applies a strict regulatory regime to the processing of genetic data.

EU Member States can according to Art. 9(4) and Recital 53 maintain or introduce further conditions than those set forth in the GDPR with regard to the processing of genetic data. Several European countries have national legislation providing even stricter requirements for the processing of genetic data than those in the DPD and the GDPR.

It is therefore essential to know which laws to comply with and where disputes should be settled. Consequently, we must consider the rules of both private, and public, international law – indeed, to an extent the legal questions that arise challenge the traditional distinction between private, and public, international law.

---

30 S.M.C. Gibbons, above n. 11, p. 177.

4.1. PUBLIC INTERNATIONAL LAW: THE NOT SO GOLDEN TRIANGLE: SOVEREIGNTY, TERRITORIALITY AND JURISDICTION

Sovereignty usually refers to a state's power and right to govern itself, to make and enforce laws within its borders. It is a descriptive term alluding to supreme power. As Colangelo puts it, the term '[s]overeignty itself offers no analytically independent reason why states have or do not have power; it simply describes the power states do have at any given moment of development of the international legal system.'[31]

Jurisdiction is an aspect of sovereignty, both coextensive and limited by a state's sovereignty.[32] However, a unified definition of 'jurisdiction' does not exist. For the purposes of this chapter, we will use the classical definition provided by Mann as a starting point; 'a State's right under international law to regulate conduct in matters not exclusively of domestic concern'.[33] The 1935 Harvard Research on International Law Draft Convention on Jurisdiction with Respect to Crime ('the Harvard Draft') is, despite it not being a treaty, considered the main framework for assessing public international law jurisdiction.[34]

The territoriality principle is the primary basis for jurisdiction not only in the Harvard Draft, but in international law since the seventeenth century.[35] Under the territoriality principle, a state has jurisdiction over acts that have been committed within its territory. This divides the world into compartments in which each sovereign state has jurisdiction within its borders.[36] Thus, there is a clear connection between sovereignty, territoriality, and jurisdiction.

Territoriality is a thorny concept in relation to cloud computing. Two issues have received particular focus. First, it can be challenging to determine the location of the cloud-based genomic data processing. This question has been subject of much debate. For example, the Article 29 Data Protection Working Party stated that:

> [C]loud computing is most frequently based on a complete lack of any stable location of data within the cloud provider's network. Data can be in one data centre at 2 pm and

31 A.J. Colangelo, 'Spatial legality' (2012) 107(1) *Northwestern University Law Review* 69–126, 106.

32 F.A. Mann, 'The Doctrine of Jurisdiction in International Law' (1964) 111 *Recueil des Cours* 30.

33 Ibid., p. 9.

34 Draft Convention on Jurisdiction with Respect to Crime (1935) 29 *The American Journal of International Law*, Supplement: Research in International Law, 439–442.

35 C. Ryngaert, *Jurisdiction in International Law*, Oxford University Press, Oxford 2015, pp. 49–100 provides a thorough explanation of the principle and its history.

36 F.A. Mann, above n. 32, p. 30.

on the other side of the world at 4 pm. The cloud client is therefore rarely in a position to be able to know in real time where the data are located or stored or transferred.[37]

Hon and Millard clarified:

> In most cases, data are usually copied or replicated to different data centres, for business continuity/backup purposes, rather than being 'moved' by being deleted from one data centre and re-created in another. Often the provider will know where a user's data fragments (e.g. for a particular application) are stored, at the data centre if not equipment level.[38]

Second, data can also be located on the territory of states that the data does not have any real substantial connection to.[39] This issue is increasingly moving to the center of the discussion.

The disclosure requests from law enforcement agencies we mentioned above can serve as an example of the challenges territoriality poses for DNA data processing in transnational cloud databases. For identification purposes in criminal cases, law enforcement agencies have shown an interest in obtaining human biological samples from biobanks in order to perform DNA testing on the material.[40] There is reason to believe that such requests will become even more frequent when the material has already been sequenced and it is possible to request access to only the relevant, limited, non-coding parts of the DNA sequence. Thus, disclosure requests from law enforcement agencies to transnational DNA databases should be expected.

Some recent cases illustrate the difficulties that may arise. In the *Yahoo! Belgium* case, the public prosecutor of Dendermonde in Belgium requested that Yahoo! disclose the identity of people who committed Internet fraud via their Yahoo! e-mail addresses. Even though Yahoo! is based in the United States without a branch or offices in Belgium, the Court of Cassation found that such disclosure is not an intervention outside Belgium's territory because Yahoo! has a business link to Belgium.[41] Similarly, a DNA cloud database operator may be based in the

---

37 Article 29 Data Protection Working Party, Opinion 05/2012 on Cloud Computing, WP 196, adopted 01.07.2012, p. 17.

38 K.W. Hon and C. Millard, 'Data Export in Cloud Computing – How can Personal Data be Transferred outside the EEA? (The Cloud of Unknowing, Part 4)' (04.04.2012), Queen Mary University of London School of Law Cloud Legal Project, p. 7 <http://www.cloudlegal.ccls.qmul.ac.uk/Research/researchpapers/55649.html> accessed 08.07.2016. Cited from C. Kuner, *Transborder Data Flows and Data Privacy Law*, Oxford University Press, Oxford 2013, p. 122.

39 D.J.B. Svantesson, 'A New Jurisprudential Framework for Jurisdiction: Beyond the Harvard Draft' (2015) 109 *American Journal of International Law Unbound* 69 <https://www.asil.org/blogs/new-jurisprudential-framework-jurisdiction-beyond-harvard-draft> accessed 08.07.2016.

40 See for instance the Norwegian Supreme Court decision in Rt. 2006 p. 90 (NOKAS).

41 *Yahoo! v. Belgium*, Belgium Supreme Court decision, Cass. P.13.2082.N.

United States, the cloud may be marketed to and used by Belgian researchers to deposit Belgian citizens' DNA data, and the database operator in the United States may receive a disclosure request from Belgian law enforcement agencies.

In the *Microsoft* warrant case, United States law enforcement wanted information associated with a specified web-based e-mail account stored on Microsoft's servers in Ireland. Microsoft argued that the US enforcement activity is extra-territorial.[42] The United States disagreed, saying that all activities required to retrieve the data can be taken from the US.[43] Both claims are possible.[44] Complying with one country's law can mean breaking another country's law. This places DNA cloud database providers in a precarious position.

To properly engage with the questions at hand, the examples above show that we need to depart from strict territoriality and instead seek alternative mechanisms for delineating rights and responsibilities in relation to DNA data being shared across borders and processed in cloud computing arrangements. We propose the contours of such a solution in section 5 below.

4.2. PRIVATE INTERNATIONAL LAW

As to private international law, questions of jurisdiction and choice of law may arise for several reasons, and the rules of recognition and enforcement may also be actualised in the context of the type of storage and processing of DNA data we discuss. Importantly, both conflicts governed by contract and matters of a non-contractual nature may arise which means that a wide scope of private international law rules need to be considered.

4.2.1. Where disputes should be settled

In the European Union, the Brussels I*bis* Regulation 1215/2012 defines which courts are competent to decide in cross-border litigation between EU Member States in cases concerning civil and commercial matters, such as data privacy.[45]

---

42 Brief for Appellant, *Microsoft Corporation v. United States* (2d Cir.); for the European Union side, see Brief of *Amicus Curiae* Jan Philipp Albrecht, Member of the European Parliament, *Microsoft Corporation v. United States of America* (2d Cir.).

43 Government's Brief in Support of the Magistrate Judge's Decision to Uphold a Warrant Ordering Microsoft to Disclose Records Within its Custody and Control, *In re A Warrant to Search a Certain E-Mail Account Controlled And Maintained by Microsoft*, 15 F. Supp. 3d 466 (SDNY 2014).

44 D.J.B. Svantesson and F. Gerry, 'Access to extraterritorial evidence: The Microsoft cloud case and beyond' (2015) 31 *Computer Law & Security Review* 478–489.

45 Regulation (EU) No. 1215/2012 of the European Parliament and of the Council of 12 December 2012 on jurisdiction and the recognition and enforcement of judgments in civil and commercial matters.

Between EFTA states and EU and EFTA states, the 2007 Lugano Convention, which is almost identical to the Brussels I*bis* Regulation, applies. If the Brussels I*bis* Regulation or the Lugano Convention do not apply, national law applies.

According to Art. 25 Brussels I*bis*, the parties can agree that a court or the courts of a Member State are to have jurisdiction to settle any dispute which have arisen or which may arise. If the parties in the choice of forum clause have chosen a third, non-EU state court, for instance a US court, in principle Brussels I*bis* does not apply.[46]

If nothing has been agreed, Art. 7 Brussels I*bis* provides a default rule in matters related to contract. The courts for the place of performance of the obligation in question are competent. That means that the courts where the cloud services were provided or should have been provided are competent.[47] Moiny illustrates the difficulties in ascertaining where a cloud service is provided or performed, concluding that it could be argued 'that the service is performed where the user normally uses the service, where the service provider supervises and manages the service, or even partially at each place', showing the importance of including an appropriate provision in the contract.[48]

In the United States, three criteria apply: (1) the state must have a long-arm statute; (2) the defendant must have certain minimum contacts with the forum; and (3) the defendant appearing in that forum cannot violate traditional notions of 'fair play and substantial justice'.[49]

Choice of forum clauses are usually part of the cloud terms of service. The choice is often either California or Washington, as both US states are home to many cloud service providers, meaning that non-US users need to be aware of US legislation and legal practices.[50]

4.2.2. *Applicable law*

Arts. 17 and 2 of the International Covenant on Civil and Political Rights make extraterritorial jurisdictional data privacy claims mandatory.[51] Each signatory

---

46 J-P. Moiny, 'Cloud and jurisdiction: mind the borders' in A.S.Y. Cheung and R.H. Weber (eds.), *Privacy and Legal Issues in Cloud Computing*, Edward Elgar Publishing, Cheltenham 2015, pp. 118–138, 124.

47 Ibid., p. 125.

48 Ibid., p. 125.

49 T. Mahler (ed.), *Coco Cloud. Confident and Compliant Clouds. First Study of Legal and Regulatory Aspects of Cloud Computing*, p. 129 <http://www.coco-cloud.eu/sites/default/files/cococloud/files/content-files/deliverables/Coco_Deliverable%20D2.2_UO_20141031(1of2).pdf> accessed 08.07.2016.

50 Ibid.

51 D.J.B. Svantesson, 'The Extraterritoriality of EU Data Privacy Law – Its Theoretical Justification and Its Practical Effect on U.S. Businesses' (2014) 53 *Stanford Journal of International Law* 53–102, 77–79.

state is obligated to provide legal protection against unlawful attacks on the privacy of people subject to its jurisdiction and those present within its territory.[52] The convention, however, does not relate to substantive data protection law, such as for instance the particular approach to data protection in the EU.[53]

In the European Union, the Rome I Regulation 593/2008 applies to contractual obligations. According to Art. 2, the Regulation has universal application, so that the law the Regulation specifies should be applied whether or not it is the law of an EU Member State.

The Rome I Regulation's point of departure is freedom of choice. A contract is governed by the law chosen by the parties according to Art. 3. If such a choice has not been made, Art. 4 designates that the law of the country where the service provider has his habitual residence will apply. Irrespective of applicable law, overriding mandatory provisions must be respected. Mandatory provisions are provisions a country regard as crucial for safeguarding its public interest, see Art. 9. The applicable law can according to Art. 21 be refused if it is manifestly incompatible with public policy.

For non-contractual obligations in civil and commercial matters, the Rome II Regulation 864/2007 applies. According to Art. 4, the point of departure is that the law of the country in which the damage occurs is applicable to a non-contractual obligation arising out of a tort/delict. For infringement of intellectual property, Art. 8 states that the law applicable shall be the law of the country for which protection is claimed.

Non-contractual obligations arising out of violations of privacy and right relating to personality, are explicitly exempt from the Rome II Regulation in Art. 1.

For data protection in the EU and EEA, the Data Protection Directive 95/46/EC applies. Article 4 lists three grounds where the national implementation of the Directive applies to the processing of personal data. These are processing in the context of the activities of an establishment of the controller on Member State territory, public international law, and use of equipment on the territory of a Member State. The territorial scope was described in the *Google Spain*[54] case as being 'particularly broad', but in the *Bodil Lindqvist*[55] case the Court of Justice of the European Union had clarified that the Directive should not be interpreted as to be applicable to the entire Internet.[56]

In May 2018, the Directive will be replaced by the General Data Protection Regulation (EU) 2016/679. Article 3 clarifies the territorial scope. In addition to

---

52 Ibid.

53 Ibid.

54 Case C-131/12, *Google Spain v. AEPD and Mario Costeja Gonzalez*, 13.05.2014.

55 Case C-101/01, *Bodil Lindqvist*, 06.11.2003.

56 C. Kuner, 'Extraterritoriality and regulation of international data transfers in EU data protection law' (2015) 5(4) *International Data Privacy Law* 235–245, 243.

establishment and public international law, the Regulation will also apply to the processing of personal data of data subjects who are in the EU by a controller or processor not in the EU, insofar as the processing is related to offering of goods or services to data subjects in the EU or monitoring of their behaviour in the EU. The territorial scope of the Regulation has far-reaching implications and can be criticised for not distinguishing between the types of data privacy rules that will apply.[57] As suggested elsewhere, a more layered approach where some, but not necessarily all, rules would apply to controllers or processors outside the EU could have been more appropriate.[58] Thus, a transnational DNA cloud database processor in the United States could have been subject to the most relevant, but not all, the EU data protection rules.

5. CONTOURS OF A SOLUTION

We are not here aiming to present a solution to the problems and issues outlined above; our aim is much more humble. All we want to do is to briefly introduce, and bring attention to, some matters that ought to be considered by anyone seeking to propose solutions to the issues we have described and discussed above, thus providing the broad contours of a potential approach going forward. We acknowledge that this is a rather eclectic selection of proposals.

5.1. THE LIMITS OF TERRITORIALITY

As discussed above, territoriality runs as a *fil rouge* through contemporary thinking on jurisdiction. However, its limitations are obvious, not least in a field such as transnational cloud databases for processing of DNA data. In light of this, one important feature of any work towards a solution will be to come up with a better jurisprudential basis for approaching the concept of jurisdiction.

One possibility, previously presented elsewhere, is to look beyond the territoriality principle to the underlying core principles, and adopt the following framework for jurisdiction:

> In the absence of an obligation under international law to exercise jurisdiction, a State may only exercise jurisdiction where:
> (1) there is a substantial connection between the matter and the State seeking to exercise jurisdiction;

57 D.J.B. Svantesson, 'Extraterritoriality and targeting in EU data privacy law: the weak spot undermining the regulation' (2015) 5(4) *International Data Privacy Law* 226–234.

58 D.J.B. Svantesson, 'A "Layered Approach" to the Extraterritoriality of Data Privacy Laws' (2013) 3(4) *International Data Privacy Law* 278–286.

(2) the State seeking to exercise jurisdiction has a legitimate interest in the matter; and
(3) the exercise of jurisdiction is reasonable given the balance between the State's legitimate interests and other interests.[59]

These 'core principles' better correspond to online reality than does the territoriality principle, and adopting these principles as the point of departure for designing rules regarding jurisdiction and applicable law will be more fruitful than clinging on to dated notions of territoriality. For example, this thinking frees from the notion that a country automatically has jurisdiction over any content stored on its territory. These core principles constitute the common core that unites public international law and private international law.[60] Ginsburg has described the approach we here outline as a 'move from an increasingly anachronistic rule, which may be producing more errors than it used to, toward a looser standard that requires careful balancing of interests'.[61]

5.2. HARMONISATION

Greater legal harmonisation internationally may be necessary if the research aims of genomic cloud databases are to be reached. Extensive cross-border scientific collaboration and data sharing requires cross-border legislation. This will also require more collaboration between regulatory authorities. Achieving a minimum data privacy standard can be realistic. As important as this will be, it will not, however, represent a complete solution. After all, even with a minimum data privacy standard, for instance the EU will likely require stricter privacy standards than the minimum requirements for processing of genetic data. For the specific purpose of genomic health care and research, one could therefore also or instead consider an international, preferably global, convention. The problem with a convention is, however, that it may create a too-rigid framework for genome technology that advances far faster than Moore's law. It can also raise questions of whether genomics should be subject to exceptional legal regulation or rather be treated similarly to health data in general. Thus, even where work is undertaken towards harmonisation, other options must be pursued in parallel.

---

59 See further: D.J.B. Svantesson, above n. 39. This approach to jurisdiction has been endorsed in the Netherlands Presidency of the Council of the EU Debriefing Conference on Jurisdiction in Cyberspace (07–08.03.2016, Amsterdam) doc. 7323/16.

60 D.J.B. Svantesson, above n. 39.

61 T. Ginsburg, 'Introduction to Symposium: Rethinking State Jurisdiction in the Internet Era' (2015) 109 *American Journal of International Law Unbound* 67 <https://www.asil.org/blogs/introduction-symposium-rethinking-state-jurisdiction-internet-era> accessed 08.07.2016.

5.3. BETTER RELATION BETWEEN REGULATION AND TECHNOLOGY

Technology, and the use of technology, are the drivers with which law and regulation try their best to keep up. This is only natural. Nevertheless, it seems to us that, not least in the context of cross-border data transfers, the Global Alliance for Genomics & Health is correct in asserting that: 'In the end, a privacy and security policy must drive the technological choices and final security architecture when sharing data among entities that may span institutional, geographic, and regulatory boundaries.'[62]

In the 1990s, Lex Informatica (or Code) was seen as a viable solution to the jurisdictional dilemmas global technological solutions pose, and it seems to be gaining traction again, now often referred to as algorithmic law. The idea is that a legal regulatory regime lacks the flexibility that the information society requires. Instead, technological rules are used as they do not rely on national borders, allow easy customisation of rules, and benefit from built-in self-enforcement and compliance-monitoring capabilities.[63] The jurisdiction of Lex Informatica is the network itself.[64] Regardless of whether Lex Informatica could be a viable solution to the processing of genomic data in the cloud, we acknowledge that a harmonious balance between technology and legislation is a necessity.

5.4. RISK MITIGATION

Similarly to the situation in other industries, some of the risks of placing DNA data in the cloud may be mitigated by ensuring adequate encryption. As recommended for example by Dove et al., '[r]esearchers should ensure that their own organization has data encryption capabilities and good management infrastructure for control over data stored on a cloud.'[65] Art. 89 GDPR requires that safeguards are in place to ensure respect for the principle of data minimisation in scientific research, mentioning pseudonymisation as one example of such a safeguard.

---

62 Global Alliance For Genomics & Health, 'Genomic and Clinical Data Sharing Policy Questions with Technology and Security Implications: Consensus Position Statements from the Data Safe Havens Task Team' (18.10.2014) <https://genomicsandhealth.org/files/public/FinalV2_Data%20Safe%20Havens%20Task%20Team_Deliverable_0.pdf> accessed 08.07.2016.

63 J.R. Reidenberg, 'Lex Informatica: The Formulation of Information Policy Rules Through Technology' (1998) 76(3) *Texas Law Review* 553–584, 572.

64 Ibid., 573.

65 E.S. Dove, Y. Joly and A-M. Tassé, 'Genomic cloud computing: legal and ethical points to consider' (2015) 23 *European Journal of Human Genetics* 1271–1278, 1274.

5.5. EDUCATION

In a 2015 determination by the Australian Privacy Commissioner, Timothy Pilgrim, a patient, was awarded a written apology and A$6,500 as a result of the patient's doctor having disclosed personal information about the patient to a law enforcement officer.[66] The officer in question had simply called the doctor and the doctor had disclosed the personal information in question.

Such examples are not rare, and while it may reasonably be presumed that those engaged in research in the DNA field generally have a better understanding of the data privacy considerations involved, one key step forward is to ensure that researchers and doctors gain an even better understanding of their legal obligations. Education in itself is not enough to ensure compliance, but education should be an integrated element of a solution.

5.6. BALANCE OF RESPONSIBILITIES

The role of ethics committees discussed above is, as noted by Reichel, one of two basic points of departure in the area of genomic research. The other is consent:

> In regards to human biological samples in research, two basic points of departure can be identified in national and international law. First, the use of human biological samples in research is conditioned on the informed consent in some form of the donor. Secondly, research on human biological samples should be placed under the review of independent research ethics committees.[67]

We acknowledge the limits to consent, which today is widely used as a basis for depositing individual level genomic data in international clouds. Data subjects (the donors) are often asked to provide their informed consent in relation to matters most lawyers do not fully understand. The impact of choice of law and choice of forum clauses are good examples of this. Such consent can therefore never be truly informed, and to pretend that it is, can only be harmful.

But we must also take care not to create an unworkable 'nanny state' where the individual no longer accepts any personal responsibility. Finding the correct balance of responsibilities is a serious challenge for regulators in this field. Dynamic consent is a promising option for creating better-informed and more understandable consents.[68]

---

66 *'EZ' and 'EY'* [2015] AlCmr 23 (27.03.2015).

67 J. Reichel, above n. 27, p. 358 (internal footnotes omitted).

68 I.B. Ljøsne, H.J.A. Teare, J. Kaye, S. Beck, H.B. Bentzen, L. Caenazzo, C. Collett, F. D'Abramo, H. Felzmann, T. Finlay, M.K. Javaid, E. Jones, V. Katic, A. Simpson and D. Mascalzoni, 'Dynamic Consent: a potential solution to some of the challenges of modern biomedical research', *BMC Medical Ethics*, 2017, 18:4.

We must ensure that consents are not misused. Inspiration for a workable 'misuse model' may perhaps be found in the 1993 EU Directive on unfair contractual terms in consumer contracts.[69] The Directive provides generally worded provisions meant to ensure that unfair terms are not upheld in consumer contracts. Importantly, those generally worded provisions are combined with detailed examples of types of terms that generally are seen as unfair. This is a highly useful structure that could be replicated in our context here. However, there is another – much less flattering – reason to take note of the 1993 Directive on unfair contractual terms in consumer contracts. One need only sign up for one of the common online services most of us use to come across terms that clearly fall within the unfair terms of the mentioned Directive, and yet they are presented to millions of European users. This tells us something important; in the end, what really matters is not only how we structure regulation in this field, it also matters that the regulation in question actually is enforced.

6. CONCLUDING REMARKS

To date, there has been a paucity of research addressing the international law issues discussed above in the context of DNA data processing in transnational clouds.[70] There is a pressing need for research on this topic. After all, the discussed technologies, and the use of the technologies, are moving forward constantly and rapidly, and the absence of a solid understanding of the legal considerations involved comes with obvious risks.

It could perhaps be suggested that the jurisdictional complexity described above – with a great number of overlapping laws from different countries being applicable to DNA databases – works to promote data privacy. After all, the jurisdictional complexity creates a degree of uncertainty for database operators, and where they wish to ensure compliance with all laws that potentially apply to them, they would rationally abide by the strictest data privacy standards to which they may be exposed. However, first of all, it is questionable that this is how the operators of DNA databases respond in practice. Furthermore, appropriate data privacy protection should be ensured by good data privacy rules, not by unclear rules of jurisdiction. The data privacy protection provided by our complex jurisdictional rules must be improved.

In the above, we have not aimed at being exhaustive on any one topic. Rather, to make the presentation accessible to a diverse audience, we have provided a brief introduction to both DNA data processing and to the legal issues. In addition, we have sought to briefly sketch some of the key considerations as we move forwards towards seeking real solutions in this field. Thus the aim of this chapter is modest, yet important.

---

69 Council Directive 93/13/EEC of 5 April 1993 on unfair terms in consumer contracts.

70 See, however, the excellent work of researchers such as J. Reichel, above n. 28.

SECTION IV

PRIVACY AND CRIME

12. REGULATING ECONOMIC CYBER-ESPIONAGE AMONG STATES UNDER INTERNATIONAL LAW

Maša Kovič Dine*

1. INTRODUCTION

A growing dependence on information and communication technologies as well as on Internet-based resources has made state actions and everyday activities of corporations unimaginable without the use of cyberspace. Cyberspace can be defined as 'the environment formed by physical and non-physical components, characterised by the use of computers and the electro-magnetic spectrum, to store, modify and exchange data using computer networks'.[1] Computer technology, cloud services and other cyberspace data storage options have enabled these actors to store mass data about their activities and access them through technological infrastructures. Additionally, the expansion in technology has changed the way companies develop their products and services, increasingly relying on information about customers' preferences, routines, likes and wishes, and thus gathering large collections of such data. While global interconnectivity and storage of information on computer networks has its benefits, it also makes it easier for unauthorised persons to manipulate such data. With the creation of proper algorithms they may deduce and access confidential information, such as corporations' trade secrets and patents, or customers' personal data and other sensitive information. Following the 2008 global economic crisis, governments have taken a more proactive role in ensuring their businesses strive in a global market. Thus, in the last decade, news stories keep surfacing of peacetime economic cyber-espionage between certain states, mostly between China and the United States.[2] This commonly occurs when one state hacks into the databases of

* Faculty of Law, University of Ljubljana. E-mail: masa.kovic-dine@pf.uni-lj.si.

1 M.N. Schmitt (ed.), *Tallinn Manual on the International Law Applicable to Cyber Warfare* (Tallinn Manual), Cambridge University Press, Cambridge 2013, p. 258.

2 See Reuters, 'China cyber espionage is more than an irritant, must stop: U.S.', 21 September 2015, <http://www.reuters.com/article/us-usa-china-idUSKCN0RL1VF20150921>; 'U.S. Report Accuses China and Russia of Internet Spying', *New York Times*, 3 November 2011,

corporations located in another state to use that data for the advantage of its own corporations and aid them in the competitive international markets.

The aim of this chapter is to crystalise the current understanding of peacetime economic cyber-espionage among states under international law, with a special reference to theft of personal and otherwise privileged data. Commencing in section 2, the chapter initially addresses the issues of legality or illegality of economic cyber-espionage under international law and analyses whether states could lawfully react to malicious economic cyber-espionage by relying on different existing international law principles and norms. Section 3 addresses the differences between traditional espionage and cyber-exploitation, which suggest a need for a separate regulation of economic cyber-exploitation at the international level. Privacy considerations related to the data stolen in economic cyber-espionage activities are presented in section 4. The possibility of applying the measures of the Agreement on Trade-Related Aspects of Intellectual Property Rights (TRIPS) to economic cyber-exploitation cases is illustrated in section 5. The main argument of the chapter is presented in section 6, which illustrates a possible analogy that could be drawn between economic cyber-exploitation and the international humanitarian law concept of pillage. Section 7 presents the differences in the perception of trans-Atlantic cyber-exploitation between the United States and the European Union. Finally, section 8 draws the conclusion with a suggestion to prohibit economic cyber-exploitation.

The author acknowledges that there are also important differences between economic cyber-exploitation and the pillage of private property and does not deny their relevance. The intention of the chapter is merely to present how this analogy can provide a few points for defining economic cyber-exploitation under international law and for regulating the trans-Atlantic theft of intellectual property between states.

2. LEGALITY OF ESPIONAGE UNDER INTERNATIONAL LAW

2.1. TRADITIONAL ESPIONAGE AND INTERNATIONAL LAW

Espionage among nations in times of both peace and war has been taking place since time immemorial. It can be defined as 'an undercover, state-sponsored intrusion into the restricted space of another state for the sake of collecting

<http://www.nytimes.com/2011/11/04/world/us-report-accuses-china-and-russia-of-internet-spying.html>; 'Chinese Army Unit is Seen as Tied to Hacking Against U.S.', *New York Times*, 18 February 2013, <http://www.nytimes.com/2013/02/19/technology/chinas-army-is-seen-as-tied-to-hacking-against-us.html>; CNN, 'Chinese Cyber Spies May be Watching You, Expert Warn', 28 August 2016, <http://www.cnn.com/2016/08/23/us/declassified-china-cyber-espionage/index.html>.

information.'[3] In essence, it represents an intrusion into one state's internal data by another state, and thus represents a violation of the principles of state sovereignty[4] and non-intervention.[5] However, there has been little interest among states to regulate espionage at the international level, as nearly all states actively practice it as part of their international security strategy. While there are some international rules limiting the scope of espionage,[6] neither customary international law nor international treaties explicitly prohibit it. However, legal scholarship has contrasting opinions on the nature of espionage, recognising it from legal to illegal, indicating the grey area of the issue. Some of these opinions on the legality of espionage will be presented below.

While the legal nature of espionage is unclear at the international level,[7] national legislations criminalised the traditional form of espionage (whether performed in time of peace or wartime) performed by individuals or entities as one of the crimes against the state. As most crimes of espionage are generally carried out on the territory of the affected state, the principle of territorial jurisdiction would allow the state to prosecute the foreign spy, if caught. However, the foreign spies as state agents may have immunity from prosecution.[8] Hence, in the past the states have merely declared them as *persona non grata*.[9] The protective principle of extra-territorial jurisdiction would allow the application of such national rules extra-territorially when the foreign spy conducts the espionage activities abroad. Under this principle, states may exercise jurisdiction over foreign nationals who have committed an act abroad, which can be deemed to be prejudicial to the security and the vital interests of the state concerned and represents a violation of the state's national laws.[10] Thus, a state may exercise this

---

3 R. Bitton, 'The Legitimacy of Spying among Nations' (2013), <http://ssrn.com/abstract=2323021>, p. 2.

4 S. Chesterman, 'The Spy Who Came in from the Cold War: Intelligence and International Law' (2006) 27 *Michigan Journal of International Law* 1081–1084.

5 C. Lotrionte, 'Countering State-Sponsored Cyber Economic Espionage under International Law' (2015) 40 *North Carolina Journal of International Law and Commercial Regulation* 443.

6 See e.g. Vienna Convention on Diplomatic Relations 1961 and Vienna Convention on Consular Relations 1969; Convention on the Law of the Sea 1982, 1833 UNTS 3, Art. 19: 'Passage of a foreign ship shall be considered to be prejudicial to the peace, good order or security of the coastal State if in the territorial sea it engages in any of the following activities … any act aimed at collecting information to the prejudice of the defence or security of the coastal State.'

7 K. Ziolkowski, 'Peacetime Cyber Espionage – New Tendencies in Public International Law' in K. Ziolkowski (ed.), *Peacetime Regime for State Activities in Cyberspace: International Law, International Relations and Diplomacy*, NATO CCD COE Publications, Tallinn 2013, p. 462; Chesterman, above n. 4, pp. 1074–1075.

8 Vienna Convention on Diplomatic Relations, 500 UNTS 95 (1961), Art. 31.

9 Lotrionte, above n. 5, pp. 460–461; D.P. Fidler, 'Economy Cyber Espionage and International Law: Controversies Involving Government Acquisition of Trade Secrets through Cyber Technologies' (2013) 17(10) *ASIL InSights*, <https://www.asil.org/insights/volume/17/issue/10/economic-cyber-espionage-and-international-law-controversies-involving>.

10 M.N. Shaw, *International Law*, 6th ed., Cambridge University Press, Cambridge 2008, pp. 666–667.

jurisdiction and initiate proceedings against the foreign spy regardless if the act is not considered an offence under the law of the spy's state and if extradition to the concerned state is refused.[11] As Shaw recognises, there are still uncertainties as to how far this principle extends in practice, and which acts it could cover.[12] This also puts into question the applicability of this principle to espionage. Since this chapter concentrates on regulating espionage at the international level, further address of the extra-territorial application of national rules is outside its scope.

Nonetheless, an attempt to criminalise hacking into computer and network systems has been made also at the international level with the Council of Europe's adoption of the Convention on Cybercrime[13] in 2001. The Convention calls on states to establish as criminal offences under their domestic law, when committed intentionally, any illegal access, illegal interception, data interference, system interference, and misuse of devices.[14] Article 2 of the Convention specifically addresses the theft of data by criminalising illegal access carried out through infringement of security measures with the intent to obtaining computer data. The Convention prohibits illegal access and interception of data and information by individuals and entities and requires from states to punish such individuals or entities under the domestic criminal code. It does not carry such a prohibition for states, hence leaving the issue of economic cyber-espionage among states unaddressed.[15]

Another set of international documents that contain measures relating to espionage are those addressing the relationship between states in times of war. These documents do not explicitly prohibit espionage, but define treatment of captured foreign spies. As the issue of the treatment of spies surpasses the scope of the chapter, the following paragraph only presents these documents. The Lieber Code,[16] drafted in 1863 by request of Abraham Lincoln for the Union Army, determined the punishment with death by hanging for a spy for the act of spying.[17] Similar positions were adopted in the 1874 Declaration of Brussels,[18]

---

11 Ibid., p. 667.

12 Ibid.

13 Convention on Cybercrime, Council of Europe, ETS 185 (2001).

14 Arts. 2–6, Convention on Cybercrime.

15 W.C. Banks, 'Cyber Espionage, Surveillance, and International Law: Finding Common Ground', keynote address delivered to the Texas A&M Law Review Symposium, 17.10.2014, <http://ssrn.com/abstract=2558155>, p. 10.

16 Instructions for the Government of Armies of the United States in the Field (the Lieber Code), prepared by Francis Lieber, LLD, Originally Issued as General Orders No. 100, Adjutant General's Office, 1863, Washington: Government Printing Office (1898), <https://ihl-databases.icrc.org/ihl/INTRO/110>.

17 Art. 88, Lieber Code.

18 International Declaration concerning the Laws and Customs of War (Declaration of Brussels), Brussels, 27 August 1874, <https://ihl-databases.icrc.org/applic/ihl/ihl.nsf/Treaty.xsp?action=openDocument&documentId=42F78058BABF9C51C12563CD002D6659>.

the first effort of codifying the laws of war.[19] Spying was permitted, but if the spy was caught, he was tried and treated according to the laws of the state whose army captured him and was recognised as a prisoner of war.[20] Later documents, such as the 1899 and 1907 Hague Conventions[21] as well as the 1949 Geneva Conventions,[22] confirmed that captured spies should be tried and punished according to the laws of the capturing state, are not recognised the status of a prisoner of war, and are to be treated with humanity.[23] These rules all apply in an international armed conflict. However, the International Committee of the Red Cross' Commentary to the 1949 Geneva Convention notes that also in non-international armed conflicts, spies should be treated humanely and can only be punished based on a judgement by a regularly constituted court.[24] It needs to be pointed out nevertheless that spies sent to steal information in times of war do not engage the international responsibility of the state that sends them, according to the Additional Protocol to the Geneva Conventions Relating to the Protection of Victims of International Armed Conflicts.[25]

In the past, states targeted by espionage did not claim that such activities were contrary to international law, nor initiated international legal proceedings against each other with regard to it. Grotius in the seventeenth century noted that sending spies in wartime is permitted by the law of nations, and that any state that refuses to use spies in wartime does so out of arrogance, rather than considering espionage illegal.[26] Oppenheim confirmed that 'all states constantly or occasionally send spies abroad, and ... it is not considered wrong morally, politically, or legally to do so'.[27] Building on this position, some authors argue

---

19 Chesterman, above n. 7, p. 1079.

20 Art. 20, Declaration of Brussels.

21 Hague Convention (II) with Respect to the Laws and Customs of War on Land and Its Annex: Regulations Concerning the Laws and Customs of War on Land (1899 Hague Convention), 32 Stat. 1803, 187 Consol. T.S. 456 (1899), <http://www.icrc.org/ihl.nsf/FULL/150?OpenDocument>; Hague Convention (IV) Respecting the Laws and Customs of War on Land and Its Annex: Regulations Concerning the Laws and Customs of War on Land (1907 Hague Convention), 36 Stat. 2277, 187 Consol. 227 (1907), <http://www.icrc.org/ihl.nsf/FULL/195?OpenDocument>.

22 Geneva Convention (IV) Relative to the Protection of Civilian Persons in Time of War (1949 IV Geneva Convention), 75 UNTS 287 (1949), <http://www.icrc.org/ihl.nsf/FULL/380?OpenDocument>.

23 1899 Hague Convention, Arts. 29, 30, 31; 1907 Hague Convention, Arts. 29, 30, 31; 1949 IV Geneva Convention, Arts. 4, 5, 64–76.

24 Geneva Convention (IV) Relative to the Protection of Civilian Persons in Time of War, Commentary of 1958, Comentary to Art. 154, International Committee of the Red Cross, <https://ihl-databases.icrc.org/ihl/COM/380-600177?OpenDocument>, p. 616.

25 Protocol Additional to the Geneva Conventions of 12 August 1949, and Relating to the Protection of Victims of International Armed Conflicts, UN Doc. A/32/144/Annex I (1977), <http://www.icrc.org/ihl>.

26 Chesterman, above n. 7, p. 1078; H. Grotius, *De Jure Belli Ac Pacis Libri* Tres 655 (1646), translation by Francis W. Kelsey (1925).

27 L. Oppenheim, *International Law: A Treatise*, H. Lauterpacht (ed.), 7th ed., Longman's, Green & Co, London 1948, Vol. I, pp. 770, 772.

that espionage is justifiable under international law as a tool for states to facilitate international cooperation.[28] Espionage permits states to verify that their neighbours are complying with their international obligations, which gives states incentives to continue to cooperate in international matters.[29] Bitton takes a step further, justifying espionage as a tool for enforcing transparency in international relations towards proximate neighbouring non-liberal states.[30] He argues that espionage prevents intervention between liberal and non-liberal governments claiming that it enables the proximate neighbouring states to know the positions and stances towards each other. It thus facilitates international trust, cooperation and stability and prevents the need of states to be constantly in a state of vigilance and preparation to forcefully respond to a threat against each other.[31]

On the contrary, some authors argue that espionage should be prohibited under international law. While acknowledging the absence of the specific rules addressing espionage under international law they believe that espionage activities violate the general international law principles of state sovereignty and non-intervention.[32]

Already the above few examples illustrate the complexity of regulating intelligence gathering among states. While it might be difficult to confirm that traditional espionage is illegal under international law, the author believes there are reasons that indicate that economic cyber-espionage with data theft, as a specific form of espionage, could be considered illegal under international law.

2.2. DEFINITION OF ECONOMIC CYBER-ESPIONAGE/ EXPLOITATION

Economic cyber-espionage, or cyber-exploitation as it is sometimes referred to, could be defined as a clandestine activity engaged in or facilitated by a foreign government against a computer system or network designed to gain unauthorised access to economic intelligence, such as proprietary information, technology or personal data, for economic advantage.[33] Simply said, economic cyber-exploitation takes place when the government of state A uses its

28 C.D. Baker, 'Tolerance of International Espionage: A Functional Approach' (2003) 19 *American University International Law Review* 1092.

29 Ibid.

30 Britton, above n. 3, p. 17.

31 Ibid., pp. 23–25.

32 R. Buchan, 'The International Legal Regulation of State-Sponsored Cyber Espionage' in A.M. Osula and H. Röigas (eds.), *International Cyber Norms: Legal, Policy and Industry Perspectives*, NATO CCD COE Publications, Tallinn 2016, pp. 3–16.

33 Canadian Security Intelligence Service, 'Economic Security' (1994), <http://www.datapacrat.com/True/INTEL/CSIS/BACK6E.HTM>.

intelligence system against a computer network of a company located in state B to access proprietary information or customers' personal information for the economic benefit of the companies in state A. Most of these hacks are not channelled towards theft of proprietary information with the intention of gaining commercial advantage of the home company over the foreign company. The intention of these attacks is to steal collections of data with consumers' personal information, to damage the foreign company's reputation or to sell the stolen data to a third party.[34] The latest example of such economic cyber-exploitation is the case of the Sony Pictures Entertainment e-mail hack, where a group of hackers suspected to work with the North Korean government targeted Sony corporate and employee data over a comedy movie referencing the North Korean leader.[35] The data theft was combined with terrorist threats, which led to the decision that movie theatres in the US would not screen the movie.[36] This decision impacted the earnings of the movie producers and movie theatres, as well as making public the private e-mail correspondence of the Sony staff with damaging content.

Economic cyber-exploitation is a special form of cyber-espionage among states. It is perpetrated in time of peace by a state or actors whose actions are attributable to the state and the target is another state and its businesses. It is considered as espionage among states, as the target are not only the businesses in another state, but also the state itself. First, the state has the interest in protecting the confidential information of its companies and its economy on the international markets. Secondly, the confidential information is stored/available on the cyber-infrastructure allocated on the territory of the targeted state. The emergence of cloud computing which enables states and companies to store data on a server that can be located worldwide does not change the above described definition of economic cyber-exploitation. The state where the targeted business is registered continues to hold interest in the protection of the confidential information and its economy. It may however complicate the question of ownership of the information and thus the state's jurisdiction for prosecution of theft. Further elaboration of this question at this early stage in the development of international law on economic cyber-espionage would be premature. Economic cyber-exploitation should not be confused with cyber-espionage between businesses, i.e. industrial espionage. Industrial espionage relates to theft of trade secrets and collections of data between private sector entities without any government involvement and is thus not subject to public international law but rather both civil and criminal law at a national level.

---

34 A. Cravero and P. Dalton, 'Digital Assets Theft: Cybersecurity' (2016) 22(3) *Computer and Telecommunications Law Review* 72.

35 S. Kirchner, 'Beyond Privacy Rights: Cross-Border Cyber-Espionage and International Law' (2014) 31(3) *John Marshall Journal of Information Technology and Privacy Law* 370–371.

36 Ibid., p. 371.

Due to their complexity, the breadth of information that can be stolen, the nature of the information stolen and the possibility of leading to a serious cyber-attack, there are appeals for economic cyber-exploitation to be regulated under public international law. The author believes that these special characteristics of economic cyber-exploitation provide an important distinction from traditional espionage and thus provide for a greater need for international regulation.

3. SPECIAL CHARACTERISTICS OF ECONOMIC CYBER-EXPLOITATION

There are five significant differences between traditional espionage and economic cyber-exploitation, which suggest a different international response to economic cyber-exploitation. This chapter focuses on economic cyber-exploitation among states and not the theft of information by individuals/entities for private benefits, which has been recognised by some states already as a cyber-crime (above, section 2.1). Hence the described differences centre on activities of hackers sponsored by states.

First, with the development of digital technology it has become much easier to steal economic information from others. The development of computer systems has enabled companies to gather information on servers for various purposes. At the same time the development of the Internet has enabled easy access to this data from unauthorised sources, which could be located in faraway places and with a hidden identity. Today a government may hire a hacker in a foreign country, who uses servers in several other countries to steal data from a company in a third country and thus fully conceal all the traces.

Not only is the theft of large collections of data today easier to carry out, it also makes a lot of sense financially. It is cheaper to access the tools and technology to carry out a cyber-attack on a foreign company and to conduct hacking activities necessary for such steeling of big data, than to conduct all the lengthy, resource demanding research to develop new products, technology and programs. Hence, states often practice economic cyber-exploitation as a cheap alternative to traditional research and development. Such theft is increasing from year to year. Latest examples of trans-Atlantic economic cyber-exploitation between states indicate that industry losses from data theft range as high as a few million dollars,[37] with a report by the Ponemon Institute pointing out that the average costs of cyber-attacks on US companies in 2012 was $8.9 million.[38]

---

37 J. Adams, 'Decriminalizing Hacktivism: Finding Space for Free Speech Protests on the Internet', George Washington University Law School (2013), <http://ssrn.com/abstract=2392945>, p. 23.

38 '2012 Cost of Cyber Crime Study: United States', Ponemon Institute (October 2012), <http://www.ponemon.org/local/upload/file/2012_US_Cost_of_Cyber_Crime_Study_FINAL6%20.pdf>, p. 1.

The former Cyber Command and NSA Director Keith Alexander called it 'the greatest transfer of wealth in history'.[39] Such theft positions the foreign companies at an advantage on the international markets and gives them a leap in technological advancements.[40]

Secondly, the breadth of data stolen is much larger than with traditional espionage. With traditional espionage, the amount of data that could be stolen was usually limited to the individual spies' ability to remember certain information or to carry the data storage devices. With the development of new technologies, these storage devices have become smaller and are able to store larger amounts of information. However, the cyberspace is even more convenient as it enables instant and unlimited access to a company's remote data storage location and thus to the intellectual property and personal information.

Thirdly, due to the possibility of using technology to mask the paths of data theft, it takes a long time to investigate such theft, leading to few conclusive answers. Cyberspace enables states to hide their actions behind anonymous hackers operating abroad and through foreign server systems, making it difficult to track the theft down to the state. Additionally, attribution to the right perpetrator is nearly impossible. Even the US Office of the National Counterintelligence Executive itself confirmed that it has not been able to attribute many of the data thefts to the state that ordered and sponsored such acts.[41]

Fourth, for all the above-mentioned reasons, cyber-exploitation may also open doors for cyber-attacks on critical governmental and corporate infrastructure, as it indicates paths for hidden access to critical data. Namely, examples of economic cyber-exploitation indicate that intellectual property is not the only information stolen. Often the thefts target companies' business strategies, data collections and research and development. With this material the foreign state may also gain direct access to important governmental infrastructure or other undisclosed governmental information such as blueprints, designs or security codes for a state's critical infrastructure. Holding such information may enable the foreign state to cause significant damage to governmental property and the functioning of the third state.

Finally, more and more of the latest cyber-exploitation cases are focused on the theft of personal data. With the Internet entering all spheres of our life, we are more commonly sharing with various companies a plethora of information from our names, addresses, e-mails, telephone to credit card numbers. Additionally, through social media, people are seemingly more willing to share with the rest of the world their 'likes', feelings, wishes and expectations. Companies gather and store this information on their customers for various reasons. While some of it

---

39 Banks, above n. 15, p. 5.

40 Lotrionte, above n. 5, p. 452.

41 Fidler, above n. 9.

is necessary for the performance of their services, other information is gathered by companies to better understand their customers and thus to improve their products and services. The theft and leaking of valuable and confidential information thus poses a double risk – a risk to businesses and a risk to individuals or entities whose data has been stolen. Data theft poses a risk to all businesses, but especially to those in industries relying heavily on their own research and development.[42] The companies receiving this data may use it for their advantage or worse, misappropriate it. Most commonly this data is published publicly with the intention to cause damage to the competing company from a foreign state.[43] However, such publishing of customers' personal data on the Internet and consequently elsewhere poses also a great risk to these individuals and brings up questions of protection of their privacy.

4. ECONOMIC CYBER-EXPLOITATION AND PRIVACY CONSIDERATIONS AT THE INTERNATIONAL LEVEL

The basic international human rights documents all protect the right to private life and privacy. When individuals submit their information to various online services from Facebook, Twitter, to Amazon, they do so voluntarily, granting these companies permission to collect and handle it for their needs (depending on the specific data collection agreements). A problem arises when this data is stolen in an economic cyber-exploitation attack and made public, like the example of the published e-mails of the Sony Picture Entertainment employees.

Article 12 of the Universal Declaration of Human Rights,[44] Art. 17 of the International Covenant on Civil and Political Rights (ICCPR),[45] as well as Art. 8 of the European Convention on Human Rights (ECHR),[46] all protect the right to privacy and private life, which encompass also the protection of personal data. The Charter of Fundamental Rights of the European Union is even more precise in this protection, as its Art. 8 specifically grants every individual the right to protection of his/her personal data,[47] additionally to Art. 7, which protects the right to private life like the other three documents. All the mentioned basic international human rights documents require the states parties to take positive actions to prevent human rights violations also by non-state actors (in this case hackers).[48] States are free to take different measures in their domestic law to

---

42 Cravero and Dalton, above n. 34, p. 71.
43 Ibid., p. 72.
44 Universal Declaration of Human Rights, UN GA Resolution 217 A (III), 10 December 1948.
45 International Covenant on Civil and Political Rights, GA res. 2200A (XXI), 21 UN GAOR Supp. (No. 16) at 52, UN Doc. A/6316 (1966); 999 UNTS 171(1967).
46 European Convention for the Protection of Human Rights and Fundamental Freedoms, ETS 5; 213 UNTS 221 (1950).
47 Charter of Fundamental Rights of the European Union, [2010] OJ C 83/389–403.
48 Kirchner, above n. 35, p. 376.

ensure the minimum standard required for by these international human rights documents. Unfortunately, the language of the relevant articles is rather vague and gives the states a lot of flexibility in implementing this obligation in their national legislations. Additionally, the scope of these documents is limited to everyone within the jurisdiction of the state party.[49] The state has to ensure that personal data is protected on its territory from being published. Relying on the principle of objective territorial jurisdiction, the state may persecute for the violation of the domestic rules on privacy protection any foreign hackers that have published the stolen personal data on a computer network located on the territory of the state.[50] Other forms of extra-territorial jurisdiction would not apply in this case. However, the special characteristics of economic cyber-exploitation set obstacles to such prosecution. First, the hacking activities are sponsored by a foreign state and thus the hackers could be considered state agents with immunities from prosecution. Secondly, cyberspace knows no borders and neither does the global market. Companies hold personal data from individuals from all over the world and the stolen personal data may be published on a computer network anywhere in the world. It can cause equally serious damage to these individuals regardless of where it is published. The Tallinn Manual on the International Law Applicable to Cyber Warfare (Tallinn Manual), a non-binding study by a group of experts examining international law rules applicable to cyber-warfare, notes that cyberspace is not a legal lacuna and that the sovereignty of a state in cyberspace is limited to the territory of that state, i.e. the cyber infrastructure allocated on its territory.[51] Thus, the state cannot prosecute hackers when the personal data is published on a computer network abroad. This further indicates a need for special regulation of economic cyber-expliotation at the international level. The issue of privacy and data protection could be a part of such a regulation.

States have been already taking a step in this direction. The European Union, which is leading in the data protection field has been trying to address the issue of economic cyber-exploitation for personal data through regulating companies' data collection and storage practices and managing risks. In July 2016, the European Council adopted the Network and Information Security Directive (NIS Directive),[52] which lays down obligations to ensure secure network and information systems and thus – *inter alia* – prevent data theft for operators of essential services, like energy, transport, health and finances, and digital service providers. The NIS Directive extends the requirement of ensuring

49 Art. 2 ICCPR; Art. 1 ECHR.

50 Tallinn Manual, Rule 2, p. 20.

51 Tallinn Manual, Rules 1 and 2, pp. 15–21.

52 The Directive entered into force in August 2016 and the Member States have 21 months to transpose it into their national laws. Directive (EU) 2016/1148 of the European Parliament and of the Council of 6 July 2016 concerning measures for a high common level of security of network and information systems across the Union, [2016] OJ L 194/1–30.

secure network and information systems to all online service providers like search engines, cloud providers, social networks, public administrations, online payment platforms and ecommerce websites. The online service providers have a new requirement to report any significant cyber incidents. The NIS Directive is also intended to increase the cooperation between the Member States on vital issues of cyber-security. This means that companies operating online will have an obligation to ensure a secure and trustworthy digital environment where data protection will be given the highest regard, by conducting prescribed risk management.[53] The aim of the Directive is to ensure that companies operating online take appropriate steps to deal with cyber-threats and theft of data, as well as to share information about these threats between EU Member States.[54] Thus, the Directive is expected to reduce the incidence of economic cyber-exploitation cases in EU.

The main document addressing data protection in the EU is the General Data Protection Regulation (GDPR)[55] adopted in April 2016 that holds strict obligations on data protection for all controllers and processors of personal data. The Regulation replaces the 1995 Data Protection Directive[56] and simplifies the data protection rules by harmonising them into one single document for the whole EU. While the Regulation entered into force on 24 May 2016, it shall apply from 25 May 2018. Until then the Data Protection Directive and its transposed measures in national legislations are valid. Article 5 of GDPR requires that all personal data be processed under strict conditions and only for a legitimate purpose. These requirements also apply to issues of cyber-security.[57] Any unauthorised access to processed data, transmission, storage and disclosure is considered a breach of the data protection rules.[58] The GDPR hence recognises as a data breach already any access to the personal data, which means any hacking into the system of a company/data processor, regardless of how the hacker and/or the state sponsoring the hacking activities uses this accessed

---

53 Proposal for a Directive of the European Parliament and of the Council concerning measures to ensure a high common level of network and information security across the Union (NIS Directive Proposal), COM/2013/048 final – 2013/0027 (COD), p. 4.

54 P. Ryan, P. Buckenham and N. Donnelly, 'EU Network and Information Security Directive: Is it possible to legislate for cyber security?', Arthur Cox, Technology and Innovation, Group Briefing, October 2014, <http://www.arthurcox.com/wp-content/uploads/2014/10/Arthur-Cox-EU-Network-and-Information-Security-Directive-October-2014.pdf>.

55 The Regulation entered into force in May 2016 and will apply from 25 May 2018. Regulation (EU) 2016/679 of the European Parliament and of the Council of 27 April 2016 on the protection of natural persons with regard to the processing of personal data and on the free movement of such data, and repealing Directive 95/46/EC (General Data Protection Regulation), [2016] OJ L 119/1–88.

56 Directive 95/46/EC of the European Parliament and of the Council of 24 October 1995 on the protection of individuals with regard to the processing of personal data and on the free movement of such data, [1995] OJ L 281/31–50.

57 Cravero and Dalton, above n. 34, p. 66.

58 Art. 4, GDPR.

data. Thus, all controllers and processors shall implement appropriate technical and organisational measures to ensure security of the processed data relevant to the appropriate risk and prevent the hackers to gain this data and process it further.[59] The Regulation offers suggestions as to the methods of protection, but these are only exemplary, as the measures taken should be appropriate to the type of data collected and the risk level.[60] The processors of personal data are given the option to choose the most appropriate method for data protection. Some of the suggestions include encryption and pseudonymisation of the personal data, as well as ensuring ongoing confidentiality, and carrying out regular testing, assessment and evaluation of the effectiveness of the technical and organisational measures for ensuring the security of the processed data.[61]

The Regulation also sets a process for notification of any data breach, which is likely to result in a risk to the rights and freedoms of natural persons.[62] Any processor is obliged to report the breach to the national supervisory authority and the controller. In cases of high risk to the rights and freedoms of the natural persons, the breach should be also notified to the concerned individuals.[63] After such a breach legal action may be taken according to the national rules of each Member State. However, in cases of economic cyber-exploitation and data breach, the difficulties with prosecution are the same as those for prosecuting foreign spies described above (above, section 2.1). Even if there is enough evidence to attribute the actions of the hackers to the sponsoring state, no legal action under this directive can be taken against it.

On the contrary, the US has refrained from regulation of personal data protection and have allowed companies and associations to regulate themselves.[64] The US Constitution and other privacy statutes regulate the government's use of personal data far more broadly and strictly than the private use of such data.[65] The focus is thus on protection of data from the US Government's exploitation. Related to that is also the fact that data privacy is not regulated with one general act at the federal level, but with numerous acts within industry sectors and at the state levels.[66] This indicates the difficulties in ensuring protection of stolen data in economic cyber-exploitation cases in the US.

Privacy rules are extremely important for data protection and can play a crucial role in ensuring that companies protect personal data from economic

---

59 Art. 32 GDPR.
60 Ibid.
61 Ibid.
62 Arts. 33 and 34 GDPR.
63 Ibid.
64 J.M. Fromholz, 'The European Union Data Privacy Directive' (2000) 18(1) *Berkeley Technology Law Journal* 461.
65 Ibid., p. 470.
66 Ibid., p. 471.

cyber-exploitation. They present a piece in the puzzle of data protection in economic cyber-exploitation cases. This piece ensures that only adequate, necessary and consented data is collected, as well as that strong data protection mechanisms are in place to prevent data theft. However, if data theft takes place, these rules are ineffective indicating an additional need for a specific regulation of economic cyber-exploitation at the international level.

5. ECONOMIC CYBER-ESPIONAGE AND THE TRIPS AGREEMENT

At the international level, the theft of proprietary information and intellectual property by individuals is already regulated by the Agreement on Trade-Related Aspects of Intellectual Property Rights (TRIPS).[67] This sets out the minimum standards of intellectual property protection that Member States of the World Trade Organisation (WTO) should adopt in their national legislations. While this does call for a universal standard on intellectual property protection, it does not address economic cyber-exploitation cases.

Nonetheless, several authors[68] and even states have considered the TRIPS Agreement as an option to protect their companies from foreign hacking. One of the benefits stressed is the WTO dispute settlement system and the possibility of bringing a case of economic cyber-exploitation before its Dispute Settlement Body.[69] The US administration noted in one of its reports on cyber-security, that it will not hesitate to use the WTO dispute settlement procedures against other states for intellectual property theft, if the bilateral negotiations with the relevant states are unsuccessful.[70] This could be understood also for economic cyber-exploitation cases. However, the report does not state which measures of the TRIPS Agreement they would base their arguments on. Moreover, there are also certain difficulties in applying the TRIPS to economic cyber-exploitation, as explained below.[71]

The first difficulty is specific to TRIPS and not connected to economic cyber-exploitation. The standards for intellectual property protection set by the

---

67 Agreement on Trade-Related Aspects of Intellectual Property Rights (TRIPS), 1869 UNTS 299 (1994).

68 S. Malawer, 'Confronting Chinese Economic, Cyber Espionage with WTO Litigation', *New York Law Journal*, 24.12.2014, <http://www.newyorklawjournal.com/id=1202712784205/Confronting-Chinese-Economic-Cyber-Espionage-With-WTO-Litigation#ixzz3MfIKeTXb>, p. 3; C.P. Skinner, 'An international law response to economic cyber espionage' (2014) 46 *Connecticut Law Review* 1165; Lotrionte, above n. 5, p. 527.

69 Fidler, above n. 9.

70 Office of the United States Trade Representative Demetrios Marantis, 2013 Special 301 Report, <https://ustr.gov/sites/default/files/05012013%202013%20Special%20301%20Report.pdf>, p. 25.

71 Malawer, above n. 68, p. 3; Fidler, above n. 9.

TRIPS are the minimum standards, which often do not satisfy the protection requests and needs of companies in developed countries. Thus, developed countries routinely adopt bilateral intellectual property protection treaties with higher protection standards[72] lowering the value and effect of TRIPS. On the other hand, developing countries find these standards too high and routinely ask for extension of the deadlines by which they must comply with the TRIPS standards,[73] mostly because through intellectual property theft they avoid spending large funds for research and development.

Secondly, the data theft carried out in cyberspace in most cases does not constitute a single intellectual property theft as recognised and covered by TRIPS, like a theft of the information for a patent, trade secrets or trade mark. As mentioned above, in most cases it includes the theft of a collection of data gathered by a company for its research and development. This stolen information can be used and manipulated in various ways to the advantage of the thief. Additionally, the latest thefts are focused on stealing personal data to simply harm the foreign company on the international markets. Furthermore, it might sometimes be impossible even to pinpoint the real perpetrator of the theft, as the stolen data might be used differently by the perpetrator than the company from which the information has been stolen.

Thirdly, Art. 3(1) of TRIPS restates the most favoured national treatment principle, which requires the state to treat foreign companies no less favourable than national companies with regard to protection of intellectual property rights.[74] The intention of this article is to afford the same protection of intellectual property rights to foreign companies as to national companies, as well as to enforce breaches of intellectual property rights. This means that a state cannot sponsor any spying activities or stealing intellectual property from foreign companies on its own territory for the benefit of its national companies. However, the TRIPS agreement nowhere discusses or addresses the theft of intellectual property rights from companies in a foreign state for the benefit of its national companies, as is the case with economic cyber-exploitation. The reason for this lies in the territorial nature of intellectual rights protection.[75] The protection of the intellectual property rights is limited to the territory of the state where they are granted.[76] Extra-territorial applicability of the protection of trade secrets and Art. 3(1) of TRIPS is not recognised and WTO Member States

---

72 E.A. Rowe and D.M. Mahfood, 'Trade Secrets, Trade and Extraterritoriality' (2014) 66 *Alabama Law Review* 82.

73 Ibid.

74 Art. 3(1) TRIPS.

75 A. Peukert, 'Territoriallity and Extraterritoriallity of Intellectual Property Law' in G. Handl, J. Zekoll and P. Zumbansen (eds.), *Beyond Territoriality: Transnational Legal Authority in an Age of Globalization, Queen Mary Studies in International Law*, Brill Academic Publishing, Leiden/Boston 2012, p. 189.

76 Ibid., pp. 189–190.

have shown no interest in expanding the territorial protection of intellectual property rights to other states.[77] Thus, under the TRIPS Agreement and Art. 3(1), a state does not have the obligation to treat foreign companies in a foreign state no less favourably than its own national companies.

There have been suggestions that discrimination referred to in Art. 3(1) with reference to economic cyber-exploitation may take place at the level of dissemination of the stolen data. Discrimination thus happens when data stolen though state-sponsored hacking activities in a foreign state is provided only to national companies and excludes foreign companies from having this information. In this case, foreign companies within the perpetrating state are objects of less favourable treatment compared to national companies. However, this argument does not address the essence of economic cyber-exploitation.[78] Nor does it grant any protection to the foreign companies from which the undisclosed information has been stolen.

An option where economic cyber-exploitation could be addressed and companies could counter the theft of their undisclosed data is Art. 39 of the TRIPS Agreement. This provision in the first paragraph calls on states to protect undisclosed information in order to ensure effective protection against unfair competition. The second paragraph additionally states that 'natural and legal persons shall have the possibility of preventing information lawfully within their control from being disclosed to, acquired by, or used by other without their consent in a manner contrary to honest commercial practices'.[79] Such information has to be secret, has to have commercial value because it is secret, and has been subject to reasonable steps under the circumstances, to be kept secret by the person lawfully in control of the information.[80] Economic information stolen through economic cyber-exploitation has the nature of undisclosed information. Economic cyber-exploitation could be regarded as contrary to honest commercial practice. Thus, the companies owning undisclosed data must have the possibility to prevent and stop infringements, as well as to recover the losses incurred.[81] Therefore, under the TRIPS Agreement, WTO Member States have to introduce into their national legislation enforcement procedures enabling prompt and effective action against infringements of intellectual property rights.[82] Due to the above-mentioned lack of extra-territorial applicability of the substance of the TRIPS Agreement, the rules on enforcement procedures should apply for theft of data within the state. However, nothing prevents a state adopting legislation that extends its jurisdiction in such cases also to foreign hackers, as does the

[77] Fidler, above n. 71; Banks, above n. 15, p. 9.
[78] Lotrionte, above n. 5, p. 530; Malawer, above n. 68, p. 4.
[79] Art. 39(2) TRIPS Agreement.
[80] Ibid.
[81] Art. 41 TRIPS Agreement.
[82] Art. 42 TRIPS Agreement.

US Economic Espionage Act (below, section 7).[83] Nonetheless, this option is inapplicable if the concerned state has not extended its jurisdiction.

All the above-mentioned leads to the conclusion that economic cyber-exploitation activities are not yet comprehensively regulated by international law. The TRIPS Agreement could provide some suggestions, but they are limited.[84]

6. ACT OF PILLAGE

A possible analogy for regulating economic cyber-exploitation at the international level could be drawn from the international humanitarian law concept of pillage. Pillage, which is prohibited under international law, and cyber-exploitation, share several commonalities.

Pillage is regarded as a forcible taking of private property by an invading or conquering party from the enemy's subjects in times of war.[85] The act of pillage is prohibited under customary international humanitarian law.[86] Looting and theft of private property have been part of war as long as espionage has been taking place among states.[87] However, for an equally long time they have been subject to prohibition and limitations.[88] The first codified prohibition was included in the Lieber Code from 1863.[89] The Hague Conventions of 1907 were the first to codify a general prohibition of pillage at the international level.[90] This was confirmed in 1949 by the Geneva Conventions[91] and extended to both international and non-international armed conflicts.[92] Though the Additional Protocol II to the Geneva Conventions refers to property of those not taking part in the armed conflict, the International Committee of the Red Cross (ICRC) has concluded that state practice does not confirm such a limitation, and prohibits pillage of any property.[93]

Pillage has also been prohibited as a war crime by international criminal law in the statutes of international criminal law tribunals. While the Statute of the

---

83 Economic Espionage Act (EEA), 18 U.S. Code § 1831 (1996).

84 Banks, above n. 15, p. 10.

85 *Black's Law Dictionary*, 5th ed., West Publishing, St. Paul MN 1979, p. 1033. V. Sancin, D. Švarc and M. Ambrož, *Mednarodno pravo oboroženih spopadov*, Littera Picta d.o.o., Ljubljana 2009, p. 101.

86 J.G. Stewart, *Corporate War Crimes: Prosecuting the Pillage of Natural Resources*, New York, Open Society Foundations 2011, p. 12; Customary International Humanitarial Law Rules, International Committee of the Red Cross, Rule 52, <https://ihl-databases.icrc.org/customary-ihl/eng/docs/v1_cha_chapter16_rule52>.

87 P.J. Keenan, 'Conflict Minerals and the Law of Pillage' 14(2) *Chicago Journal of International Law* 533.

88 Ibid.

89 Lieber Code, above n. 16, Art. 44.

90 Hague Conventions of 1907, above n. 21, Art. 47.

91 Geneva Convention (IV), above n. 22, Art. 33(2).

92 Additional Protocol II to the Geneva Conventions (1977), Art. 4(2)(g).

93 Stewart, above n. 86, p. 12.

International Criminal Tribunal for the former Yugoslavia[94] prohibits pillage of public and private property, the Statute of the International Criminal Court (ICC)[95] prohibits pillaging of 'a town or place even when taken by assault' and the Statute of the International Criminal Tribunal for Rwanda[96] prohibits any act of pillage. This confusion regarding which acts of pillage are prohibited under international law has been again solved by the ICRC, which recognises that there exists both a general prohibition of pillage, as well as a prohibition of pillage of certain kinds of property (cultural property, property of the wounded and sick persons, property of persons deprived of liberty). The ownership of the pillaged property is irrelevant, as under international customary law, pillage occurs whether the looted property belongs to private persons, to communities or to the state.[97]

The ICC Elements of Crimes,[98] a document that defines international crime in the Statute of the ICC, defines five key legal components of the act of pillage. These are: (1) the perpetrator appropriated certain property; (2) the perpetrator intended to deprive the owner of the property and appropriated the property for personal or private use; (3) the appropriation was without the consent of the owner; (4) the conduct took place in the context of international or non-international armed conflict; and (5) the perpetrator was aware of factual circumstances that established the existence of an armed conflict.[99] With regard to these elements of crime, Stewart notes that the ICC definition in point 2 with reference to 'for personal and private use' contradicts both historical and modern interpretations of the offence.[100] He points to the decision of the Special Court of Sierra Leone in the *Prosecutor v. Brima et al.*[101] case, where the Court declared that 'the requirement of "private or personal use" is unduly restrictive and ought not to be an element of the crime of pillage'.[102] Stewart derives that the majority of the war crimes jurisprudence defines pillage simply as appropriation without the consent of the owner.[103]

Considering the majority position on the definition of the pillage, several common characteristics with economic cyber-exploitation can be drawn. First,

94 Statute of the International Criminal Tribunal for the former Yugoslavia, Art. 3(e).
95 Statute of the International Criminal Court, Art. 8(2)(b)(xvi) and (e)(v).
96 Statute of the International Criminal Tribunal for Rwanda, Art. 4(f).
97 Commentary of 1958, Convention (IV) relative to the Protection of Civilian Persons in Time of War, Geneva, 12 August 1949 (ICRC Commentary of 1958, Art. 33, International Committee of the Red Cross), <https://ihl-databases.icrc.org/applic/ihl/ihl.nsf/1a13044f3bbb5b8ec12563fb0066f226/36bd41f14e2b3809c12563cd0042bca9>).
98 International Criminal Court, Elements of Crimes, CC-ASP/1/3 at 108, UN Doc. PCNICC/2000/1/Add.2 (2000).
99 ICC Elements of Crimes, Art. 8(2)(b)(xvi).
100 Stewart, above n. 86, p. 20.
101 *Prosecutor v. Brima et al.*, Case No. SCSL-04-16-T, Judgment (2007).
102 Ibid., para. 754.
103 Stewart, above n. 86, p. 21.

the perpetrator appropriated certain property. Foreign governments resorting to economic cyber-exploitation appropriate data from companies located in third states. Secondly, the perpetrator intended to deprive the owner of the property. When foreign governments hire hackers to hack into the security space of a company located in a third state they clearly hold a direct intent for such actions. Hacking into a foreign company's security system and network, stealing intellectual property along with personal data cannot be performed without intent. As already described above, too much planning, thinking, deception, and hiding traces has to be exercised for such stealing to be accidental. Additionally, when the perpetrator wants to harm the foreign company and publishes the personal data online, it is clear that the intent for such actions is present. Thirdly, the appropriation is carried without the consent of the owner. The fact that the foreign government has to resort to hackers to gain the wanted data, alone indicates that the appropriation of this data is without the consent of the third state. Should the third state consent to giving the intellectual property or collected data from its companies, there would be no need for disguised gathering of this data.

The fourth and fifth element of the definition of the war crime of pillage are not common to economic cyber-exploitation, as these acts are carried out in time of peace. Namely, pillage can only occur in armed conflict, as it is regarded as a war crime. This is logical, as it is physically nearly impossible for a foreign state to carry out the act of pillage in a third state in time of peace, without its forces being physically present on the territory of the third state. If the foreign state forces are gathering private property of a third state with the consent of the third state, then there is no armed conflict and this does not constitute the act of pillage as defined by international humanitarian law. As economic cyber-exploitation is taking place in cyberspace, national borders or national territory does not limit the actions of hackers. The hackers do not need to be present on the territory of the foreign company to carry out the act of stealing data. Hence their actions can be carried out both in times of war as in times of peace. Thus, it is physically impossible to satisfy the requirement of armed conflict per se. Economic cyber-exploitation may take place also in an international armed conflict or an internationalised non-international armed conflict. However the armed conflict is not an element of economic cyber-exploitation, but rather an external factor. Moreover, the first definition of the act of pillage from the Lieber Code prohibited any 'pillage or sacking, even after taking a place by main force.'[104] This means that it was recognised from the initial codifications of the prohibition of pillage that it can take place even after or apart from the fighting necessary to take or defend a location,[105] noting that the connection to the armed conflict is lax.

---

104 Keenan, above n. 87, p. 534.

105 Ibid.

However, as ICRC notes, the intention of the prohibition of pillage is to spare people the suffering resulting from the destruction of their real and personal property.[106] This intention is the most relevant part of the prohibition of pillage. It is common to the prevention of economic cyber-exploitation, where the intention is to spare the companies the suffering from the loss of their intellectual property and data. Hence, the relevant elements of the prohibition of pillage can be considered in the design of the measures regulating economic cyber-exploitation in international law.

Additionally, the requirement of an armed conflict in the definition of the act of pillage defines the perpetrator, which is a foreign state (international armed conflict) or a rebel group, which is in most cases a proxy for a foreign government[107] (non-international armed conflict). However, more often than not, the perpetrator of the act of pillage is not a foreign state but a company collaborating with a warring army or having the authorisation for such pillage by the warring army.[108] With economic cyber-exploitation among states, as discussed in this chapter, the perpetrator is also a foreign state or more precisely a hacker/group of hackers hired by the foreign state.

The commonalities between economic cyber-exploitation and pillage of natural resources provide a cause for regulating economic cyber-exploitation at the international level. Since pillage is regulated, the majority of common elements call for regulation of economic cyber-exploitation. Even more so, as cyber-exploitation may open the doors to cyber-attacks, as described above, and may also be the source of warfare.

7. ECONOMIC CYBER-EXPLOITATION AMONG STATES

International economic cyber-exploitation for trade secrets and personal data, mostly from US companies, is a growing occurrence. Lately, media has been full of reports that the Chinese government has been orchestrating data theft activities against US companies.[109] Such theft compromises the competitiveness of US companies in China and globally.[110] A report by Virginia-based cyber-security firm Mandiant identifies a special large unit of hackers run by the Chinese People's Liberation Army that carries out these trans-Atlantic cyber-thefts.[111]

---

106 ICRC Commentary of 1958, Art. 33.
107 Ibid., pp. 21–22.
108 Ibid., p. 34.
109 Fidler, above n. 9.
110 Malawer, above n. 68, p. 1.
111 L.C. Baldor, 'US Ready to Strike Back on China Cyberattacks', *Yahoo News*, 19 February 2013, <https://news.yahoo.com/us-ready-strike-back-china-cyberattacks-224303045--finance.html>.

Some 150 US companies from 20 different sectors were victims of large data theft by this unit.[112] Some studies indicate that the US companies lost over $250 billion in information loss and another $114 billion in related expenses in 2012 alone from economic cyber-exploitation.[113] The White House Administration has publicly confirmed the information theft, pointing at the Chinese Government for at least enabling it.[114] The Chinese Government, however, denies its involvement in these cyber-attacks and claims it too is a victim of hacking, some of which may be traced back to the US State Department.[115]

In 2010, Chinese hackers penetrated into a US company holding security tokens for over 760 US companies, and compromised their security information.[116] Thus, they were able to access the data and secure information from companies and organisations like the European Space Agency, the Inter-American Development Bank, eBay, Google, Facebook, and others.[117] Economic cyber-exploitation not only affects the competitive advantage of one state's companies, but also affects the state's job market. A McAfee study found that an average of $100 billion loss from economic cyber-espionage in the US would lead to 508,000 lost jobs in the US alone.[118]

However, in May 2014 the US Government responded to the increasing number of cyber-exploitation events and the US Department of Justice indicted five Chinese military officers in *United States v. Wang*[119] for hacking into the servers of a few major American companies and thus for the first time filing criminal charges against foreign nationals for economic cyber-exploitation.[120] The Chinese officers are accused of stealing of confidential and proprietary technical and design specifications, stealing network credentials, stealing e-mails and installing malware. No further proceedings have yet taken place. However, China is not the only offending state, as some reports also indicate Russia, France, Iran and Israel.[121]

---

112 Fidler, above n. 9.

113 Lotrionte, above n. 5, p. 451.

114 Ibid., p. 452.

115 Ibid.

116 J. Brenner, 'The New Industrial Espionage' (2014) 10(3) *The American Interest*, <http://www.the-american-interest.com/2014/12/10/the-new-industrial-espionage/>.

117 B. Krebs, 'Who Else was Hit by the RSA Attackers?', *Krebs on Security*, <http://krebsonsecurity.com/2011/10/who-else-was-hit-by-the-rsa-attackers/>.

118 'The Economic Impact of Cybercrime and Cyber Espionage', report by the Centre for Strategic and International Studies, McAfee (2013), <http://www.mcafee.com/es/resources/reports/rp-economic-impact-cybercrime.pdf>, p. 4.

119 *United States of America v. Wang Dong, Sun Kailiang, Wen Xinyu, Huang Zhenyu, Gu Chunhui*, Criminal No. 14-118, United States District Court for the Western District of Pennsylvania (Pittsburgh).

120 Malawer, above n. 68, p. 2; Nakashima and Wan, 'U.S. Announces First Charges against Foreign Country in Connection with Cyberspying', *Washington Post*, 19 May 2014.

121 Brenner, above n. 116.

Additionally, the Obama Administration has adopted the Administration Strategy on Mitigating the Theft of US Trade Secrets[122] to address the continuing trade theft. The strategy mostly focuses on domestic actions from promoting best practices in trade secret protection and enhancing domestic law enforcement to setting up a deterrence system, which entails maintaining and strengthening and offensive capacity.[123] The strategy does not however promote international action. It only calls for diplomatic discussions with foreign partners on the need to prevent economic cyber-exploitation.[124]

Similarly, the European Union adopted a cyber-security strategy in 2013.[125] However, this strategy does not have much in common with the US strategy. The reason for this lies in the differing policy positions regarding cyber-security due to differing political, social and cultural norms.[126] The same reasons apply also to differing data protection strategies. The EU strategy focuses on building capacities to resist cyber-attacks, to recover from them and to combat cyber-crime. Its objective is to create a unified EU policy for cyberspace directed on comprehensive protection for assets and people.[127] It emphasises the strengthening systemic resilience and resistance to attack and fraud.[128]

Nonetheless, the issue of economic cyber-exploitation is an area where both the US and the EU can work together in promoting a common solution. This is a win-win solution for both, as both have more to benefit from an international regulation on economic cyber-exploitation than to lose. Namely, companies in both the US and the EU are being targeted by foreign states for data theft. As presented above, this leads to serious financial consequences for the industries, the job market and also generally on the economy in these states.

---

122 White House, *Administration Strategy on Mitigating the Theft of U.S. Trade Secrets*, Executive Office of the President of the United States (2013), <https://www.whitehouse.gov//sites/default/files/omb/IPEC/admin_strategy_on_mitigating_the_theft_of_u.s._trade_secrets.pdf>.

123 Fidler, above n. 9; A. Bendiek, *Tests of Partnership: Transatlantic Cooperation in Cyber Security, Internet Governance and Data Protection*, RSW Research Paper, Stiftung, Wissenschaft und Politik, Berlin 2014, p. 6.

124 Fidler, above n. 9.

125 Joint Communication to the European Parliament, the Council, the European Economic and Social Committee and the Committee of the Regions, Cybersecurity Strategy of the European Union: An Open, Safe and Secure Cyberspace, JOIN(2013) 1 final, Brussels, 07.02.2013, <https://eeas.europa.eu/policies/eu-cyber-security/cybsec_comm_en.pdf>.

126 S. Ulgen, 'Cyberspace: The new transatlantic frontier', EurActive.com, January 2016, <http://www.euractiv.com/section/digital/opinion/cyberspace-the-new-transatlantic-frontier/>.

127 Bendiek, above n. 123, p. 19.

128 Ibid., p. 6.

8. CONCLUSION

Many governments are resorting to some sort of economic cyber-exploitation for various reasons. With the development of Internet technologies, it has become easier and more inexpensive to carry out data theft. The benefits of such theft result in an important competitive advantage on the globalised market. At the same time, such theft causes serious damage to the company being perpetrated, mostly in the loss of profit and a loss of years of research and development. Hence, there is a need to address the economic cyber-exploitation at the international level.

As the topic is a relatively new issue in international law, few attempts at regulation have been made, mostly due to the fact that all states resort to some sort of espionage. Hence espionage in not considered illegal under international law. On the other hand, the consequences of the failure to regulate economic cyber-exploitation are serious, rendering a need for its regulation at the international level. Economic cyber-exploitation is characteristically similar to pillage under international humanitarian law. Thus the law on prohibition of pillage could provide a basis for designing the regulation on economic cyber-exploitation and prohibit such activities. Additionally, the law on prohibition of pillage is customary international law codified in several international treaties and recognised by the whole international community. Hence, its acknowledgment could provide the necessary consensus needed among the states for the adoption of an international economic cyber-exploitation document. Especially, it could provide a bridge between the US and EU, which have substantially different views on the need to address cyber-security and data protection, the US focusing on domestic law enforcement and the EU on building capacity to resist hacking activities.

Theft is theft, however it is carried out and whatever the information that is stolen. When economic cyber-exploitation is taking place among states, an international response is necessary.

INVITED COMMENT

13. TERRORISM AND PAEDOPHILIA ON THE INTERNET

A Global and Balanced Cyber-Rights Response Is Required to Combat Cybercrime, Not Knee-Jerk Regulation*

Felicity GERRY QC**

1. INTRODUCTION

> *[A]s the Internet erases the distance between countries, we see growing efforts by terrorists to poison the minds of people like the Boston Marathon bombers and the San Bernardino killers.*[1]

A recent budget bill in the United States, which used an unconventional procedural measure to bring a controversial cyber-surveillance bill to the floor, contained the word 'cyber' 423 times.[2] It was observed that the word 'increasingly connotes a malware arms race that nobody wins'.[3] This chapter takes a critical look at international instruments, some selected legislation and

* Taken in part from the author's papers and collaborative research.

** Queen's Counsel, London, Leeds and Darwin; Senior Lecturer, Charles Darwin University, Australia. E-mail: felicity.gerry@cdu.edu.au.

1 Address to the Nation by the President of the United States (06.12.2015) <www.whitehouse.gov/the-press-office/2015/12/06/address-nation-president>.

2 R. BRANDOM, 'Congress snuck a surveillance bill into the federal budget last night', *The Verge* (16.12.2015) <http://www.theverge.com/2015/12/16/10288182/cisa-surveillance-cyber-security-budget-proposal> accessed 06.01.2016.

3 A. ROBERTSON and S. O'KANE, 'The Cyberbudget of the Cyberunited Cyberstates of Cyberamerica', *The Verge* (16.12.2015) <http://www.theverge.com/2015/12/16/10307822/every-cyber-in-the-2016-omnibus-budget-bill> accessed 06.01.2016.

case law to better understand how cyber law is dealt with globally against a background of concerns over balancing freedom with regulation of the Internet. It discusses the use of terrorism and paedophilia as excuses for regulation of the Internet and considers whether human rights standards are being safeguarded as individual states legislate to regulate use of the Internet. Taking a particular focus on an international legal analysis in the context of freedom of expression, freedom of information, surveillance and right to privacy issues, this chapter is approached from the following perspectives: the regulation of criminal activity online, consideration of data privacy relations, jurisdictional issues in the context of cyber evidence, balancing regulation with the freedom of expression (both generally and in relation to political dissent) and balancing the protection of the privacy of victims in the wider context of transnational organised crime. It is necessarily an overview of such huge topics and is therefore set against the background of three areas of criminal law:

1. the release of the draft cybercrime law for Cambodia in 2014;
2. using technology to combat human trafficking;
3. extra-territorial jurisdiction.

These areas involving investigation, jurisdiction and legislation in the context of cyber law and technology are discussed in the context of the human rights framework. However, the chapter seeks to also explore the Internet as a tool for liberation where there are dangers in the context of terrorist and online sexual grooming and abuse.

2. CYBER-COMMUNICATION

It has been said that to enjoy the wonders that come from global communication, we have to put up with some of the 'terrible aspects' and, on this topic, Kashmir Hill reported on President Obama's address to the US nation following attacks in Paris, France and San Bernardino, California in 2015.[4] Hill noted that the President effectively blamed the Internet both by highlighting online grooming and radicalisation, and by suggesting that law enforcement solutions come from making it 'harder for terrorists to use technology to escape from justice.' Hill reported that during a press briefing the next day, the White House secretary clarified that while the President 'believes in the importance of strong encryption',

[4] K. Hill, 'Let's Stop Blaming 'The Internet' For Terrorism', *The Huffington Post* (14.12.2015) <http://www.huffingtonpost.com/entry/internet-terrorism_566ed1dee4b0fccee16f1960?ncid=tweetlnkushpmg00000017> accessed 07.01.2016.

we 'don't want terrorists to have a safe haven in cyberspace.' Hill also noted that such sentiment was echoed by presidential candidates Donald Trump who had said, 'We're losing a lot of people because of the Internet' and Hillary Clinton who had suggested we need to 'deny [would-be terrorists] online space' and 'shut off their means of communicating'.[5]

Such statements do not begin to address complications in attempting to regulate the Internet and are contrary to the provision of wide access to digital communication. This is generally considered to enhance democracy, particularly by providing global citizens with access to information and networks, which would not otherwise be easily available. The ease with which people communicate every day is effectively enabled by six features identified by Helen Roberts in her research paper for the Australian Parliament as long ago as 1995:

- the lack of centralised control;
- the difficulty of controlling the spread of information;
- the availability of encryption;
- the world-wide nature of the Internet;
- the difficulty of determining the originator of information which is anonymous or pseudonymous; and
- the unfamiliarity of policy makers with the technology and the fluid nature of the technology.[6]

Internet regulation lies at the centre of conflicting ideas around globalisation and jurisdictional hybridity to such an extent that it becomes impossible to map the multifaceted overlapping doctrinal and practical issues. The literature on the difficulty of regulation in this context is vast and engages fundamental jurisprudential thought.[7] However, noting in particular the potential for children to access unsuitable material together with strong right-to-privacy issues, Roberts recommended that

> Legislation on pornography and copyright should be technology neutral and not effectively more restrictive in the Internet environment than for other communication technologies ... technological solutions would be most effective in censoring material unsuitable for children. Not only should blocking devices be available as an optional extra but a code of practice or legislation could require that each commercial service offer a channel blocking feature to parents.

---

5 Ibid n 6.

6 H. Roberts, *Can the Internet be regulated?*, Research Paper 35 1995–96, Australian Parliament <http://www.aph.gov.au/About_Parliament/Parliamentary_Departments/Parliamentary_Library/pubs/rp/RP9596/96rp35> accessed 07.01.2016.

7 P.S. Berman, *Global Legal Pluralism: a jurisprudence of law beyond borders*, Cambridge University Press, New York 2012, pp. 23–57.

She did not suggest widespread regulation as a form of law enforcement. Citizens using what she called 'the new medium', she concluded, 'require less complex law' to maintain the 'free speech culture of the Internet, in combination with the implied freedom of communication' thus tipping the balance in favour of what are considered to be human rights, in particular free speech.

It follows that, although the context and the concepts are vast, we need to continue to consider not so much cybercrime, but the effective protection of cyber rights for the vast majority of the global populace who use the Internet for legitimate means and to navigate the potential for global harmonisation in this context.

3. CYBER RIGHTS

Human rights are protected through both international and regional treaties, which are intended to be reflected in domestic provisions. Global efforts have been made to protect human rights, particularly the freedom of expression and privacy rights. These can be used to exemplify the necessity for balance between state security and rights to freedom of expression and privacy. The right to privacy is intrinsically linked to the freedom of expression, as it allows individuals to express themselves without fear of retribution.[8] This is particularly important on the Internet, where anonymity is part of the culture.

All states assume obligations under international law to respect, to protect and to fulfil human rights. Human rights issues exist in a data context just as much as anywhere else. David Lyon has commented that

> The Snowden revelations about National Security Agency surveillance, starting in 2013, along with the ambiguous complicity of internet companies and the international controversies that followed provide a perfect segue into contemporary conundrums of surveillance and Big Data.[9]

He notes three major issues: the intensification by states of surveillance by expanding interconnected datasets and analytical tools, the use of predictive analytics for pattern-discovery is used to justify unprecedented access to data and what he calls 'the ethical turn' as an 'urgent mode of critique' defining privacy

---

8 F. La Rue, *Promotion and protection of all human rights, civil, political, economic, social and cultural rights, including the right to development*, Report of the Special Rapporteur on the promotion and protection of the right to freedom of opinion and expression, para. 24, A/HRC/23/40 (17.04.2013) <http://www.ohchr.org/Documents/HRBodies/HRCouncil/RegularSession/Session23/A.HRC.23.40_EN.pdf>.

9 D. Lyon, 'Surveillance, Snowden, and Big Data: Capacities, consequences, critique' (July 2014) *Big Data and Society* <http://bds.sagepub.com/content/1/2/2053951714541861> accessed 07.01.2016.

in the context of disembodied images of both computing and legal practices fuelling surveillance.[10] The dangerous consequence is the loss of rights-based discourse in the online context in favour of regulation against a background of seemingly urgent threats arising from modern forms of conflict manifesting in multifaceted and individualised physical attacks, inevitably devised and facilitated by technology and pictured more vividly in political rhetoric than codes for cyberspace or alternative dispute resolution.

In the search for the ever more elusive harmony of legislative processes in the context of Internet use, it is useful to reflect on where states have been able to achieve some general cooperation: in the era post twentieth-century global conflict, concepts of global cooperation and unity were enshrined in the Universal Declaration of Human Rights (UDHR). Its preamble recognises that 'the equal and inalienable rights of all members of the human family are the foundation of freedom, justice and peace in the world'.[11] It was developed at a time when current data usage and data collection could not have been envisaged, but it demonstrated how basic principles could be affirmed by multiple countries across the globe when in near history many had nothing in common ideologically and most had been engaged in active physical warfare, surveillance and technological development of weaponry. The dangers from states to each other were vitiated by some global agreement on future dispute resolution. The UDHR is sufficiently widely drafted to allow for changes in global behaviour, the potential for modern conflict as well as growth in global trade and communication. The focus on people's rights not national interest is the core issue. In the search for global cooperation, it always bears repeating that the UDHR does not ignore the potential for individual differences, nor does it expect movement to some unachievable similarity ignoring diverse language and culture. It sets out some basic and agreed human rights.

In July 2012, the UN Human Rights Council adopted a resolution affirming the application of those rights online, especially freedom of expression. This resolution confirmed that both Art. 19 of the UDHR and Art. 19 of the International Covenant on Civil and Political Rights (ICCPR)[12] are 'applicable regardless of frontiers and through any media of one's choice'[13] and that any attempt by governments to illegitimately censor or block Internet content would

10 Ibid.

11 Universal Declaration of Human Rights, GA Resolution 217A (III), UN GAOR, 3rd Session, 183rd Plenary Meeting, UN Doc. A/810 (10 December 1948) (Preamble).

12 Art. 19(2) provides: 'Everyone shall have the right to freedom of expression; this right shall include freedom to seek, receive and impart information and ideas of all kinds, regardless of frontiers, either orally, in writing or in print, in the form of art, or through any other media of his choice.'

13 UN Human Rights Council, 'The promotion, protection and enjoyment of human rights on the Internet', para. 1, A/HRC/20/L.13 (29.06.2012).

be incompatible with those instruments.[14] More recently, on 20 June 2014, the Council called upon all states to address the protection of these common standards in laws that pertain to the Internet.[15]

The real question is how to maintain those common standards when terrorist attacks and child abuse online are used to fuel attempts to control the Internet and to change the way we approach rights specifically in an online context.

4. CYBER FREEDOM

According to the former UN Special Rapporteur Frank La Rue, privacy is the 'presumption that individuals should have an area of autonomous development, interaction and liberty, a "private sphere" with or without interaction with others, free from State intervention and from excessive unsolicited intervention by other uninvited individuals.' This right also extends to the individual capability to 'determine who holds information about them and how is that information used.'[16] Furthermore, the right infers that 'individuals are able to exchange information and ideas in a space that is beyond the reach of other members of society, the private sector, and ... the State.' Communications should remain secure, i.e. 'individuals should be able to verify that their communications are received only by their intended recipients, without interference or alteration, and that the communications they receive are equally free from intrusion.' If individuals wish to be anonymous in their communication, this must be preserved so that individuals may 'express themselves freely without fear of retribution or condemnation'.[17]

A report by the Office of the UN High Commissioner for Human Rights reiterated that any '[state] surveillance measures must not arbitrarily or unlawfully interfere with an individual's privacy, family, home or correspondence; Governments must take specific measures to ensure protection of the law against

---

14 Ibid.

15 UN Human Rights Council, 'The promotion, protection and enjoyment of human rights on the Internet', para. 5, A/HRC/26/L.24 (20.06.2014) ('Calls upon all States to address security concerns on the Internet in accordance with their international human rights obligations to ensure protection of freedom of expression, freedom of association, privacy and other human rights online, including through national democratic, transparent institutions, based on the rule of law, in a way that ensures freedom and security on the Internet so that it can continue to be a vibrant force that generates economic, social and cultural development').

16 F. La Rue, *Promotion and protection of all human rights, civil, political, economic, social and cultural rights, including the right to development*, Report of the Special Rapporteur on the promotion and protection of the right to freedom of opinion and expression, A/HRC/23/40 (17.04.2013).

17 Ibid.

such interference'.[18] Mass surveillance by governments, by its very nature, creates an interference with the right to privacy since 'the collection and retention of communications data amounts to an interference ... whether or not those data are subsequently consulted or used'.[19] So we can see that there are common standards in the context of human rights which ought to apply in the online context.

Against that background of rights-based obligations and the current tensions, there was a small triumph for freedom of speech over mandatory Internet filtering in a US Supreme Court ruling in 2009. The *New York Times* reported on the judgment as follows:

> A 10-year campaign to censor the Internet ended last week when the Supreme Court refused to step in and save the Child Online Protection Act. Everyone can agree on the need to protect children from sexually explicit online material, but this misguided law tried to do it in ways that infringed on too much constitutionally protected free speech.

It continued: 'Congress had passed the Child Online Protection Act in 1998 after the Supreme Court had struck down an even broader law regulating online indecency'. The 1998 Act imposed civil and criminal penalties, including up to six months in prison, for offering commercial material online that was 'harmful to minors'. Under the topic 'Freedom of Speech and Expression' the report emphasises the findings of the court that the legislation violated the First Amendment in a number of ways and that the law's purpose could be better achieved, 'with less damage to free expression, if parents used filtering software to keep objectionable material away from children'. The then Bush administration were pushing for more restrictions in relation to online pornography based on legitimate interests in keeping sexually explicit material away from children which clearly 'cannot be done through a sweeping censorship regime'.[20] The essence of the judgment and the news reports giving primacy to the protection of rights over Internet regulation in the context of sexual conduct is not so clear in the context of terrorism and online radicalisation so predictions that Congress would not 'rush to take up online indecency again' were only correct in part in

18 Report of the Office of the United Nations High Commissioner for Human Rights, 'The right to privacy in the digital age', para. 15, A/HRC/27/37 (30.06.2014).

19 Ibid., para. 20; see also, *Weber and Saravia v. Germany*, App. no. 54934/00 (ECtHR, 2006), para. 78; *Malone v. UK*, App. no. 8691/79 (ECtHR, 1984), para. 64. (Both of these ECtHR cases indicate that even the mere possibility of communications information being captured creates an interference with the right to privacy.)

20 'A Win for Free Speech Online', Editorial, *New York Times* (26.01.2009) <http://www.nytimes.com/2009/01/27/opinion/27tue2.html?th&emc=th&_r=0>.

that the rush to regulate the Internet is now discussed in the context of violent terrorist conduct rather than abusive conduct by child abusers.

5. CYBER REGULATION

It does not take too much to see that the Internet is not a separate community for the world of cyberspace. The types of conduct being discussed are not new, although the manner in which abuse and conflict manifests itself and is conducted with the assistance of technology occurs in a way that could not have been envisaged before the World Wide Web. The global nature of the connected world therefore creates a new global legal conundrum and raises issues of governance. Cybercrime laws need to balance international criminal law principles with competing issues of sovereignty in the context of the online global community. What follows are some practical suggestions and proposals for some global solutions to address the larger issue of global compliance of international human rights law pertaining to the Internet and cybercrime in the specific contexts that is the focus of this chapter.

It is axiomatic that separate legislative responses by disparate nations are unlikely to achieve the balance required to maintain human rights standards at global level unless the legislative response follows a set of globally agreed and balanced principles. The standards of human rights protection anticipated by the UDHR and protected in the International Covenant on Civil and Political Rights (ICCPR) and other international instruments clearly need to be met in relation to Internet and data usage. Universal human rights are guaranteed by international law in the forms of treaties, customary international law, conventions, and other sources of international law. Most states promise to comply with their international law obligations by upholding principles of universality and equality, by ensuring both the equality of citizens, and by enabling equal access to justice. Those state promises are currently reflected in the growing spread of what has become known as the 'right to be forgotten' which, as set out below, pass the decision making processes to corporate entities and therefore raise the level of importance of global governance which exists outside of national legislative responses. As individual nations legislate, questions arise as to where the power lies to censor the Internet and who is making the decisions, how those decisions are made and what mechanisms will function to challenge decision making. In the context of child abuse such concerns arise both in the context of covering up criminal behaviour and anonymity of those accused and acquitted. They are emotional issues that need a principled and balanced solution. Blanket restrictions could easily affect not just the rule of law but also how the law is seen to function, and public perception of criminal behaviour. The overlapping nature of law in the global operation of the Internet challenges traditional positivist views on territoriality and exposes the near impossibility of isolationist approaches. The need to capture transnational legal concepts which arise from practical global public challenges requires decision-making based on solid doctrinal foundations rather than emotional reaction.

If we accept that the Internet can be used to combat human rights abuses and that the Internet can be, equally, harnessed to interfere with rights and generate inequality, then we expose the balance that needs to be struck by states and global commercial technological corporates. It is important to recognise that there is no one international instrument dealing with rights and responsibilities on the Internet. In the absence of such a document, individual countries legislate against a background of other international instruments. Research from the various papers from which this chapter is drawn expose inconsistencies in international and domestic approaches to both freedom of expression and privacy and surveillance issues which have the potential to create global tension if not addressed in the near future. On a practical level, the fear of cyber-terrorism and cyber-abuse fuelling decisions by individual states based on their own national interest and ideology rather than global harmony even though individual legislative responses in the Internet context inevitably affect other countries and regimes. The scope for conflict is enormous and the likely risk to individual rights and freedoms high. There are many discussions to be had in the context of global governance where industry standards can function outside the laws of individual states and territories. The legal contribution here is international agreement on principles to be applied to best reflect human rights and the need to combat specific cybercrimes.

6. CYBER SURVEILLANCE

The Internet is now a global information infrastructure and provider of commercial services as a result of the widespread adoption of browsers making information accessible to users across the globe. Access to the Internet is liberating and educational; however, it must be acknowledged that it has also been used a great deal to facilitate cybercrime of many types, including the most serious in nature. As we have seen, the prevalence of cybercrime is then used as a justification for intrusive surveillance and over-regulation.[21] Human Rights Watch has concisely summarised the issues and guided the way to a set of principles:

> Intrusive surveillance and over regulation threaten privacy rights of individuals … Governments should only be able to call for information relating to an individual's

[21] F. Gerry and N. Berova, 'The rule of law online: Treating data like the sale of goods: Lessons for the Internet from OECD and CISG and sacking Google as the regulator' (2014) 30(5) *Computer Law and Society Review* 481.

> private life for the public interest. Any relevant legislation must specify the precise circumstances for accessing private individual's information. In addition, the right to information requires governments to allow free flow of information … A decision to block access to online materials should be subject to the highest level of scrutiny, with a burden on the government to demonstrate that censorship would effectively avert a threat of irreparable, imminent, and weighty harm, and that less extreme measures are unavailable as alternatives to protect the state interest at issue.[22]

The major issue in any cybercrime law is balancing competing interests on an individual, corporate, government and global level. It is notable that a leaked draft cybercrime law for Cambodia, which did not appear to take these factors into account, does not appear to have been brought into force, although that does not, of itself, mean that draconian legislative responses are not still planned.

The proposed Cambodian cybercrime law was drafted in such a way that it would be ineffective as a tool to combat online crime, its terms were misleading, beyond mere issues of translation, and it had real potential to restrict the media, communication by social media and individual freedom. The structure and contents were such that rights were inhibited, policing was inappropriate and the legislation, if enacted, could be used to target human rights activists/NGOs. The draft restricted legitimate acts of expression and communication and violated an individual's right to privacy. The leaked version also failed to properly deal with child exploitation online and other cybercrime. If enacted it was a dangerous instrument and required significant amendment to comply with Cambodia's international obligations. In that particular example, the extraterritorial effect of some draft provisions would have been unenforceable and the provisions for punishment inconsistent with global approaches to access to information and conversely to child abuse online. Cambodia's draft cybercrime law highlighted how one state cannot approach cybercrime from an isolationist perspective by drafting provisions creating a dangerous drift away from human rights standards towards blanket Internet regulation.[23]

7. CYBER CHANGE

The speed of technological changes outpaces social and legal changes so that laws that are too specific quickly become obsolete. In a very short space of time, much of the world has moved from telephones to smart phones, desktop computers

---

22 Human Rights Watch, '"Race to the Bottom": Corporate Complicity in Chinese Internet Censorship' (10.08.2006) 5 <http://www.hrw.org/reports/2006/china0806/3.htm>.

23 F. Gerry and C. Moore, 'A slippery and inconsistent slope: How Cambodia's draft cybercrime law exposed a dangerous drift away from human rights standards' (2015) 31(5) *Computer Law and Security Review* 628–650.

to laptops to tablets to inventions like Google Glass. Now there are cyborgs and artificial intelligence.[24] The latest fears in relation to state-sponsored surveillance involves the effects of analytics and how people are losing their freedom to choose through powerful suggestions made based on previous usage. The slower pace of changing domestic law means that criminal laws and regulations, such as fraud, online abuse, stalking, and also laws regulating privacy, defamation and other communications, are at risk of being left far behind or are reactive in a piecemeal and ineffective way and reports of governments sidestepping their own legislative procedures abound particularly in relation to what data has been collected, retained, used and abused. The examples are numerous: metadata storage, co-traveller analytics, hacking devices and undersea cables, remote controlled operations of iProducts, surveillance of lawyers' privileged communications and documents,[25] direct access to servers of multinational corporations without the consent of the service provider. The list goes on and on and the actions have been largely achieved due to ineffective control of intrusive state behaviour. Justifications for such data collection and retention have tended to vary from inevitability to combating conduct by terrorists and paedophiles.[26] State concerns about online abuse and terrorism are legitimate, but over-regulation is the most likely conduit for inhibiting freedoms. These competing issues demonstrate the need for agreed overarching legal principles, applicable just as much for the protection and freedom of the individual as it is to the role of the state to regulate criminal conduct.

8. CYBER LAW

States have attempted to enact laws to address such Internet-related issues, with varying degrees of success. Some states directly censor and control the Internet,[27] while others place the responsibility for enforcing the law in the hands of the trade organisations who stand to gain from their enforcement.[28] Research on Cambodia's leaked draft cybercrime law highlights just one example

---

24 F. Swain, 'Beyond human: How I became a cyborg', *BBC* (online) (08.01.2014) <http://www.bbc.com/future/story/20140107-how-i-became-a-cyborg>.

25 O. Kerr, 'Did the NSA really help spy on U.S. lawyers?', *The Washington Post* (online) (16.02.2014) <http://www.washingtonpost.com/news/volokh-conspiracy/wp/2014/02/16/did-the-nsa-really-help-spy-on-u-s-lawyers/>.

26 N. Mokoena, 'Censor the Internet? Yes or No?', *News24* (online) (17.09.2012) <http://www.news24.com/MyNews24/Censor-the-Internet-Yes-or-No-20120917>.

27 SCS, 'Why South Korea is really an Internet dinosaur', *The Economist Explains Blog* (10.02.2014) <http://www.economist.com/blogs/economist-explains/2014/02/economist-explains-3>.

28 E. Black, 'WCIT, TPP, Russia PNTR: Growing Recognition of Internet Freedom As A Trade Issue', *Forbes* (online) (19.12.2012) <http://www.forbes.com/sites/edblack/2012/12/19/wcit-tpp-russia-pntr-growing-recognition-of-Internet-freedom-as-a-trade-issue/>.

of state legislative responses to complex criminal issues around online conduct, exposing a dangerous global drift by all states from the necessary common human rights standards in the context of global cyber law in favour of prioritising state surveillance over all Internet users rather than targeted investigative responses. States' commitment to common human rights standards requires the formulation of a balanced set of cyber laws and procedures to combat cybercrime and improve cyber security, without compromising human rights in all states. Our Cambodian research proposed the immediate formulation of a global panel of experts with a view to the creation of uniform global cyber law construct: an international convention which was in fact envisaged by the OECD in the context of privacy over three decades ago. In the US, the legal academic Henry Perritt proposed some time ago that a model code of cyberspace law be enacted by the United Nations. Inconsistencies in international and domestic approaches to jurisdiction, investigation, freedom of expression and privacy and surveillance issues have the potential to create increased global tension far more than terrorism or paedophilia (which have been around for centuries) if not addressed in the near future. In the context of global cyber regulation human rights standards must be safeguarded if there is to be a balanced rule of law online.

The importance of wide governing principles relating not just to states but to those commercial enterprises now heavily involved in Internet editing in the context of what has become known as the 'right to be forgotten' as material is removed from simple Internet searches. January 2016 saw Russia's 'Right to be Forgotten Law', signed by President Putin, enter into force. The law imposes an obligation on search engines that disseminate advertisements targeted at consumers located in Russia to remove search results listing information on individuals where such information is unlawfully disseminated, untrustworthy or outdated.[29] The criteria are not well defined. Hogan Lovells' lawyers, Natalia Gulyaeva and Maria Sedykh, predicted that it would be applied to 'websites registered using a Russian top-level domain (.su, .ru, .rf); and websites and advertisements that are in the Russian language (including where the website has another non-Russian top level domain)', but it is not clear what scrutiny there will be or how the matter will be subject of any rights-based challenge.[30]

The apparent global roll-out of a perceived 'right to be forgotten' was originally highlighted by the Court of Justice of the European Union (CJEU) decision in *Google Spain SL v. Agencia Española de Protección de Datos*

---

[29] N. Gulyaeva and M. Sedykh, 'Russian "Right to be Forgotten" Law: Update' (24.12.2015) *Chronicle of Data Protection*, Hogan Lovells, <http://www.hldataprotection.com/2015/12/articles/consumer-privacy/russian-right-to-be-forgotten-law-update/> accessed 07.01.2016.

[30] Ibid.

(AEPD).[31] This decision required Google to enforce a 'right to be forgotten', effectively making Google responsible for Internet regulation by removing links, which allow access to material the subject of application. It did not apply to all of Google's operations, which perhaps explains the Russian legislation, but it has highlighted again the piecemeal and geographically localised legal issues, which can have global effect. It also highlights the level of control in the hands of commercial organisations, now followed by legislation in Russia with other countries inevitably following suit without any discussion on a harmonised approach. Thousands of applications have been received and are being processed. The system is meant to ensure that the material remains but becomes harder to find and is not pushed up the search engine rankings. Evaluating any rights-based approach becomes a difficult but important exercise and requiring such organisations to apply a set of globally agreed principles would at least be a step to requiring some sort of legitimate governance.

The legal issues do not just arise in the context of access to information by the public but also to the ability for state parties and litigants to access otherwise private or commercially sensitive information. The recent *Microsoft* case has raised concern about cross-jurisdictional evidence collection when a US judge issued a warrant for production of the contents of a server based in Ireland without reference to traditional mutual legal assistance treaties.[32] The consequences of such litigation and judicial responses led to significant consideration of new jurisdictional approaches to legislation dealt with in one of the papers on which this chapter is based. Concepts focusing not on national boundaries, but on connection between the litigants and the material, are now worthy of discussion, not to allow ever-increasing access by governments but to ensure there are guiding principles publicly identifiable and subject to scrutiny of application. Similar concerns have now been raised over a European decision that employers can read employees' personal e-mails.[33] In all such cases the balance needs to be found between private and state and commercial interests but in the cyber context there is an added value in global governance through effective systems with guiding principles.

Thus, it becomes clear that states cannot effectively legislate in the context of cyber law alone and, if they do, the practical reality is that such legislation will

---

[31] Case C-131/12, *Google Spain SL v. Agencia Española de Protección de Datos (AEPD)* (CJEU, 13.05.2014).

[32] *In the Matter of a Warrant to Search a Certain E-Mail Account Controlled and Maintained by Microsoft Corporation*, F. Supp. 2d. No. 13 Mag. 2814, 2014 WL 1661004, at *11 (SDNY Apr. 25, 2014) 8–9 <http://www.nysd.uscourts.gov/cases/show.php?db=special&id=398>.

[33] L. Hughes, 'Bosses can snoop on workers' private emails and messages, European court rules', *The Daily Telegraph* (13.01.2016) <http://www.telegraph.co.uk/technology/internet/12096847/Bosses-can-snoop-on-workers-private-emails-and-messages-European-court-rules.html> accessed 18.01.2016.

require circumvention at some point when factual circumstances demonstrate a principled and necessary reason to do so. The solution at least appears to be to achieve the harmonisation of national legislations related to privacy, as envisaged by the OECD in the 1970s, through the establishment of an international convention which deals with the applicable international human rights principles, including privacy rights, but also focusing on the whole of the cyber context in an enforceable and acceptable way. Data privacy was also a key element in the *Microsoft* cloud case. While in that case we saw a clash between the European emphasis on data privacy on the one hand, and US calls for efficient law enforcement on the other hand, the reality is, as the research exposes, both more nuanced and more complex.

Privacy is typically negatively affected by both cyber law, and attempts to address cybercrime,[34] so attempts to protect against, and investigate, cyber law, may involve methods that are in themselves invasive of privacy. Balancing the protection of privacy with the need to effectively address cyber law is always going to be easier with an overarching set of principles that fundamental human rights can provide. On 20 June 2014, the Council called upon all states to address the protection of these common standards in laws that pertain to the Internet[35] and, in relation to the protection of individual privacy, UN Special Rapporteur, Frank La Rue has said that communications should remain secure, i.e. 'individuals should be able to verify that their communications are received only by their intended recipients, without interference or alteration, and that the communications they receive are equally free from intrusion.' If individuals wish to be anonymous in their communication, this must be preserved so that individuals may 'express themselves freely without fear of retribution or condemnation.'[36] Here we can again refer to the mentioned report by the Office of the UN High Commissioner for Human Rights, which as noted emphasises that 'surveillance measures must not arbitrarily or unlawfully interfere with an individual's privacy, family, home or correspondence; Governments must take specific measures to ensure protection of the law against such interference.'[37] The collection and retention of communications data amounts to an 'interference ... whether or not those data are subsequently consulted or used.'[38]

34 *Submission by the Australian Privacy Foundation In response to the House of Representatives Standing Committee on Communications' Cyber Crime Inquiry* (06.08.2009) <https://www.privacy.org.au/Papers/Cybercrime-090805.doc>.

35 UN Human Rights Council, above n. 15, § 5.

36 Ibid., para. 23.

37 Report of the Office of the United Nations High Commissioner for Human Rights, 'The right to privacy in the digital age', para. 15, A/HRC/27/37 (30.06.2014) <http://www.ohchr.org/EN/HRBodies/HRC/RegularSessions/Session27/Documents/A.HRC.27.37_en.pdf>.

38 Ibid., para. 20; See also, *Weber and Saravia v. Germany*, above n. 19.

9. CYBER PROTECTION

If we are considering global conventions and/or the balancing exercise that an individual judge has to engage in, then it is important to remember that this right is a qualified right and can be restricted, per Art. 19(3) ICCPR. The requirement of a limitation to be 'provided by law' requires that the law should be 'formulated with sufficient precision' to enable an individual to regulate his or her conduct accordingly and it must be made accessible to the public.'[39] The law must also 'provide sufficient guidance to those charged with their execution to enable them to ascertain what sorts of expression are properly restricted and what sorts are not.'[40] Any restriction must be proportionate to the protective aim and must be the least intrusive measure.[41] This principle of proportionality must also account for the form of the expression, including its means of dissemination.[42]

The protection of individuals however does not mean the *over*-protection of individuals. Technology is increasingly cited, as the Presidential address shows, as the solution to global cybercrime, and is particularly under consideration in investigative action in the context of the global human trafficking framework.[43] Human trafficking is a particularly interesting area for examining data usages to combat human rights abuses as it not only relates to the coercive and exploitative movement of peoples, but is linked to commercial exploitation through forced labour and to ownership through slavery, which is also linked to funding terrorism. Here, perpetrators utilise technological forms as means of recruiting and controlling their victims and investigators use technology to combat the criminal conduct.[44] In the middle is the human whose rights are infringed by

---

39 Human Rights Committee 102nd session: CCPR/C/GC/34 General Comment No. 34, para. 25 (07.01.2017) <http://www2.ohchr.org/english/bodies/hrc/docs/GC34.pdf>. See also, Communication No. 578/1994, *de Groot v. The Netherlands*, Views adopted on 14 July 1995.

40 Ibid.

41 Ibid.

42 Ibid.

43 Human trafficking is a highly lucrative industry that extends to all corners of the globe. The phrases 'human trafficking', 'slavery' and 'forced labour' are used interchangeably but essentially amount to exploitation for profit and power. The potential profits from human exploitation are huge. In a 2012 survey by the International Labour Office it was estimated that 20.9 million men, women and children were in forced labour globally, trafficked for labour and sexual exploitation or held in slavery-like conditions.

44 M. Latonero, G. Berhane, A. Hernandez, T. Mohebi and L. Movius, 'Human Trafficking Online: The Role of Social Networking Sites and Online Classifieds' (2011) *Technology and human trafficking* <https://technologyandtrafficking.usc.edu/report/> accessed 25.07.2015; M. Latonero, J. Musto, Z. Boyd, E. Boyle, A. Bissel, K. Gibson and J. Kim, 'The rise of mobile and the diffusion of technology-facilitated trafficking', USC Annenberg Center on Communication Leadership and Policy, 2012 <http://technologyandtrafficking.usc.edu/2012-report/#.VbtgbHt5efQ> accessed 25.07.2015; J. Musto, 'The posthuman anti-trafficking turn: Technology, domestic minor sex trafficking, and augmented human–machine alliances' in K.K. Hoang and R. Salazar Parreñas (eds.), *Human trafficking reconsidered: Rethinking the problem, envisioning new solutions*, International Debate Education Association 2014.

both sides. Links are made between exploiters, purchasers and victims, but also the circulation of information regarding how to engage in criminal activity.

The growing interest in finding ways to 'exploit technology' with a view to more effectively disrupt global human trafficking networks has facilitated the recording, storage and exchange of victims' information after being identified as such by the very authorities who perceive themselves as saviours not exploiters but, in terms of human rights, the effect on the victim can be almost as significant as the physical or technological coercion by traffickers.[45] The transnational, multi-dimensional and highly adaptive character of human trafficking renders the possibilities for using technology endless and the risks requiring acknowledgement and assessment having regard to the fundamental rights of both the victims and other individuals who may collaterally be affected. The rush to monitor phone calls and e-mails of suspected terrorists without prior authorisation[46] and concern over human exploitation by terrorist organisations was seemingly prioritised over both national legislative provisions and overarching human rights principles.[47] Litigation post-breach is not the solution, and justification or excuses based on terrorist conduct or human exploitation cannot justify the fundamental undermining of the rule of law by which society is naturally and legally regulated. A state that ignores the rule of law is a far worse enemy than a terrorist organisation of paedophile ring and draconian Internet regulation proposed by governments in the wake of recent atrocities will not increase our safety or allow us to lead more peaceful, harmonious lives.[48]

10. CONCLUSION

As 'cyber' as a word increasingly embeds itself in our international psyche, and the use of technology is invariably transnational, criminal conduct cannot be efficiently controlled unless worldwide international cooperation is established and individual protections are maintained through rights-based observance, publicly and commercially. In order to protect an individual's rights to freedom

---

45 M. Thakor and D. Boyd, 'Networked trafficking: Reflections on technology and the anti-trafficking movement' (2013) 37 *Dialectical Anthropology* 277–90.

46 'France adopts controversial surveillance Act', *Privacy Laws and Business* (11.08.2015) <www.privacylaws.com/Int_enews_11_8_15> accessed 21.08.2015.

47 L. Shelley, 'ISIS, Boko Haram, and the Growing Role of Human Trafficking in 21st Century Terrorism', *The Daily Beast* (26.12.2012) <http://www.thedailybeast.com/articles/2014/12/26/isis-boko-haram-and-the-growing-role-of-human-trafficking-in-21st-century-terrorism.html> accessed 21.08.2015.

48 D. Guppy, 'The West must defeat a far worse enemy than radical Islam', *The Spectator* (05.01.2016) <http://blogs.spectator.co.uk/2016/01/the-west-must-defeat-a-far-worse-enemy-than-radical-islam/> accessed 07.01.2016.

of expression, information, and right to privacy, uniform law and policy and global governance in the cyber context should be developed. The standards of human rights protection anticipated by international instruments need to be met in relation to Internet and data usage. In the absence of one international instrument dealing with rights and responsibilities on the Internet, individual countries choose how to legislate against a background of other international instruments; some follow and others do not. At present, public statements by organisations such as Google and Microsoft suggest there is corporate concern about responsibility for individual liberty, but CEOs change and shareholders can influence corporate ideology so restrictive laws, regulations and policies are prioritised by nations. In much more radical recommendations, Helen Roberts's paper suggested to the Australian Parliament that there could be 'cyberspace virtual courts, which would be more attuned to network customs and would be able to mete out punishment enforceable in the Internet'.[49] To achieve such an end would require a set of principles to be applied. She suggested more use of alternative dispute resolution to react to the need for speed in Internet cases. The non-conflict possibilities are significant and worth the effort in order to resolve issues on an international basis and can be achieved by taking a cyber-rights rather than a cybercrime approach.

---

49 Roberts, above n. 6.

INVITED COMMENT

14. UNDERSTANDING THE PERPETUATION OF 'FAILURE'

The 15th Anniversary of the US Terrorist Finance Tracking Programme

Anthony AMICELLE*

Surveillance, ancient reality, only becomes modern traceability when it is performed within an organized system, whose extension suggests that it is a genuine societal project, pursued by private powers as much as public powers. ... Traceability implies three elements: It would require traces and thus a medium to identify them; it would require traces registration mechanism; finally it would require a structure to process and analyse them in order to draw conclusions. Without this type of organisation – which implies a certain voluntarism – traces exist, traceability does not.[1]

As a government technology of people and things, traceability is not as such a state monopoly, and certainly not a counterterrorism specificity.[2] Indeed, the three elements of traceability are united in a range of social, commercial, professional, health care and food safety configurations, to name a few. Studies have underlined the historicity and multiple uses of traces related to objects and subjects acting and/or circulating in the physical world or the cyberspace. With these remarks, it is worth noting that contemporaneous security programmes with dataveillance capabilities for counterterrorism purposes are extensively based on traceability. Apart from the emphasis on signal intelligence (SIGINT) arising from the 2013 US National Security Agency (NSA) surveillance scandal, the abbreviation FININT highlights another type of security configuration,

* Centre international de criminologie comparée (CICC), École de criminologie, Université de Montréal. E-mail: anthony.amicelle@umontreal.ca.

1 M.-A. HERMITTE, 'La traçabilité des personnes et des choses. Précaution, pouvoirs et maîtrise' in P. PEDROT (ed.), *Traçabilité et responsabilité*, Economica, Paris 2003, p. 3.

2 D. TORNY, 'La traçabilité comme technique de gouvernement des hommes et des choses' (1998) 44 *Politix* 51–75.

among the myriad of acronyms used to distinguish various sources and methods of intelligence.

With reference to FININT, US Treasury officials in particular have promoted 'the development of a new discipline for acquiring and analyzing financial intelligence' for numerous years, especially with the Terrorist Finance Tracking Program (TFTP).[3] According to Juan C. Zarate, the first assistant secretary of the Treasury for terrorist financing and financial crime:

> financial intelligence can be defined in many ways. In its broader sense, financial intelligence is any bit of information – however acquired – that reveals commercial or financial transactions and money flows, assets and capital data, and the financial and commercial relationships and interests of individuals, networks, and organizations. Such information can come in a variety of forms – crumpled receipts found in terrorist safe houses, the detail ledgers of hawaladars, suspicious transaction reports from banks, and transnational wire-transfers records. ... The right information about the sender or recipient of funds can open a window on broader networks or identify unseen ties. If it is timely and specific enough, such intelligence can help disrupt terrorist acts.[4]

On the one hand, a significant part of financial strategies against terrorism have mainly reinforced and transformed former mechanisms such as anti-money laundering policies. Alongside this classic process of adaptation of pre-existing measures, original initiatives have also emerged, starting with the TFTP that was formally introduced in October 2001.

> After the terrorist attacks on September 11, 2001, the United States Department of the Treasury initiated the Terrorist Finance Tracking Program (TFTP) to identify, track, and pursue terrorists – such as Al-Qaida – and their networks. The U.S. Treasury Department is uniquely positioned to track terrorist money flows and assist in broader U.S. Government efforts to uncover terrorist cells and map terrorist networks here at home and around the world.[5]

The conditions for the existence of such a security programme with global dataveillance capabilities have been well-known since the public disclosure of the TFTP in 2006 and the related EU–US controversy.[6] It consists of mobilising large quantities of digital traces generated by a particular form of cross-border communication, e.g. financial digital traces in relation to interbank

---

3 J.C. Zarate, *Treasury's war. The unleashing of a new era of financial warfare*, Public Affairs, New York 2013, p. 46.

4 Ibid., pp. 46–48.

5 US Treasury, *Resource Center: Terrorist Finance Tracking Program (TFTP)*, Washington DC, 2016.

6 L. Amoore, M. De Goede and M. Wesseling, 'Data wars beyond surveillance: Opening the black box of SWIFT' (2012) 5(1) *Journal of Cultural Economy* 49–66.

communication. Based on a set of relations above, beyond and below the national, the financial security programme contributes to the production of surveillance and intelligence from a traceability apparatus of financial transactions. The three elements of traceability are reunited in the name of counterterrorism with the articulation of three contemporaneous processes, e.g. the digitisation of interbank communications, the transnationalisation of financial intelligence and, last but not least, the hybridisation of traces management practices. Indeed, the secondary use of financial digital traces has been the result of a hybridisation process between state and non-state practices that set out the broad outline of a transnational bureaucracy of traceability. TFTP combines features of both SWIFT (Society for Worldwide Interbank Financial Telecommunication) – the 'private' administrator of international financial circulation – and US Treasury, a 'public' administrator of economic and financial activities.

While the development of such state/business configurations in security highlights citizens' powerless position in current democratic regimes, it also underlines the geographical materiality of mass dataveillance. Indeed, state actors such as US officials do not need to take control over sovereign territories connected with global communication networks in order to be in a powerful informational position. They must ensure access to targeted data storage sites within their national territory or they must be able to 'tap' the international communication machinery through 'the placement of interceptors on the large fibre-optic cables connecting the different hubs of the Internet'.[7] As a fundamental pillar of the financial system, far from being de-territorialised, SWIFT relies heavily on physical sites which are highly concentrated geographically, both in the US and Europe. This traditional location of globally oriented communication infrastructures thus contributes to destabilising trans-Atlantic and international relations in light of the principle of equality between sovereign entities in terms of information exchange.[8] The capacity to transform unilaterally the transnational space of interbank communication into a field of financial dataveillance in the name of counterterrorism remains highly controversial, especially in the European Union. Apart from privacy concerns, the added value of such security programmes is still challenged. In light of available sources, TFTP concrete results do not coincide with the official legitimation narrative in terms of pre-emption via the triptych of 'identification, tracking and networks mapping' of 'terrorists

---

7 Z. Bauman, D. Bigo, P. Esteves, E. Guild, V. Jabri, D. Lyon and R.J.B. Walker, 'After Snowden: Rethinking the impact of surveillance' (2014) 8 *International Political Sociology* 122; D. Bigo, G. Boulet, C. Bowden, S. Carrera, E. Guild, N. Hernanz, P. De Hert, J. Jeandesboz and A. Scherrer, 'Open season for data fishing on the Web: The challenges of the US PRISM programme for the EU' (2013) 292 *CEPS Policy Briefs* 1–10.

8 A. Amicelle, 'The EU's paradoxical efforts at tracking the financing of terrorism. From criticism to imitation of dataveillance' (2013) 56 *CEPS Liberty and Security Series* 1–19.

suspects'.[9] Consequently, one key question has emerged for several years: why does this kind of security programme with global dataveillance capabilities persist, regardless of failures to achieve stated goals against terrorism?

Here, I would like to explore three hypotheses in relation to the terrorist finance tracking programme that could be extended to US, European and trans-Atlantic security programmes with dataveillance capabilities.

First, the *function-creep* hypothesis. As with other disclosures of US programmes through public media, members of European Parliament and European data protection authorities have hypothesised that digital traces of international communications were massively collected and processed for multi-tasking purposes. In other words, they challenged the counterterrorist purpose of the security programme. They expressed concerns about the possibility of economic and industrial espionage with the access to strategic transactions and commercial information about European companies. Despite US government denials, this potentiality was a recurrent cause for deep concern until the 2010 trans-Atlantic agreement. Contrary to Edward Snowden's surveillance revelations on NSA practices, there has been no practical example demonstrating cases of economic or political espionage.

Second, the hypothesis of *symbolic capital*. The TFTP represents a critical issue at stake for the US Treasury regarding power relationships in the US national security field. Indeed, this kind of security programme-related database is seen as a key resource by and for social actors seeking recognition in a specific social space. Whether it was fully envisioned at the beginning, or formulated *ex post*, this reflection has been made very clear. Juan C. Zarate emphasised that the TFTP was

> also the story of the small group of officials from the Treasury Department and other government agencies who engineered this new brand of financial power. These strategies were designed under the radar, with the clear mission to revamp the way financial tools were used. They served also to resurrect a Treasury Department that was struggling to remain relevant to national security issues. … We envisioned a day when the Treasury Department would become central to core national security debates, and that's exactly what happened. … The reality was that Treasury had been a minor institutional player in the world of terrorism until 9/11.[10]

The hypothesis of TFTP as symbolic capital for federal agencies has gained traction following the attempt by NSA agents to hack the new SWIFT server in Switzerland, to access to international financial messages without the mediation

---

[9] A. Amicelle, '(Il)légitimité du renseignement financier. Usages transnationaux de la traçabilité des flux de capitaux' (2014) 47(2) *Criminologie* 77–104.

[10] Zarate, above n. 3, p. xi.

of the US Treasury TFTP.[11] After 15 years, the programme also illustrates traditional struggles for acquiring or safeguarding spheres of competence associated with budget, resources and symbolic power.

Third, the *information question* hypothesis. Like many other US security programmes with global dataveillance capabilities, the TFTP raises with great acuity the information question in trans-Atlantic and international relations, relating to 'power asymmetries as a consequence of differential dissemination of information or, at least, access inequalities to information producing devices'.[12] While the 2010 trans-Atlantic agreement has caused a slight rebalancing in power relationships between the European Union and the United States, the situation has remained unchanged for more than 180 non-EU countries connected to the SWIFT network. US Treasury agents have accessed personal information of millions of third countries' citizens, residents and companies without relying on foreign counterparts nor being constrained by foreign legislation. This form of inequality between sovereign entities in relation to security programmes such as the TFTP is acknowledged and partly promoted both in the US and the European Union: 'Based on the TFTP, it has been possible to obtain information on U.S. and EU citizens and residents suspected of terrorism or terrorist financing in third countries where requests for mutual legal assistance were not responded to in a timely manner'.[13] This kind of security programme makes it possible for users and beneficiaries to avoid foreign contingencies in security and intelligence such as diplomatic and judicial vicissitudes or technical, relational and operational difficulties. This aspect seems to strongly contribute to the continuity of the programme.

Although those non-mutually exclusive hypotheses do not exhaust the possibilities of understanding social, political and economic dynamics at work, they raise questions regarding US, EU and trans-Atlantic security programmes with global dataveillance capabilities in light of power relations in national and transnational fields of security.

---

11 European Parliament, Press release, 'MEPs call for suspension of EU–US bank data deal in response to NSA snooping', Brussels 2013; P. Schmuck, 'Pourquoi la NSA a espionné un village thurgovien', *Le Matin* (12.09.2013), <http://www.lematin.ch/suisse/Pourquoi-la-NSA-a-espionne-un-village-thurgovien-/story/18340039>.

12 D. Linhardt, 'La "question informationnelle". Éléments pour une sociologie politique des fichiers de police et de population en Allemagne et en France' (2005) 29 *Déviance et Société* 259.

13 European Commission, *Joint Report from the Commission and the U.S. Treasury Department regarding the value of TFTP Provided Data*, Brussels 2013, p. 6.

SECTION V

PRIVACY AND TIME

INVITED COMMENT

15. DOES IT MATTER WHERE YOU DIE?

Chances of Post-Mortem Privacy in Europe and in the United States

Iván SZÉKELY*

When people compare the differing concepts of data privacy in Europe and the United States, along with the different systems of legal and practical protection associated with them and the respective frameworks of informational self-determination, they invariably think of the privacy rights of living persons. One of the reasons they do this is because in public thinking, the notion of privacy is closely bound up with the actual life circumstances, expectations and rights of living persons, and the value represented by privacy is, manifestly or latently, important for people who are alive. The other reason is that in most of the countries where data protection rights have been enacted, the concept of personal data is limited to information associated with living persons. Nevertheless, one's personal uniqueness, or unique personality if you like, does not vanish with death: for the relatives and the personal friends, as well as the professional community and cultural memory, or indeed in a broader sense for society as a whole, the essence of a human being is more than the biological functioning of an organism, and it lives on after the stoppage of the biological machine. We ought to picture this as a comet in the sky: the radiant nucleus represents the human essence of a living person, and its long tail symbolises the personality left behind after death: as time passes, this remnant of personality becomes less and less linked to the human essence of the deceased, in much the same way that the end of the comet's tail gradually melts into the dark sky.[1]

* Vera and Donald Blinken Open Society Archives (OSA), Central European University (CEU). E-mail: szekelyi@ceu.edu.

[1] For the archivist's perspective on the subject, see I. SZEKELY, 'The Four Paradigms of Archival History and the Challenges of the Future' in M. MERVIÖ (ed.), *Management and Participation in the Public Sphere*, IGI-Global, Hershey PA 2015, p. 28. The metaphor was originally put forward by Laszlo Majtenyi.

1. THE LEGAL LANDSCAPE

Some of the problems concerning the protection and regulation of the gradually impersonalised information relating to deceased persons are adequately resolved by the traditional institutions of law, both within the national frameworks and in the international context: two examples – important on account of their financial implications, besides anything else – are intellectual property right and copyright. The bequest of persons living in today's networked society includes informational items the legal regulation of which is currently underway, although the formation of a unified approach to it is admittedly still further down the road. By contrast, the issue of the extension of data privacy beyond death has remained unresolved, and at best constitutes a grey zone within the law: it forms one of the increasingly important constituent elements of a manifold legal requirement, which the specialist literature has in the past few years come to describe as 'post-mortem privacy', and which includes 'the right of a person to preserve and control what becomes of his or her reputation, dignity, integrity, secrets or memory after death'.[2] This is what makes it worthwhile to ponder over such questions as whether there has been, or could be, or will always be, a difference between the respective concepts and possible realisations of post-mortem privacy concepts of the two continents.

As a subset of privacy,[3] data privacy belongs to the category of personality rights, and as such, it is rooted in different traditions on the opposite sides of the Atlantic, and the underlying ideas, social and legal traditions are also different. It is no use that on the surface technological convergence exacts policy convergence – as Colin Bennett predicted back in the 1980s – the law conserves the underlying traditions and these become important in every controversial case, when either the resolution of the controversy requires a court ruling or the enactment of new legislation becomes necessary in the course of legal development.

In countries with a common law system one cannot really speak of 'personality rights' in the same comprehensive sense that one can in relation to

---

2 L. Edwards and E. Harbinja, 'Protecting Post-Mortem Privacy: Reconsidering the Privacy Interests of the Deceased in a Digital World' (2013) 32(1) *Cardozo Art and Entertainment* 101–147.

3 In the era of datafication, more and more privacy-related areas have come to constitute data management problems, yet data privacy (or to use the European equivalent, data protection) merely forms a subset of the complete phenomenon of control over personal integrity, or the protection against harmful influences on personal integrity. Passing through a body scanner of the latest generation, for example, may not constitute data management in the strictest sense; nevertheless, it may be intrusive and humiliating for those whose religious or other convictions conflict with the display of the quasi-nude human body.

European countries following the continental law system. Those rights, which in continental or civilian law belong to the category of personality rights, will cease to apply after death in the countries of common law. In the case of a deceased person, the legal definitions of defamation or damage to good reputation become meaningless – in contrast with the deceased's economic rights, such as copyright or the right to own property, which the legal successors will inherit and continue to practice. By contrast, respect for personality rights has a long history in Europe. In Germany in particular, the right to human dignity is regarded as the cornerstone of the entire legal system, one that gives rise to all the other human and personality rights (including informational self-determination): the mother of all such rights, so to speak. The German courts have declared in several rulings[4] that the inviolability of human dignity does not end with death, and it is the duty of the state to guarantee continued protection in this area.

But of course, the difference between the two legal systems cannot be described in such a simple manner. The United Kingdom, one of the countries with a common law system, is also a member of the European Union and, consequently, was obliged to incorporate the provisions of the European Convention of Human Rights in its legal system. One of the consequences that resulted from this can be seen in the way the British courts have ruled in cases related to the use of pictures of celebrities and others (included deceased persons) in the 2000s: without actually extending the protection of personality rights beyond death, they limited the commercial or trademark-type marketing of the visual representations of persons.[5] And as for the US, the different states set up legal protections of various degrees in reaction to the growing market in celebrity images, although in some states these rights also applied to ordinary citizens and were extended to the protection of personal images after death. Nor do the countries with continental system of law represent a uniform position: unlike in Germany, in France, for example, the 'personal' aspect of personality rights is distinguished from the 'economic' aspect, only recognising the extension of the latter (for example, the right to marketing the pictures of celebrities). In the legal case regarding a book published about the private life of President Mitterand after his death, the French Court of Cassation clearly stated that the right to privacy ends with the death of the person concerned.[6]

---

4 See for example the *Mephisto* (BVerfGE 30, 173) and *Marlene Dietrich* (BGH 1 ZR 49/97) cases.

5 See for example *Irvine v. Talksport Ltd.* (P.M. Bryniczka, '*Irvine v. Talksport Ltd.*: Snatching Victory from the Jaws of Defeat – English Law Now Offers Better Protection of Celebrities' Rights' (2004) Spring, *Sports Lawyers Journal* 171–194; E.K. Oke, 'Image Rights of Celebrities in the Digital Era: Is There a Need for the Right of Publicity in Ireland?' (2014) 4(1) *Irish Journal of Legal Studies* 92–117.)

6 *SA Editions Plon v. Mitterand*, (Cour de Cassation, JCP 1977. II. 22894). For more detail see Edwards and Harbinja, above n. 2.

The central element of European data protection legislation is personal data, defined as any data relating to an identified or identifiable natural person. Although the guiding international documents, the EU's data protection directive and the Council of Europe's (CoE) data protection convention do not specifically state that only living persons can possess personal data, this is how it is interpreted everywhere – in the EU Member States and the signatory countries of the CoE. Some countries even explicitly include this among the definitions accompanying their data protection laws.[7] By contrast, some other countries – by way of exception – have legal provisions in force, which subordinate the handling of a deceased person's personal data to the instructions of a surviving relative, and occasionally even to the previously recorded directions of the data subject.[8] In summary, we may conclude, therefore, that the existing EU data protection laws do not protect the data of deceased persons, and in fact the new General Data Protection Regulation (GDPR) of the EU, which will directly apply in all Member States from May 2018, expressly excludes data referable to deceased persons from the category of personal data (although it leaves the possibility open for Member States to formulate their own rules in this regard).[9]

2. CONVERGING TECHNOLOGIES, DIVERGING POLICIES

The fact that people increasingly tend to share aspects of their lives on the Internet, on various other social media, and that they are also inclined to store their personal informational goods on the net, lends a pressing actuality to the above, seemingly theoretical issues. According to an estimate from 2012, a total

7 Sweden: 'Personal data: All kinds of information that directly or indirectly may be referable to a natural person who is alive' (s. 3, Personal Data Act (1998:204, <http://www.dataprotection.eu/pmwiki/pmwiki.php?n=Main.SE>)); UK: 'personal data means data which relate to a living individual who can be identified...' (s. 1, Data Protection Act 1998, <http://www.legislation.gov.uk/ukpga/1998/29/pdfs/ukpga_19980029_en.pdf>).

8 In Estonia, for example, the Personal Data Protection Act of 2003 decrees that '[t]he consent of a data subject [to the processing of his/her personal data] shall be valid during the life of the data subject and thirty years after the death of the data subject, unless the data subject has decided otherwise.' Estonia, Personal Data Protection Act of 2003, <http://www.legaltext.ee/text/en/X70030.htm>.

9 Regulation (EU) 2016/679 of the European Parliament and of the Council of 27 April 2016 on the protection of natural persons with regard to the processing of personal data and on the free movement of such data, and repealing Directive 95/46/EC (General Data Protection Regulation): 'This Regulation should not apply to data of deceased persons. Member States may provide for rules regarding the processing of data of deceased persons.' Recital 27 of the preamble.

of 375,000 Facebook users die annually in the US alone,[10] while other estimates put the same figure at 580,000, with the corresponding figure for the worldwide population estimated at 2.89 million.[11] The bequests of these people contain a growing number of virtual items, e-mails, files stored in the cloud and avatars. In some cases, the material value dominates in these virtual legacies (for example, credits collected in online games, or domain names), while in other cases the values associated with the personality of the deceased are more important (one example is the content of the deceased person's online communications), but in most cases both elements are present.

Any user with good common sense might think that the fate of these virtual legacies basically is in the hands of the service providers, and the law has only limited space to manoeuvre here – and they would not be far from the truth. This is so, firstly, because the price the users pay for the seemingly free services is the sale and marketing of their data and personality, which the service providers determine from the position of unilateral power (formally through a contract to which users agree by signing it). Secondly, because the system handles the users' data, and the associated users' profiles, in the way the programmers originally designed it – in Lessig's words, 'Code is law'.

But there are several other aspects that have lent the issue of post-mortem privacy a pressing actuality: one is the 'eternal memory' suggested by the visionaries of information society (briefly stated, the Internet does not forget and, therefore, all information will be preserved and become available everywhere and for everybody), and the plan designed to prevent this from happening, i.e. the provocatively named 'Right to be Forgotten' campaign (or of late, 'Right to Erasure'). Nor should we forget that nowadays more and more advanced and intelligent virtual personalities have come to represent the people who are active on the Internet, and some of these virtual personalities have the capability of autonomous actions as well as of interaction with other entities, including writing e-mails, chatting, bidding in auctions, etc. These intelligent entities may remain active after the death of the actual person concerned, and may continue with their activities, thus extending the personality of the deceased, prolonging its virtual life, so to speak.

In view of the ongoing globalisation and policy convergence, one would expect the large service providers (the vast majority of which are based in the US anyway) to be carrying out very similar policies in managing the deceased persons' data (accounts, profiles, files). Actually, we see precisely the opposite: Yahoo's

---

10 J. Mazzone, 'Facebook's Afterlife' (2012) 90 *North Carolina Law Review* 1643–1685, <http://www.leggioggi.it/wp-content/uploads/2012/10/SSRN-id2142594.pdf>.

11 N. Lustig, '2.89m Facebook Users Will Die in 2012, 580,000 in the USA', <http://www.nathanlustig.com/2012/06/06/2-89m-facebook-users-will-die-in-2012-580000-in-the-usa/>.

'No Right of Survivorship' clause excludes the survival of contents about deceased users, along with those uploaded by them; Facebook users can opt to have their profiles either deleted or preserved, and their passwords released or withheld (memorialisation request); the certified legal heir can deactivate a deceased's Twitter account (without the option of discovering its content); in exceptional cases, Google may release data and e-mails (but will not give out passwords), in response to a bequest procedure; Microsoft Hotmail releases the contents to the official executor of a will (but not to the legal heirs); Instagram originally claimed ownership of all photos uploaded by users (although it retracted that claim in response to strong protests in 2012); Blizzard (the operator of the World of Warcraft) has not recognised its users' digital property rights from the start; while in the case of Linden Labs (Second Life), digital properties can be inherited. One the more recent developments has been the 'Inactive Account Manager' option, introduced in 2013 by Google: this offers users the choice to determine the future fate of the data and contents related to their profile.

On the surface, therefore, it would appear that, instead of being fragmented along the continental division of legal and social traditions, these divergent policies are rooted in the philosophies and business models of service providers. At the level of details, however, the differences remain important, as the respective 'natural sense' of justice and socio-cultural traditions of the two continents continue to play a role even in this rapidly changing and increasingly globalised world of ours, and all this is reflected in the legal tendencies, the rulings of court cases and the reasoning of the judges. On that basis, an important conceptual difference seems to be emerging between the two continents, one that Harbinja has called attention to in several of her studies published in recent years.[12]

In the US, policy-makers tend to look for a solution in the direction of the commodification and propertisation of deceased persons' data; this is indicated by the model law adopted by the Uniform Law Commission,[13] which applies the rules of proprietary and inheritance rights to digital properties in the name of technology neutrality. Legislation testifying to such an approach already exists in certain states of the US. Nevertheless, some influential American civil

12 E. Harbinja, 'Does the EU data protection regime protect post-mortem privacy and what could be the potential alternatives?' (2013) 10(1) *SCRIPTed* 19–38, <https://script-ed.org/article/eu-data-protection-regime-protect-post-mortem-privacy-potential-alternatives/>; Edwards and Harbinja, above n. 2.

13 Uniform Law Commission, Uniform Fiduciary Access to Digital Assets Act, <http://www.uniformlaws.org/shared/docs/Fiduciary%20Access%20to%20Digital%20Assets/2014_UFADAA_Final.pdf>.

rights organisations[14] were strongly critical of the model: they argued that since digital legacies were not analogous to physical bequests, they should therefore be treated differently: a large part of the data are accumulating without the awareness of the data subjects, the privacy rights of third parties are also a matter of concern in digital legacies, and the inclusion of guardians in such probate proceedings would be especially dangerous. By contrast, theorists in Europe strive to find solutions in line with the preservation of human dignity and information rights, as these would be more befitting to the European system of values. These solutions ought to make it clear that the ideas of personal integrity and personal freedom are crucially important considerations in the handling of personal data and that the commercial trading and the transfer of ownership of such data would be incompatible with all that. (We should point out, however, that in some respect the documents of the European data protection reform seem to move away from such a purely rights-based approach and show certain signs of propertisation, as is the case with the rules of data portability,[15] for example.)

3. PROSPECTS FOR THE FUTURE DECEASED

In 2014 the organisers of the annual international Computers, Privacy and Data Protection (CPDP) conference dedicated a separate panel to the question of post-mortem privacy.[16] The European participants of the debate made optimistic statements about the possibility of creating the legal framework of post-mortem privacy in the foreseeable future. The imminent European data protection reform, as we saw, has failed to show any sign of this for the moment. In any case, if there is any chance of it happening at all, it is more likely to happen in Europe, where some kind of a legislation, not necessarily within the framework of data protection legislation but through some other instruments of law, might follow, on the basis of which a person within his lifetime might be able to have control over the future fate of his or her private information, or a surviving relative might be able to practise this right, and that this right may hopefully be based on the intangible attributes of human essence, rather than on the propertisation and commercial marketing of human qualities.

---

14 Center for Democracy and Technology (CDT), American Civil Liberties Union (ACLU), Electronic Frontier Foundation (EFF), Consumer Action CDT et al., 'Civil Liberty Organizations Respond to the Uniform Fiduciary Access to Digital Assets Act' (12.01.2015), <https://cdt.org/files/2015/01/Joint-Letter-re-ULC-Bill-general-statement-2-FINAL.pdf>.

15 See GDPR Art. 20 (esp. s. 2.).

16 'Post-mortem Privacy: Exploring Deceased's Privacy in a Digital World', <http://www.cpdpconferences.org/archive.html>.

The past few decades have seen the publication of a number of popular books that offered lists of countries and member states ranked according to being the most advantageous from the viewpoint of setting up new companies, taxation, taking out insurance policies, getting married, retiring, etc. We are still a long way from the stage where similar books could be published about the best countries in which to conclude our lives, if we care about having continuing protection for our personality and privacy after death. But when the publication of such books eventually becomes timely, their content and approach will certainly be different for Europe and the US.

INVITED COMMENT

16. THE RIGHT TO BE FORGOTTEN, FROM THE TRANS-ATLANTIC TO JAPAN

Hiroshi MIYASHITA*

1. THE TRANS-ATLANTIC DEBATE

In the wake of the EU General Data Protection Regulation and the ruling of the Court of Justice in the European Union (CJEU) in *Google Spain*, the right to be forgotten has become one of the most controversial topics in data protection around the globe. For instance, the right to be forgotten has been described as 'a form of censorship, one that would most likely be unconstitutional if attempted in the United States'.[1]

It is well described that 'Americans want to be famous while the French want to be forgotten'.[2] Forgetfulness with legal enforcement may be a beauty of privacy, but may also be a threat to the free flow of information. The right to be forgotten without thinking of free speech is dangerous, and the free flow of information in the Internet without privacy protection is savage.

Considering the debate between the EU and the US on the right to be forgotten, this chapter aims to clarify the ongoing debate and issues on the right to be forgotten in Japan, including some judicial decisions, the legislative debate and the standard of delisting.

---

* Faculty of Policy Studies, Chuo University, Japan. E-mail: hmiya.64r@g.chuo-u.ac.jp.

1 JONATHAN ZITTRAIN, 'Don't Force Google to "Forget"', *New York Times*, 14 May 2014, p. A29.

2 JEFFREY ROSEN, 'The deciders: the future of privacy and free speech in the age of Facebook and Google' (2012) 80(4) *Fordham Law Review*, 1533.

2. JUDICIAL DECISIONS IN JAPAN

2.1. FOR THE RIGHT TO BE FORGOTTEN

On 22 December 2015, Saitama District Court, in a case seeking the delisting of a criminal case of child prostitution, three years earlier, held that 'even the criminal, who was broadcasted and known to the society on his or her arrest, has the right to respect for his or her private life as a right to personality ... and "the right to be forgotten" of the previous criminal the society, depending on the nature of the crime'.[3] In this case, the court particularly considered the difficulty of deleting information on the Internet in modern society in light of the interest of rehabilitation.

As another example, on 9 October 2014, Tokyo District Court declared that Google should delist 122 search results of the plaintiff who used to belong to a group with a bad reputation.[4] The court found that 'it is obvious that even the titles and the snippets themselves constitute infringement of the data subject's right to personality'. And Google users do not have a legitimate interest in searching websites including the obvious infringement of the right to personality of others. Consequently, 'Google should be regarded as a controller of the website and has the obligation to delete the search results'. This is the first decision of delisting, admitting the right to be forgotten, in Japan.

The attorney for the plaintiff, Tomohiro Kanda, mentioned that he referred to the logic of the judgment in the *Google Spain* case by the Court of Justice of the European Union.[5] It is more efficient to request the search engine companies rather than the original web operators to delete the no longer relevant words. It is reasonable to think that search result pages containing the infringement of the right to personality should be identified as Google's infringement of the right to personality. According to Kanda, minor criminal records can be requested to be deleted after three to five years in his experience in the Tokyo District Court.[6]

In another more controversial case, Tokyo District Court on 8 May 2015 ordered Google to erase the search results regarding breach of professional responsibility of a doctor, since this had been nine years previously. The case was appealed by Google.

---

3 Saitama District Court, Decision on 22 December 2015, Hanreijiho no. 2282 p. 78 (2016).

4 Decision by Tokyo District Court, 9 October 2014 (unpublished). See Tomohiro Kanda, 'Case on the request of the preliminary injunction to delete the search results of Google', in Yoshimichi Okuda (ed.), *Internet Society and the Right to be Forgotten*, Gendaijinbunsya, 2015, p. 112 (in Japanese).

5 Case C-131/12 *Google Spain SL and Google Inc. v. Agencia Española de Protección de Datos (AEPD)* (CJEU, 13 May 2014).

6 Kanda, above n. 4, p. 135.

2.2. AGAINST THE RIGHT TO BE FORGOTTEN

There have been different conclusions from other decisions in Japan. Tokyo High Court on 12 July 2016 reversed the Saitama District Court's 'right to be forgotten' decision, saying that 'in our country, both the requirements and effects of the right to be forgotten are not clear because of no explicit provision of law'.[7] The High Court dismissed the claim of a right to be forgotten, saying that '"right to be forgotten" as a part of the right to personality ... should not be considered independently from the right to honour and privacy as a part of right to personality'.

A further example can be seen in the Kyoto District Court, on 7 August 2014, where the court dismissed a request to delist search results in Yahoo Japan.[8] The plaintiff had been arrested under the Nuisance Ordinance for peeping with small cameras concealed in his sandals. The court's formula was whether (1) the search results have social legitimate significance, and (2) the contents and the means of displaying the search results are unlawful. The court held that the search results of this incident did not violate the plaintiff's privacy, because 'it passed only one year and half after arresting and the incident drew social attention and was public interest'. And 'its contents and the means of the search results are not unlawful because Google just displayed URLs and a part of the contents of the original websites'. The Osaka High Court also rejected the appeal on 18 February 2015.[9] The High Court showed sympathy of the importance of rehabilitation of the plaintiff, but the incident was one of social interest and only two years had elapsed since the arrest.

On 31 January 2017, the Supreme Court of Japan held that criminal information on child prostitution in the search results cannot be deleted. According to the Court, it is permissible to delete search results when the interest in an individual's privacy obviously overrides the reason for providing the search results. The Court did not mention the 'right to be forgotten'.

3. DELISTING STANDARD

3.1. TORTS AND RIGHT TO BE FORGOTTEN

In Japan, the basic logic of the right to be forgotten is based on Art. 709 Civil Code under the torts principle, rather than the Act on the Protection of Personal Information.[10] Article 709 provides that '[a] person who has intentionally or

---

7 Tokyo High Court, Decision of July 12, 2016 (unpublished). See Hiroshi Miyashita, 'Taking "right to be forgotten" seriously' (2016) 741 *Hogaku Seminar* 1.

8 Kyoto District Court, Judgment of 7 August 2014, Westlaw Japan 2014 WLJPCA08076001.

9 Osaka High Court, Judgment of 18 February 2015, LEX-DB 25506059.

10 Act on the Protection of Personal Information. English translation available at <http://www.ppc.go.jp/files/pdf/280222_amendedlaw.pdf> accessed 25.08.2016.

negligently infringed any right of others, or legally protected interest of others, shall be liable to compensate any damages resulting in consequence'. The courts have repeatedly held that Art. 709 implicitly contains the right to personality, such as right to privacy or right to honour.[11] Under Japanese law, the right to privacy in Japan is implicitly protected as a fundamental human right under Art. 13 of the Constitution.[12] Constitutional provisions can only apply to government action, whereas the Civil Code applies to private parties.[13] This is why the logic of the right to be forgotten may be interpreted from the right to personality, with the indirect influence of the constitutional right to privacy, since the Civil Code applies to private search engine companies.

3.2. BALANCING

In the case of unwanted disclosure of private facts, the courts use the *ad hoc* balancing test between the right to personality and the other rights or interests, particularly freedom of expression. As a classic example, the Tokyo District Court in 1964 interpreted Art. 709 Civil Code as 'the right to privacy is recognised as the legal or protection or the right so as not to be disclosed of private life'.[14] Since then, the Supreme Court has used an ad-hoc balancing test between 'the disadvantage of the victim by the possible injuries and the disadvantage of the intruder by the injunction, in light of the social position of the injured person and the nature of the injury'.[15]

The landmark decision to consider the right to be forgotten in Japan is about the interest of rehabilitation. The plaintiff had been sentenced to three years in prison due to a charge of bodily injury. Twelve years later, a famous novelist had used the real name of the plaintiff in his work of nonfiction. The question was whether the plaintiff's previous criminal conviction should be forgotten in the novel. The Supreme Court on 8 February 1994[16] held that one's embarrassing past, including facts relating to a criminal record, could not be made public if the legal interest in not being publicised outweighed the public interest. The Court took into account the person's later life as well as the historical and social importance of the event, the significance of the parties, and the meaning of using

11 See e.g. Supreme Court, Judgment of 11 June 1986, Minshu vol. 40 no. 4 p. 872.

12 'All of the people shall be respected as individuals. Their right to life, liberty, and the pursuit of happiness shall, to the extent that it does not interfere with the public welfare, be the supreme consideration in legislation and in other governmental affairs' (Art. 13 Constitution).

13 The Supreme Court seems to take the position that right to privacy is a part of the right to personality. See Supreme Court, Judgment of 12 December 1973, Minshu vol. 27 no. 11 p. 1536.

14 Tokyo District Court, Judgment of 28 September 1964, Hanreijiho vol. 385, p. 12.

15 Supreme Court, Judgment of 24 September 2002, Hanreijiho vol. 1324 p. 5.

16 Supreme Court, Judgment of 8 February 1994, Minshu vol. 48 no. 2 p. 149.

the person's real name. In conclusion, the Court upheld the privacy infringement argument, due to the disturbance to the plaintiff's social rehabilitation and his new life environment, which is understood as 'interest of forgetfulness'.[17] The Court's approach is consistent with the constitutional value of being respected as individuals by not allowing republication of the forgetting past.

In the Japanese context, freedom of expression has a high constitutional value, but 'it is not always prevailing with other interests'. It is true that some Japanese scholars insisted that the search engines contribute to the freedom of expression and the right to know.[18] Yet, it is important to realise that the *Google Spain* case does not directly balance between freedom of expression and the right to privacy and data protection. The CJEU ruling is based on the balancing between data protection right and 'not only the economic interest of the operator of the search engine but also the interest of the general public in finding that information upon a search relating to the data subject's name'.[19]

3.3. STANDARD-MAKING

We have seen some concrete progress for supporting the right to be forgotten. First, Yahoo Japan publicised the criteria for delisting on 30 March 2015.[20] According to the delisting factors, Yahoo Japan will consider (i) the attribution of the information and (ii) the nature of the information. As for the attribution of the information, information relating to public figures, representatives of corporations and famous people should be regarded as of high public interest. On the other hand, information on minors should be treated as having a strong demand for privacy protection. As for the nature of the information, sexual pictures, physical details, victims of crime or bullying victims are categorised as requiring privacy protection. On the contrary, previous illegal activities including criminal offences and punishment records generally merit a strong demand for public interest. Some information regarding place of birth requires special consideration due to the sensitive discriminatory issues encountered by Burakumin (an outcast group living in certain areas at the bottom of the social order in the past) in Japan. Compared with the report on the right to be forgotten

---

17 Atsushi Omura, 'Gyakuten jiken' (2010) 356 *Hogaku Kyoshitsu* 128.

18 See e.g. Shigenori Matsui, *Constitutional Theory of the Internet*, Yuhikaku, 2014, p. 257; Satoshi Narihara, 'Debate situation of right to be forgotten in Japan, US and Europe', (2015) December *Administration and Information System* 54. See also Eugene Volokh and Donald M. Falk, 'First Amendment Protection for Search Engine' (2012) 8 *Journal of Law, Economic & Policy* 883.

19 CJEU, *Google Spain* case, para 97.

20 Yahoo Japan, Policy on the receiving requests of non-display of search results, 30 March 2015 (in Japanese).

by Google Advisory Council, Google considers passage of time and source for delisting, which were not included in the Yahoo Japan's report.[21]

Secondly, in July 2015 the Ministry of Internal Affairs and Communications published a Report on the measures on the flow of personal and user information on the Internet.[22] The Report touches on the CJEU ruling and refers to the Article 29 Data Protection Working Party's opinion in November 2014 for 13 issues to be considered for delisting.[23]

Thirdly, in Japan, the Internet Service Providers enjoy some immunity against liability under the Providers' Immunity Law.[24] The Act provides some immunity under certain conditions, such as no knowledge of illegal information for damage compensation on the Internet, the voluntary guidelines give concrete examples for deleting personal information on the web, distinguishing public figures from private persons, and types of personal information.

If search engines function globally, it is necessary to take a step for the global implementation of delisting.[25] If search engines have different standards of delisting, it is necessary to take a step for the uniform standard for delisting. At the same time, it is important to take into account that privacy is heavily influenced by cultural and social norm of each region and over time.

4. TECHNICAL ISSUES

In Japan, right to be forgotten litigation concerns at least two technical legal issues, apart from the main issue of standards of delisting. First, in light of the search engine liability, it is controversial whether the search engines are liable for the mechanical and automatic search results, whose contents are originally came from a third party. Unlike section 230 of the US Communications Decency Act of 1996, which gives a broad immunity for the intermediary, there is no explicit provision for the search engines' liability for the delisting injunction in Japan.

---

21 See Google, Advisory Council, 'The Advisory Council to Google on the Right to be Forgotten', February 2015.

22 Ministry of Internal Affairs and Communications, Report on the measures of flow of personal and user information in the Internet, July 2015 (in Japanese).

23 Article 29 Data Protection Working Party, Guidelines on the implementation of the Court of Justice of the European Union judgment on *Google Spain and inc v. Agencia Española de Protección de Datos (AEPD) and Mario Costeja González*, C-131/12, 26 November 2014.

24 Act on the Limits of Liability for Damages of Specified Telecommunications Service Providers and the Right to Request Disclosure of Identification Information of the Senders. English translation available at <http://www.soumu.go.jp/main_sosiki/joho_tsusin/eng/Resources/laws/Compensation-Law.pdf>.

25 See Brendan Van Alsenoy and Marieke Koekkoek, 'Internet and Jurisdiction after *Google Spain*: the Extraterritorial Reach of the Right to be Listed' (2015) 5(2) *International Data Privacy Law* 105.

Some courts in Japan consider that 'the title and snippet themselves are the expression by the search engines',[26] who should be liable for their republication. Others see that 'search engines themselves do not express illegally, nor do they control the webpages'.[27]

Secondly, in terms of the effect of delisting, it is not clear to what extent the judgement of delisting reaches in domains and territory. In a preliminary injunction on 19 March 2012 in the case of Google auto complete suggesting a man's name with criminal convictions, the Tokyo District Court ordered Google to erase the suggested words in both '.com' and '.jp' domains, a request which Google refused to obey.

Thirdly, the Personal Information Protection Commission, newly established in January 2016, is expected to receive requests from the users' complaints of delisting. Yet, unlike the EU data protection authority, it is doubtful that the Japanese Commission has such a power over delisting, since the Act on the Protection of Personal Information does not specify the lodging of complaints to the Commission. It should also be borne in mind that, in practice, due to the limited resources, data protection authorities may not protect the fundamental right to data protection in their enforcement jurisdiction at the borders of their respective nations.[28]

We have seen the divisiveness of the judicial decisions on the right to be forgotten in Japan. Yet, it is easy to recognise the demand for the right to be forgotten. According to the official statistics, Tokyo District Court received 711 injunction requests relating to Internet issues in 2013, whose number had drastically increased from only 33 injunction requests in 2009.

5. LEGISLATIVE DEBATE

The Act on the Protection of Personal Information was amended in September 2015 to include an obligation of erasure of personal data without delay where such data is not necessary for the original purpose (Art. 19). This new provision is understood as not the data protection rights, but efforts of the data controller. Since the Act on the Protection of Personal Information is regarded as a 'charter of fundamental duties' for data controllers, rather than a 'charter of fundamental rights' for data subjects, the courts may be unlikely to refer to this Act to protect the right to be forgotten.

---

26 Tokyo High Court, Decision of 12 July 2016, Hanrei Times no. 1429 p. 112.

27 Tokyo District Court, Judgment of 18 February 2010, Westlaw 2010WLJPCA02188010. See also Tokyo High Court, Decision of 15 January 2013 (unpublished).

28 Christopher Kuner, *The Court of Justice of the EU Judgment on Data Protection and Internet Search Engines*, LSE Law, Society and Economy Working Papers 3/2015, p. 22.

During the law reform debate in the Diet (Parliament), the Prime Minister said on 27 March 2015:

> The legislation on the right to be forgotten has been debated in EU. In Japan, there is no explicit provisions on the right to be forgotten; namely the right to delete or erase the unnecessary personal information by the certain period of time passage. Yet, there are cases where the personal data can be deleted or erased under the defamation or infringement of the right to personality. The Government of Japan carefully observes the EU developments.

There is no concrete legislative process so far to provide for the right to be forgotten, but the right to be forgotten debate may be connected with Japan's new 'revenge porn' law of 2014.[29]

6. TIME AND PRIVACY

Human beings forget, but the Internet does not. This is why forgetting is commonly demanded as a legal right in the twenty-first century. If personality itself is partly shaped by the digital personality in this connected world, it is reasonable to protect the digital personality with forgetfulness.

Time is an essential component of privacy.[30] In an opinion by the Advocate General in a case of data retention, it is reasonably observed that privacy and 'historical' time are intertwined.

> If the principle of retaining all that personal documentation for a certain period of time is considered lawful, it remains to ask whether it is inevitable, that is to say, necessary, for it to be imposed on individuals over a period which covers not only 'the present time' but also 'historical time'.[31]

In this sense, the right to be forgotten is the counter-measure for the Internet unforgotten memory to restore the human nature of forgetting. In Japan, more judicial rulings based on the Supreme Court decision in 2017 and the standard-making for delisting by the Personal Information Protection Commission are expected on this issue, taking into account the trans-Atlantic discussions.

---

29 Act on the Prevention of Victimisation resulting from Providing the Personal Sexual Image Records. See Shigenori Matsui, 'The criminalization of revenge porn in Japan' (2015) 24(2) *Washington International Law Journal*, 289.

30 See Jed Rubenfeld, *Freedom and Time*, Yale University Press, 2001, p. 254.

31 Case C-293/12 *Digital Rights Ireland and Seitlinger and Others* (CJEU, 12 December 2013), opinion of Advocate General Cruz Villalón, para. 147.

PART II

THEORY OF PRIVACY

17. IS THE DEFINITION OF PERSONAL DATA FLAWED?

Hyperlink as Personal Data (Processing)*

Jakub MÍŠEK**

1. INTRODUCTION

The system of personal data protection is mostly built on the premise of prevention.[1] The law affects any natural or legal person who works with personal data, which means a person who processes such data.[2] The term 'personal data' and its exact meaning is therefore the cornerstone of the whole system.[3] Once anyone processes this special kind of data, which the law sees as personal, they fall within the framework of Directive 95/46/EC and are bound to perform all the duties of a data controller, unless one of a small number of exceptions applies to them. Directive 95/46/EC is a preventive tool. It protects privacy by preventing abuse of personal data.[4] It is based on the idea that processing personal data in accordance with the rules minimises the risk of harm to privacy. This idea was also acknowledged by the Court of Justice of the European Union (CJEU) in several recent cases, e.g. the *Google Spain* case[5] and

* This chapter was presented as a working paper at the Fourth Göttinger Research Forum on Law and ICT/IP 2015. I would like to express my gratitude to Zsolt Balogh for his valuable commentary. This chapter was created with the support of Masaryk University Grant No. MUNI/A/0947/2015.

** Institute of Law and Technology, Faculty of Law, Masaryk University. E-mail: jkb.misek@mail.muni.cz.

1 See R. GELLERT, 'Understanding Data Protection as Risk Regulation' (2015) 18(11) *Journal of Internet Law* 8.

2 As will be more thoroughly described later, 'processing of personal data' is a very broad term.

3 See R. POLČÁK, 'Getting European Data Protection Off the Ground' (2014) *International Data Privacy Law* 282–289.

4 See Recitals no. 26 et seq. of Directive 95/64/EC.

5 Para. 66 of Decision C-131/12. 'First of all, it should be remembered that, as is apparent from Article 1 and recital 10 in the preamble, Directive 95/46 seeks to ensure a high level of protection of the fundamental rights and freedoms of natural persons, in particular their right to privacy, with respect to the processing of personal data (see, to this effect, *IPI* EU:C:2013:715, paragraph 28).'

the *Rynes* case,[6] where the Court stated that a high level of protection of the right to privacy, with respect to processing of personal data, must be ensured.

This chapter examines how the core concepts of 'personal data' and 'personal data processing' evolved over the years when the Directive has been applicable, and aims to test the system's stability. The hypothesis is that the definitions of these concepts are too broad. Thus, the data protection law regulates such kinds of data that the system cannot actually handle. Therefore, the only way to maintain the system is not to enforce the rules.

1.1. DEFINITION OF PERSONAL DATA

For testing the hypothesis, it is necessary to start from the very basic concepts. European Directive 95/46/EC (hereinafter referred to as 'the Directive') defines the term 'personal data' quite broadly as 'any information relating to an identified or identifiable natural person'.[7] The person whose data are processed is called 'data subject' and Art. 2 also states that an identifiable person is a natural person 'who can be identified, directly or indirectly.' That is followed by a non-exhaustive list of examples of information that can be used for identification, including identification number and information about a person's physical, physiological, mental, economic, cultural or social identity. It is important to stress that the Directive is based upon the principles formulated in the early 1980s.[8] In the first proposal of the Directive, in 1990, Art. 3 para. 1 uses the same definition of the term personal data as the final version.[9] It is therefore safe to assume that the current system is grounded in the ideas and technology paradigm of the late 1980s. The examples stated in the Directive thus reflect this period's conception of what could lead to the identification of a person, and they can serve only as an interpretation aid through that.

In 2007, the Article 29 Data Protection Working Party (WP29) published an opinion on the concept of personal data, interpreting the notion of 'personal data' itself. The opinion defines four elements which must all apply for this term to apply and for information to fall into the scope of the Directive.

---

6 Para. 27 of Decision C-212/13. 'As is clear from Article 1 of that directive [95/46/EC] and recital 10 thereto, Directive 95/46 is intended to ensure a high level of protection of the fundamental rights and freedoms of natural persons, in particular their right to privacy, with respect to the processing of personal data (see *Google Spain and Google*, C-131/12, EU:C:2014:317, paragraph 66).'

7 Art. 2(a) of Directive 95/46/EC.

8 See OECD, *Thirty years after: The OECD privacy guidelines* (2011), <http://www.oecd.org/sti/ieconomy/49710223.pdf> accessed 30.06.2016.

9 Proposal for a Council Directive concerning the protection of individuals in relation to the processing of personal data, COM (90) 314 final, SYN 287 and 288, Brussels, 13 September 1990, <http://aei.pitt.edu/3768/1/3768.pdf> accessed 30.06.2016.

The elements are as follows: the first element is 'any information'; the second element is 'relating to'; the third element 'identified or identifiable' [natural person]; and finally the fourth element is 'natural person.'

The first and the fourth elements do not need to be elaborated upon in detail here, as they are not problematic for our case. However, the second and the third should be discussed further. When it comes to the 'relating to' part, WP 29 says that in general, this is fulfilled when the information is 'about the individual'.[10] The opinion then divides this concept into (yet another) three elements, and if none of them are fulfilled in the given case, then the information is not relating to the person and therefore, it is not personal data. The first element is 'content', which is a case where the information is about the individual in the common meaning of the word (e.g. the results of a medical analysis or the traffic and location data of electronic communication). The second element is 'purpose':

> [The] 'purpose' element can be considered to exist when the data are used or are likely to be used, taking into account all the circumstances surrounding the precise case, with the purpose to evaluate, treat in a certain way or influence the status or behaviour of an individual.[11]

Finally, the last element is 'result'. If the use of information is likely to have an impact on an individual, then the information is relating to them. These subjective concepts of purpose and result are quite sensible ones: they ensure that only such information which could cause harm, and should therefore be regulated by the law falls within the scope of the Directive. Unfortunately, as will be elaborated in detail later, the recent decisions of CJEU do not allow for a 'subjective approach to personal data' interpretation.

The 'identified or identifiable' element is represented by a question whether the information can be used to identify a natural person, directly or indirectly. Directly identifying personal data are such types of information that can be used for identification immediately, without any additional information. An example of that can be a very specific surname of a person; their position; a unique identification number; and so on. Indirectly identifying personal data are such types of information which are not sufficient for the identification of a person but can be used for such purpose when connected with additional information.[12] In the end, this means that according to the Directive, personal data can be defined as any information which leads, or could lead, to the identification of a specific

---

10 Article 29 Data Protection Working Party Opinion No. 4/2007 on the concept of personal data, WP 136, p. 9 <http://ec.europa.eu/justice/data-protection/article-29/documentation/opinion-recommendation/files/2007/wp136_en.pdf> accessed 30.06.2016.

11 Ibid., p. 10.

12 Ibid., pp. 13–14.

natural person. This very broad scope is confirmed by Recital 26 of the Directive, which states:

> [The] principles of protection must apply to any information concerning an identified or identifiable person, whereas, to determine whether a person is identifiable, account should be taken of all the means likely reasonably to be used either by the controller or by any other person to identify the said person.[13]

Even though the recital is not legally binding, it may serve as a useful aid in the interpretation process. The main advantage of this broad definition approach is its technological neutrality. Regardless of the form the identifying information assumes, it is still within the scope of the Directive. On the other hand, this approach brings about one major disadvantage. Today's technology enables us to process large datasets and connect different kinds of information in a way, which had never been possible before. It means that almost any information could be used for the identification of a natural person, and so virtually any information can be seen as personal data within the scope of the Directive.[14]

According to Tikk's summary, the unique combination of information, which as a whole constitutes a possibility for the identification of an individual, is essential.[15] In other words, the context of the information is the cornerstone of the process of indirect identification. It is necessary to emphasise that both the original information (which is not sufficient for identification on its own) and the information which creates the context are personal data in the scope of the Directive from the very beginning of their life cycle. Information does not become personal data. When it can be used for the identification of a person at any time in the future, it has been personal data from the very beginning of its existence. In fact, data controllers do not have to know that they are processing personal data. Indirectly identifiable personal data are personal data from an objective point of view, regardless of the controller's knowledge. This concept is called the 'objective approach to the personal data definition'. However, it is quite problematic, as it causes a great lack of legal certainty.

An objective approach to the personal data definition is closely connected with the preventive function of personal data protection and the systematic

---

13 Recital 26 of Directive 95/46/EC.

14 This is caused primarily by indirectly identifying personal data. A good example is the well-known *Netflix* case, which proved that it is sufficient to know a specific person's rating of six movies and the time these ratings were made with a two-week tolerance to achieve a 99% probability of their identification. (See P. Ohm, 'Broken Promises of Privacy: Responding to the Surprising Failure of Anonymization' (2009) 57(6) *UCLA Law Review* 1720.) In this example case, all of the mentioned information – the name of the movie, its rating and the date of the rating – counts as personal data within the scope of the Directive.

15 E. Tikk, 'IP Addresses subject to personal data regulation' in E. Tikk and A.M. Talihärm (eds.), *Legal & Policy Proceedings 2010* [online], Cooperative Cyber Defence Centre of Excellence, Tallinn 2010, p. 28.

focus on the data itself. Its roots can be found in the line of argument in recent cases before the CJEU. The Court has specified multiple times, e.g. in the *Google Spain* case[16] and in the *Rynes* case,[17] that a high level of protection of the right to privacy, with respect to the processing of personal data, must be ensured. This position has been stipulated very strongly. The division between directly and indirectly identifying personal data is in fact only doctrinal. The Directive does not distinguish between them in any way when it comes to rights and duties. The more information is in the scope of the Directive, the more persons are considered data controllers and have a duty to comply with it. That means that it helps to ensure better protection and prevention of harm for data subjects.

The CJEU has stated that in order to ensure a high level of protection of privacy, all 'derogations and limitations' must be minimal.[18] Understanding certain kinds of information as non-personal data when they are not in the right context at that specific moment[19] means taking them out of the scope of the Directive and, therefore, derogating the protection. The risk of harm arising from the connection of seemingly unrelated data is a real problem.[20] After all, Recital 26[21] of the Directive does not offer any assistance in drawing a line between 'this information is personal data' and 'it is too unreasonable to use this information for identification, and therefore it is not personal data'.

In the light of the court decisions mentioned above, which have overruled otherwise valid interpretations of WP 29, it is necessary to conclude that the objective approach to personal data is currently prevalent. This approach was confirmed in the CJEU by the Opinion of Advocate General Campos Sánchez-Bordona in Case C-582/14, *Patrick Breyer v. Bundesrepublik Deutschland*, regarding the question whether an IP address is personal data. The Advocate General stated that:

> It might even be accepted ... that the dynamic IP address only becomes personal data when the Internet service provider receives it. However, it would then have to be accepted that that classification was applied retroactively, as regards the period of retention of the IP address, and therefore the IP address regarded as non-existent if it has been retained beyond the period which would have been permitted had it been classified from the outset as personal data. If that approach is adopted it will bring about a result contrary to the spirit of the legislation on the protection of personal data. The reason that the retention of such data is justified only temporarily would be circumvented by any delay in determining the relevance of a quality which is inherent

16 Case C-131/12, *Google Spain*, para. 66.
17 Case C-212/13, *Rynes*, para. 27.
18 Ibid., para. 28.
19 That means that the data controller does not know at the time that the data is indirectly identifying personal data.
20 See for example above n. 14, pp. 1701–1777.
21 It is not binding and furthermore can be read both ways.

> that data from the outset: their potential as a means of identifying – by themselves or together with other data – a natural person. For that purely logical reason, it is more reasonable to attribute that nature to the data from the outset.[22]

The upcoming European data protection legislative framework, the General Data Protection Regulation (GDPR), does not address this issue. To the contrary, it leaves it untouched, because the new definition of personal data in the GDPR is almost identical with the one in the Directive. Article 4, paragraph 1 reads as follows:

> 'personal data' means any information relating to an identified or identifiable natural person ('data subject'); an identifiable natural person is one who can be identified, directly or indirectly, in particular by reference to an identifier such as a name, an identification number, location data, an online identifier or to one or more factors specific to the physical, physiological, genetic, mental, economic, cultural or social identity of that natural person.[23]

1.2. HYPERLINK AND PERSONAL DATA

A hypertext link, hyperlink or just link for short, is a method of reference used in information technologies. It allows the user to follow the link directly to another document or its specific part. In this chapter, hyperlinks are considered primarily within the scope of the Internet. A hyperlink consists of an anchor, which is the location in the source document,[24] from which the hyperlink can be followed, and address, which denominates the target document or its specific part. A hyperlink can be hidden, but usually it is somehow typographically highlighted. The target address is however usually concealed in the source code.

This chapter analyses the issue of whether a hyperlink constitutes processing of the personal data that can be found in the target document.[25] This would more often be the case for the so-called 'deep hyperlinks', which target a specific document, than those hyperlinks that only target a home page. In this case, the document itself is not important; only the content of the target document, since the document itself cannot be considered personal data.[26] A good illustrating

22 Opinion of Advocate General Campos Sánchez-Bordona in Case C-582/14, para. 78.

23 Regulation (EU) 2016/679 of the European Parliament and of the Council of 27 April 2016 on the protection of natural persons with regard to the processing of personal data and on the free movement of such data, and repealing Directive 95/46/EC (General Data Protection Regulation).

24 It can be a word, a picture, a place in the picture, or even a whole document, like a web page, which automatically redirects the user to another web page.

25 A target document is a specific document to which the hyperlink leads.

26 Case C-141/12, *YS v. Minister voor Immigratie, Integratie en Asiel.*

example would be a target such as is a web page of Mrs Lindqvist. At this site, she has published information about her 18 colleagues, e.g. their full names, jobs, and hobbies. The act of linking to that webpage would be a processing of the personal data contained in it. If the website also contained sensitive data falling within the scope of Art. 8 of the Directive 95/46/EC, like the medical status of these colleagues or their religious beliefs, then this act of linking would be processing of sensitive personal data.

There are two possibilities of how the link could fall within the scope of the Directive. The first possibility is that the link itself is personal data; the second is that the link is only a processing of personal data contained in the target document.

1.2.1. Hyperlink as personal data

The question in this part is whether a hyperlink should be considered personal data on the basis that it targets personal data in another document. To decide whether a hyperlink falls within the scope of the Directive, we shall use the test proposed in the WP 29 Opinion No. 4/2007, on the concept of personal data. The first step is to decide whether a hyperlink can be considered information. The Directive states that it may be any information, which ensures quite a large scope of the provision. A basic hyperlink consists of two pieces of information. The first one is the anchor and the way it should be displayed to the user; the second one is the address of the target. Therefore, a hyperlink is information. It does not matter that it is the kind of information, which can be processed directly by, or at least with the aid of, a computer. First, the Directive takes automatised processing of data into account.[27] Secondly, the use of a computer for hyperlinks would undoubtedly be a case of means, which are reasonable to be used, in the meaning of Recital 26 of the Directive. Based on these arguments, it should be concluded that hyperlink is information.

The second element is whether the information is related to the data subject. When it comes to the 'content' part of the relation condition, it is highly dependent on the context of the link. If the anchor is a name of a person and the targeted document is their personal page on a social network, then the link is definitely related to the data subject. However, even if it is just a group of letters and numbers, it is very easy to create the context merely by following the link. Once the context is created, it is evident whether the link is related to a natural person or not. In fact, this is quite a similar situation as in the case of indirectly identifying information. In this scenario, it should be considered even

[27] E.g. Art. 2(b) of the Directive.

stricter because it is quite easy to connect the information (a link and its context) together.[28] The second condition is therefore also met.

The third element is that the natural person in question must be identified or identifiable. This condition heavily relies on the character of information present in the targeted document. If the content of the targeted document contains personal data, then the person is identifiable.[29] This reasoning is applicable also for the fourth element: that subject in question is a natural person. We can therefore conclude that both conditions are met under certain circumstances.

As apparent from the previous paragraphs, a hyperlink is a piece of information that can lead to the identification of a data subject. Therefore, it should be considered personal data within the scope of the Directive and the data processing rules apply on it. Naturally, only links that lead to target pages containing personal data can be seen as personal data (processing). However, as stated in the previous part of this chapter, it can be quite difficult to determine with certainty that a target document does not contain personal data, due to the very broad scope of the 'personal data' concept. This situation causes a lack of legal certainty.

1.2.2. Hyperlink as personal data processing

This scenario considers the question of whether creating, posting or using a hyperlink could be deemed processing of the personal data are contained in the target document. The Directive defines processing of personal data in Art. 2(b) as follows:

> processing of personal data ('processing') shall mean any operation or set of operations which is performed upon personal data, whether or not by automatic means, such as collection, recording, organization, storage, adaptation or alteration, retrieval, consultation, use, disclosure by transmission, dissemination or otherwise making available, alignment or combination, blocking, erasure or destruction.

Just as in the case of 'personal data', the definition in this case is also very broad. It states that processing is anything that is done with personal data.[30] It also

28 It is not necessary to discuss the 'purpose' and 'result' elements of this part, because, as described earlier, the CJEU has denied the subjective interpretation approach to personal data. Purpose matters, once the information is within the scope of the Directive, but it is not important when it comes to the decision whether it falls within the scope.

29 Otherwise it would not be personal data in the first place.

30 This notion is also valid for the GDPR, since a definition of data processing present in Art. 4, para. 2 reads as follows: '"processing" means any operation or set of operations which is performed on personal data or on sets of personal data, whether or not by automated means, such as collection, recording, organisation, structuring, storage, adaptation or alteration,

offers a list of examples, which includes 'dissemination or otherwise making available'. The question is whether linking to personal data can be considered dissemination or making the data available.

There seems to be a strong analogy with the intellectual property law, esp. authors' rights, and the communication of a protected work to a public. In the *Svensson* case (C-466/12), the CJEU stated that a hyperlink could be considered a manner of communication of a work to a public. However, in that specific instance, this was not the case, because the protected work was already publicly available and thus there was no 'new public'.[31] The 'new public' doctrine is not relevant in cases of personal data protection. It is clear from the line of argument in the CJEU *Google Spain* case (C-131/12) that every act of processing (dissemination) of data is significant for the processing of personal data, regardless of whether the recipient had a chance to see the data on its own before.[32] From the analogy of personal data and the IP law, we can see that a hyperlink can be used as a means of dissemination of content that is present in the targeted document, although the analogy is not perfect.

One of the questions answered in the *Google Spain* decision was whether the method conducted by an Internet search engine[33] is a processing of the personal data which are present on the indexed third party's web pages and in other documents on the Internet. In paragraph 28 of the decision, the Court said:

> it must be found that, in exploring the internet automatically, constantly and systematically in search of the information which is published there, the operator of a search engine 'collects' such data which it subsequently 'retrieves', 'records' and 'organises' within the framework of its indexing programmes, 'stores' on its servers and, as the case may be, 'discloses' and 'makes available' to its users in the form of lists of search results. As those operations are referred to expressly and unconditionally in Article 2(b) of Directive 95/46, they must be classified as 'processing' within the meaning of that provision, regardless of the fact that the operator of the search engine also carries out the same operations in respect of other types of information and does not distinguish between the latter and the personal data.

This paragraph expressly states that offering a list of search result is 'making personal data available'. A list of search results consists of a number of hyperlinks. The visible elements of the list are the anchors of hyperlinks, to which addresses of target documents are connected. This situation offers an interpretation that the

retrieval, consultation, use, disclosure by transmission, dissemination or otherwise making available, alignment or combination, restriction, erasure or destruction.'

31 Case C-466/12, *Svensson*, para. 30.

32 Indexing of content and linking to it is a different data processing with different purposes than the original publication of the content on the third party web page. See para. 29 of the decision.

33 Indexing of third party web pages and offering results based on the end user's query.

CJEU silently acknowledged hyperlinking as processing of personal data present in targeted documents. Therefore, it is important to examine how independent the steps of search engine operation, described in the judgment, are.

It is not entirely clear from paragraph 29 whether all the mentioned steps must be conducted to classify the activity of a search engine operator as personal data processing. The hypothesis is that each of the steps is sufficient on its own. To confirm this, we should analyse the life cycle of data processed during the search engine operation and compare it to the simple act of linking to the target document. Article 2(b) of the Directive lists actions mentioned by the Court as independent examples. When the search engine indexes a document containing information *A*,[34] it makes a copy of information *A* on its servers. Let us call this copy *A'*. This action is the 'collecting', 'retrieving' and 'recording' of personal data. Information *A'* is disassembled into words, which are indexed and 'stored' in a specific manner, so that the program can reversely track their source. When the end user uses the search function, the search engine conducts a search in the stored *A'* data. Then it offers the user a list of hyperlinks which target third party web pages of other documents based on the result of the search. In the light of the decision, this operation is 'disclosing' or 'making available' of personal data. However, it must be noted that the disclosed information is not *A'* but the original information *A*. The end user will never see the inside of the search engine. The user will not be shown what the information *A'* looks like. Instead, the result is a hyperlink to the web page containing information *A*. In this aspect, disclosing search results is technically the same thing as a simple hyperlink. Therefore, under the premise that 'disclosing' or 'making available' in itself is personal data processing, hyperlinking should be interpreted as a processing of personal data which are present in the targeted document. This opinion was also implicitly confirmed by the CJEU decision.

An interesting result of this interpretation is that the person who provides the hyperlink is, in fact, processing personal data which are absolutely out of their sphere of control.

1.2.3. Comparison of the two approaches and their consequences

The two above-mentioned approaches to the relationship of the hyperlink and personal data yield the same result. Both these approaches are strictly dependent on the content of the targeted document. Publishing a hyperlink which targets a document containing personal data is processing of personal data. Therefore, this action is governed by the rules laid down in the Directive. The person who

[34] For the sake of the analysis, it is assumed that information *A* is personal data in the form of a text.

provides the link is a data controller because they determine the purpose of the processing of personal data (their dissemination).[35] The household exemption (Art. 3, para. 2 of the Directive) is not applicable in this case, because the processing of personal data is aimed into the public space.[36] As data controller, they would have to fulfil the duties which arise from the Directive. In the light of technical reality, these duties may seem quite absurd. The controller would have to have a legal reason for data processing (probably processing for legitimate interest of the controller, as granted by Art. 7(f) of the Directive). Apart from that, the controller would also have to inform the data subjects about the processing (a duty with which even search engines are unable to comply).

The results of some of these duties might differ depending on whether we understand a hyperlink as personal data or only as a processing of personal data. One such case would be for example the obligation to make the data accessible for the data subject. In the first case, this data would be the link. In the second case, it would be a copy of the target page, or maybe, ironically, only the link once again, because that is what this technology does – provides access to information.

In the end, there is little practical difference between the two possible interpretations. Nevertheless, in my view, the interpretation in which a hyperlink is only a processing of personal data is more advisable. It is simpler and less absurd then the 'hyperlink is personal data' variant. There are no new personal data, just a new way of processing the old. The only problem with this interpretation is that the controller processes data, which are entirely out of their control. Therefore, they cannot fulfil some controller duties; for example deleting the data when the processing is illegitimate. However, they can stop the processing by simply removing the hyperlink from the source document.

Finally, what is the status of the end user, meaning someone who uses the link? Their situation depends heavily on in the context in which the hyperlink is used. Internet browsing on a personal device should be covered by the household and personal activity exemption[37] most of the time. However, this may not apply when the browsing is conducted in the course of activities aimed at the public, in their place of employment, and in other situations which are considered to be

---

35 In this chapter, it is assumed that the question of purpose determination is evaluated objectively, which means based on the result ('there is a processing'). Another possibility would be that the controller would have to determine the purpose knowingly, which would be a subjective approach. It would mean that if the person in question had no intention to process personal data, they would not be considered a data controller. Google tried to use this argumentation in the *Google Spain* case, but it was denied by the court. However, this approach could be beneficial for the whole personal data protection system. Its detailed analysis is beyond the scope of this chapter.

36 See the CJEU decisions in Case C-101/01, *Lindqvist* and Case C-212/13, *Rynes*.

37 Art. 3, para. 2 of the Directive.

out of the scope of the exemption. The practical impacts of this situation only show the absurdity of the current state of the rules.

1.2.4. *Practical example*

A specific example of the problems mentioned above can be the use of hyperlinks in the process of publishing open data.[38] The final goal is the so-called 'linked data'. This concept consists of providing information in the way that datasets link to each other. This is very beneficial both for the providers of public sector information, who do not have to make their copies of the related dataset, as well as for the user, who has access to a vast amount of information from one place.

If the creation and publication of a hyperlink are a processing of personal data, then the provider of open data, who coded in their dataset links that target another dataset containing personal data, needs to have a legal justification for this data processing. They have to fulfil all the duties which arise from the Directive, unless they are entirely sure that there are no personal data present in the target document. In some cases, this might simply be technically impossible, since the provider does not have control over the targeted dataset. It must be noted that this is not a failure. It is a purpose of such open data solutions not to have control over datasets created by other public bodies and only to link them together. However, in this case, it could lead to an inability to fulfil the data protection legal duties, especially in instances, when the targeted datasets change regularly.[39]

It should be emphasised that open data can have serious impacts on the privacy of data subjects. Protecting links as personal data processing might be quite a reasonable approach in this case. It is necessary to be careful and to publish only as few directly identifying information as possible as open data.

Open data have value only when there is a software application which can use them properly. These applications usually work within the server–client architecture, meaning that the end user uses a web-based application, or an application in their electronic device, which connects the application with the developer's server and downloads the data from it. Nowadays, most developers download datasets from the servers of open data providers, store them on their servers and let the users connect to them. If the datasets contain personal data, this is definitely a processing of personal data. However, it is also possible to write the client application in such a way that it connects directly to the servers of

[38] Open data means providing the public sector information in a way which is easily processed and reusable.

[39] In specific cases, the provider might not even know that the targeted data are personal data. This is due to the low legal certainty when it comes to indirectly identifying personal data.

open data providers and downloads data from there. That is very similar to how hyperlinks work. In this case, the application developer would still be considered a personal data controller because creating links in the end user application is in fact dissemination of personal data or, as is stated in the *Google Spain* case, 'making personal data available.'

1.3. DISCUSSION AND CONCLUSION

The analysis showed that hyperlinking to a document containing personal data should be considered a processing of personal data and is therefore covered by the Directive. This interpretation can be reasonable in certain situations, as was mentioned in the practical example of linked data. At the same time, it is very demanding for data controllers,[40] since they must fulfil all the duties laid down by the Directive. In accordance with that, this situation is very demanding for law enforcement agencies as well. Data protection authorities (DPAs) must ensure that controllers comply with the law. Unfortunately, too often these duties are impossible to be fulfilled. For example, the controller cannot be reasonably obliged to respect the information duty (Art. 11 of the Directive) or to have a legal reason to process sensitive data (Art. 8)[41] when it comes to hyperlinking.[42] If we want the system to function properly, these situations should also be enforced. However, DPAs turn a blind eye to such cases for many practical reasons.[43] Therefore, it is an empty norm; the law is not efficient. From a Kelsenian view, it is non-existent. This might not be a problem were DPAs to proceed systematically on the basis of expressed *de minimis* conditions. However, this is not the case and therefore their decision-making seems random.

There are two possible solutions to the problem. The first one consists of narrowing the input of the data protection system. That would mean specifying

40 There, data controllers might not even realise that they are, in fact, data controllers.

41 This would be the case of linking to a webpage containing sensitive personal data, like information about the religious beliefs of the data subjects.

42 This problem can be seen even in the example of the *Google Spain* case. No matter how necessary the ruling was to stop indexing in reasonable situations, it has *de jure* made all web search engines' actions illegal. The Court offered Art. 7(f) of the Directive to legitimise this processing – legitimate interests pursued by the controller or by a third party or parties to whom the data are disclosed, except for cases where such interests are overridden by the interests or fundamental rights and freedoms of the data subject (paras. 73 and 74 of the decision). This, however, applies only to 'normal personal data' and not to sensitive personal data. Art. 8 of the Directive does not offer such legitimisation ground. Thus, since it is certain that search engines index pages containing sensitive personal data, their operation is breaching the law.

43 To mention just two of them: it would shut down the Internet (because these duties cannot be fulfilled in technological reality) and the DPAs do not have the manpower to enforce the rules.

more precisely what kind of data should be protected so that only the data that could cause real harm fell within the framework of the regulation. A benefit of this solution would be lowering the demands on data controllers,[44] simplifying the whole system, and enabling the DPAs to focus on cases that threaten privacy. This solution would, however, present some drawbacks. The major one is the fact that the legislator would have to set either a general rule, which would be hard to interpret, or to create an enumerative list of what are considered 'safe kinds' of otherwise personal data. A general rule would probably lead to a decrease of legal certainty, at least for the time before establishing a stable decision practice in courts. An enumerative list would nullify the principle of technology neutrality, which would undermine the flexibility of the law and its capacity to react to technological development. This solution would mean a real complication for the legal framework, especially in the field of data protection, which is on the frontier of the clash of law and new technologies. As can be seen in the example of Directive 95/46/EC, a technology-neutral approach has allowed the Directive to remain quite applicable, even after such a long time and considering such great technology development since it was amended. Maintaining a technology-neutral legislative framework for the future is important. Another drawback of an enumerative list is that it would increase the possibility of false negatives: a situation when the system lets cases go unnoticed, although they could cause a real harm to the privacy. Measuring possible harm for the future is difficult and this solution would constitute an unreasonable exception in the system, in which all exceptions should be as narrow as possible, as the CJEU has stated multiple times.

The second possible solution lies in narrowing the output of the system. Once the application of the personal data legal framework activates, the system should evaluate whether it is reasonable to apply all the legal duties of a controller. If the possible harm was low, then only certain duties would be necessary. However, the current personal data protection is binary, which constitutes, in fact, the biggest problem: it is all or nothing.[45] The best way to apply this second possible solution would be to evaluate specific duties of the controller and place them in several categories. At this point, it is possible to follow up on a concept proposed by Dan Svantesson: the so-called 'layered approach'.[46] The categories, or layers, of controllers' duties, would be activated based on the risk level of the ongoing data

44 Or more precisely, on subjects operating with data, who would cease to be be data controllers.

45 This statement is valid not only for extraterritorial application of the law, as claimed by Svantesson in D. Svantesson, 'The (uncertain) future of online data privacy' (2015) 9(1) *Masaryk University Journal of Law and Technology* 138–139. It is a universal feature of the system.

46 Similarly, as mentioned above in n. 45, this concept can be used not only in extraterritorial application, as Svantesson suggests, but also in national application. For more, see ibid.; D. Svantesson, 'A "layered approach" to the extraterritoriality of data privacy laws' (2013) 3(4) *International Data Privacy Law*.

processing. Where there was a minimal or no risk of harm, only the most basic duties would have to be fulfilled.[47] For example, that would be the obligation to cooperate with the data subject and to provide them with information about the processing or to cease the data processing if it constitutes an unreasonable violation of the right to privacy or personal data protection. Where the risk was somewhat higher, more obligations would have to be followed by the data controller. These might include obtaining a legal reason for the processing and keeping the data secure. Generally speaking, the higher the risk, the heavier the duties.[48] There is a clear economic factor included as well: data controllers would not have to spend an unreasonable amount of money and manpower to fulfil all the legal duties in low-risk data processing cases.

This solution comes with some difficulties. It would take the time to establish a widely accepted scale of risks which would help the data controllers to assess easily how risky their ongoing processing is. The proposed solution, without such a tool, would only cause more chaos and legal uncertainty than good. Evaluating the risk would consist not only of the process of the data processing itself. Other factors, like the nature of the data controller,[49] could be included in the consideration as well. However, the creation of a practical tool of this kind could be achieved by a careful and systematic law interpretation conducted by the DPAs and courts.

As can be seen from this chapter, the current European Directive 95/46/EC does not offer many possibilities to individualise the different kinds of data processing based on the risk of harm. There are several provisions in the GDPR that reflect risk-based approach or that can be interpreted and used this way. The following provisions can serve as an example:

- Article 11, which reads as follows: 'If the purposes for which a controller processes personal data do not or do no longer require the identification of a data subject by the controller, the controller shall not be obliged to maintain, acquire or process additional information in order to identify the data subject for the sole purpose of complying with this Regulation.' This provision frees the controller from the information duty when it is unreasonable to fulfil it. It effectively solves one of the problems of the current system, as described above.
- Article 14, para. 5(b) which, once again, allows the controller not to fulfil their information duty, if it is impossible or if it requires a disproportionate effort to do so.

---

47 Or possibly almost none of them.

48 Similarly see D.J. Solove, 'Privacy Self-Management and the Consent Dilemma', p. 1903, <http://papers.ssrn.com/abstract=2171018> accessed 30.06.2016.

49 For example, universities and research institutions could have a lighter mode for processing for the purpose of research, because one can assume them to have a certain moral standard.

- Article 19 constitutes an obligation to communicate any rectification or erasure of personal data to the third parties to whom the data were disclosed, unless this proves impossible or requires a disproportionate effort.
- A risk-based approach is clearly present in data security issues. Article 32 states: 'Taking into account the state of the art, the costs of implementation and the nature, scope, context and purposes of processing as well as the risk of varying likelihood and severity for the rights and freedoms of natural persons, the controller and the processor shall implement appropriate technical and organisational measures to ensure a level of security appropriate to the risk.'
- Duties to have data protection impact assessments, prior consultations, and data protection officers (Arts. 35, 36, 37 et seq.) are bound only in cases of specific types of data processing, which are considered to be riskier.

It can be seen from the above-mentioned examples that the GDPR has involved elements of the risk-based approach to individualise different kinds of data processing. There are two problems, at least at this point: the first one is that the most of such possibilities apply only in case of high-risk data processing. Only liberation from information duty can be used as an aid for low-risk data processing.[50] The second problem is that all these necessary derogations, which can be used to make the whole system more functional, are now only on the paper. The usefulness of the GDPR depends on how its provisions will be interpreted by national amendments, DPAs, and courts. It is necessary to proceed with a great caution in this case.

Finally, to answer the question posed in the title of this chapter: no, the definition of personal data is not flawed. It is technology-neutral, and it allows us to unfold the great preventive possibilities of the data protection legal framework. However, the rest of the system needs to be adjusted in a way that allows it to function properly. In a way in which the rules can and will be enforced logically, meaningfully and systematically.

50 The absence of further possible derogations also means, for example, that the operation of Internet search engines is still *stricto sensu* illegal under the GDPR. See above n. 39.

18. BIG DATA AND 'PERSONAL INFORMATION' IN AUSTRALIA, THE EUROPEAN UNION AND THE UNITED STATES*

Alana MAURUSHAT** and David VAILE***

1. INTRODUCTION

Information that can be associated with an identifiable individual is given special treatment in law in many countries. This 'personal information', as it is called in Australia, attracts the coverage of privacy and data protection law. The scope of the information that fits within the relevant definition varies between jurisdictions, and is a core concern of this chapter.[1]

Information, which cannot be associated with an identifiable individual in the way defined in a particular jurisdiction, escapes such classification as

---

* The authors are grateful for contributions from Stephen Wilson on an earlier draft, and the assistance of interns at the Cyberspace Law and Policy Community at the Faculty of Law, University of New South Wales. We are also grateful for the constructive suggestions provided by the peer reviewers and editors. This chapter does not represent the views of the 'Data to Decisions Cooperative Research Centres' (D2D CRC) Programme.

** Faculty of Law, University of New South Wales. E-mail: a.maurushat@unsw.edu.au.

*** Faculty of Law, University of New South Wales; Law School, Deakin University. E-mail: d.vaile@unsw.edu.au.

1 A survey of the terms used in 30 countries reportedly found a 'lack of consensus'; CHEUNG, A., 'Re-personalizing personal data in the cloud', in CHEUNG, A. and WEBER, R. (eds.), *Privacy and Legal Issues in Cloud Computing*, Edward Elgar Publishing, Cheltenham 2015, p. 69. Australian researchers have identified variations even among the Australian jurisdictions: BURDON, M. and TELFORD, P., 'The Conceptual Basis of Personal Information in Australian Privacy Law' (2010) 17(1) *eLaw Journal: Murdoch University Electronic Journal of Law* 15, <https://elaw.murdoch.edu.au/index.php/elawmurdoch/article/viewFile/41/15> and recommend reconsiderations of the UK's Booth Review suggestions; see BOOTH, S. ET AL., 'What are 'Personal Data'? A Study Conducted for UK Information Commissioner', Information Commissioner's Office, 2004, <http://www.ico.gov.uk/upload/documents/library/corporate/ research_and_reports/final_report_21_06_04.pdf>.

'personal'.[2] It can then be dealt with under often less restrictive controls outside of privacy and data protection law such as contractual restrictions on data scraping imposed by data owners, or issues involving copyright clearance. This has significant implications for both data subjects (whose information is less protected) and data custodians (who face fewer regulatory constraints).[3] Privacy and data protection laws typically only apply when data or information is linked to a person, or is capable of the identification of a person. If Big Data items or records do not fall within the relevant legal definition of categories such as 'personal information', 'personal data' or their equivalent, they are not subject to privacy law in a given jurisdiction, so there are fewer rules for their use and transfer. Where information is 'personal' there are a variety of methods that are used, in particular in data analytics, to make the information non-identified. The terms for these methods include 'anonymous', 'pseudonymous', 'de-identified', 'depersonalised', 'data minimisation' and 'not personal data'.

Although the technology practices known as 'Big Data' raise many important privacy issues, this paper focuses on their effect on questions about whether a particular record or data set is considered 'personal' and therefore 'about' an identifiable individual. We survey definitions of personal data or information (or their equivalent) in jurisdictions including Australia, the United States and the European Union in the context of identifiability and Big Data.

The divergence of the definitions used in the jurisdictions helps explain some of the differences in how they respond to Big Data developments – and to the challenges that Big Data tools may pose for legal systems.

This chapter commences with a look at what constitutes Big Data, and methods of de-identification within Big Data analysis. The next section addresses the differing definitions of 'personal information' and its equivalents in Australia, the US and Europe. We then offer a short comparative section before addressing the question: to what degree does the ability to de-identify information push Big Data practices out of or into the scope of 'personal information' and hence into privacy legislation? Legal developments in Australia, the US and particularly the EU are considered.

---

2 For instance, information that cannot be associated with or related to an identifiable individual is 'anonymous' and escapes regulation by the European Data Protection Directive, discussed below.

3 Some commentators have observed that the distinction is too much a 'bright line', all or nothing; it may preferable to consider more information as potentially personal but only apply a subset of requirements to those where risks do not warrant the full set of legal protections. See Kuan Hon, W., Millard, C. and Walden, I. 'The problem of "personal data" in cloud computing: what information is regulated? – The cloud of unknowing' (2011) 1(4) *International Data Privacy Law* 211, 225.

2. BIG DATA, DE-IDENTIFICATION AND RE-IDENTIFICATION

'Big Data' is a popular term coined to describe an emerging phenomenon of data manipulation and analysis on a much larger scale, and with more sophisticated methods, than were previously common with traditional structured data systems like relational databases. It encompasses techniques such as 'data mining' and 'predictive analytics', but it is more than this. As one commentator put it, 'the real revolution is not in the machines that calculate data, but in data itself and how we use it.'[4]

While there is no agreed or rigorous definition of 'Big Data', it commonly refers to new ways of addressing the rapidly increasing volume and complexity of information subject to collection and manipulation by computers.[5] 'Big Data' is often used alongside 'cloud computing' to refer both to the vast amounts of data, and to the software methods developed to extract information and exploit the new 'data lakes' for diverse uses (we refer below to Big Data software and tools as 'BD tools' to distinguish them from the data sets).

One difference from traditional data practices is that Big Data is often not collected for a particular use or specific purpose; for this reason, it can become more useful as new potential applications emerge from continued evolution of BD tools and data sets.[6] However, use of data for a purpose other than that for which it was collected often creates tension as personal data should not be collected or used any more than is necessary for the purpose of which it was collected.

Big Data can also involve the collection of vast amounts of unconnected and disparate data, and the application of 'machine learning' pattern-matching and related techniques to discern correlations in it and propose associations and responses. Attempting to predict and pre-empt patterns of human or system behaviour is both the most ambitious promise of Big Data (in the form of 'predictive analytics'[7] or 'prescriptive analytics'),[8] and also its most controversial potential over-reach.

---

4 Mayer-Schönberger, V. and Cukier, K., *Big Data: A Revolution that will Transform How We Live, Work, and Think*, John Murray Publishers, London 2013, p. 7.

5 Its origin is often attributed to industry analyst Laney, D.'s influential paper, '3D Data Management: Controlling Data Volume, Velocity, and Variety', The Meta Group (online), 6 February 2001, <http://blogs.gartner.com/doug-laney/files/2012/01/ad949-3D-Data-Management-Controlling-Data-Volume-Velocity-and-Variety.pdf>.

6 This raises the significance of apparently non-personal data sets. See Scassa, T., 'Geographical Information as "Personal Information"' (08.08.2010), <http://ssrn.com/abstract=1689639>.

7 Predictive analytics harms already has a well-developed literature: see Crawford, K. and Schultz, J., 'Big Data and Due Process: Toward a Framework to Redress Predictive Privacy Harms' (2013) 55(93) *Boston College Law Review* 93–128, <http://ssrn.com/abstract=2325784>. On the practical challenges, see Le, L. et al., 'On predictability of rare events leveraging social media: a machine learning perspective', eprint arXiv:1502.05886, February 2015.

8 Associating alternative decision choices with the prediction of outcomes; van Rijmenam, M., 'The Future of Big Data: Prescriptive Analytics Changes the Game', *Data Informed*, June 2014,

While the information used in Big Data applications need not be related to identifiable individuals, there is much interest on those applications that do use data sets potentially connected with identifiable individuals, whether from the point of collection or after analysis and manipulation.

Data does not need to be fully categorised or identified ahead of time for it to be taken up and harnessed by BD tools, nor do the required rules or associations need to be specified before take-up. This flexibility is one of the key differences from traditional, more structured data systems. They can also selectively strip or discard certain attributes during uptake, including those that facilitate linking particular data items to particular individuals. For this reason, Big Data is often touted as supporting the useful features of enabling 'de-identification', and also of enabling the extraction of valuable and useful insights from de-identified data sets.[9]

'De-identification' is the removal, stripping or obfuscation of directly identifying elements from a data record or set such that the result can no longer be associated or linked with a particular individual.[10]

<http://data-informed.com/future-big-data-prescriptive-analytics-changes-game/>; Bertsimas, D. and Kallussee, N. 'From Predictive to Prescriptive Analytics', *eprint arXiv*:1402.5481, February 2014, <http://arxiv.org/abs/1402.5481>. This will be of relevance to the insurance industry, *inter alia*. Swedloff, R. 'Risk Classification's Big Data (R)evolution' (2014) 21*Connecticut Insurance Law Journal* <http://ssrn.com/abstract=2566594>.

9 This is of great interest in fields such as biomedical research, where research ethics often requires forms of de-identification. Medical researchers are concerned to minimise the privacy impact of re-identification technologies, although this is tempered by a preference to avoid adverse impact on research procedures, and disagreements on methods. See O'Keefe, C., et al., 'Individual privacy versus public good: protecting confidentiality in health research' (2015) 34 *Statist. Med.* 3081–3103; Wu, F., 'Defining Privacy and Utility in Data Sets' (2013) 84 *University of Colorado Law Review* 1117, <http://ssrn.com/abstract=2031808>; Isasi, R. et al., 'Identifiability and Privacy in Pluripotent Stem Cell Research' (2014) 14(3) *Cell Stem Cell* 427–430. There are varying levels of sensitivity to the potential impact of re-identification on subjects, and opinions differ as to the extent of the risk, but there seems to be a consensus that data tools do increasingly lower the barrier to re-identification in this field. El Emam, K. et al., 'De-identification Methods for Open Health Data: The Case of the Heritage Health Prize Claims Dataset' (2012) 14(1) *Journal of Medical Internet Research*, e33, <http://www.jmir.org/2012/1/e33>. See also Hrynaszkiewicz, I. et al., 'Preparing raw clinical data for publication: guidance for journal editors, authors, and peer reviewers' (2010) *British Medical Journal*, <http://www.bmj.com/content/340/bmj.c181>.

10 Office of the Australian Information Commissioner (OAIC), *Information policy agency resource 1: De-identification of data and information* (2014), <http://www.oaic.gov.au/information-policy/information-policy-resources/information-policy-agency-resources/information-policy-agency-resource-1-de-identification-of-data-and-information>. See, for a practical example, Wasserman, L. and Zhou, S., 'A statistical framework for differential privacy' (2010) 105(489) *Jour. of American Stat. Assoc.* 375–389, <http://arxiv.org/abs/0811.2501>.

While a detailed discussion of general de-identification methods is beyond the scope of this paper one could note that such methods, as presented by Hon et al., include:

- deleting or omitting 'identifying details', for example names;
- substituting code numbers for names or other direct identifiers (this is pseudonymisation, effectively);
- aggregating information, for example by age group, year, town;
- 'barnardisation' or other techniques introducing statistical noise, for example differential privacy techniques with statistical databases;
- provide unique hash values to data; or
- some combination of these methods.[11]

Technical measures for de-identification or anonymisation of Big Data profiling are also evolving, and may have implications if put into practice.[12] Data collected in one jurisdiction may be classified as personal information and therefore require de-identification, while the same data in another jurisdiction may not require de-identification. Databases are seldom confined and established based on the jurisdiction of a person. This may mean that companies will choose to apply the highest privacy standard to data and de-identify all data, or conversely, they may choose the lowest threshold and either not de-identify or use a less robust de-identification technique.

3. DEFINITIONS OF INFORMATION CAPABLE OF IDENTIFYING A PERSON

Different jurisdictions use different terminology to describe information that falls within the coverage of their privacy and data protection rules, and different definitions to articulate the tests for inclusion.

---

11 For more information, see Kuan Hon, W., Millard, C. and Walden, I., 'The problem of "personal data" in cloud computing: what information is regulated? – The cloud of unknowing' 2011 1(4) *International Data Privacy Law* 211, 214–216.

12 See for example, Al Musallam, M. and Al Muhatdi, J., 'De-correlating User Profiles: Exploring Anonymity Tools', MEDES 14, Proceedings of the 6th International Conference on Management of Emergent Digital EcoSystems, ACM, 15 September 2014, 220–222. They note that users are not only identifiable through explicitly disclosed data but also through aggregate analysis of meta-data – i.e. data about their communication patterns with services – and investigate the role of meta-data in user profiling, to find out the sources of meta-data and what they can reveal about a user. They argue that meta-data are indeed personal information, and discuss privacy-via-anonymity as a means of anonymising user profiles.

Terms of interest for us include 'personal information' (PI) in Australia and Asia-Pacific Economic Cooperation (APEC), 'personally identifiable information' (PII) in the US, and 'personal data' (PD) in the EU and Organisation for Economic Co-operation and Development (OECD).

The definitions determine whether certain data items are caught under the particular privacy and data protection regime. The issue is one of 'reasonableness' of steps which could be taken for a person associated with the data to become identifiable, and the impact of improvements in Big Data tools on that question into the future. Most of our focus is on the Australian position but we refer to US and EU considerations, and their particular terms.

3.1. 'PERSONAL INFORMATION' (PI) IN AUSTRALIA

Prior to amendments in 2012 (which came into force in March 2014), the definition of 'personal information' in section 6 of the Privacy Act 1988 (Cth) was as follows:

> '*personal information*' means information or an opinion (including information or an opinion forming part of a database), whether true or not, and whether recorded in a material form or not, about an individual whose identity is apparent, *or can reasonably be ascertained, from the information or opinion* [emphasis added].

The Australian Law Reform Commission's Report on Privacy recommended that the definition of 'personal information' be changed. Recommendation 6–1 proposed that 'the Privacy Act should define 'personal information' as 'information or an opinion, whether true or not, and whether recorded in a material form or not, about an identified or reasonably identifiable individual'.[13]

After amendments in the Privacy Amendment (Enhancing Privacy Protection) Act 2012 (Cth), the definition of 'personal information' was subtly changed by the omission of the words requiring that identity be ascertainable 'from the information or opinion'. The definition inserted now reads:

> *personal information* means information or an opinion about an identified individual, or an individual who is reasonably identifiable:
> (a) whether the information or opinion is true or not; and
> (b) whether the information or opinion is recorded in a material form or not.

[13] ALRC Report 108, *For Your Information: Australian Privacy Law and Practice*, 2008, <http://www.alrc.gov.au/publications/6.%20The%20Privacy%20Act%3A%20Some%20Important%20Definitions/what-%E2%80%98personal-information%E2%80%99>.

The Explanatory Memorandum (EM) states that the new definition was adopted to be more consistent with the APEC Privacy Framework ('9. Personal information means any information about an identified or identifiable individual')[14] and other international instruments. The EM does not refer explicitly to the relevant instruments, but it appears likely to mean the revised OECD Privacy Guidelines,[15] Council of Europe Convention 108 and EU Directive, such that international jurisprudence will be more relevant to the Privacy Act 1998 (Cth).[16]

The effect of the omission in the new Act is to make it marginally clearer that the question of identifiability can take into account information other than the original information itself. If there had been any doubt that the steps one might be permitted to take to identify a person from a piece of information could involve referring to other information, this appears to have been removed.[17]

The rather terse revised definition in the 2012 Act is expanded upon by Guidelines from the regulator and the Office of the Australian Information Commissioner (which subsumed the Privacy Commissioner's office in 2010).

3.1.1. OAIC Australian Privacy Principles Guidelines

The OAIC's Australian Privacy Principles Guidelines is the main document on this topic. It covers the revised and renamed Privacy Principles in the amended version of the Privacy Act in force from 2014. These Guidelines offer guidance on whether an individual is 'reasonably identifiable' from particular information about that individual at section B.91, saying this will depend on:

- the nature and extent of the information;
- the circumstances of its receipt;
- who will have access to the information;
- other information either held by or available to the APP entity[18] that holds the information;

---

14 APEC Secretariat, *APEC Privacy Framework*, APEC#205-SO-01.2 (approved at 16th APEC Ministerial Meeting, Santiago, Chile, 17–18 November 2004), 2005, p. 5, [9] and note to [9], <http://publications.apec.org/publication-detail.php?pub_id=390>.

15 'OECD Privacy Guidelines', Pt. I of *OECD Privacy Framework*, OECD, revised 2013, p. 9, <http://oecd.org/sti/ieconomy/oecd_privacy_framework.pdf>. This updated the original 1980 OECD model. See below for details of the other instruments.

16 Explanatory Memorandum, Privacy Amendment (Enhancing Privacy Protection) Bill 2012, Item 36. 60, <http://parlinfo.aph.gov.au/parlInfo/download/legislation/ems/r4813_ems_00948d06-092b-447e-9191-5706fdfa0728/upload_pdf/368711.pdf>.

17 The Explanatory Memorandum suggests, in the Introduction to Sch. 1, that in the new Act 'The proposed definition does not significantly change the scope of what is considered to be personal information.'

18 APP is the Australian Privacy Principles. An APP entity is an organisation subject to the Australian Privacy Principles found in the Privacy Act 1988 (Cth).

- whether it's possible to identify the individual using resources available to the person or entity that holds or has access to the information;
- if the information is publically released, whether a reasonable member of the public who accesses that information would be able to identify the individual.[19]

Section B.92 addresses the question, 'in whose eyes should the information be reasonably identifiable?' The answer: the person or entity that holds or has access to the information.[20]

The guidelines offer the example of a licence plate number. A layperson is unlikely to have the resources to identify the owner of the licence plate and thus would not be holding personal information. However, a car registration agency would most likely be able to use their database to identify the owner, which would make the licence plate personal information if held by them, or by an individual with access to the database.

3.1.2. Factors affecting 'identifiability' and reasonableness

We consider next some of the factors which potentially affect the interpretation of the 'reasonableness' requirement in the new Australian definition, with comments about related factors from other jurisdictions. The new definition as referenced in the explanatory memorandum refers to an individual who is 'reasonably identifiable':

> Whether an individual can be identified or is reasonably identifiable depends on context and circumstances. While it may be technically possible for an agency or organisation to identify individuals from information it holds, for example, by linking the information with other information held by it, or another entity, it may be that it is not practically possible. For example, logistics or legislation may prevent such linkage. In these circumstances, individuals are not 'reasonably identifiable'. Whether an individual is reasonably identifiable from certain information requires a consideration of the cost, difficulty, practicality and likelihood that the information will be linked in such a way as to identify him or her.[21]

---

19 Office of the Australian Information Commissioner, *APP Guidelines*, 'Reasonably Identifiable', Chapter B. Key Concepts, [B.91–94], Version 1.2, March 2015, <https://www.oaic.gov.au/resources/agencies-and-organisations/app-guidelines/chapter-b-app-guidelines-v1.2.pdf>.

20 This does not address whether the information would be personal information if it fell into the hands of another entity with better resources. Information may not be PI when collected by one entity with few resources, but could become PI in future if it could be accessed or possessed by another entity which had more effective sources of ancillary identifying information or tools.

21 Explanatory Memorandum, Privacy Amendment (Enhancing Privacy Protection) Bill 2012, re: Sch. 1, Item 36.

A number of other factors need to be considered when addressing 'identifiability'. The APP Guidelines state that other attributes could contribute to identifiability. They also offer some generic guidance on what 'reasonably' means:

> B.105 'Reasonable' and 'reasonably' are not defined in the *Privacy Act*. The terms bear their ordinary meaning, as being based upon or according to reason and capable of sound explanation. What is reasonable is a question of fact in each individual case. It is an objective test that has regard to how a reasonable person, who is properly informed, would be expected to act in the circumstances. What is reasonable can be influenced by current standards and practices.[22]

In a related set of Guidelines on mobile privacy, without more directly expressly dealing with 'reasonableness', OAIC notes that what constitutes personal information will vary

> depending on what can reasonably be ascertained in a particular circumstance, but may include:
> - photographs
> - Internet Protocol (IP) addresses, Unique Device Identifiers (UDIDs) and other unique identifiers in specific circumstances
> - contact lists, which reveal details about the contacts themselves and also a user's social connections
> - voice print and facial recognition biometrics, because they collect characteristics that make an individual's voice or face unique
> - location information, because it can reveal user activity patterns and habits.[23]

The Victorian Privacy Commissioner also offers guidance on the reasonableness test.

In one Victorian case, it was argued that the identity of a partner of a research participant could be reasonably ascertained by the researcher from questions and answers provided by her partner, in conjunction with cross-matching her telephone number with electronic white pages in order to ascertain her name and address. Victoria Civil and Administrative Tribunal (VCAT) found that this process of cross-matching research databases with external databases would 'involve taking more than moderate steps', and was not satisfied that the complaint

---

22 Office of the Australian Information Commissioner, *APP Guidelines*, 'Reasonable, Reasonably', Chapter B. Key Concepts, [B.105] 22. The cases of *Jones v. Bartlett* [2000] HCA 56 [57]–[58] (Gleeson CJ) and *Bankstown Foundry Pty Ltd v. Braistina* [1986] HCA 20 [12] are cited.

23 Office of the Australian Information Commissioner, 'Mobile Privacy. A better practice guide for mobile app developers', 2014, 4, <https://www.oaic.gov.au/agencies-and-organisations/guides/guide-for-mobile-app-developers>.

was about 'personal information' within the meaning of the Information Privacy Act 2000 (Vic.).[24]

However, where steps may be unreasonable at the time of making a hypothetical analysis, there is potential for reduction of this burden into the future. As online data systems become more ubiquitous, functional and powerful, especially Big Data systems or those based in an easily upgraded Cloud,[25] the onerousness or expense of the steps required to identify someone starting from a given information item may reduce over time.

A range of meta-data items like IP addresses may fit within the new Australian PI definition with no fundamental difficulty. One commentary suggests examples when IP addresses may constitute personal information:

- where a person has a permanent IP address;
- when a record previously made by the website operator exists and is accessible; or
- when (dynamic) IP address generated by dial-up ISPs can be linked to the log books of the ISP (only permissible in limited circumstances, and a warrant may be necessary);
- if the information could be linked to an individual at some future time, it would still be information about a person who would be reasonably identifiable in the future.[26]

Characteristics of a website and how it might be accessed must also be taken into account in determining whether or not an IP address can be deemed personal information (e.g. when access to the site is via a proxy server or anonymising software, it may be impossible to identify an individual by any means, thus the IP address would not be classified as personal information).

Whether certain meta-data items, like IP and other device addresses, are about an individual who is reasonably identifiable will depend on the context. Factors are discussed in detail below.

3.1.2.1. Cost, and cost reduction over time

The APP Guidelines say individuals are not reasonably identifiable where identification is technically possible but the steps required to identify the

---

24 Office of the Victorian Privacy Commissioner, 'Whether identity is apparent or can be reasonably ascertained', *Guidelines to Victoria's Information Privacy Principles*, ed. 3, November 2011, p. 11, <https://www.cpdp.vic.gov.au/images/content/pdf/privacy_guidelines/OVPC%20Guidelines%20to%20the%20IPPs%20Edition%203%202011.pdf>.

25 Cloud services are very often offshore and perhaps out of easy reach of local regulators. See Vaile, D., 'The Cloud and Data Sovereignty after Snowden' (2014) 2(1) *Australian Journal of Communications and the Digital Economy*, <http://telsoc.org/ajtde/2014-03-v2-n1/a31>.

26 CCH, 'Are IP Addresses "personal information"?' *Australian Privacy Commentary* [¶15–120], 17 November 2014.

individual are 'excessively time-consuming or costly in all the circumstances', to the point where there is 'almost no likelihood of it occurring'.[27] This suggests 'reasonably identifiable' depends on the capability of the person or entity holding the information.

3.1.2.2. Reliance on information other than the item itself

The Australian definition of PI in force from 2014 drops the earlier apparent requirement that the identity be ascertainable '*from the information [itself]*', although OIAC Guidelines suggest that a capacity to refer to other information was arguably covered by the definition before 2014. It is now clearly permissible to rely on external information, not just the information in question, for the identifiability assessment.

A recent determination by the Australian Information Commissioner confirms that the new definition of personal information is broad enough to catch information that needs to be processed alongside external information sources (though it hints that this may have already been the case):

> The main textual difference between the current and the new definitions is that the new definition will not explicitly require that an individual be identifiable 'from the information or opinion'. Information in a government document can qualify as 'personal information' even though some additional action – such as an Internet search or data-matching – must be undertaken to identify an individual. However, it is probable that the current definition applies in those circumstances, and that the change will merely resolve any doubt.[28]

For example, in some circumstances an IP address will be PI in Australia; the APP Guidelines recommend erring on the side of finding PI if there is doubt.[29]

3.1.3. 'Not reasonably identifiable' – guidance?

The ALRC recommended in 2008 that the Privacy Commissioner provide a Guidance document on the meaning of 'not reasonably identifiable', to assist in delimiting the scope of 'personal information'. This does not appear to have borne fruit – there is no such Guidance document on this negative term.

---

27 Office of the Australian Information Commissioner, *APP Guidelines*, 'Meaning of "reasonably identifiable"', Chapter B. Key Concepts, [B.93], Version 1.2, March 2015.

28 *'BA' and Merit Protection Commissioner* [2014] AICmr 9 (30 January 2014), [44] <http://www.austlii.edu.au/au/cases/cth/AICmr/2014/9.html>.

29 Office of the Australian Information Commissioner, *APP Guidelines*, 'Reasonably Identifiable', Chapter B. Key Concepts, [B.94], Version 1.2, March 2015 <https://www.oaic.gov.au/resources/agencies-and-organisations/app-guidelines/chapter-b-app-guidelines-v1.2.pdf>.

While references to 'reasonably identifiable' are included in the commentary in the omnibus APP Guidelines (apart from section B.93 these include few examples of items that are outside the limits of 'reasonableness'), they refer mostly to the principle that the other information or knowledge held by the person with access to the information in dispute may change the 'personal' nature of this information by enabling identification when used in combination.[30]

3.1.4. Consideration of the scope of 'personal information'

The Information Commissioner's determination in *Ben Grubb v. Telstra Corporation Ltd*, a request for a person's telecommunications meta-data held by their service provider, was decided on the definition of 'personal information' in effect pre-2014.[31]

It concluded, partly on the basis of a Parliamentary Joint Committee on Intelligence and Security report,[32] that:

> The process of ascertainment of an individual's identity involving inquiries from and cross-matching against different network management and records management systems is not only possible, but is in fact a process that Telstra already puts into practice, not only for network assurance purposes but also in responding to large numbers of requests for metadata by law enforcement agencies and other regulatory bodies.[33]

On this basis, the network meta-data, including the IP address, was found to be 'personal information'.

This decision was reversed on appeal in *Telstra Corporation Limited and Privacy Commissioner* in the AAT.[34] Deputy President Forgie placed significant weight on the now deleted words 'identity is apparent, or can reasonably be ascertained, *from the information or opinion*'; and also the previous practice, before the meta-data retention scheme, of not retaining meta-data for more than 30 days or so.

Deputy President Forgie's conclusion that in this case the information item fell outside the definition is also based on the notion that the communications network meta-data that is triggered by and relates to a person's phone call or

---

30 Ibid., [B.92].

31 *Ben Grubb v. Telstra Corporation Ltd* [2015] AICmr 35 (1 May 2015) <http://www.austlii.edu.au/au/cases/cth/AICmr/2015/35.html>.

32 *Report of the Inquiry into Potential Reforms of Australia's National Security Legislation*, Parliamentary Joint Committee on Intelligence and Security, tabled 24 June 2013.

33 In *Telstra Corporation Ltd and Privacy Commissioner* (2015) 254 IR 83, [2015] AATA 991, (18 December 2015) [82], <http://www.austlii.edu.au/au/cases/cth/AATA/2015/991.html>. See also Swinson, M., 'Putting the 'Personal' Into Personal Information' (2016) 13(2) *PrivLB* 45.

34 Ibid.

Internet connection[35] is not 'about' the individual, but instead is only 'about the way in which Telstra delivers the call or the message', it is 'about the service it provides to Mr Grubb but not about him'.[36] The IP address was considered to be 'not *about* the person but *about* the means by which data is transmitted from a person's mobile device over the Internet and a message sent to, or a connection made, with another person's mobile device'.[37] In addition, the fact that some IP addresses are not allocated *permanently* to a person's device, but dynamically assigned for a shorter time and work to ensure communications intended for a person's device get to them reliably for that time, was seen to be another reason to find IP addresses are not information 'about' a person.[38]

Given that IPv4 address exhaustion and Carrier-Grade Network Address Translation (CG-NAT) will apply dynamic allocation and sophisticated multiplexing of IP addresses to an increasing proportion of all online connections, but the meta-data derived from this process is acceptable as core information retained for surveillance and identification of individuals, it seems anomalous to decide that merely technically upgrading beyond an older simpler, static allocation model to a faster one would remove the necessary connection with the caller.[39]

Finally Forgie noted that the amendment to the 'Telecommunications Interception and Access Act by the Data Retention Act which came into force 13 October 2015', deeming certain information (much of the communications meta-data in question, including certain IP addresses) to be 'personal information' and thus about an individual, should not apply here because the amendment was not yet in force.[40] Section 187LA(2) Telecommunications (Interception and Access) Act 1979 (Cth) states:

> Information that is kept under this Part, or information that is in a document kept under this Part is taken, for the purposes of the *Privacy Act 1988*, to be personal information about an individual if the information relates to: (a) the individual; or (b) a communication to which the individual is a party.[41]

---

35 Data that is now retained to enable law enforcement and national security agencies to later identify and track the communications of certain individuals.

36 *Telstra v. Privacy Commissioner*, above n. 33, [112].

37 Ibid., [113] (emphasis added).

38 Ibid., [113].

39 Huston, G. [chief scientist, APNIC], 'What is Metadata, and Why Should I Care?', *The ISP Column* (blog), August 2014, <http://www.potaroo.net/ispcol/2014-08/metadata.html>.

40 See for instance Telecommunications (Interception and Access) Amendment (Data Retention) Act 2015, s. 3, Sch. 1, Item 1H which added the following note to the definition of 'personal information' in s. 6(1) of the Privacy Act: 'Note: Section 187LA of the Telecommunications (Interception and Access) Act 1979 extends the meaning of personal information to cover information kept under Part 5-1A of that Act.'

41 It is unclear to what degree s. 187LA TIA Act would imply that IP addresses or similar meta-data items of a type potentially affected but which were *not* actually collected for data retention purposes would be considered to be PI; and whether it would have effect for purposes

Note that this recent amendment uses the broader EU DPD and OECD test of 'relates to' an individual, rather than the narrower APEC and Privacy Act term 'about', as discussed below. And in (b) it also explicitly includes a category of the type excluded by Forgie, 'information relate[d] to ... a communication'.

The Privacy Commissioner appealed the AAT decision to the Federal Court in 2016, with a decision expected in early 2017. Whatever the outcome of this further litigation, the impact of the AAT decision against recognition of IP address and other telecommunications meta-data as PI is likely to be limited by its application to the narrower pre-2012 amendment version of the definition of PI, its reference to a superseded pre-retention scheme retention model, and also its predating the effect of section 187LA TIAA, which now confirms that significant components of telecommunications meta-data are PI in Australia for its purposes, using language that contradicts Forgie DP's rejection of information related to a communication as compatible with it being PI.

It would also be interesting to have further expert analysis and judicial consideration of the implications of the dynamic IP allocation methods used in telecommunications in the second decade of the twenty-first century, rather than the static methods common in the last decades of the preceding one, and whether the legislation was intended to be technologically specific to the latter when the former fulfils the same function. If increases in complexity, velocity, variety or volume of meta-data are enough to break a legal nexus between the data and the individual, this will have significant consequences for regulation of Big Data, which has all these attributes.

3.2 'PERSONAL INFORMATION' (PI) IN THE APEC PRIVACY FRAMEWORK

The APEC Privacy Framework was the only international source cited explicitly by the Australian 2012 amending Bill's Explanatory Memorandum when it noted that the new definition in part arises from a desire for consistency with international provisions.

APEC's Framework uses the term 'personal information', and offers a definition that focuses on identifiability. It is however very short, but potentially internally inconsistent within the document itself. At [9] it says personal information is 'information *about* an identified or identifiable individual' (emphasis added). But the note beside [9] gives an alternate meaning: '[PI] is information *that can*

other than data retention. (Such a retention-dependent outcome could create difficulties in application of this new section; given the limited transparency of the retention scheme, it may be difficult for an individual to know if a particular packet, channel or data stream meta-data item was retained, or was of a type retained.) It may also be anomalous if a user's IP address were characterised as PI for one purpose but not for another closely related one.

be used to identify an individual' (emphasis added). This inconsistency could create doubt about whether information about an identifiable individual, but not usable for identifying that person, would be included.[42]

The note to [9] also says that PI includes 'information that would not meet the criteria of identifying an individual alone, but when put together with other information would identify an individual'. This clarifies that it is not only the information itself that can enable identification.

However, while the APEC framework is a source for the revised Australian definition, in particular its use of 'about' rather than 'related to', and may support its move to 'identifiable' from 'individual whose identity can be ascertained', it offers little guidance on important questions such as:

- the degree of access to the other information required, or whose access is relevant to consider: only the initial data collector or custodian, or any entity that gains access?
- whether 'reasonableness' is a criterion (its absence may imply not), and what 'reasonable' might mean (how onerous do steps to use other information have to be before they fall outside the definition?)
- whether future re-identifiability needs to be considered, or only re-identifiability at say, the time of collection.

Its internal inconsistency is also puzzling. It has also been criticised more generally as offering little support for high privacy standards where they already exist.[43]

The APEC Privacy Framework is thus relevant, and clearly influenced the new Australian definition, but it ultimately creates as many questions as answers on the question of the proper scope of 'personal information'.

3.3. 'PERSONALLY IDENTIFYING INFORMATION' (PII) IN THE US

Unlike the EU definitions of personal data discussed below, the US situation is much more inconsistent.

---

42 APEC Secretariat, *APEC Privacy Framework*, APEC#205-SO-01.2, 2005, p. 5, [9] and note to [9], <http://publications.apec.org/publication-detail.php?pub_id=390>.

43 Greenleaf, G., 'Five years of the APEC Privacy Framework: Failure or promise?' (2009) 25(1) *Computer Law & Security Review* 28–43. 'The "Pathfinder" projects seem[ed] to be developing toward a generalised version of the US Safe Harbor scheme [which authorised what would otherwise be unlawful transfer of personal information from the EU to the US because the US is recognised as not having 'adequate' protections for EU DPD compliance purposes].'

While the US Privacy Act of 1974 regulates the collection of personal information by federal government agencies, there is no overarching federal law regulating private entities. Some states have their own laws, such as California's Online Privacy Protection Act of 2003.

> Neither federal nor state law agrees on a single term that identifies the basic category of personal information. … U.S. law is far from settled on [the term 'personally identifiable information'] to identify the underlying concept to which it refers.[44]

Schwartz and Solove describe three common approaches to defining personal information. These are

1. the 'tautological' approach;
2. the 'non-public' approach; and
3. the 'specific types' approach.

While the approaches are not limited to US definitions and could be applied more generally, for our purposes we are only using them in the US context. One reason is that US privacy law is complex, dense and often conflicting as different industries are regulated differently than others. As such, we are adopting the approach of Schwartz and Solove for this section to better make sense of the field in general.

The 'tautological' approach to US privacy law simply defines 'personal' as meaning any information that identifies a person. For example,

> The *Video Privacy Protection Act* (VPPA) neatly demonstrates this model. The VPPA, which safeguards the privacy of video sales and rentals, simply defines 'personally identifiable information' as 'information which identifies a person.' For purposes of the statute, information that identifies a person is PII and falls under the statute's jurisdiction once linked to the purchase, request, or obtaining of video material.[45]

The 'non-public' approach defines personal information by focusing on what it is not, rather than what it is, excluding from its protected scope any information that is publicly accessible or that is purely statistical. 'Instead of saying that PII is simply that which identifies a person, the non-public approach draws on concepts of information that is publicly accessible and information that is purely statistical.'[46]

---

44 Schwartz, P. and Solove, D., 'Reconciling Personal Information in-the United States and European Union' (2014) *California Law Review* 877–916, 888, <http://ssrn.com/abstract=2271442>.

45 Schwartz, P. and Solove, D., 'The PII Problem: Privacy and a new concept of Personally Identifiable information' (2011) 86 *New York University Law Review*, 1829.

46 Ibid., p. 1830.

The third approach is to list 'specific types' of data that constitute personal information. If information falls into a specified or listed category, it becomes personal information under the statute. State data breach notification laws take this approach.[47] Prominent definitions of PII are considered below.

3.3.1. *HIPAA*

While the most often used term is 'personally identifiable information' (PII), there are variations on terminology and meaning. So for instance the US Health Insurance Portability and Accountability Act (HIPAA) refers to 'individually identifiable health information', which is:

> [I]nformation that is a subset of health information, including demographic information collected from an individual, and:
> 1. Is created or received by a health care provider, health plan, employer, or health care clearinghouse; and
> 2. Relates to the past, present, or future physical or mental health or condition of an individual; the provision of health care to an individual; or the past, present, or future payment for the provision of health care to an individual; and
>   i) That identifies the individual; or
>   ii) With respect to which there is a reasonable basis to believe the information can be used to identify the individual.[48]

The phrasing of this medical records provision has parallels to PI in the Australian context, but this is not widely used outside of health insurance, and it appears in practice that even HIPAA works on a fixed set of 18 data items which are considered identifiable elements, and everything else falls outside of this category.[49] (Most of these would fall outside the meta-data category.)

3.3.1.1. GAO

The most widely used and mainstream definition for PII appears to be from the Government Accountability Office (GAO). The GAO's definition is:

> PII is – any information about an individual maintained by an agency, including

---

[47] Schwartz and Solove, above n. 44, p. 889.

[48] 12 45 CFR § 160.103, summarised in *HIPAA Administrative Simplification,* Regulation Text, 15, 26.03.2013, <http://www.hhs.gov/hipaa/for-professionals/privacy/laws-regulations/>.

[49] Narayanan, A. and Shmetikov, V., 'Privacy and Security – Myths and Fallacies of "Personally Identifiable Information"' (2010) 53(6) *Communications of the ACM*, <http://www.cs.utexas.edu/~shmat/shmat_cacm10.pdf>.

> (1) any information that can be used to distinguish or trace an individual's identity, such as name, social security number, date and place of birth, mother's maiden name, or biometric records; and
> (2) any other information that is linked or linkable to an individual, such as medical, educational, financial, and employment information.[50]

This makes no mention of telecommunications or location meta-data, or similar data types.[51] There have however been longstanding recommendations for such items to be recognised as at least potential PI.[52]

3.3.2. *Office of Management and Budget*

The US Department of State[53] refers to an Office of Management and Budget (OMB) definition of PII from 2007:

> Information that can be used to distinguish or trace an individual's identity, such as their name, Social Security number, biometric records, etc., alone, or when combined with other personal or identifying information which is linked or linkable to a specific individual, such as date and place of birth, mother's maiden name, etc.[54]

The Manual pointing to this definition gives the following examples of PII that must be reported if breached:

(1) personnel or payroll information;
(2) social security numbers and/or passport numbers;
(3) date of birth, place of birth and/or mother's maiden name;
(4) medical information;

---

50 Memorandums 07-16 and 06-19. GAO Report 08-536, 'Privacy: Alternatives Exist for Enhancing Protection of Personally Identifiable Information', May 2008, <http://www.gao.gov/new.items/d08536.pdf>.

51 For discussion, see Porter, C., 'De-Identified Data and Third Party Data Mining: The Risk of Re-Identification of Personal Information' (2008-2009) 5(1) *Shidler Journal of Law, Commerce & Technology* 1–8; Omer, T. and Polonetsky, J., 'Big Data for All: Privacy and User Control in the Age of Analytics' (2013) 11(5) *Northwestern Journal of Technology and Intellectual Property* [xxvii]–274.

52 McIntyre, J., 'Balancing Expectations of Online Privacy: Why Internet Protocol (IP) Addresses Should be Protected as Personally Identifiable Information' (2010) 60(3) *DePaul Law Review* 2011, <http://ssrn.com/abstract=1621102>.

53 US Department of State, *Foreign Affairs Manual*, 5 FAM 463, 'Definitions', 2014, <http://www.state.gov/documents/organization/85694.pdf>. This also offers a survey of other relevant Acts, directives and guidance at 5 FAM 462.1 and 462.2.

54 Office of Management and Budget, *Safeguarding Against and Responding to the Breach of Personally Identifiable Information*, M-07-16 (22.05.2007), <https://www.whitehouse.gov/sites/default/files/omb/memoranda/fy2007/m07-16.pdf>.

(5) law enforcement information that may identify individuals, including information related to investigations, arrests, convictions, or sentencing;
(6) department credit card holder information or other information on financial transactions (e.g., garnishments);
(7) passport applications and/or passports; or
(8) biometric records.

3.3.3. *Data breach*

The California Senate Bill 1386, which was the first data breach law, is another example: its definition of personal information includes specific types such as social security numbers, driver's licence numbers, financial accounts, but not, for example, e-mail addresses or telephone numbers (perhaps in part because of its special focus).[55]

Most states have data breach notification laws with varying definitions of personal information, and what types of information fall within the scope of the legislation.[56]

3.3.4. *Children's Online Privacy Protection Act*

The Children's Online Privacy Protection Act (COPPA), by contrast, defines Personal Information by a 'specific types' list:

> Individually identifiable information about an individual collected online, including
> - a first and last name;
> - a home or other physical address including street name and name of a city or town;
> - an e-mail address;
> - a telephone number;
> - a Social Security number;
> - any other identifier that the Commission determines permits the physical or online contacting of a specific individual; or
> - information concerning the child or the parents of that child that the Web site collects online from the child and combines with an identifier described in this paragraph.[57]

---

55 California Senate Bill 1386, 2002, <http://www.leginfo.ca.gov/pub/01-02/bill/sen/sb_1351-1400/sb_1386_bill_20020926_chaptered.pdf>.

56 Maurushat, A., Bolton, M. and Vaile, D., 'Data Breach Notification Goes Global' forthcoming *Privacy International Bulletin* (2016).

57 15 USC 91, Children's Online Privacy Protection Act, 1998–2000, <https://www.law.cornell.edu/uscode/text/15/chapter-91>.

This would appear to exclude IP addresses or other meta-data, including location data, unless directly linked by the collecting site to one of the named identifiers.

3.4. DE-IDENTIFICATION

As discussed above, 'de-identification' has been a widely practised method of moving information out of the PII category in the US, using various data obfuscation methodologies. This is apparently on the assumption that there is only a fixed small set of data items that can be used to identify a person, and if you deal with them, what you have left is no longer 'identifiable'.[58]

This assumption is coming under increasing scrutiny, in part because the de-identification methods relied on simplistic fixed data sets prone to breaking when faced with the more sophisticated, open-ended tools of big data.[59] As noted by Narayanan and Shemitikov,

> The versatility and power of re-identification algorithms imply that terms such as 'personally identifiable' and 'quasi-identifier' simply have no technical meaning. While some attributes may be uniquely identifying on their own, any attribute can be identifying in combination with others.[60]

However, this caution from the technical community may not have weakened the attachment in business and some US government circles to the notion that there can be sets of meta-data, or indeed other data that are not capable of supporting identifiability, despite their origin with a person.[61]

---

58 See for instance a now-deprecated approach in Sweeney, L., 'Achieving k-anonymity privacy protection using generalization and suppression' (2002) 10(05) *International Journal on uncertainty, Fuzziness, and Knowledge-Based Systems* 557–570, <https://epic.org/privacy/reidentification/Sweeney_Article.pdf>.

59 See for example, Chin, A. and Klinefelter, A., 'Differential Privacy as a Response to the Reidentification Threat: The Facebook Advertiser Case Study' (2012) 90(5) *North Carolina Law Review*; UNC Legal Studies Research Paper No. 2062447, <http://ssrn.com/abstract=2062447>.

60 Narayanan, A. and Shmetikov, V., 'Privacy and Security – Myths and Fallacies of "Personally Identifiable Information"' (2010) 53(6) *Communications of the ACM*. For another practical example, see Porter, C., 'De-Identified Data and Third Party Data Mining: The Risk of Re-Identification of Personal Information' (2008) 5 *Shidler J.L. Com. & Tech.* 3, <http://www.lctjournal.washington.edu/Vol5/a03Porter.html>.

61 For another perspective, working back from the identification of the risk that data protection law is supposed to defend against, see Eloïse, G., 'If Personal Information is Privacy's Gatekeeper, then Risk of Harm is the Key: A Proposed Method for Determining What Counts as Personal Information' (2013) 24(1) *Albany Law Journal of Science and Technology*, <http://ssrn.com/abstract=2334938>.

3.5. 'PERSONAL DATA' (PD) IN EUROPE AND THE OECD

The European data protection framework includes a Council of Europe convention based on an OECD Guideline, and several EU directives. They are considered below with comments on relevant divergences.

3.5.1. *CoE Convention 108*

The 1981 Council of Europe (CoE) Convention for the Protection of Individuals with regard to Automatic Processing of Personal Data,[62] also known as Convention 108, offered its important definition of 'personal data' in Art. 2(a):

> 'personal data' means any information relating to an identified or identifiable individual ('data subject')

There are several differences from the current Australian definition of 'personal information'.

- Convention 108 refers to information 'relating to' rather than 'about' an individual, as in the Australian definition of PI. While very similar, 'relating to' is potentially broader than 'about'.[63]
- It uses the term 'data' rather than the Australian and US term 'information', belying its origins in controls on digital information processing. But for the

[62] Convention for the Protection of Individuals with regard to Automatic Processing of Personal Data, ETS 108, 28 January 1981, Strasbourg, <http://conventions.coe.int/Treaty/en/Treaties/Html/108.htm>.

[63] See Burdon, M. and McKillop, A., 'The Google Street View Wi-Fi Scandal and Its Repercussions for Privacy Regulation' (2013) 39(3) *Monash University Law Review* 702. They note that 'the *Privacy Act's* definition of personal information is therefore more constricted in its application because the removal of 'relates to' narrows the situations in which information can identify an individual. A MAC [Media Access Control, a hardware network interface] address is a good case in point as it is a device identifier rather than an individual identifier. In that sense, it is not information "about" an individual, but it can clearly be information that "relates" to an individual.' They also say 'the principle reason for the use of "about" as opposed to "relates" appears to be consistent with the APEC Privacy Framework', at 712. See also Nouwt, S., 'Reasonable Expectations of Geo-Privacy?' (2008) 5(2) *SCRIPTed* 376 for a discussion from the perspective of the EU definition and 'related to' a person <https://pure.uvt.nl/ws/files/1024811/NouwtScriptEd5_2.pdf>. Nouwt observes that the Article 29 Working Party Opinion 4/2007 discussed below posits that when information is given 'about' a particular person, this information has a 'content' element, one of three possible elements under a 'relates to' test; another is a 'purpose' element: 'Finally, despite the absence of a "content" or "purpose" element, information can relate to an individual when the "result" of using the information has an impact, minor or major, on the individual's rights and interests. An example is the monitoring of a taxi's positions by a taxi company using a satellite location system. The content is not related to a person but to a car and the purpose is not to evaluate the taxi driver's performance. However, this system can have an impact on the taxi drivers and therefore this data is subject to [EU] data protection rules.'

purpose of analysing its application to data processing techniques, as in this paper, the potentially broader scope of 'information' is probably of limited significance.

- It uses 'identified or identifiable individual' rather than the new Australian definition of 'identified individual, or an individual who is reasonably identifiable'.[64] The Australian qualifier 'reasonably' is not in the Convention version.

3.5.2. *OECD Privacy Framework*

The OECD Privacy Framework, in its July 2013 revision of the original 1980 Guidelines governing the Protection of Privacy and Transborder Flows of Personal Data (Privacy Guidelines), contains a definition of 'personal data' at [1(b)] on page 13 in identical terms to the Convention 108 definition above.[65] Australia is also a member of the OECD, and its privacy law derives from the 1980 source, as do most of those in Europe.

3.5.3. *EU Data Protection Directive*

There is also a 'personal data' definition from the Data Protection Directive 95/46/EC ('DPD'), which is the key source for EU law. 'Personal data' in Art. 2(a) of the DPD means:

> any information relating to an identified or identifiable natural person ('data subject'); an identifiable person is one who can be identified, directly or indirectly, in particular by reference to an identification number or to one or more factors specific to his physical, physiological, mental, economic, cultural or social identity.[66]

The broad definition of PI in the DPD is refined in its Recital 26:

> whereas to determine whether a person is identifiable, account should be taken of all the means likely reasonably to be used either by the controller or by any other person to identify the said person;

---

64 The 2012 Explanatory Memorandum to the Privacy amendment bill, cited above, confirms this change was done to be more consistent with international instruments. While the OECD version was not mentioned explicitly, it is clearly a critical influence on the current Australian text.

65 Specifically in OECD Privacy Guidelines, Pt. I of *OECD Privacy Framework*, revised 2013, 13, <http://oecd.org/sti/ieconomy/oecd_privacy_framework.pdf>.

66 Directive 95/46/EC of the European Parliament and of the Council of 24 October 1995 on the protection of individuals with regard to the processing of personal data and on the free movement of such data, [1995] OJ L 281/31.

> whereas the principles of protection shall not apply to data rendered anonymous in such a way that the data subject is no longer identifiable;
>
> whereas codes of conduct within the meaning of Article 27 may be a useful instrument for providing guidance as to the ways in which data may be rendered anonymous and retained in a form in which identification of the data subject is no longer possible. [line breaks added]

Recital 26 extends the definition by referring to potential identification by 'any other party', rather than just the 'controller'. In this it is broader than say, the UK law discussed below.

The Recital 26 test for de-identification is that the subject is 'no longer identifiable', and that 'identification ... is no longer possible'. This does not specify whether the potential for future identifiability is covered, but the 'no longer possible' formulation suggests a more permanent expectation than uses of the term 'de-identified' to cover effectively temporary anonymisation in research, discussed above.

3.5.3.1. Transfers and schemes

The Directive restricts the transfer of personal data to other countries. Personal data may be transferred only to countries with an 'adequate level of protection' of privacy. The *Schrems* case[67] confirmed that the US does not offer such a level of adequate protection.[68] In doing so the European Court of Justice held that the EU/US Safe Harbour agreement was a breach of EU human rights law. The US Safe Harbour scheme was recently replaced by a newly negotiated 'Privacy Shield'.[69] It is unknown whether the European courts will view the new Privacy Shield as adequately protecting privacy.[70]

---

67 Case C-362/14, *Maximillian Schrems v. Data Protection Commissioner* (CJEU, 6 October 2015).

68 'Regarding the practical consequences of the CJEU judgment, the Working Party considers that it is clear that transfers from the European Union to the United States can no longer be framed on the basis of the European Commission adequacy decision 2000/520/EC (the so-called "Safe Harbour decision"). ... transfers that are still taking place under the Safe Harbour decision after the CJEU judgment are unlawful.' Article 29 Working Party, Statement, 16 October 2015, <http://ec.europa.eu/justice/data-protection/article-29/press-material/press-release/art29_press_material/2015/20151016_wp29_statement_on_schrems_judgement.pdf>.

69 For a summary of the changes from Safe Harbor, see Connolly, C., 'Implementation of the new EU–US Privacy Shield', Galexia (online), March 2016, <http://www.galexia.com/public/research/articles/research_articles-art57.html>.

70 See litigant's commentary: Baker, J., 'Why Safe Harbor 2.0 will lose again', *Ars Technica* (online), 3 February 2016, <http://arstechnica.com/tech-policy/2016/02/interview-safe-harbour-2-0-will-lose-again-argues-max-schrems/>.

3.5.4. *EU e-Privacy Directive*

Directive 2002/58/EC concerning the Processing of Personal Data and the Protection of Privacy in the Electronic Communications Sector[71] mostly adopts the definitions in the DPD, above, in Art. 2, so it introduces no alternative term.

It deals with relations of customers of telecommunications services with various entities. Articles 5 and 6 prohibit telecommunication providers and ISPs from generally providing identifying information about their customers, which reduces the feasibility of using this data for general re-identification purposes. But Art. 15 offers a number of exceptions. In *Promusicae v. Telefonica*,[72] the European Court of Justice decided Art. 15 does not preclude Member States from imposing an obligation on the part of access providers to release identifying information to holders of IP addresses in the context of civil proceedings (for instance, copyright infringement cases). However, Lundevall-Unger and Tranvik note the Court did not discuss whether or not the existence of legal obstacles should impact on assessment of the identifiability of IP addresses in the hands of Internet Service Providers or industry organisations like Promusicae.[73]

3.5.5. *Article 29 Data Protection Working Party Guidance*

The EU's independent Article 29 Data Protection Working Party provides guidance and interpretation for EU data protection law. Several of its opinions are relevant here.

In 2007 the EU's Article 29 Data Protection Working Party offered Opinion 4/2007 (WP 136)[74] on the concept of 'personal data' in the DPD. This included the consideration of the term 'personal data' in the case of *Bodil Lindqvist* (C-101/01).[75] The European Court of Justice decided there that 'referring, on an internet page, to various persons and identifying them by name or by other means, for instance by giving their telephone number or information regarding their working conditions and hobbies, constitutes the processing of personal data'.[76]

---

71 Directive 2002/58/EC of the European Parliament and of the Council of 12 July 2002 concerning the processing of personal data and the protection of privacy in the electronic communications sector (Directive on privacy and electronic communications), [2002] OJ L 201/37–47.

72 Case C-275/06, *Promusicae v. Telefonica* (CJEU, 29 January 2008).

73 Lundevall-Unger, P. and Tranvik, T., 'IP addresses–Just a Number?' (2011) 19(1) *International Journal of Law and Information Technology* 53–73, 57, fn. 17.

74 Article 29 Data Protection Working Party, Opinion 4/2007 on the concept of 'personal data' in the DPD, WP 136, 20 June 2007, <http://ec.europa.eu/justice/policies/privacy/docs/wpdocs/2007/wp136_en.pdf>.

75 Case C-101/01, *Bodil Lindqvist* (CJEU, 6 November 2003).

76 See Opinion 4/2007, p. 6. For analysis, see also 'EU – What is Personal Data?' *Technology, Media & Telecommunication News*, Linklaters, 1 October 2008, <http://www.linklaters.com/Publications/Publication1403Newsletter/PublicationIssue20081001/Pages/PublicationIssueItem3513.aspx>.

Their analysis of the definition of 'personal data' breaks down the definition into four building blocks. These are:

1. 'any information'
2. 'relating to'
3. 'an identified or identifiable'
4. 'natural person'

Example No. 15 on pages 16–17 outlines the Working Party's consideration of whether IP addresses constitute 'data relating to an identifiable person'. The meaning of 'directly or indirectly identifiable' is covered at pages 12–13. The Working Party concluded:

> Unless the Internet Service Provider is in a position to distinguish with absolute certainty that the data correspond to users that cannot be identified, it will have to treat all IP information as personal data, to be on the safe side.

The 2007 Article 29 Opinion also considers when an individual is identifiable in light of 'all the means likely reasonably to be used either by the controller or by any other person to identify the said person'. This requires a range of factors to be considered, including the purpose of the information, the structure of the processing, the advantage to the data controller, the interests of the individual and the risk of technical or organisational failures. It also covers use by entities other than the 'controller'. The extent of relevant means are set broadly, so a third party in possession of, for instance, an IP address might apply through the courts to an ISP in order to identify the name and address of the subscriber attached to an IP address. An IP address in the hands of any party must be regarded as potentially personal data.

An earlier Article 29 Opinion 2/2002[77] had also addressed the narrower issue of IP address as potential 'personal data'. The subsequent debate with Google's Fleischer was 'one of the few public debates to date concerning IP addresses as personal data'.[78] Opinion 2/2002 said that it was 'now widely recognised that an IP address – and a fortiori a unique identification number integrated in the address – can be considered as personal data in the sense of the legal framework.'[79]

77 Article 29 Data Protection Working Party, 'The Use of Unique Identifiers in Telecommunications Terminal Equipment: the Example of IPv6', Opinion 2/2002, WP 58, 30 May 2002, <http://ec.europa.eu/justice/policies/privacy/docs/wpdocs/2002/wp58_en.pdf>.

78 Litvinov, A., 'The Data Protective Directive as Applied to Internet Protocol (IP) Addresses: Uniting the Perspective of the European Commission with the Jurisprudence of Member State' (2013) 45 *George Washington International Law Review* 579.

79 Communication of the Commission on the Organisation and Management of the Internet Domain Name System of April 2000, COM(2000) 202, and documents adopted by the

Opinion 2/2002 also referred to EC Directive 97/66 on the processing of personal data and the protection of privacy in the telecommunications sector, and the possibility for individuals to restrict the identification of 'calling and connected' addresses, invoking RFC 3041 of the Internet Engineering Task Force (IETF)[80] as evidence that it was already technically feasible to avoid reliance on fixed device identifiers like MAC addresses and use an arbitrary and dynamic IP address for outgoing connections to offer support for anonymity, if desired.[81]

Pseudonymised, coded and 'anonymous' data was considered in Opinion 4/2007. A pseudonym is an identifier that uniquely applies to one entity, but is not linked to other identifiers such that the person can be easily linked to the record. Coded data is similar, and widely used in medical research, as noted above: traditional identifying items like name and address are removed and stored in a secure lookup table, and a code with random or non-significant content is added in their place, with access to the lookup table being the only way to re-associate the data with a known individual.[82] 'Anonymous' data is assumed to not be reasonably able to be linked to an identified individual; there are generally no lookup tables, although there may be random record identifiers.

If this pseudonymisation or coding can be reversed to identify the individual, by the data controller or anyone else, it is likely to be 'personal' data. Attempts to anonymise and de-identify data are increasingly looked on with caution, in part because of demonstrated failures, and in part because of the advent of more sophisticated big data methods of re-identification.[83]

Article 29 Data Protection Working Party, in particular 'Privacy on the Internet – An integrated EU Approach to On-line Data Protection', WP 37, 21 November 2000, <http://ec.europa.eu/justice/data-protection/article-29/documentation/opinion-recommendation/files/2000/wp37_en.pdf>.

80 IETF, 'Privacy extensions for stateless address autoconfiguration in IPv6', January 2001, <https://tools.ietf.org/html/rfc3041>.

81 This discussion was anticipating conversion to the larger IPv6 address space, sadly not yet complete in 2016. The subsequent exhaustion of the IPv4 address space while it continues to be used complicates Network Address Translation re-use of IPv4 addresses, but the issues are still relevant. See Huston's comment above.

82 This is a major method in medical research. Wilson, P., 'Legal issues of data anonymisation in research' (2004) 328 *BMJ* 7451, <http://www.bmj.com/content/328/7451/1300>.

83 See for instance European Union Agency For Network And Information Security (ENISA), 'Privacy by Design in Big Data: An Overview of Privacy Enhancing Technologies in the Era of Big Data Analytics' (December 2015). See also, Charkow, B., 'Control over the De-Identification of Data' (2003) 21(1) *Cardozo Arts & Entertainment Law Journal* 195–228, 223; and Ohm, P., 'Broken Promises of Privacy: Responding to the Surprising Failure of Anonymization' (2009-2010) 57(6) *UCLA Law Review* 1701–1778. For a counter view on the new EU Regulation and de-identification, see Omer, T., 'Privacy Law's Midlife Crisis: A Critical Assessment of the Second Wave of Global Privacy Laws' (2013) 74(6) *Ohio State Law Journal* 1217–1262.

3.5.6. *National implementation example: UK Data Protection Act 1998*

UK law is generally consistent with EU principles in this area, but the language is somewhat different, and there are some inconsistencies. Section 1(1) of the UK's Data Protection Act 1998 states:

> 'Personal data' means data which relate to a living individual who can be identified – (a) from those data, or (b) from those data and other information which is in the possession of, or is likely to come into the possession of, the data controller, and includes any expression of opinion about the individual and any indication of the intentions of the data controller or any other person in respect of the individual.

Compared to the DPD, the UK statute:

- refers to 'data', not 'information';
- adds a requirement that the individual be living;
- uses 'can be identified' instead of 'identified or identifiable'; and
- uses a different formulation focusing on information in or likely to come into the possession of the 'data controller' rather than 'directly or indirectly' using types of information.

The Information Commissioner's Office has a guide, 'Determining what is personal data', that includes an Appendix C on 'Information "anonymised" for the purposes of the Directive' and a discussion about identifiability, which tends to accept that reasonable attempts to de-identify will be effective.[84]

A UK Court of Appeal case, *Durant*, added two extra requirements to the DPD block 2 above, 'relating to' an individual, including a required connection with 'biographical significance', and suggested that even database records retrievable by the subject's name might not be 'personal data'.[85]

The Article 29 Working Party regarded *Durant* as compromising the protection afforded to individuals by the Data Protection Directive without these two extra tests for 'personal data', and as a result the European Commission considers the UK to have failed to implement the Directive adequately.[86]

---

84 ICO, 'Determining what is personal data', 2012, <https://ico.org.uk/media/for-organisations/documents/1554/determining-what-is-personal-data.pdf>.

85 *Durant v. Financial Services Authority* [2003] EWCA Civ 1746, [26]–[31]. The narrow interpretation was relied upon by cases such as *Deer v. University of Oxford* [2015] EWCA Civ 52, [2015] ICR 1213 (6 February 2015).

86 For more on this topic, see Bygrave, L., *Data Privacy Law: An International Perspective*, Oxford University Press, Oxford 2014. As to the continued relevance of EU privacy law in UK post-Brexit, see Wood, S., 'GDPR still relevant for the UK', Information Commissioner's Blog, 7 July 2016, <https://iconewsblog.wordpress.com/2016/07/07/gdpr-still-relevant-for-the-uk/>.

On the other hand, dealings with data to anonymise it may have the protection of law in the UK (a tribunal has ruled that anonymisation is 'processing'),[87] while WP 136 is unclear on the point, having not discussed it and left it unresolved.

3.5.7. *New EU General Data Protection Regulation*

Moves to reform existing EU law on data protection and introduce the General Data Protection Regulation (GDPR), proposed by the European Commission in 2012, concluded in 2016.[88] The reform package includes both the GDPR and the Data Protection Directive for Police and Criminal Justice Authorities (DPD-PCJA),[89] which regulates law enforcement entities separately. It updates and replaces the earlier data protection rules based on the 1995 DPD, and a 2008 Framework Decision for the police and criminal justice sector.[90] Our main aspect of interest is the 'personal data' definition.

In Art. 4(2) of the new regulation, 'personal data' means 'any information relating to a data subject', and the latter is separately defined, below. This split into two definitions retains the core language from the DPD of 'information relating to' a person.

'Data subject' means:

> an identified natural person or a natural person who can be identified, directly or indirectly, by means reasonably likely to be used by the controller or by any other

87 *All Party Parliamentary Group on Extraordinary Rendition v. The Information Commissioner & The Ministry of Defence* [2011] UKUT 153 (AAC) (APGER), [127], cited in Kuan Hon, W., Millard, C. and Walden, I., 'The problem of "personal data" in cloud computing: what information is regulated? – The cloud of unknowing' (2011) 1(4) *International Data Privacy Law* 211, 214, <http://idpl.oxfordjournals.org/content/1/4/211.short>.

88 Regulation (EU) 2016/679 of the European Parliament and of the Council of 27 April 2016 on the protection of natural persons with regard to the processing of personal data and on the free movement of such data, and repealing Directive 95/46/EC (General Data Protection Regulation), [2016] OJ L 119/1–88. The key elements of the revised data protection regime proposed by the European Commission and agreed by the European Parliament and Council are explained in European Commission, 'Questions and Answers – Data protection reform', Fact sheet, 21 December 2015, <http://europa.eu/rapid/press-release_MEMO-15-6385_en.htm>.

89 Directive (EU) 2016/680 of the European Parliament and of the Council of 27 April 2016 on the protection of natural persons with regard to the processing of personal data by competent authorities for the purposes of the prevention, investigation, detection or prosecution of criminal offences or the execution of criminal penalties, and on the free movement of such data, and repealing Council Framework Decision 2008/977/JHA, [2016] OJ L 119/89–131.

90 Council Framework Decision 2008/977/JHA which addresses police and judicial cooperation in criminal matters, and includes rules for exchanges of personal data, including national and EU databases and transmissions to competent authorities and private parties for purposes of prevention, investigation, detection or prosecution of criminal offences, or execution of criminal penalties. Council Framework Decision 2008/977/JHA of 27 November 2008 on the protection of personal data processed in the framework of police and judicial cooperation in criminal matters, [2008] OJ L 350/60–71.

> natural or legal person, in particular by reference to an identification number, location data, online identifier or to one or more factors specific to the physical, physiological, genetic, mental, economic, cultural or social identity of that person.[91]

Compared to the DPD, there is a change from 'identifiable' to 'can be identified'.

It includes a new pair of data types, 'location data' and 'online identifiers', and adds 'genetic' to the list of factors specific to the person. The others are wide enough to potentially encompass behavioural biometric traits like eyeball movement, keyboard typing cadence and other potential collectable online Big Data about user interactions.

By explicitly including both 'location data' (which could be expected to include the telecommunications meta-data generated by mobile and fixed devices interacting with wireless base stations and other location-sensitive elements) and 'online identifiers' (which could encompass credentials generated by such devices), it seems more likely that a wide range of communications meta-data will fall within the latest EU definition than under the DPD.

The new phrase 'by means reasonably likely to be used' appears to be a form of the earlier 'reasonableness' test, although it also introduces a 'likelihood' element. This may have the effect of reducing consideration of identification by the use of, say, unauthorised or fraudulent means, if these are possible but rare (although if online fraud or data breach continues to proliferate, such means could presumably become 'reasonably likely to be used').

The new phrase 'by the controller or *by any other natural or legal person*' explicitly contemplates other parties as those whose capacity to identify must be assessed, and includes corporate entities (and perhaps even AI bots if and when they get legal personhood) amongst them.

And finally like the Directive, the GDPR allows transfers across borders when the personal data will receive 'an adequate level of protection.' Under the Regulation, as well as the Directive, the goal is to protect the fundamental right of data protection on a global basis. This extraterritorial application continues the potential for conflict between EU and US characterisations of various forms of meta-data as either 'personal' or not, and for disputes over the 'adequacy' of protection in EU citizen data in a cloud hosted in, or by entities from, jurisdictions like the US where it may be subject to third party Big Data analysis.[92]

---

91 GDPR.

92 Hunton & Williams, 'The Proposed EU General Data Protection Regulation – A guide for in-house lawyers, *Hunton Regulation Tracker* (June 2015), <https://www.huntonregulationtracker.com/files/Uploads/Documents/EU Data Protection Reg Tracker/Hunton_Guide_to_the_EU_General_Data_Protection_Regulation.pdf>. The recent case of *Microsoft v. USA* (US Ct of Appeals, 2nd Circuit, 14-2985, 14 July 2016) may have reduced the risk of US warrants permitting access to EU citizens' e-mails hosted in Ireland, and thus improved adequacy a little, but questions remain over the 'adequacy' of the new 'Privacy Shield' arising after the earlier *Schrems* case over NSA access to EU Facebook user data in Ireland: see Albrecht, J.-P. and Schrems, M., 'Privacy

4. COMPARING THE FRAMEWORKS

4.1. AUSTRALIA AND US

As noted above, the Australian PI definition appears to be broader than the US PII because of the explicit and implicit recognition that information other than the data in question can play a role in determining identifiability for Australian purposes.

IP addresses and other meta-data identifiers could be PI in some circumstances. The characterisation in the US of, say, an IP address as PII is however disputed and frequently rejected.

For instance a US federal district court in Washington state held that an IP address is not PII because it 'identifies a computer rather than a person.'[93] This has echoes of the AAT Australian ruling in *Telstra v. Privacy Commissioner*, above, although in that case it was the means of communication, not the computer, that was identified.[94] While there is some similarity on this point, it is worth noting that the *Telstra* case may well have come to a different conclusion if conducted under current law and practice.

4.2. AUSTRALIA AND EU

Given the various European definitions of PD noted above, it is difficult to compare the Australian PI definition, but it generally appears to quite similar in concept. In particular, both accept that you can have recourse to external data sources in the course of reasonable efforts to identify from a given sample of information; and that the capacity of others to use such external data is relevant, not just the activities of the data collector or current holder.

External data may include meta-data like an IP address, but both presumably contemplate access to other stores of data, perhaps even including face recognition based on large data sets.

Shield: The new EU rules on transatlantic data sharing will not protect you', *Irish Times*, 12 July 2016, <http://www.irishtimes.com/opinion/privacy-shield-the-new-eu-rules-on-transatlantic-data-sharing-will-not-protect-you-1.2719018>.

93 Baker, W. et al., 'The changing meaning of "personal data"', *IAPP Privacy Academy*, Baltimore, 30 September 2010, <https://www.privacyassociation.org/resource_center/the_changing_meaning_of_personal_data>.

94 *Telstra v. Privacy Commissioner* [2015] AATA 991 (on appeal), discussed above, where an IP address was considered to be 'not *about* the person but *about* the means by which data is transmitted from a person's mobile device over the internet and a message sent to, or a connection made, with another person's mobile device' [113] (emphasis added). (Since the events covered in this ruling a statutory amendment deemed IP address to be PI for certain purposes.)

4.3. US AND EU

As with PI, there appear to be significant differences in scope between PD (as used in Europe) and PII (as mostly used in the US). This is not surprising: Mayer-Schönberger notes that the US and Europe, holding fundamentally differing views about privacy and the necessary legal protection to be afforded to citizens, have developed quite different data protection regimes:

> The EU created a comprehensive framework that establishes privacy as a fundamental right to be protected proactively by government. The United States, on the other hand, adopted a patchwork of legislation that relies primarily on industry self-regulation with some protection through the courts, consistent with its view of privacy as a qualified right and its suspicion of governmental intrusion.[95]

The systems' divergent treatment of information in situations where it is merely *identifiable* but the individuals to whom the data relates are not currently *identified* has a significant outcome. It leads to key differences between what falls within the definitions. In a significant part of US privacy law, such information would fall outside privacy regulation.[96]

This is arguably too restrictive of the scope of data protection, and it may for instance encourage US-based online behavioural marketing operators to underestimate the potential impact their tracking may be considered to have in other jurisdictions (EU) where it would fall into the 'personal' category. (See discussion below.)

As to the question of whether PI can cover communications meta-data, like an IP address or other temporary or permanent device identifiers, the European usage which accepts that IP addresses can be PD contrasts sharply to the approach taken in the United States under laws such as COPPA where, a decade ago, the Federal Trade Commission (FTC) considered whether to classify even static IP addresses as personal information, but ultimately rejected the idea out of concern that it would unnecessarily increase the scope of the law.[97]

In the past few years, the FTC began however to suggest that IP addresses should be considered PII for the same reasons as their European counterparts. Indeed in a recent consent decree, the FTC included within the definition of 'non-public, individually-identifiable information' an 'IP address (or other

---

95 Mayer-Schönberger, V., 'No Choice: Trans-Atlantic Information Privacy Legislation and Rational Choice Theory' (1999) *George Washington Law Review* 67.

96 See Schwartz, P. and Solove, D., 'Reconciling Personal Information in-the United States and European Union' (2014) *California Law Review* 877–916, 880.

97 Baker, W. and Matyjaszewski, A., 'The changing meaning of "personal data"' (2011) 11(3) *The Privacy Advisor*, International Association of Privacy Professionals, p. 18, <https://iapp.org/media/pdf/publications/advisor04_11_print.pdf>.

"persistent identifier")'. The HIPAA Privacy Rule also treats IP addresses as a form of 'protected health information' by listing them as a type of data that must be removed from personal health information for de-identification purposes.[98]

5. CONCLUDING REMARKS

In this chapter we have examined how differing definitions of 'personal information' or its equivalent are problematic for transborder data flows, and in particular for Big Data analytics. At first glance it may not be obvious to the reader, and certainly to a non-expert in the field, how differing definitions of personal information and their effects on Big Data analytics relate to challenges to democracy. The answer is simple yet also complex. Big Data shapes democracy. Big Data is about privacy, data protection, security, freedom of expression, and civil liberties and protected human rights in general. One way to prevent some misuses of Big Data and to improve the protection of personal information is through de-identification. Yet de-identification is not required in many instances, or the transborder nature of data sharing complicates the field. When is de-identified required? What must be de-identified? Is this effective in protecting privacy? How are other human rights protected, such as the right not to be discriminated against and the right to freedom of expression (and in some jurisdictions the right of anonymous speech)? These notions are all intertwined. This chapter has not sought to answer these questions but has pursued, the modest aim of illustrating the complexities alone that exist in interpreting personal information across borders.

We also noted how Council of Europe's Convention 108 on data protection has become a *de facto* international standard for trans border data protection issues. EU courts and governing bodies continue to push the boundaries of the trade-off between gains to be made from Open Data and Big Data on the one hand, and privacy and data protection risks on the other, as seen in the decision of *Schrems* with its global impact on transnational data flow policies. Questions about identifiability and when information becomes 'personal' feature at the core of these regulatory developments, and extend into far-flung jurisdictions like the US and Australia.

Significant work remains to be done on the implications of Big Data including those on privacy issues beyond identification, on discrimination, on the impact on other civil liberties such as freedom of expression and association, and more. The next step is for further public empirical studies on these various risks, including the part played by the uncertainties around identification explored in this chapter.

---

[98] McBride, S. et al., 'Privacy and Security in a Ubiquitous Health Information Technology World', in McBride, S. and Tietze, M. (eds.), *Nursing Informatics for the Advanced Practice Nurse*, Springer, New York 2016, p. 350.

19. BLENDING THE PRACTICES OF PRIVACY AND INFORMATION SECURITY TO NAVIGATE CONTEMPORARY DATA PROTECTION CHALLENGES

Stephen Wilson*

1. INTRODUCTION

The relationship between European privacy regulators and predominantly American technology businesses can seem increasingly fraught. A string of adverse (and sometimes counter intuitive) privacy findings against digital businesses – including the 'Right to be Forgotten', and bans on biometric-powered photo tag suggestions – have left some wondering if privacy and IT are fundamentally at odds. Technologists may be confused by these regulatory developments, and as a result, uncertain about their professional role in privacy management.

Several efforts are underway to improve technologists' contribution to privacy. Most prominent is the Privacy by Design movement (PbD). A newer discipline of 'privacy engineering' is also striving to emerge. Yet a wide gap still separates the worlds of data privacy regulation and systems design. Privacy is still not often framed in a way that engineers can relate to. Instead, PbD's generalisations overlook essential differences between security and privacy, and at the same time, fail to pick up on substantive common ground, like the 'Need to Know' and the principle of Least Privilege.

There appears to be a systematic shortfall in the understanding that technologists and engineers collectively have of information privacy. IT professionals routinely receive privacy training now, yet time and time again, technologists seem to misinterpret basic privacy principles, for example by exploiting personal information found in the 'public domain' as if data privacy

* Constellation Research. E-mail: swilson@lockstep.com.au.

principles do not apply there,[1] or by creating personal information through Big Data processes, evidently with little or no restraint.[2]

Engaging technologists in privacy is exacerbated by the many mixed messages which circulate about privacy, its relative importance, and purported social trends towards promiscuity or 'publicness'.[3] For decades, mass media headlines regularly announce the death of privacy.[4] When US legal scholars Samuel Warren and Louis Brandeis developed some of the world's first privacy jurisprudence in the 1880s, the social fabric was under threat from the new technologies of photography and the telegraph. In time, computers became the big concern. The cover of *Newsweek* magazine on 27 July 1970 featured a cartoon couple cowered by mainframe computers and communications technology, under the urgent upper case headline, '*IS PRIVACY DEAD?*'.[5] Of course it's a rhetorical question. And after a hundred years, the answer is still no.

This chapter reviews how engineers tend collectively to regard privacy and explores how to make privacy more accessible to technologists. As a result, difficult privacy territory like social networking and Big Data may become clearer to non-lawyers, and the trans-Atlantic compliance challenges might yield to data protection designs that are more fundamentally compatible across the digital ethos of Silicon Valley and the privacy activism of Europe.

2. WHAT ENGINEERS UNDERSTAND ABOUT PRIVACY

Privacy is contentious today. There are legitimate debates about whether the information age has brought real changes to privacy norms or not. Regardless, with so much personal information leaking through breaches, accidents, or digital business practices, it's often said that 'the genie is out of the bottle', meaning privacy has become hopeless. Yet in Europe and many jurisdictions,[6]

[1] See 'Google's wifi misadventure, and the gulf between IT and Privacy', <http://lockstep.com.au/library/privacy/googles-wifi-misadventure-and>.

[2] See 'What stops Target telling you're pregnant?', <http://lockstep.com.au/blog/2012/03/07/target-tells-youre-pregnant>.

[3] J. Jarvis, *Public Parts*, Simon & Schuster, New York 2011.

[4] See for example 'Privacy is dead, tech evangelist tells entrepreneurs', *InDaily*, 14 June 2016, <http://indaily.com.au/news/business/2016/06/14/privacy-is-dead-tech-evangelist-tells-entrepreneurs>; 'Privacy Is Dead: What You Still Can Do to Protect Yourself', *The Huffington Post*, 27 August 2015, <http://www.huffingtonpost.com/adam-levin/privacy-is-dead-what-you_b_8047530.html>; and 'Privacy is dead, says Mark Zuckerberg, even for his unborn daughter', *Digital Trends*, 8 October 2015, <http://www.digitaltrends.com/social-media/mark-zuckerberg-daughter-vr>.

[5] R. Boeth, 'The Assault on Privacy', *Newsweek*, 27 July 1970.

[6] G. Greenleaf, 'Sheherezade and the 101 Data Privacy Laws: Origins, Significance and Global Trajectories' (2014) *J.L. Inf. & Sci.* 23, 4.

privacy rights attach to Personal Information no matter where it comes from. The threshold for data being counted as Personal Information (or equivalently in the US, 'Personally Identifiable Information') is low: any data about a person whose identity is readily apparent constitutes Personal Information in most places, regardless of where or how it originated, and without any reference to who might be said to 'own' the data (see section 3.2 below). This is not obvious to engineers without legal training, who have formed a more casual understanding of what 'private' means. So it may strike them as paradoxical that the terms 'public' and 'private' don't even figure in laws like Australia's Privacy Act.

Probably the most distracting message for engineers is the well-intended suggestion 'Privacy is not a Technology Issue'. In 2000, IBM chair Lou Gerstner was one of the first high-profile technologists to isolate privacy as a policy issue.[7] The same trope (that such-and-such 'is not a technology issue') is widespread in online discourse. It usually means that multiple disciplines must be brought to bear on certain complex outcomes, such as safety, security or privacy. Unfortunately, engineers can take it to mean that privacy is covered by other departments, such as legal, and has nothing to do with technology at all.

In fact all of our traditional privacy principles are impacted by system design decisions and practices, and are therefore apt for engagement by information technologists. For instance, IT professionals are liable to think of 'collection' as a direct activity that solicits Personal Information, whereas under technology-neutral privacy principles, indirect collection of identifiable audit logs or database backups should also count. This and many other subtle interactions between security and privacy are discussed by Wilson.[8]

Yet the most damaging thing that technologists hear about privacy could be the cynical idea that 'Technology outpaces the Law'. While we should not underestimate how cyberspace will affect society and its many laws borne in earlier ages, in practical day-to-day terms it is the law that challenges technology, not the other way round. The claim that the law cannot keep up with technology is often a rhetorical device[9] used to embolden developers and entrepreneurs. New technologies can make it easier to break old laws, but the legal principles in

---

7 See 'IBM Names Harriet P. Pearson as Chief Privacy Officer', IBM press release, 29 November 2000, <https://www-03.ibm.com/press/us/en/pressrelease/1464.wss>. Gerstner said: 'At its core, privacy is not a technology issue. It is a policy issue. And the policy framework that's needed here must involve the information technology industry, the private sector in general and public officials'. He was right. Privacy is less about what we do with information than *what we don't do*. Technology alone can't often prevent the re-use or over-use of personal data, and we always need backup rules and procedures that continue to protect people if and when the technology fails.

8 S. Wilson, 'Mapping privacy requirements onto the IT function' (2003) 10(1) *Privacy Law & Policy Reporter*.

9 L.B. Moses, University of New South Wales (personal communication, 2014).

most cases still stand. If privacy is the fundamental 'right to be let alone',[10] then there is nothing intrinsic to technology that supersedes that right. It turns out that technology-neutral privacy laws framed over 30 years ago[11] are powerful against very modern trespasses, like wi-fi snooping by Google[12] and over-zealous use of biometrics by Facebook.[13] So technology in general might only outpace policing.

3. REORIENTATING HOW ENGINEERS THINK ABOUT PRIVACY

One of the leading efforts to inculcate privacy into engineering practice has been the 'Privacy by Design' movement. 'PbD', as it is commonly known, is a set of guidelines that originated in the 1990s with the then privacy commissioner of Ontario, Ann Cavoukian. The movement sets out to embed privacy 'into the design specifications of technologies, business practices, and physical infrastructures'.[14] PbD is basically the same good idea as building in security, or building in quality, because to retrofit these things too late in the design lifecycle leads to higher costs and disappointing outcomes.

Privacy by Design attempts to orientate technologists to privacy with a set of simple callings:

1. Proactive not Reactive; Preventative not Remedial
2. Privacy as the Default Setting
3. Privacy Embedded into Design
4. Full Functionality – Positive-Sum, not Zero-Sum
5. End-to-End Security – Full Lifecycle Protection
6. Visibility and Transparency – Keep it Open
7. Respect for User Privacy – Keep it User-Centric.[15]

---

10 S. Warren and L. Brandeis, 'The right to privacy' (1890) *Harvard Law Review* 193–220.

11 Organisation for Economic Cooperation and Development, 'Privacy Principles' (1980), <http://oecdprivacy.org>.

12 Office of the Australian Information Commissioner, 'Google Street View Wi-Fi Collection: Statement from Australian Privacy Commissioner, Timothy Pilgrim', 7 August 2012, <https://www.oaic.gov.au/media-and-speeches/statements/google-street-view-wi-fi-collection>.

13 HmbBfDI Hamburg Commissioner for Data Protection and Freedom of Information, 'Proceedings against Facebook resumed' (2012), <https://www.datenschutz-hamburg.de/fileadmin/user_upload/documents/PressRelease-2012-08-15-Facebook_Proceedings.pdf>.

14 See <https://www.ipc.on.ca/english/Privacy/Introduction-to-PbD>.

15 A. Cavoukian, *Privacy by Design – The 7 Foundational Principles*, Information and Privacy Commissioner of Ontario, Toronto 2011, <https://www.ipc.on.ca/english/Privacy/Introduction-to-PbD>.

PbD is a well-meaning effort, and yet its language comes from a different culture to engineering. The PbD maxims rework classic privacy principles without adding much to the work of designers.

The most problematic aspect of Privacy by Design is its idealism. PbD responds to the cynicism of some national security zealots who see privacy as outdated[16] with the pat assertion that privacy should be a 'positive sum' game. But privacy is actually full of contradictions and competing interests, and we need to be more alert to this. The Collection Limitation principle for example can contradict the security or legal instinct to always retain as much data as possible, in case it proves useful one day. Disclosure Limitation can conflict with usability, because Personal Information may be siloed and less freely available to other applications. And above all, Use Limitation can restrict the revenue opportunities that digital entrepreneurs might otherwise see in all the raw data they are privileged to have gathered. Instead of naïvely asserting that privacy can be maximised along with any other system objective, it is better that engineers be aware of the trade-offs that privacy can entail, and that they be equipped to deal with real world compromises implied by privacy just as they do with other design requirements. Privacy can take its place in engineering along with all the other real world considerations that need to be carefully weighed, including cost, usability, efficiency, profitability, and security.

Given that engineering has a lot to do with precision, the best way to start bridging the gap between law and technology is with technicalities, not the generalisations of PbD. Too often, casual intuitions about privacy in daily experience are carried over into the way we approach information systems. We should seek to correct instances where informal ideas lead to misunderstandings in how engineers tackle privacy. The following sections highlight some of these.

3.1. PRIVACY IS NOT SECRECY

There is a preoccupation at large with anonymity, which infects how engineers approach privacy. For example, the grassroots 'CryptoParty' movement[17] is organised around a heady belief that privacy means hiding from the establishment. CryptoParties spread a message of resistance, and teach participants how to use tools like the *Tor* private browser and the *PGP* encryption application.

Most so-called 'Privacy Enhancing Technologies' (PETs) are really more about secrecy. Engineers most often look to implement privacy in their work through encryption and access control – both being methods that prevent

---

16 See the comment by NSA security consultant Ed Giorgio that 'privacy and security are a zero-sum game' (L. Wright, 'The Spymaster', *The New Yorker*, 21 January 2008).

17 See <http://www.cryptoparty.in>.

information from being accessed by unauthorised persons. However, encryption is not compatible with mainstream life online, for we rarely know in advance all the parties that we wish to have access to our data. If we wish to shop on the web, use a credit card, tweet, share photos or hang out on Google, we simply cannot encrypt everything; we need to expose a great deal of information, and instead of controlling access on a fine-grained basis, we need those who receive information to treat it with restraint. Thus privacy needs to be appreciated as the protection required when our affairs are *not secret*.

3.2. DEFINING PERSONAL INFORMATION

In engineering, a great deal hinges on the definitions. In data privacy around the world, a reasonably consistent definition of Personal Information or Personal Data is found. In the United Kingdom, Personal Data is 'data which relate to a living individual who can be identified'.[18] In Germany, Personal Information is 'any information concerning the personal or material circumstances of an identified or identifiable individual'.[19] In Australia, Personal Information is 'information or an opinion about an identified individual, or an individual who is reasonably identifiable'.[20]

In the United States, the term *Personally Identifiable Information* (PII) is preferred but has a similar definition to the terms above; for example, the US federal government uses PII to mean:

> information that can be used to distinguish or trace an individual's identity, either alone or when combined with other personal or identifying information that is linked or linkable to a specific individual.[21]

Thus in much of Europe, the USA and elsewhere, data can constitute *Personal Information* if it is inherently identifiable, or alternatively, if it can be *combined* with any other reasonably available data to cause the person concerned to be identified. That is, the data *fragments* can be regarded as personal even if a larger sum of information is required to achieve identification. The definitions are all about the prospects of identification occurring.

Engineers can be surprised by the implication that so much routine operational data counts as Personal Information, such as event logs and analytics. They also need to know that Personal Data need only be *identifiable* and not uniquely

[18] See <https://ico.org.uk/for-organisations/guide-to-data-protection/key-definitions>.
[19] See <https://clientsites.linklaters.com/Clients/dataprotected/Pages/Germany.aspx>.
[20] See <https://www.oaic.gov.au/privacy-law/privacy-act>.
[21] US General Services Administration, <http://www.gsa.gov/portal/content/104256>.

identifying. Thus IP addresses are widely treated as Personal Information.[22] The precautionary definition makes good sense from a security perspective; engineers usually appreciate that if identifiable data merits protection, steps should be taken before the data is actually identified.

3.3. INDIRECT COLLECTION

Technology-neutral privacy legislation does not specifically define the term 'collection'. So while collection might be associated intuitively with forms and questionnaires, we need to interpret the regulations more broadly. 'Collect' is not necessarily a *directive* verb, so *collection* can be said to have occurred, sometimes passively, *whenever Personal Information appears in an IT system*. Therefore the creation or synthesis of new Personal Information counts as a form of indirect collection. And so if data analysis (or Big Data; see below) can deliver brand new insights about identifiable people, like the fact a shopper may be pregnant,[23] then those insights merit more or less the same protections under privacy law as they would had the shopper filled out a form expressly declaring she is pregnant. Likewise, if automatic facial recognition (such as that of Facebook's *tag suggestions* feature) leads to names being attached to previously anonymous photos in databases, then that new Personal Information must be said to have been *collected*, thereby requiring the collector to adhere to applicable privacy principles.[24]

This is what would have been expected when data privacy principles were first framed decades ago.[25] If an organisation holds Personal Information, then, absent specific consent to the contrary from the individuals concerned, the organisation should hold as little PI as possible, confine itself to PI needed for an express purpose, refrain from re-purposing PI, and let individuals know what PI is held about them.

These principles ought to apply regardless of how the organisation came to have the Personal Information; that is, whether the collection was direct or indirect. Even data obtained from the 'public domain' such as wi-fi transmissions should be subject to privacy protections. As noted, the qualifiers 'public' and 'private' do not operate in Australia's Privacy Act. As we shall see, many new technologies which have emerged long after traditional privacy laws, provide

---

22 W. Baker and A. Matyjaszewski. 'The changing meaning of "personal data"' (2011) 11(3) *The Privacy Advisor*, International Association of Privacy Professionals.

23 C. Duhigg, 'How Companies Learn Your Secrets', *New York Times*, 16 February 2012.

24 S. Wilson and A. Johnston, 'Facebook's Challenge to the Collection Limitation Principle', *Encyclopedia of Social Network Analysis and Mining*, Springer, 2014.

25 OECD, above n. 11.

new ways for Personal Information to be collected or created, but these new information pathways do not of themselves obsolete the old privacy principles.

4. BIG DATA AND PRIVACY

The term 'Big Privacy' has been coined to emphasise that a special response may be needed to address the impact of Big Data. Cavoukian and Reed, two prominent advocates, have described 'Big Privacy' as 'Privacy by Design writ large, i.e the application of the seven principles of Privacy by Design, not only to individual organisations, applications, or contexts, but to entire networks, value chains, and ecosystems'.[26] But there must be more to Big Data privacy than simply redoubling our efforts. After all, regular privacy protections already address 'entire networks, value chains, and ecosystems'.

Big Data and the 'Internet of Things' challenge a particular philosophy in privacy that users should be granted 'control' over 'their' data. Most Personal Information today is probably collected behind our backs by complex web services, well beyond any practicable user control. The unwitnessed collection of PI will be hugely exacerbated by the explosion of direct collection points (such as wearable computers, network-connected devices, 'smart' appliances, and sensors spread throughout the built environment). Furthermore, Big Data is capable of creating fresh PI from mundane raw data in non-obvious ways. Thus it seems increasingly unlikely that individuals can even grasp what information is being collected about them, let alone meaningfully control it.

Big Data also exposes the limitations of 'ownership' as a privacy mechanism. Innovators and entrepreneurs who have invested so heavily in these new technologies will understandably claim to own the outputs of their algorithms, and to me they do have a reasonable case. But nowhere does the term 'ownership' appear in Australia's Privacy Act for example.[27] Data privacy applies to all identifiable information, irrespective of who 'owns' it. And in recognition of the way that Big Data can produce fresh Personal Information, the Australian Privacy Commissioner has started referring to 'collection by generation'.[28]

---

26 A. Cavoukian and D. Reed, *Big Privacy: Bridging Big Data and the Personal Data Ecosystem through Privacy by Design*, Information and Privacy Commissioner of Ontario, 2013, <https://www.ipc.on.ca/site_documents/PbDBook-From-Rhetoric-to-Reality-ch3.pdf> accessed 28.03.2016.

27 Privacy Amendment (Enhancing Privacy Protection) Act (2012), Commonwealth of Australia.

28 See 'Guide to big data and the Australian Privacy Principles Consultation Draft', May 2016, <https://www.oaic.gov.au/resources/engage-with-us/consultations/guide-to-big-data-and-the-australian-privacy-principles/consultation-draft-guide-to-big-data-and-the-australian-privacy-principles.pdf>.

The realisation that synthetic Personal Information is subject to privacy provides clearer understanding of many current controversies. While on their face, some European privacy rulings may take engineers by surprise (especially in America), many of these cases may be better understood as logical applications of privacy regulations to subtle information flows, this leading to improved trans-Atlantic understanding. Some cases follow.

4.1. 'DNA HACKING'

In 2012, researchers at MIT's Whitehead Institute for Biomedical Research used new statistical techniques to work out the names of anonymous DNA donors whose genomes had been published in the 1000 Genomes Project.[29] The trick was to take named DNA samples from public online genealogy databases and look for matching sequences of genes, to measure the probability that genes had come from identified ancestors. This work was ostensibly a well-meaning proof of re-identification, and it is indeed important to test the limits of ambitious claims that data can be anonymised (such promises lie at the heart of genomics projects and the UK National Health Service's ambitions to open electronic medical record systems to researchers). And yet the de-identification demonstration was itself a technical violation of the privacy of 1000 Genomes Project volunteers.

The scientists and engineers at the Whitehead Institute evidently did not see that recording a person's name against what had been anonymous data represents a fresh collection of Personal Information. The concept of 'collection by creation' is coming into explicit use.[30] Even if the consent form signed for the original DNA donation disclaims the possibility of absolute anonymity, if a third party does re-identify the donor, then they are collecting Personal Information of the donor, albeit indirectly. The new collection logically requires its own consent; the original disclaimer does not apply when third parties take data and process it beyond the original purpose for collection. De-identification demonstrations should probably be subjected to ethics approval, just as they would if they were taking information directly from the people concerned.

American genetics researchers conducting this sort of work across the Atlantic, or in any international context, should review European data collection

---

29 J. Bohannon, 'Genealogy databases enable naming of anonymous DNA donor' (2013) 339(6117) *Science* 262.

30 Australian privacy regulators have started referring to this as 'collection by creation'; see the May 2016 consultation draft document 'Guide to big data and the Australian Privacy Principles', <https://www.oaic.gov.au/resources/engage-with-us/consultations/guide-to-big-data-and-the-australian-privacy-principles/consultation-draft-guide-to-big-data-and-the-australian-privacy-principles.pdf>.

principles, and consider for themselves the implications of identifying DNA samples by synthetic means.

4.2. THE RIGHT TO BE FORGOTTEN

The Right to be Forgotten (RTBF) is a somewhat unfortunate misnomer for a data control measure decided recently by the European Court of Justice.[31] RTBF creates a mechanism by which individuals who feel that particular old search results are inaccurate and unjust can apply to search engine operators to have those results removed (or delisted) from name-search results. There is no absolute right to have offending searches blocked; each application is reviewed on its merits. Thus the new rule does not seek to censor the past as some have claimed[32] but rather to restore some of its natural distance.

Search algorithms are no simple window into an objective past. Rather, they aggregate material from an immense public matrix, and sort and prioritise it according to each user's history as well as the search provider's own business priorities. Search results differ markedly across users, from one month to the next, and from place to place. This variability is a result of profiling, because search algorithms actually represent an effort by Internet companies whose main business is to sell advertising, to calculate what users are truly interested in. Search is a form of machine learning; over time, the accuracy of searches is improved globally but also locally, as feedback is collected about how individuals respond to results. Thus web search allows businesses like Google to get to know us better. As such, search algorithms are massive generators and collectors of synthetic Personal Information, and should be subject to data privacy laws. The Right to be Forgotten can be seen to as a straightforward application of those laws in Europe. If a piece of Personal Information served up by the search algorithm is inaccurate or irrelevant, then the algorithm is in conflict with the Collection Limitation and Data Quality Principles.

Search should be seen not as some passive reproduction of matters in the 'public domain' but a special type of Big Data product. If today's search algorithms can reveal Personal Information that until now has been effectively impossible to find, then big information companies should play a part in helping to temper the unintended privacy consequences.

---

31 M. Reicherts, 'The right to be forgotten and the EU data protection reform: Why we must see through a distorted debate and adopt strong new rules soon', European Commission (2014), <http://europa.eu/rapid/press-release_SPEECH-14-568_en.htm>.

32 See 'Wikipedia founder: EU's Right to be Forgotten is "deeply immoral"', *Daily Telegraph*, 6 August 2014, <http://www.telegraph.co.uk/technology/wikipedia/11015901/EU-ruling-on-link-removal-deeply-immoral-says-Wikipedia-founder.html>.

4.3. SECURITY MEETS PRIVACY

Security and privacy are awkward bedfellows. People often say they're different but as discussed, there is a widespread misconception that privacy means secrecy, and in turn, engineers are liable to restrict their privacy thinking to encryption as a means to hide Personal Information, rather than constrain the way it flows according to privacy principles.

A broader privacy perspective, beyond secrecy, may be engendered in security professionals by appealing to a number of traits in common between privacy and security practices. If these were better appreciated, we should be able to more firmly locate technological accountability for privacy within organisations, and we should see more effective interdisciplinary collaboration on privacy.

1. Conventional wisdom holds there is no such thing as perfect security; with finite resources, any real world information system may one day fail. Similarly, privacy is never perfect. If we get a piece of privacy engineering wrong, it is not the end of the world; there is always room for continuous improvement. And because privacy is more about restraint than secrecy, there are grounds for optimism in the face of any breach. For instance, Personal Information released into the public domain or into the wrong hands still enjoys certain legal protections, at least in the 100 or more countries with data protection laws.[33] Therefore engineers can get over the widespread fatalism that it is too late to implement privacy controls.
2. Nothing is ever certain, in neither technology nor the law. Technologists often demand certainty in the interpretation of privacy laws, and can be frustrated by the judgement calls that appear in the definitions of Personal Information. And yet engineers and security professionals are at home with probabilities. Uncertainty is what risk management is all about. Privacy and security can be usefully joined by treating problems like re-identification as information system risks. As shown by de-identification demonstrations, anonymity is fragile. But it is not actually essential to privacy. We can treat re-identification as a risk, seek to estimate its likelihood, and put reasonable safeguards in place to mitigate it.
3. Security professionals know all too well the Principle of Least Privilege; namely that users and computer modules should only have access to the information and resources necessary for their legitimate purposes. Privacy practitioners will recognise this as the intellectual cousin of the Use and Disclosure Principles. The lay person likely knows this as the 'Right to Know'. This principle is not absolute but requires that good judgement be

---

33 Greenleaf, above n. 6.

exercised in the way that information is allowed to flow to those who need it. Thus privacy and security have this in common: information needs to be shared to be useful, but there must be limits.

4. Excessive personal information is fast becoming a liability for many businesses, as data breaches escalate. For instance, when the US Office of Personnel Management was attacked in June 2015, it was found that employment and family records going back 15 years were stolen.[34] It is doubtful that such old data really had to be kept online; had it been archived, the impact of the breach would have hugely reduced. Here's a clear case where privacy and security interests are aligned.

5. CONCLUSION: RULES TO ENGINEER BY

We tend to sugar-coat privacy. Advocates try to reassure harried managers that 'privacy is good for business' but the same sort of slogan was ineffective in connection with the quality movement in the 1990s. In truth, what's good for business is peculiar to each business. It is plainly the case that some businesses thrive without paying much attention to privacy, or even by mocking it.

Let's not shrink from the reality that privacy creates tensions with other objectives of complex information systems. Engineering is all about resolving competing requirements. If we are serious about 'Privacy by Design' and 'Privacy Engineering', we need to acknowledge the inherent tensions, and equip real designers with the tools and the understanding to optimise privacy alongside all the other complexities in modern information systems.

A better appreciation of the definition of Personal Information and of technology-neutral data privacy rules should help to at least demystify European privacy rulings on matters such as facial recognition and the Right to be Forgotten. Trans-Atlantic data protection relationships at the practical engineering level can improve when there is common understanding. The treatment of privacy can then be lifted from a defensive compliance exercise, to a properly balanced discussion of what each organisation is seeking to get out of the data it has at its disposal.

---

34 See 'Hacking of Government Computers Exposed 21.5 Million People', *New York Times*, 9 July 2015, <http://www.nytimes.com/2015/07/10/us/office-of-personnel-management-hackers-got-data-of-millions.html>.

20. IT'S ALL ABOUT DESIGN

An Ethical Analysis of Personal Data Markets*

Sarah Spiekermann**

Personal data is a core asset in the digital economy. It is an enabler of many online business models[1] and is traded as a commodity on data markets. Every day a company like BlueKai states to run over 75 million auctions of personal profiles stemming from over 750 million users worldwide. Personal data collection and trading has become so common that Meglena Kuneva, the former European Commissioner for Consumer Protection, described personal data as 'the new oil' in the digital economy.

However, personal data markets are not fully legitimised and sustainable in their current form, for various reasons: one is that people whose data assets are being traded are largely excluded from the market: 'Consumer ignorance leads to a data market in which one set of parties does not even know that negotiation is taking place.'[2] Second, personal information markets risk undermining peoples' privacy and hence harm a legal right. To date many people are still unaware of the degree of erosion of their privacy. The privacy threat is not as present to ordinary users as some privacy scholars might think.[3] However, this situation is changing. Whistle-blowers like Edward Snowden and others help making people aware of the threatening practices of the data world. Surveys suggest that a rising share of people become more concerned over time.[4]

---

* This chapter, originally written for this volume, has been subsequently re-printed in: Wolfie Chirstl and Sarah Spiekermann, *Networks of Control – A Report on Corporate Surveillance, Digital Tracking, Big Data & Privacy*, Facultas Verlag, Wien, September 2016 <http://crackedlabs.org/en/networksofcontrol>.

** Institute for Management Information Systems, Vienna University of Economics and Business (WU), Vienna, Austria. E-mail: sspieker@wu.ac.at.

1 Anderson, C., *Free – The Future of Radical Price*, Random House Business Books, London 2009.

2 Schwartz, P.M., 'Property, Privacy, and Personal Data' (2004) 117(7) *Harvard Law Review* 2078.

3 Oetzel, M.C., and Gonja, T., 'The Online Privacy Paradox: A Social Representations Perspective,' *Human Factors in Computing Systems*, ACM, Vancouver, Canada, pp. 2107–2112.

4 Fujitsu, 'Personal data in the cloud: A global survery of consumer attitudes', Tokyo 2010.

In addition to these legal and user-related challenges around personal data markets, some economic reason speaks against them in their current design. First, the quality of data assets is often too poor. Many companies have to live on what they can spy on rather than accessing high-quality and timely user data. Second, data-driven business models are politically and ethically unstable leading to high legal risks and costs. And third, the potential damage done to a brand can be considerable, when true data handling practices come to light.

Against the background of these challenges, the typical European answer is to pass new legislation to better protect citizens. And in fact, the EU has introduced a new General Data Protection Regulation, the GDPR, which was published in April 2016, requiring companies to considerably overhaul their data collection and processing operations. In the United States, scholars have started a debate whether personal data might be considered as a kind of property so that citizens have more rights in the trade of their data.[5] And the White House published a Bill of Privacy Rights that goes beyond the original Fair Information Practices often considered as a privacy guideline in the US.[6]

Whenever such regulatory efforts are undertaken, ethical arguments are playing a core role justifying protection efforts and arguments. For instance, privacy is often related to dignity or free speech. Yet, at the same time, and to my best knowledge, no systematic ethical analysis of personal data markets exists. This is a pity, because ethical theory allows for a very systematic, holistic and critical analysis of personal data markets. It allows recommendations to be derived for personal data market design. It also makes clear that the protection of personal data is not only a matter of privacy protection, but also one of knowledge and power asymmetries, of quality in human relationships, of personal duty as well as humanity's long-term ability to flourish. Ethical analysis is very powerful for helping to understand the implications of personal data markets.

Philosophy has equipped us with various approaches to take wise and good decisions. I propose three of them in particular as worthwhile applying to personal data markets: the Utilitarian calculus, which is the original philosophy underlying modern economics;[7] the Kantian duty perspective, which has been a cornerstone for what we historically call the Enlightenment;[8] and finally Virtue

---

5 Samuelson, P., 'Privacy as Intellectual Property?' (2000) 52 *Stanford Law Review* 1125–1173; Schwartz, above n. 2.

6 The White House, 'Consumer Data Privacy in a Networked World: A Framework for Protecting Privacy and Promoting Innovation in a Global Digital Economy', Washington DC 2012.

7 Mill, J.S., 'Utilitarianism' (1863) in A. Ryan (ed.), *Utilitarianism and Other Essays*, Penguin, London 1987.

8 Kant, I., *An Answer to the Question: 'What Is Enlightenment?'* (1784), Penguin, London 2009.

Ethics, an approach to life that originates in Aristotle's thinking about human flourishing and has seen considerable revival over the past 30 years.[9]

1. A SHORT UTILITARIAN REFLECTION ON PERSONAL DATA MARKETS

The Utilitarian calculus, which originates in works by John Stuart Mill, is an attempt to weigh the beneficial and harmful consequences of an artefact.[10] Utilitarian thinking focuses our analysis on the *market* for personal data. It extracts its positive and negative effects on long-term value generation for organisations, people, society and investors.

1.1. FINANCIAL BENEFITS

From a Utilitarian perspective, monetary value is considered a benefit. Investors and organisations collecting personal data can monetise it and certainly have a 'plus' on their Utilitarian balance sheet. Yet, as game theory has shown for decades, purely one-sided benefits of players are normally perceived as unfair on markets where supply and demand need to meet sustainably.[11] And so, if companies or data brokers continue leveraging the benefits of personal data trading without data subjects' active share in the profits, they might see a destabilisation of their business in the medium or long term. Behavioural economics clearly suggests that people or 'data subjects' would need to adequately profit from personal data markets as well.

1.2. KNOWLEDGE AND POWER

If we can assume satisfactory profit sharing mechanisms are found at some point, then on economic grounds personal data markets appear quite advantageous. Yet, to be rational, Utilitarianism embeds a more holistic decision spectrum than just financial benefits. So let's take another important value created in personal data markets, which is likely to be impacted by personal data markets: knowledge extractable from Big Data. So far, the knowledge created about people's behaviour is asymmetrical. In our current personal data market

---

9 MacIntyre, A., *After Virtue: A Study in Moral Theory*, 2nd ed., University of Notre Dame Press, Notre Dame, IN 1984.

10 Mill, above n. 7.

11 Tisserand, J.-C., 'Ultimatum game: A meta-analysis of the past three decades of experimental research' (2014) *Proceedings of International Academic Conferences*, International Institute of Social and Economic Sciences.

design, knowledge has become a powerful value from which only a few service monopolies benefit; for instance data brokers like Acxiom, BlueKai, and large data collectors, such as Google, Apple or Facebook. Hence, the social 'utility points' potentially created through Big Data knowledge is counterbalanced by the drawback of power asymmetries.

Power asymmetries breed distrust and undermine cooperation. In personal data markets they are observable in two forms: between economies, and between corporates and people. First, most European economies don't have powerful data brokers. Their legal frameworks have not allowed for the rise of this phenomenon. As a result, they don't benefit from a potential knowledge aggregation inherent in personal data markets. The result is a rising political tension between the US and EU on this matter. Secondly, people don't know how much corporates know about them. People don't learn anything about themselves from the knowledge that others hold about them, and are, in addition, exposed to potential manipulation and economic disadvantages.[12] So, summing up, the utility created through personal data markets' knowledge potential is neutralised (or even negatively outweighed) by power asymmetries and their consequences.

Political and technical design could change this calculus! If it was possible to build personal data markets as symmetrical knowledge structures, in which people got full insight into what companies know about them, societies might become more knowledgeable and thoughtful. What would happen if Facebook was willing to give me feedback on the entire data pool they hold about me, telling me not only about the raw data they have, but also what my data tells them about me. Who am I am psychologically, emotionally as well as socially according to their current analytical models? The learning I might have from this insight could be highly beneficial for me as an individual. I might grow and become more humble upon such honest feedback. However, I might also be so shocked about myself that I would like to ensure nobody knows about all of this except me. I might demand choice and control over my data as a result. As a European I might also prefer to have my data stored and processed in Europe. Taken together: If the political and technical design of personal data markets assured two-sided knowledge and symmetry of power, including the granting of exit and control rights, then 'knowledge-creation' could be seen as a heavy positive on the Utilitarian balance sheet.

1.3. BELONGINGNESS AND QUALITY OF HUMAN RELATIONS

Knowledge, power and money are not all we care about. Other crucial values for consideration in a Utilitarian calculus are the importance of honest and free

12 Christl, W., 'Kommerzielle Digitale Überwachung im Alltag', Cracked Labs – Institut für Kritische Digitale Kultur, Vienna 2014.

communication between humans and our need for belongingness. Some parts of this belongingness can be nourished through our exchanges with others online. How do current data markets play into this dimension?

The digital realm has a huge potential for honest communication. Scientists talk about a 'disinhibition effect' online.[13] People tend to be more willing to say what they think online and overcome their possible shyness. Except for excesses of disinhibition (i.e. trolling behaviour), people's opening-up behaviour can be considered as a positive side of the Web. It can add to people's inner peace, freedom and chances to find friends. In virtual worlds for instance it has been recognised that sometime friendships develop which are more honest and straightforward from the start.[14] However, currently, data markets are designed such that they systematically monetise our personal exchanges and sell and analyse our relational data. Being in a virtual world I can never be sure that my behaviour and my discussions there with others will not be analysed, monitored, sold or added to a negative profile. As a result, the darker or idiosyncratic part of my identity cannot be expressed or strive online. I hold myself back. Facebook studies conducted at WU Vienna have shown that over 90 per cent of the users on the social network 'think twice' before they post something about themselves.[15]

Holding oneself back in the way it is done today may just be the start. As personal data markets advance and people become more aware of being watched or of their communication potentially being used against them, it might be that strategic communication could become the norm online. Even more so, if personal data markets allowed people to make money on their data and their online conversations, communication could become strongly calculus-driven. Already today, people engage in a kind of 'impression management' online. Trying to trick machines into paying higher prices for keywords used in artificial communication online might seem far-fetched these days, but cannot be excluded as a potential scenario. If this happened, then the human relationships involved in this online communication could seriously suffer as a result.

Such negative effects could be mitigated through good technical design. If we ensured truly private rooms in the digital realm where our data was neither monitored nor sold, but instead encrypted, anonymised and deleted (when no longer useful to the individual), then we could have more honest and deliberate communication online; potentially building very truthful relationships on digital platforms. The digital realm could contribute to our freedom and autonomy where needed.

---

13 Suler, J., 'The Online Disinhibition Effect' (2004) 7(3) *Cyber Psychology & Behavior* 321–326.

14 Yee, N., *The Prometheus Paradox*, Yale University Press, New Haven 2014.

15 Futurezone, 'This is how Austrian Facebook users tick!' in *Futurezone – Technology News*, Kurier.at, Vienna 2012.

Taken together, a few short Utilitarian value reflections on personal markets show that their ethicality depends crucially on their technical and political design. Unfortunately, their currently observable design with one-sided financial gains, knowledge asymmetries and lack of privacy undermine their ethicality from a Utilitarian perspective. Utilitarian philosophy is only one angle to think about the ethicality of an act or a phenomenon. As outlined above, other philosophical perspectives can complement Utilitarian reasoning. Therefore, the next section is going to look at personal data markets from a deontological perspective.

2. A SHORT DEONTOLOGICAL REFLECTION ON PERSONAL DATA MARKETS

The word 'deontology' has roots in *deon*, a Greek word that stands for duty. Deontology is a philosophy of obligation, and flourished in eighteenth-century Europe. One of the main thinkers of deontology was Immanuel Kant (1724–1804). Kant, a German philosopher, is regarded as one of the most influential thinkers of the Enlightenment. He wanted to create a universal justification for moral actions. In order for moral justifications to be rational, he argued that the consequences of an act might be too much subject to the volatile ideas of human happiness and could therefore not serve as a reliable moral guideline. So he effectively questioned the Utilitarian kind of reasoning I have used above.

A moral obligation, which he called a 'categorical imperative', can be justified only by something that is a universal principle in itself. Kant formulated a *Categorical Imperative* that all more specific actions should conform to. The first part of this imperative read as follows: 'Act only in accordance with that maxim through which you can at the same time will that it become a universal law'.[16] Note the use of the word 'maxim' here. For Kant, maxims are not just values that one can try to live up to. Instead, maxims are a kind of subjective law or 'principle of action' that can be universalised and upon which one has the *duty* to act. Take the example of having the maxim to never lying to anyone. *Wanting* to tell the truth would not be enough for Kant. In Kant's sense, I have the duty to never lie or to always tell the truth ('Act *only* according to that maxim'). Why is Kant so strict? Because of the ethical confidence we can then have in our surroundings. If the above maxim would be a universal law then we could fully trust that anyone tells the truth.

Kant also argued that there should be a universal principle that guides our considerations on what are worthwhile maxims: this is that in our maxims human beings should always be treated as ends in themselves and never only

---

16 Kant, I., 'Groundwork for the Metaphysics of Morals' (1785) in M.J. Gregor and A.W. Wood (eds.), *Practical Philosophy*, Cambridge University Press, New York 1999, p. 73, 4:421.

used as a means to something. For this reason, he completed his Categorical Imperative with a second part that stressed human dignity: 'So act that you use humanity, whether in your own person or in the person of any other, always at the same time as an end, never merely as a means'.[17]

Thinking about 'duties', it becomes clear that only individual human beings can really hold them. So in Kant's philosophy, maxims are always *subjective* principles that are supposed to be held by a person; notably by the person who is supposed to take an ethical decision. When a person needs to make an ethical decision, Kant reasons that she should behave as if she would not only decide for herself, but as if she was a 'universal lawmaker'. Note the difference between Utilitarianism and Deontology in this regard: Utilitarianism allows to reason at an abstract level, weighing pros and cons of something without taking any actual *subjective* stance. For instance, we can argue that the pros of personal data markets are more knowledge, but the cons are more power asymmetries. The argument is valid, but the individual decision maker or lawmaker or analyst of personal data markets that is formulating this argument is not personally touched or involved in this observation in any way. He or she does not perceive any duty to anyone upon the analysis, just analysing personal data markets 'neutrally'. As a result, the Utilitarian decision maker is engaging in an exercise that Thomas Nagel has critically referred to as practising 'a view from nowhere'.[18]

Kant in contrast requires ethical decisions to be taken from a personal position that involves subjective principles. If we want to use the Categorical Imperative to ethically judge on personal data markets, then we therefore need to put ourselves in the shoes of a concrete person who is personally involved with the object of analysis. When it comes to personal data markets this could be any fictitious person who is involved in them. Ideally however we chose a person who is in fact coming close to being a true 'universal lawmaker' in these markets. This could be a person who is running a personal data market, such as Scott Howe, current president and CEO of Acxiom, Lawrence J. Ellison, head of Oracle and BlueKai, or someone else in a comparatively powerful position. To make the following reasoning didactically entertaining I allow myself to engage in the deontological analysis of personal data markets by taking Scott Howe of Acxiom as an exemplary 'universal lawmaker' who could be asked to decide on the ethicality of practices that his proprietary personal data company engages in.

The maxim of Scott Howe could be to have Acxiom engage in or abstain from certain ways of data collection, aggregation, analysis, sharing and monetisation. From a deontological perspective the question is what universal law Scott wants for himself and others. He needs to personally want that the data-activities in which Acxiom engages should always and everywhere take place in the way *he*

---

17 Ibid., p. 80, 4:429.

18 Nagel, T., *Der Blick von Nirgendwo*, Suhrkamp, Frankfurt/Main 1992.

designs them for his company (or signs them off). For this purpose it is crucial to discuss personal data markets' practices one by one. Potential duties arising with data collection are very different from duties relevant in data aggregation or analysis. Deontological analysis forces us to look at all market activities separately. I will do so in the following only for the activity of data collection.

Scott Howe could theoretically hold the maxim 'Always collect the data of the people such that the people do *not* know what has happened (because they are not asked for their explicit and informed consent).' But deontological ethics questions whether such a position is realistic. Deontological analysis seeks to understand whether Scott Howe can really want such conduct to become a universal law. Instead of taking a 'view from nowhere' the philosophical theory demands to reflect on what the CEO would want for himself first. So, would Scott Howe want to have his own personal data collected without his knowing? How much time would he want to invest into reading and understanding terms and conditions? What intimate data would he want to have collected at all about his personal life and the lives of his friends? I would presume that rationally and in his own self-interest Scott Howe can actually not want that the data Acxiom processes about himself be collected without his conscious and explicit knowing and free consent. In contrast, it seems rational that Scott How would want his personal data to be collected only with his fully conscious, informed and explicit consent by parties he engages with. Ethics from a deontological perspective demands that Scott's duty resides in now applying this subjective principle to his corporate decisions. If we think this to the end, Scott and his team at Acxiom would now need to think about how to make informed and conscious ethical data collection possible from a technical and organisational perspective. Many potential actions could be taken. For instance, Acxiom could require its data suppliers to proof that data subjects' consent was given for all the purposes that Acxiom wants to process the data for. It might for this purpose support standards for controlled and policy-based data flows.[19] It might offer end-users access to its databases[20] and allow for dynamic consent procedures.[21] It might only work with partners that are certified for fair data collection practices, etc. I do not want to expand here on the full list of potential actions Acxiom could engage in to enable Scott Howe's maxim. But what we see from the line of arguments is that

19 Casassa Mont, M., Pearson, S. and Bramhall, P., 'Towards Accountable Management of Identity and Privacy: Sticky Policies and Enforceable Tracing Services', HP Laboratories, Bristol 2003.

20 European Parliament and the Council of Europe, Directive 95/46/EC of the European Parliament and of the Council of 24 October 1995 on the protection of Individuals with regard to the processing of personal data and on the free movement of such data, [1995] OJ L 281/31.

21 Kaye, J., Whitley, E.A., Lund, D., Morrison, M., Teare, H. and Melham, K., 'Dynamic consent: a patient interface for twenty-first century research networks' (2014) *European Journal of Human Genetics* 1–6.

the ethical reflection leads into organisational and technical design measures taken to fulfil the maxim.

Can we conclude that as a result of such efforts data collection is ethically fine from a deontological perspective? Unfortunately, not yet fully.

According to deontological thinking, ethical judgements need to consider the second formula of the categorical imperative as well. This formula asks whether people serve *only* as a means to an end. Are they only a means in the data collection process to reach a certain end? The answer to this question is straightforward: If we use people just as a means to get their signature under a data-sharing contract, then the second formula of the categorical imperative is not fulfilled. This is what happens mostly today. People's notice and choice (if it is granted) does not aim to easily inform people and have them actively and consciously participate in personal data markets.[22] By contrast, often people are just used to give their signature so that companies then have a free ticked to use their data and make money. Current data collection may be fine from a legal perspective, but from a duty-ethical perspective it is not.

So what would be Scott Howe's duty to fulfil the second part of the Categorical Imperative? One strategy could be to position the data collection process in a different way than is being done today. It is possible to view data collection as a means of deliberate participation in the crafting of a better world that thrives on more knowledge (see above) and that sees less fraud. Personal data markets can give people the opportunity to participate and share in these goals. Companies like Acxiom could collect data from fully conscious individuals who are willing to share their data for explicit causes. The key to this path is one thing though: people would need to *autonomously* buy into these goals. Autonomy is a key to Kant's understanding of ethical conduct.

Autonomous consent to data collection would mean that, first, data subjects would need to learn about all of the purposes pursued with their data and they would then need to consent to these one by one. Most importantly, this fine-grained consent would need to be given freely. Data subjects today are often forced into data sharing, because if they deny sharing, they are denied service delivery. Such enforcement for data sharing contradicts Kant's Categorical Imperative. Enforcement can also be very subtle; i.e. psychological pressure can be put on people by repeating mantras to them, such as 'sharing is caring', etc. Data collectors would need to abstain from any of such manipulative tactics. They would need to be very frank, and let the people decide as they want to. They would need to be ready to forgo many opportunities for collecting data from people who simply don't want to share. And they would need to be willing to provide non-sharers with service just as much as anyone else. Only if data collecting companies act this way do they enter the ethical white-zone, at least from Kant's deontological perspective.

---

22 SCHWARTZ, above n. 2.

3. A SHORT VIRTUE-ETHICAL REFLECTION ON PERSONAL DATA MARKETS

The virtue-ethical approach to decision-making and behaviour is a twentieth-century rediscovery of Aristotelian philosophy.[23] Virtue-ethical thinking focuses on the long-term flourishing of people; a flourishing that might become affected by certain behaviours, technology, or the existence of personal data markets. In Aristotle's view a virtuous life is a necessary condition for flourishing; or achieving what he calls eudemonia (often translated as 'wellbeing'). Two concepts are particularly constitutive of virtuousness, and enable eudemonia: these are arête and phronesis.[24]

Arête stands for an excellent character, expressed in well-balanced behaviour towards oneself and others (golden-mean behaviour). Aristotle pulls out the nature of arête in his *Nicomachean Ethics* where he describes a number of concrete virtues such as courage, temperance, high-mindedness, veracity, generosity, etc.[25] These virtues are examples, which illustrate the meaning of arête. A noteworthy aspect of arête is that virtuous behaviour is generally *not instrumental* to anything. Instead it is driven by an inner compass for what is right and good. The world of literature and film is full of examples for arête: for instance fairy tale character Cinderella, Jane Bennett in Jane Austin's novel *Pride and Prejudice*, or the protagonist Jake Sully in James Cameron's film *Avatar*.

A core virtue leading to people's flourishing (also called eudemonia) is phronesis. Phronesis stands for practical wisdom. It is the knowledge and ability of a person to take right and just decisions. Phronesis is *not* about rules that can directly be applied (such as legal regulations). Instead phronesis implies to recognise in a situation what it is that does justice to the virtues, to persons, and goods involved. Phronetic leaders are good in prioritising the right actions and recognising a relatively complete spectrum of consequences; including the 'soft' or long-term consequences of decisions for virtues, persons and goods. Phronesis seems vital for instance to do make good judgements on the utilitarian weights of the costs and benefits of personal data markets that I outlined above in the Utilitarian analysis.

The core virtue ethical question for personal data markets is *focusing now on the users*. It asks whether the technical, social and economic manifestations of data markets will be influencing people's lives such that they impede or hinder them to become the kind of person that possesses arête and phronesis. Could

23 Aristotle, *Magna Moralia*, Clarendon Press, Oxford 1915; Aristotle, *Nichomachean Ethics* Cambridge University Press, Cambridge 2000; Hursthouse, R., *On Virtue Ethics*, Oxford University Press, Oxford 1999; MacIntyre, above n. 9.

24 Hursthouse, R., 'Virtue Ethics' in E.N. Zalta (ed.), *The Stanford Encyclopedia of Philosophy*, The Metaphysics Research Lab, Stanford 2012.

25 *Nichomachean Ethics*, above n. 23.

personal data markets lead to subtle unconducive conditions of oppression that bar people from cultivating their virtues and develop phronesis and arête? In doing so, could they impede people's flourishing in any way? In the words of Lisa Tessman: Could personal data markets create a condition of 'systemic constitutive bad luck'?[26]

How can virtue ethics be applied to personal data markets? To do so it is necessary to envision a concrete person (actor) who might live in a future world in which personal data markets strive. Lets take a fictitious person called Bill, who is seriously overweight and has therefore started to use a health-tracking device. The device measures his weight, transpiration, heart rate, cholesterol, fat, steps and movements made in a day, calories, body posture, etc. Bill has acquired the device as part of his plan to do a lot of sports to bring his body back into a healthy condition. Yet, this plan turns out to be extremely hard, and the device's data suggests that Bill's plan has failed.

Projecting today's technical architectures into the future, all or most of Bill's data would probably flow uncontrolled to the health app provider, who might sell it on to share the data with third parties, including insurance companies, data brokers, employers, etc. The health app service might be for free, but it is very likely that Bill's data then turns against him. His health insurance rating might go up more steeply than expected. The responses to his application for a new job as a sales rep might be poorer than he expected. Bill cannot know that his health app data is behind this 'systemic constitutive bad luck.' The virtuousness of his character might not be directly impacted by the fact that invisible forces make life more difficult for him. However, what could happen is that he turns sour. Bill's chances to live a good life, and to benefit from the flourishing his good character actually deserves, are dwindling. These circumstances might lead to a character change in Bill, who might turn from a positive person into a frustrated one that is not good to live with. That said, it could also be that his character is extremely resistant and that his person and behaviour do not change much when faced with a data-world driving his life into a negative spiral. Virtue ethical analysis projected into a likely future gives no definite answers.

However, let us take a step back from Bill and look at society at large: we must ask the question how an economy and society evolves in which people start feeling discriminated upon their data profiles. Their feelings and perceptions towards anyone they meet (e.g. employers), the state, or any service they use (e.g. health apps) might be increasingly marked by distrust and ambiguity. People will probably start presuming that the vis-à-vis knows more about them than they do about him; that no matter where they turn, they confront a knowledge asymmetry that puts them into a weaker position than they could be

26 Tessman, L., *Burdened Virtues – Virtue Ethics for Liberatory Struggles*, Oxford University Press, Oxford 2005.

in if there was no data-sharing. If this evolution is permitted to happen, we will see a society reigned by distrust and lack of loyalty, or as Hume anticipated it: a society in which everyone is everyone's else's wolf. This is indeed a very negative virtue ethical outlook.

A second scenario should also be considered, because above I have been reflecting on personal data markets in which people receive property rights to their data. In this scenario, Bill would be well aware that his health data would be shared, and with whom and under what conditions. Let us say that Bill is not too rich. Therefore he has made a deal with the health app provider, and licensed out the usage of his health data for the next five years to come. He also strikes a deal with his health insurance company that receives the data, tracks his progress and allows him in return a discount on the cost of health insurance over the next five years. At first sight, this looks much better than the kind of opaque data-world we are in right now. Bill actually might have taken a prudent decision by selling his data, because this deal motivates him to a certain degree to really change his fitness behaviour. By experience he might foresee himself not persisting with a fitness plan unless he is under some financial pressure to succeed. When Bill meets his insurance companies he knows what they know and they can talk about it. Loyalty and trust increases over the knowledge symmetry.

However, there is still a serious virtue ethical risk in this scenario: what happens if Bill loses weight and becomes quite sportive within a year? He has reached his health goals. He has formed a good health-habitus. But still he is forced to continue sharing his data. He is not allowed to stop using the health device, as he would naturally want to. Instead, he is forced to continue using it and bravely upload his data. Naturally, he will become aware of the fact that he sells himself, or parts of himself. He realises that he has made a deal of himself. If such awareness arises, I don't expect it to be very healthy for Bill's perception of the self. He might start seeing himself with different eyes. To a certain extent he might see himself as a virtual prostitute. And probably he will start hating the service provider, the insurance provider and all those parties who deprive him of his liberty to use or not use objects as he likes to. If data deals are designed such that people cannot easily opt out of them, liberty is most likely to suffer. And people who have sold their digital identity might lose faith in their own virtuousness. Their behaviour could start to become instrumental instead of natural. Virtue would suffer. At least this is a possibility.

The kind of envisioning of the future that is necessary for virtue ethical analysis is of course speculative. The true effects might come out completely differently. Still, they are likely and in technology design and policy making it is finally only this exercise of informed anticipation and envisioning that allows us to make virtuous decisions.[27]

---

[27] Nonaka, I., Toyama, R. and Toru, H., *Managing Flow – A Process Theory of the Knowledge-Based Firm*, Palgrave Macmillan, New York 2008.

4. CONCLUSION

Taken together, I would argue that my short analysis here suggests that personal data markets can have negative ethical implications. They must therefore be regarded with caution. That said, the technical and legal design of personal data markets has a great impact on the ethicality of these markets. With the right design and a careful crafting of technical and organisational mechanisms, the long-term liberty of people can be maintained. In particular, it must be ensured that people can exit data deals at any time and that such exits will not lead to negative consequences for them. Personal data should never become an asset that people are forced to sell.

PART III

ALTERNATIVE APPROACHES TO THE PROTECTION OF PRIVACY

21. EVALUATION OF US AND EU DATA PROTECTION POLICIES BASED ON PRINCIPLES DRAWN FROM US ENVIRONMENTAL LAW

Mary Julia EMANUEL*

1. INTRODUCTION

Like all international regulatory agreements, creating standards of trans-Atlantic data protection that satisfy all parties is no easy feat. As seen with the recent *Schrems* case striking down the Safe Harbour Agreement, we are far from finding an appropriate arrangement that works. Although US Federal Trade Commissioner Julie Brill argued that the US and EU share 'an overwhelming degree' of principles and goals, it is an objective fact that the EU demands high standards for the personal data protection of its citizens.[1] The US model of self-regulation and 'sector specific … regulatory fragmentation' does not mesh with the systematic coverage required by the EU.[2] While the standards of the European Union will remain the 'benchmark' for other countries to meet, that is not to say that there are no lessons to be learned from the United States at all; they just are not in the realm of data protection, but rather environmental protection.[3] In fact, robust comparisons can be made to how we conceptualise both data and the environment, as well as how the initial regulatory schemes of the two arenas have developed. In turn, this comparison also allows us to anticipate what the second iteration of data protection should look like by understanding how environmental protection developed in the United States after the initial wave of regulations in the 1960s and 1970s.

---

* H. John Heinz III College, Carnegie Mellon University. E-mail: memanuel@andrew.cmu.edu; maryjuliae@gmail.com.

1 BRILL, J., 'Bridging the Divide: A Perspective on U.S.–EU Commerical Privacy Issues and Transatlantic Enforcement Cooperation' in H. HIJMANS, H. KRANENBORG (eds.), *Data Protection Anno 2014: How to Restore Trust?*, Intersentia, Antwerp 2014.

2 MARCINKOWSKI, B.M., 'Privacy Paradox(es): In Search of a Transatlantic Data Protection Standard' (2013) 74(6) *Ohio State Law Journal* 1167–1194.

3 Ibid.

Making sure that public policy is able to effectively regulate the newest technology has been one of the biggest challenges of the past century, and will certainly only increase in difficulty and importance in the coming decades. Policies, for better or worse, are often implemented incrementally, which makes it almost impossible to cover the almost exponential increases in technological capabilities and applications. Rapid advancement puts the public, including policy-makers, at a disadvantage for understanding the technological changes impacting their lives. This dichotomy between the reality of the problem and comprehension (or lack thereof) describes the state of privacy policy since its inception. While this problem is true for all kinds of policy, it is especially relevant to technology regulation.

Privacy policy in regard to data protection has been increasingly necessary in the post-World War II rise in governmental programmes, consumerism and technological innovation.[4] The desire, as well as the capacity, to collect and store information had not previously existed on the scale that we talk about now, but the growth of social welfare programmes, insurance companies and other public and private sectors greatly enlarged the incentives to do so.[5] At the same time, it became possible to convert record-keeping systems from paper to more convenient electronic databases. These trends were not seen as harmful at first, as the available technology was relatively rudimentary and it would have been impossible to predict how information could be shared and analysed before the Internet. The lack of a foreseeable threat did not make it seem necessary to create strict regulations, and this precendent of less regulation became the standard in privacy policy-making.

It is quickly becoming apparent that something must be done to close the gap between possible threats to privacy and the relevant regulations. New methods and applications for data collection, such as the Shangai city government's use of a 'public credit score' to reward or penalise citizens for their behaviour based on government data,[6] are being developed at a breath-taking pace, and although there have been minimal consequences so far, this may not always be the case. Dennis Hirsch likens the so-called 'Information Revolution' to the Industrial Revolution of the nineteenth century, which saw both a total transformation of society with many economic benefits, but also an 'unprecedented level of environmental degradation'.[7] Because privacy is often seen as an individual concern, this comparison may not be immediately apparent. However, privacy

---

4 Nehf, J.P., 'Recognizing Societal Value in Information Privacy' (2003) 78 *Washington Law Review* 1–92, 28, <http://ssrn.com/abstract=1989235>.

5 Ibid.

6 Schmitz, R., 'What's Your "Public Credit Score"? The Shanghai Government Can Tell You', *NPR*, 3 January 2016, <http://www.npr.org/sections/parallels/2017/01/03/507983933/whats-your-public-credit-score-the-shanghai-government-can-tell-you>.

7 Hirsch, D.D., 'Protecting the Inner Environment: What Privacy Regulation Can Learn from Environmental Law' (2006) 41 *Georgia Law Review* 4, <http://ssrn.com/abstract=1021623>.

is a societal issue; there are actually many parallels that can be drawn between the two fields.

This chapter will build on Hirsch's proposal that lessons from environmental protection can be related to privacy policy. Focusing specifically on the data protection aspect of privacy, I will examine three concepts – the right-to-know, impact assessment, and opting in – that are a part of American environmental law to see how they could be applied. I will also evaluate the extent to which these concepts are already present in relevant US and EU legislation. In order to properly determine this, it is important to first understand the history of privacy protection, both as it is conceptualised and regulated, in the US and Europe.

1.1. A BRIEF HISTORY OF US PRIVACY POLICY

The Fourth Amendment of the US Constitution gives people the right to be secure 'in their persons, houses, papers and effects, against unreasonable searches and seizure'.[8] It also requires warrants to be issued only when there is a probable cause and only for a specific place, person, or thing.[9] Many Americans have assumed that the Fourth Amendment would extend to cover citizens from data collection practices invading their digital spaces as well. However, Supreme Court rulings have showed that their definition of privacy covers information that is in 'complete secrecy', and once information is out, or given to a third party, then it is not a violation of the Fourth Amendment for the Government to use it.[10] In this way the government can use records from phone companies, Internet companies, bank records, credit card companies, hotels, cable companies, employers and landlords to gather a 'digital dossier' on an individual.[11] Although the pieces of information themselves are not harmful alone, together they can be used to distinguish and identify a person by their habits, purchases, lifestyle and beliefs, which can lead to discrimination or even persecution.

Concerns about privacy did not reach the United States Government until 1965, when a 'Federal Data Center' was considered, but ultimately was dismissed after concerns that the centralisation of data would lead to citizens being treated 'as data entries rather than human beings'.[12] While there was no centralisation, data was still collected to facilitate efficiency of the government agencies, which later could be gathered electronically using the Internet. Nine years later, a bill that would become the Privacy Act of 1974 was introduced that would have created an authority to enforce standards in both private and public sectors; it

---

8 US Const. Amend. IV.

9 Solove, D.J., 'Digital Dossiers and the Dissipation of Fourth Amendment Privacy', (2002) 75 *Southern California Law Review* 1117, <http://ssrn.com/abstract=313301>.

10 Ibid., p. 1134.

11 Ibid., p. 1084.

12 Nehf, above n. 4, p. 28.

also required that an individual be notified when their information was released or shared and let individuals access and change their personal files.[13] This bill was inspired by the US Department of Health, Education and Welfare's 1973 report, *Records, Computers and the Rights of Citizens*, that laid out the so-called Fair Information Practice Principles that advocated a rudimentary data protection framework.[14] These principles would go on to also be included in guidelines issued by the Federal Trade Commission, which are not enforceable on their own under law.[15] The prospects of this bill surviving in its original form plummeted when the private sector regulations were dropped during the legislative process. Although the first draft of the presented bill treated privacy as a social concern, its opposition in Congress argued that privacy was an individual concern, and the resulting legislation, the Privacy Act of 1974, was a lowest common denominator policy that did not have jurisdiction outside federal agencies and did not create a regulatory body to allow for enforcement or guarantee compliance.[16]

In hindsight, the leniency of the Privacy Act of 1974 allowed for the practice of data mining to be considered acceptable by not requiring a federal oversight body to be necessary for reviewing new uses of collected data. In 1979 the Department of Health, Education and Welfare (HEW) implemented Project Match, a programme that compared the records of federal employees to records of individuals receiving welfare, in an attempt to reduce fraud. Although the Privacy Act technically did not allow for information to be used for additional unrelated purposes without affirmative consent, Project Match did not follow this rule – allowing similar programmes to do the same in the future.[17] Governmental agencies tripled the number of computer matches by 1984, driven by the increased capabilities of computers and continued adaption of the computer matching technology by federal agencies.[18] This practice began to attract the attention of the public, and Congress passed the Computer Matching and Privacy Protection Act (CMPPA) in 1988.[19] Like the Privacy Act, Nehf points out that it too failed to secure data protection – the primary impact was 'not to limit but to legitimize computer database sharing in the federal government'.[20]

The failure of constructing an overarching privacy policy resulted in some smaller legislation being passed over specific issues: the pre-existing Fair Credit Reporting Act of 1970 covers credit reports, the Family Educational Rights and Privacy Act of 1974 covers student records and the Driver's Privacy Protection

---

13 Ibid., p. 30.

14 US Department of Health, Education, and Welfare, *Records, Computers, and the Rights of Citizens: Report of the Secretary's Advisory Committee on Automated Personal Data Systems*, July 1973.

15 Federal Trade Commission, *Privacy Online: A Report to Congress*, 1998.

16 Nehf, above n. 4, p. 31.

17 Ibid., p. 34.

18 Ibid., p. 35.

19 Computer Matching and Privacy Protection Act, 5 USC §552a (1994).

20 Nehf, above n. 4, p. 35.

Act of 1994 (DPPA) covers motor vehicle records.[21] Some laws that seem to be written in the public's interest, like the Cable Communications Policy Act, Electronic Communications Privacy Act (ECPA), Video Privacy Protection Act (VPPA) and Telephone Consumer Protection Act (TCPA) allow for the disclosure of information to marketing and other companies.[22] Nehf claims that there is 'virtually no regulation of the collection and disclosure of information on the Internet'.[23]

1.2. A BRIEF HISTORY EUROPEAN PRIVACY POLICY

Data privacy in the EU has been a much more unified and successful effort, due in part to the relatively new institutions of the European Union encouraging less political stagnation. Individual efforts by European countries were wildly varied in scope and success, and there is not much of a history of unified privacy policy until after creation of the European Union. To get a sense of the efforts beforehand, the first international effort can be traced back to the Universal Declaration of Human Rights (UDHR) in 1948, which promises no 'interference with his privacy, family, home, or correspondence, nor attacks upon his honor and reputation'.[24] The UDHR was the first time that legal protection of privacy was considered in an international context. Four decades later, the Organization of Economic Cooperation and Development (OECD) produced guideline recommendations for data privacy protection including notice, purpose, consent, security, disclosure, access and accountability.[25] The Council of Europe adopted these guidelines at the Convention for the Protection of Individuals with regard to Automatic Processing of Personal Data in 1981.[26] The US also endorsed the OECD's recommendations officially, but took no steps to implement them.[27]

While most European countries passed legislation following the Convention, the need for a more concrete and harmonised data-protection policy was recognised in the international community. Unlike in the US, a comprehensive framework, rather than incremental individual legislation, concerning data

---

21 Fair Credit Reporting Act, 15 USC §1681–1681u; Family Educational Rights and Privacy Act of 1974, 20 USC §1232g; Driver's Privacy Protection Act of 1994, 18 USC §2721.

22 Cable Communications Policy Act, 47 USC §551; Electronic Communications Privacy Act, 18 USC §2501, et seq.; Video Privacy Protection Act, 18 USC §2710–11; Telephone Consumer Protection Act, 47 USC 227.

23 Nehf, above n. 4, p. 46.

24 UDHR 1948, Art. 12.

25 Moshell, R., '... And Then There Was One: The Outlook for a Self-Regulatory United States Amidst a Global Trend Toward Comprehensive Data Protection' (2005) 37 *Texas Tech Law Review* 5.

26 Council of Europe, Convention for the Protection of Individuals with Regard to Automatic Processing of Personal Data, *Council of Europe Treaty Series 108*, Council of Europe, Strasbourg 1981.

27 Moshell, above n. 25, p. 5.

protection was pursued. Directive 95/46/EC incorporated the ideas of the OECD into a framework for European data-protection law with eight main principles: 'purpose limitation, data quality, data security, sensitive data protection, transparency, data transfer, independent oversight, and individual redress'.[28] The first ensures that data is collected and used for the original purpose, and that it is only kept as long as it is needed; data quality mandates that information is 'kept accurate and updated'.[29] Data security promises that normal data will be protected when transported and analysed, while sensitive data protection would keep the most potentially controversial information (race, sexual preference, religion, etc.) from being released.[30] Transparency would facilitate knowledge about 'collection methods, intended use of data, and identification of the data collector' and data transfer to third parties would be restricted without permission from the individual.[31] Data protection is to be supervised independently, and individuals can request records of their information on file and 'pursue action' against collectors who do not follow the other principles.[32] Data protection is also a 'fundamental right' promised in Art. 8 of the Charter of Fundamental Rights of the European Union and in Art. 16(1) of the Treaty on the Functioning of the European Union.[33]

These principles laid the groundwork to protect EU citizens much more comprehensively than anything in the United States. The EU adopted the General Data Protection Regulation (GDPR) in 2016 to replace the relatively outdated Data Protection Directive, as well as a new Police and Criminal Justice Data Protection Directive, but both have two years to be fully implemented in all Member States. These reforms aim to increase the effectiveness, harmonisation and relevancy of the data protection framework, and will be discussed in the third section of this chapter.

1.3. THE DANGERS OF SURVEILLANCE

As Neil Richards says, 'other than a vague threat of Orwellian dystopia, as a society we don't really know why surveillance is bad'.[34] An often used argument

---

28 Directive 95/46/EC of the European Parliament and of the Council of 24 October 1995 on the protection of individuals with regard to the processing of personal data and on the free movement of such data, [1995] OJ L 281/31.

29 Moshell, above n. 25, p. 7.

30 Ibid., p. 7.

31 Ibid., p. 7.

32 Ibid., p. 7.

33 European Commission, *Communication from the Commission to the European Parliament, the Council, the European Economic and Social Committee, and the Committee of Regions on Safeguarding Privacy in the Connected World, A European Data Protection Framework for the 21st Century*, 25 January 2012, COM(2012) 11 final, p. 2.

34 Richards, N.M., 'The Dangers of Surveillance' (2013) *Harvard Law Review* 1934, <http://ssrn.com/abstract=2239412>.

in defence of data collecting is that it only harms those who are doing things that they should not be doing. However, this argument incorrectly considers privacy as an individual issue rather than a social one, a distinction that will be explained later in this chapter. Solove gives three ways that information gathering is dangerous: the first is that its use can make governments more totalitarian, in that knowing more about people's private lives can 'significantly increase the extent to which the government can exercise social control'.[35] The second harm is that data collection can inhibit civil liberties of expression as individual decision-making is often altered if they know their actions are being recorded.[36] The last threat mentioned is that data collection will give more power 'towards a bureaucratic machinery that is poorly regulated and susceptible to abuse' and can lead to government exploitation of information.[37]

A more distant and bureaucratic relationship between the government and those it governs decreases the amount of power individuals have over their own lives.[38] History has proven that governments will value national security over privacy time and time again – including the deportations and rounding up of over 10,000 suspected Communists by the FBI under J. Edgar Hoover in the Red Scare of the 1920s, and the gathering of information on 'personal and sexual relationships' of members of the women's liberation movement, civil rights activists, and of critics of the Vietnam War, to discredit them in the 1960s and 1970s by the FBI and the CIA.[39] Information was painstakingly gathered before the digital age on dissent groups in order to gain power over them, and the databases available over every citizen would allow anyone's right to express their opinion to be used against them by linking their political beliefs or interests with their private lives.

1.4. RECOGNISING PRIVACY AS A SOCIETAL CONCERN

The three dangers of data collection laid out by Solove are just some of the consequences of such actions that encroach on individual's digital privacy. It is important to realise that these three impact the society to which they apply as a whole. In contrast, the few existing privacy laws and discussion that surrounds them talk about the loss of privacy as impacting only the individual. For example, many of the policy alternatives deem self-regulation to be satisfactory, and the market failure of these types of programmes is evidence that they do not effectively regulate data collection. James P. Nehf takes 'characteristics of

35 Solove, above n. 9, p. 1102.
36 Ibid., p. 1103.
37 Ibid., p. 1105.
38 Ibid., p. 1106.
39 Ibid., p. 1107.

environmental concerns' from a casebook on environmental regulation edited by Robert V. Percival to more broadly define aspects of societal problems to illustrate how privacy fits that theoretical conception better.[40] The transition from viewing all problems as just impacting individuals to how they affect groups of people is important because the effects can be hard to measure on an individual level, but can be obvious on a larger scale. Nehf uses Percival's work on cementing distinct societal benefits and applies them to information privacy.[41]

The six characteristics are 'involuntary and unavoidable risk', 'difficulty in identifying individual harm', 'obstacles tracing injury to its cause', 'inadequacy of money damages', 'externalities' and 'non-economic value in preventing the harm'.[42] Inescapable risk is a clear part of environmental problems, like air or water pollution, and can easily be applied to data collection that affects every member of modern society.[43] Although it is possible to lower risk somewhat by individual action, the bulk of the threat is unavoidable. The exact dangers that come from data protection are clearly hard to identify at first as pointed out earlier, and assessing the harm to each individual is even more challenging. However, just as it is impossible to quantify the exact number of minutes an individual will lose from their life due to air pollution, it is still seen as a threat to be concerned about. In the same way, data protection should be considered a higher priority than its current status. In the same way, pointing out the specific polluter or company collecting individual would be tedious and ultimately would have little impact on the problem as a whole. Alternatively, Nehf also gives five characteristics of individual concern: 'voluntarily assumed risk', 'discoverable injury', 'fewer tracing obstacles', 'economic injury predominates' and 'fewer external costs'.[44] Comparing the two sets of criteria, it is clear that privacy concerns fit the societal concerns model much more appropriately than of individual concern.

Just as environmental protection and data collection concerns can be conceptualised in the same way, so can the solutions. Environmental issues have always existed, even before they were classified as such with the introduction of specific regulations. However, digital privacy only goes back as far as the technology has existed – a much shorter period of time. Therefore, there has been more time for environmental law to develop compared with privacy protection law. Technology policy-makers would benefit from learning from the mistakes and successes in environmental management in order to escape some of the pitfalls in the development of environmental law.

---

40 Nehf, above n. 4, p. 60.
41 Nehf, above n. 4, p. 60.
42 Ibid., pp. 60–62.
43 Ibid., p. 60.
44 Ibid., pp. 62–63.

2. THREE PROPOSALS BASED ON CONCEPTS OF AMERICAN ENVIRONMENTAL POLICY

Environmental degradation has been a consequence of human actions since the dawn of civilisation, but it increased drastically with the Industrial Revolution and even more so after World War II. In the US, any sort of environmental regulation was based mostly in common law, with the few exceptions that actually protected private interests. Crises such as the burning of the Cuyahoga River spurred public concern that peaked with Earth Day of 1970. The political pressure resulted in waves of important regulations being implemented – passing the National Environmental Policy Act (NEPA), Clean Air Act and establishment of the Environmental Protection Agency all happened in 1970.[45] Other important regulations such as the Clean Water Act, Toxic Substances Control Act, Comprehensive Environmental Response, Compensation and Liability Act (CERCLA), Emergency Planning and Community Right-to-Know Act (EPCRA) are just a few parts of the policies passed before 1990 that established the architecture guiding environmental protection.[46]

If we were to place the current state of global privacy protection development on its equivalent of the American environmental protection timeline, it would be the early 1960s. Although there have been increasingly more public concerns about privacy, critical awareness has not been reached, and due to the virtual nature of data collection, may never on its own without a crisis. In one of the first papers comparing data protection policy to environmental policy, Hirsch argued that privacy policy could learn from the 'command-and-control' regulations of first generation environmental management and skip to ways of approach that are 'more cost-effective and adaptable'.[47] What he fails to realise is the second generation regulations improve ways of reducing degradation within a framework that was created in the first round of policies, and these kinds of fundamental structuring legislation still needs to be created for privacy protection. Just as reducing pollution, risk assessment, conservation, and establishing the right-to-know were identified as some of the goals for subsequent environmental policies in the 1970s, now is the time to distinguish cohesive and comprehensive steps to secure the many facets of privacy protection globally.

I will suggest three concepts – right-to-know, impact assessment and 'opt-in' (affirmative consent) – that have worked in US environmental protection that should be implemented to increase transparency, accessibility and accountability in the privacy arena. The EU and the US are in different stages of formulating

---

45 National Environmental Policy Act, 42 USC §§4321–4370h; 42 USC 7401 et seq.

46 Federal Water Pollution Control Act, 33 USC §§1251–1387; Toxic Substances Control Act, 15 USC §§2601–2692; Comprehensive Environmental Response, Compensation and Liability Act, 42 USC §§9601–9675.

47 Hirsch, above n. 7, p. 8.

and adapting relevant legislations, but there are lessons both governments can learn from American environmental law. In the following sections I will discuss the success of the existing environmental policy, how it should be adapted to fit privacy concerns and how US and EU policies compare to the suggested ideal.

2.1. RIGHT-TO-KNOW

2.1.1. The Emergency Planning and Community Right-to-Know Act of 1986

The Emergency Planning and Community Right-to-Know Act of 1986 was designed to give communities more information about chemical risks and develop more robust state and local governments' emergency response plans.[48] Emergency response became a priority after the 1984 disaster at a Union Carbide pesticide manufacturing plant in Bhopal, India that released 40 tons of methyl isocyanate, exposing over 500,000 people to the poisonous gas.[49] The only other Union manufacturing plant was in West Virginia, and despite having temporarily closed the US facility to make it safer after the Bhopal accident, the reopened plant leaked methyl isocyanate and aldicarb oxime, two highly dangerous gases, just three months later.[50] These horror stories brought political salience to increasing transparency about chemical hazards. Besides the primary responsibilities relating to increasing emergency preparedness, the EPCRA also requires that any facility must document and alert agencies when they have hazardous chemicals over a specific threshold, and submit relevant material safety data sheets (MSDS) forms.[51]

While the provisions under EPCRA are meant to make emergency responses easier, the data protection right-to-know needs to extend even farther in applicability, and should also modeled after several other laws that are not specific to environmental protection, but work in junction with the environmental arena for complete coverage. Replicating how the Occupational Safety and Health Act (OSHA), EPCRA, Toxics Release Inventory, Hazardous Materials Transportation Act and Hazardous Communication Standard work together will be crucial for privacy policy to increase transparency and public knowledge. The Occupational Health and Safety Act of 1970 requires that employees have access to MSDS for hazardous chemicals to inform them about 'potential health effects of exposure and how to avoid them'.[52] Employees have

---

48 Schierow, L.-J., 'The Emergency Planning and Community Right-to-Know Act (EPCRA): A Summary', Congressional Research Office, 2012, p. 1.
49 Ibid., p. 2.
50 Ibid., p. 2.
51 Ibid., p. 3.
52 Ibid., p. 2.

the right to access exposure records about themselves and employees working in similar conditions under OSHA's Hazard Communication Standard. The EPCRA expands on OSHA by requiring the MSDS be released to local planning committees (LEPC), state emergency response commission (SERC) and the EPA.[53] EPCRA also establishes the Toxics Release Inventory under section 313, which is released annually to the public.[54] For each chemical, the facility must disclose 'general category of use (manufactured, processed, etc.), treatment or disposal methods used, and amount released to the environment or transferred off-site'.[55] In addition to manufacturing regulations, there are also standards for transportation monitored by the Department of Transportation. The Hazardous Materials Transportation Act of 1975 regulates exchange of hazardous materials by requiring both ends of the exchange to be registered (with some exceptions) and that the material must be 'properly classed, described, packaged, marked, labeled, and in conditions for shipment'.[56] The Department of Transportation also maintains its own list of hazardous materials in the Library Pipeline and Hazardous Material Safety Administration.

2.1.2. Establishing the right-to-know in the data protection arena

Hazardous materials are a surprisingly suitable substitute for personal data. Both have the potential to be dangerous, either accidentally or maliciously, if not guarded carefully, but the collection or manufacturing of either can be beneficial, and more importantly, is inevitable. Based on the previously considered regulations, the ideal data protection right-to-know legislation will encompass informative data sheets, right to access exposure to each kind of data, and information about transportation or accessibility of each kind of personal information. The parallel MSDS – perhaps a proposed name could be PISDS, for personal information safety data sheet – could be applicable for each kind of action that would collect and store different kinds of information, whether it be visiting a website, filling out a survey, or registering with a rewards saver card at a grocery store. These would go beyond a standard privacy policy by being succinct and explicit by design. Because data collection goes beyond occupational safety, the data sheets could serve the general public by being available in a database online. Companies would have the same responsibility of the employers to provide equivalent information similar to the Hazardous Communication Standard to let individuals know about the records and amount of exposure of their personal information if requested.

---

53 Ibid., p. 2.
54 Ibid., p. 3.
55 Ibid., p. 3.
56 49 CRF 171.2(a).

The exchange of information could also learn from hazardous materials by requiring both the buyer and seller to be registered with the authoritative agency. Data sharing would be tracked, so individuals could see that information collected from one source (that was recorded) was used for another purpose if given to a different buyer (hopefully with consent from the individual, as discussed later). Requiring the disclosure of private information would tear down the veil of secrecy that surrounds the market for 'Big Data' and allow informed analyses to be developed for privacy impact assessments and educated decisions about opting in to data collection programmes, the other two suggestions of this chapter. Although this type of system does not currently exist, it certainly could be developed in the near future.

2.1.3. Evaluation of relevant US policy

The US government does not offer its citizens the 'right-to-know' anything about the collection of personal information. The closest it has come to something similar was the California Right to Know bill (AB 1291) that was introduced in 2013, and only gave consumers the right to access their own information and all third parties that obtained the data, but would not limit collection, use, or sharing of the information.[57] However, this bill was not passed. The Obama administration introduced a Consumer Privacy Bill of Rights in 2015 styled after the guidelines from the OECD that would include the right to transparency and access, but it is unlikely that the bill will make it through Congress.[58] Once a data protection framework giving these rights to American citizens is passed, PISDS could increase public knowledge about the ways their personal information is being used.

2.1.4. Evaluation of relevant EU policy

Officially, Directive 95/46/EC offers EU citizens access to all the information they could need – notice of collection, disclosure of the collector and access to the records about them, with the knowledge that data can be used only for the original purpose unless consent is given. However, in practice these rights are not always apparently available. Consultation shows that the public do not

---

57 Reitman, R., 'New California "Right to Know" Act Would Let Consumers Find Out Who Has Their Personal Data – And Get a Copy of It' (2013); 49 U.S.C. Title 49, subchapter III, chapter 51.

58 Denvil, J. 'Insights on the Consumer Privacy Bill of Rights Act of 2015' (2015) *HL Data Protection* <http://www.hldataprotection.com/2015/03/articles/consumer-privacy/insights-on-the-consumer-privacy-bill-of-right-act-of-2015/>.

feel that they are 'in control of their data', are not 'properly informed' of how and by whom their data is processed, or 'how to exercise their rights online'.[59] Section 1 Arts. 11 and 14 GDPR reinforce the 'obligation on controllers to provide transparent and easily accessible and understandable information' upon collection of the data.[60] However, the Regulation does not explicitly call for mechanisms of increasing the consumer's understanding of the implications of the data collection. My suggestion of creating PISDS could fill this gap by giving the public a meaningful way to consent.

2.2. IMPACT ASSESSMENTS

2.2.1. The National Environmental Policy Act of 1970

The National Environmental Policy Act (NEPA) was the first major piece of environmental legislation adopted by the US Government in 1970 and has since become a model for countries around the world for requiring environmental impact assessments. NEPA is mandatory for all federal governmental agencies to submit evaluations for how a project will affect the environment. It is a multi-step process all projects must go through, including those that will not have an impact. Under Title 1, there are three end results: categorical exclusion (CatEx), no impact found resulting in a 'finding of no significant impact' (FONSI), or an environmental impact statement (EIS).[61] A categorical exclusion is reserved for actions that do not have 'significant effect on the human environment'.[62] If a proposal does not fall under the established CatEx for the specific agency, an environmental assessment is conducted to see if an EIS is necessary by providing evidence and facilitate either a FONSI or EIS by including the purpose, possible alternatives and relevant agencies for consultation in making the decision.[63] Finally, if necessary an EIS is prepared with any environmental impacts of the proposal, including adverse and unavoidable ones, possible alternatives, relationship between short- and long-term consequences, and secondary effects to provide policy-makers with information about the costs associated with a

---

59 European Commission, above n. 33, pp. 4–5.

60 European Commission, *Proposal for a Regulation of the European Parliament and of the Council on the protection of individuals with regard to the processing of personal data and on the free movement of such data (General Data Protection Regulation)*, 25 January 2012, COM(2012) 9 final, p. 8.

61 Environmental Protection Agency, *National Environmental Policy Act (NEPA)*, <http://www.epa.gov/compliance/nepa/> accessed 01.05.2015, para. 5.

62 40 CFR §1508.4.

63 40 CFR §1508.9.

proposal.[64] Public comments also encouraged and are required to be taken into consideration and included in the EIS.[65]

2.2.2. *NEPA as a model for privacy impact assessment*

As asserted by Dariusz Kloza, impact assessments have gained 'worldwide importance in the field of privacy' as they are a pre-emptive, rather than reactive, type of strategy.[66] Privacy Impact Assessments (PIAs) are not a new idea, the concept goes back to the 1990s and have been in practice for at least a decade in some countries.[67] The ideal PIA should be of compulsory nature that is mandatory by law, have different tiered outcomes, include public comments, and be easily available to the public.[68] The PIA process needs to be a part of all projects of the government, even if the proposal does not impact privacy. As the authors of the PIAF Project believe, in order to make sure that all organisations include a PIA when developing new plans, a PIA should be 'mandated by law' and have sanctions in order to deter non-compliance.[69] Just as NEPA has CatEx and environmental assessments to make sure an EIS is necessary, the PIA procedure should include a 'threshold' analysis to make privacy impact assessments only drawn out to completion when necessary to eliminate waste of resources.[70] The process should also include an open comment period for the public to weigh in on how a proposed action could affect them. In a field that often comes close to threatening personal liberties, the fact that 'public participation is intrinsic to democratic governance' should not be forgotten.[71] Finally, a 'public register' of PIAs could make the information available to the general public as well as experts involved in the PIA process to gain experience from past assessments.[72]

All federal projects have to go through the NEPA process – each proposal has to prove that the potential effects of the programme will not harm the environment, and take the consequences into consideration if there are any. The broad applicability of NEPA should be brought to future privacy impact assessments by having any proposals that may involve information submit an assessment in order to evaluate more possible threats to privacy. Environmental

64 Environmental Protection Agency, above n. 61, para. 8.

65 Ibid., para. 12.

66 Kloza, D., 'Public Voice in Privacy Governance: Lessons from Environmental Democracy' in *Know Right 2012. Knowledge Rights – Legal, Societal and Related Technological Aspects. 25 years of Data Protection in Finland*, Österreichische Computer Gesellschaf, Vienna 2013, p. 3.

67 PIAF Project, *Recommendations for a privacy impact assessment framework for the European Union* (2012), p. 5.

68 Ibid., pp. 7–29.

69 Ibid., p. 9.

70 Ibid., p. 24.

71 Kloza, above n. 66, p. 7.

72 PIAF Project, above n. 67, p. 20.

impact assessments have been proven to be valuable tools in gathering and analyzing information prior to decision-making, and privacy impact assessments should build off of the working model to fit their own needs.

2.2.3. Evaluation of relevant US policy

Privacy impact assessments are mandated under the E-Government Act of 2002 for government agencies for all programmes that 'use personally identifiable information', with this being defined as 'any information that permits the identity of an individual to be directly or indirectly linked'.[73] The assessment must be reviewed by a chief information officer, be made public, and send a PIA to the Director for every system that requests funding.[74] However, many are exempt from being made public in order to 'protect classified, sensitive, or private information' relevant to the assessment.[75] The compliance-only orientation of the PIA has made the agencies do what is mandated – only 56 per cent of the 24 major federal agencies had fully functional and operating PIA policies in 2009.[76] An absence of public involvement in the PIAs is another fault of the American process.[77] The fact that agencies are encouraged to publish them after the budget has already been negotiated – making the PIA a 'retrospective evaluation' that renders it useless.[78]

Roger Clarke states that 'US federal agencies conduct PIAs in name only' and that the 'US remains a wasteland' policy-wise.[79] To change this, a specific data protection impact assessment framework should be implemented in the US. If based off the current PIAs, legal consequences for non-compliance should be added, and make them mandatory for all proposed actions that could affect data protection. Privacy threshold analyses do exist in name, but in their current form do not serve their purpose. The NEPA standard of tiered outcomes would make sure that all possible actions are covered, with CatEx, privacy threshold analysis and DPIA being the three possible outcomes of the assessment process.

2.2.4. Evaluation of relevant EU policy

Privacy impact assessments have been utilised in Europe, but have not been uniformly adopted by all the member states or the European Union. The notion

---

[73] PIAF Project, *PIAF: A Privacy Impact Assessment Framework for data protection and privacy rights* (2011), p. 9.
[74] Ibid., p. 10.
[75] Ibid., p. 10.
[76] Ibid., p. 135.
[77] Ibid., p. 136.
[78] Ibid., p. 136.
[79] Ibid., p. 137.

was entertained by the Article 29 Working Party in a proposal concerning EU Radio-Frequency (RFID) PIA in 2011, proposed in a DPIA framework for smart-metering systems in 2012, and now a DPIA is included in the GDPR.[80] Article 35 states that the controller will 'carry out an assessment of the impact' when 'processing operations present specific risks' including information ranging from economic situation to genetic data.[81] Even though the risks are laid out in the article, making a data protection impact assessment necessary for only some processes leaves room for DPIAs to not be carried out when they should. It would be more comprehensive to follow the NEPA standard and require all proposed actions to go through the process, and have the irrelevant ones end early from a CatEx in order to make sure that an assessment was at least considered for any action. The NEPA framework would make future DPIAs more efficient and effective.

2.3. OPT-IN PRIVACY POLICY

2.3.1. Mineral rights and the value of 'opting in'

Having more information available like PIAs and PISDSs would allow the public to have a more comprehensive understanding of the value of their personal information, which is absolutely necessary for a functioning 'opt-in' model of data sharing. While privacy concerns have traditionally handled first in an 'opt-out' model that requires individuals to stop an action affecting them, it is possible to have a system that would require consent before gathering information. The concept of mineral rights in the United States is the perfect illustration of how alternate ownership policies can occur, despite going against the norm. The usual standard is that 'all mineral resources belong to the government', and that all extraction or selling of a resource must be approved beforehand.[82] Due to the colonial and expansionist/frontier history of the United States, mineral rights are reserved originally for the owners of the surface by the early Homestead Acts.[83]

When a property owner has both the surface rights and mineral rights, it is known as a 'fee simple estate'.[84] An estate can have 'severed' mineral rights if the federal government originally claimed them, as it often did after the Stock-Raising Homestead Act of 1916, or if the owner sells the mineral rights and

---

80 PIAF Project, above n. 67, p. 5.

81 European Commission, above n. 60, p. 10.

82 King, H. (no date), *Mineral Rights | Oil & Gas Lease and Royalty Information* <http://geology.com/articles/mineral-rights.shtml>, para. 2.

83 Ibid., para. 4.

84 Ibid., para. 2.

retains the surface rights.[85] Another possibility is fractional ownership, where an owner has a percentage of the minerals: 'a 50 percent ownership means that the owner is entitled to half of the minerals'.[86] Ownership can even be divided by the types of minerals on one piece of property. Companies sometimes lease from the owner for a certain amount of time, where they pay the owner for the lease and 'royalty payments' – a percentage of the production value of produced minerals.[87] Mineral rights cover a variety of highly valuable of resources including fossil fuels, gemstones, metal ores and other minerals.[88] Owners of mineral rights have many paths to choose about how to manage their property, whether it be maintaining complete control and forgoing any monetary benefits, selling them to make a large profit, or coming to a leasing agreement that is somewhere between the first two options. If you define personal information as property of an individual, it is not hard to imagine a similar system to be used for the exchange of data in which the individual has control over their own personal information and the power to sell it to companies in exchange for direct compensation. This system would allow those who do not mind giving up their privacy to benefit from the market demand for personal information and allow others to retain their privacy.

2.3.2. Consumer benefits from data collection

It would be erroneous to proclaim that no benefits that the consumer can gain from sharing information with companies. Sovern shares an anecdote about how women's catalogues began being addressed to him, after using catalogues to buy clothes for his children after his wife died.[89] He was initially grateful to be able to save time shopping for his daughters, but was not pleased that the companies selling women's clothes had bought his name from the companies from which he had bought children's clothing, as he 'did not need to be reminded about [his] wife's death by receiving catalogues that should have come to her'.[90] It is not that all consumers want to keep all their information private, but that they want control: their names 'sold to some companies but not others'.[91]

At first glance it can seem like consumers are not concerned with threats to their privacy, as they do not usually opt-out when the option is available to them. However, the serious lack of information about the extent to which data is

---

85 Fitzgerald, T., *Understanding Mineral Rights*, 2017, p. 1 <http://store.msuextension.org/publications/outdoorsenvironmentandwildlife/MT201207HR.pdf>.

86 Ibid., p. 2.

87 Ibid., p. 3.

88 Ibid., p. 4.

89 Sovern, J., 'Opting in, Opting Out, or No Options at All: The Fight for Control of Personal Information' (1999) 74 *Washington Law Review* 1074.

90 Ibid., p. 1074.

91 Ibid., p. 1074.

collected, the options to avoid the process, or the harms of having their privacy infringed on keep consumers from being able to make educated decisions. Coase's theorem about social costs predicts that if people value privacy more than what companies value that information, then they will pay to keep it private, and that if businesses value the information more than the people value their privacy, then people will not want to pay to stop companies from doing so.[92] Because of the information asymmetry, the latter condition is the default case – people do not see the value in paying companies to stop collecting their data. However, in an opt-in system, the pressure would be on the companies to convince people that giving out their information is worth giving up privacy.

Back when the main invasion of privacy was junk mail, about 50 per cent of individuals in the US did not know about any of the existing programmes to keep their names off mailing lists in 1996.[93] This is not an accident; companies often 'intentionally hi[d]' practices from consumers in order to 'limit the potential for consumer action'.[94] Sovern quotes Paul Schwartz's argument that a monopoly equilibrium occurs when people think their information is being protected, but businesses know this is not the case.[95] When consumers believe their records are safe, there is no market incentive for sellers to 'compete on the basis of how much security they provide', but an opt-in system would force companies to do just that.[96]

The multiple ways that mineral rights can be passed between the individual and the companies should be replicated in future data collection opt-in programmes. Having information from the other proposed actions would allow people to make more informed decisions about how they want to release their information. Those who are interested in the benefits of selling or leasing access to their personal information could do so, and those who are not could keep the information private. An opt-in system would allow Coase's theorem run its true course instead of being hindered by market failure. It is important to note that giving back the ownership of individual's personal information would not need to be modeled after the slightly archaic system of mineral rights completely. Personal information has been collected and traded by data brokers for years; the idea here is to return the control to the individual. In fact, there have been some companies such as Datacoup, Handshake and Meeco that already anticipate this shift disrupting the market – they reward their customers in exchange for collecting and selling their personal information to other companies.[97]

92 Ibid., p. 1071.
93 Ibid., p. 1076.
94 Ibid., p. 1078.
95 Ibid., p. 1079.
96 Ibid., p. 1079.
97 Secorun Palet, L., 'Privacy or Profit? These Firms Want To Help You Sell Your Data', *NPR*, 9 September 2014, <http://www.npr.org/2014/09/09/346981606/privacy-or-profit-these-firms-want-to-help-you-sell-your-data>.

The transaction of data is still the same: generated by consumers and sold to third-parties, but the customers are consenting to the transaction and benefit from it.

The tangibility of the physical world makes opting in an inherent part of mineral rights. If a company were to start drilling in a place where they did not own the mineral rights, the owner would immediately reprimand them. Companies do not try to develop land without permission, but this is the equivalent of the concept of inferred consent. It should not be appropriate for companies to use personal information if explicit approval is not given. The standard of affirmative consent concerning data will give individuals more control of what is shared, with whom, and in what way.

2.3.3. *Evaluation of relevant US policy*

As with the right-to-know proposal, the concept of an 'opt-in' policy is so far removed from American political thought that it can be almost impossible to realistically conceive. The only existing notion would again be the Obama Administration's Consumer Privacy Bill of Rights, which would effectively bring American data protection up to speed with the EU's Directive 95/46/EC. It promises seven principles: individual control, transparency, respect for context, security, access and accuracy, focused collection and accountability.[98] The suggested individual control element would give American consumers control over the data they share and 'how companies collect, use, or disclose' this personal information.[99] It would also give Americans the ability to easily withdraw or limit consent over the use of their own data.[100] Other pillars of the bill include basic rights to transparency and keeping data from being used for other purposes without informing the consumer. While the Consumer Privacy Bill of Rights would certainly be a step in the right direction for securing data protection for American citizens, it would not require programmes to be opt-in. In fact, it explicitly states that 'infer[ring] consent' is acceptable, instead of making affirmative consent the standard.[101]

2.3.4. *Evaluation of relevant EU policy*

Like the previous evaluations, although Directive 95/46/EC seemed to require consent as proposed above, the implementation of this concept did not translated

[98] White House Office, 'Consumer Data Privacy in a Networked World: A Framework for Protecting Privacy and Promoting Innovation in the Global Digital Economy', Executive Office of the President, 2012, p. 10.

[99] Ibid., p. 11.

[100] Ibid., p. 11.

[101] Ibid., p. 17.

as well as imagined. Although the Directive stated that personal data would only be processed if consent was 'unambiguously given', the exceptions in the document significantly lessened this promise.[102] In public consultation periods during the development of the General Data Protection Regulation, stakeholders made it known that the current policy was too 'fragment[ed]' and needed to be more harmonious throughout the EU.[103] However, in the recently adopted GDPR, the language states that consent needs to be 'given by a clear affirmative act' that confirms a 'freely given, specific, informed and unambiguous' decision by the subject for all processing purposes. Furthermore, the 'right to erasure' in section 3 Art. 17 allows an individual the right of 'erasure of personal data relating to them' if the original purpose of collection has passed; the subject may withdraw consent if they object to the processing of the data.[104] This new 'right to be forgotten' gives individuals greater control over the personal data around them. However, the biggest increase of control would be the distinction of need for explicit, rather than ambiguous, consent in practice as well as on paper.[105] The implementation of the Regulation in 2018 will show whether the new stronger language is more successful than the previous Directive.

3. CONCLUSION

Although the comparison is justified, it is a little optimistic to pronounce the global state of data protection now to be in the same situation as environmental protection in the 1960s, because such a claim would mean that change is just around the corner. It is just as likely that Hirsch is right and a more apt comparison would be to the Industrial Revolution, which could become a self-fulfilling prophecy if no checks are put in place against the rapid advancement of data collection technology. We look back now at the nineteenth century and lament the primary forests that could have been saved if there had been any concept of ecological conservation. The same could be true of today – we are at a crossroads. The importance of privacy has been proven by the John Muirs of the field, but is nowhere near accepted as a universal value. Although not impenetrable, the European Union already has the foundation and track record of considering data protection to be worth securing, and is certainly on a path that will make future threats to privacy easier to combat. Watching the adoption and implementation of the new GDPR by the EU Member States will certainly be a significant learning experience for the data protection policy arena. On the other side of the spectrum, the United States seems adamant that interests

[102] Directive 95/46/EC, above n. 28.
[103] European Commission, above n. 60, p. 3.
[104] Ibid., p. 7.
[105] Ibid., p. 8.

like economic growth will come before privacy concerns. There is no reason to wait for the virtual equivalent of a hundred Santa Barbara oil spills to convince the American public and government to see the value of privacy. The concepts discussed are already accepted as valid in the context of the environmental, and can be used to make data protection seem less outlandish by proving they have a basis in American law.

In regards to formulating successful privacy protection, there is no reason to reinvent the wheel. The broad societal concepts discussed in this chapter – right-to-know, impact assessment and an opt-in approach – have proven to be appropriate ways to approach environmental policies, and each should be considered as valuable tools when crafting data protection. In the incremental climate of the United States, it is feasible to introduce one of the ideas independently of each other and build on the success of the first to advocate for more protection in future efforts. In the EU, tweaking the already existing legislation in the ways discussed in this paper – more explicit adherence to 'the right to know', following the NEPA framework for impact assessments, and requiring affirmative consent when opting-in – should be included in proposals at the next possible opportunity to make the framework more comprehensive. Implementing the GDPR will make the gaps of its coverage visible, and thus a new iteration of policy can begin. Securing accountability, transparency, and user control concerning data protection now is essential for effective conservation of privacy as the policy arena will only become more complicated in the future.

22. FLAGRANT DENIAL OF DATA PROTECTION

Redefining the Adequacy Requirement

Els De Busser*

1. POINT OF DEPARTURE

Given the reality of the 'information society' worldwide, this is an arena in which we must play the game and we have to recognize that others may make the rules.[1]

The author of this quote is George B. Trubow, well-known US privacy and information law expert, describing the US position in 1992, a time during which EU institutions were drafting Directive 95/46/EC.[2] The latter introduced the adequacy requirement obliging non-Member States to have an adequate level of data protection, without which no personal data exchange with the EU was allowed. Trubow recognised that the US data protection system would not pass this adequacy test, in particular regarding the purpose limitation principle known in the US as the secondary use limitation, or function creep.

After the entry into force of the EU's first legal instrument on data protection, Directive 95/46/EC – on the protection of personal data processed for activities within the scope of Community law, largely corresponding with commercial activities – the adequacy requirement was copied into the Council of Europe's 2001 Additional Protocol to the Data Protection Convention (2001 Additional Protocol).[3] Later it was also copied into EU Framework Decision 2008/977/JHA

* The Hague University of Applied Sciences. E-mail: E.deBusser@hhs.nl.

1 G.B. Trubow, 'European Harmonization of Data Protection Laws Threatens U.S. Participation in Trans Border Data Flows' (1992–1993) 13(1) *Northwestern Journal of International Law and Business* 176.

2 Directive 95/46/EC of 24 October 1995 on the protection of individuals with regard to the processing of personal data and on the free movement of such data, [1995] OJ L 281.

3 1981 Convention for the Protection of Individuals with regard to the Automatic Processing of Personal Data, ETS No. 108 and 2001 Additional Protocol, ETS No. 181.

on data protection in criminal matters (2008 Framework Decision).[4] This means that both EU and Council of Europe (CoE) Member States may have to assess the adequate level of data protection of a third state requesting for personal data. The term 'Member States' will in this contribution thus refer to EU or CoE Member States. For the sake of argument, abstraction is made of the fact that the adequacy requirement is not applied for all data transfers[5] and that not all CoE Member States have ratified the 2001 Additional Protocol. This chapter focuses on the (need for an) adequacy rule itself, and not its application.

The adequacy requirement has given rise to a variety of issues in the EU. Often these concerned issues related to inconsistencies in application.[6] Most recently the adequacy requirement was questioned by Austrian national Maximillian Schrems in his complaint against the Irish Data Protection Authority regarding Facebook's transfer of personal data from the EU to its US-based servers. One of the questions brought up in the complaint was whether the adequacy assessment from the Safe Harbour framework – based on a Commission decision of 2000 – was still valid after former NSA contractor Edward Snowden shed a different light on US data processing in 2013. The Court of Justice in this case delivered a landmark ruling by declaring the Safe Harbour framework invalid, while also endorsing the monitoring of third states' systems after the European Commission delivers an adequacy assessment; in particular, when amendments made to such systems could influence the outcome of an adequacy assessment.[7] The Commission reacted rather quickly to the *Schrems* judgment, with a list of alternative bases for data transfers to the US, stressing that it is still committed to the goal of a renewed and sound framework for trans-Atlantic transfers of personal data.[8] Questioning the validity of an adequacy assessment brings up the question whether the adequacy requirement as such is a useful and workable condition. This question does not imply that legal requirements should be removed once complicated issues come to the surface. Yet, if legislative amendments or secret programs on data processing in the third state affect an existing adequacy decision to such an extent that the continuation of transborder data flows is compromised, how can we solve the issue while still holding on to this requirement? We could rely on the third state to inform us of any substantial changes in legislation that could affect the adequacy decision, but this will not solve the problem of secret data processing programmes as was the case with the NSA. Constant monitoring of legislative and policy movements in all third

---

4 Framework Decision 2008/977/JHA on the protection of personal data processed in the framework of police and judicial cooperation in criminal matters, [2008] OJ L 350.

5 See E. De Busser, 'The Adequacy of an EU-US Partnership', in S. Gutwirth et al., *European data protection: in good health?*, Springer, Dordrecht 2011, pp. 185–202.

6 Ibid.

7 Case C-362/14, *Schrems v. Data Protection Commissioner* ECLI:EU:C:2015:650.

8 COM(2015)566 final, 06.11.2015.

states with which EU and Member States' authorities have ongoing transborder data flows is unrealistic.

In true devil's advocate fashion, the question should be asked whether the adequacy requirement as such is still needed. In today's information-based society, in which Internet, cloud servers and smart phones allow data to cross borders in a nanosecond, does adequacy still have a place? Should the EU forget about it altogether or just loosen its grip and let the smooth flow of data prevail over solid data protection standards? Is it even reasonable to oblige other states to commit to the EU data protection standards? A search for answers to these questions is undertaken in this contribution.

Discussions on the adequacy rule have filled many pages and the requirement as such has occupied many scholars' minds; however, one stone has so far been left unturned, and that is the comparison with extradition. International information exchange and extradition of individuals are to a large extent similar in structure and in criteria. In particular the fulfilment of human rights based requirements imposed by the requested state without the requesting state's prior agreement is a parallel that could help answer the aforementioned questions. The fact that extradition to third states has brought about more case law than information exchange should facilitate testing the limits of the adequacy rule. The objective of this contribution is to (re-)define the limits of the adequacy requirement by weighing human rights protection against the smooth transborder flow of data in the context of data transfers from Member States to third states. In view of this objective, as a first step the similarities and differences between transborder data flows on the one hand, and the extradition of an individual on the other, are examined. This is necessary to test the relevance of the comparison and the exercise described above. In a second stage, the human rights aspect is scrutinised. More specifically, in this stage the circumstances are studied under which a transborder data transfer or a transfer of persons is made dependent on the respect for specific human rights (further: the human rights requirement). An additional feature is that the human rights meant here are comprised in a legal instrument that was not ratified by the state that requested the data. Evidently, this leads to two extra questions: what are the risks and consequences of non-compliance with this human rights criterion by the requesting state? And lastly, which state is responsible for the respect for human rights as a prerequisite for a transborder data flow or the extradition of an individual?

2. REASONS FOR USING EXTRADITION IN REDEFINING ADEQUACY

The reasons why in this contribution a parallel is drawn between the prerequisite of an adequate level of data protection in international information exchange on the one hand, and the requirements associated with extradition on the other, are explained in this section. International information exchange and extradition of individuals have many similarities. In particular the fulfilment of human rights based requirements imposed by the requested state without the requesting state's prior agreement is a parallel that could help answer the aforementioned questions. The fact that extradition to third states has brought about more case law in comparison with information exchange should facilitate testing the limits of the adequacy rule.

2.1. INTERSTATE COOPERATION

Both international information exchange and extradition are forms of interstate cooperation involving the transfer of either personal data or a person for the purpose of an investigation, prosecution or execution of a sentence in the recipient state. In both cases, it occurs that this recipient state is a state outside the EU and outside Europe. This means chances are high that the recipient or requesting state is a state that did not ratify the legal instrument that provides in the requirements in the first place.

As the adequacy requirement is a part of the EU and CoE data protection standards, it makes interstate cooperation dependent on the recipient state fulfilling a condition that it did not formally endorse. Interstate cooperation could occur with a third state that agrees with the data protection standards of the CoE and even has a similar system in place but simply has not – yet – ratified the CoE Data Protection Convention, for other reasons. The US is however an example of a third state that has a fully different data protection system in place and is not expected to ever ratify the Data Protection Convention due to the profound legal amendments this would cause in the national US legal system. Thus, the US should provide in an adequate level of data protection to receive personal data from an EU Member State or agency. This is the extraterritorial effect of our data protection standards. Looking into the rationale of the adequacy requirement means looking into the protection of the EU single market. Considering the EU's development as an economic union and the fact that information including personal data is the bread and butter of businesses, the adequacy requirement was deemed necessary to avoid a circumvention of the protection offered by Directive 95/46/EC when exporting data to countries with lower or no data protection guarantees and a possible re-import to the EU.[9] In addition, free circulation of information should be ensured.[10] It is a reality that free movement of persons – one of the basic freedoms of the EU – also brings with it free movement of crime. For that reason, cross-border exchange

9 European Commission, 'Analysis and impact study on the implementation of Directive EC 95/46 in Member States', 2003, p. 31.

10 2001 Additional Protocol, ETC 181, Explanatory Report, at 24.

of information is crucial in preventing, detecting, investigating and prosecuting criminal offences. In as far as personal data are concerned and in as far as data are concerned that were received by one Member State from another Member State, the 2008 Framework Decision was enacted. Also this legal instrument contains rules on an adequate level of data protection for third states before they can receive personal data for the purpose of criminal investigations.

Free movement of crime also makes interstate cooperation rise in transferring persons. Extradition for the purpose of prosecution or executing a sentence has increased in the past decades together with growing cross-border crime rates. Fulfilling a requirement that a state did not ratify is equally a feature of several national laws on extradition. Extradition shall be refused if the procedure in the requesting state is contrary to the ECHR. Contrary to popular belief, this is not a binding rule in multilateral conventions though.[11] Since the ECHR is ratified by all CoE Member States but is not open to ratification by third states, all extradition procedures with third states depend on the third state fulfilling a requirement they did not ratify. Obviously, this does not mean that third states are unable to fulfil the prerequisite of an ECHR-compliant procedure; it merely means they are confronted with a *conditio sine qua non* they never formally agreed to.

I am drawing the parallel between extradition and the exchange of personal data; hence I compare the human rights requirement from the extradition context to the adequacy requirement from the data protection context. Both requirements show a fundamental difference in their *raison d'être*. The adequacy requirement was specifically designed to enable cooperation with states that did not ratify the basic legal instrument on personal data protection, the CoE Data Protection Convention; whereas the human rights requirement is also applied in other contexts such as mutual assistance in criminal matters. Still, both function as grounds for refusing interstate cooperation: if the requesting state does not have an adequate level of data protection, exchange of personal data will in principle not take place. If the requesting state does not guarantee proceedings that respect human rights, the person may in principle not be extradited. I write 'in principle' because both requirements can be derogated from. These exceptions will be a significant part of this contribution.

2.2. PROTECTED INTERESTS AND HUMAN RIGHTS

Both the adequacy requirement and the human rights requirement function as grounds for refusal of interstate cooperation, but do these requirements protect

---

11 C. Van den Wyngaert, 'Applying the European Convention on Human Rights to Extradition: Opening Pandora's Box?' (1990) 39(4) *The International and Comparative Law Quarterly* 758.

the interests of the state or the interests of the individual involved? Apart from discussions on whose interests are protected by the speciality rule, it should be clear that the human rights requirement in extradition cases protects the interests of the individual concerned. In fact, there is a clear trend in extradition laws since 1948 towards increased protection of human rights of persons.[12] The adequacy requirement may be a requirement that is only activated when cooperation between states occurs, the interests that it protects are those of the individuals concerned.

Based on the profound implications that the act of being extradited to another state would have on a person's life, one would expect extradition treaties to contain a ground for refusal based on human rights compliance. They don't. No explicit general rule states that extradition should be compatible with human rights.[13] It is the ECtHR's jurisprudence however that brought clarity, with the landmark judgment in the *Soering v. UK* case in 1989.[14]

Even though international information exchange and extradition both involve the protection of specific human rights, the types of human rights they protect are not the same.[15] Information exchange when involving personal data typically requires safeguarding the right to a private life. Since the entry into force of the EU Charter of Fundamental Rights in 2009, one could argue this should be the right to data protection alongside the right to a private life. Kuner hit the nail on the head when he wrote that data protection seems to be an 'emerging' fundamental right that has at the present time not yet gained full recognition under public international law, but may do so in the future.[16]

Extradition procedures and the test of ECHR-complying procedures in the requesting state typically involve the right to life and prohibition of torture or inhuman or degrading treatment or punishment. The right to a fair trial is at first sight not included since the extradition process does not itself qualify as criminal proceedings, yet it can lead to a rejection of extradition requests when the requesting state has demonstrated not to live up to fair trial standards. More on this question follows in a further part of this contribution.

Academics have often reflected on the existence of a hierarchical relationship between human rights protection and the obligation to extradite, with the conclusion being that the answer depends on the human right that is at stake.[17] Since extradition procedures lead to an individual being transferred for the purpose of prosecution or a sentence, requiring the requesting state to comply

12 M.C. Bassiouni, *International Extradition Law*, Oxford University Press, Oxford 2014, p. 6.

13 European Commission, above n. 9, p. 758.

14 ECtHR, *Soering v. UK*, App. no. 14038/88, A/161.

15 European Commission, above n. 9, pp. 764 et seq.

16 C. Kuner, 'Extraterritoriality and the Fundamental Right to Data Protection', *EJIL Talk*, 16.12.2013.

17 European Commission, above n. 9, p. 761 and H. van der Wilt, 'On the Hierarchy between Extradition and Human Rights', in E. De Wet and J. Vidmar (eds.), *Hierarchy in International Law: The Place of Human Rights*, Oxford Scholarship Online, 2012, pp. 158–160.

with certain standards means that our – i.e. European or ECHR – human rights have an extraterritorial effect. This is not the case for all human rights though. When reading through the ECHR three categories of human rights become visible. The distinction is based on whether and in how far one can derogate from these rights. Derogating from human rights is regulated under Art. 15 ECHR and only allowed in time of war or other public emergency threatening the life of the nation provided that measures taken are limited to what is strictly required by the exigencies of the situation and provided that such measures are not inconsistent with its other obligations under international law. The 'highest' category of human rights are those that form an exception to this exception, meaning that even in emergency circumstances no exceptions can be made of the right to life, the prohibition of torture or inhuman or degrading treatment, the prohibition of slavery and the principle of legality.[18] Even when another exception is still made for deaths resulting as lawful acts of war, these qualify as absolute or non-derogable rights. The second category are the human rights that may only be restricted in emergency circumstances, not in normal circumstances, and contain the right to personal freedom and the right to a fair trial.[19] A last category is made up of the human right that can be restricted also in normal circumstances, nevertheless under specific conditions. The right to a private life falls within this category. If no restrictions to this right were allowed, no business transactions or criminal investigations could take place, let alone transborder data flows to third states. Whenever in accordance with the law and limited to what is necessary in a democratic society in the interests of national security, public safety or the economic well being of the country, for the prevention of disorder or crime, for the protection of health or morals, or for the protection of the rights and freedoms of others, restrictions to the right to privacy are acceptable.

When extraditing an individual to a third state where he or she faces a real risk of receiving the death penalty or being subjected to torture, the extradition may not take place. The conclusion can be different though when the right to fair trial is considered, in the sense that the requested state bears to a certain extent the responsibility for the fairness of the criminal proceedings the extradited person will face after his or her transfer. What is now the equivalent of this primacy of non-derogable rights over the obligation to extradite in information exchange? Does the adequacy requirement have a similar effect of prevailing over a state's commitment to cooperate and transfer personal data? Since the right to a private life – that the ECtHR relied on in its jurisprudence[20] dealing with data protection questions – can be restricted for the purpose of prevention of disorder or crime, the answer is most likely no when criminal investigations

---

18 In the ECHR these are Arts. 2, 3, 4§2 and 7.

19 Arts. 5 and 6.

20 *Inter alia*, ECtHR, *Amman v. Switzerland*, App. no. 27798/95, ECHR 2000-II and ECtHR, *Rotaru v. Romania*, App. no. 28341/95, ECHR 2000-V.

are concerned. In commercial activities however, recent jurisprudence by the Court of Justice of the European Union (CJEU) has shed exciting new light on the matter. Also this is a topic I will deal with in a subsequent part of this chapter.

2.3. TRUST

Similar to every form of interstate cooperation, international information exchange and extradition call for a certain level of trust. In order to send personal data or a person to a third state, the requested state should have trust in the requesting state not to misuse the data for other purposes or to prosecute the extradited person for other offences than those stated in the request. The so-called speciality rule protects the interests of the requested state when extraditing a person but also the person's rights. Agreeing with an extradition for a specific offence means that the requested state did not invoke any grounds for refusal in that particular case. If the requesting state afterwards prosecutes the extradited person for another offence, the requested state never had the chance to check whether any grounds for refusal could be applicable such as prosecution for a political offence. Similarities with the principle of purpose limitation in data protection are rather strong. When processing personal data, the data processor is not allowed to use the data for any other purpose than the purpose the data were collected for unless it concerns a compatible purpose or unless an exception applies. This also goes in cross-border data transfers to third states. Both the speciality rule and the purpose limitation principle can be derogated from when consent is given by the requested state or the person concerned.

2.4. JURISPRUDENCE

Reasons for testing the limits of the adequacy requirement by relying on extradition lie in the longer tradition and thus wider availability of jurisprudence on the latter. The increase in mobility of individuals since decades led to an increase in cross-border crime, cross-border criminal proceedings and extradition procedures. A steeply growing development is equally visible in information distribution. Personal data crosses jurisdictions with nearly every action – purchasing items, booking flights or hotel rooms, communicating, saving and exchanging documents and pictures, etc. – an individual takes. Add to that all the personal data that Internet and app users are willing to voluntarily share on social media and other services. One would think this automatically leads to a waterfall on fresh case law dealing with data protection and privacy related questions. Nonetheless, with the exception of a few landmark cases on data protection, in extradition we can still look at a much longer list of jurisprudence to rely on.

This is due not only to the longer tradition of extradition and the fact that personal data cases are often settled out of court, although the latter seems to be changing after some high-profile cases.[21] Also a significant amount of individuals whose personal data have been misused will never even notice this has happened. If one does discover an abuse, only in the most serious of cases will a complaint be submitted to the competent authority.[22]

3. USING THE PERIMETERS OF EXTRADITION FOR DATA PROTECTION

In the previous section the similarities and differences between the adequacy requirement in the context of data exchange and the human rights requirement in the context of extradition were examined. Even though the protected interests may not correspond fully, examining them will assist in testing the limits of adequacy. The larger amount of jurisprudence in the context of extradition will serve that function as well. Aspects of interstate cooperation and the concept of trust show strong parallels between the two requirements. I continue examining interstate cooperation in the next step of this analysis.

Interstate cooperation has a variety of aspects fed by a long tradition of diplomatic traffic, drafting and negotiating treaties and also preventing and resolving conflicts. Analysing a specific part of cooperation and touching upon conflicting obligations automatically brings up questions on how to prevent conflicts. In the context of extradition, van der Wilt distinguished four strategies that states rely on to avoid conflict situations.[23] These are also relevant for the context of information exchange and data protection and can offer some clarity in the adequacy debate between the EU and the US. I therefore use the avoidance techniques described by van der Wilt to take a further step in using extradition perimeters for the purpose of information exchange.

---

21 See for example: E. Edwards, 'Increase seen in law suits for failing to protect personal data', *The Irish Times*, 26.03.2015, <http://www.irishtimes.com/business/increase-seen-in-law-suits-for-failing-to-protect-personal-data-1.2154537> and P. Herbert, 'Max Mosley search results case settled by Google', 22.05.2015, <http://www.hamlins.co.uk/max-mosley-search-results-case-settled-by-google-2>.

22 To illustrate this: the Eurobarometer survey on data protection conducted in 2015 revealed that six out of ten persons did not know the public authority in their country that is responsible for protecting their rights regarding personal data. Yet, more than two-thirds of respondents who felt that they did not have complete control over their personal data said that they were concerned about this lack of control. Special *Eurobarometer* 431 – 'Data Protection, European Commision, Directorate-General for Justice and Consumers', 2015, pp. 12 and 51.

23 H. van der Wilt, 'On the Hierarchy between Extradition and Human Rights', in E. De Wet and J. Vidmar (eds.), *Hierarchy in International Law: The Place of Human Rights*, Oxford Scholarship Online 2012, p. 151 et seq.

3.1. AVOIDANCE STRATEGIES

States typically rely on one of four strategies attempting to avoid conflict with other states. Relying on the rule of non-inquiry and the separation of powers doctrine, states can claim that their courts are not allowed to investigate another state's administration of criminal justice and ignore the issue exists. Secondly, the requesting state could also offer the requested state assurances that no risk of human rights violation exists. A third strategy could be to enable redress in case of a human rights violation and a fourth method means turning to the person involved for sufficient evidence of a risk of ill-treatment.[24] The common foundation that van der Wilt rightfully recognises for these avoidance techniques – and basically the reason why these strategies exist in the first place – is the fact that a refusal of extradition triggers state responsibility while a human rights infringement is only a possibility. In other words, states open their proverbial umbrella attempting to shift responsibility towards a probability.

Van der Wilt described these strategies for avoiding possible conflicts in extradition, a form of interstate cooperation that often makes emotions run high, but the four methods are equally relevant in information exchange between Member States and third states.

3.1.1. *Negated and assumed adequacy*

It is hardly likely that the rule of non-inquiry would be relied upon in transborder data flows to avoid conflict. Even if the European Commission could theoretically pass for the executive branch of the EU institutions, the Commision received the competence in accordance with Directive 95/46/EC to examine the level of data protection in a third state.[25] What could indirectly qualify as an example of non-inquiry is the negation of the adequacy requirement in several trans-Atlantic agreements. In its cooperation agreement with the US, Eurojust incorporated a rule that no general restrictions for processing of data with respect to the legal standards of the receiving party may be imposed as a condition for delivering information.[26] This can – and should – be read as a denial of any adequacy requirement, since the requirement is nothing else but a condition without which information should not be transmitted. Moreover, it is a restriction with respect to the third state's legal standards on processing the received data, and it is a general restriction. The EU–US MLA Agreement that was signed in

24 Ibid., p. 151.

25 Member States' authorities are in accordance with Directive 95/46/EC also mandated to make adequacy assessments and in accordance with the 2008 Framework Decision they have exclusive competence to do so.

26 The precise text of the provision includes the term 'generic': Art. 10, Agreement between Eurojust and the United States of America, 06.11.2006.

2003[27] included a copy of the provision prohibiting general restrictions. The EU–US Agreement on the use and transfer of passenger name records to the US Department of Homeland Security (PNR Agreement)[28] and the EU–US Agreement on the exchange of financial messaging data for the purpose of the Terrorist Finance Tracking Programme (TFTP Agreement)[29] both provide in assumed adequacy by stating that the receiving US authority is deemed to ensure an adequate level of data protection for the processing of data in accordance with the agreement. Still, no full adequacy assessment was made prior to these agreements.

An important caveat should be made, though. The rule of non-inquiry and the above described negation and assumption of adequacy have a different rationale. While non-inquiry is based on sovereignty and separation of powers, both negated and assumed adequacy are the result of negotiations between EU and US authorities searching a compromise between two different data protection legal frameworks and still trying to ensure the smooth flow of information. It is thus more a matter of tipping the balance in favour of undisturbed data transfers; although the outcome is the same: the fact that the third state's system may harbour risks for unfair data processing is not thoroughly examined before data transfers are carried out.

3.1.2. *Assurances*

What is significantly more likely to be used by states trying to avoid the adequacy requirement causing conflict is receiving assurances from the third state that the personal data in question will be processed in a fair and just way. Diplomatic assurances are a frequently used mechanism in interstate cooperation, especially in extradition cases.[30] It is important to note that these are also often met with skepticism based on the smoke and fire analogy.[31]

---

27 Agreement 25 June 2003 on mutual legal assistance between the European Union and the United States of America, [2003] OJ L 181/34–42.

28 Agreement between the United States of America and the European Union on the use and transfer of passenger name records to the United States Department of Homeland Security, [2012] OJ L 215/5.

29 Agreement between the European Union and the United States of America on the processing and transfer of Financial Messaging Data from the European Union to the United States for the purposes of the Terrorist Finance Tracking Program, [2010] OJ L 195/5–14.

30 For an overview, see B. Van Ginkel and F. Rojas, 'Use of Diplomatic Assurances in Terrorism-related Cases. In Search of a Balance between Security Concerns and Human Rights Obligations', Expert Meeting Paper International Centre for Counter-Terrorism, The Hague 2011.

31 See J. Silvis, 'Extradition and Human Rights. Diplomatic Assurances and Human Rights in the Extradition Context', Lecture presented at Council of Europe, PC-OC Meeting, 20.05.2014, pp. 16–17.

In the context of commercial activities the now annulled Safe Harbour framework listed commitments US companies voluntarily signed in order to enable data processing activities in the EU. In the context of criminal investigations two examples come to mind in the trans-Atlantic cooperation: the above-mentioned EU–US PNR Agreement and the EU–US TFTP Agreement.

In the case of commercial activities, the Safe Harbour framework was the compromise found after the proposed Directive 95/46/EC concerned many US companies doing business in the EU. It basically is a list of assurances to avoid conflicts erupting from the US data protection framework not being adequate from an EU perspective. The European Commission adopted a decision in 2000 confirming that the Safe Harbour framework presented an adequate level of data protection in accordance with the Directive. It is this decision that was annulled in October 2015 after the Irish High Court turned to the CJEU for a preliminary ruling. The referral was triggered by a complaint originating from Austrian citizen Maximillian Schrems. Schrems claimed that after the leaks by Edward Snowden in 2013 and the data processing programmes disclosed by these leaks and operated by the US National Security Agency, the US data protection legal system could no longer be rubber-stamped as adequate and the Commission decision of 2000 should be declared void. Additional feature in this case was the entry into force of the Charter of Fundamental Rights in the EU legal system[32] since Art. 8 of the Charter introduced for the first time a genuine right to data protection besides the right to a private life in Art. 7.

The CJEU declared the Commission's adequacy decision invalid. In its ruling the Court referred to the fact that EU legislation involving interference with fundamental rights must lay down clear and precise rules governing the scope and application of a measure and imposing minimum safeguards. Legal provisions are not limited to what is strictly necessary when they authorise, on a generalised basis, storage of all the personal data of all the persons whose data has been transferred from the EU to the US without any differentiation, limitation or exception being made in the light of the objective pursued and without an objective criterion by which to determine the limits of access to the data and of its subsequent use, for purposes which are specific, strictly restricted and capable of justifying the interference which access to the data and its use entail.[33] From the point of view of the assurance technique, a particularly interesting aspect of the Court's decision in the *Schrems* case is the suggestion that after an adequacy decision the Commission should engage in periodical checks to verify whether the adequacy finding is still factually and legally justified.[34] Monitoring any amendments to the already checked third states' systems makes sense when

32 [2000] OJ C 364.

33 Case C-362/14, *Schrems v. Data Protection Commissioner* ECLI:EU:C:2015:650, 91–92.

34 Ibid., 76.

assurances were provided but the state in question changes its legislation. A meaningful argument against monitoring is first of all the boom in monitoring mechanisms of the past years on several levels: EU, CoE and UN. No doubt these are highly respectable efforts for improving legal frameworks in specific fields of interest, yet one could wonder what the risk is of inflation of monitoring mechanisms or monitoring fatigue. Member States' authorities and international institutions could soon be doing more monitoring than substantial legislative work. Another argument relates to the *Schrems* case and the fact that monitoring the US data protection legal framework would have not revealed the secret programmes that were used.

The so-called SWIFT scandal was uncovered by journalists in 2006 revealing covert transfers of financial messaging data from Belgian-based company SWIFT to the US Treasury.[35] The Belgian data protection authority concluded that SWIFT did not fulfil the relevant legal obligations transferring the data in accordance with the US Treasury's administrative subpoenas. Following these findings and considering the importance of the data transfers for investigating the financing of terrorist activities, the US Treasury negotiated assurances with the EU in 2007.[36] In 2010 after SWIFT made changes to its technical infrastructure, these were replaced by an actual agreement known as the TFTP Agreement.

Difficult discussions between EU institutions and US authorities on the transfer of passenger name record (PNR) data from EU airlines to the US Department of Homeland Security involving the use of a push or pull mechanism, the amount of data transferred and the retention period, first led to a set of assurances called 'undertakings'.[37] Also in this case, an agreement was later concluded containing these assurances.[38]

The avoidance technique of assurances seems to be rather popular in the trans-Atlantic cooperation covering personal data transfers. Not that this is a bad thing. Organising transfers between such fundamentally different data protection frameworks, this may be the only way. Nonetheless, this should be done with due regard for the essential safeguards incorporated in both systems,

---

35 See E. Lichtblau and J. Risen, 'Bank Data Is Sifted by U.S. in Secret to Block Terror,' *New York Times*, 06.06.2006, and Commissie voor de Bescherming van de Persoonlijke Levenssfeer (Privacy Commission Belgium), Decision 09.12.2008.

36 EU-US Exchange of Letters on SWIFT and the Terrorist Finance Tracking Programme, [2007] OJ C 166/17–27. These representations were published in the US in 72 Federal Register 204, 23.10.2007, p. 60054.

37 Commission Decision of 14 May 2004 on the adequate protection of personal data contained in the Passenger Name Record of air passengers transferred to the United States' Bureau of Customs and Border Protection, [2004] OJ L 235/11–14; Annex Undertakings of the Department of Homeland Security Bureau of Customs and Border Protection (CBP), [2004] OJ L 235/15–22.

38 Agreement between the United States of America and the European Union on the use and transfer of passenger name records to the United States Department of Homeland Security, [2012] OJ L 215/5.

such as necessity and proportionality. The latter was stressed by the CJEU in the above-mentioned *Schrems* case.[39]

3.1.3. *Legal remedies*

A third avoidance technique is reliance on redress mechanisms or legal remedies. Extradition decisions could be taken more easily when the requesting state assures that remedies are available in case a human right infringement should occur.[40] This can only be confirmed in the context of information exchange and data protection. In fact the presence of redress mechanisms is listed as one of the aspects to include in an adequacy assessment. Redress was also the Achilles heel of the trans-Atlantic data transfers so far. Should EU citizens have information that their personal data are processed in an inadequate manner by US authorities, the 1974 US Privacy Act is only applicable to US citizens and residents, extending no rights to EU citizens.[41] On 10 December 2016, a general EU–US agreement for the protection of personal data exchanged for the purpose of criminal investigations entered into force after receiving approval from the European Parliament.[42] The European Commission made the final conclusion of the agreement dependent on the adoption of the Judicial Redress Act by the US Congress, which is a fact since 24 February 2016.[43] The Judicial Redress Act aims at extending the relevant provisions of the Privacy Act to EU citizens. More on this new development in section 3.2.

3.1.4. *Evidence*

Van der Wilt pointed out that in the relationship between extradition and human rights, delivering evidence of potential ill-treatment is one of the most difficult issues. Due to what is at stake, the threshold is high, as there should be specific reasons for believing that the person involved is personally in danger of being subjected to ill-treatment.[44] Yet the human rights infringement is still a risk or eventuality, just like the potential unfair processing of transferred personal data.

---

39 Case C-362/14, *Schrems v Data Protection Commissioner* (CJEU, 2015), 93.

40 van der Wilt, above n. 17, p. 169.

41 5 USC §552a(a)(2). See also EP Report, 2013/2188(INI), 21.02.2014.

42 Council Decision (EU) 2016/2220 of 2 December 2016, on the conclusion, on behalf of the European Union, of the Agreement between the United States of America and the European Union on the protection of personal information relating to the prevention, investigation, detection, and prosecution of criminal offences, [2016] OJ L 336/1–13.

43 Judicial Redress Act of 2015, Pub.L. 114–126.

44 van der Wilt, above n. 17, p. 171.

Moreover, it is an eventuality that would happen on the territory of the third state involved but based on standards that this third state may not have ratified. How can one assess the risk of having one's personal data processed in an unfair manner when this processing is done on the territory of a third state and is regulated in the legal order of that state?

The questions concerning the risk of unfair processing and delivering evidence of such risk are inherently connected to the extraterritorial effect of European human rights and data protection standards. This subject is dealt with in the following section.

3.2. REAL RISK

The *Soering* judgment indeed introduced the first standards one should apply when speaking of human rights requirements and the risk of ill-treatment in the state that requested extradition. Several other cases and rulings followed in which the ECtHR gave further indications on how to deal with this potential human rights infringement in the requested state. The question now arises whether we can use the Court's findings in delineating the perimeters of the adequacy requirement for data transfers to third states. Obviously, the ECHR does not contain the right to data protection, so we need to rely on the jurisprudence on the right to a private life for this analysis.

In fact, what we want to know here is whether it is appropriate for Member State authorities or the European Commission to scrutinise the processing of personal data in the third state before a transfer of personal data is agreed and, whether a transfer can be denied based on potential unfair processing of the data in the third state. Looking at the ECtHR's jurisprudence on the extraterritorial effect of human rights in the context of extradition, essential findings on the fair trial rights from Art. 6 ECHR can be used for drawing the perimeters of the adequacy requirement. In principle, Art. 6 does not have an extraterritorial effect but under certain conditions, the ECtHR has recognised that a Member State may refuse extradition based on the unfairness of criminal proceedings in the third state. For this reason, I will examine whether we can use the same criteria defined by the Court in its extradition jurisprudence for the adequacy requirement in data transfers to third states.

The fact that it is Art. 6 ECHR on fair trial rights in criminal proceedings that is used as the benchmark here, does not mean that these findings are only valid for data transfers for the purpose of criminal investigations. What is examined in this part is under which circumstances a transfer of personal data can be denied based on what could happen with the data post-transfer, regardless of the purpose for which the data were transferred.

The ECHR does not include a rule requiring the Member States to impose their standards on third states, meaning that Member States do not need to verify the fairness of a trial to be held in a third state before deciding on extraditing an individual.[45] Yet, when two cumulative criteria are fulfilled, Member States can and should deny cooperation. These criteria are found in the ECtHR's rulings on the matter. First, the ill-treatment in the third state needs to reach the threshold of a flagrant denial of justice. Second, there should be a real risk the individual involved will be the subject of ill-treatment and this is for the applicant to prove. Applying these two criteria in cases where unfair processing of personal data is the ill-treatment, means that a flagrant denial of fair processing should be proven.

It was in the *Soering* judgment that the ECtHR for the first time recognised the flagrant denial of justice standard. Defining the test that is now established in its jurisprudence, the Court relies on the fact that a trial is manifestly contrary to the rights of Art. 6 ECHR or the principles embodied therein.[46] An infringement of these rights that is so fundamental that boils down to a destruction of the very essence of these rights.[47] The test is therefore rather stringent and further precisions are lacking. Nevertheless, a handful of examples from the Court's case law are available. These include trials that are summary in nature while also disregarding the rights of the defence,[48] deliberate and systematic refusal for a person detained in a foreign country to have access to a lawyer,[49] and use in criminal proceedings of statements obtained by torture of the suspect or another person.[50]

Finding an equivalent of the test for the area of data protection, processing that is manifestly contrary to the applicable standards of data processing should be the criterion. A denial of necessity and proportionality by collecting a mass amount of personal data then comes to mind since a bulk collection of data that has no nexus with a specific criminal investigation denies the existence of necessity and proportionality in the first place. Lacking judicial or administrative remedies for reacting against a data protection infringement would be a relevant example as well, especially in light of the current EU–US cooperation in which the so-called umbrella agreement on data exchange for law enforcement purposes was frozen for as long as the US had not adopted the Judicial Redress Act introducing judicial remedies to EU citizens.

On 24 February 2016 President Obama signed the Act,[51] an event that was referred to by European Commissioner for Justice Jourová as a historical achievement and one that paved the way for the signature of the EU–US

---

45 Council of Europe, European Court of Human Rights, 'Guide on Article 6 – Right to a Fair Trial (criminal limb)', 2013, p. 53.

46 *Othman (Abu Qatada) v. UK*, App. no. 8139/09, §259, ECHR 2011.

47 Council of Europe, European Court of Human Rights, above n. 45, p. 53.

48 *Bader and Kanbor v. Sweden*, App. no. 13284/04, §47, ECHR, 2005.

49 *Al-Moayad v. Germany*, App. no. 35865/03, §101, ECHR 2007.

50 *Othman (Abu Qatada) v. UK*, App. no. 8139/09, §267, ECHR 2011.

51 Judicial Redress Act of 2015, Pub.L. 114–126.

umbrella agreement on data exchange in criminal matters.[52] Bearing this latest development in mind, one could state that the lacking of judicial redress for EU citizens in the US is no longer an issue. However, the newly signed Judicial Redress Act is only referring to 'covered countries or organizations' and 'covered persons'. A designation by the Attorney General and the publication thereof in the Federal Register is needed before a country or a regional economic integration organisation – the latter seems to refer to the EU – can benefit from the provisions of this act. Moreover, the conditions under which such designation is to be made include an American version of the adequacy requirement: the country or organisation first needs to have either entered into an agreement with the US providing in appropriate privacy protections for information shared for the purpose of preventing, investigating, detecting or prosecuting criminal offences or an effective sharing of information for these purposes and with appropriate privacy protections in place should be established. Additionally, the transfer of personal data for commercial purposes between the country or organisation and the US should be permitted and the policies on transferring data for commercial purposes of the country or organisation should not materially impede the national security interests of the US. It seems that the US still gave itself enough latitude to retrace their steps if necessary. Also, the US legal system is from an EU point of view not the easiest to understand. The 1974 Privacy Act that would be opened up to foreigners following the entry into force of the Judicial Redress Act, protects the privacy of 'records'.[53] The term has some similarities with personal data as used in the EU but its interpretations can be deceiving for EU citizens, as well as the many exceptions included the Privacy Act. In all, it may seem a groundbreaking achievement that EU citizens will be given judicial remedies before US courts in case of irregular processing of their data; in reality it will be rather demanding for an EU citizen to first, find out about

52 Statement by Commissioner Věra Jourová on the signature of the Judicial Redress Act by President Obama, 24.02.2016, <http://europa.eu/rapid/press-release_STATEMENT-16-401_en.htm>. Council Decision (EU) 2016/2220 of 2 December 2016, on the conclusion, on behalf of the European Union, of the Agreement between the United States of America and the European Union on the protection of personal information relating to the prevention, investigation, detection, and prosecution of criminal offences, [2016] OJ L 336/1–13.

53 5 USC §552a(a)(4): 'means any item, collection, or grouping of information about an individual that is maintained by an agency, including, but not limited to, his education, financial transactions, medical history, and criminal or employment history and that contains his name, or the identifying number, symbol, or other identifying particular assigned to the individual, such as a finger or voice print or a photograph.' The Guidelines interpreting the Privacy Act added that the meaning of 'record' does not correspond to the meaning given to the term in the conventional sense or as used in automatic data processing. It refers to the tangible or documentary (as opposed to a record contained in a person's memory) carrier of personal information. This means it does not necessarily correspond to the meaning of the term 'computer record' or even 'file'. See Office of Management and Budget (OMB) Guidelines, Privacy Act, 40 Fed. Reg., 09.07.1975, pp. 28951–28952.

the irregular processing and second, understand the US laws well enough for making a successful case before the competent US court.

A second limb of the flagrant denial of justice test developed by the ECtHR is delivering evidence of the risk of ill-treatment. According to the Court the same burden of proof should apply in extradition cases as in the examination of extradition and expulsions under Art. 3 ECHR on the prohibition of torture and inhuman or degrading treatment or punishment. This means that it is the applicant who should bring forward evidence proving that there are substantial grounds for believing that, if extradited to the requesting state in question, he would face a real risk of being subjected to a flagrant denial of justice. The government of that state could attempt to prove this is not the case.[54] Based on the ECtHR's case law, risk is determined by examining the foreseeable consequences of transferring an individual to the requesting state, taking his personal circumstances and the situation in the requesting state into account. Obviously, those facts are of principal importance that are known or ought to have been known to the requested state at the time of the transfer.[55]

Making assessments of a flagrant denial of justice based on foreseeable consequences is a burdensome task, especially when controversial issues such as torture, inhuman or degrading treatment are concerned or other forms of ill-treatment of individuals that states wish to keep covered. The secrecy surrounding the treatment of extradited individuals led to cases where crucial facts only came to light after the transfer.[56] In the *Al-Saadoon and Mufdhi v UK* case, the ECtHR stated that such information can still be regarded.[57]

3.3. NEW LIMIT FOR THE ADEQUACY REQUIREMENT

Several aspects of the previous sections of this chapter have equivalents in data protection and the adequacy procedure. Data processing, in particular when done for the purpose of intelligence analysis, has been revealed by Edward Snowden to have taken place in secret in the US. The covert programmes used by the NSA and other authorities collected personal data in bulk and breached the necessity and proportionality principle that is considered to be a basic data protection standard in the EU. In the *Schrems* ruling, the CJEU confirmed this by stating that

> Legislation is not limited to what is strictly necessary where it authorises, on a generalised basis, storage of all the personal data of all the persons whose data has been

54 *Inter alia Othman (Abu Qatada) v. UK*, App. no. 8139/09, §272, ECHR 2011.
55 *Al-Saadoon and Mufdhi v. UK*, App. no. 61498/08, §125, ECHR, 2010.
56 Silvis, above n. 31, p. 7.
57 *Al-Saadoon and Mufdhi v. UK*, App. no. 61498/08, §125, ECHR, 2010.

> transferred from the European Union to the United States without any differentiation, limitation or exception being made in the light of the objective pursued and without an objective criterion being laid down by which to determine the limits of the access of the public authorities to the data, and of its subsequent use, for purposes which are specific, strictly restricted and capable of justifying the interference which both access to that data and its use entail.[58]

European Commision Decision 2000/520 that labelled the Safe Harbour framework as offering an adequate level of data protection was declared void by the CJEU in this judgment. Interestingly, this decision also included a provision referring to the imminent risk of grave harm to data subjects as one of the reasons for suspending data transfers to an organisation that has signed the Safe Harbour framework.[59]

What is needed to decide on a flagrant denial of justice is a manifest breach of the fair trial rights and evidence of a real risk of ill-treatment. All of these aspects have equivalents when data protection is concerned. This means a conclusion can be drawn regarding the question whether the adequacy requirement can be treated the same way as the human rights requirement in extradition cases. In other words, is it appropriate for a state to examine and assess another state's level of data protection based on standards that the requesting state did not ratify? Making the analogy with the flagrant denial of justice and the criteria used by the ECtHR for its assessment, the conclusion can be drawn that for transfers of personal data to third states, it is appropriate for a state to examine the third state's level of data protection on a real risk for a flagrant denial of data protection. Evidence for potential ill-treatment should be delivered by the data subject who claims his personal data have been unfairly processed in the third state.

4. CONCLUSION: A FLAGRANT DENIAL OF DATA PROTECTION

States have the essential task and duty of protecting individuals based on human rights legal instruments and at the same time engaging in cooperation with other states based on bilateral or multilateral treaties and conventions. Tension between the protective and the cooperative functions are especially apparent in extradition cases.[60] The past few years have shown that such tension does not just exist in the transfer of persons but also in the transfer of personal data from EU Member States to third states, especially the US. In extradition cases, the

---

58 Case C-362/14, *Schrems v. Data Protection Commissioner*, ECLI:EU:C:2015:650, 93.

59 Art. 3 of Decision 2000/520/EC, [2000] OJ L 215/7.

60 Silvis, above n. 31, p. 1.

requested state has the right to check the legal order of the requesting state when a real risk of flagrant denial of justice exists. For the purpose of redefining the limits of the adequacy requirement in data exchange by relying on the human rights protection in extradition caes, I applied the test of a flagrant denial of justice on the transfer of personal data from Member States to third states. This analysis resulted in a flagrant denial of data protection test.

The flagrant denial of data protection test would mean that a Member State has the right to refuse cooperation with a third state when the legal order of the latter has been examined and its processing of personal data was found to be manifestly contrary to fair data processing. In other words, the tension between protection and cooperation stops when denial of data protection is flagrant.[61] Provided that the data subject can deliver evidence that there is a real risk for flagrant denial of data protection, the transfer can be suspended or refused. The concept of fair data processing refers to the standards of the CoE's Data Protection Convention. These may not technically be human rights nonetheless the ECtHR has referred to data protection when examining the human right to a private life. In addition, the EU Charter recognised the right to data protection as an independant fundamental right.

Bulk collection of personal data combined with a denial of judicial redress is the unfortunate conclusion of EU–US data transfers of the past years. The combination of the two can – and in my opinion should – be seen as a flagrant denial of data protection triggering the end of trans-Atlantic data transfers. This conclusion may be after the fact, considering the annulment of the European Commission's adequacy decision in October 2015 and considering that the Commission also demanded the enactment of a new Judicial Redress Bill in the US Congress in order to create legal certainty and enforcement of data protection of EU citizens before US courts. Now that has been done, this does not mean it is a reason to celebrate. It is important now that the European Commission secures the designation by the US Attorney General for all EU Member States to be covered by the Judicial Redress Act. Even though the US has in the past expressed criticism on the adequacy requirement in the European data protection legal framework, it is rather ironic that this newest piece of legislation introduces a similar requirement demanding appropriate privacy protections.

As a side note, it is important to stress that this test can be used in the exchange of personal data with other third states as well. Since many data processing companies have their main seat in the US, we tend to focus on that particular state even though states such as China, Russia and Saudi Arabia – states involved in trade relations with European Member States – could also have difficulties passing the adequacy test.

---

61 See, *mutatis mutandis*, *Drozd and Janousek v. France and Spain*, App. no. 12747/87, §110, ECHR 1992.

Was it pretentious of the EU to require an adequate level of data protection from third states before transferring personal data considering that third states did not ratify the data protection standards? Referring again to the protection and cooperation functions, I think not. Balancing the two by using the flagrant denial of data protection test could however help in understanding the seriousness of the situation and in finding the limits of the adequacy requirement. Having started this chapter with a quote by George B. Trubow, it is appropriate to end it with another of his thoughts:

> It will be ironic, indeed, if Europe's insistence on the protection of human rights causes this country to pay some real attention to informational privacy in both the public and private sectors. Usually we are in the position of lecturing other nations about the sanctity of fundamental human rights; in the informational privacy dimension we are the ones who must be lectured.[62]

[62] Trubow, above n. 1, p. 175.

23. A BEHAVIOURAL ALTERNATIVE TO THE PROTECTION OF PRIVACY*

Dariusz Kloza**

1. INTRODUCTION

The frankest and freest and privatest product of the human mind and heart is a love letter; the writer gets his limitless freedom of statement and expression from his sense that no stranger is going to see what he is writing. Sometimes there is a breach-of-promise case by and by; and when he sees his letter in print it makes him cruelly uncomfortable and he perceives that he never would have unbosomed himself to that large and honest degree if he had known that he was writing for the public.

Mark Twain (c. 1906)[1]

I.

On 7 February 2016 Joseph ceased to use what had once been his private e-mail account. He has never used any of the mainstream e-mail providers such as

* I have discussed 'behaviour' as an alternative privacy protection with many of my mentors, colleagues and friends around the world and I am indebted to all of them. In particular, I thank – in alphabetical order – Irina Baraliuc, Marcin Betkier, István Böröcz, Roger Clarke, Michał Czerniawski, Paul De Hert, Philippa Druce, Raphaël Gellert, Jake Goldenfein, Graham Greenleaf, Barry Guihen, Mireille Hildebrandt, Lucas Melgaço, Marit Moe-Pryce, Vagelis Papakonstantinou, Cristina Pauner Chulvi, Dan J.B. Svantesson, Matt Szafert and Nigel Waters for their extensive comments on an earlier version of this chapter. I am grateful for an exchange of views on a dedicated seminar *Encryption and other 'behavioural' alternatives for privacy protection*, held at the Swinburne University of Technology, Melbourne, Victoria, Australia on 19 April 2016, and in particular to Claudy Op den Kamp and Monika Žalnieriūtė. I thank two anonymous peer-reviewers for their suggestions. Finally, I am grateful to the Faculty of Law of Bond University, Gold Coast, Queensland, Australia for providing me time and space that allowed me to research and write this chapter. I further gratefully acknowledge financial support for that purpose received from the Fonds Wetenschappelijk Onderzoek – Vlaanderen (FWO).

** Research Group on Law, Science, Technology and Society, Vrije Universiteit Brussel; Peace Research Institute Oslo. E-mail: dariusz.kloza@vub.ac.be.

[1] *The Autobiography of Mark Twain*, Vol. 1, ed. H.E. Smith (2010); <http://www.marktwain project.org>.

Google, AOL, Apple or Yahoo. Instead, he opened this particular e-mail account at one of the major nationwide providers in the country Y, situated in Europe, where he was born and where he lived at that time. That particular e-mail account required a paid subscription, though its annual fee was rather negligible. In return, it offered a mailbox free from annoying advertisements, which – in the early years – came attached to the bottom of each message. Joseph trusted this provider that his e-mail account would be free of any commercial spying and similar practices, which – from Joseph's point of view – were unwanted. (He could not recall ever buying anything suggested by any advertisement, no matter how persuasive they were.)

Back in 2006 it was a conscious choice dictated by an idealistic desire to avoid dominant multinational companies, fuelled largely by the cyberpunk literature and movies of Joseph's childhood. Although Joseph has never been a 'digital native' – i.e. someone who grew up already surrounded by emerging technologies, and thus having acquired, almost automatically, high-tech literacy skills – he has quickly become 'tech-savvy' and these technologies have fascinated him ever since. When he was around ten years old his parents bought him his first personal computer and this way he has witnessed the most of the technological progress of 1990s. His fascination, at that stage, was rather romantic: his enthusiasm grew with each new own discovery. (To the extent that he too was initially captivated by Barlow's *Declaration of the Independence of Cyberspace*,[2] which – Joseph claims – for him shed new light on Schiller's '*deine Zauber binden wieder*').[3] In his elementary school he learned to code a couple of computer programming languages. Some 20 years later, he claims, he can 'speak fluently only HTML' (Hyper Text Markup Language). In the golden age of cyberspace, together with a fellow student at the university, he even had run a blog devoted to the intersection of law and technology. The web archives nowadays have 'thankfully forgotten it'.

Yet his fascination for technology has never been unconditional. He certainly has never blindly trusted technology. For instance, being a frequent traveller, he always carries with him some cash in a 'hard currency', because credit cards might unexpectedly stop working. He always covers the keyboard of the terminal while typing in his personal identification number (PIN). While travelling, some of his credit cards once or twice were skimmed and his bank blocked further transactions on its own initiative. Joseph was glad that his money was safeguarded, but also equally annoyed that he was deprived of access to his funds until he came back to his country of residence and received a new card in a

---

2 J.P. Barlow, *Declaration of the Independence of Cyberspace*, Davos, 8 February 1996, <https://www.eff.org/cyberspace-independence>.

3 A passage from Friedrich Schiller's *Ode to Joy* (*An die Freude*, 1795). In the majority of translations to English interpreted as 'your magic binds again [reunites]'.

bank branch. Having, under social pressure, once signed up to a major social networking site and having kept it for a few years, he quit after falling victim to a data breach.

With the passage of time, Joseph has changed his desktop computer for a laptop and a dial-up connection to broadband wireless. He was using his private e-mail account predominantly for casual discussions with family and friends, sporadic online shopping and travel reservations. Sometimes his e-mail conversations would concern intimate facts concerning himself or his family and close friends. From time to time he exchanged views on delicate subjects and politics, sometimes explored in a very sarcastic way. However, these conversations have never amounted to anything illegal or otherwise illicit. Nevertheless, Joseph assumed his private communications were secure enough and – in the early years – he did not employ any extra layers of protection such as encryption or anonymisation. The only exceptions to this were services encrypted by default, e.g. online banking. He would make sure his anti-virus software and its database were up-to-date. In general, he had been using relatively strong passwords, changed periodically, so – at the end of the day – he had been sleeping rather well.

As the technology progressed and the equipment became more affordable, Joseph increasingly accessed his e-mails on multiple devices, e.g. on home and office computers. Put simply, it was both convenient and useful. Technically speaking, this involved subscribing to the IMAP (Internet Mail Access Protocol) communication protocol, which allows for synchronisation among these devices, yet keeping copies of all e-mails not only on each device, but also on the server. At a certain point, using the IMAP protocol became beneficial further for backup purposes. There was a time when backup was of little concern for Joseph. At home, he has had in his possession an external hard drive and he would make a backup copy once in a while. At work, he would avoid any cloud computing services and he would access his professional Dropbox account – demanded by his employer – solely via a website, thus avoiding the need to install a specific application on his laptop and avoiding any accidental upload. However, once while boarding a plane, his backpack accidentally dropped onto the ground, causing significant damage to his laptop, including a permanent loss of some data.

In the meantime, Joseph has progressively become aware and conscious of both the benefits and drawbacks of innovation and emerging technologies, of their impact on his life and the lives of others in society. Eventually, dealing with these technologies has become a part of his professional life. He called it *la déformation professionnelle*. Joseph is not a conservative, quite the contrary, but he sees that a tiny number of things were better in the past and he views some reasonable degree of 'offline-ness' as one of those.

Joseph would use his mobile phone until the device ceases to function. (His last mobile phone served him for six years and – while obtaining a new one – he lamented that nowadays his options were limited almost entirely to smart phones.) Determined to make do, he decided not to enable any 'smart' functionality and would use his phone solely for calling and texting. With the phone he currently possesses, he is still able to take out its battery while attending important meetings. (For such meetings, he leaves his tablet in the office.) He would put a removable sticker on the laptop built-in camera. He would reject the majority of loyalty programmes, short of those of airline alliances, his guilty pleasure. In his web browser, he would enable a do-not-track functionality, install a blocking application for advertisements and an add-on to blur his Internet Protocol (IP) address. He would use unorthodox search engines and erase his browsing history and cookies every few days.

He would prefer reading on paper than on his tablet. Each year, on holidays, he would disconnect entirely for a couple of weeks. He would not even touch a keyboard of any device. He calls it a 'digital detox'. While travelling, he would decline to use any navigation device and instead would consult a pocket map or ask someone for directions. (He once lamented that the generation just a decade younger than him had lost the sense of directions and 'these days they cannot find their way without Google Maps'.)

On 7 February 2016 a new surveillance law entered into force in country Y. This piece of law constituted a part of a broader reform process pursued by a new far-right government, elected just a few months earlier. Not going into details, certain law enforcement agencies of that government became empowered to read too much – in Joseph's opinion – of his communications, without any concrete reason or adequate safeguards. In particular, due to deliberate vagueness of legal provisions, these agencies became allowed to access any data stored at any server within the borders of the country Y. Because Joseph was using the IMAP protocol and because a copy of his data was kept on a server, these agencies could access *de facto* the entirety of his e-mail communication. While Joseph would assume, even dangerously, that similar practices debated or introduced in truly democratic countries would be genuinely used to fight against serious crime and terrorism, there exists a critical threat that these new surveillance powers in country Y, the country of his passport, could be used also to undermine the political opposition, now or in the future. Even though Joseph no longer lives there – together with many of his fellow citizens, also those living abroad – he finds what this new government does is pretty much undemocratic. Being born in Eastern Europe and being aware of atrocities committed in the past by the Gestapo, NKWD, Bezpieka, Securitate or Stasi – just to name a few – many of these with the aid of information collected by these security services, Joseph felt 'cruelly uncomfortable'.

When in 2013 Edward Snowden revealed spying practices carried out by the US National Security Agency, Joseph was rather glad his e-mail provider was not compromised. However, a few of Joseph's friends have used mainstream providers such as Google, and this way some of his e-mails could have been spied on. However, he had nothing to do with American politics and actually not that much correspondence has been exchanged that way. Thus this did not trouble him greatly. Yet both these developments – in the US and, subsequently, in the country of his passport – eventually convinced him he needed some extra steps to protect his interests.

On 7 February 2016 Joseph therefore ceased to use this particular private e-mail account. He did not think he had any other choice. The law in country Y has been used instrumentally to legitimise the abuse of power. First, the 'cost' of going to a constitutional court to challenge the law, assuming it was possible and that it would make any change, constituted an entry barrier. Second, he could not encrypt for himself his e-mails already stored on the server. In practice, he changed the modern IMAP to the old-fashioned Post Office Protocol 3 (POP3) and downloaded all the e-mails to his own device, automatically deleting the totality of their copies from the server. Still, this has not been a perfect solution: he cannot exclude backup copies, kept by the provider in the course of normal business practice, finding its way to the wrong hands. (In point of fact, this e-mail account still remains active as some of his relatives, colleagues and friends might not yet know his new e-mail address. He intends to close down the old one within a year or so.)

He has not abandoned the idea of having an e-mail account for purely private purposes; quite the contrary. Some ideas came by word of mouth and – after some market research – he opted for a provider offering end-to-end encryption, no 'back doors', 'key escrows' or similar practices, whose servers are located in a jurisdiction believed to be free from the peeping eyes not only of businesses but also of governments. Even with a lawful court order, such a service provider could hand over only encrypted data that cannot be read without a key. Even if the data were hacked or leaked, they would reveal a string of meaningless zeros and ones. And it would be difficult to compel him to hand over the decryption keys. He has eventually trusted that this provider would actually do what it claims. Joseph likes to believe he partakes in a bigger movement. With his friends and colleagues, who are well-read in information and communication technologies, he has begun looking for effective means to protect privacy. Such debates recently concern alternatives for secure cloud storage of data or instant messaging. They still have not found what they are looking for.

II.

The story of Joseph is true and I know him personally.[4] His story has inspired me to ponder on the gradual failure of existing arrangements – i.e. modalities (like

---

[4] The name has been changed. 'Joseph' was chosen because 'J.' in 'Edward J. Snowden' stands for 'Joseph'. It was Mireille Hildebrandt with her chronicle of Diana's 'onlife world' (M. Hildebrandt, *Smart Technologies and the End(s) of Law: Novel Entanglements of Law and Technology*, Edward Elgar Publishing, Cheltenham 2015, pp. 1–7) who inspired me to start too with a story. The concluding sentence is adapted from U2 and their song 'I still haven't found what I'm looking for' (Clayton/Evans/Hewson/Mullen; 1987). I particularly thank Barry Guihen for his advice in giving account to Joseph's story.

the law), actors and dynamics between them – to *adequately* protect individual and collective interests, including privacy.

In our world, that is to say, the Western world, it is expected that the tripartite foundation of our societies – democracy, fundamental rights and the rule of law (in the Anglo-Saxon world) or *Rechtsstaat* (in continental Europe)[5] – would *adequately* protect individuals, the society and their respective, and sometimes contradictory, interests against abuse. This duty to protect adequately has multiple aspects. It first and foremost requires establishing a dedicated system of protection. It further includes drawing a 'thin red line' whenever these various interests diverge or conflict. It includes holding the state accountable for its own actions and inactions. It requires the state to ensure relevant actors within its jurisdiction partake in providing this adequate protection and to hold these actors accountable for that.[6] Some forms of protection are exclusive for the state, e.g. criminal justice or national security. Some others are 'shared', i.e. the state offers some protection in a form of e.g. enforceable legal rights, but a lot of room for manoeuvre is nevertheless left for individual choice. According to the belief of individual's freedom, she is to choose whether, when and how to be protected, thus complementing the system of protection. It is further expected that democracy, fundamental rights and the rule of law (*Rechtsstaat*) would ensure that both the public authorities (governments at all levels, independent regulatory authorities, etc.) as well as private actors, this including organisations and other individuals, would not interfere or invade, unless strictly necessary yet with some safeguards offered, with individual and collective interests. It is also expected that public authorities would operate on the basis of the law and within its limits, far from arbitrariness, while realising their public mission, including the provision of prosperity, safety and security, among others. This ideal is applicable to the entirety of political life. It includes both individual and collective interests and privacy is one of them. In some instances, the existing arrangements do their job excellently. In some other instances, these arrangements do not live up to the expectations vested therein. Put simply, in those instances the existing arrangements – i.e. modalities, actors and dynamics between them – have failed to *adequately* protect diverse interests and the protection of privacy is one of them.

---

5 Drawing boundaries between these four concepts lies beyond the scope of this chapter. Cf. further e.g. J. Waldron, 'The Rule of Law and the Importance of Procedure' in J. Fleming (ed.), *Getting to the Rule of Law*, New York University Press, New York 2011, p. 3.

6 This is a reference to the concept of 'system responsibility'. Cf. e.g. P. De Hert, 'Systeemverantwoordelijkheid Voor de Informatiemaatschappij Als Positieve Mensenrechtenverplichting' in D. Broeders, C. Cuijpers and J.E.J. Prins (eds.), *De Staat van Informatie*, Amsterdam University Press, Amsterdam 2011, pp. 33–95; P. De Hert, 'From the Principle of Accountability to System Responsibility? Key Concepts in Data Protection Law and Human Rights Law Discussions' (2011) *Proceedings of the Data Protection Conferences 2011 Budapest*, Budapest, pp. 95–96.

The protection of interests such as privacy is to a large extent achieved by means of regulation and the key modality of regulation is that of law. However, the law may sometimes be unable to offer any protection, the protection offered might be insufficient, the law might simply lack common sense or, worse, might be used instrumentally to approve an undemocratic practice. Resorting to other means to fill in the gap often brings only moderate consolation. As a result, people have less and less trust in the existing arrangements as well as in those who regulate (e.g. parliaments), execute these regulations (e.g. governments) and – sometimes – adjudicate (e.g. courts of law). The story of Joseph's private e-mail account illustrates this perfectly: initially, the law offered him no practical, effective or efficient protection from the peeping eyes of multinational companies, but he was still free to *choose* another e-mail provider, with a different business model, in another country with a different set of laws. For some years such a solution was acceptable to him as – even though later on the National Security Agency (NSA) in the United States (US) could have read these few e-mails extracted from his friends' accounts – he did not perceive it as an invasion crossing his own 'thin red line'. The main reason was that he had nothing to do with US politics. However, when the law in more and more countries, including the country of his passport, has been used to sanction the almost unlimited and warrantless searching powers of law enforcement authorities, this was too much for him. This threat – that someone could be reading his e-mails without his knowledge, sometimes without really good reason and that this might be used against him, now or later – touched upon him, his identity and dignity and he *chose* to cease using that particular e-mail account. Instead, he *chose* to subscribe to a provider offering encrypted services, accepting all consequences of his choice.

What Joseph did is to resort to his own *behaviour* to protect his interests, including his privacy. He chose to undertake certain actions or inactions to protect – when he was aware of threats and he understood them – those of his interests he considered vital and directly relevant to his personhood, even though his choice did not make his life easier. (He faced the truth that the more secure, the less available and less easy to use the service is.)

The use of behaviour to protect own interests is nothing new. In this setting, behaviour has a long history. For example, when trust in a messenger could not be sustained, it is Julius Caesar who has been credited with inventing perhaps the first, simplest and most widely known cryptography technique: in his private correspondence he would use a substitution cipher. He would write 'three letters back', i.e. replace the letter D by A, E by B, etc. However, the way in which behaviour is used nowadays to protect privacy, the reasons for that and their implications are rather new and thus merit academic attention. In this contribution I would like to explore the phenomenon of *behavioural means of privacy protection* as a reaction to the failure of the existing arrangements to offer *adequate* protection thereof.

III.

The structure of this chapter is rather simple. Section 2 overviews contemporarily available privacy protections and these could be of a regulatory (and in particular legal), organisational and technological nature. Section 3 analyses the inadequacies of these protections. I start with the underlying problem of the protection of privacy – i.e. the irreversibility of harm – and I next discuss main reasons for such inadequacies in each category of protections. In particular, I argue that contemporary regulatory protections are inadequate because they do not offer practical, effective and efficient protection; they do not keep pace with the ever-changing nature of the society, their needs and desires, on the one hand, and of innovation and technology, on the other; they are often used instrumentally to pursue specific political goals; and such a usage leads to the diminishment of public trust. These early parts give a succinct overview of the many avenues available to protect privacy. They subsequently argue that despite this multiplicity of ways, in some instances, contemporarily available privacy protections do not live up to the expectations vested therein. (I use a lot of examples and a reader in a hurry might safely omit them.) Therefore section 4 introduces the notion of behavioural means of privacy protection as a response to these inadequacies. Based on my own experience, lengthy discussions and observations, I overview their history, offer an early typology thereof and spell out their characteristics, conditions for their successful application and problems they might cause. Section 5 concludes this chapter by arguing for the recognition of behavioural protections as a standalone and legitimate means of privacy protection. It further speculates on side effects these protections might cause (e.g. chilling effect and social exclusion) and on the boundaries between their use and abuse. So far as possible, this chapter is accurate to end of November 2016.

In this chapter, I refrain from defining what 'privacy' and 'personal data protection' (or 'data privacy') are or what they do. I also refrain from distinguishing one from the other.[7] For the sake of ease for the reader, I use

---

[7] The distinction between 'privacy' and 'data protection' is based on the *method* by which they perform their function in the society. As Gutwirth and De Hert put it, 'the history and the practice of democratic constitutional states … always reveal the use and articulation of two distinct constitutional or legal tools. On the one hand, there are tools that tend to guarantee non-interference in individual matters and the *opacity of the individuals*. On the other hand … tools that tend to organise and guarantee the *transparency and accountability of the powerful*. These two instruments have the same ultimate objective, namely the limiting and controlling of power, but they realise this ambition in a different way, from a different perspective' (S. Gutwirth and P. De Hert, 'Regulating Profiling in a Democratic Constitutional State' in M. Hildebrandt and S. Gutwirth (eds.), *Profiling the European Citizen. Cross-Disciplinary Perspectives*, Springer, Dordrecht 2008, p. 275; emphasis in original). The former is conceptualised as 'privacy', the latter – 'personal data protection' or 'data privacy'. Cf. further e.g. G. González Fuster, *The Emergence of Personal Data Protection as a Fundamental Right of the EU*, Springer, Dordrecht 2014.

'privacy' to signify both. Instead, I discuss solely the *means* of their protection, as I have axiomatically assumed that both merit protection. The reader would nevertheless see I that tend to understand 'privacy' as a human right in the European sense, but this does not exhaust its other possible meanings. I use the term 'protections' (in plural) to denote the wide range of regulatory, organisational, technological and behavioural means (modalities) available for keeping privacy 'safe from harm and injury'.[8] After introducing Christopher Hood's theory of governance in section 2, 'protections' are interchangeably used with 'tools'. Conversely, by using 'protection' (in singular) I deploy its natural meaning.

2. TOOLS FOR PRIVACY PROTECTION

2.1. REGULATORY TOOLS

2.1.1. Legal tools

What means are currently available for the protection of privacy? In other words, what means the various stakeholders – from a layman on the street to those who regulate, to those who handle information, to those who oversee compliance – have at their disposal to protect privacy, either their own, either of others? Here I am not interested in what the object of protection is (I have named it 'privacy' and refrained from defining it but already assumed it is worth protecting), I am least interested in who has to protect (it shall suffice for my purposes to assume each of the above-listed stakeholders has to play some role) or where the protections originate from (e.g. formal political arenas),[9] but rather I am interested in the mechanisms of protection; in other words: how? I have been inspired by the classic *The Tools of Government* by Christopher

8 Oxford Dictionary of English.

9 In order to get the most complete understanding of any theory of regulation, many commentators argue that not only the ways how regulation is achieved matter, but also those who regulate (actors) and relations (dynamics) between them (cf. e.g. C.D. Raab and P. De Hert, 'Tools for Technology Regulation: Seeking Analytical Approaches Beyond Lessig and Hood' in R. Brownsword and K. Yeung (eds.), *Regulating Technologies. Legal Futures, Regulatory Frames and Technological Fixes*, Hart Publishing, Oxford 2008, pp. 263–285). Other commentators supplement these with processes of regulation (constituent steps or tasks) and venues ('institutional locations where authoritative decisions are made') (cf. e.g. J.R. Turnpenny, A.J. Jordan, D. Benson and T. Rayner, 'The Tools of Policy Formulation: An Introduction' in A.J. Jordan and J.R. Turnpenny (eds.), *The Tools of Policy Forumulation: Actors, Capacities, Venues and Effects*, Edward Elgar, Cheltenham 2015, pp. 8–12; F.R. Baumgartner and B.D. Jones, *Agendas and Instability in American Politics*, University of Chicago Press, Chicago 1993, p. 32). An analysis of the many theories of regulation from these perspectives lies outside the scope of this chapter.

Hood, who was interested in the 'tools' – 'such as tools for carpentry and gardening' – that government has at its disposal for governance, i.e. for 'shaping our lives'. His systematisation is useful to make sense of the complexity of available protections, allowing to choose the best means in the given situation and in the given time, implicitly facilitating their scrutiny.[10]

Theoretically speaking, nowadays privacy can be protected by regulatory (legal), organisational and technological means. By 'regulation', I deploy its political science meaning, that is 'sustained and focused control exercised by a public authority over activities valued by the community',[11] 'the ability of A to get B to do something that B would not otherwise do, or not do something B would normally do',[12] or 'the intentional use of authority to affect behaviour of a different party according to set standards, involving instruments of information-gathering and behaviour modification'.[13] All these definitions focus on different aspects of regulation, but indisputably all have one element in common: that regulation is 'a way of controlling society'.[14] (These definitions are silent as to the ultimate goal of regulation and implications resulting therefrom. I will come back to this point below, at section 3.2.1.3.)

When regulation *does* protect privacy, it does so in two ways, and the former comprises the latter. In a very general sense, the mere fact privacy is regulated constitutes a form of protection to an individual and to the society on a condition that such was the ultimate goal of regulation. It could set its boundaries or spell out conditions for a justifiable interference with one's interests. This is a broad understanding. In a more concrete sense, the regulatory framework for privacy can contain some particular elements – like individual rights, security measures and remedies – whose main role is either to make sure 'nobody gets hurt' or – should something bad happen – victims may seek justice. This is a narrow understanding. It spells out for example the tools available to those who wish to protect their own interests.

When regulation *does not* protect privacy, it does so in the same two ways. A privacy matter might deliberately not be regulated while it normally should have been. Alternatively, regulation might sanction a practice infringing individual's privacy without any safeguards. These might result for example in a far too broad access to personal information. Finally, a tool to protect privacy may not exist, may not offer any efficient level of protection (i.e. an illusion thereof) or may not be available in a given situation. Perhaps this is not an incontestable

10 C.C. Hood, *The Tools of Government*, Macmillan, London 1983, pp. 2–11. Cf. also: C. Hood and H. Margetts, *The Tools of Government in the Digital Age*, Palgrave Macmillan, Basingstoke 2007.

11 P. Selznick, 'Focusing Organisational Research on Regulation' in R. Noll (ed.), *Regulatory Policy and the Social Sciences*, University of California Press, Berkeley 1985, p. 363.

12 A. Freiberg, *The Tools of Regulation*, Federation Press, Sydney 2010, p. 84.

13 J. Black, 'Rebuilding the Credibility of Markets and Regulators' (2001) 3(1) *Law and Financial Markets Review* 1–2.

14 Hood, above n. 10, p. 4.

example, but the need to remove or reduce public access to personal information that is claimed no longer relevant for the society resulted in the coinage of the 'right to be forgotten'.

Regulatory tools are perhaps the most widespread in the privacy universe and the law is their main manifestation. Formally speaking, the sources of law can range from (1) international treaties, legislation and other forms of rulemaking, to (2) case law (adjudication), (3) legal doctrine and (4) legal custom, to (5) general principles of law and equity.[15] The regulation of privacy and tools for its protection originate predominantly from the first three sources.

The protection of privacy by rulemaking is usually tripartite. First, it is a fundamental right recognised both in international and supranational human rights instruments as well as in virtually all national constitutions in Western democratic states. Constitutionalisation of privacy protection traces back as early as to the Enlightenment movements, starting perhaps with the Fourth Amendment to the Constitution of the United States (1789) protecting against unreasonable searches and seizures by the federal government. The twentieth century brought the legal conceptualisation of privacy as a human right. In the aftermath of the atrocities of World War II, privacy became protected by international instruments, such as 1948 Universal Declaration of Human Rights (Art. 12) (non-binding) and 1966 International Covenant on Civil and Political Rights (Art. 17), and regional instruments, such as 1950 European Convention (Art. 8) on Human Rights and its 1969 American counterpart (Art. 11) (but *not* in its 1981 African counterpart, at least not directly). Most recently, the European Union (EU) bound itself with the Charter of Fundamental Rights (2009), recognising separately the right to privacy (Art. 7) and to personal data protection (Art. 8). There are also 'sector-specific' instruments, such as the 1989 Convention on the Rights of the Child (Art. 16). All in all, basic privacy rules are situated at the top of the hierarchy of legal norms and therefore touch upon the essential principles of a national legal system.[16]

Second, privacy and its protections are a *direct* object of regulation, either by civil, criminal and administrative branches of law. A patchwork of common law torts of privacy emerged after Warren and Brandeis' influential article 'The Right to Privacy'.[17] Such a civil action, regardless of the label it bears, is nowadays widely recognised in the majority of jurisdictions. Some other jurisdictions even criminalise behaviour violating privacy.[18] All in all, these means of protection

---

15 Cf. Art. 38 of the Statute of the International Court of Justice: 'The Court … shall apply: international conventions, … international custom, … the general principles of law recognized by civilized nations; … judicial decisions and the teachings of the most highly qualified publicists of the various nations ….'

16 S. Gutwirth, *Privacy and the Information Age*, Rowman & Littlefield, Lanham MD 2002, p. 32.

17 S. Warren and L. Brandeis, 'The Right to Privacy' (1890) 4(5) *Harvard Law Review* 193–220.

18 Cf. P. De Hert, 'The EU Data Protection Reform and the (Forgotten) Use of Criminal Sanctions' (2014) 4(4) *International Data Privacy Law* 262–268.

took the shape of a liability for some form of wrongdoing. These are therefore retroactive in principle.

When a single piece of law – be in an act of parliament or other statutory instrument – regulates privacy, it deals with a single aspect of privacy and most often it is the regulation of privacy when personal information is being handled. (I, of course, generalise here.) They bear, in English, names such as 'Privacy Act' or 'Data Protection Act'. Nowadays such laws can be found in more than a hundred jurisdictions.[19] Such laws surfaced for the first time in Europe in 1970s and gradually became more common around the world. The earliest legal statutes – those of Western Germany's Hesse in 1970, Sweden in 1973 and of West Germany (federal) in 1977 – were legislated as a response to the gradual increase of processing of information with the aid of a computer within government and large private organisations (as only these entities needed and could have afforded to at the time).[20] Their focus changed over time, from countering the inhumane information processing (first generation), to vesting some rights in an individual (second) and in particular the right to self-determination (third), to strengthening the position of an individual and regulations of specific sectors (fourth generation).[21]

Regulation of data privacy at the international and regional levels dates back to 1980 with the Organization for Economic Co-operation and Development (OECD) issuing their non-binding data protection Guidelines, revised in 2013.[22] In 1981 the Council of Europe opened for signature its 'Convention 108',[23] a first-ever binding treaty that is now adhered to by more than 50 jurisdictions worldwide and aspiring, after nearly completed modernisation, to lay a foundation for a global standard.[24] In 1990 the UN issued their, obviously non-binding, guidelines for the regulation of computerised personal data files.[25]

---

19 G. Greenleaf, 'Sheherezade and the 101 Data Privacy Laws: Origins, Significance and Global Trajectories', 2013, pp. 2–10.

20 V. Mayer-Schönberger, 'Generational Development of Data Protection in Europe' in P. Agre and M. Roteberg (eds.), *Technology and Privacy: The New Landscape*, MIT Press, Cambridge MA 1997, p. 221.

21 Ibid., pp. 219–241. Each of Mayer-Schönberger's generations of data protection laws reflect the defence against the prevailing threat of that time. This could be compared with Clarke's 'eras of dataveillance': the era of justifiable centralisation (1940–80), of unjustified centralisation (1980–2000) and of dispersed power (from 2000 onwards) (R. Clarke, 'The Eras of Dataveillance', 1994, p. 1, <http://www.rogerclarke.com/DV/NotesDVEras.html>).

22 OEDC, *Guidelines governing the Protection of Privacy and Transborder Flows of Personal Data*, Paris, 11 July 2013, <http://www.oecd.org/sti/ieconomy/oecd_privacy_framework.pdf>.

23 Council of Europe, *Convention for the Protection of Individuals with regard to Automatic Processing of Personal Data*, Strasbourg, 28 January 1981, ETS 108.

24 G. Greenleaf, 'The Influence of European Data Privacy Standards Outside Europe: Implications for Globalization of Convention 108' (2012) 2(2) *International Data Privacy Law* 68–92; G. Greenleaf, '"Modernising" Data Protection Convention 108: A Safe Basis for a Global Privacy Treaty?' (2013) 29(4) *Computer Law and Security Review* 430–436.

25 United Nations, General Assembly, *Guidelines for the regulation of computerized personal data files*, A/RES/45/95, New York, 14 December 1990.

All in all, these laws usually spell out conditions for the handling of personal information as well as both empower individuals with regard to the handling of their data and offer protection against abuses thereof. In this sense, they combine proactive and retroactive elements. The protection they afford is – to a large extent – compulsory, i.e. stakeholder cannot waive it by agreement, a practice well known for example in contract law. They protect individuals by channelling the legitimate use of their personal data by others, i.e. both public authorities and private sector organisations. They empower individuals by vesting in them information and control over how their information is handled as well as they offer protection and remedies against abuses. For example, like many data privacy legal frameworks worldwide, the 1995 Data Protection Directive in the European Union gives a catalogue of rights that an individual can invoke and these include the right to access her data, to rectify any wrong or incomplete information, to object processing on certain lawful grounds and to seek remedy for damages and harm suffered. The Directive further protects her against being subject to an automated decision-making. With the progress of time, this catalogue is often being expanded. For example, the 2002 e-Privacy Directive, within its scope of application, introduced a data breach notification. In 2016 the General Data Protection Regulation not only universalised such notification but it also added e.g. the right to de-listing and to data portability. These laws are binding and compliance therewith is strengthened by a variety of sanctions; the most severe would be a punishment combined with invalidity (*lex plus quam perfecta*).

These laws I have overviewed above constitute a form of primary legislation and they are usually supplemented by a plethora of other forms of regulation by law.[26] For example, Moshell considers four legal means in this context: comprehensive, sectorial, self-regulation of privacy and 'privacy technologies'.[27] These could equally be binding or not (i.e. soft law). In the latter case, they constitute a set of norms for which no structural enforcement is foreseen and compliance depends solely on the will and/or rational calculations of regulated actors.

Third, privacy and its protections are an *indirect* object of regulation. Many of legal provisions outside the typical boundaries of (data) privacy law deal in one or another way with privacy and its protection. *De lege lata*, international anti-terrorism arrangements or free trade agreements in which the need for sharing personal information necessitated safeguards for individuals and their personal data. (Or a lack of such safeguards, in case of which it is a form of regulation that does *not* protect privacy.) If I look at an individual, in case of a violation, she can normally seek relief by complaining to the body that handles

[26] C. Bennett and C.D. Raab, *The Governance of Privacy: Policy Instruments in Global Perspective*, MIT Press, Cambridge MA 2006.

[27] R. Moshell, '... And Then There Was One: The Outlook for a Self-Regulatory United States Amidst a Global Trend Toward Comprehensive Data Protection' (2005) 37 *Texas Tech Law Review* 366–367.

her data, to a relevant supervisory authority or to a court of law, national or – in a few situations – supranational.[28] When she resorts to a public enforcement machinery, her 'complaints and cases can be handled within various domains of law, ranging from administrative (if applicable) to civil and criminal law; the use of one does not usually preclude the use of any other'.[29] For example, a prohibition in the criminal procedure to disclose to the public the names of the accused and of experts and witnesses, among others, can be invoked to protect their privacy too.[30] The control of mergers and acquisitions of businesses running on personal data often has implications for privacy protection.[31] Yet the most pertinent use is perhaps made of consumer law and especially of a class action. The recently filled in reference for a preliminary ruling to the Court of Justice of the EU (CJEU; Luxembourg Court) asks the question whether the use of a social networking site for purposes *both* private and professional qualifies its user as a consumer. If so, she could benefit from protective jurisdiction rules offered by EU private international law and sue a service provider headquartered in another country in the jurisdiction of her domicile.[32]

De lege ferenda, tools for privacy protection are constantly being called for – as a response to the inadequacies of existing ones – and subsequently developed. The discourse thus far has most often looked at other branches of law for an inspiration on how to protect best various aspects of privacy. These include property law,[33] private international law (conflict of laws), consumer law,[34]

---

28 A. Galetta and P. De Hert, 'The Proceduralisation of Data Protection Remedies under EU Data Protection Law: Towards a More Effective and Data Subject-Oriented Remedial System?' (2015) 8(1) *Review of European Administrative Law* 123–149.

29 D. Kloza and A. Galetta, 'Towards Efficient Cooperation between Supervisory Authorities in the Area of Data Privacy Law', Brussels Privacy Hub Working Papers, Brussels 2015, <http://www.brusselsprivacyhub.org/Resources/BPH-Working-Paper-VOL1-N3.pdf>, p. 10.

30 I am referring to a recent scandal in the Polish media (January 2017) in which the public television 'broadcasted', with a few instances of delay, a hearing at a court of law, without withholding the names of any person involved therein, thus breaching the criminal procedure (cf. Art. 355ff Code of Criminal Procedure; Act of 6 June 1997, as amended, OJ No. 89, Item 555) and the press law (cf. Art. 13(1) Press Law; Act of 26 January 1984, as amended, OJ No. 5, Item 24).

31 Cf. the most recent example: P. Teffer, 'EU wants to know if Facebook lied about Whatsapp', *EU Observer*, 20 December 2016, <https://euobserver.com/digital/136359>. Cf. also European Data Protection Supervisor, 'Privacy and competitiveness in the age of big data. The interplay between data protection, competition law and consumer protection in the Digital Economy', Brussels, March 2014, <https://secure.edps.europa.eu/EDPSWEB/webdav/site/mySite/shared/Documents/Consultation/Opinions/2014/14-03-26_competitition_law_big_data_EN.pdf>.

32 Case C-498/16, *Maximilian Schrems v. Facebook Ireland*.

33 Cf. e.g., N. Purtova, *Property Rights in Personal Data: A European Perspective*, Kluwer Law International, The Hague 2011.

34 Cf. e.g., A. Galetta, D. Kloza and P. De Hert, 'Cooperation among Data Privacy Supervisory Authorities: Lessons From Parallel European Cooperation Mechanisms', Brussels–London–Warsaw–Castellón, 2016, pp. 38–62, <http://www.phaedra-project.eu/wp-content/uploads/PHAEDRA2_D21_final_20160416.pdf>.

competition law,[35] contract law[36] and criminal justice,[37] among others, but it is environmental law that probably has attracted the most of attention.[38]

Both direct and indirect regulation of privacy and of its protections owes much to the jurisprudence of the courts of law at all levels, like the Supreme Court of the United States, the European Court of Human Rights (ECtHR, Strasbourg Court),[39] CJEU[40] or advisory and standard-setting bodies, such as the Article 29 Working Party in the EU[41] or the annual International Conference of Data Protection and Privacy Commissioners (ICDPPC). This picture would not be complete without international organisations, networks of regulators, civil society organisations and academia. In 2015, the United Nations (UN) Human Rights Commission created for the first time the position of a Special Rapporteur on the Right to Privacy,[42] but even earlier calls asked for a specific, dedicated UN agency for the protection of privacy.[43]

---

35 Cf. e.g. D. Kloza and A. Mościbroda, 'Making the Case for Enhanced Enforcement Cooperation between Data Protection Authorities: Insights from Competition Law' (2014) 4(2) *International Data Privacy Law* 120–138.

36 Cf. L.A. Bygrave, *Internet Governance by Contract*, Oxford University Press, Oxford 2015.

37 Cf. e.g. P. De Hert and A. Willems, 'Dealing with Overlapping Jurisdictions and Requests for Mutual Legal Assistance While Respecting Individual Rights. What Can Data Protection Law Learn from Cooperation in Criminal Justice Matters?' in P. De Hert, D. Kloza and P. Makowski (eds.), *Enforcing Privacy: Lessons from Current Implementations and Perspectives for the Future*, Wydawnictwo Sejmowe, Warsaw 2015, pp. 48–76, <http://www.phaedra-project.eu/wp-content/uploads/phaedra1_enforcing_privacy_final.pdf>.

38 Cf. J. Nehf, 'Recognizing the Societal Value in Information Privacy' (2003) 78 *Washington Law Review* 1–92; D.D. Hirsch, 'Protecting the Inner Environment: What Privacy Regulation Can Learn from Environmental Law' (2006) 41(1) *Georgia Law Review* 1–63; D. Kloza, 'Public Voice in Privacy Governance: Lessons from Environmental Democracy' in E. Schweighofer, A. Saarenpää and J. Böszörmenyi (eds.), *KnowRight 2012. Knowledge Rights – Legal, Societal and Related Technological Aspects. 25 Years of Data Protection in Finland*, Österreichische Computer Gesellschaft, Vienna 2013, pp. 80–97. Cf. also Emanuel, Ch. 21, in this volume.

39 Cf. R. Gellert and S. Gutwirth, 'The Legal Construction of Privacy and Data Protection' (2013) 29(5) *Computer Law & Security Review* 522–530.

40 Cf. J. Kokott and C. Sobotta, 'The Distinction between Privacy and Data Protection in the Jurisprudence of the CJEU and the ECtHR' (2013) 3(4) *International Data Privacy Law* 222–228; G. Zanfir, 'How CJEU's "Privacy Spring" Construed the Human Rights Shield in the Digital Age' in E. Kużelewska, D. Kloza, I. Kraśnicka and F. Strzyczkowski (eds.), *European Judicial Systems as a Challenge for Democracy*, Intersentia, Antwerp 2015, pp. 111–126.

41 Cf. Y. Poullet and S. Gutwirth, 'The Contribution of the Article 29 Working Party to the Construction of a Harmonised European Data Protection System: An Illustration of "Reflexive Governance"?' in O. De Schutter and V. Moreno Lax (eds.), *Human Rights in the Web of Governance: Towards a Learning-Based Fundamental Rights Policy for the European Union*, Bruylant, Brussels 2010, pp. 253–294.

42 United Nations, Human Rights Council, Resolution 28/16, <http://www.ohchr.org/EN/Issues/Privacy/SR/Pages/SRPrivacyIndex.aspx>.

43 P. De Hert and V. Papakonstantinou, 'Three Scenarios for International Governance of Data Privacy: Towards an International Data Privacy Organization, Preferably a UN Agency?' (2013) 9(3) *I/S: A Journal of Law and Policy for the Information Society* 272–324. Cf. also De Hert and Papakonstantinou, Ch. 25, in this volume.

2.1.2. *Not only law regulates*

However, not only law regulates. There is a wide repertoire of means, instruments and techniques that are used in regulating social behaviour.[44] Most classically, in his toolkit for regulation, Hood first distinguished 'detectors' and 'effectors'. The former are meant to obtain information and the knowledge gathered that way will constitute a basis for governmental action executed with the help of the latter. Second, in 'detecting' and 'effecting' government possesses four types of resources: nodality (i.e. information), treasure (i.e. financial resources), authority (i.e. legal power) and organisation (i.e. human resources, materials, equipment).[45]

But it was Lawrence Lessig who, among law and technology scholars, offered a classic theory of regulation. His 'pathetic dot theory' looks at constrains of human behaviour. Lessig distinguishes four modalities that regulate human behaviour: law, social norms, market, and architecture (code).[46] The novelty of his theory, at the time it was proposed in 1990s, was that the computer code regulates similarly to architecture and thus 'regulation in cyberspace may be perfectly achieved through modifications to software codes'.[47] Both physical architecture and computer code constrain some behaviour by making other behaviour possible or impossible. Equally, as one enters a room through a door (sometimes, through a window, but that is not a standard behaviour), one may equally need some credentials to log in to a certain online service. (One may try to hack it, but that is not a standard behaviour either.)

More generally, political scientists like Morgan and Yeung classify modalities of regulation in five categories: command and control (i.e. rule-based coercion), competition and economic instruments (i.e. 'competitive forces arising from rivalry between competing units', like taxes, charges or subsidies), consensus (i.e. co-regulation or self-regulation), communication (i.e. persuasion and education) and techno-regulation (code) (i.e. elimination of undesired behaviour by 'designing out the possibility for its occurrence').[48] Freiberg goes further and distinguishes six main modalities, i.e. economic tools, transactional regulation, authorisation, structural regulation (i.e. manipulation of physical environment), informational regulation and legal regulation.[49] In comparison with modalities mentioned earlier, Freiberg considers transactional regulation and authorisation as standalone. By transactional means he understands 'regulation by contract, grant agreement or other financial arrangement' made in the public interest. This

---

44 B. Morgan and K. Yeung, *An Introduction to Law and Regulation: Text and Materials*, Cambridge University Press, Cambridge 2007, p. 79.

45 Hood, above n. 10, pp. 2–6.

46 L. Lessig, *Code Version 2.0*, Basic Books, New York 2006, pp. 121–123, <http://www.codev2.cc/download+remix/Lessig-Codev2.pdf>.

47 Morgan and Yeung, above n. 44, p. 102.

48 Ibid., pp. 79–149.

49 Freiberg, above n. 12, pp. 84–87.

form of regulation is based not on public authority exercised by the government, but on the equality of parties, known from contract law.[50] By authorisation he understands the power of the government to 'authorise, permit, allow or recognise or legitimate a particular activity, status or premises'.[51]

All these theories converge and what actually matters is 'picking the' right tool(s) 'for the job' and 'for the times'.[52] These tools are not mutually exclusive, each of them can be used for diverse purposes, each produces the best effects in different contexts, and each has their own advantages and disadvantages as well as benefits and dangers.[53]

2.2. BEYOND REGULATION[54]

2.2.1. Organisational protections

Regulatory means do not exhaust the available toolkit of privacy protections. There exists a wide repertoire of organisational and technological means. Such measures are applied in many domains of life, from airports (e.g. security screening) to road traffic (e.g. speed limits), but – for my purposes – it is the theory of information security that is illustrative.[55] Specialists in the field would usually claim that information security is about protecting 'confidentiality, integrity and availability of information assets, whether in storage, processing, or transmission'.[56] In other words, they would talk about a classical model of the 'CIA triad', in which each element represents a fundamental objective of information

50 Ibid., p. 132.

51 Ibid., p. 141.

52 Hood, above n. 10, pp. 7–11.

53 D. Kloza, N. van Dijk and P. De Hert, 'Assessing the European Approach to Privacy and Data Protection in Smart Grids. Lessons for Emerging Technologies' in F. Skopik and P. Smith (eds.), *Smart Grid Security. Innovative Solutions for a Modernized Grid*, Elsevier, Waltham MA 2015, p. 31.

54 I am particularly indebted to Roger Clarke for his guidance on this matter.

55 The notion of 'security' has multiple meanings. For example, scholars of international relations usually work with a definition of 'security' that involves 'the alleviation of threats to cherished values' (P.D. Williams, *Security Studies: An Introduction*, Routledge, Abingdon 2012, p. 1), affecting – according to one typology – five sectors: military, political, social, economic and environmental (B. Buzan, *People, States and Fear: The National Security Problem in International Relations*, University of North Carolina Press, Chapel Hill 1983). For computer scientists, 'information' is one of those 'cherished values' and for them 'security' is about minimising 'the risk of exposing information to unauthorised parties' (H.S. Venter and J.H.P. Eloff, 'A Taxonomy for Information Security Technologies' (2003) 22(4) *Computers and Security* 299). Various aspects of security are in diverse relations with 'data privacy'. In particular, while 'security' of personal data is a requirement of 'data privacy', 'security' of a state is channelled by 'data privacy'. In the former type of relations, 'security' is at the service of 'data privacy', in the latter – 'security' is usually confronted with 'data privacy'.

56 M.E. Whitman and H.J. Mattord, *Principles of Information Security*, Cengage Learning, Boston 2012, p. 8.

security. Confidentiality refers to the restriction of access to information only to those who are authorised to use it, integrity – to the assurance that information has not been altered in an unauthorised way and availability – to the assurance that the service will be available whenever it is needed.[57]

The 'CIA triad' is clearly a data-centric security model, yet it is often criticised for simplicity, as more it at stake when it comes to the security of information handling. This created a critical need to coin alternatives to the 'CIA triad' and the many proposals developed include, *inter alia*, the 'Parkerian Hexad',[58] the 1992 OECD security guidelines (revised 2002 and 2015),[59] national manuals – such as 'Engineering Principles for Information Technology Security' (2004) by the US National Institute of Standards and Technology (NIST),[60] 'Information Security Manual' by the Australian Signals Directorate (ASD) (2016),[61] '10 Steps to Cyber Security' by the UK's National Cyber Security Centre (2016)[62] – and, eventually, the ISO 27001 series of standards.[63] Each of them usually expand the 'CIA triad' by adding further principles and among these models the one offered by the NIST is perhaps the broadest, listing 33 such principles, adding e.g. an assumption of insecurity (principle no. 6) and the ease of use (principles nos. 12–15).

The principles of information security – such as the CIA triad – are effectuated by particular, concrete safeguards and controls.[64] They are meant to successfully counter attacks, reduce risk, resolve vulnerabilities and otherwise improve the security of information.[65] According to one classification, they could be proactive (i.e. aiming at avoidance, deterrence and prevention of a threat), reactive (detection of, recovery after and insurance against a threat)

---

57 M. Rhodes-Ousley, *Information Security The Complete Reference, Second Edition*, McGraw-Hill, London 2013, pp. 85–86.

58 D.B. Parker, *Fighting Computer Crime*, Scribner, New York 1998, pp. 230–239.

59 OECD, *Guidelines for the Security of Information Systems and Networks*, Paris 2002, <http://www.oecd.org/sti/ieconomy/15582260.pdf>; OECD, *Digital Security Risk Management for Economic and Social Prosperity: OECD Recommendation and Companion Document*, Paris 2015, <http://www.oecd.org/sti/ieconomy/digital-security-risk-management.pdf>.

60 G. Stoneburner, C. Hayden and A. Feringa, 'Engineering Principles for Information Technology Security (A Baseline for Achieving Security)' (2004) *NIST Special Publication 800-27 Rev A.*, <http://csrc.nist.gov/publications/nistpubs/800-27A/SP800-27-RevA.pdf>, pp. 6–22.

61 Australian Signals Directorate, *Australian Government Information Security Manual*, Canberra 2016, <http://www.asd.gov.au/infosec/ism/index.htm>.

62 National Cyber Security Centre, *10 Steps to Cyber Security*, London 2016, <http://www.ncs.gov.uk/guidance/10-steps-to-cyber-security>.

63 International Organization for Standardization, *ISO/IEC 27001 – Information security management*, Geneva 2009–2013, <http://www.iso.org/iso/home/standards/management-standards/iso27001.htm>.

64 The distinction between these two terms in information security literature is rather problematic. While some general meaning was asserted to 'controls', the more accurate term would be 'safeguards' because 'controls' are 'second-level safeguards that ensure that intended safeguards are actually in place and working' (Roger Clarke in a private correspondence, September 2016).

65 Whitman and Mattord, above n. 56, p. 10.

as well as non-reactive, i.e. tolerance.[66] According to another, they could be of organisational or technological nature.

Organisational means concern the set-up of an entity handling information. An organisation, at a *general* level, would usually resort to e.g. procedural (administrative) safeguards, such as internal policies, standards and guidelines spelling out rules, roles and responsibilities for handling information. It would as well resort to physical, 'bricks and mortar' security of premises and of equipment handling information, such as fences, doors and locks. Security would receive adequate attention at the senior level of an organisation, e.g. by a dedicated officer with oversight powers. Staff would be continuously updated on developments in the area and information handling systems would be kept up-to-date and continuously tested against vulnerabilities. Eventually, backup copies would be made and business continuity strategies would be put in place. Seemingly trivial issues such as the provision of supporting utilities (e.g. energy supply or cooling system) and protection against the fire belong to this category too.

At a more *concrete* level, an organisation would e.g. employ restrictions as to the physical or temporal access to information. It would differentiate access thereto depending on a given, clearly defined role of a member of staff. It might restrict access to some particular workstations. An organisation would further employ multi-factor authentication with 'strong' passwords, comprising a combination of lower- and upper-case letters, numbers and signs, supplemented by other forms of identification, e.g. a token. It would decentralise all data storage (i.e. 'you don't put all your eggs in one basket'). Ultimately, it would register all the information handling operations. Such a log is vital for the purposes of accountability yet it also allows to look for patterns for anomalies, e.g. whether an employee accesses database outside normal hours of business and whether it was justified. All in all, a lot of security in practice is about 'logical access restrictions'.[67]

The same organisation, at a *product* level, would aim at ensuring security 'by design'. This idea shares parallels with 'Privacy by Design' (cf. below, in this section) by departing from a paradigm that security is 'not an afterthought' and 'it has to be an integral part of any development project'.[68] In a classical understanding, 'implementation without security flaws' can be guided by eight foundational principles,[69] i.e.:

1. Economy of mechanism: keep the design as simple and small as possible.
2. Fail-safe defaults: base access decisions on permission rather than exclusion.

---

66 R. Clarke, 'Practicalities of Keeping Confidential Information on a Database With Multiple Points of Access: Technological and Organisational Measures', 1992, <http://www.anu.edu.au/people/Roger.Clarke/DV/PaperICAC.html>.

67 Ibid.

68 P. Siriwardena, 'Security by Design' (2014) 58 *Advanced API Security* 11–31.

69 J. Saltzer, and M. Schoeder, 'The Protection of Information in Computer Systems', 1974, sec. 1, <http://web.mit.edu/Saltzer/www/publications/protection/>.

3. Complete mediation: every access to every object must be checked for authority.
4. Open design: the design should not be secret.
5. Separation of privilege: where feasible, a protection mechanism that requires two keys to unlock it is more robust and flexible than one that allows access to the presenter of only a single key.
6. Least privilege: every program and every user of the system should operate using the least set of privileges necessary to complete the job.
7. Least common mechanism: minimise the amount of mechanism common to more than one user and depended on by all users.
8. Psychological acceptability: it is essential that the human interface be designed for ease of use, so that users routinely and automatically apply the protection mechanisms correctly.

The narrative of a data-centric security model would be normally applicable to the protection of privacy as long as personal information is being handled. (Note that organisational measures are not exclusive to data privacy, e.g. medical doctors normally receive each of their patients individually in an examination room behind closed doors. This is meant to protect aspects of privacy other than personal data.)[70] In many jurisdictions, security of data being handled is a requirement of data privacy law. Yet, contrary to the popular belief amongst the specialists in the field, information security does not equal data privacy, as for the latter there is more at stake.

Translating all these into the privacy universe, organisational protections include methods, techniques and measures such as:

- Privacy by Design (PbD);[71]
- privacy impact assessment (PIA),[72] privacy risk management and other evaluative techniques;

---

70 Cf. below n. 195.

71 The writings on each of these methods are voluminous and thus only basic 'textbooks' will be cited here. The concept of Privacy by Design was coined in 1990s by Ann Cavoukian, then Information and Privacy Commissioner of Ontario, Canada and is best described on a dedicated website, <http://www.privacybydesign.ca>. Cf. further esp. A. Cavoukian, *Privacy by Design in Law, Policy and Practice. A White Paper for Regulators, Decision-Makers and Policy-Makers*, Information and Privacy Commissioner, Ontario, Toronto 2011, pp. 6–13.

72 There are many definitions of privacy impact assessment. One of the most comprehensive is the following: a PIA is a systematic, continuous as well as reasonably accountable, transparent and participatory activity of analysing (identifying, evaluating and proposing measures for mitigation of) consequences (positive and negative; intended and unintended) of a single initiative (*sensu largo*) on (a) given benchmark(s), if this initiative presents significant risks to the benchmark(s), with a view to support the informed decision-making as to the deployment of this initiative and its scale, constituting a means to protect the benchmark(s). Cf. further e.g. R. Clarke, 'Privacy Impact Assessment: Its Origins and Development' (2009) 25(2) *Computer Law & Security Review* 123–135; R. Clarke, 'An Evaluation of Privacy Impact Assessment Guidance Documents' (2011) 1(2) *International Data Privacy Law* 111–120; D. Wright,

- privacy seals and certification;[73]
- privacy icons (pictograms);[74]
- privacy standardisation;[75]
- privacy audits;
- appointment of a dedicated senior officer to oversight privacy matters, e.g. data protection officer (DPO), as it is known in Europe, or Chief Privacy Officer (CPO), as known in the Americas.

2.2.2. *Technological protections*

Technological protections are rather self-evident. Their generic categories can include, for example, access controls (e.g. two-factor authentication) and the use of cryptography as well as a wider range of measures against malware and otherwise hostile software (i.e. detection and eradication), against hostile takeover of an information system (i.e. firewalls) or against the insecurity of remote connections, e.g. virtual private networks (VPN).[76] These protections build on a premise that technology can invade individual interests but it can equally be used to counter such an invasion.

Translating all these into the privacy universe, technological protections manifest themselves predominantly by the so-called Privacy Enhancing Technologies (PETs). PETs constitute a 'system of [information and communications technologies] measures protecting informational privacy by eliminating or minimising personal data thereby preventing unnecessary or unwanted processing of personal data, without the loss of the functionality of the information system'.[77] The concept of PETs was put together in 1995 in a join research paper of Canadian and Dutch data protection authorities and

---

'The State of the Art in Privacy Impact Assessment' (2012) 28(1) *Computer Law & Security Review* 54–61; D. Wright and P. De Hert (eds.), *Privacy Impact Assessment*, Springer, Dordrecht 2012; P. De Hert, D. Kloza and D. Wright, 'Recommendations for a Privacy Impact Assessment Framework for the European Union', Deliverable D3 of the PIAF [A Privacy Impact Assessment Framework for data protection and privacy rights] project, Brussels/London 2012, <http://piafproject.eu/ref/PIAF_D3_final.pdf>; Kloza, van Dijk and De Hert, above n. 53, pp. 11–47).

73 Cf. e.g. R. Rodrigues, D. Barnard-Wills, D. Wright, P. De Hert and V. Papakonstantinou, *EU Privacy Seals Project. Inventory and Analysis of Privacy Certification Schemes*, Publications Office of the European Union, Luxembourg 2013, pp. 100–116.

74 Cf. e.g. M. Hansen, 'Putting Privacy Pictograms into Practice: A European Perspective' (2009) 154 *GI Jahrestagung* 1703–1716.

75 Cf. e.g. P. De Hert, V. Papakonstantinou and I. Kamara, 'The Cloud Computing Standard ISO/IEC 27018 through the Lens of the EU Legislation on Data Protection' (2016) 32(1) *Computer Law & Security Review* 16–30.

76 R. Clarke, 'The Prospects of Easier Security for Small Organisations and Consumers' (2015) 31(4) *Computer Law and Security Review* 538–552.

77 G.W. van Blarkom, J. Borking and J. Olk, *Handbook of Privacy and Privacy-Enhancing Technologies. The Case of Intelligent Software Agents*, College Bescherming Persoonsgegevens, The Hague 2003, p. 33.

originally was concerned with protecting privacy by pseudo-identities.[78] These technologies can be applied both by those who handle data and by those whose data are being handled (i.e. end-user PETs). The toolkit of PETs has expanded significantly ever since and nowadays it considers the application of categories technologies such as:

- de-identification of information: anonymisation, and especially randomisation (such as noise addition, permutation and differential privacy) and generalisation (such as aggregation, K-anonymity and L-diversity);[79]
- pseudonymisation;
- cryptography, including strong, end-to-end encryption, be it symmetric, asymmetric or fully homomorphic;[80]
- (multi-factor) identification, authentication and authorisation;
- decentralisation;
- techniques for data erasure;
- techniques for un-linkability and non-traceability;
- protection against malicious software (malware), e.g. anti-virus software;
- specific protocols, e.g. Platform for Privacy Preferences (P3P).[81]

Some other catalogues of PETs focus on practical tools that a layman on the street can apply, for example:[82]

- device-management tools, e.g. live operating systems, file encryption and erasing software, password vaults;

78 Ibid., p. 36; R. Hes and J. Borking, *Privacy-Enhancing Technologies: The Path to Anonymity.* Achtergrondstudies En Verkenningen. Registratiekamer, 1995, <https://www.ipc.on.ca/images/Resources/anoni-v2.pdf>.

79 Cf. Article 29 Working Party, *Opinion 05/2014 on Anonymisation Techniques*, WP 216, Brussels, 10 April 2014, pp. 11–19, 27–37, <http://ec.europa.eu/justice/data-protection/article-29/documentation/opinion-recommendation/files/2014/wp216_en.pdf>.

80 Cf. C. Gentry, 'Fully Homomorphic Encryption Using Ideal Lattices' (2009) 19 *Proceedings of the 41st Annual ACM Symposium on Symposium on Theory of Computing STOC 09*, 169–178.

81 Cf. <http://www.w3.org/P3P>.

82 R. Clarke, 'Key Factors in the Limited Adoption of End-User PETs', 2014, <http://www.rogerclarke.com/DV/UPETs-1405.html>, fig. 1. The Electronic Privacy Information Center (EPIC) offers an *Online Guide to Practical Privacy Tools*, <https://epic.org/privacy/tools.html>, the Electronic Frontier Foundation (EFF) offers a *Surveillance Self-Defence Kit*, <https://ssd.eff.org/en>, the Centre for Internet and Society at Stanford University offers, in the form of a wiki, 'a list of free technologies aimed at empowering Internet users to gain better control over their data', <http://cyberlaw.stanford.edu/wiki/index.php/PET>, and Douglas Crawford has recently published his *Ultimate Privacy Guide*: <https://www.bestvpn.com/the-ultimate-privacy-guide>.

- traffic-related tools, e.g. Internet anonymisers, Virtual Private Networks (VPNs), proxy servers, firewalls, anti-malware software;
- web-related tools, e.g. web browser ad-ons, cookie/cache/Internet history cleaners, privacy friendly search engines and social networking sites;
- email-related tools, e.g. e-mail encryption, alternative e-mail accounts, anonymous remailers;
- other communications-related tools, e.g. secure instant messaging, Voice over Internet Protocol (VoIP) and video messaging; temporary mobile phones;
- other, e.g. alternative currencies or blind digital signatures.

This classification is obviously not watertight and when all protections work together, the distinction between them is rather nominal. Each of the three categories of protection – regulatory, organisational and technological – complement each other and often overlap. (One particular protection measure might belong to more than one type.) Further, these protections are interrelated and affect each other: regulation (e.g. laws or standards) may require the use of specific organisational and technological measures. For example, the recently passed GDPR in the EU requires a form of PIA to be conducted for certain information handing and further mandates data privacy to be protected 'by design'. In some instances, both organisational and technological can have a regulatory effect, in a sense of Lessig's 'pathetic dot theory' – they make certain actions or inactions (im)possible by requiring or ruling out some other. While regulatory protections are offered top-down, i.e. usually from the state, the organisational and technological are usually offered bottom up, i.e. from non-state actors. Finally, diverse protections would find diverse applications among various stakeholders. An organisation would pursue the goals of Privacy by Design and to that end would conduct a privacy impact assessment. A layman on the street would be rather interested in secure instant messaging software, offering strong, end-to-end encryption. Should she decide to discontinue using a particular service, she would exercise her right to object the processing of personal data.

3. INADEQUACIES OF CONTEMPORARILY AVAILABLE TOOLS FOR PRIVACY PROTECTION

3.1. INTRODUCTION: IRREVERSIBILITY OF HARM

The underlying problem of privacy protection is that of the irreversibility of harm. It manifests itself clearly with the informational aspect (type) of privacy. The mere fact a piece of *personal* information is being handled – be it collected, analysed, stored and destroyed, or whatever else operation thereon – constitutes an interference with and – possibly – a threat to the interests of an individual and, in some instances, to those of a society.[83] (The best way to protect individuals and societies would be not to handle any information at all. Under such a paradigm, our societies would never work.) Such a piece of information might be disclosed without any good reason or authorisation, it might be used against the will of that person, thus in any case creating some degree of harm. Equally it all might go well: all handling would be secure enough and conducted in an interest of that particular person or in an interest of a given society, causing no harm of any nature nor scale to anybody. But, equally, it might all go wrong: a piece of information might be used against someone or may be revealed to a person, or perhaps worse, to a society, not intended to know it. Information once released, especially in the digital era, will circulate freely and would never be erased. Therefore, in this sense, a disclosure of personal information is irreversible. It follows that the consequences of such a disclosure rarely can be repaired, therefore making privacy harms irreparable. I hasten to explain that here I understand 'harm' rather broadly. Even if damage can largely be repaired with money, the significance of *mental* harm is much higher and no compensation can provide any relief thereto.

For example, I find ironic the famous battle Mr Mario Costeja fought in 2010–2014 to have some of his personal information removed from a search engine listing. In 1998, 'an announcement mentioning his name appeared [in one of the major Catalan newspapers] for a real-estate auction connected with attachment proceedings for the recovery of social security debts'.[84] The case 'has been fully resolved for a number of years and that reference [thereto] was now entirely irrelevant'.[85] It would probably be forgotten if the publisher had not decided to digitalise the archives of a newspaper, make them publicly available on the Internet and – what is crucial here – searchable by a machine.

---

83 Cf. further the classical 'interference argument' by Adalbert Podlech coined in 1970s when the Western German doctrine of personal data protection was growing mature: '... jede Erhebung, Speicherung, Verarbeitung und Weitergabe personenbezogener durch Träger öffentlicher Gewalt in einem formellen Verfahren ein Eingriff in das durch Art. 2 Abs. 1 [Grundgesetz] gewährleistete informationelle Selbstbestimmungsrecht ist' (in essence: on the grounds of the German Constitution, any formal handling of personal data by public authorities constitutes an interference with the right to informational self-determination). A. Podlech, 'Das Recht auf Privatheit' in J. Perels (ed.), *Grundrechte als Fundament der Demokratie*, Suhrkamp, Frankfurt am Main 1979, p. 55. The concept of informational self-determination entered the Western German legal system with the famous 1983 population census decision of the Federal Constitutional Court (Bundesverfassungsgericht). BVerfG, Urteil des Ersten Senats vom 15. Dezember 1983, 1 BvR 209/83 u.a. – *Volkszählung*. Cf. further G. Hornung and C. Schnabel, 'Data protection in Germany I: The population census decision and the right to informational self-determination' (2009) 25 *Computer Law and Security Review* 84–88. I thank Frederik Zuiderveen Borgesius for bringing this matter to my attention.

84 Case C-131/12, *Google Spain SL, Google Inc. v. Agencia Española de Protección de Datos (AEPD), Mario Costeja González* (CJEU, 13 May 2014), §14.

85 Ibid., §15.

Notwithstanding the Luxembourg Court ruling in his favour,[86] nowadays putting the name of Mr Costeja into this particular search engine yields roughly 20,000 results.[87] Not only was his information searchable before he entered the courtroom, but the media attention the case received made the specific piece of information, which he wanted to hide, more widely known than before. Given the relevance of the Court's ruling, the Spanish data protection authority (DPA) found the facts behind the case to be in the public interest. This authority therefore eventually denied him a right to de-list, at a search engine, the many links to contents commenting on the case.[88] As a result, Mr Costeja's case sits comfortably in the category of the 'Barbara Streisand effect', i.e. a phenomenon in which an attempt to hide something produces exactly the reverse effect, facilitated by the use of technology.[89]

The Court of Justice has created – or interpreted? – 'the right to be forgotten' (or rather 'the right to de-listing'), yet the efficiency of such a right today is highly questionable. This has to do with the way information and communications technologies (ICTs) function.[90] They work by copying information, by doing it fast and – normally – by allowing anybody to do so; this is their primary *modus operandi*. These copies are multiple, untraceable and thus uncontrollable. Asking a service provider, like Google, to remove certain links from its search engine results is efficient as it removes a major access point to the contested piece of information. But it does not remove this piece of information from a server on which it is stored. (In that case, it is a website of a newspaper which digitalised its archives.) Nor does it remove this information from proxy servers, from backup servers or from webpages archives. Google complies with the ruling and – upon receipt of a justified request – removes information from the results when these are sought from within the European territory. Accessing Google from e.g. Australia has produced unfiltered results. Mayer-Schönberger once famously advocated for an expiration date on a piece of information, as a solution to the problem of the infinite memory of ICTs.[91] Immediately a market has been

86 Ibid.

87 As of the end of September 2016.

88 Agencia Española de Protección de Datos (AEPD), Resolución No. R/02179/2015, Madrid, 14 September 2015, <http://www.agpd.es/portalwebAGPD/resoluciones/tutela_derechos/tutela_derechos_2015/common/pdfs/TD-00568-2015_Resolucion-de-fecha-14-09-2015_Art-ii-culo-16-LOPD.pdf>.

89 E. Morozov, *The Net Delusion: The Dark Side of Internet freedom*, Public Affairs, New York 2012, pp. 120–123.

90 I set aside here the debate on the impact of the right to be forgotten on the freedom of expression as this is a separate matter. Cf. further J.P. Mifsud Bonnici and A.J. Verheij, 'On Forgetting, Deleting, de-Listing and Starting Afresh!' (2016) 30(1–2) *International Review of Law, Computers & Technology* 1–4.

91 V. Mayer-Schönberger, *Delete: The Virtue of Forgetting in the Digital Age*, Princeton University Press, Princeton 2009, pp. 171–173.

created for that: in 2011 a German company X-Pire offered software that added a self-destruction feature to one's pictures.[92]

My point is that the law – or, broader, regulation – is helpless in such a situation. I am aware it is a strong statement. It cannot normally forbid digitalisation of written media like newspapers (it is against the freedom of expression and a few other freedoms and liberties), it cannot compel multinational companies outside a given jurisdiction to obey (extraterritorial jurisdiction is still relatively limited, despite recent attempts to extend the territorial scope of data privacy laws),[93] and it cannot prohibit media from reporting on a pending court case (again, the freedom of expression). Mr Costeja resolved to regulatory protections, but the law does not solve his problem now, nor is it capable of solving it in any foreseeable future. Other types of protections – organisational and technological – were of little use in his situation. The conclusion must be that the contemporarily available tools for privacy protection are inadequate.

3.2. INADEQUACIES

3.2.1. Regulatory tools

3.2.1.1. Inefficiency of contemporary regulation

How do the inadequacies of contemporarily available regulatory protections manifest themselves? I see these inadequacies as having at least a four-fold nature. First, it is the *inefficiency* of contemporary regulation, including the law. Second, it is the inability to keep pace with societal and technological developments. Third, it is the instrumental use of regulation. Fourth and finally, it is the diminishment of public trust.

The narrative of human rights is perhaps the most useful starting point to illustrate the inefficiency of contemporarily available regulatory protections. The European Convention on Human Rights confers on the individuals a number of enforceable human rights and the one that interests me here is the right to privacy.[94] The enjoyment of any rights conferred by the said Convention

92 Cf. <http://petapixel.com/2011/01/17/x-pire-software-adds-a-self-destruct-feature-to-your-digital-photos>.

93 Cf. e.g. L. Moerel, 'The Long Arm of EU Data Protection Law: Does the Data Protection Directive Apply to Processing of Personal Data of EU Citizens by Websites Worldwide?' (2011) 1(1) *International Data Privacy Law* 28–46; D.J.B. Svantesson, *Extraterritoriality in Data Privacy Law*, Ex Tuto Publishing, Copenhagen 2013; and P. De Hert and M. Czerniawski, 'Expanding the European Data Protection Scope beyond Territory: Article 3 of the General Data Protection Regulation in Its Wider Context' (2016) 6(3) *International Data Privacy Law* 230–243.

94 Convention for the Protection of Human Rights and Fundamental Freedoms, Rome, 4 November 1950, ETS 5.

is governed by a number of 'meta-principles'. First and foremost, its opening Article declares that the contracting parties 'shall secure to *everyone* within their jurisdiction the rights and freedoms defined [in the] Convention'.[95] Then the Convention goes on, enumerating 11 substantive rights and Art. 8 deals with the right to privacy. A wide range of 'meta-principles' comes back from Art. 13 onwards: itself, this provision proclaims the right to effective remedy, Art. 14 prohibits discrimination,[96] Art. 15 allows for limited derogations in the time of emergency, Art. 16 restricts political activity of non-citizens, Art. 17 prohibits the abuse of rights and Art. 18 puts limits on the restriction of rights. The subsequent Articles of the Convention establish the European Court of Human Rights and define its functioning. Finally, Art. 53 states that the Convention does not restrict the level of protection, i.e. it does not limit or derogate any right if national laws and/or other international instruments provide for a higher standard of protection.

Subsequent 'meta-principles' have been added by the judges in Strasbourg. On a numerous occasions and most recently in *Nježić and Štimac v. Croatia* (2015), the Court held that the 'object and purpose of the Convention as an instrument for the protection of individual human beings require that [its provisions] be interpreted and applied so as to make its safeguards *practical* and *effective*'.[97] With my collaborators, I have argued elsewhere that such a protection must also be *efficient*. While effectiveness indicates a 'possibility or capability of producing a result', efficiency goes a step further and indicates a possibility or capability of 'functioning or producing effectively and with the least waste of effort'.[98] In *X and Y v. the Netherlands* (1985), the Strasbourg Court held that a state can 'in certain circumstances' be 'responsible for the acts of third parties', thus adopting the German doctrine of *Drittwirkung* to European human rights.[99] In result, the state is obliged to afford practical and effective protection to all individuals within its jurisdictions, be it its relations with individuals (vertical effect) or in relations between the individuals themselves (horizontal effect).

Translating these to the privacy universe, the currently available regulatory protections often do not live up to these standards. Looking solely at the example of the EU data privacy regulation, the 1995 Data Protection Directive[100] fell victim to many troubles stemming from EU decision-making, suffering from a lack of sufficient quality as well as complexity, slowness and being 'hostage to

95 Emphasis mine.

96 Cf. also Art. 1 of Protocol No. 12 to the ECHR.

97 *Nježić and Štimac v. Croatia*, App. no. 29823/13 (ECtHR, 9 April 2015), §61. Emphasis added.

98 Kloza and Galetta, above n. 29, p. 4. Collins English Dictionary, <http://www.collinsdictionary.com>.

99 *X and Y v. the Netherlands*, App. no. 8978/80 (ECtHR, 26 March 1985), §33.

100 Directive 95/46/EC of the European Parliament and of the Council of 24 October 1995 on the protection of individuals with regard to the processing of personal data and on the free movement of such data, [1995] OJ L 281/31–50.

the lowest common denominator'.[101] The Directive was a political compromise build upon diverse experience of several EU Member States with regulating the processing of personal data.[102] Furthermore, its dual aim of establishing internal market and protecting fundamental rights eventually caused doubts as to the validity of its legal basis.[103] Despite the Directive offering significant protections at the time of its enactment and transposition deadline (1998), compared *avant la lettre*, it has quickly become outdated.

A proposal for its replacement in entirety – i.e. the General Data Protection Regulation – was tabled in January 2012, predominantly to keep pace with the development of emerging technologies,[104] and signed into law in April 2016.[105] Despite great enthusiasm about the proposed text, expressed initially as a 'Copernican revolution'[106] and eventually as 'still a sound system for the protection of individuals',[107] many commentators observed that either the new Regulation would not solve existing problems or it would create new ones. Blume, for example, speaks of an 'illusion of a higher level of protection' that would result from the entry into force of GDPR.[108] Koops, highly critical, further argues that the direction of the data protection reform is fundamentally flawed for at least three reasons: (1) the individual's control over their data is a delusion, (2) so too is the conception that the reform simplifies the law, and (3) an attempt of comprehensiveness, i.e. to regulate all in a single statute, has failed.[109] Anecdotally, in a private conversation held in mid-2015 in Brussels, a representative of an office of a DPA in Europe joked that she would move to Morocco once the GDPR was passed, as Morocco would then offer a higher level of protection of privacy. The truth is most probably somewhere

---

101 J. Zielonka, *Is the EU Doomed?*, Polity, Cambridge 2014.

102 Mayer-Schönberger, above n. 20, pp. 234–36.

103 O. Lynskey, 'From Market-Making Tool to Fundamental Right: The Role of the Court of Justice in Data Protection's Identity Crisis' in S. Gutwirth, R. Leenes, P. De Hert and Y. Poullet (eds.), *European Data Protection: Coming of Age*, Springer, Dordrecht 2013, pp. 59–84.

104 Proposal for a Regulation of the European Parliament and of the Council on the protection of individuals with regard to the processing of personal data and on the free movement of such data (General Data Protection Regulation), Brussels, 25.01.2012, COM(2012) 11 final.

105 Regulation (EU) 2016/679 of the European Parliament and of the Council of 27 April 2016 on the protection of natural persons with regard to the processing of personal data and on the free movement of such data, and repealing Directive 95/46/EC (General Data Protection Regulation), [2016] OJ L 119/1–88.

106 C. Kuner, 'The European Commission's Proposed Data Protection Regulation: A Copernican Revolution in European Data Protection Law' (2012) 11(6) *Privacy and Security Law Report* 1–15.

107 P. De Hert and V. Papakonstantinou, 'The New General Data Protection Regulation: Still a Sound System for the Protection of Individuals?' (2016) 32(2) *Computer Law & Security Review* 179–194.

108 P. Blume, 'The Myths Pertaining to the Proposed General Data Protection Regulation' (2014) 4(4) *International Data Privacy Law* 269–273.

109 B.-J. Koops, 'The Trouble with European Data Protection Law' (2014) 4(4) *International Data Privacy Law* 250–261.

in-between. Davies recently reflected on the GDPR's final version that 'in spite of shortcomings, disappointments and lost opportunities, [it] should provide a more robust infrastructure of rights protection'.[110]

Regulatory inefficiencies could be also demonstrated by examining the quality of legal norms. Many legal instruments suffer from complexity and difficulty-to-navigate, making them 'anything but straightforward'[111] and the EU data protection law is no exception. It is hard not to recall Fuller's classical 'eight ways to fail to make law', i.e. his conditions of good law-making:

> The first and most obvious lies in a failure to achieve rules at all, so that every issue must be decided on an *ad hoc* basis. The other routes are: (2) a failure to publicise, or at least to make available to the affected party, the rules he is expected to observe; (3) the abuse of retroactive legislation, which not only cannot itself guide action, but undercuts the integrity of rules prospective in effect, since it puts them under the threat of retrospective change; (4) a failure to make rules understandable; (5) the enactment of contradictory rules or (6) rules that require conduct beyond the powers of the affected party; (7) introducing such frequent changes in the rules that the subject cannot orient his action by them; and finally, (8) a failure of congruence between the rules as announced and their actual administration.[112]

Kuner has applied these to the European data protection law as in force in 1998, concluding the lack of rules to address certain problems, lack of public awareness of data privacy law, lack of clarity, contradiction of rules and failure of congruence between the rules and their administration.[113]

3.2.1.2. Ever-changing nature of the object of protection and of the context

The second reason to judge the contemporarily available regulatory protections as inadequate is the *ever-changing* nature of both the object of protection and the context in which the protection of this object is sought. Innovation and technology are regulated for two reasons. First, we want to stimulate the progress of both, and thus – indirectly – the progress of society in general. This objective justifies all public funding for research and development or all public efforts to create a stimulative environment for technology companies and start-ups, e.g. by reducing red-tape or offering affordable loans. Second, we want to eliminate or at least minimise those consequences of innovation and technology that we

110 S. Davies, 'The Data Protection Regulation: A Triumph of Pragmatism over Principle?' (2016) 3 *European Data Protection Law Review* 290–296, <http://edpl.lexxion.eu/data/article/10075/pdf/edpl_2016_03-006.pdf>.

111 J. Zielonka, *Is the EU Doomed?*, Polity, Cambridge 2014, p. 40.

112 L.L. Fuller, *The Morality of Law*, Yale University Press, New Haven 1964, p. 39.

113 C. Kuner, 'The "Internal Morality" of European Data Protection Law', 2008, pp. 10–15, <http://ssrn.com/abstract=1443797>.

consider negative, and thus – indirectly – eliminate or minimise harm of any nature to society and each individual member thereof, preferably before it occurs. This objective thus justifies all public transportation safety and security rules, e.g. speed bumps, although their efficiency might merit a separate discussion.

Following this perspective, regulation can be interpreted as an activity of putting a 'thin red line' between what we, as a society, want or desire and what we do not want nor desire. Such regulation would have been easy if innovation and technology, the society and their needs and desires, were of a *constant* nature. Conversely, they constantly *change*. They both progress on their own pace and these do not necessarily synchronise nor converge. Both the society and innovation and technology develop faster than regulation. Moore's Law is a perfect example thereof: Moore's predication that the number of transistors in a dense integrated circuit doubles approximately every two years have 'transformed computing from a rare and expensive venture into a pervasive and affordable necessity',[114] causing – at the same time – a need to re-invent (a lot of) the law. The question whether the regulation of cyberspace – at the time when these technologies were emerging – requires a dedicated branch of law caused in the late 1990s a seminal debate on the 'law of the horse'.[115] Furthermore, in the early 2000s, globalisation proved regulation solely at a national level to be inefficient, thus leading Beck to conclude that global risks require global responses.[116] To add to this complication, what a given society needs or desires is not static and what is acceptable varies by cultures, contexts and time.

3.2.1.3. Instrumentalisation of regulation

The third reason for inadequacy is the *instrumentalisation* of regulation, including the law. I have analysed in section 2 that those who regulate have at their disposal a wide repertoire of tools for that purpose. Therefore the act of regulation requires a *choice* of an appropriate tool or of a combination of tools that would fit the purpose sought in a given context and in a given time. Such a choice is never simple and the main criterion of its evaluation is that whether a choice made is good or not.

Those who regulate have a complex decision to make if they want their choices to be judged good. Hood suggests four canons of good application of

---

114 G.E. Moore, 'Cramming More Components onto Integrated Circuits' (1965) 38(8) *Electronics* 82–85. Cf. <http://www.intel.com/content/www/us/en/silicon-innovations/moores-law-technology.html>.

115 F.H. Easterbrook, 'Cyberspace and the Law of the Horse' (1996) *University of Chicago Legal Forum* 207–217; L. Lessig, 'The Law of the Horse: What Cyberlaw Might Teach' (1999) 113(2) *Harvard Law Review* 501; L. Lessig, *Code and Other Laws of Cyberspace*, Basic Books, New York 1999.

116 U. Beck, 'The Cosmopolitan Condition: Why Methodological Nationalism Fails' (2007) 24(7–8) *Theory, Culture & Society* 286–290. I thank Paul De Hert for bringing this matter to my attention.

these tools.[117] Some prior examinations – to a reasonable extent – of available alternatives would precede the selection of tools to regulate. Next, the tool chosen would match the regulatory goal pursued. The choice would not be 'barbaric', in a sense it would satisfy ethical criteria to which a given society subscribes, and – finally – would not waste resources in order to achieve the goals pursued.[118]

Each of these criteria, however objective they might look *prima facie*, would always involve an aspect of politics. For example, the combination of tools available for achieving a regulatory goal 'runs into billions or even trillions if one assumes no incompatibilities or mutual exclusivities'. The catalogue changes over time: new tools are being added and others are being abandoned. A fully rational review of alternatives is thus rather impossible in any finite time.[119] Furthermore, similarly to regulatory goals pursued, tools for regulation are not value-free. While some might be used for both 'good' and 'bad' purposes – and thus the context of their application matters – some other clearly belong to the latter category. Here Hood gives an example of an atomic bomb.[120] It follows that there is no intrinsically good tool for regulation. Therefore those who regulate would base their choices on their experience as well as considerations of ideological and economical aspects that are political in their nature. This in any case does not make their choices simpler: few societies subscribe to a single moral code. Instead, societies have adopted a variety of different ethical and ideological standards. Efficiency of their choices is not only about using least possible resources (time, money, manpower) but also about imposing least burden on those who are regulated. Eventually, their choices will judged against political criteria of legitimacy (if the public accepts decisions without having to be coerced) and accountability (if and how those who regulate can justify their choices).[121]

Despite such complexity in choosing the right tool for regulation, there are instances in which politics will play a decisive role in such a choice. Here I understand 'politics' in its derogatory meaning, as an act 'in the interests of status or power … rather than as a matter of principle'.[122] Those who regulate usually have a well-defined political agenda to achieve and this would determine their choices of tools. In other words, tools of regulation will be then used instrumentally and regulation would become a 'servant of politics'.[123]

---

117 Hood, above n. 10, p. 133.

118 Ibid., pp. 132–152.

119 Ibid., pp. 134–135.

120 Ibid., p. 140.

121 Morgan and Yeung, above n. 44, pp. 221–301.

122 Oxford Dictionary of English.

123 K. de Vries and N. van Dijk, 'A Bump in the Road. Ruling Out Law from Technology' in M. Hildebrandt and J. Gaakeer (eds.), *Human Law and Computer Law: Comparative Perspectives*, Springer, Dordrecht 2013, pp. 89–121; S. Gutwirth, P. De Hert and L. De Sutter, 'The Trouble with Technology Regulation from a Legal Perspective. Why Lessig's "Optimal Mix" Will Not Work' in R. Brownsword and K. Yeung (eds.), *Regulating Technologies*, Hart Publishers, Oxford 2008, pp. 193–218.

Translating these to the privacy universe, tools of regulation might be used equally to protect or to intrude privacy. It is equally possible that a deliberate choice not to regulate or a failure to regulate, such as due to carelessness, may result in an intrusion into privacy for which no protection is available.

3.2.1.4. Diminishing trust in those who regulate, handle information and oversee

This brings me to the fourth and last identified inadequacy of regulatory protections and it is the *diminishing trust* in those who regulate, those who handle information and those who oversee these two.

Trust plays a crucial role in the functioning of social life. If one trusts, she grants some other person or people some discretionary power over something and thus accepts 'some amount of risk for potential harm in exchange for the benefits of cooperation'.[124] In the theory of democracy, when people have 'given up into the hands of the society, and therein to the governors', they have done so 'with this express or tacit trust, that it shall be employed for their good'.[125] On a daily basis, trust is 'an elementary fact of social life':[126] 'If I am unwilling to trust that the strangers I meet on the street will not mug me, I will be unable to leave my house'.[127] Similarly, when people have to trade in goods or services, they would prefer that their business partners would refrain from undesirable behaviour.[128] Therefore the main role of trust is to 'reduce social complexity'[129] by 'ruling out possible, but undesirable and unfavourable, future actions of other people or organisations'.[130]

With the rise of democracy, people have established trust in those who govern them in a belief that 'the government is capable of bringing about desired outcomes'[131] or – at least – such a government would cause no harm. Yet there is a discrepancy between theory and practice. In late 2016 Eurobarometer reported that only some one-third of Europeans trust in the European Union, and only 27 per cent of them trust in their national governments.[132] Surveys of American public opinion in 2015 suggest that trust in the federal government

---

124 M.E. Warren, *Democracy and Trust*, Cambridge University Press, Cambridge 1999, p. 1.

125 J. Locke, *Second Treatise of Government*, 1690, sec. 1.

126 N. Luhmann, *Trust and Power*, Wiley, Chichester 1979, p. 4.

127 Warren, above n. 124, p. 4.

128 D. Gefen, 'E-Commerce: The Role of Familiarity and Trust' (2000) 28 (6): *Omega* 729.

129 Luhmann, above n. 126, p. 4.

130 Gefen, above n. 128, p. 728.

131 M.J. Hetherington, *Why Political Trust Matters. Why Trust Matters.* Princeton University Press, Princeton 2004, p. 5.

132 European Commission, *Standard Eurobarometer 85: Public opinion in the European Union*, July 2016, p. 14.

varies from 19 per cent to 51 per cent.[133] Only 37 per cent of Australians trusted their government in Canberra, and 75 per cent of them claim their federal government fails to contribute to greater good.[134] Such trust diminishes with each misstep of public authorities and the disclosures in 2013 about global mass surveillance practices played here a vital role. In their aftermath, only 6 per cent of American adults say they are 'very confident' that government agencies can keep their records private and secure, while another 25 per cent say they are 'somewhat confident'.[135]

These surveys clearly indicate the insufficient trust in those who regulate, those who handle information and those who control these two. This lack of trust can have multiple reasons, and one of those is the lack of adequate oversight. The concepts of democracy, the rule of law (*Rechtsstaat*) and fundamental rights require that the judicial branch oversees the activities of two other branches, i.e. legislative and executive. (And that higher instances of this judicial branch oversee the lower instances.) In particular, courts of law are required to respect standards of an open and transparent environment, where cases, reasoning and decisions are made public, unless there is a good reason to keep it secret. This secrecy is rather exceptional and to be interpreted rather narrowly. This way the society trusts in the practice of courts, confident that these institutions would deliver justice.

I can think of a few examples from the privacy universe to illustrate my point. The Foreign Intelligence Surveillance Court (FISC or, colloquially, FISA Court) was established in 1978 to 'hear applications for and grant orders approving electronic surveillance anywhere within the United States'.[136] The FISA Court is composed of 11 judges sitting *ex parte* to hear from only one side in the case – an agency of a federal government, such as the National Security Agency (NSA). Its deliberations are kept secret and its decisions are rarely made public, short of some statistical data. (These statistics reveal that the FISA Court almost never denies any request for electronic surveillance.)[137] When a request is denied, a

---

133 Pew Research Center, 'Beyond Distrust: How Americans View Their Government', November 2015 <http://www.people-press.org/2015/11/23/1-trust-in-government-1958-2015>.

134 Edelman, *Trust Barometer: Australia*, 2015, <http://www.edelman.com.au/wp-content/uploads/2015/02/2015-Edelman-Trust-Australia-Results.pdf>.

135 G. Gao, 'What Americans Think about NSA Surveillance, National Security and Privacy', Pew Research Center, 2015, <http://www.pewresearch.org/fact-tank/2015/05/29/what-americans-think-about-nsa-surveillance-national-security-and-privacy/>.

136 50 USC 1803(a)(1).

137 In 2015, the federal law enforcement agencies made 1499 applications to the FISA Court of which 1457 included requests for authority to conduct electronic surveillance. One application was withdrawn. The Court did not deny any applications in whole, or in part. The FISC made modifications to the proposed orders in 803 applications. Thus, the Court approved collection activity in a total of 1456 of the applications to conduct electronic surveillance. Cf. US Department of Justice, Assistant Attorney General, letter dated 28 April 2016, <https://www.justice.gov/nsd/nsd-foia-library/2015fisa/download>.

federal agency can request a Court of Review for reconsideration. That is known to have happened only a handful of times in the FISA Court's history and no case has ever been taken to the Supreme Court of the United States. It is not clear either if any of the service providers against whom the orders for electronic surveillance are made are able to appear before such this Court.[138] This secrecy combined with almost automatic approval of request caused the Court to bear the brunt of heavy criticism, even being nicknamed 'a kangaroo court with a rubber stamp'.[139]

But not only courts of law are set up to oversee handling personal information. It is a part of each data privacy legal framework that a jurisdiction designates one or more agencies, independent of the government, to oversee compliance with data privacy laws. Such agencies – called privacy commissioners in some jurisdictions, and data protection authorities (DPAs) in others – play multiple roles. Their role of an ombudsman interests me the most. In this role, an authority acts on behalf of an alleged victim of a violation because she normally is in a less favourable position. This usually has to do with the lack of legal expertise and resources, in particular money. European statistics show that only one-third of the population is aware of such an agency in their country, and of those a half would prefer such an agency to deal with their problem.[140] I could not find any statistics discussing trust in DPAs, yet I will use four examples to illustrate my point how the inability to lead the office can diminish the trust vested in those oversight bodies.

The Office of the Privacy Commissioner of Australia, established in 1988, was joined in 2010 with its freedom of information (FoI) and information policy counterparts, previously held by Australian Ombudsman, to form the Office of the Australian Information Commissioner (OAIC). Three commissioners headed the newly created bureau and those for FoI and privacy reported to the Information Commissioner. In 2014 the federal government in Canberra attempted to abolish the OAIC altogether and to move the Privacy Commissioner to a position within the Australian Human Rights Commission. (The FoI and information policy portfolios were meant to return to the Ombudsman.) The government could not pass the reform legislation in the upper chamber of the federal Parliament and this created a political limbo hitherto unresolved. The government instead withdrew most of the Office's funding, forcing it to dismiss some of its staff and close its Canberra premises. The Information Commissioner, John McMillan, before his resignation in June 2015, was reported to work from home. In result, from 2015 the Privacy Commissioner also acts

138 E. Lichtblau, 'In Secret, Court Vastly Broadens Powers of N.S.A.' (2013) *International New York Times*, p. 1.

139 S. Ackerman, 'Fisa Chief Judge Defends Integrity of Court over Verizon Records Collection', *The Guardian*, 06.06.2013, <https://www.theguardian.com/world/2013/jun/06/fisa-court-judge-verizon-records-surveillance>.

140 European Commission, *Special Eurobarometer 431: Data protection*, 2015, pp. 51–57.

as interim Commissioner for FoI and information policy, being reappointed for the two other offices for three-month periods. Only September 2016 saw the permanent appointment of the incumbent Privacy Commissioner Timothy Pilgrim for a fixed term as Information Commissioner.[141] (I too had a lot of difficulties in putting this level of complication in a single paragraph.)

The Australian example is not isolated. When in January 2014 Peter Hustinx finished his second term as the European Data Protection Supervisor (EDPS), a data protection authority for European Union's institutions, agencies, bodies and offices, his successor could not be chosen for almost a year. After the first public vacancy notice in July 2013,[142] an inter-institutional 'selection board' found that all shortlisted candidates were lacking enough experience.[143] No new vacancy notice followed immediately after. The situation was unprecedented as the post had to be filled in in the middle of the reform process of the EU data privacy law, in which the office of the EDPS was a vivid commentator, working to ensure fulfilment of the EU fundamental right to personal data protection. Commentators frequently asked as to the explanation for the reasoning of the selection board as well as for overall transparency of the process, dubbing the whole process a 'political football'.[144] Hustinx expressed his concerns an open letter stating 'this uncertainty and the possibly long delays that may be involved … are likely to harm the effectiveness and the authority of the EDPS over the coming months'.[145] Their demands were never satisfied. Simply a second vacancy notice was issued in May 2014 with a one-month deadline[146] and the post was filled in on 4 December 2014 by a joint decision of the European Parliament and the Council.[147]

The EDPS story is linked to the story of the Inspector-General for the Protection of Personal Data (GIODO), the Polish DPA. On 4 December 2014 the incumbent Polish Inspector-General, Wojciech R. Wiewiórowski, was elected for the post of Assistant EDPS in Brussels. The vacancy in Warsaw was not filled until mid-April 2015. A candidate can be proposed e.g. by a group of members of parliament and thus the majority has initially proposed the candidacy of Mirosław Wróblewski, who later on withdrew it. The reasons for that remain unclear, yet the media speculated that the parliamentary group proposed this candidate without prior consultation with then prime minister, Ewa Kopacz.

---

141 I thank Roger Clarke for bringing this matter to my attention.

142 [2013] OJ C 219A/1–5.

143 J. Fleming, 'Pressure Grows over EU Data Watchdog Replacement', *EurActiv.com*, 09.01.2014, <http://www.euractiv.com/section/ustice-home-affairs/news/pressure-grows-over-eu-data-watchdog-replacement/>.

144 C. Kuner, 'The Baffling Case of the Headless EDPS', *IAPP Privacy Perspectives*, 15.01.2014, <https://iapp.org/news/a/the-edps-mess/>.

145 Cf. <https://secure.edps.europa.eu/EDPSWEB/webdav/site/mySite/shared/Documents/EDPS/PressNews/News/14-01-07_Letter_to_EC_PH_EN.pdf>.

146 [2014] OJ C 163A/6–9.

147 [2014] OJ L 351/9.

Assuming the media were right, there is no constitutional requirement for such a consultation, thus such a delay can be only seen as a part of a political game. The subsequent candidate proposed by the parliamentary majority, Edyta Bielak-Jomaa, won the support of the lower chamber on 9 April 2015, yet in grotesque proceedings. The voting was held in the middle of the night, with MPs giving no attention whatsoever to the presentation of the candidates and observing party discipline when it came to the very moment of voting.[148] The upper chamber confirmed the nomination on 16 April.

Yet perhaps the most remarkable story about trust in DPAs is that of Hungary. From its establishment in 1992 until 1 January 2012, the functioning of the Hungarian authority followed an ombudsman model and it was set up as the Parliamentary Commissioner for Data Protection and Freedom of Information. A vivid debate at to the merits of such an arrangement was concluded with the entry into force of the new Constitution. Among many changes it brought, the post of the Parliamentary Commissioner was abolished and a new authority was set up, outside a national legislature, to fulfil the functions of a DPA. In result, the incumbent Commissioner András Jóri was forced to vacate his office. This caused a few Hungarian NGOs to complain to the European Commission, which monitors the compliance of the Member States with the EU law, that the premature termination of his mandate breached EU data privacy law. In order to act independently, a DPA must be assured that its term in office will not be cut short, other than for a few narrowly interpreted exceptions. The European Commission shared these views and launched before the CJEU an action against Hungary for its failure to fulfil this obligation.[149] There was no surprise when the Luxembourg Court ruled that

> Hungary compelled [the Commissioner] to vacate office in contravention of the safeguards established … to protect his term of office, thereby compromising his independence … The fact that it was because of institutional changes that he was compelled to vacate office before serving his full term cannot render that situation compatible with the requirement … of independence for supervisory authorities.[150]

I cannot help but conclude this argument with a reference to the socio-psychological theory of procedural justice. It holds that people pay attention not only to the outcome of proceedings (distributive justice) but also the way of arriving at a given outcome.[151] In other words, they care if the proceeding

---

148 J. Wątor, 'Poseł Z Kartką Na Czole', *Gazeta Wyborcza*, 10.04.2015, <http://wyborcza.biz/biznes/1,100897,17733132,Posel_z_kartka_na_czole.html>.

149 A. Jóri, 'The End of Independent Data Protection Supervision in Hungary – A Case Study' in S. Gutwirth, R. Leenes, P. de Hert and Y. Poullet (eds.), *European Data Protection: Coming of Age*, Springer, Dordrecht 2013, pp. 395–406.

150 Case C-288/12, *Commission v. Hungary* (CJEU, 8 April 2014), §59.

151 T.R. Tyler, 'Procedural Justice and the Courts' (2008) 44 *Court Review* 26.

were fair[152] and they are more likely to accept the outcome, even if unfavourable to them. The idea of procedural justice is based on four building blocks: voice (participation), neutrality, respect and trust. In particular, people infer whether those who decide upon them or represent them listen and consider their views, whether they 'are being honest and open about the basis for their actions; are trying to do what is right for everyone involved; and are acting in the interests of the parties, not out of personal prejudices'.[153] Tyler coined these conditions having courts of law in mind. I hold these are equally applicable to oversight bodies and this includes data privacy supervisory authorities. The few examples I have discussed above allow me to add in this context the conditions of transparency, stability, continuity and independence as major factors of public trust. The experience of the Australian, European, Polish and Hungarian DPAs teaches that both legislature and executive need to take these bodies seriously. The conclusion must be that trust in such oversight bodies is significantly diminished when public authorities ignore them, underestimate their role or treat them instrumentally, as enablers of political goals or disablers of political opponents.

3.2.2. *Organisational tools*

I have made only a mention of privacy impact assessments (PIAs) in section 2.2 as one of organisational tools to protect privacy. Their in-depth analysis lies outside the scope of this contribution but it shall suffice for my purposes to assume that PIAs are considered an adequate, broadest and – so far – most mature response to the challenges technology and globalisation prosed to the protection of privacy. Much of their success depends on the quality of the process of assessment. Let me use the critique of PIAs to illustrate the point that organisational measures have too their limits in delivering adequate protection.[154]

152 R. Hollander-Blumoff, 'Just Negotiation' (2010) 88(2) *Washington University Law Review* 381.

153 Tyler, above n. 151, pp. 30–31.

154 For a critical analysis of other organisational measures, cf. e.g. S. Gürses, C. Troncoso and C. Diaz, 'Engineering Privacy by Design' (2011) *Computers, Privacy & Data Protection (CPDP 2011)*, Brussels, pp. 1–25, <https://www.cosic.esat.kuleuven.be/publications/article-1542.pdf>; M. Hildebrandt and L. Tielemans, 'Data Protection by Design and Technology Neutral Law' (2013) 29(5) *Computer Law and Security Review* 509–521; D. Wiese Schartum, 'Making Privacy by Design Operative' (2016) 24(2) *International Journal of Law and Information Technology* 151–175 (concerning Privacy by Design); and R. Rodrigues, D. Wright and K. Wadhwa, 'Developing a Privacy Seal Scheme (That Works)' (2013) 3(2) *International Data Privacy Law* 100–116; R. Rodrigues, D. Barnard-Wills, P. De Hert and V. Papakonstantinou, 'The Future of Privacy Certification in Europe: An Exploration of Options under Article 42 of the GDPR' (2016) 869 *International Review of Law, Computers & Technology* 1–23 (concerning privacy seals).

Before PIAs are even performed, they often meet with opposition arguing they would constitute another unnecessary regulatory burden, adding to already overgrown bureaucracy, causing unnecessary expenditure and delays in the decision-making process and in the implementation of a project. Opponents would not omit underlining the complexity of the assessment process in practice, difficulties it brings, combined with a lack of practical experience and minimal or non-existent guidance from those who require a PIA to be conducted. Proponents of PIAs lament that they are often performed perfunctorily and used instrumentally, both to the detriment of the protection of privacy.[155] PIAs are only a tool to support decision-making and thus they do not prevent privacy-intrusive projects from being implemented. A PIA final report might suggest not to implement a project or a part thereof, but nevertheless the decision-makers would approve it as they would perceive the risk worth taking.[156] Or worse, they would perform a PIA solely to fulfil the regulatory requirement but nevertheless would proceed with the implementation of the project.

Next, policies mandating PIAs are often criticised for their narrow scope, i.e. even when the performance of PIA is required by law, the requirements set forth are too narrow and too nuanced to deliver any adequate level of protection. It is further not expected that public authorities or businesses would perform a PIA when not required to do so by the law or otherwise incentivised. This narrowness manifests itself in a limited list of privacy-intrusive projects subjected to PIA. For example, the GDPR requires a form of PIA to be performed – at a minimum – when an individual is subjected to surveillance and decision-making based on profiling, when her sensitive data (such as medical records) are handled on a large scale and when public areas are systematically monitored. To further narrow this list, there exist plenty of exceptions allowing for avoidance of a PIA, such quantitative determinants as 'large scale', 'systematic' or 'extensive'. It is inevitable that those who handle information would attempt to define their projects in a way permitting to escape this regulatory requirement.[157] Yet the feeling is that there are plenty of other types of privacy intrusions resulting from data handlings that merit their subjection to a privacy impact assessment. Furthermore, with the ever-changing nature of society, and innovation and technology, a narrow and prescriptive catalogue of privacy-intrusive actions subjected to PIAs is rather counter-productive.

When PIAs have been performed, they usually lack transparency, i.e. the whole process is opaque and its final results are difficult if not impossible to find. Multiple stakeholders legitimately fear the disclosure of state secrets, trade secrets and otherwise privileged information, yet they fail to acknowledge the existence of certain solutions thereto, e.g. the removal of such information from a

155 De Hert, Kloza and Wright, above n. 72, p. 9.
156 Kloza, van Dijk and De Hert, above n. 53, p. 32.
157 I thank Colin J. Bennett for bringing this to my attention.

public version of their PIA final reports. For instance, the Canadian federal audit of PIAs carried out revealed that only a minority of the stakeholders audited were regularly posting and updating the results of PIA reports to their external websites. Just as the public reporting on PIAs was lacking in completeness, so too was it lacking in quality.[158]

Even when the law requires a PIA process to consult external stakeholders, PIAs actually carried out give it limited scope or make it meaningless.[159] Again a Canadian example: many commentators observed that PIAs performed there seldom involve public consultation, opinion polling or other means of gauging the privacy values of the public. The end product tends to resemble a compliance checklist and does not require documentation of deliberations.[160] Systemically, PIAs are often performed too late, when the design of a project cannot be meaningfully influenced to protect privacy, and are equally often misunderstood by their confusion with audits. (While the *modus operandi* of PIAs is to influence the design of a project, thus being an *ex ante* tool, audits are meant to verify compliance once the project has been deployed, and perhaps, concluded, thus being *ex post* tools.) Finally, there is a popular conviction that once a PIA is completed, all privacy problems are solved for good. But, as time passes, both projects undergo changes and so do societal and technological contexts in which these projects are deployed. Thus PIAs often fail to be understood as a continuous process, to the detriment of privacy protection.

3.2.3. *Technological tools*

As with the critique of privacy impact assessments, I will use the criticism of the end-user Privacy Enhancing Technologies (PETs) in general, and of encryption in particular, to illustrate the shortcomings of technological tools for privacy protection.

The classical critique of PETs is four-fold. The first is that PETs are not for everyday users and this largely explains their limited adoption. They are designed predominantly for people who perceive the need to use technology to protect their privacy against incursions by public authorities, businesses and other individuals, and against unsafe and hostile technologies. Therefore the most likely adopters would include e.g. senior public officials and business executives whose work is particularly sensitive, victims of a crime and political activists, such as dissidents or whistle-blowers.[161] The second critique is that of usability (ease of use). The

158 J. Stoddart, 'Auditing Privacy Impact Assessments: The Canadian Experience' in D. Wright and P. De Hert (eds.), *Privacy Impact Assessment*, Springer, Dordrecht 2012, p. 434.

159 Kloza, above n. 38, pp. 80–97.

160 R. Bayley and C. Bennett, 'Privacy Impact Assessments in Canada' in D. Wright and P. De Hert (eds.), *Privacy Impact Assessment*, Springer, Dordrecht 2012, p. 183.

161 Clarke, above n. 82, pt. 4.3.

use of PETs is rather laborious: from learning how to use them to launching each individual tool each time it is needed. PETs do not come in a single software package, but rather each individual PET is a standalone tool. For example, there is normally different software to encrypt the contents of a hard drive and different software to encrypt e-mail communications. To add to this complexity, the use of such software is rather difficult for first-comers.[162] The third critique is that usability is not the sole criterion. Assurance, or trust in a particular encryption technology, seems to be the missing link.[163] The fourth and final criticism is that PETs are mostly research artefacts rather than tools designed for people to use.[164]

Encryption as a PET shares a lot of general critique of PETs but also has a few drawbacks on its own. The first critique is that there is no cryptographic technique that is absolutely unbreakable. The unbreakability depends on three factors cumulatively, i.e. the strength of the encryption algorithm, the length of the encryption key (128-bit-key is nowadays a bare minimum) and the security of the key management (to be kept separately in a safe and secure location).[165] The easiest way to break a cryptosystem is to try all possible keys (i.e. exhaustive key search), thus eventually guessing correctly, yet at a great expense of time and other resources. Further, implementations of encryption may contain accidental errors or deliberate 'back doors'.[166] Finally, cryptography constitutes a dual-use technology, being capable of both civilian and military applications. It is thus subjected to regulation, with certain jurisdictions either restricting or prohibiting its use, import and export or controlling the setting of international encryption standards.[167] The 1996 Wassenaar Arrangement,[168] currently

---

162 A. Whitten and J.D. Tygar, 'Why Johnny Can't Encrypt. A Usability Evaluation of PGP 5.0' in L. Cranor and G. Simson (eds.), *Security and Usability: Designing Secure Systems That People Can Use*, O'Reilly, Sebastopol CA 2005, p. 699.

163 S. Fahl, M. Harbach, T. Muders, M. Smith and U. Sander, 'Helping Johnny 2.0 to Encrypt His Facebook Conversations Categories and Subject Descriptors', *Symposium on Usable Privacy and Security (SOUPS)*, ACM, Washington DC 2012, p. 11.

164 Clarke, above n. 82, pt. 4.1.

165 W. Hon, C. Millard and I. Walden, 'The Problem of 'Personal Data' in Cloud Computing: What Information Is Regulated? The Cloud of Unknowing, Pt. 1', Legal Studies Research Paper 75/2011, London 2011, p. 23.

166 S. Gürses and B. Preneel, 'Cryptology and Privacy in the Context of Big Data' in B. Van Der Sloot, D. Broeders and E. Schrijvers (eds.), *Exploring the Boundaries of Big Data*, Amsterdam University Press, Amsterdam 2016, pp. 62–66.

167 J. Ball, J. Borger and G. Greenwald, 'Revealed: How US and UK Spy Agencies Defeat Internet Privacy and Security', *The Guardian*, 06.09.2013, <https://www.theguardian.com/world/2013/sep/05/nsa-gchq-encryption-codes-security>.

168 Arrangement on Export Controls for Conventional Arms and Dual-Use Goods and Technologies, Wassenaar 1996; cf. esp. the dual-use list, cat. 5, pt. 2, <http://www.wassenaar.org/wp-content/uploads/2016/07/WA-LIST-15-1-CORR-1-2015-List-of-DU-Goods-and-Technologies-and-Munitions-List.pdf>. Cf. also Council Regulation (EC) No. 428/2009 of 5 May 2009 setting up a Community regime for the control of exports, transfer, brokering and transit of dual-use items, [2009] OJ L 134/1–269, currently under revision, cf. COM(2016) 616 final.

comprising 42 jurisdictions, is perhaps most known example of multilateral export control regime.[169] Finally, criminal laws might require individuals to surrender cryptographic keys to law enforcement, yet the suspect might resort to the privilege against self-incrimination.[170]

Encryption nevertheless survives most of the above-mentioned criticism and is thus considered an efficient technology to protect information in a digital environment. In the aftermath of the 2013 Snowden disclosures about the global mass surveillance practices, multiple stakeholders resorted, *inter alia*, to the widespread use of strong, end-to-end encryption without the possession of the key by any intermediary or manufacturer. In a 2013 questions and answers session with *The Guardian*, Snowden himself advised: 'Encryption works. Properly implemented strong crypto systems are one of the few things that you can rely on.'[171]

4. THE BEHAVIOURAL ALTERNATIVE

4.1. HISTORY

> *That the individual shall have full protection in person and in property is a principle as old as the common law; but it has been found necessary from time to time to define anew the exact nature and extent of such protection.*[172]

Resorting to one's own behaviour to protect certain interests is perhaps as old as humanity and attempts of that type to secure communications offer a fascinating example to illustrate my point. In the era of verbal communications, the mere invention of writing made all communications secret, at least initially, as not many people were able to read. Human messengers, if they were to carry a written message, were chosen from among illiterates, a practice still known in the nineteenth century.[173] As the skill of writing became more widespread, additional precautions were needed to ensure secrecy.[174] Thus cryptography, i.e.

---

169 B.-J. Koops, *The Crypto Controversy: A Key Conflict in the Information Society*, Kluwer Law International, The Hague 1999, pp. 97–113.

170 Ibid., pp. 167–200; B.-J. Koops, 'Commanding Decryption and the Privilege Against Self-Incrimination' in C.M. Breur, M.M. Kommer, J.F. Nijboer and J.M. Reijntjes (eds.), *New Trends in Criminal Investigation and Evidence*, Intersentia, Antwerp 2000, pp. 437–438.

171 G. Greenwald, 'Edward Snowden: NSA Whistleblower Answers Reader Questions', *The Guardian*, 17.06.2013, <https://www.theguardian.com/world/2013/jun/17/edward-snowden-nsa-files-whistleblower>.

172 Warren and Brandeis, above n. 17.

173 D.J. Solove, *Understanding Privacy*, Harvard University Press, Cambridge MA 2008, pp. 61–65.

174 A.C. Leighton, 'Secret Communication among the Greeks and Romans' (1969) 10(2) *Technology and Culture* 140.

the art and science of making communications unintelligible to all except the intended recipients, was invented and since antiquity has been widely used in politics and warfare. Julius Caesar used one of the earliest known cryptographic systems. Around 50 BC Caesar wrote to Cicero using a cipher that shifts the Latin alphabet three places to the right and wraps the last three letters back onto the first three letters.[175] But, equally in politics and warfare, the adversary wants to read a cryptic message. Therefore cryptanalysis, i.e. reading secret messages and uncovering the cryptographic system utilised, played a vital role in the conclusion of many conflicts. The recovery of an Enigma machine from a sinking Nazi submarine, and breaking its code by Polish mathematicians, is believed to have been a turning point in World War II.[176] Both cryptography and cryptanalysis progressed with the advent of computers, crowned with Diffie's and Hellman's revolutionary development of asymmetric cryptography in 1976.[177]

Surprisingly, when sophisticated cryptography combined with a plethora of other cutting-edge measures employed to protect digital communications fails, a return to simplicity might be more fruitful. I found entertaining a piece of news brought by *The Guardian* in 2014 when – in the aftermath of the Snowden revelations – reportedly both Russian and German secret services ditched their computers and returned to the use of mechanical, analogue typewriters.[178] At least a piece of information would remain in a predetermined, finite number of easily traceable copies, assuming photocopies were not made.

Nevertheless, secrecy of communications is not only a domain of politics and warfare. Messages have been concealed and coded also for purely private purposes. To take a most mundane example, for generations children have kept their secrets in diaries secured with padlocks, or in a hiding place known only to them. Similarly, they use their own key-language (idioglossias) to communicate with peers, so that their parents or unwelcome colleagues cannot learn the contents of their communications. To take the most prominent example, only a handful of readers would not be familiar with the encryption software called 'Pretty Good Privacy', or 'PGP'. It has been widely used since the 1990s, especially in e-mail communications, and is to a large extent based on Diffie's and Hellman's invention. The idea is that anyone with a *public* key of a particular addressee can lock a message addressed to her. The addressee is the only person

175 D. Luciano and G. Prichett, 'Cryptology: From Caesar Ciphers to Public-Key Cryptosystems' (1987) 18(1) *The College Mathematics Journal* 1–2.

176 Ibid., p. 3; M. Rejewski, 'How Polish Mathematicians Broke the Enigma Cipher' (1981) 3(3) *Annals of the History of Computing* 213–234.

177 W. Diffie and M.E. Hellman, 'New Directions in Cryptography' (1976) 22(6) *IEEE Transactions on Information Theory* 644–654; D. Kahn, 'Cryptology Goes Public' (1979) 58(1) *Foreign Affairs* 153–154.

178 P. Oltermann, 'Germany "May Revert to Typewriters" to Counter Hi-Tech Espionage,' *The Guardian*, 2014.

knowing her *private* key, so she and only she herself can unlock the message and read its contents.[179]

4.2. TYPOLOGY

How do people adjust their behaviour to protect privacy? I hasten to explain to the reader that the typology I propose here is my first attempt to classify and make sense of behavioural tools for privacy protection. I also re-emphasise this typology grew up from my own experience, observations and discussions with relatives, friends and colleagues rather than from any specific scientific method. It is thus meant to be an invitation to further discussion, which – it is hoped – would help to render this toolkit as complete as possible.

Behavioural tools for privacy protection could be used *individually*, by a person concerned, normally in her own personal interest, or *collectively*, by a societal group, usually in their own collective interests. These protections could include a wide range of *actions* and *inactions*. They might *directly* target the objective of privacy protection or might target some other objective, thus *indirectly* adding to the protection of privacy. Behavioural tools are usually scalable: people might be engaging in such actions or inactions on a *permanent* or *temporary* basis, or at *regular intervals* (e.g. 'digital detox'). They might employ different behaviour in their *professional* (at work) and *private* life (at home). They might engage for their own benefit (i.e. *inward* tools) or for the benefit of other people (e.g. their relatives and friends, their social group or even the society at large; *outward* tools).

The spectrum of behavioural tools opens with *non-engagement*, i.e. the choice not to use certain services. The first sub-category is *non-participation* and it starts with small daily choices, ranging to essential, more drastic decisions. Initially, people would cease to use services or service providers notorious for invading their privacy. In the latter instance, this might amount to conscious avoidance of particular brands. It might further amount to avoidance of services or service providers originating from particular countries that are not considered trustworthy. (Some people would test or experiment with these services and providers before.) Some people would perform certain transactions offline instead of online. If there was an option to pay cash for theatre tickets for a performance in the neighbourhood, they would go to the box office instead ordering them on a website. People would refuse to give their postcode for statistical purposes (a common practice in some supermarket chains). Some people, as a matter of principle, would not use social networking sites (Facebook or Google Plus), or would use some of them for professional reasons only, e.g.

179 Cf. <http://www.pgpi.org/doc/pgpintro>.

LinkedIn or Twitter. I have known people who have ceased to use them. Some people do not possess or use a mobile phone or – a few more – do not use any 'smart' functionalities thereof. I have known people who disconnect from all digital services for a given period of time, celebrating e.g. 'digital detox' or 'National Day of Unplugging'.[180] I have also known people who still use paper agendas and diaries for planning their time. (The latter, I was told, is partially because 'we slowly but consequently lose our ability to handwrite'.)[181]

The second sub-category of non-engagement is *non-disclosure* and it concerns partaking in a wide spectrum of services, but having first carefully chosen *which* information, *if ever*, to disclose, *how* to disclose or which sub-services to subscribe in, and to *what extent*. It is an attempt to meaningfully partake in services with no or only minimal, selective disclosure of information. Non-disclosure, similarly to non-participation, starts with trivial daily choices. I have known people who would never set-up an account for just a single online transaction or would never opt-in for any newsletters while buying goods or services over the Internet. (It is a common practice of ticket-selling intermediaries or airlines to offer to 'become a member' and to subscribe to newsletters with 'best offers ever'.) People would uninstall software when they no longer need it, even when they used it only once or twice. I have known people who install a mobile application of Uber each time they need to use its services; such a need must arise for them rather sporadically. They might opt for a pre-paid mobile phone bought with cash over a subscribed one – still available in some countries – and thus making it easy to change, should the need arise (cf. 'burner phones'). When paying with a pseudonymous currency, e.g. Bitcoin, they would hide their IP number and use a new address each time they send and receive a new payment. They would exchange cash for crypto-currencies in a dedicated bank machine. I have known people who provide their office address for delivery of goods bought online, catalogues and 'less important' correspondence as a means to avoid disclosing their home address. I have also known people, especially youngsters, who set up their social networking sites to display different contents to different groups, i.e. their classmates see different photos than their parents.

The spectrum continues with the protection of the security and secrecy of activities as well as the obfuscation of the mere fact thereof (*concealment*). Here people would resolve to *technological* and – to a lesser extent – *organisational* means. However, what qualifies these two types as behavioural tools is the way these are assessed, chosen and used. Further, it is the way these means create and

---

180 Cf. <http://nationaldayofunplugging.com>.

181 Statement on file with the author. Some inspiration for such temporary disconnection from the digital world might have come from a documentary movie *Finding Paul Miller* (2013); cf. P. Miller, 'I'm Still Here: Back Online after a Year without the Internet', *The Verge*, 01.05.2013 <http://www.theverge.com/2013/5/1/4279674/im-still-here-back-online-after-a-year-without-the-internet>.

change habits of their users. People would first enquire and assess whether a given means would offer them the protection they seek. As there exist replacements for the vast majority of technologies (e.g. there are a few alternatives to a major online maps provider), they would choose predominantly those whose main aim is to protect privacy. Often they would use them in addition to the other technologies used, e.g. they might install a specific add-on into their web browser. (The sole aim of these additional technologies might be to protect security of information and then their security features are at a service of privacy.) People would prefer technologies offered by providers originating from countries with laws more supportive for individual privacy or providers who store information of their clientele in such jurisdictions. (I have nevertheless known people who, having obtained a new mobile device, would each time wipe out its memory and install a trusted operating system, even at the pain of losing warranty.) It has become a common practice, after the 2013 Snowden disclosures, for Europeans to choose European organisations whose servers are located on the Old Continent, thus making them 'NSA-proof'.[182] Certain organisations made their business model on this criterion of geographic location. In other words, geography matters and people would 'shop' for a favourable forum. People who have specific background would prefer open source technologies as they would build their trust therein on the verification the software code whether it actually delivers the promised protections. A trust in a technology or its providers is usually enhanced with clear privacy policies and 'social contracts'. (For example, in such a 'contract', the Tor Project claimed it would never 'implement front doors or back doors into [their] projects'.)[183]

When people start using e.g. end-to-end, military-grade encryption of their e-mails, they would often change the way they read and write these. They would access their e-mail account solely via website, which they would open only in a web browser offering a strong preservation of anonymity, e.g. Tor. For some other services, they would force their browser to connect only using a secure connection (i.e. the HTTPs protocol), they would set it up to clear browsing history and cookie files at the end of each session or they would enable a 'do-not-track-me' functionality and disable any form of geo-location. There are further instances when complex security, secrecy and obscurity are necessary, for example whistle-blowers. They might use particular technologies only for a single purpose, e.g. an e-mail account to communicate with one person, and this each time with the use of a so-called live operating system.

People might further re-organise their daily habits to protect their privacy. They might conceal and diffuse their identity. The use of pseudonyms, such as nicknames, anonymisation of web searches, by the use of dedicated search

---

182 Wojciech R. Wiewiórowski coined this term.

183 Cf. <https://blog.torproject.org/blog/tor-social-contract>.

engines, and anti-malware software are the simplest example here. They would opt for an anonymous travel card in a city, if possible, even if this option is more expensive. They would refuse to accept a 'smart meter' to calculate their energy consumption. People might use different service accounts – e.g. multiple e-mail addresses and logins for instant messengers – for different purposes, e.g. professional reasons or online shopping. They would use dedicated software to ensure erasure of data from a hard drive, should these data no longer be needed, or to remove traces of their activities ('digital footprint') from the Internet.[184]

On some rare occasions, people would protect the security and secrecy of their activities by resolving to classical methods of cryptography (writing code) and steganography (concealing information within other non-secret information). They might develop some keywords and nicknames with specific meaning asserted that is known only to a closed circle of people. (They might pay attention not to mention any names; *nomina sunt odiosa*.) They might speak a rare, foreign language (e.g. in public spaces) or even invent and speak a new one; the latter would be extremely rare. They might simply call instead or type on an instant messenger since voice – at the current level of technology development – is still more difficult for a machine to meaningfully analyse than any computer-typed text. Or – the simplest solution – they would not discuss a given matter in any public space.

People would ultimately resort to organisational, 'bricks and mortar' means, such as coverage (hiding) and obliteration. For example, people would place removable stickers on the lens of their laptop's built-in video camera and microphone. ('Removable' as they from time to time would actually use the camera.) In their houses, windows would be coverable with curtains or blinds. When entering a password on a device, they would cover they keyboard, similarly to typing in a PIN number on a credit card terminal. They would recycle only shredded documents, if they contained any valuable information, e.g. health records or bank statements. (Some people would burn them in a fireplace.) At home, they would keep their passport – and other documents embedded with radio-frequency identification (RFID) devices – in a cover capable of blocking its detection and interaction therewith. Even simply while walking at an airport, people would hide, cover or just turn over their boarding passes and passport so that nobody can guess or read their names and nationalities.[185] If a battery is still removable from their mobile devices, they would take it out during meetings they perceive to be sensitive, otherwise they would hold them e.g. in a microwave.

The spectrum of behavioural tools closes with a wide range of *proactive* tools. While the previously discussed tools are predominantly aimed at reducing

---

184 Cf. <http://www.abine.com/deleteme> or <http://www.deseat.me>.

185 A lot can be read from merely a front cover of a passport and from its colour.

threats to privacy, these aim to increase the level of privacy protection. People would engage in protest when their collective interest is threatened, e.g. a mass surveillance practice is to be put in place in a given jurisdiction. One of the earliest examples of significant protest aiming at safeguarding privacy was held in the Netherlands in 1971 and targeted a national census. Never again would such a comprehensive survey of the entire population be held in the country.[186] More recently, in 2008 the Dutch protested against a compulsory roll-out of smart meters in the entire country. As a result of public outrage, the relevant bill was amended in the parliament to accommodate privacy safeguards.[187] These developments are believed to have inspired the introduction of privacy safeguards in the energy sector at EU level.[188] As a case in point, August 2016 saw the beginning of public outrage against the lack of anonymity of a national census in Australia. This protest gained popularity especially after the hashtag *#CensusFail* went viral on Twitter and the registration website went down.[189]

People might organise themselves in advocacy groups and in particular set up dedicated non-governmental organisations (NGOs). I can immediately think of some global players such as the Electronic Frontier Foundation (EFF),[190] some 'regional' players like the European Digital Rights [EDRi][191] and 'national ones', like *Digital Rights Ireland*,[192] *Fundacja Panoptykon*[193] in Poland or *La Quadrature du Net* in France.[194]

Finally, people might engage in *awareness-raising*. Parents would teach their children about basic aspects of security while using the Internet. Whistle-blowers might contribute to the enhancement of protection should their disclosures bring a change therein. Ethical ('white-hat') hacking, i.e. breaking into protected systems and networks to test and assess their security, although at the limits of moral acceptability, closes the spectrum of collective tools.

---

186 C. Bennett, *The Privacy Advocates. Resisting the Spread of Surveillance*, MIT Press, Cambridge MA 2008, pp. 134–137.

187 Cf. e.g. C. Cuijpers and B.-J. Koops, 'The "Smart Meters" Bill: A Privacy Test Based on Article 8 of the ECHR. Study Commissioned by the Dutch Consumers' Association', Tilburg 2008, <http://www.consumentenbond.nl/morello-bestanden/pdf-algemeen-2008/onderzoek_UvT_slimme_energi1.pdf>; C. Cuijpers and B.-J. Koops, 'Smart Metering and Privacy in Europe: Lessons from the Dutch Case' in S. Gutwirth, R. Leenes, P. De Hert and Y. Poullet (eds.), *European Data Protection: Coming of Age*, Springer, Dordrecht 2013, pp. 269–293; Kloza, van Dijk and De Hert, above n. 53.

188 S. Goel, Y. Hong, V. Papakonstantinou and D. Kloza, *Smart Grid Security*, Springer London 2015, pp. 46–57.

189 Cf. <https://censusfail.com>.

190 Cf. <http://www.eff.org/secure-messaging-scorecard>.

191 Cf. <http://edri.org>.

192 Cf. <https://www.digitalrights.ie>.

193 Cf. <http://panoptykon.org>.

194 Cf. <http://www.laquadrature.net>.

Table 1. An early typology of behavioural tools for privacy protection

<table>
<tr>
<td rowspan="3">- Individual
- Collective</td>
<td rowspan="3">- Inaction
- Action</td>
<td rowspan="2">Direct</td>
<td>- Non-engagement
• Non-participation
• Non-disclosure
• Selective disclosure</td>
<td rowspan="3">- Temporary
- Permanent
- Regular intervals</td>
<td rowspan="3">- Professional
- Private</td>
<td rowspan="3">- Inward
- Outward</td>
</tr>
<tr>
<td>- Secrecy, security and concealment
• Technological means
• *Forum shopping*
• *Trust seeking*
• End-user PETs
• Encryption
• Pseudonymisation
• Anonymisation
• Cryptography
• Steganography
• Organisational means
• Coverage (hiding)
• Obliteration</td>
</tr>
<tr>
<td>Indirect</td>
<td>- Protest
- Advocacy
- Awareness-raising
- Whistle-blowing
- (White hat) hacking</td>
</tr>
</table>

4.3. IMPLICATIONS

4.3.1. Characteristics

An attempt to offer an early typology of behavioural tools for privacy protection has brought me to offer some general observations about their inherent features. A careful reader would immediately note that these tools are predominantly addressed to a layperson on the street, seeking for a new means to safeguard her interests. This does not exclude other stakeholders, such as private organisations, from adopting some of behavioural protections. These behavioural tools are useful predominantly to protect privacy when personal data are being handled.[195]

[195] There are plenty of conceptualisations of types (or of the scope) of 'privacy'. From a chronological viewpoint, the modern understanding of privacy started with 'the right to be let alone' as defined by WARREN and BRANDEIS, above n. 17, pp. 193–220. The scholarship on privacy continues e.g. with Westin's four states of privacy: solitude, intimacy, anonymity and reserve (A.F. WESTIN, *Privacy and Freedom*, Atheneum, New York 1967), Posner's economic critique of privacy (R. POSNER, 'The Right of Privacy' (1978) 12(3) *Georgia Law Review* 393–422) and Regan's recognition of its societal value (P. REGAN, *Legislating Privacy: Technology, Social Values and Public Policy*, University of North Carolina Press, Chapel Hill 1995,

Again, their applicability to data privacy does not exclude their usefulness for the protection of types of privacy, e.g. the one of body or association. Behavioural tools have been coined in a response to privacy threats posed by globalisation and technological development and thus they are predominantly applicable to the digital world. They are most useful if applied *ex ante*, i.e. before information is disclose or, broader, any privacy threat materialises itself. They are thus predominantly of a preventive nature. Finally, behavioural protections are not limited by the territoriality of regulation. In other words, contrary to the regulatory tools, but alike to organisational and technological ones, behavioural tools know no geographical boundaries for their application.

4.3.2. Conditions

I can immediately think of at least four conditions for a successful application of behavioural tools for privacy protection. The first condition is to be *aware* of a privacy threat itself and of a possibility to make certain choices and undertake certain actions or inactions to avoid or minimise such threat.

An individual who resolves to behavioural tools must be 'genuinely alarmed'[196] and – to a large extent – need to be a 'proficient users' of new

pp. 212–243), among others. More recent attempts to conceptualise include Clarke (R. Clarke, 'Introduction to Dataveillance and Information Privacy and Definitions of Terms', 1997, <http://www.rogerclarke.com/DV/Intro.html>) who initially distinguished four types – privacy of the person, of personal data, of personal behaviour and of personal communication – and supplemented them in 2013 with privacy of personal experience. Later, Finn, Wright and Friedewald enlarged this catalogue by the privacy of thoughts and feelings, of location and space, of association (R.L. Finn, D. Wright and M. Friedewald, 'Seven Types of Privacy' in S. Gutwirth, R. Leenes, P. De Hert and Y. Poullet (eds.), *European Data Protection: Coming of Age*, Springer, Dordrecht 2013, pp. 3–32). In parallel, Rössler distinguished three types: decisional, informational and local privacy (B. Rossler, *The Value of Privacy*, Wiley, Cambridge 2005, pp. 86–142) and Solove observed four major types of handlings of personal data that might cause harm to individual: information collection, processing, dissemination as well as invasion (Solove, above n. 173, pp. 10–11). Most international human rights instruments, drafted in 1950s and 1960s, distinguish four broad aspects of the right to privacy: private life, family life, home and communications. The broad scope of privacy was confirmed by the European Court of Human Rights who ruled that it is 'not possible or necessary to attempt an exhaustive definition' of privacy (*Niemietz v. Germany*, 1992). Most recently, Koops et al. have 'structure[d] types of privacy in a two-dimensional mode, consisting of eight basic types of privacy (bodily, intellectual, spatial, decisional, communicational, associational, proprietary, and behavioural privacy), with an overlay of a ninth type (informational privacy) that overlaps, but does not coincide, with the eight basic types' (B.-J. Koops, B. Clayton Newell, T. Timan, I. Škorvranek, T. Chokrevski and M. Galič, 'A Typology of Privacy' (2016) 38 *University of Pennsylvania Journal of International Law* 1–76). I quote here these various conceptualisations merely to demonstrate both the wide scope of the notion of privacy as well as the complexity in its delimitation.

196 J. Franzen, 'Imperial Bedroom', *New Yorker*, 12.10.1998, pp. 48–53.

technologies.[197] In practice, a good deal of behavioural protections would be used by 'knowledgeable and obsessive enthusiasts' or – in other words – 'geeks'.[198]

The level of awareness in the society about privacy threats and measures available to counter them is, however, insufficient. On the one extreme, there are people who were born and risen in the digital era – i.e. 'digital natives'[199] – and for them the question how to navigate amongst emerging technologies is rather obsolete. On the other extreme, there are 'digitally divided' or 'digitally excluded' people. Because of their lack of digital literacy, vulnerabilities or language barriers, they are unable to fully enjoy digital technologies. Despite the problem of 'digital divide' being of predominantly temporal nature and despite breeze familiarity of digital technologies amongst 'digital natives', the problem is that still not everybody knows *enough* to identify and evaluate privacy threats and to act thereon. And even amongst those who know, their awareness is rather inaccurate and insufficient.[200]

The vast majority of Europeans see 'disclosing personal information as an increasing part of modern life', yet they are not sufficiently aware of the ways in which to protect their privacy.[201] Individuals are often 'uninformed and confused' and hence often 'misinterpreting their own behaviour'.[202] It is still a common practice that people click 'I agree' without giving even the slightest thought that they are consenting to a certain practice of data handling and that such a practice might run counter to their interests. Europeans lack further information on the available remedies in case something goes wrong.[203] They are often unaware of the existence of a national data protection authority (DPA) that could offer them assistance in such a situation.[204] All in all, the privacy universe forgets that – although people usually claim they care about 'privacy', and even if they really do so – in practice they often have their attention taken up by 'more immediate problems: jobs, shelter, health, education, food, water'.[205] Despite people increasingly bringing digital education from homes and schools,

---

197 Moshell, above n. 27, p. 367.

198 Oxford Dictionary of English.

199 M. Prensky, 'Digital Natives, Digital Immigrants' (2001) 9(5) *On the Horizon* 1.

200 J.B. Rule, *The Politics of Privacy: Planning for Personal Data Systems as Powerful Technologies*, Elsevier, New York 1980, p. 184.

201 European Commission, *Special Eurobarometer 359: Attitudes on Data Protection and Electronic Identity in the European Union*, Brussels 2011, p. 5.

202 G. González Fuster, 'How Uninformed Is the Average Data Subject? A Quest for Benchmarks in EU Personal Data Protection' (2014) 19 *IDP. Revista de Internet, Derecho y Política* 99.

203 FRA, 'Access to Data Protection Remedies in EU Member States', Publications Office of the European Union, Luxembourg 2011, pp. 32–34.

204 European Commission, above n. 201, p. 174.

205 J. Cannataci, intervention at the Computers, Privacy and Data Protection (CPDP) Conference, Brussels, 25.01.2017.

it is rather basic and thus still more is needed.[206] I have observed multiple efforts undertaken to raise awareness. For instance, European authorities organise on an annual basis a data protection day on 28 January and their Asian-Pacific counterparts engage annually in 'Privacy Awareness Week' in early May. I have further observed the question of privacy protection being dealt with in popular culture. Recent motion pictures, such as *Erasing David* (2010), Laura Poitras' documentary *Citizenfour* (2014) – and the 2015 Academy of Motion Picture Arts and Sciences' Oscar for the best documentary it won – as well as Oliver Stone's recent biopic *Snowden* (2016), have contributed significantly to the increase in public understanding of privacy problems. (I set aside any evaluation of their artistic value.)

The second condition for a successful application of behavioural tools is that of *proximity*. An individual would resort to behavioural tools when she perceives the threat as directly relevant for safeguarding her own interests or interests of a social group she belongs to. Such a perception is highly subjective, contextual and rarely consistent. This is so because the appropriate level of privacy protection is only something that can be decided at an individual level and according to the highly variable instincts about what is, and is not, intrusive or sensitive.[207] An anecdote to illustrate my point: when I moved to study in Copenhagen, the otherwise perfect apartment where I was supposed to live had no curtains to cover the windows. When I asked the landlady to provide them in the flat, she – immediately and without any hesitation – wondered if I had something to hide. Initially her reaction surprised me, but later on I thought that her own perception of privacy was legitimate. She might not have anything to hide. But I did not have anything to expose to the neighbours on the opposite side of the street. My viewpoint here was equally legitimate. Eventually, curtains appeared in the windows.

The third condition concerns the *gravity* of a threat. People would engage in behavioural tools when the threat – in their perception – is sufficiently significant. As with the criterion of proximity, human perception of gravity of a privacy threat highly depends both on the context and on their judgement. Translating this to the privacy universe, for example, a whistle-blower risking lifetime sentence for her disclosures – at the end of the day, she is never sure whether she would be recognised as a whistle-blower in a given jurisdiction and whether she would be asserted with the protection due – would be predominantly concerned about the safety and security of herself and her mission.[208] She would resort to

---

206 G. González Fuster, D. Kloza and P. De Hert, 'The Many Faces of Privacy Education in European Schools' in G. González Fuster and D. Kloza (eds.), *The European Handbook for Teaching Privacy and Data Protection at Schools*, Intersentia, Cambridge 2016, p. 15.

207 Bennett, above n. 186, pp. 210–214.

208 P. De Hert and D. Kloza, 'WikiLeaks, Privacy, Territoriality and Pluralism. What Does Matter and What Does Not?', Tilburg Institute for Law, Technology and Society Blog, 2011, <http://www.vub.ac.be/LSTS/pub/Dehert/Dehert_361.pdf>.

advanced encryption techniques to share otherwise classified information at her disposal. Outlets such as WikiLeaks or SecureDrop of the Freedom of the Press Foundation have created and described sophisticated channels for transmitting information.[209] Furthermore, that few people feel the same about risk every day of their lives makes it more complicated. As people grow older, wiser, richer or poorer – and as the society and technology progress – people's perception of what risk is and their aversion to taking risk will shift, sometimes in one direction, sometimes in the other.[210]

The final condition is that of *usability*. The easiness of use might play a decisive role in the choice of behavioural tools for privacy protection. The problem is well known with from the criticism of the end-user PETs.[211] If any new tools require sophisticated knowledge, experience and a good deal of effort and patience to apply in practice, their applicability would find application only amongst determined 'geeks'. In practice, a perfect choice of such technologies is, obviously, not possible, and thus people are left with a dilemma between more protection at the detriment of usability or less protection yet better usability.

4.3.3. Problems

Behavioural tools for privacy protection are not unproblematic. I fear that their use might bring negative social implications such as chilling effect, lower quality of service and even exclusion. Put simply, people might choose not to engage in certain services capable of intruding their privacy that are otherwise rather legitimate. The chilling effect on the freedom of speech – e.g. not expressing own views as these might be used against the speaker – is perhaps the most obvious example. I have known people in certain countries who prefer not to have political opinion as this might put their lives in danger. Translating this to the privacy universe, I have known people who would not access someone else's profile on a social networking site when this site registers and discloses who has viewed it to the latter person. But this is not an isolated example: I might like and I might find useful some level of artificial intelligence of an instant messenger from a major service provider. Yet their practices of handling personal data have instantly dampened my enthusiasm for this type of innovation. I did not subscribe. By remaining faithful to the means of communication chosen earlier, which have proven their reliability, the quality of my digital experience might be diminished. Furthermore, people resorting to behavioural tools for privacy protection might exclude themselves from some parts of social life. For example,

---

209 Cf. <https://wikileaks.org/#submit> and <https://securedrop.org>.

210 P.L. Bernstein, *Against the Gods: The Remarkable Story of Risk*, Wiley, New York 1998, p. 263.

211 Cf. above section 3.2.3.

I do not have any account on any 'private' social networking site. (Except for professionally oriented Twitter and LinkedIn accounts.) I do not feel that I need it or that – by excluding myself – I lose something. My choice was dictated by many reasons and the protection of my privacy is only one of them. However, in extreme cases, this choice of mine excludes me from social activities procured with the use of such a platform. If people use such sites for example to invite guests for a housewarming party, I might not receive an invitation, unless these people send me an e-mail or make a phone call. Other people might judge me anti-social. Overall, I feel such a price is worth paying.

I further fear that the usage of behavioural tools might be abused and that, as a consequence, certain stakeholders might 'strike back'. The state might consider these tools counterproductive to its efforts in e.g. maintain national security and thus it might attempt to restrict their use. (Encryption would be the most pertinent example here; I return to it below.) Equally businesses might find these protections running contrary to their interests. (Let me illustrate this point by recalling some websites, usually media outlets, which 'refuse' to work if an add-block software continues to run).

The problem of 'striking back' can been seen from the perspective of international human rights law. It sets forth certain limitations for the enjoyment of rights and for their restriction. First and foremost, there exist limits as to the exercise of own privacy. 'Privacy' is not a limitless concept and the law reflects that. The right to privacy could be interfered with on a condition such interference is legal, proportionate, necessary in a democratic society and serves a legitimate aim. Further, staying within the legal discourse, rights are not meant to be abused and the law reflects that too. On the other side, those who attempt to interfere with 'privacy' not only have to respect the above-mentioned limitation criteria but also must interpret these limitations narrowly. In other words, *in dubio pro libertate*. Thus each attempt to interfere with privacy and each new type of its protection cannot escape the compliance with these conditions.

I found the example of the usage of encryption and attempts to counter it illustrative as to the quest for equilibrium between two legitimate yet seemingly competing interests at stake – e.g. national security versus individual privacy. Technologies of cryptography are, by definition, capable of good and bad. Information may be encrypted to safeguard legitimate secrets or to help to blow the whistle. It also may be encrypted to ensure that the plotting of an illicit action is not undermined. Here is the crypto controversy: the accommodation of the conflicting interests of privacy and information security, on the one hand, with the interests of law enforcement and national security, on the other.[212] While some commentators call for 'a right to encrypt personal information

[212] Koops, above n. 169, p. 2.

effectively',[213] some jurisdictions consider limiting its use in the name of national security, e.g. France and Germany.[214] I share the conviction that to ban entirely the use of encryption or to significantly undermine its effectiveness – e.g. by introduction of 'back doors' or 'key escrows' – would be disproportionate. It might even render encryption meaningless. At the end of the day, nobody questions the need for national security, but the question is rather how?

I eventually fear that – as with cryptography – certain behavioural tools would meet the same fate: their use will be confronted with their abuse. There is no straightforward answer. Each development – be it a disclosure of a secret, a political dispute, a voice in a debate or a note to a case – helps to delineate borders between their legitimate use and abuse. This question of use versus abuse may be answered in two ways. Looking from the ethics point of view, different schools of ethics might provide diverse answers, arguing either for individual (i.e. privacy) or collective interests (i.e. national security) to prevail. Looking from the viewpoint of democracy, the rule of law (*Rechtsstaat*) and fundamental rights viewpoint, a more formal, i.e. procedural, answer might arrive. Nevertheless, such an answer will never escape a moral judgement.

5. CONCLUSION

This contribution has been an invitation to consider an alternative type of privacy protections – behavioural. I have observed that 'the way in which one acts or conducts oneself' sometimes has a dedicated goal of safeguarding one's own privacy.[215] It all started with a contestation with a friend of mine that 'you too cover your laptop camera with a sticker'. This observation opened a vivid discussion with family, friends and colleagues. I have concluded that certain individual choices, actions and inactions aimed at privacy protection – i.e. behavioural tools for privacy protection – do not necessarily fit into the three types of protections existing thus far, i.e. regulatory, organisational and technological. Therefore it was logical to coin a new type of protections, analyse its emergence, typology and implications.

I have then concluded that these new behavioural tools have emerged in response to the inadequacies of contemporarily available protections. I have observed that – even with my own laptop camera – I have covered it with a removable sticker because neither regulation efficiently prohibits abusive

---

213 M. Kirby, 'Privacy Protection, a New Beginning: OECD Principles 20 Years on' (1999) 6(3) *Privacy Law and Policy Reporter* 25–34.

214 B. Cazeneuve, *Initiative franco-allemande sur la sécurité intérieure en Europe*, Paris, 26.08.2016, <http://www.interieur.gouv.fr/Le-ministre/Interventions-du-ministre/Initiative-franco-allemande-sur-la-securite-interieure-en-Europe>.

215 Oxford Dictionary of English.

global mass surveillance practices nor there exists software, in which I can have confidence, to ensure that the laptop camera does not operate without my prior knowledge and consent. I have subsequently learned about a friend of mine, whom I nicknamed here Joseph, who had to cease to use one of his private e-mail addresses as a way of protecting himself against abusive surveillance practices, because neither existing organisational nor technological protections could have helped him.

These behavioural tools for privacy protection are by no means a silver bullet to the privacy problem. They do not aim to replace the three types of protections tools existing thus far. They rather aim at supplementing and completing them. The proposition that solely a single type of protective measures cannot achieve privacy protection remains valid. Behavioural tools are addressed to those individuals who are conscious of both their privacy and threats thereto, who perceive these threats as directly relevant for them (and the societal group they belong to) and who consider these threats as significantly dangerous for them (and to these groups). Yet these tools are often less easy to apply in practice. A careful reader would further conclude these protections know no jurisdictional boundaries, are predominantly applicable to informational aspect of privacy when challenged by digital technologies and produce best effects if applied *ex ante*. I have focused on individuals and their privacy, but I cannot exclude other stakeholders making choices, undertaking actions and inactions to protect privacy, their own or others, and – further – their other interests. But this is a subject matter for separate analysis.

This contribution has been an invitation to stakeholders – from the layman on the street and the computer 'geek' to those who regulate, handle information to those who oversee compliance, having diverse roles and responsibilities – to consider behavioural tools as a standalone and legitimate means of privacy protection. The way in which I have presented this novelty here is, obviously, not final. With the ever-changing nature of the society and technology, this new type of tools would require re-visiting and re-conceptualising, should the need arise.

24. THE FUTURE OF AUTOMATED PRIVACY ENFORCEMENT

Jake Goldenfein*

The contours of privacy law often evolve in response to excessive or inappropriate government surveillance. Since the 1765 proto-privacy decision of *Entick v. Carrington* addressing unwarranted searches of documents and private property by the English executive,[1] judges have continued to advance or produce new privacy protecting limitations on law enforcement. However, the manner in which privacy law might respond to the 2013 Edward Snowden revelations regarding the startling surveillance capabilities of various nation states is somewhat uncertain.[2] The goal of this chapter is therefore to evaluate certain proposals as to how privacy law might react to contemporary law enforcement surveillance techniques. In particular, this chapter explores ideas around *automated* privacy enforcement and the articulation of individual protections from profiling into the telecommunications infrastructure.[3]

While remaining broadly supportive of proposals involving automation and informatics, and believing strongly in the need to reconsider the media of legal transmission and relations in the contemporary technological environment, this chapter questions the achievability of automated privacy solutions to law enforcement surveillance both technically and politically. In particular, the possibility of creating systems that could be deployed at web-scale, and of developing automated approaches capable of achieving an acceptable balance between effectively constraining inappropriate surveillance and completely forbidding those law enforcement practices – a seemingly untenable political position – remain unclear. Rather than acquiescing to the overwhelming difficulty of the task however, the chapter outlines some paths of further inquiry that might assist in directing future research in the area.

* Swinburne Law School, Swinburne University of Technology. E-mail: jgoldenfein@swin.edu.au.

1 *Entick v. Carrington* (1765) 19 How. St. Tr. 1029.

2 Glenn Greenwald, *No Place to Hide*, Metropolitan Books 2014.

3 See for example Mireille Hildebrandt and Bert-Jaap Koops, 'The Challenges of Ambient Law and Legal Protection in the Profiling Era' (2010) 73(3) *The Modern Law Review* 428.

1. CHARACTERISING CONTEMPORARY LAW ENFORCEMENT SURVEILLANCE

Although there are multiple forms of high-technology surveillance used in law enforcement and security, this chapter focuses on automated *profiling* technologies. It is worth briefly explaining some basic features of those surveillance exercises in order to better understand suggestions as to how they might be constrained by law. While law enforcement (and indeed law itself) are taken to have always been information technologies, it is argued here that the technologies of law enforcement are becoming increasingly automated. Law enforcement surveillance, especially as performed in 'high' or political policing that focuses on calculating criminal propensity and pre-empting future conduct,[4] increasingly operates through the collection (or interception), retention and algorithmic processing of information stored across multiple databases. As these techniques and practices become more sophisticated and automated, greater reliance is placed on information processing such as data mining, predictive analytics and other artificial intelligence techniques, deployed at mass-scale, to detect patterns 'hidden in the data'[5] for the purpose of flagging or identifying individuals as suspicious. Over time therefore, traditional law enforcement surveillance techniques have been supplemented (or supplanted) by technologies that aggregate and concatenate large sets of 'transactional' data into probability relationships for the sake of generating inferences about criminal propensity. Although the efficacy of these systems at preventing criminal activity has been challenged, they are unquestionably highly sophisticated technical formations that produce significant consequences for individuals.

It should be noted that these complex surveillance practices operate not only in the highly clandestine environments of security and intelligence surveillance. 'Low-level' data mining by quotidian police forces also occurs under the rubric of 'predictive-policing',[6] and automated high-level surveillance techniques continually filter down into routine police operations. As Jenny Hocking

4 See for example Jean-Paul Brodeur, 'High Policing and Low Policing: Remarks About the Policing of Political Activities' (1983) *Social Problems* 507, 516; also see Jean-Paul Brodeur, 'High and Low Policing in Post-9/11 Times' (2007) 1(1) *Policing* 25 for an update of the argument.

5 Louise Amoore, 'Algorithmic War' (2009) 41(1) *Antipode* 49, 55–56.

6 See for example Walter Perry et al., 'Predictive Policing: The Role of Crime Forecasting in Law Enforcement Operations', Rand Corporation, 2013. More routine exercises analyse information already available to law enforcement, such as incident, health, prison administration, and intelligence files, as well as existing clinical instruments used by corrections agencies, in order to classify individuals according to risk. In other words, routine law enforcement predictive analytics still operate on categories of information within the purview of statistical probability.

described as early as 2004, there is a 'slow and steady shift in the security bureaucracy away from an "exceptional" – and hence marginalised structure, toward an incorporation of its key elements into the broader criminal justice process.'[7] It therefore seems sensible to anticipate growing deployment of technologies used to predict the identity of criminal perpetrators in regular police operations, and accordingly to canvas ideas for how they might be meaningfully regulated.

2. THE UTILITY OF EXISTING LEGAL MECHANISMS

There have been some legal challenges to these types of surveillance exercises under existing privacy regimes such as Art. 8 of the European Convention of Human Rights, the right to the protection of personal data in the EU Charter of Fundamental Rights, and the US Constitution's Fourth Amendment.[8] At this stage there is conflicting jurisprudence as to whether mass surveillance and profiling is a judicially acceptable activity – at least in the law enforcement context. In the case of *Szabó v. Hungary*,[9] for example, the European Court of Human Rights, while finding that the particular Hungarian surveillance exercise in question violated the right to private life in Art. 8, did not impose a requirement of 'reasonable suspicion' on government use of mass surveillance technologies, such as would prohibit 'mass' or suspicionless surveillance – although this case is now on appeal to the Grand Chamber. On the other hand, the DRIPA decision (i.e. concerning the UK's Data Retention and Investigatory Powers Act 2014) has suggested indiscriminate data retention, even by law enforcement and security agencies, may be impermissible.[10] Further, while automated processing and decision-making is subject to the European General Data Protection Regulation,[11] it is unclear what effect this will have on law enforcement and security surveillance because of applicable derogations and exceptions,[12] as well as questions over the degree to which those surveillance exercises operate

7 Jenny Hocking, *Terror Laws: Asio, Counter Terrorism and the Threat to Democracy*, UNSW Press 2004, p. 157.

8 Some cases are yet to be finalised or are on appeal, see for example *Human Rights Organisations v. United Kingdom* (submission on the facts available: <https://www.amnesty.org/en/documents/ior60/3222/2015/en/>), *Obama v. Klayman* (2015) No. 14-5004, and *ACLU v. Clapper* (2015) No. 13-3994.

9 *Szabó and Vissy v. Hungary* App. no. 37137/14 (ECtHR, 12 January 2016).

10 Cases C-203/15 and C-698/15, *Tele2 and Watson* (CJEU, 21 December 2016).

11 Regulation (EU) on the protection of natural persons with regard to the processing of personal data (2016/679), [2016] OJ L 119 (General Data Protection Regulation).

12 Mireille Hildebrandt, *Smart Technologies and the End(s) of Law*, Edward Elgar Publishing 2015, p. 197. See also for example General Data Protection Regulation Arts. 2(2), 9(2) and 23(1).

on 'personal' or 'private' information.[13] According to Paul de Hert and Vagelis Papakonstantinou,[14] the draft Police and Criminal Justice Data Protection Directive was similarly flawed.[15] There thus appears to be relative consensus that no existing legal regime adequately addresses automated profiling by law enforcement,[16] and that impending reforms are unlikely to significantly affect that position. Some have argued that, in the context of profiling, this is because the process by which data becomes knowledge needs to be subject to regulation and limitation, not simply the data itself.[17] For example, Mireille Hildebrandt claims that rather than rendering the data constituting an individual profile accessible, the legal goal should be transparency – to 'reveal the *logic* behind the production of a profile.'[18]

3. ARTICULATION INTO INFRASTRUCTURE

In several texts, Hildebrandt has elaborated how that approach might manifest as a functional constraint on profiling.[19] However, a key dimension of her proposal, and the element of most interest for this chapter, is that legal protection from profiling involve the articulation of that protection into the telecommunications

---

13 See for example Mireille Hildebrandt, 'Defining Profiling: A New Type of Knowledge?' in Mireille Hildebrandt and Serge Gutwirth (eds.), *Profiling the European Citizen: Cross-Disciplinary Perspectives*, Springer 2008, p. 17, and Ronald Leenes, 'Mind my step?' in Mireille Hildebrandt and Serge Gutwirth (eds.), *Profiling the European Citizen: Cross-Disciplinary Perspectives*, Springer 2008, p. 197.

14 Paul De Hert and Vagelis Papakonstantinou, 'The Police and Criminal Justice Data Protection Directive: Comment and Analysis' (2012) 22(6) *Computers and Law Magazine of SCL* 1, 3.

15 Proposal for a Directive of the European Parliament and of the Council on the Protection of Individuals with Regard to the Processing of Personal Data by Competent Authorities for the Purposes of Prevention, Investigation, Detection or Prosecution of Criminal Offences or the Execution of Criminal Penalties, and the Free Movement of Such Data, COM (2012) 10 (25 Janurary 2012), <http://eur-lex.europa.eu/LexUriServ/LexUriServ.do?uri=COM:2012:0010:FIN:EN:PDF> (11 PVLR 200, 1/30/12).

16 See for example Lee Bygrave, 'Minding the Machine: Article 15 of the EC Data Protection Directive and Automated Profiling' (2000) 7(4) *Privacy Law and Policy Reporter* 67; Clive Norris and Xavier L'Hoiry, 'What do they Know? Exercising Subject Access Rights in Democratic Societies' at 6th *Biannual Surveillance and Society Conference*, 24–26 April 2014; also see Mireille Hildebrandt, 'Legal Protection by Design: Objections and Refutations' (2011) 5(2) *Legisprudence* 223, 236 where she says in respect of Art. 12: 'Since it is technically impossible to provide such access in a way that is comprehensible for ordinary citizens, the normativity that is inherent in the computational infrastructure overrules the normativity of the written law.'

17 See for example Hildebrandt, above n. 13, Hildebrandt and Koops, above n. 3, and Leenes, above n. 13, 197.

18 Hildebrandt, above n. 13.

19 Ibid. and see for example Hildebrandt, above n. 3.

infrastructure itself.[20] Hildebrandt thus offers an idea of 'ambient law', which calls for the expression of legal rights into 'the digitally enhanced environment because human rights such as privacy, due process and non-discrimination lack effective remedies if they are only articulated as written law.'[21] This reflects the idea that law as a technology of the script 'has reached the limits of its protective powers',[22] and requires transformation at the level of its 'mode of existence' in order to retain its efficacy and sustain its identity when operating within contemporary (pre-emptive) communications environments and infrastructures.[23] Cornelia Vismann and Martin Krajewski have offered similar comment, arguing '[t]raditionally, the law has dominated the reality of word and image to a degree unequalled by any other performative system. Now, however, with the advent of the computer legal fictions must compete with digital virtuality.'[24] Together, those claims elucidate how, because modern law developed in the context of text and the printing press, it struggles to adequately 'couple'[25] with and regulate the present social milieu, which is interdependent on an evolved and automated technical ecology. Arguably, the same can be said of the application of law to the constraint of law enforcement surveillance, a socio-technical system that has become increasingly automated, and operates (partially) in a divergent media format from law and legal process. The idea of articulating appropriate protection into the telecommunications infrastructure therefore becomes an interesting possibility for alternative modalities of constraining law enforcement surveillance.

4. AUTOMATED PRIVACY ENFORCEMENT

There are some examples from computer science research that might offer insight into how legal protection from law enforcement profiling could be articulated into a telecommunications infrastructure. These are instances of privacy policy and access control languages that could potentially be used

---

20 Another element of Hildebrandt's suggestion involves a 'critical transparency right' to facilitate 'smart opacity' (Hildebrandt and Koops, above n. 3, p. 450). That is, 'technological devices that can translate, for the citizen, what profiling machines are doing' (Serge Gutwirth and Mireille Hildebrandt, 'Some Caveats on Profiling' in Serge Gutwirth et al. (eds.), *Data Protection in a Profiled World*, Springer 2010, pp. 31, 39), that are designed in such a way to be 'visible and contestable' (Hildebrandt and Koops, above n. 3, p. 456). But this was not necessarily conceptualised to be applicable to law enforcement profiling.

21 Hildebrandt, above n. 12, p. 224.

22 Hildebrandt and Koops, above n. 3, p. 450.

23 Hildebrandt, above n. 12, pp. 159, 224.

24 Cornelia Vismann and Markus Krajewski, 'Computer Juridisms' (2007) 29 *Grey Room* 90, 92.

25 Gunter Teubner, 'Regulatory Law: Chronicle of a Death Foretold' (1992) 1 *Social & Legal Studies* 451, 470 describing the process by which law regulates social systems.

to constrain automated profiling by prohibiting certain types of decision-making (such as the application of a profile to a particular individual) by a law enforcement agency under certain conditions. In other words, these approaches could potentially inform code-based constraints on algorithmic surveillance at the point of data processing. In an ideal case, these should not be technologies that merely inform data controllers about legal limitations, nor forms of 'techno-regulation' (using technical artefacts to implement legal rules),[26] but rather an 'automation' of the technologies of law to address the automated technologies of law enforcement. That said, defining the 'legality' or 'lawful' character of legal technology, i.e. articulating the difference between 'techno-regulation' and technical enunciations of law, is a question beyond the scope of this chapter.[27] Accordingly, the focus here is on other measures of feasibility such as technical and political possibility.

One example of an access control/privacy language comes from a collaboration between the Ontario Information and Privacy Commissioner and IBM, which modelled the Canadian Freedom of Information and Protection of Privacy Act[28] into a machine-readable programming language called EPAL – Enterprise Privacy Authorisation Language.[29] This is effectively an 'authorisation scheme'[30] defining permissible digital action with categories for: data users, actions, data categories, purposes, conditions and obligations. Vocabularies for these categories are created, which are subsequently 'ordered into hierarchies to express what requested data accesses are allowed or denied, and under what conditions'.[31] These include what resources are being requested, what operations are being performed on the resource and the purpose of the request.[32]

Another programming language based on similar ideas is XACML (which has been described as a specialised variant of XML),[33] that includes some potentially useful extra functionality, and has since become a standard in the

---

26 See for example Roger Brownsword, 'Code, Control and Choice: why East is East and West is West' (2005) 25(1) *Legal Studies* 1, 2.

27 See for example Serge Gutwirth discussing Kyle McGee's work on Latour in Serge Gutwirth, 'Providing the Missing Link: Law after Latour's Passage' in Kyle McGee (ed.), *Latour and the Passage of Law*, Edinburgh University Press 2015, pp. 122, 141.

28 Freedom of Information and Protection of Privacy Act RSO 1990 (C.F. 31).

29 For technical details see Paul Ashley, Satoshi Hada et al., 'Enterprise Privacy Authorisation Language (EPAL 1.2), (10.11.2003), <https://www.w3.org/Submission/2003/SUBM-EPAL-20031110/>.

30 Paul Ashley, Satoshi Hada et al., 'The Enterprise Privacy Authorisation Language (EPAL) – How to Enforce Privacy throughout an Enterprise', <http://www.w3.org/2003/p3p-ws/pp/ibm3.html>.

31 Ibid.

32 Anne Anderson, 'A Comparison of Two Privacy Policy Languages', Sun Microsystems, 2005, p. 3, <http://dl.acm.org/citation.cfm?id=1698182>.

33 Russel Kay, 'How to – XAMCL', *Computerworld*, 19.05.2003, <http://www.computerworld.com/article/2570927/app-development/xacml.html>.

field.[34] This includes descriptions for additional categories like *environment*, and a more complex mechanics around *purpose* including descriptions of both purpose of collection and purpose of request. According to its creators, these features give XACML the capacity for more specificity and complexity than EPAL.[35] A potentially more significant difference however, is the way XACML handles vocabularies. XACML can support attributes that are instances of XML,[36] meaning the vocabulary attributes (like purpose and user category) can be defined outside XACML itself, potentially facilitating interoperation with external XML information and data sets.

Another language has even been proposed that can supposedly transcribe privacy rules according to Helen Nissenbaum's concept of 'contextual integrity'.[37] This includes vocabularies for *roles*, *contexts*, *types of information* (category/nature/class), *appropriateness*, who the *subject* of the information is, as well as *positive* and *negative* norms, and *temporal* logic that can enable policies to permit information flows in virtue of past actions – that is, operate on sequences of communications.[38]

All of these (existing and proposed) approaches encounter conceptual problems when directed to the constraint of automated profiling. The first issue relates to these languages, in some instances, attempting to formalise already existing privacy legislation. It has been argued that, in certain situations, replicating or translating existing legislative regimes into formal representations is neither possible nor desirable. As Bert-Jaap Koops and Ronald Leenes note, hard-coding data protection law, for instance, would involve more than simply transforming and representing rules.[39] It requires negotiating the complex bureaucracy of the European data protection system, as well as formalising ideas that are intended to function with a degree of informality. That is, while 'purpose' specification for instance, plays a significant role in measuring the permissibility of information transfers under data protection law, this is in reality a highly discretionary concept, requiring a discretionary interpretation of action in the spatio-temporal world. Although the languages described above include vocabularies for purpose (and XAMCL can even compare purpose of collection and purpose of request), because all possible attributes for the 'purpose'

34 'A Brief Introduction to XACML', 14.03.2003, <https://www.oasis-open.org/committees/download.php/2713/Brief_Introduction_to_XACML.html>.

35 Anderson, above n. 32; note XACML was initially developed by Sun Microsystems who published her paper.

36 Ibid., p. 21.

37 Adam Bath et al., 'Privacy and Contextual Integrity: Framework and Applications', *2006 IEEE Symposium on Security and Privacy*, 21–24.05.2006, <http://web.cs.iastate.edu/~hridesh/teaching/610/06/02/papers/barth.pdf>.

38 Ibid.

39 Bert-Jaap Koops and Ronald Leenes 'Privacy Regulation Cannot be Hardcoded. A critical comment on the "Privacy by Design" provision in data-protection law' (2014) 28(2) *International Review of Law, Computers & Technology* 159, 161.

vocabulary need to be specifically defined, they are a long way from covering the field of possibly relevant 'purposes', and are, for example, incapable of making the crucial assessment of relationship between primary and secondary purposes. Further, the contextual integrity approach, for example, not only relies on formal definitions of highly discretionary (and open textured) concepts but seeks to represent very high levels of social nuance – something human agents often fail to achieve. The difficulty stems from all of these languages requiring that vocabularies be defined in each domain of operation. That is, for each of these languages, the vocabulary terms must be specified such that the language can parse whether the values of each *attribute* (vocabulary term) in an authorisation decision satisfy the conditions for access specified in the policy without processing the semantic meaning of the attributes.[40] While semantic meaning is generated in each specific domain of operation, those semantics are not domain-independent, meaning that each time a vocabulary is applied to new data sources, the syntax needs to be redefined. There are therefore difficulties in scaling such an approach from an intra-organisational level like a particular bureaucracy or business enterprise as contemplated by EPAL, to defining vocabularies for data dispersed throughout the web, and created in large variety of circumstances. Law enforcement profiling occurs on that vast scale, operating on data produced, recorded, stored and processed in multiple contexts. XAMCL improves this to a certain extent through interoperability with external XML elements, but still requires defined attributes for any elements processed through the system.

There has, however, been research into the use of 'semantic web' technologies in a privacy protecting system that could potentially apply at web-scale and in the context of law enforcement and security profiling. For instance, the Transparent Accountable Data Mining Initiative (TAMI) developed at MIT[41] has been working on programs to measure the permissibility (legality) of data mining activities in law enforcement and security for some time. Using parallel but transparent data mining techniques, TAMI operators estimate outcomes to evaluate the legality of data mining exercises. The tools used by the TAMI group attempt to identify the origins of actions, any factually incorrect antecedents, any impermissible sharing of data, and any inferences used for impermissible purposes. They do this by duplicating information processing through the 'inferencing engine', 'truth maintenance system', and 'proof generator' of the counter-profiling system to produce an audit trail. As noted, the technical distinction of TAMI's approach is the use of 'Semantic Web' reasoning for the purpose of 'tagging and classifying data at Web scale',[42] which could potentially address the issues identified above.

---

40 Anderson, above n. 32, p. 4.

41 D.J. Weitzner, H. Abelson, T. Berners-Lee et al., 'Transparent Accountable Data Mining: New Strategies for Privacy Protection' (2006) *MIT CSAIL Technical Report* 1.

42 Ibid., p. 2.

Unlike the EPAL/XAMCL approach, the TAMI approach does not involve real-time access control, but rather could be used to facilitate an *ex post* prohibition on automated surveillance on the basis of parallel, accountable 'counter-profiling'. Although this introduces questions of compliance – it might still be useful especially if such a system were used prior to the 'identification' of a profile flagged as suspicious if reaching that decision breaches certain 'legal' (technical) conditions. However, it is yet to be determined the degree to which such 'semantic' technologies are truly effective in this context, and it is worth taking into account Luciano Floridi's argument that 'sematic-web' is probably better described as 'machine-readable web'[43] technology, as it is not capable of parsing semantic 'meaning', but rather is based on 'data description languages'.[44] Irrespective of description, at this stage, these technologies are yet to live up to their promise. Nevertheless, if some of the technical difficulties were overcome, for instance if semantic web technology significantly advanced, or a more narrowly focused approach was developed that, as far as possible, excluded any discretionary or semantic concepts (i.e. avoided the necessity of defining attributes for 'purpose'), but still carried legal authority and legitimacy (such as a piece of legislation produced in 'propositional' logic, directed precisely at data mining by law enforcement agencies, in which the normative dimensions of legal instruments are expressed in calculable form), there are other fundamental difficulties that must still be overcome. These go beyond the classic criticisms of legal expert systems, for instance, that there are 'extra-logical factors' at play in law due to law's being 'embedded in social and political context',[45] that law's entanglement with language becomes, from a computer programming perspective, too great a problem of 'open texture'[46] and 'semantic indeterminacy',[47] or that self-executing rule enforcement elides the possibility of resistance,[48] informality and flexibility,[49] and diminishes the separation of powers.[50] Along

43 Luciano Floridi, *The Fourth Revolution: How the Infosphere is Reshaping Human Reality*, Oxford University Press 2014, p. 160.

44 Ibid., p. 161.

45 Andrew Grienke, 'Legal Expert Systems: a Humanistic Critique of Mechanical Legal Influence' (1994) 1(4) *Murdoch University Electronic Journal of Law* 35, 40.

46 Marek Sergot, 'The Representation of Law in Knowledge Based Systems' in Trevor Bench-Capon (ed.), *Knowledge Based Systems and Legal Applications*, Academic Press Ltd 1991, pp. 3, 25.

47 Grienke, above n. 45, p. 44.

48 Ryan Calo, 'Code, Nudge, or Notice?' (2014) 99 *Iowa Law Review* 773, 781; see also Mireille Hildebrandt, 'Prefatory Remarks on Part 1: Law and Code' in Mireille Hildebrant and Jeanne Gaakeer (eds.), *Human Law Computer Law: Comparative Perspectives*, Springer 2013, pp. 13, 15.

49 Vaios Karavas and Gunther Teubner, 'www.companynamesucks.com: The Horizontal Effect of Constitutional Rights Against "Private Parties" within Autonomous Internet Law' (2005) 12(2) *Constellations* 262, 274.

50 Calo, above n. 48, p. 781.

with problems of technical possibility, there are pressing questions as to whether these approaches might be legally, institutionally or politically achievable. For example, developing an approach that avoids discretionary concepts like 'purpose' or reasonableness requires a radical rethinking of the criteria on which privacy decisions are based.

Identifying those criteria requires understanding the elements of automated surveillance and profiling deemed sufficiently objectionable to warrant legal intervention. As it appears unlikely that these technologies will be excluded entirely from the law enforcement toolkit, one sensible approach might be to forbid profiling based on poor automated interpretations of data (not false positives, but the risk of false positives on the basis of how an algorithm processes data). It is unclear as to how that might be achieved however. One potentially useful analysis of automated data processing comes from Justin Clemens and Adam Nash, who describe the ontological character of digital data as being defined by the endless decontextualising and recontextualising of data through protocol-based negotiations and manipulations between storage state and display state that 'severs any link to the data's semantic source'.[51] Arguably then, an automated privacy approach should enforce fidelity of the interpretations generated by automated decision-making systems to the phenomena the data is supposed to represent.

Could it be possible to write technical iterations of law that restrict the decontextualisation and recontextualisation of data using 'context' vocabularies in a manner capable of addressing the way in which raw data is linked and interpreted such as to narrow the spectrum of 'possibilities' the profiling software is permitted to compute? An approach based on context specification could possibly show sensitivity to the meaning-making modulations that occur as data moves from original transaction to storage to display in law enforcement surveillance software, however it is not clear whether the notion of 'context' could be sufficiently emptied of semantic value, more than, for example, 'purpose'? However, even if it were technically achievable, would such an approach not be tantamount to entirely forbidding the function of automated and algorithmic surveillance technologies, which operate precisely by reading meaning into otherwise semantically barren data through concatenation with other data points? In other words, on what basis could you create syntactic vocabularies capable of dealing with data created through navigations of the digital realm writ large that are useful for limiting law enforcement profiling, without being so effective as to forbid the process wholesale? The political reality of the contemporary 'security' state is unlikely to capitulate to so pronounced a reduction in capabilities. This difficulty of identifying a criterion that can

---

[51] Justin Clemens and Adam Nash, 'Being and Media: Digital Ontology after the event of the end of media' (2015) 24 *The Fibreculture Journal* 6.

facilitate balance may explain why there are as yet so few workable suggestions for system architectures capable of realistically automating enforcement of privacy against law enforcement surveillance.

Being unable to perceive a feasible solution at this stage does not, however, indicate total futility. Indeed, the law enforcement surveillance practices that are presently regulated by Art. 8 of the European Convention or data protection, for instance, continued for many years prior to the formulation of any legal constraint. Further, the necessity of both: a limitation on contemporary law enforcement surveillance, and a reconsideration of law's mediality in the contemporary technological environment, remain highly compelling. We need to acknowledge that the computer is no longer 'a matter of law, which poses certain problems for the legal order',[52] but rather that the computer, the network, code, and programming logic are increasingly becoming the modes and media of legal transmission, and the materiality of 'law's media dependency'.[53] Although Hildebrandt's and other approaches for 'legal protection by design' represent a possible change, not only in the form of law, but possibly also the 'nature' of law, it may be necessary to acknowledge the possibility of plurality in legal nature, or plural legal natures, in order to maintain law's efficacy. Accordingly, rather than rule out automated legal technologies, the more productive approach may be to identify some preliminary questions that must be answered in order to assist in the future development of appropriate technical and socio-technical systems that could have utility for defining technical legal normativity.

5. QUESTIONS FOR FURTHER RESEARCH

The analysis above raises several fundamental questions around the possibility of implementing automated legal (and specifically) privacy technologies. This chapter has already looked briefly at the questions of technical feasibility as well as what criteria an automated system might employ to limit automated profiling. However, there are other pressing questions, including: investigation into the point at which an automated legal constraint might or should apply; whether it is preferable to constrain profiling systems at the point of decision-making or rather only to prevent the identification of 'flagged' profiles; how automated approaches might be practically developed, implemented and enforced; as well as the potentially problematic politics of automated legal applications.

Whether we should be focusing efforts to constrain surveillance at the stage of data collection, data processing, or after a profiling decision is made

---

52 Vismann and Krajewski, above n. 24, p. 92.

53 Vaios Karavas, 'The Force of Code: Laws Transformation Under Technological Conditions' (2009) 10 *German Law Journal* 463, 474.

requires further investigation. One rationale for not limiting the data available for processing at first instance is that, potentially, the more data stored and processed the better the 'quality' of the profiling decision. Another is that, depending on the data itself and how it is stored and tracked, a large quantity of the data processed in automated profiling systems may not be 'identifiable'. That raises the question of whether there should be specific rules about the circumstances in which 'flagged' profiles might be subsequently identified by law enforcement agencies. This is a separate question to the degree that data linkage is contemplated in the definition of 'personal information'.[54]

Determining a preferable approach might require considering another preliminary question of whether it might be appropriate to apply a legal intervention only when 'consequences' for individuals are generated. For instance, if an automated profiling exercise results in an individual receiving a particular designation with respect to criminal propensity, but nothing further occurs in the spatio-temporal realm, should that be sufficient to provoke the application of a legal constraint? Are consequences for individuals only possible if a profile is identified? This raises the question of whether there is a meaningful distinction between 'informing' and 'acting' that should be used to interpret how these systems interact with the world and how we perceive their potential impact? Is it problematic to characterise the selection of a suspicious subject as an 'action' itself? Following Ryan Calo, I would argue that if we characterise 'acting' not by a physical mechanism but by effect, by the possibilities and experiences generated and elided,[55] selecting an individual as suspicious *is* a 'decision' and a way of acting on the world. However, there are some who would argue that such a decision only has material effect through 'integrating that finding into a criminal investigation process'.[56] But how do we characterise the integration of predictive analytics into an investigation? Does there need to be a subsequent 'intervention'? This then raises further questions around whether purely automated action has the same impact on individuals as action mediated by human intelligence and agency – a question that requires very serious consideration at a general level.

Another question concerns how these kinds of legal technologies might be delivered, implemented and enforced. Could appropriate software be created by (or on behalf of) parliament, and the code effectively implemented as a piece of legislation? Should a law require the use of that code, or should the code itself be a 'legal' artefact? Should profilers be required under law to use these approaches or permitted to implement independently created algorithms coupled with

54 Case C-582/14, *Breyer v. Bundesrepublik Deutschland* (CJEU, 19 October 2016).
55 Ryan Calo, 'Robotics and the Lessons of Cyberlaw' (2015) 103 *California Law Review* 513, 531.
56 Perry, above n. 6, 108.

sufficient, accountable technical auditing? Not 'code as law' but 'law as code'. Julie Cohen has discussed the use of algorithmically-mediated compliance mechanisms in regulatory markets,[57] but there has been no discussion of such approaches being produced or mandated by legislatures. Other issues concern how accountability could be ensured considering the intellectual and technical expertise required to access and understand the operation of those systems?[58] Do we need to train 'legal coders' and teach 'legal algebra'?[59] Should algorithms that are too complex or opaque to be audited for accountability be prohibited?

A final consideration is the political rationality that might be instantiated, not by automated surveillance technologies, but by the automated legal constraints of those technologies. Could implementation of automated legal rules (even if in order to constrain other rights diminishing activities) be indulging in a potentially totalitarian exercise? Any effort to control outcomes by eliminating contingency carries an 'insanity proper to logic'.[60] Surely self-executing, self-legitimating legal rules risk raising the same spectre of totalitarian control – arguably with very direct consequences for individual liberty and autonomy? It is likely that we need to start thinking more closely about how the differences between natural and synthetic agents (i.e. humans and machines), and the actions they take, may implicate political rationality, and pay close attention to the relationship between specific *technologies* of law and political outcomes.

6. CONCLUSION

Hopefully this contribution will provoke further research in this area. The intention has not been to argue against the possibility of automated privacy enforcement or high-level legal informatics, but rather to enquire into why these approaches have not materialised into functional examples. It may be that the production of entirely machine-readable constraints is not possible (without substantial technological advances). It may be that achieving a balance between the protection of individual rights and efficacy of a surveillance system is neither possible nor politically tenable. That is, it might not be possible to

---

57 Julie Cohen, 'The Regulatory State in the Information Age' (2016) 17(2) *Theoretical Inquiries into Law* 1, 27–28.

58 See for example Mark Andrejevic, 'Surveillance in the Big Data Era' in Kenneth Pimple (ed.), *Emerging Pervasive Information and Communication Technologies (PICT): Ethical Challneges, Opporutnities and Safeguards*, Springer 2014, p. 68.

59 As suggested by Lucien Mehl, 'Automation in the Legal World: From the machine processing of legal information to the law machine' in *Mechanisation of Thought Processes* (1959) Vol. 2, pp. 755, 767.

60 Jacques-Alain Miller, 'Jeremy Bentham's Panoptic Device' (1987) 41 *October* 3, 7.

eliminate only the objectionable elements of automated profiling – at least not with existing technological approaches. There are numerous questions across various registers that need answering. Some are specific to questions of automated privacy enforcement, some pertain more generally to law and automation, and some implicate broader ontological and political questions. Hopefully, faced with recognition of the true scale and potential of law enforcement surveillance (as well as other applications of automated decision-making), our understanding of the relationship between law and automation will rapidly improve.

25. MOVING BEYOND THE SPECIAL RAPPORTEUR ON PRIVACY WITH THE ESTABLISHMENT OF A NEW, SPECIALISED UNITED NATIONS AGENCY*

Addressing the Deficit in Global Cooperation for the Protection of Data Privacy

Paul De Hert** and Vagelis Papakonstantinou***

1. INTRODUCTION

While the protection of privacy is a global concern,[1] the new technologies or methods of processing of personal data – such as big data, the Internet of Things, cloud computing, or smartphone applications – might easily drive to despair any legislator attempting to apply local jurisdictional approaches to personal data processing. This is because this type of processing is by design addressed directly to individuals anywhere in the world, treating national borders as irrelevant.

Quite contrary to what is urgently needed, an entrenchment attitude may be identified even in regional and global data privacy models devised today at the level of the European Union (EU), the Council of Europe (CoE) and the Organisation for Economic Co-operation and Development (OECD). At state

* An earlier version of this contribution appeared as: Paul De Hert and Vagelis Papakonstantinou, 'Why the UN should be the world's lead privacy agency?', *IAPP Privacy Perspectives*, 28 April 2016, <https://iapp.org/news/a/why-the-un-should-be-the-worlds-lead-privacy-agency>.

** Research Group on Law, Science, Technology and Society (LSTS), Vrije Universiteit Brussel; Tilburg Institute for Law, Technology, and Society (TILT), Tilburg University. E-mail: paul.de.hert@uvt.nl.

*** Research Group on Law, Science, Technology and Society (LSTS), Vrije Universiteit Brussel. E-mail: vpapakonstantinou@mplegal.gr.

1 See, for example, 'Privacy will hit tipping point in 2016', *CNBC*, 9 November 2015, <http://www.cnbc.com/2015/11/09/privacy-will-hit-tipping-point-in-2016.html>.

level, an increased interest in data privacy has been identified, with more than 100 countries having by now enacted some sort of data protection law within their respective jurisdictions.[2] However, this does not necessarily mean that they all approve of and subscribe to, for example, the EU model or any other of the above available global models. Regulatory approaches are diverging, failing to reach out to each other. Even compatibility among them is hard to achieve, as the recent Privacy Shield saga[3] demonstrates. While the right to data privacy is globally acknowledged as an important safeguard for individuals in the digital era, the way to protect it is understood differently in different parts of the world. To avoid legal fragmentation, it appears that global cooperation and coordination is imperative. However, the ways to achieve it vary considerably, and seemingly insurmountable obstacles lie ahead.

While the question whether an international treaty or convention, which would constitute the obvious policy option, is a viable solution has already been addressed in theory, mostly towards the negative,[4] some hope may come from the United Nations (UN). In July 2015, the UN Human Rights Council appointed Professor Joseph Cannataci as its first-ever Special Rapporteur on the right to privacy. His mandate is, among others, to gather information, identify obstacles, take part in global initiatives and raise awareness.

In order to address this global deficit in cooperation, the authors believe that a new, specialised UN agency for the protection of data privacy needs to be established.[5] We believe that the World Intellectual Property Organization (WIPO) could serve as useful inspiration to this end. The role of the global regulatory text of reference for data privacy, corresponding to the Paris and Berne Conventions within the global system for intellectual property protection, could be held by the UN Guidelines for the Regulation of Computerized Personal Data Files.[6] Despite their age, we believe that, if modernised, they could achieve global consensus and attain the basic data privacy purposes, constituting the global lowest common denominator.

---

2 See Greenleaf, G., 'Global Data Privacy Laws 2015: 109 Countries, with European Laws Now a Minority' (2015) 133 *Privacy Laws & Business International Report*, February 2015; UNSW Law Research Paper No. 2015-21, <http://ssrn.com/abstract=2603529>.

3 See, indicatively, Bracy, J., 'EU Member States approve Privacy Shield', *IAPP Tracker*, 8 July 2016, <https://iapp.org/news/a/eu-member-states-approve-privacy-shield/>.

4 Kuner, C., 'An International Legal Framework For Data Protection: Issues and Prospects' (2009) 25 *Computer Law & Security Review*.

5 De Hert, P. and Papakonstantinou, V., 'Three Scenarios for International Governance of Data Privacy: Towards an International Data Privacy Organization, Preferably a UN Agency?' (2013) 9(3) *I/S A Journal of Law and Policy for the Information Society*.

6 As adopted by General Assembly resolution 45/95 of 14 December 1990 (the 'UN 1990 Guidelines').

In the following section of this chapter, section 2, we briefly outline the deficit in global cooperation to the detriment of the level of data protection afforded to individuals. Then the UN initiatives for the global protection of data privacy are discussed (section 3). We then suggest that a new, specialised UN agency for data privacy be established, and we identify its potential benefits (section 4). Finally, we compare such an initiative with the WIPO and global intellectual property protection model that, to our mind, could serve as a useful role model for the development of a similar, global UN system for the protection of data privacy (section 5).

2. THE DEFICIT IN GLOBAL COOPERATION FOR THE PROTECTION OF DATA PRIVACY

It has become by now a self-evident truth that new personal data processing models transcend national borders and pay no respect to national jurisdictions. Because they are ultimately connected with the Internet, which enables the provision of services or the sale of products from anyone to anyone, anywhere in the world, new business models and technologies to serve them are designed exactly around this requirement: to be able to serve a global clientele directly, without local representatives, from a single location somewhere on the globe. It is in this light that recent technologies such as cloud computing, smartphone applications or geolocation services need to be viewed. It is by design that they disregard local legal regimes and constraints. This trend is not expected to change in the future. If one wished to add another trend to the picture, it would be that of ubiquitous processing: the continuous processing of information performed in the background, without individuals necessarily being aware of it. The Internet of Things broadly falls within the same category. If correlated with the internationalisation trend above, we would end up with ever-increasing volumes of personal data being transmitted directly by individuals, to be collected and processed anywhere in the world.

At the same time, the equally demanding security-related personal data processing requirements ought not be overlooked. International crime, as well as international terrorism, have made the global cooperation of national law enforcement authorities necessary, which is ultimately connected to the requirement that personal data be exchanged seamlessly among them.

In view of the above, international coordination of legal regimes is urgently needed in order to provide individuals anywhere in the world with adequate protection of their rights. From their point of view, individuals engage in mainstream activities from the comfort of their homes or offices: they navigate the Internet, make purchases and use global services. The background of the global personal data processing involved in these simple and straightforward activities largely escapes them. In other words, they are unaware (or at least do not fully grasp the implications) of their personal data being transmitted and processed anywhere (and by anyone) in the world. Being accustomed in their everyday (offline) lives to traditional legal systems and regimes, which provide for protection locally, they expect a similar level of protection while online. Consequently, the legal system needs to provide them with adequate means to do so. For the time being this has not been the case. The legal tools placed at the disposal of individuals in order to protect their right to data privacy until today have grossly failed to provide any meaningful protection against cross-border incidents.

This deficit is attributable to the legal regimes for the protection of data privacy that are in effect across the globe today. Rather than converging in order to address the internationalisation of personal data processing described above, differences in data privacy legal approaches across the globe have become increasingly entrenched over the past few years. In the EU, the model initially introduced by Directive 95/46[7] is furthered by its successor, the General Data Protection Regulation (GDPR)[8] that will come into effect in May 2018. Notwithstanding the strict and formal requirements it places upon EU Member States when it comes to personal data processing (application of processing principles, requirement for a legal basis for the processing, monitoring by a data protection authority), its approach towards international personal data transfers is straightforward: third countries, in order to be able to exchange personal data with EU Member States, need to adhere to the EU model through one of its provided alternatives.[9] Although these alternatives may come in different formats, their underlying idea is that third countries will need to accept and apply an equivalent to the EU approach on personal data processing. Such an approach may sound rigid or outright incompatible to the legal frameworks of several countries around the globe, which could explain the fact that over the past 20 years, only a handful of countries have been awarded with *adequacy* status by the European Commission.

A level of flexibility is allowed for in the Convention of the Council of Europe, which also is undergoing a modernisation process aimed at amending its text, which dates back to 1981.[10] Its Member States, which include all of the EU

---

7 Directive 95/46/EC of the European Parliament and of the Council of 24 October 1995 on the protection of individuals with regard to the processing of personal data and on the free movement of such data.

8 Regulation (EU) 2016/679 of the European Parliament and of the Council of 27 April 2016 on the protection of natural persons with regard to the processing of personal data and on the free movement of such data, and repealing Directive 95/46/EC (General Data Protection Regulation).

9 See Chapter V the General Data Protection Regulation.

10 See Council of Europe, Modernisation of Convention No. 108, <http://www.coe.int/t/dghl/standardsetting/dataprotection/modernisation_en.asp>.

Member States but also several other countries as well, are required to implement an admittedly more relaxed model than that of the EU, due to the lack of many processing formalities present in the EU regulatory framework. A further difference involves the fact that the Council of Europe data privacy model never hid its ambition to become the global data privacy standard[11] – which indeed may constitute a possible, and perhaps even welcome, development, as will be discussed in the analysis that follows. In this context, it should be noted that the CoE Convention allows for ratification of its text by non-Members as well. While until recently, third countries used this option as a preparation exercise to seek an *adequacy* finding by the EU, the modernisation process has revealed a new dynamic for the Council of Europe efforts, with numerous countries being found at various ratification stages.

Other instruments in the field, such as the OECD Guidelines[12] or the Asia-Pacific Economic Cooperation (APEC) Privacy Framework, are not binding. However, they too contribute to the picture of global fragmentation because they do not aim at compatibility, or even interoperability, with the above two (binding) regulatory instruments. This lack of a firm regulatory approach has permitted the development and proliferation of a multitude of 'soft law' approaches, which may take the form of anything between regional case-specific rules and regulations (for example, the Berlin Group),[13] international standards (for example, the International Standards Organisation),[14] international *fora* (for example, the International Conference of Data Protection and Privacy Commissioners), or global cooperation initiatives (for example, the Madrid Resolution).[15] All of the above, while welcome in promoting the global data privacy idea, unavoidably take place in, and aim to fill gaps in, the global regulatory void. The lack of a firm, globally acknowledged legal framework on data privacy makes all such initiatives appear disconnected from the real legal world, in the sense of granting rights and extracting obligations.

What we are therefore faced with is a diverging, rather than converging, approach on international data privacy. On the one hand, technologies and individuals act globally, disregarding any local notion such as legal jurisdiction,

11 See Greenleaf, G., '"Modernising" Data Protection Convention 108: A Safe Basis for a Global Privacy Treaty?' (2013) 29(4) *Computer Law & Security Review*.

12 OECD Guidelines on the Protection of Privacy and Transborder Flows of Personal Data, 2013.

13 International Working Group on Data Protection in Telecommunications, <https://datenschutz-berlin.de/content/europa-international/international-working-group-on-data-protection-in-telecommunications-iwgdpt>.

14 See, for example, De Hert, P., Papakonstantinou, V. and Kamara, I., 'The New Cloud Computing ISO/IEC 27018 Standard Through the Lens of the EU Legislation on Data Protection' (2016) 32 *Computer Law & Security Review*.

15 International Standards on the Protection of Privacy with regard to the processing of Personal Data, Madrid, 5 November 2009.

court systems or data protection authorities. On the other hand, the legal instruments in effect disregard this reality, each one sticking to its own regulatory model: rather than trying to build regulatory bridges, each international organisation or country concerned seeks to export, if not impose, its own model onto others. A point in the not too distant future may easily be imagined when a truly global data breach or other data protection incident (Internet social networks are, after all, enterprises that may, at some point in the future, go bankrupt) will make all too obvious the shortcomings of this approach to each, mostly unsuspecting, Internet user on the globe.

3. PAST AND RECENT UN INITIATIVES IN THE DATA PRIVACY FIELD

Until today, the UN has not been particularly interested in global data privacy matters. With regard to protection of the general right to privacy, Art. 17 of the International Covenant on Civil and Political Rights of 1966,[16] and in particular its Comment No. 16,[17] as well as Art. 12 of the Universal Declaration of Human Rights[18] set the basic regulatory framework. Specifically with regard to data privacy, the UN issued in 1990 its Guidelines and, after a long period of silence, on 1 July 2015, at the alleged insistence of the civil society,[19] the UN appointed a Special Rapporteur on the Right to Privacy. Professor Joseph Cannataci took up this role on 1 August 2015.

This approach, while pointing in the right direction, appears limiting with regard to the contemporary global personal data processing environment. The UN Guidelines actually belong to the first generation of international data protection regulatory documents[20] and are in need of modernisation. The installation of a Special Rapporteur, while an important development in itself, is not enough. The Special Rapporteur role is a part-time, not fully UN-supported role. Even under its current, mostly consulting, mandate, the Special Rapporteur will struggle to execute it satisfactorily with his current infrastructure. On the

---

16 'No one shall be subjected to arbitrary or unlawful interference with his privacy, family, home or correspondence, nor to unlawful attacks on his honour and reputation.'

17 General Comment No. 16, Art. 17 (the right to respect of privacy, home and correspondence, and protection of honour and reputation), UN Human Rights Committee, HRI/GEN/Rev9 (Vol.1), 8 April 1988.

18 'No one shall be subjected to arbitrary interference with his privacy, family, home or correspondence, nor to attacks upon his honour and reputation. Everyone has the right to the protection of the law against such interference or attacks.'

19 See 'UN Human Rights Council creates Special Rapporteur on right to privacy', International Justice Resource Center, 22 April 2015, <http://www.ijrcenter.org/2015/04/22/un-human-rights-council-adopts-resolution-to-create-special-rapporteur-on-the-right-to-privacy/>.

20 De Hert and Papakonstantinou, above n. 5.

other hand, global data privacy matters are complex issues, constantly in flux. They cannot possibly be followed by a single person or even a small team of experts, regardless of their best intentions.[21] In addition, they ultimately involve concrete cases, where individuals whose rights are infringed or data controllers wishing to process data in new ways ask for specific guidance and assistance. A watchdog function alone is not enough (and, in any event, is better carried out by civil society organisations). In other words, data privacy has an administrative nature that resembles better the subject matter of UN specialised agencies (the WIPO, the International Labour Organization, the World Bank, the International Monetary Fund) rather than that of UN Special Rapporteurs (freedom of opinion and expression, freedom of religion or belief, independence of judges and lawyers, migrants, minority issues).

4. SUGGESTING THE ESTABLISHMENT OF A NEW, SPECIALISED UN AGENCY ON DATA PRIVACY

The foregoing explains our belief that an adequate response would be for the UN to establish a new, specialised agency aimed at the protection of data privacy. UN specialised agencies

> are autonomous organizations working with the United Nations. All were brought into relationship with the UN through negotiated agreements. Some existed before the First World War. Some were associated with the League of Nations. Others were created almost simultaneously with the UN. Others were created by the UN to meet emerging needs.[22]

So far, the UN has operated 15 specialised agencies, including the World Intellectual Property Organisation, whose example could be followed in the case of data privacy as well, as will be demonstrated in the analysis that follows.

The mandate for such a new UN specialised agency could be similar to the one already in effect for its Special Rapporteur on Privacy. Its terms of reference, meaning the regulatory framework to be applied by such a new UN agency, need not be a comprehensive, detailed set of rules immediately after its establishment. A number of options are possible. While the authors have a preference for the UN 1990 Guidelines to be updated, alternatives could be to draft an additional protocol to Art. 17 of the Covenant, or to adopt the Council

---

21 In EU terms, the office of the European Data Protection Supervisor (EDPS) may serve as a good sample, or measure, for this task.

22 Cf. <http://www.un.org/en/sections/about-un/funds-programmes-specialized-agencies-and-others/index.html>.

of Europe Convention in one form or another. We believe that what is important here is the establishment of a new UN agency *per se*. Consequently, emphasis need not be placed, at least at the beginning, on devising a robust data privacy legal framework for it to apply. Instead, a global lowest common denominator regulatory framework, wherever this is to be found, could be used as a starting point, in order for regulatory work to start taking place at an international, rather than regional, level.

The benefits of establishing such a new UN agency would be substantial. First, such an agency would offer data privacy a global point of reference. Currently, different regions in the world cannot even agree on terminology, with Europeans speaking about data protection, others about data privacy, and a smaller, but no less important, group categorising everything under the general right to privacy. Similarly, individuals who believe that their rights have been infringed, particularly outside their national borders, need to navigate a multitude of agencies and authorities in order to find a remedy. A common point of reference provided by an organisation accessible to all, even if it would ultimately only refer the matter to competent national authorities, would be an indispensable contribution in a fragmented, and largely non- or even miscommunicating, global environment.

A second contribution would be the placement of the data privacy discussion on its proper basis. No agreement is found globally whether data privacy constitutes a basic human right or not – and, if so, whether it is independent from the right to privacy. While things are beginning to crystallise in the EU, elsewhere data privacy is viewed as an online business competitive advantage, or the means to equip electronic commerce with public trust.[23] Other countries fear that the data privacy discussion may affect adversely their information technology industry. A new UN agency would address this controversy by firmly placing protection within the UN and, thus, within the human rights context.

A third contribution would be the organisation's potential role as a global convergence mechanism. At present there exists no formal international forum for achieving convergence among the various data privacy models in effect across the globe. International instruments in effect today (the EU Regulation, the CoE Convention, the OECD Guidelines and the APEC Framework) unfortunately have not incorporated permanent administrative mechanisms with the mandate to achieve, if not coherence, at least basic understanding in their texts. On the contrary, lack of such mechanisms demonstrates regulatory competition and a struggle for global domination. A UN agency would provide the self-evident forum for such a mechanism to operate on a permanent basis.

---

23 See, for example, Online Trust Alliance (OTA), 'Social Media and eCommerce Sites Lead in Security and Privacy', 6 June 2012, <https://otalliance.org/news-events/press-releases/social-media-and-ecommerce-sites-lead-security-and-privacy>.

Finally, the new UN agency could act as the international last recourse, assuming the role of the global go-to organisation for these data subjects who may feel that their data privacy right has been infringed and who do not benefit from a national data protection authority (or, as the recent case in the UK has demonstrated, they do benefit from such an authority but feel that their views need to be heard elsewhere as well).

5. THE WIPO MODEL AS USEFUL GUIDANCE TOWARDS THE ESTABLISHMENT OF A UN SYSTEM FOR THE GLOBAL PROTECTION OF DATA PRIVACY

In our view, there exist definite parallels between 1873 in intellectual property law and 2016 in data privacy law. In particular, the need for international protection and the inability to conduct normal business otherwise were identified for each legal system at these respective dates. In the WIPO's words,[24] the Paris Convention, in 1883, was 'the first major step taken to help creators ensure that their intellectual works are protected in other countries' that came about only when

> the need for international protection of intellectual property (IP) became evident when foreign exhibitors refused to attend the International Exhibition of Inventions in Vienna, Austria in 1873 because they were afraid their ideas would be stolen and exploited commercially in other countries.

This is a more or less accurate description of global personal data processing circumstances met today: individuals are desperate to be assured that their personal data are protected in other countries, wherever the Internet has made it possible for their data to be freely and immediately transmitted. At the same time, exports of personal data are grossly curbed by the application of the EU *adequacy* criterion. In one or another way, this wording may be found in other international instruments as well, culminating in today's fragmented world of haves (data privacy national legislation) and have-nots – the latter being in essence penalised by the former by means of exclusion of any business involving personal data transfers.

The WIPO is, in its own words, 'a self-funding agency of the UN, with 188 member states'. It was established by means of a Convention (the WIPO Convention of 1967) but replaced its predecessor, the United International Bureaux for the Protection of Intellectual Property, which was established as

24 See <wipo.int>.

early as 1893, in order to administer the Paris and Berne conventions. While the details of these two instruments are of no relevance to the purposes of this analysis, it could be noted that the Berne Convention was the result of a campaign by Victor Hugo and his association of authors, and that each text has been amended several times (approximately every 15–20 years, since their release in 1883 and 1886, respectively). Consequently, they came as the result of a users' campaign (perhaps in the equivalent of today's civil society), and their finalisation was neither an easy nor a finite task. The WIPO was not set up as a UN specialised agency; however, it became one shortly after its establishment, in 1974.[25]

At any event, the WIPO mandate[26] could be applied *mutatis mutandis* in the data privacy context as well. After all, it does not lie far away from the mandate of the UN's Special Rapporteur on Privacy established today. Indeed, a new UN data privacy agency would need to promote data privacy purposes and issues globally, in cooperation with all other international organisations already active in the field. It would also be empowered to ensure administrative cooperation among the various data privacy national agencies to be found across the globe. Other tasks entrusted to the WIPO today (for example, the running of the patent cooperation treaty or the international trademark system) could be paralleled within the new UN agency on data privacy scope: running a global certification system, for these global data controllers that would need one, or offering an alternative dispute resolution mechanism. Because of the technical character of both rights, the scope of work for these international agencies entrusted with the task to promote their purposes and monitor their application in practice could constantly develop, following technological or other developments in their respective fields.

While a detailed roadmap on the establishment of a new UN specialised agency on data privacy would have to take into account internal UN procedures, we believe that the WIPO case could provide useful background to this end. There are two basic options for the establishment of a UN specialised agency: either setting up a new international organisation outside the UN and then

---

25 Although it is beyond the scope of this chapter to address the limitations or criticisms of WIPO, the following could perhaps serve as indicative literature in this regard: May, C., *The World Intellectual Property Organisation – Resurgence and the Development Agenda*, Routledge 2007; Cordray, M.L., 'GATT v. WIPO' (1994) 76 *J. Pat. & Trademark Off. Soc'y* 121; Boyle, J., 'A Manifesto on WIPO and the future of Intellectual Property' (2004) 9 *Duke Law & Technology Review*.

26 'The objectives of the Organization are: (i) To promote the protection of intellectual property throughout the world through cooperation among States and, where appropriate, in collaboration with any other international organization; (ii) to ensure administrative cooperation among the intellectual property Unions'. Convention Establishing the World Intellectual Property Organization, Art. 3.

applying for special organisation status within the UN (as was the case with the WIPO), or creating a new agency directly by the UN. In our mind, the second solution, the direct establishment of a new agency by the UN, is preferable – and the existing Secretariat of the Special Rapporteur could provide a useful starting point in this regard. Establishment of a new international organisation outside the UN could prove impossible in practice because it would essentially require a self-initiated new international convention on data privacy. Even if this was accomplished, there would presumably exist an intermediate period when it would antagonise existing (UN, Council of Europe, etc.) structures on data privacy. On the other hand, direct establishment of a new agency by the UN, equipping it with an existing UN regulatory framework (the amended Guidelines of 1990 or a new additional protocol) or using in one way or another the Council of Europe Convention would avoid any conflicts of interest among the organisations concerned and would signal in a positive way to everybody the UN resolution to engage, and dominate, the field globally.

6. CONCLUSION

The UN has remained idle on the issue of data privacy since 1990, therefore missing significant developments, including the Internet as well as the global war against terrorism. The world today is a very different place than it was in 1990, when the UN's last attempt to regulate on this issue took place. What then constituted a problem of a closed number of countries that were experimenting with new technologies now has global implications affecting directly the everyday lives of people living in industrialised countries, in the developing world, as well as people receiving humanitarian assistance. The processing of personal information has culminated in an independent human right, on a par with any other rights on the list, whose adequate protection occupies a leading position on concerns expressed by individuals anywhere in the world regardless of the different predicaments they may be in. It is therefore time for the UN to become active in the field once again.

The UN responded to these conditions by establishing a new Special Rapporteur on Privacy. This appointment is important, and the person entrusted with this role has already undertaken positive steps towards successful execution of his mandate. However, in this chapter we question whether this is enough. Incremental progress may be a cautious and reasonable approach but does little to address pressing global data privacy issues. A global problem affects everyone on a daily basis, international cooperation among the legal instruments at hand is not only missing but not even planned for, and regional half-measures aimed at resolving each new problem (the right to be forgotten against Internet searches, technical standards against cloud computing, etc.) only soothe but do not heal the wounds. A new UN specialised agency is urgently needed.

To this end, useful guidance may be provided by the UN model for the global protection of intellectual property: the World Intellectual Property Organisation is a specialised UN agency entrusted with the global protection and promotion of intellectual property rights. This model was initiated more than 100 years ago when cross-border problems not unlike the ones identified today in the data privacy field made international cooperation and the establishment of a global system of protection imperative. After decades of experimenting, the incorporation of a new, specialised UN agency was considered the preferred way forward; the WIPO thus joined the UN in 1970 and holds a similar role to what could be envisaged for a new UN specialised agency on data privacy.

In our opinion, the establishment of a new UN specialised agency does not necessarily require a robust new international treaty on data privacy. The legal framework that could support its operation, at least in the short term, is more or less already available: the amended UN Guidelines of 1990 could undertake this role, or, a new additional protocol to Art. 17 of the Covenant. What should be aimed at initially is flexibility and inclusiveness, even at the expense of effectiveness of protection. Effectiveness of protection is an abstract term perceived differently across the world. The UN model would not replace already existing national ones. It would formulate the global common lowest data privacy denominator. However, it would be a standard applicable by everyone.

INVITED COMMENT

26. CONVENTION 108, A TRANS-ATLANTIC DNA?

Sophie KWASNY*

The Convention for the protection of individuals with regard to automatic processing of personal data[1] ('Convention 108') was opened for signature in Strasbourg on 28 January 1981[2] and came into force on 1 October 1985. Thirty-five years after its opening for signature, the Convention applies to 50 countries.

Convention 108 is unique. It was unique over three decades ago, and remains the only legally binding international instrument in the field of data protection. Its legally binding force is a key element that makes it unique, but it is not the only one. Another key characteristic of Convention 108 is its unmatched potential for global reach: Convention 108 is open to any country in the world.

Is this opening to the world, aimed at affording protection to individuals when data concerning them flow across borders and oceans, with a particular focus on the trans-Atlantic dimension examined here, the result of genetic instructions which guided its development? Or is it instead the result of a genetic mutation or the result of the use of genetic engineering techniques?

Convention 108 was conceived, and delivered, with the idea that data protection should respect the principle of international free flow of information. Its trans-Atlantic nature in fact pre-dated the Convention itself, deriving from the identity of its parents and in the hopes they vested in the Convention.

On the life scale of an international treaty, a few decades of life amounts only to infancy, and the trans-Atlantic hopes that have started to materialise only recently are to be considered in a longer-term perspective, with a promising future.

* Data Protection Unit, Council of Europe. E-mail: sophie.kwasny@coe.int.

1 More information on Convention 108: <http://www.coe.int/en/web/conventions/full-list/-/conventions/treaty/108>.

2 28 January has been known for the past ten years as a 'data protection day', on an initiative of the Council of Europe to mark the anniversary of Convention 108, and is also celebrated outside Europe as 'privacy day'.

1. CONVENTION 108, TRANS-ATLANTIC AT BIRTH

The Committee that drafted Convention 108 had in its mandate the clear instruction 'to prepare a Convention for the protection of privacy in relation to data processing abroad and transfrontier data processing'.[3] It 'was instructed to do so in close collaboration with the Organisation for Economic Co-operation and Development, as well as the non-European member countries of that organisation, having regard to the activities which OECD was carrying out in the field of information, computer and communications policy.'[4]

The 'OECD, as well as four of its non-European member countries (Australia, Canada, Japan and the United States) were represented by an observer on the Council of Europe's committee.'[5]

While many other multilateral Conventions of the Council of Europe are titled 'European' Conventions, the drafters of Convention 108 decided not to use the European adjective in the title of the Convention, precisely to highlight the open nature of the instrument and 'to underline that there ought to be ample scope for accession to it by non-European States'.[6]

Accession to the Convention by non-Member States of the Council of Europe is regulated by Art. 23 of the Convention, which prescribes that:

> After the entry into force of this Convention, the Committee of Ministers of the Council of Europe may invite any State not a member of the Council of Europe to accede to this Convention by a decision taken by the majority provided for in Article 20.d of the Statute of the Council of Europe and by the unanimous vote of the representatives of the Contracting States entitled to sit on the committee.

As emphasised in the Explanatory Report[7] to the Convention, the immediate intention of the drafters was to enable accession by the four non-European countries already mentioned, that had participated in the work of the drafting Committee.

The drafters of the Convention had already envisaged accession to Convention 108 by, notably, the United States. A vision aimed at securing the protection of individuals in full respect of the principle of free flow of information.

Louis Joinet, Chair of the Committee that drafted the Convention, had underlined the emerging power constituted by information, the related risk of restrictions on transborder data flows, and strived to deliver an international instrument that would contribute to providing a legal solution to this emerging concern.

---

3 Explanatory Report to Convention 108, §13.
4 Ibid., §14.
5 Ibid., §15.
6 Ibid., §24.
7 Ibid., §10.

> Information has an economic value and the ability to store and process certain types of data may well give one country political and technological advantage over other countries. This in turn may lead to a loss of national sovereignty through supranational data flows.[8]

2. DEFINITELY MORE TRANS-ATLANTIC 30 YEARS LATER

Despite an early active trans-Atlantic exchange at the drafting stage of Convention 108, participation in the work of Convention 108 by representatives from the western side of the Atlantic would not start before the beginning of the third millennium.

Trans-Atlantic participation in the work related to Convention 108 currently involves several countries from the Americas (Canada, Mexico, Uruguay and the US), as well as the regional network of Ibero-American data protection authorities.

Uruguay currently is the sole trans-Atlantic partner to have committed to be legally bound by the Convention, being party to it, while Canada, Mexico and the US participate as observers.

2.1. CANADA

Canada is the 'oldest' trans-Atlantic participant in the work of the Consultative Committee of Convention 108. It has been involved since 2004 under the status of observer foreseen in Art. 18.3 of Convention 108 regarding the composition of the Committee. To only refer to its most recent participation since the 30th anniversary of Convention 108, Canada attended the Plenary meetings of the Consultative Committee in 2011 and 2014. Its participation was ensured by a representative of the Ministry of Justice.

2.2. MEXICO

Mexico is the latest trans-Atlantic participant in Convention 108. It was granted observer status during the 33rd Plenary meeting of the Consultative Committee of Convention 108 (Strasbourg, 29 June to 1 July 2016), having previously participated in all meetings of the *ad hoc* committee on data protection entrusted with the task of finalising the modernisation of Convention 108. Mexico's

---

8 Louis Joinet, statement before the OECD Symposium on transborder data flows and the protection of privacy, Vienna, 20–23 September 1977.

participation was ensured by representatives of its data protection authority (*Instituto Nacional de Transparencia, Acceso a la Información y Protección de Datos Personales* – INAI) and of the Ministry of Foreign Affairs.

2.3. URUGUAY

Uruguay's became a fully fledged Party to the Convention on 1 August 2013. Uruguay was not only the first trans-Atlantic Party to Convention 108, but also the first non-Member State of the Council of Europe to accede to it. It has since regularly attended the annual Plenary meetings of the Consultative Committee. Uruguay also participated in all four meetings of the *ad hoc* committee on data protection held in 2013, 2014 and 2016, represented by its data protection authority (*Unidad Reguladora y de Control de Datos Personales* – URCDP).

2.4. UNITED STATES

After the early involvement of the United States in the life, or rather pre-life, of Convention 108, nearly three decades passed before a formal relation was established between Convention 108 and the US.

At the beginning of 2010, the Consulate General of the US requested that the US Government be granted observer status in the Consultative Committee of Convention 108. This status was granted in February 2010, thus allowing formal participation of the US representatives in the meetings of the Consultative Committee of Convention 108. US representatives attended several annual Plenary meetings (2010, 2011 and 2012) of the Consultative Committee of Convention 108, as well as several meetings of the Bureau of the Consultative Committee.

The US furthermore took part as observer in the 2013 and 2014 meetings of the *ad hoc* Committee on data protection, taking an active interest in the modernisation of Convention 108. Participation of the US in the meetings was ensured by representatives of multiple governmental sectors and institutions, i.e. by the Executive Office of the President, the Department of Homeland and Security, the State Department and/or the Federal Trade Commission.

It is important to note that the US, as Party to another Council of Europe treaty, could decide to follow a similar path in the field of data protection. After having contributed to its drafting, the US signed the Convention on cybercrime at its opening for signature in Budapest on 23 November 2001,[9] and ratified it

[9] Convention on Cybercrime, ETS 185. Cf. further: <http://www.coe.int/en/web/conventions/full-list/-/conventions/treaty/185>.

five years later with an entry into force in January 2007. The US acceded to the 'Budapest Convention' despite the difficulty raised by some of the provisions (in particular in light of the First Amendment's free speech principles)[10] and the concerns raised at the time by civil rights organisations. In February 2012 President Obama and his Administration released a framework for protecting consumer data privacy and promoting innovation in the global economy. The framework included a 'Consumer Privacy Bill of Rights', presented as 'a blueprint for privacy in the information age' which, while underlining the importance of 'improving global interoperability' remained silent as to any significant step of the US towards an international treaty in the field.

The calls of European Union (EU)[11] institutions, and the domestic action of civil society organisations (the US Privacy Coalition called for the US Government to support Convention 108 and proposed a resolution for the US Senate aiming at US accession to Convention 108)[12] should eventually be heard, considering in particular the precedent of the Budapest Convention, and the complementarity of both instruments in a human rights context.[13]

2.5. THE IBERO-AMERICAN NETWORK OF DATA PROTECTION AUTHORITIES (*RED IBEROAMERICANA DE PROTECCION DE DATOS*)

The rules of procedure of the Consultative Committee of Convention 108 also provide for the participation of non-state observers with a view to enabling the contribution to the work of the Committee of a wide range of actors (civil society and private sector representatives). The *Red* was granted observer status in 2009 and has since participated in meetings of the Committee, usually represented by its Presidency.

---

10 Diane Rowland, Uta Kohl and Andrew Charlesworth, *Information Technology Law*, 4th ed., Taylor & Francis, 2011.

11 See item 6 of the press release of 27 November 2013 and related Communication on 'Rebuilding Trust in EU–US Data Flows', <http://europa.eu/rapid/press-release_IP-13-1166_en.htm> and item 119 of the report of the European Parliament on 'the US NSA surveillance programme, surveillance bodies in various Member States and their impact on EU citizens' fundamental rights and on transatlantic cooperation in Justice and Home Affairs', <http://www.europarl.europa.eu/sides/getDoc.do?type=REPORT&reference=A7-2014-0139&language=EN>.

12 See <https://epic.org/privacy/intl/coeconvention/>.

13 See the penultimate conclusion of the Chair of the June 2014 'Conference on Article 15 safeguards and criminal justice access to data', <http://www.coe.int/t/dghl/cooperation/economiccrime/Source/Cybercrime/CyberCrime@Octopus/3021_art15Conf_Conclusions_v1e.pdf>.

3. A NEW LANDSCAPE: THE COMMITTEE OF CONVENTION 108

The Consultative Committee of Convention 108 which gathers all signatories and observers to the Convention (circa 70 participants in total)[14] is a unique forum of cooperation and exchange. Not only in the fact that it is neither a governmental committee, nor a committee of data protection authorities, but a mix of both, providing a balanced and nuanced take on current challenges. The geographic variety of its participants also enables a rich and diverse perspective on the topics discussed (such as, during the last Plenary meeting of the Committee, the automatic exchange of tax data, big data, passenger name records (PNR), health data, right to private life and freedom of expression, data processing in a law enforcement context, legal basis of cooperation between data protection authorities).

The Committee is not solely a forum of cooperation and exchange (see in particular the provisions of the Convention on mutual assistance); its policy-making role is also to be acknowledged as sectorial, and tailored guidance of the principles of the Convention has been provided in a number of fields under the impetus and productive work of the Committee.[15]

As was the case in the late 1970s and 1980s, parallel work undertaken in the Council of Europe (the modernisation of Convention 108) and in the OECD (revision of the Guidelines on the Protection of Privacy and Transborder Flows of Personal Data)[16] in 2010 and the following years enabled closer exchanges between both organisations and respective experts.

4. TO ULTIMATELY TRANSCEND ALL BORDERS

Article 12 of Convention 108 on 'transborder flows of personal data and domestic law' provides for the free flow of data between Parties to the Convention. 'The aim of this article is to reconcile the requirements of effective data protection with the principle of free flow of information, regardless of frontiers ….'[17]

---

14 Fifty parties plus observers.

15 Recommendations of the Committee of Ministers of the Council of Europe in the field of data protection are prepared by the Consultative Committee (see e.g. the latest one, Recommendation (2015)5 on the processing of personal data in the context of employment). Other Recommendations can be consulted at <http://www.coe.int/dataprotection>.

16 For more information on the OECD privacy framework and the revision of the 1980 Guidelines see: <http://www.oecd.org/internet/ieconomy/privacy-guidelines.htm>.

17 Explanatory Report to Convention 108, §62.

The authors of the Convention were concerned that

> controls may interfere with the free international flow of information which is a principle of fundamental importance for individuals as well as nations. A formula had to be found to make sure that data protection at the international level does not prejudice this principle.[18]

The 1981 text of Convention 108 was complemented in 2001 by an additional protocol to the Convention, regarding supervisory authorities and transborder data flows,[19] to specifically address the issue of data flows to non-state parties, allowed on the basis of the condition of an 'adequate' protection.

> The flow of information is at the very core of international co-operation. However, the effective protection of privacy and personal data also means that there should in principle be no transborder flows of personal data to recipient countries or organisations where the protection of such data is not guaranteed.[20]

In the context of the modernisation of Convention 108, the objective remains the facilitation of the free flow of information regardless of frontiers in full guarantee of an appropriate[21] protection of individuals. This protection has to be of such quality as to ensure that human rights are not adversely affected by globalisation and transborder data flows.

Data flows between Parties to the Convention remain free and cannot be prohibited, to the exception of what is now proposed, which corresponds to a change occurred since 1981: restrictions regarding flows of personal data relating to 'Parties regulated by binding harmonised rules of protection shared by States belonging to a regional organisation',[22] as is notably the case for the Member States of the EU. All members of the EU are also Parties to Convention 108 and the respective legal frameworks (the EU framework derives from Convention 108 and, as was expressly underlined in Directive 95/46, gives substance to and amplifies the principles of Convention 108) need to remain compatible and consistent.

The value of Convention 108 from an EU perspective is precisely linked to the adequacy[23] scheme of the EU, as underlined in Recital 105 of the General

---

18 Ibid., §9.

19 More information on the Additional Protocol at: <http://www.coe.int/en/web/conventions/full-list/-/conventions/treaty/181>.

20 Explanatory Report to the 2001 Additional Protocol, §6.

21 The use of the word 'appropriate' instead of 'adequate' aims at distinguishing the European Union's adequacy scheme (see n 20) from that of Convention 108.

22 See modernisation proposals: <https://rm.coe.int/CoERMPublicCommonSearchServices/DisplayDCTMContent?documentId=09000016806a616c> or at <http://www.coe.int/data-protection>.

23 See Art. 45 of the General Data Protection Regulation.

Data Protection Regulation (GDPR) of the EU.[24] This recital, in relation to Art. 45.2.c of the GDPR, states that the 'third country's accession to the Council of Europe Convention of 28 January 1981 for the Protection of Individuals with regard to the Automatic Processing of Personal Data and its Additional Protocol should be taken into account' by the European Commission when assessing the level of protection.

5. CONCLUSION

It remains to be seen if the hopes and visions of the fathers of the Convention and the benefits of accession to it[25] will lead to a continuation of the regular increase in the number of Parties, as was the case over past decades, with a clear impetus towards globalisation since the thirtieth anniversary of Convention 108. This impetus, and the shift in the geographic balance of the Parties to the Convention, may well be a further incentive to accession.

Presently, accession by several African countries is pending (Cape Verde, Morocco and Tunisia have already been invited to accede to Convention 108 and are in the process of finalising their ratification procedure), countries of other regions of the world are participating as observers (Australia, South Korea, Indonesia), and others have expressed interest in either requesting observer status or joining the Convention.[26]

For over ten years there have been calls for global standards in the field of data protection.[27] There are several paths to strengthen the recognition at global level of the data protection principles and one of those paths clearly is the increase in the number of Parties to Convention 108.

This increase does not need to follow a 'region-by-region' approach, as is actually demonstrated by recent accessions to the Convention, which would tend to make it look, at this particular moment in time, more trans-Mediterranean than trans-Atlantic. Interest in the Convention is witnessed across the globe,

---

24 Regulation (EU) 2016/679 of the European Parliament and of the Council of 27 April 2016 on the protection of natural persons with regard to the processing of personal data and on the free movement of such data, and repealing Directive 95/46/EC (General Data Protection Regulation).

25 See Graham Greenleaf, 'Balancing Globalisation's Benefits and Commitments: Accession to Data Protection Convention 108 by Countries Outside Europe', 23 June 2016, <http://papers.ssrn.com/sol3/papers.cfm?abstract_id=2801054>.

26 Burkina-Faso is the latest non-European country having expressed interest in acceding to the Convention and its request is to be considered by the Committee of Ministers.

27 See the 2005 Declaration of Montreux of the International Conference of Data Protection and Privacy Commissioners (ICDPPC), <https://icdppc.org/wp-content/uploads/2015/02/Montreux-Declaration.pdf>.

based on a trans-Atlantic spirit, as much as a trans-Mediterranean or trans-Pacific one: countries are interested in forming part of a recognised space within which common data protection principles are enforced.

Convention 108 was born in Europe, conceived and moulded by individuals from several regions of the world who were dedicated to providing a legal framework that would protect people and respect the free flow of information. The further development of the Convention will eventually reveal its profound nature, and demonstrate whether its open character, including in its trans-Atlantic dimension, is a dominant gene capable of taking over its original European identity.

CONCLUSION

27. LANDSCAPE WITH THE RISE OF DATA PRIVACY PROTECTION

Dan Jerker B. SVANTESSON* and Dariusz KLOZA**

1. INTRODUCTION

It's true that not a day passes without new pieces of paper entering the Registry, papers referring to individuals of the male sex and of the female sex who continue to be born in the outside world ....
José Saramago, *All the Names* (1997)[1]

... a splash quite unnoticed
this was
Icarus drowning
William C. Williams,
'Landscape with the fall of Icarus' (1962)[2]

Perhaps the most common interpretation of Pieter Bruegel the Elder's painting *Landscape with the fall of Icarus* highlights popular ignorance of and indifference to the drowning of Icarus.[3] In Greek mythology, Daedalus and his son Icarus attempted to fly with the aid of wings they had made of both feathers and wax. Icarus recklessly flew too close to the sun, his wings melted and he drowned in the sea.[4] In Bruegel's painting, Icarus has already fallen, but he and his sad fate are hardly noticed. He disappears in the richness of the landscape shown, the crew

* Centre for Commercial Law, Faculty of Law, Bond University. E-mail: dan_svantesson@bond.edu.au.

** Research Group on Law, Science, Technology and Society, Vrije Universiteit Brussel; Peace Research Institute Oslo. E-mail: dariusz.kloza@vub.ac.be.

1 JOSÉ SARAMAGO, *All the Names*, trans. M.J. COSTA, Harvill Press, London 2013, p. 1.

2 WILLIAM C. WILLIAMS, 'Landscape with the fall of Icarus' in *Pictures from Brueghel and other poems: collected poems 1950-1962*, New Directions, New York 1962, p. 4.

3 Musées royaux des Beaux-Arts de Belgique, Brussels, *La chute d'Icare*, inv. 4030; 73.5 x 112 cm. Bought from the Sackville Gallery, London, in 1912; <https://www.fine-arts-museum.be/fr/la-collection/pieter-i-bruegel-la-chute-dicare>.

4 ROBERT GRAVES, *The Greek Myths*, Penguin Books, London 1955, ch. 92; OVID, *Metamorphoses*, trans. R. HUMPHRIES, Bloomington, London 1955, 8.183–8.235.

of a ship sailing by has not reacted to his fall and – as Bruegel's contemporary fellows would have said – the farmer goes on ploughing.[5]

Despite both the authenticity of the painting and its dominant interpretation being questioned,[6] we have found this masterpiece of Bruegel a suitable allegory for our concluding idea for this book. The underlying observation that stands out from our reading of the foregoing 26 chapters to this volume is that of the entanglement of *data privacy* in the entirety of trans-Atlantic relations. Yet we have observed that in these relations the *protection* of data privacy – to a large extent – recklessly falls victim of ignorance and indifference, similarly to the fate of Icarus as painted by Bruegel.

We have explained in our Preface that our main impetus for this book had been the Snowden *affaire*. We have aimed with this book to explore the *status quo* of trans-Atlantic data privacy relations challenging the notions of democracy, the rule of law (*Rechtsstaat*) and fundamental rights. The resulting anthology gives a snapshot of the 'hottest' issues as they look at the end of 2016. Hanneke Beaumont's sculpture *Stepping Forward* – seen as an allegory of a brave leap of faith into the unknown – gave further impetus to reflect also on the future of these relations.[7] We have thus re-read this book, spotted 'hot' topics and added a few of our own comments, ultimately offering a few modest suggestions as to the future of trans-Atlantic data privacy relations. Therefore, following the popular interpretation of Bruegel's masterpiece – with the kind permission of the Musées royaux des Beaux-Arts de Belgique – we have reproduced *Landscape with the fall of Icarus* on the front cover of this book. As a *clin d'œil*, we have titled this concluding chapter 'Landscape with the Rise of Data Privacy Protection'.

2. GENERAL OBSERVATIONS

2.1. NOVELTY OF THE CONCEPT OF DATA PRIVACY AND A GROWING NATURE THEREOF

A number of themes stand out when reading the 26 contributions we have had the pleasure of working with. Let us begin with a few all-encompassing observations.

---

5 This phrase in Dutch – '... en boer, hij ploegde voort' ('... and the farmer, he went on ploughing') – popularised by a 1935 Werumeus Buning's poem *Ballade van den boer*, has become in the Low Countries a widely accepted proverb pointing out people's ignorance. Cf. Johan W.F. Werumeus Buning, *Verzamelde gedichten*, Querido, Amsterdam 1970, pp. 185–187.

6 Cf. esp. Lyckle de Vries, 'Bruegel's 'Fall of Icarus': Ovid or Solomon?' (2003) 30(1/2) *Simiolus: Netherlands Quarterly for the History of Art* 5–18.

7 Cf. Preface, in this volume.

The underlying reflection about data privacy is that of the *dynamism* of this concept. It might sound trivial *prima facie* – in fact, many aspects of life are dynamic – but this dynamism is caused by the relative novelty of data privacy, its uncharted scope and expeditiously growing nature. In terms of the law, the legal conceptualisation of data privacy is only 40–50 years old. This book confirms that many aspects thereof have not yet matured, and this includes even the very basic definitions. For example, having read the chapters of *Míšek*, *Maurushat & Vaile* and *Wilson*, we cannot help but recall the 2003 landmark judgment of the Court of Justice of the European Union (CJEU) in *Lindqvist*, delimitating the scope of European data privacy law,[8] its 2016 decision in *Breyer*, ruling on the grounds of the 1995 Data Protection Directive[9] that a dynamic Internet protocol (IP) address constitutes personal data,[10] or the pending, very similar case before the Federal Court of Australia that is to decide whether, on the grounds of the Privacy Act 1988 (Cth),[11] 'personal information' includes metadata.[12] Higher-level courts are repeatedly being asked for authoritative definitions and this phenomenon has become frequent in the privacy universe.

We have started in the Preface with a story on inspirations for this book. Yet beyond their usefulness for our purposes, such diverse events – judgments of senior courts, international treaties, legislation and political and societal developments at numerous levels – crystallise the definition of data privacy, its scope, legal construction and permissible and acceptable interferences. It is an ongoing discourse, i.e. a careful consideration, in which multiple and – quite often – opposing viewpoints meet, with a view to make a determination that might be applied in practice. In this way the conversation on data privacy is maturing. This body of knowledge on data privacy that is being created is a product of trial and error. All this leads to the continuous re-definition, re-conceptualisation and re-delineation of boundaries of data privacy and its protection. These developments help make clear, for example, whether and when global mass surveillance practices can be considered 'OK' ('OK' stands here for an umbrella term for 'fair', 'ethically sound', 'optimal', 'just', 'acceptable', etc.).

In the same Preface, we stated our ambition for this book not to be just another publication on the Snowden *affaire*. Yet as many as 12 out of 26 contributions in one way or another make reference to it and discuss the extent to which the *affaire* is capable of altering the privacy universe. Regardless of

---

8 Case C-101/01, *Bodil Lindqvist v. Åklagarkammaren i Jönköping* (CJEU, 6 November 2003).

9 Directive 95/46/EC of the European Parliament and of the Council of 24 October 1995 on the protection of individuals with regard to the processing of personal data and on the free movement of such data, [1995] OJ L 281/31–50 (hereinafter: 1995 Data Protection Directive).

10 Case C-582/14, *Patrick Breyer v. Bundesrepublik Deutschland* (CJEU, 19 October 2016).

11 Privacy Act 1988, No. 119, 1988 as amended.

12 Federal Court of Australia, Victoria Registry, *Privacy Commissioner v. Telstra Corporation Ltd*, Case VID38/2016; cf. also the determination by the Australian Privacy Commissioner in *Ben Grubb and Telstra Corporation Ltd* [2015] AICmr 35 (1 May 2015).

its actual impact, the Snowden *affaire* has inserted itself into the perspective on data privacy as a phenomenon developed in reaction to the many threats to individual and collective interests posed by global mass surveillance practices. All in all, the growth of 'privacy' as a concept owes much to the development of invasive technologies. It was the need to address the widespread popularity of photo cameras that inspired Warren and Brandeis in 1890 to coin their famous 'right to be let alone'.[13]

2.2. THE RAPID AND CONTINUOUS CHANGE OF DATA PRIVACY, ITS DIAGNOSES AND SOLUTIONS

However, this is not to say that once data privacy comes of age, it would from then on remain constant. On the contrary, the ever-changing nature of society, of its needs and desires, on the one hand, and of innovation and technology on the other, continuously necessitates a *re-think* of the concept of data privacy and of the system of its protection. In the privacy universe, things change rapidly. Many commentators recall here Collingridge's 'dilemma of control' – i.e. it is hard to regulate something so unpredictable as technology[14] – and give evidence of the 1995 Data Protection Directive that 'lived' for only 21 years until the General Data Protection Regulation (GDPR)[15] was passed (if we look at their respective enactment dates). The need up to keep pace with technological and societal developments necessitated the revision of the law.

To further illustrate our point: we finished the Preface to this book in early September 2016. This concluding chapter was written in late November 2016. (It was a conscious choice for us to re-visit all 26 submissions while the publisher was typesetting the book and, in parallel, to write these remarks.) Over the period of these two months, on the European side of the Atlantic alone, we have witnessed multiple events impacting trans-Atlantic data privacy relations, and these include:

- the lodging with the CJEU of two actions for annulment of the Privacy Shield framework on the grounds of its incompatibility with the EU fundamental rights (16 September[16] and 25 October, respectively);[17]

---

13 Samuel D. Warren and Louis D. Brandeis, 'The right to privacy' (1890) 4 *Harvard Law Review* 193–220.

14 David Collingridge, *The Social Control of Technology*, St. Martin's Press, New York 1980, p. 17.

15 Regulation (EU) 2016/679 of the European Parliament and of the Council of 27 April 2016 on the protection of natural persons with regard to the processing of personal data and on the free movement of such data, and repealing Directive 95/46/EC (General Data Protection Regulation), [2016] OJ L 119/1–88.

16 Case T-670/16, *Digital Rights Ireland v. Commission*, CJEU.

17 Case T-738/16, *La Quadrature du Net and Others v. Commission*, CJEU.

- a Swiss referendum on the new surveillance law that has received 65.5 per cent of popular support; the federal government had argued that 'the new measures would allow Switzerland to "leave the basement and come up to the ground floor by international standards"'(25 September);[18]
- the Investigatory Powers Tribunal in the United Kingdom ruling on the incompatibility of British mass surveillance practices between 1998 and 2015 with Art. 8 of the European Convention on Human Rights (ECHR)[19] (17 October);[20]
- the Walloon initial veto to the proposed Comprehensive Economic and Trade Agreement (CETA) between the EU and Canada, predominantly due to the failure of negotiating process to satisfy democratic requirements (17 October);[21] Belgium withdrew its veto on 27 October, having attached to CETA a declaration giving it certain agricultural concessions and – more importantly for our analysis – promising to refer to the CJEU the compatibility of CETA's investor dispute settlement provisions with the EU Treaties, this including the Charter of Fundamental Rights;[22]
- presidential elections in the US, after which – media speculate – the new administration might intensify global mass surveillance practices to the detriment of the principles of democracy, the rule of law and fundamental rights (8 October);[23]
- the French Constitutional Council declaring the unconstitutionality of a key clause of the 2015 surveillance law,[24] which had allowed wiretapping without oversight, since the provision in question constituted a 'manifestly disproportionate infringement' (21 October);[25] or

---

18 Le Conseil fédéral suisse, *Votation no 607, Résultats finaux officiels provisoires, Loi fédérale du 25.09.2015 sur le renseignement (LRens)*, <https://www.admin.ch/ch/f/pore/va/20160925/det607.html>; 'Switzerland votes in favour of greater surveillance', *The Guardian*, 25 September 2016, <https://www.theguardian.com/world/2016/sep/25/switzerland-votes-in-favour-of-greater-surveillance>.

19 Convention for the Protection of Human Rights and Fundamental Freedoms, Rome, 4 November 1950, ETS 5.

20 Investigatory Powers Tribunal (IPT), *Privacy International v. Secretary of State for Foreign and Commonwealth Affairs et al.*, [2016] UKIPTrib 15_110-CH, Judgment of 17 October 2016, §101.

21 'Le Parlement wallon a opposé son veto à l'adoption du Ceta', *France24*, 17 October 2016, <http://www.france24.com/fr/20161017-belgique-parlement-wallon-veto-adoption-ceta-tafta-union-europeenne-bruxelles>.

22 Statement (No. 37) by the Kingdom of Belgium on the conditions attached to full powers, on the part of the Federal State and the federated entities, for the signing of CETA; 13463/1/16, http://data.consilium.europa.eu/doc/document/ST-13463-2016-REV-1/en/pdf.

23 Spencer Ackerman and Ewen MacAskill, 'Privacy experts fear Donald Trump running global surveillance network', *The Guardian*, 11 November 2016, <https://www.theguardian.com/world/2016/nov/11/trump-surveillance-network-nsa-privacy>.

24 Loi n° 2015-912 du 24 juillet 2015 relative au renseignement, JORF n° 0171 du 26 juillet 2015, p. 12735.

25 Conseil Constitutionnel, Décision n° 2016-590 QPC, 21 October 2016. Authors' translation.

- the UK passing into law the Investigatory Powers Act 2016, nicknamed 'Snooper's Charter', whose surveillance provisions have been dubbed 'draconian and too intrusive' by civil liberties advocates (16 November).[26]

The solutions currently in place to protect individual and collective interests related to data privacy offer a sufficient degree of protection in many situations, yet in many other situations still more is needed. Further, where solutions are currently satisfactory, they might quickly become outdated. When this is the case, the need for more (or less) protection, if ever, must be first diagnosed. Such a diagnosis often indicates that something *does not* work. The many problems of data privacy are well known: 'the kinds of mass surveillance Snowden has revealed at the NSA do not work and also carry major risks for ordinary citizens'[27] or – to paraphrase Saramago from the epigraph – 'not a day passes' without businesses doing nasty things with their customers' information.[28] In their contributions to the present book, *Kovič Dine* observes a need for an 'international response' to economic cyber-exploitation among states, and *Gerry* – in a similar vein – criticises the lack of global arrangement for effectively fighting 'cybercrime'. Finally, *Amicelle* joins the critics of global mass surveillance practices and – using the example of the US Terrorist Finance Tracking Programme – asking 'why does this kind of security programme ... persist regardless of failures to achieve the stated goals concerning terrorism'? Positions concluding that something *does* work are much less popular, but nevertheless they exist (cf. *Swire* and *Czerniawski*).

Alternatively, such an analysis can suggest there is a gap that urgently needs to be filled. The passage of time, for example, seems to be such undiagnosed need for more (or – alternatively – less) privacy protection. The reading of *Székely* questions whether and how much 'privacy' should be asserted for a person after their death? He even projects that comparisons would be made in a quest for 'the best countries to conclude our lives, if we care about having continuing protection for our personality and privacy after death'. How much privacy should be provided to an individual when a piece of their personal information loses its societal relevance? *Miyashita* sheds light on the influence of European 'right to be forgotten' (or a 'right to de-listing')[29] on the Japanese judiciary and concludes that 'human beings forget, but the Internet does not. This is why forgetting is universally demanding as a legal right in the twenty-first century'.

---

26 Warwick Ashford, 'Investigatory Powers Bill looks set to become law', *Computer Weekly*, 17 November 2016, <http://www.computerweekly.com/news/450403089/Investigatory-Powers-Bill-looks-set-to-become-law>.

27 David Lyon, *Surveillance After Snowden*, Polity Press, Cambridge 2015, p. vii.

28 Above n. 1.

29 Case C-121/12, *Google Spain SL and Google Inc. v. Agencia Española de Protección de Datos (AEPD) and Mario Costeja González* (CJEU, 13 May 2014).

Finally, *Spiekermann* makes, to our knowledge, the first comparative analysis of the ethical nature of personal data markets. There is scope for abuse when personal data are seen as an economic asset, generated by identities and individual behaviours, tradable in exchange for e.g. higher quality services and products. Having looked at them through the perspectives of utilitarianism, deontology and virtue-ethics, she diagnoses the critical need for 'careful crafting of technical and organisational mechanisms' of such markets. Such crafting must include a possibility to opt-out with no negative consequences in order for personal data markets to maintain their ethicality.

When the diagnosis is more mature, we observe that a wide spectrum of concrete proposals to increase the level of privacy protection has already been tabled. The bravest ideas include, for example, a plea to change the paradigm of cross-border transfers of personal data from 'adequacy' to a 'flagrant denial of protection'; an adaptation of a 'death row phenomenon' ground for refusal, a concept well known in extradition law (*De Busser*). More modest ideas suggest looking at other branches of law and policy, especially in the area of environmental protection, for an inspiration on how to protect best the many aspects of data privacy. This plea emerged in the early 2000s (e.g. Nehf[30] and Hirsh)[31] and is renewed in this volume by *Emanuel*. Among her propositions, she argues for the US legal concept of 'mineral rights' in property to be adapted to the needs and reality of the privacy universe as it might increase individual choice and control over their personal data. Even though consumers are rewarded in pecuniary terms, 'in exchange for collecting and selling their personal information', she considers this approach fair as individuals 'are consenting to the transaction and benefit from it'. *Emanuel* underlines the importance of choice in data privacy, whose consequences for such a transaction, including their unpredictability, must be fully understood.

Further, *Kloza* makes a suggestion to acknowledge and explore a new, fourth category of privacy protections – behavioural – alongside the three categories already well established, i.e. regulatory (legal), organisational and technological. He claims existing arrangements do not offer enough protection and resorting to own behaviour would offer some consolation. Finally, *Goldenfein* evaluates the enforcement of data privacy by means of technology and – more concretely – by automation. He gives the examples of authorisation schemes such as the Enterprise Privacy Authorisation Language (EPAL) and semantic web technologies such as the Transparent Accountable Data Mining Initiative (TAMI). Although these particular approaches 'have not materialised into

---

30 James Nehf, 'Recognizing the Societal Value in Information Privacy' (2003) 78 *Washington Law Review* 5.

31 Dennis Hirsch, 'Protecting the Inner Environment: What Privacy Regulation Can Learn from Environmental Law' (2006) 41(1) *Georgia Law Review* 1–63.

functional examples', he concludes this field is 'still in its relative infancy' and pleas for further 'research into automation of legal rights'.

Others look for more formal solutions. For example, *De Hert & Papakonstantinou* argue for the creation of a body of the United Nations (UN) to foster data privacy protection at an international level. They extend their early proposal from 2013,[32] arguing that only an international organisation is capable of effectively setting 'the global tone and minimum level of protection'. They recall the UN involvement in data privacy protection from 1966 (i.e. the International Covenant on Civil and Political Rights)[33] to the 1990 Guidelines concerning computerised personal data files[34] and evaluate it as rather obsolete and insufficient. The UN commitment was renewed with the 2015 appointment of the first special rapporteur on the right to privacy[35] and the adoption of the 2016 resolution on the right to privacy in the digital age.[36] They argue the recently revived UN involvement could constitute a solid basis for the establishment of an international data privacy agency.

In her contribution to the present book, *Kwasny* struck the same chord as earlier e.g. Greenleaf[37] and foresees that the Council of Europe's 'Convention 108'[38] – from its inception open to any country in the world – could become a standard beyond the geographical borders of Europe. However, we agree with Kuner that realisation of any such proposition would be a laborious exercise, requiring many factors to be taken into consideration, e.g. form, contents and institutional set-up.[39]

---

32 Paul De Hert and Vagelis Papakonstantinou, 'Three Scenarios for International Governance of Data Privacy: Towards an International Data Privacy Organization, Preferably a UN Agency?' (2013) 9 *I/S: A Journal of Law and Policy for the Information Society* 272–324.

33 International Covenant on Civil and Political Rights, New York, 16 December 1966. Cf. Art. 17.

34 United Nations guidelines concerning computerized personal data files, New York, 14 December 1990.

35 Cf. <http://www.ohchr.org/EN/Issues/Privacy/SR/Pages/JoeCannataci.aspx>.

36 United Nations, General Assembly, *The right to privacy in the digital age*, resolution A/C.3/71/L.39, New York, 31 October 2016, <http://www.un.org/ga/search/view_doc.asp?symbol=A/C.3/71/L.39>.

37 Graham Greenleaf, '"Modernising" data protection Convention 108: A safe basis for a global privacy treaty?' (2013) 29(4) *Computer Law and Security Review* 430–436; Graham Greenleaf, 'The influence of European data privacy standards outside Europe: implications for globalization of Convention 108' (2012) 2(2) *International Data Privacy Law* 68–92.

38 Convention for the Protection of Individuals with regard to Automatic Processing of Personal Data, ETS 108, Strasbourg, 28 January 1981, <http://conventions.coe.int/Treaty/en/Treaties/Html/108.htm>.

39 Christopher Kuner, 'An international legal framework for data protection: Issues and prospects' (2008) 25(4) *Computer Law & Security Review* 307–317.

2.3. ENTANGLEMENT OF DATA PRIVACY IN THE ENTIRETY OF TRANS-ATLANTIC RELATIONS

On a more conceptual level, we observe that data privacy is *entangled* with any aspect of trans-Atlantic relations. Be it national security or international trade, questions ranging from cross-border transfers of money with the aid of financial institutions to civil aviation to international trade, the provision of digital services or the enforcement of intellectual property rights would always raise an issue of data privacy. This is a direct consequence of globalisation and the growth of the quaternary economy, which runs on handling information. (Many have dubbed this phenomenon as 'data' being the 'new oil' or the 'fourth industrial revolution'.)

In consequence, the governance of such relations always affects, to various degrees, the protection of data privacy. Its impact could be either direct (cf. e.g. 2016 Privacy Shield),[40] either indirect (e.g. 2012 EU–US agreement on the use and transfer of Passenger Name Records).[41] In the latter case, the main objective of an arrangement is different than the regulation of data privacy, but nevertheless, such an arrangement touches thereon. In any case, data privacy has become an indispensable ingredient of contemporary international relations. The question remains as to the level of protection of data privacy that could be afforded as a result of dynamics between multiple actors on the international arena.

2.4. *INTERMEZZO: AUDIATUR ET ALTERA PARS*[42]

Finally, we have observed that a vast majority of contributions to this book diagnose some form of defect in trans-Atlantic data privacy relations and the authors of these contributions – either explicitly, either implicitly – argue for stronger protection of data privacy. Consequently, there are only few chapters that conclude the *status quo* of such relations is 'OK' and not much should be changed. (The contributions of *Swire* and *Czerniawski* stand out in this category. Yet the reader should note that nobody has argued for *less* data privacy.) Therefore, some readers might see this book as a form of advocacy for *more* data privacy. We hasten to recall our earlier point that 'privacy' is being created by discourse and thus we explain that our intentions here were purely academic,

40 Commission Implementing Decision (EU) 2016/1250 of 12 July 2016 pursuant to Directive 95/46/EC of the European Parliament and of the Council on the adequacy of the protection provided by the EU–US Privacy Shield, [2016] OJ L 207/1–112 (hereinafter: Privacy Shield).

41 Agreement between the United States of America and the European Union on the use and transfer of passenger name records to the United States Department of Homeland Security, [2012] OJ L 215/5–14.

42 Latin for 'let the other side be heard as well'.

i.e. to provide an objective account with a critical comment. However, this book is a result of a call for papers supplemented by a few invited contributions, and simply we have not received, even for consideration, contributions arguing otherwise. We acknowledge this shortcoming of this book and we would have liked to see authors with opposite viewpoints, as long as their contributions satisfy the academic criteria of ethics and quality. (Consequently, we would not have liked to see any form of lobbying in the present book.)

3. SPECIFIC OBSERVATIONS

3.1. REGULATION OF CROSS-BORDER DATA FLOWS

Let us now move to some more concrete themes that stand out when reading this book. The debates on trans-Atlantic data privacy relations concentrate on a few critical topics. Perhaps the most obvious, but perhaps equally the most important theme is the regulation of cross-border flows of personal data. Six chapters of this book are devoted to this matter (*Weber*, *Schweighofer*, *Lindsay*, *Swire*, *Vermeulen* and *Doneda*). The tension between the societal usefulness of such transfers, not to say the need for them, on the one hand, is contrasted with the societal usefulness of, not to say the need for, data privacy on the other hand. The need for restricting cross-border data flows is obvious: the value of domestic data privacy protection is severely undermined when personal data are exported without adequate safeguards. At the same time, it is equally clear that there are societal functions that are critically dependent on cross-border data flows. *Doneda* further observed that in many jurisdictions in Latin America, the proliferation of data privacy regulation, which allows for such transfers, brought positive effects as it led these counties to search for 'innovative ways of making its own economy more competitive'.[43] Other jurisdictions around the world follow this trend, with a view to receive and – nowadays – maintain the 'adequacy' of the level of protection to the EU standards.

In the past two years, much ink has been spilled over the regulation of transborder data flows between the EU and the US. This saga seems to be never-ending. The 2000 Safe Harbour arrangement[44] was found in October 2015 not to be offering the adequate level of protection of data privacy. In July 2016 the very similar Privacy Shield framework replaced it. The new European

43 These countries constitute the vast majority of members of *La Red Iberoamericana de Protección de Datos* (RIPD), cf. <http://www.redipd.es>.

44 Commission Decision of 26 July 2000 pursuant to Directive 95/46/EC of the European Parliament and of the Council on the adequacy of the protection provided by the safe harbor privacy principles and related frequently asked questions issued by the US Department of Commerce, [2000] OJ L 215/7–47.

'adequacy decision' has been severely criticised for its illusion of protection – i.e. insufficiency, lack of credibility and misleading character (*Vermeulen*). *Lindsay* further observed that Privacy Shield 'necessarily embodied compromises between the parties' and the arrangement 'cannot disguise the hallmarks of haste', and not even a year has passed before two actions for annulment have been lodged with the CJEU.[45]

The main underlying problem is that 'the US privacy protection regime is not functionally equivalent to [this] in Europe'.[46] The contemporarily dominant narrative of data privacy law at the European Union level is that of fundamental rights. *Wiewiórowski*, Assistant European Data Protection Supervisor (EDPS), argued in the Foreword to this book that

> the European Union regards itself as a distinct political entity, which is not a federation of Member States, but it is held together ... with a 'unique, invisible glue'. This connection is grounded with shared goals. One of them ... is a unique obligation to protect personal data. Stating that everyone has the right to the protection of personal data concerning them, the European Union feels obliged to observe how safe is the data both held in its territory and transferred outside thereof.

From 2009, the Charter of Fundamental Rights of the European Union (CFR)[47] guarantees two separate rights to privacy and personal data protection. It is a qualitative change from the predominantly economic narrative that was driving the harmonisation of national data privacy laws in early 1990s. While then the main idea was to harmonise the diverse laws in the EU Member States in order to ensure the free flow of personal data, this qualitative change came with the jurisprudence of the CJEU which emphasised the fundamental rights dimension of data privacy. The entry into force of the Lisbon Treaty (2009), to which the Charter of Fundamental Rights forms a part, concluded this development.[48]

This is structurally and essentially different from the narrative in the United States. Only a few readers would disagree with *Swire* that both the EU and the US are constitutional democracies built on the same shared values. Yet this observation is valid only on the most abstract level and – when it comes to data privacy – the devil lies in the detail. Contrary to the EU, the constitutional protection of data privacy in the US is far from being comprehensive (e.g. the

---

45 Above nn. 16 and 17.

46 Colin J. Bennett, 'So Who is Actually "Shielded" by the Privacy Shield?', 2016, <http://www.colinbennett.ca/data-protection/so-who-is-actually-shielded-by-the-privacy-shield>.

47 [2012] OJ C 326/391–407.

48 Cf. further e.g. Orla Lynskey, 'From Market-Making Tool to Fundamental Right: The Role of the Court of Justice in Data Protection's Identity Crisis' in Serge Gutwirth, Ronald Leenes, Paul De Hert and Yves Poullet (eds.), *European Data Protection: Coming of Age*, Springer, Dordrecht 2013, pp. 59–84; Gloria González Fuster, *The Emergence of Personal Data Protection as a Fundamental Right of the EU*, Springer, Dordrecht 2014.

Fourth Amendment to the US Constitution protections only against 'searches and seizures' originating from the federal government) and the homologue of the 1995 EU Data Protection Directive, i.e. Privacy Act of 1974, has been found 'ineffective in curbing government data processing'.[49] The Snowden *affaire* only demonstrated further the insufficiency of the protections available. The subsequent actions of the US Congress and the President – *Swire* lists 24 'significant actions to reform surveillance laws and programmes' – no matter how plausible, did not alter the essence of the US data privacy regime.[50]

The next underlying problem is that both sides at the negotiating table – the European Commission and the US Secretary of Commerce – have been fully aware not only of the structural differences between their respective data privacy regimes but also of the practice of the US regime. Yet their awareness has not been reflected in policy-making. These differences existed equally in 2000 (when the first adequacy decision was issued) and 2013 Snowden *affaire* only confirmed them. Advocate General Ives Bot, in his opinion to the *Schrems* case heard by the Luxembourg Court, observed that after 2013 the trans-Atlantic data privacy relations have changed significantly. Despite the European Commission being 'aware of shortcomings in the application of [the Safe Harbour decision]', it 'neither suspended nor adapted that decision, thus entailing the continuation of the breach of the fundamental rights of the persons whose personal data was and continues to be transferred under the safe harbour scheme'.[51] The CJEU judgment in *Schrems* resulted in the European Commission revisiting in late 2016 all 'adequacy decisions' issued thus far. The relevant jurisdictions would now be 'check[ed] periodically whether the finding relating to the adequacy … is still factually and legally justified' with a view to suspend or limit the free flow of personal data thereto should the need be.[52]

The Commission was equally aware of the many inadequacies of the final text of the Privacy Shield framework – at the end of the day the Commission's officials follow the debate, in the media or in academia. Nevertheless, an 'adequacy decision' was issued. (We refrain from commenting here on the legal technique of the whole arrangement – a voluntary self-certification of compliance to the

49 Francesca Bignami, *The U.S. Privacy Act in Comparative Perspective*, European Parliament, 2007, <http://www.europarl.europa.eu/hearings/20070326/libe/bignami_en.pdf>.

50 For the comprehensive overview, cf. e.g. Nadezhda Purtova, *Property rights in personal data: a European perspective*, Kluwer Law International, Alphen aan den Rijn 2012, pp. 92 et seq.

51 Case C-362/14, *Maximillian Schrems v. Data Protection Commissioner*, Opinion of Advocate-General Bot (CJEU, 23 September 2015), §95.

52 Commission Implementing Decision (EU) 2016/2295 of 16 December 2016 amending Decisions 2000/518/EC, 2002/2/EC, 2003/490/EC, 2003/821/EC, 2004/411/EC, 2008/393/EC, 2010/146/EU, 2010/625/EU, 2011/61/EU and Implementing Decisions 2012/484/EU, 2013/65/EU on the adequate protection of personal data by certain countries, pursuant to Article 25(6) of Directive 95/46/EC of the European Parliament and of the Council, [2016] OJ L 344/83–91. Cf. esp. Recital 8.

rules set out in a unilateral, regulatory instrument with seven annexes, mostly an exchange of polite letters, printed in the Official Journal of the European Union on 112 pages.) Put simply, 'law depends on it being taken seriously'[53] and this whole EU–US transborder data flows saga cannot be regarded as 'taken seriously'.

Therefore we sympathise with *Schweighofer*'s proposition for a bilateral treaty – in the meaning of public international law – on personal data transfers for 'commercial' purposes. Such a treaty would govern these transfers and would restrict access of US law enforcement authorities to personal data exchanged, providing sufficient legal remedies in case of violation. This would constitute a qualitative change from the Safe Harbour or the Privacy Shield arrangements as this way 'the procedural guarantees can be placed at a much higher level: from administrative law to U.S. federal treaty law and thus gets binding nature'. *Schweighofer* yet recognises the minimal chances of realisation as 'the U.S. government is not willing to change its position to data protection regulation'.

However, such a treaty is not unimaginable. From 2006 the EU and the US have a long track record of bilateral treaties – in the meaning of public international law – on personal data transfers for the 'law enforcement' purposes. These include, for example, multiple iterations of agreements on Passenger Name Records and Terrorist Finance Tracking Programme. In June 2016 both parties signed the so-called Umbrella Agreement on the protection of personal data exchanged in the context of prevention, investigation, detection, and prosecution of criminal offences.[54] It now awaits the consent of the European Parliament in order to be ratified after having been backed by the Parliament's Civil Liberties Committee on 24 November 2016.[55] We are thus of the opinion that nothing precludes that the Privacy Shield 'elevated' to the level of an international treaty complements the Umbrella Agreement. (We refer here only to the form of such an arrangement, refraining from commenting on the actual contents of any such arrangement.)

3.2. TERRITORIAL REACH OF DATA PRIVACY LAW

A second recurring theme we see is the question of *jurisdiction* and *applicable law*. *Bentzen & Svantesson* in their chapter overviewed 'which laws to comply

---

53 Peter Blume, 'Dan Jerker B. Svantesson, Extraterritoriality in Data Privacy Law [Review]' (2014) 4(2) *International Data Privacy Law* 171.

54 Cf. <http://ec.europa.eu/justice/data-protection/files/dp-umbrella-agreement_en.pdf>.

55 European Parliament, 'EU–US deal on law enforcement data transfers backed by Civil Liberties Committee', press release 20161124IPR53009, Strasbourg, 24 November 2016, <http://www.europarl.europa.eu/news/en/news-room/20161124IPR53009/eu-us-deal-on-law-enforcement-data-transfers-backed-by-civil-liberties-committee>.

with and where disputes should be settled' when information arising from deoxyribonucleic acid (DNA) is being handled in transnational computing clouds. Although they discuss a particular type of data handling, their observation about 'jurisdictional complexity' is valid for the entire universe of privacy. Nevertheless, they claim such a complexity, from one perspective, can be regarded as a positive phenomenon. In the times of uncertainty, those who handle personal data will opt for compliance with the strictest standards in line with the popular adage 'better safe than sorry'.

A moderate degree of extraterritoriality of data privacy law is necessary in order to efficiently protect individuals and their interests in the digital, interconnected and globalised world when their data are being handled. In the absence thereof, the system would have gaps, allowing for example 'forum shopping' to the detriment of data privacy protection. We therefore observe that the extreme attachment to territoriality-thinking is counter-productive to the efficiency of such protection in the cross-border setting. Using the location of the server as the jurisdictional focal point has been discredited in most legal fields, but in the context of data privacy law such territoriality-based thinking is still widespread.

As a proof of this point, *Czerniawski* argues in his chapter that the jurisdictional scope in the 2016 General Data Protection Regulation,[56] based on targeting and market access trigger, seems to be more reasonable for the territorial applicability of the EU personal data protection law than the out-dated, pre-Internet 'use of equipment' criterion determining the applicably of the 1995 Data Protection Directive. (His argument does not concentrate on the place of establishment criterion or the redirection to EU law by international law.) As nowadays almost any technological artefact could constitute 'equipment', e.g. a cookie file, this approach results in jurisdictional overreach. In other words, the EU laws currently in force could be invoked even when there is no real connection between those who handle personal data and an individual in the EU or these laws could be invoked when remedies are impossible to enforce. Therefore the new Regulation sets relatively clear limits to its extraterritorial scope, thus adding to legal certainty. Despite *Czerniawski*'s analysis being rather formal, it writes itself into the bigger dilemma of how to ensure legal certainty in the 'length' of the 'arm of the EU data protection law'[57] together with the efficient protection of individuals.

In *Czerniawski*'s conclusion, the territorial scope of the General Data Protection Regulation would require relevant authorities on both sides of the Atlantic not only to monitor the handling of personal data or, should the need be,

---

56 Above n. 15.

57 L. Moerel, 'The Long Arm of EU Data Protection Law: Does the Data Protection Directive Apply to Processing of Personal Data of EU Citizens by Websites Worldwide?' (2011) 1 *International Data Privacy Law* 33.

to co-operate to enforce their data privacy laws. It would also require to, simply, raise awareness: 'although you are a US business, you might fall into the scope of the GDPR!'. The absence of these measures might lead to a situation in which the Regulation would become a 'whim of Europeans': uncharted, unenforceable and thus ignored beyond European borders.

3.3. FREE TRADE AGREEMENTS AND DATA PRIVACY

A third recurring theme is free trade agreements and data privacy. This book analyses this matter from two viewpoints. One of them is the role of *multi-stakeholderism*. The discussions about the regulation of data privacy usually lack the voice of those who 'endure'.[58] The public is often either omitted from deliberations (intentionally or not), either not willing to partake therein. The calls to include public voice in the regulation of data privacy in a meaningful way – or even in the regulation of technology and innovation – are not new *per se*.[59] In this volume, *Meyer & Vetulani-Cęgiel*, building on the fall of the multilateral Anti-Counterfeiting Trade Agreement (ACTA) in 2012 discuss, *inter alia*, the neglected public voice in free trade negotiations. In the case of ACTA, they concluded that the relevant dialogue 'certainly could not be described as open and participatory'. As far as *transparency* is concerned, they have observed some progress with the negotiation process of subsequent agreements, such as the EU–US Transatlantic Trade and Investment Partnership (TTIP) and multilateral Trade in Services Agreement (TiSA), where the European Commission's Directorate General for Trade publishes, on dedicated websites, non-confidential updates on the progress of the negotiations.[60]

As the public voice in free trade negotiations is often neglected, so is the protection of data privacy in free trade agreements. *Greenleaf* has surveyed the existing and proposed bilateral and multilateral free trade agreements to see how they limit the operation of data privacy laws. Attempts to relax the restrictions on cross-border data flows or to prohibit the handling of certain categories of

---

58 In the context of environmental protection, Rachel Carson popularised Jean Rostand's argument that 'the obligation to endure gives us the right to know'. Cf. RACHEL CARSON, *Silent Spring*, Penguin Books, London 1962, p. 30.

59 Cf. e.g. COLIN J. BENNETT, *The Privacy Advocates. Resisting the Spread of Surveillance*, MIT Press, Cambridge MA 2008; DAVID WRIGHT, RAPHAËL GELLERT, SERGE GUTWIRTH and MICHAEL FRIEDEWALD, 'Minimizing Technology Risks with PIAs, Precaution, and Participation' (2011) 30 *IEEE Technology and Society Magazine* 47–54; DARIUSZ KLOZA, 'Public voice in privacy governance: lessons from environmental democracy' in ERICH SCHWEIGHOFER, AHTI SAARENPÄÄ and JANOS BÖSZÖRMENYI (eds.), *KnowRight 2012. Knowledge Rights – Legal, Societal and Related Technological Aspects. 25 Years of Data Protection in Finland*, Österreichische Computer Gesellschaft, Vienna 2013, pp. 80–97.

60 For TTIP, cf. <http://ec.europa.eu/trade/policy/in-focus/ttip>, and for TiSA, cf. <http://ec.europa.eu/trade/policy/in-focus/tisa>.

data solely on local servers ('data localisation') constitute the most prominent examples. He eventually compares such agreements to a pact with the devil in which data privacy is bartered for the promised benefits of the liberalisation of trade. However, as he quotes Spiros Simitis, 'this is not bananas we are talking about':[61] data privacy not only enjoys fundamental rights protection, but also is not ethically neutral and therefore cannot be easily merchandised.

Eventually, *Schaake*, a Member of the European Parliament, gives her nine suggestions for how to shape of free trade negotiations when these intersect with innovation and technology, especially highlighting that such agreements must not result in a reduction of the level of protection of fundamental rights. She further sees an opportunity to 'improve digital rights' or to set 'information and communications technologies (ICT) standards'.

No matter how participatory and transparent the negotiating process of a free trade agreement is and no matter how much these agreements advance or limit data privacy protection, what further scares people with the recently negotiated free trade agreements is their *comprehensiveness*. There are good reasons to be afraid of a potential abuse of – to give a few examples – federated identities, national identity cards, centralised databases, non-anonymous censuses and uniform privacy policies of global technology giants. *Greenleaf* joins the many commentators in viewing any free trade agreement as an easy way to 'smuggle' regulatory solutions otherwise impossible.[62] This threat is elevated to another level with free trade agreements that aim at addressing all trade-related aspects of bilateral or multilateral relations between states.

Comprehensive free trade agreements touch upon matters ranging from international trade, sanitary and phytosanitary measures, customs and trade facilitation, subsidies, investment, trade in services, entry and stay of natural persons for business purposes, mutual recognition of professional qualifications, domestic regulation (licensing, etc.), financial services, international maritime transport services, telecommunications, electronic commerce, competition policy, privileged enterprises, public procurement, intellectual property, regulatory cooperation, to trade and sustainable development, labour and environment. (Data privacy is entangled with some of these matters.) We deliberately reproduced here the entire list of substantive matters of the Comprehensive Economic and Trade Agreement (CETA) – by copying the captions of its relevant chapters – to give the reader a glimpse of the Agreement's complexity.[63] In all the comprehensiveness of

---

[61] As cited in: Lee A. Bygrave, 'International agreements to protect personal data' in James B. Rule and Graham Greenleaf (eds.), *Global Privacy Protection: The First Generation*, Edward Elgar, Cheltenham 2008, p. 15.

[62] Cf. also Czerniawski, Ch. 10, in this volume.

[63] Eventually, the text of the CETA spans 1,528 pages, comprising 30 chapters (230 pages) and an uncountable number of annexes (1,298 pages), full of technical jargon. It took us around four hours just to browse it. Cf. <http://trade.ec.europa.eu/doclib/docs/2014/september/tradoc_152806.pdf>.

such agreements, there is a reasonable fear that data privacy matters can often be interwoven with other matters and can frequently be 'blurred' among them to the detriment of its protection.

3.4. REGULATION OF ENCRYPTION

A fourth recurring theme is the *regulation of encryption*. No chapter in this book treats this matter directly and exhaustively, although a few authors do deal with it in passing. The problem was observed already in the early days of the popular use of the Internet. In particular, *Gerry* recalls the 1995 Helen Roberts' report to the Australian Parliament on the regulation of the Internet, in which the latter has foreseen 'the availability of encryption' as a regulatory challenge.[64] Like with many technologies, the problem lies in the ambivalence of the use of encryption: it could be used both for good and bad purposes.

It is thus not surprising the state has always been interested in having, at its disposal, a possibility to decrypt the contents of a message for national security and similar purposes. Early 'crypto-wars' have oscillated around 'key escrows' (a regulatory requirement for users and/or technology developers to obligatory deposit decryption keys with law enforcement bodies) or – later – import/export controls and the use of 'back doors' (a way of bypassing encryption for these bodies). The demand for keys was for many years a dominant policy of the United States, nowadays abandoned. (*Weber* although recalls a recent development of such nature in China.) The Snowden *affaire* demonstrated that the third solution became a widespread practice for all digital communications that is not publicly available. That is to say, 'back doors' have been frequently used to access any information that has been otherwise protected by a password, regardless if encrypted or not. It was not surprising that the use of encryption proliferated around the world. The terrorist attacks in Paris, France on 13 November 2015 drew public attention to the drawbacks of the use of encryption, as allegedly these attacks had been plotted with the use of encrypted instant messaging software.[65]

At the same time, encryption was heralded as an adequate means of protecting data privacy against abusive practices of both public authorities and businesses. It is therefore not surprising that a market for encrypted services – e-mail, cloud computing or instant messaging software – proliferates. In this book, *Bentzen & Svantesson* suggest 'adequate encryption' could mitigate risk of

---

64 Helen Roberts, 'Can the Internet be regulated?,' Australian Parliament, Research Paper No. 35, 1995, <http://www.aph.gov.au/About_Parliament/Parliamentary_Departments/Parliamentary_Library/pubs/rp/RP9596/96rp35>.

65 Danny Yadron, 'Does Encryption Really Help ISIS? Here's What You Need to Know', *The Wall Street Journal*, 4 December 2015, <http://blogs.wsj.com/digits/2015/12/04/does-encryption-really-help-isis-what-you-need-to-know>.

handling DNA information in a computer cloud. Yet *Wilson* observes correctly 'we simply cannot encrypt everything'; there are instances when our life would not function if all were encrypted.

The regulation of encryption – or, more accurately, the limitation of its use – once again entered the political agenda. All in all, these developments beg a question whether the use of encryption and restrictions thereof conform to the requirements of democracy, rule of law (*Rechtsstaat*) and fundamental rights.

One of the very first attempts to legally safeguard the use of encryption was a 1999 plea of Justice Michael Kirby, the leading author of the 1980 OECD Guidelines on the Protection of Privacy and Transborder Flows of Personal Data, to include 'a right to encrypt personal information effectively' in their revision in the future.[66] (Eventually, their revision, concluded in 2013, contains nothing about encryption.)[67] The General Data Protection Regulation does not take any particular stance on the use of encryption, except for heralding it as a security measure.[68] In July 2016 Buttarelli, European Data Protection Supervisor (EDPS), commenting on the launch of the reform process of the ePrivacy Directive,[69] struck a similar chord: 'The new rules should also clearly allow users to use end-to-end encryption (without "back-doors") to protect their electronic communications. Decryption, reverse engineering or monitoring of communications protected by encryption should be prohibited'.[70] We, however, do not support such a black and white approach. There are situations, although very few, in which encrypted contents must be decrypted.

3.5. REGULATION OF WHISTLE-BLOWING

We mentioned in the Preface that the Snowden *affaire* had two dimensions: (1) the relationship between a layman on the street and the state, and (2) the

66 Michael Kirby, 'Privacy protection, a new beginning: OECD principles 20 years on' (1995) 6(3) *Privacy Law Policy Report* 25–34.

67 Earlier, the OECD issued Guidelines for Cryptography Policy in 1997. They address the need to access encrypted data for public security purposes, suggesting the use of 'third trusted party' to deposit the encryption key.

68 Regulation (EU) 2016/679 of the European Parliament and of the Council of 27 April 2016 on the protection of natural persons with regard to the processing of personal data and on the free movement of such data, and repealing Directive 95/46/EC (General Data Protection Regulation), [2016] OJ L 119/1–88; Art. 32.

69 Directive 2002/58/EC of the European Parliament and of the Council of 12 July 2002 concerning the processing of personal data and the protection of privacy in the electronic communications sector (Directive on privacy and electronic communications), [2002] OJ L 201/37–47 (hereinafter: ePrivacy Directive).

70 EDPS, *Preliminary EDPS Opinion on the review of the ePrivacy Directive (2002/58/EC)*, Opinion No. 5/2016, Brussels, 22 July 2016, <https://secure.edps.europa.eu/EDPSWEB/webdav/site/mySite/shared/Documents/Consultation/Opinions/2016/16-07-22_Opinion_ePrivacy_EN.pdf>.

relationship between the states at the international level. Actually, there is also a third dimension: the relationship between a *whistle-blower and the state*. The point of departure here is the legal qualification of the actions of a whistle-blower. In the US, where the history of whistle-blowers disclosing misconduct of the federal government is rather remarkable (cf. e.g. Daniel Ellsberg disclosing the 'Pentagon Papers' in 1971), whistle-blowers end up being charged under the Espionage Act of 1917,[71] which many commentators judge as denying fair trial.[72] Edward Snowden's situation is no different. On 14 June 2013 – on the sixth day after *The Guardian* and other newspapers made public his revelations – he was criminally charged with espionage. It is therefore no surprise that in 2015 the Council of Europe called on 'the United States of America to allow Mr Edward Snowden to return without fear of criminal prosecution under conditions that would not allow him to raise the public interest defence'.[73]

We see in whistle-blowing – and in other recognised forms of civil disobedience – a commanding tool to exercise public control over state's power and over the abuse thereof. As such, these merit protection by the law and should be both exercised and limited – similarity to the 'right to encrypt' – in accordance with requirements of the rule of law (*Rechtsstaat*), fundamental rights and democracy.

A good deal of the answer to the questions of encryption or whistle-blowing lies in the principle of proportionality as known predominantly from fundamental rights law. This legal principle has many faces, bears a lot of uncertainties and thus has been widely contested. Yet – thus far – it seems to be the tool that allows drawing a 'thin red line' between competing interests, as its *modus operandi* permits to 'ask the right questions'. Born 'in eighteenth and nineteenth-century Prussia as a limit on the nascent growth of the administrative state in the absence of democratically imposed constraints', the principle of proportionality 'has an important role to play in filling this gap in contemporary circumstances' (*Lindsay*). In order both to better protect individuals and to ensure legal, 'commercial' and 'political' certainty, *Lindsay* claims, the principle still needs to be 'appropriately defined and rigorously applied'. He further vests the proportionality test in the courts of law, as – in the time of emergency – these 'are the main candidate for imposing limits on state power', yet bearing in mind the danger of 'judicial over-reach'. We agree, yet we also see the principle of proportionality widely used in the parliaments, where the relevant testing

---

71 Espionage Act of 1917, Public Law 65-24, 18 USC §792.

72 Daniel Ellsberg, 'Snowden would not get a fair trial – and Kerry is wrong', *The Guardian*, 30 May 2014, <https://www.theguardian.com/commentisfree/2014/may/30/daniel-ellsberg-snowden-fair-trial-kerry-espionage-act>.

73 Council of Europe, Parliamentary Assembly, *Improving the protection of whistle-blowers*, Resolution 2060 (2015), Strasbourg, 23 June 2015, <http://assembly.coe.int/nw/xml/XRef/Xref-DocDetails-en.asp?FileID=21931&lang=en>.

is a genuine part of *ex ante* studies and evaluations of any regulatory measure proposed. This way, a good deal of the work of a court of law would be done long before such a measure is even applied.

4. A FEW MODEST SUGGESTIONS AS TO THE FUTURE SHAPE OF TRANS-ATLANTIC DATA PRIVACY RELATIONS

This essay-style chapter has highlighted the most 'hot' issues at the end of 2016 in which the protection of data privacy on both sides of the Atlantic touches upon the notions of democracy, rule of law (*Rechtsstaat*) and fundamental rights. Some of these issues can easily be translated into a few modest suggestions as to the future shape of trans-Atlantic data privacy relations. Therefore, we conclude therewith:

1. The answer to Snowden *affaire* – and more broadly: to global mass surveillance practices – lies in the concept of the rule of law (*Rechtsstaat*) *sensu largo*. It is not sufficient to establish rules on national security, free trade or transborder personal data flows with due respect for formal and procedural requirements. The contents, and the application, of these laws must also conform to the same substantive standards.
2. Regulation of data privacy is a global concern. As Beck puts it, 'no nation can cope with its problems alone', implying that global risks require global responses.[74] Ideas for a worldwide convention on data privacy or for an international organisation overseeing its regulation are not new. Yet they would work smoothly only when substantive laws converge and this would not be a case in the foreseeable future. What is understood as 'privacy' in Europe is different from the understanding in other parts of the world. Even within Europe, perceived by many as having homologous views on 'privacy', its perception is not uniform. (For example, the Scandinavian openness of public life, manifested by public access to individual tax records, is not shared in the rest of the continent. Allowing for such differences is simply respectful for diverse cultural and legal heritages.) Achieving an international consensus beyond the mere need for the protection of privacy (with possible agreement on the most obvious topics) and enacting it into binding legal norms is rather difficult to imagine. It would be not only formally difficult to achieve but also might be detrimental to the diversity of cultural and legal heritages. Thus, we remain sceptical as to the success of

[74] Ulrich Beck, 'The Cosmopolitan Condition: Why Methodological Nationalism Fails' (2007) 24(7–8) *Theory, Culture & Society* 288.

such all-encompassing, global-reaching proposals for a (binding) standard on data privacy regulation.

3. A reminder: regulation of data privacy is a serious matter. To once again quote Simitis: 'this is not bananas we are talking about'.[75] 'Privacy' is both a fundamental right and an ethical concern that requires adequate and efficient protection. It is also a central matter in the information economy and the importance of data privacy as an enabler, and as an obstacle, to economic growth must be part of the calculation. So must be the centrality of data privacy in security practice – be it national or urban. The legal principle of proportionality is to guide the drawing of a 'thin red line' between such competing interests. In parallel, legal certainty warrants smooth operation of both information economy and security practices.
4. It will sound trivial, but new data privacy problems will be emerging every day and new solutions thereto will be proposed at an almost equal pace. What is required is a transparent, multi-stakeholder and critical debate as to linking these problems with appropriate solutions.
5. The public voice should be carefully and meaningfully listened to in the regulation of data privacy, regardless whether data privacy is a direct object of regulation (such as transborder data flows) or indirect (such as governance of free trade). Many legal frameworks in multiple domains require asking the public at large and/or their representatives (e.g. national parliaments, regional councils, non-governmental organisations, etc.) to express their views (e.g. environmental law). We argue for this phenomenon not only to become a standard in governance of technology and innovation – this including data privacy, but also to ensure that their views are actually taken into account.
6. New, comprehensive free trade agreements set up a dangerous, wrong precedent. This is not an opposition to free trade, but rather a plea – from a formal viewpoint – for a 'stepping stone' rather than a 'stumbling block' policy. Further, many commentators discussed the need for more transparency and more public participation – in other words, for more democracy – and we cannot but agree with them. We just add here a plea for 'slow' politics and some 'sectorial' approach. In bilateral and multilateral relations, the reduction of tariffs should be a subject matter of one arrangement, and investment partnership of other arrangement.
7. The EU and US data protection regimes – for 'commercial' purposes – cannot be bridged simply by means of 'adequacy decisions'. Declaring the US regime 'adequate' in the EU will always infringe the EU Charter of Fundamental Rights. Any such move will be judged as political, acting in a particular interest of sustaining the digital market for the price of

[75] Above n. 61.

deterioration of fundamental rights. It will only bring more work for the judges of the CJEU in Luxembourg. We do not have yet any golden means for the EU–US cross-border data flows problem, pointing out only that the means of 'adequacy decisions' should be abandoned in order for a serious, durable solution respecting EU fundamental rights to be put in place. A bilateral treaty in the meaning of public international law could constitute an appropriate means to that end.

8. It has long been recognised that the territoriality focus that characterises our current paradigm is a poor fit with the reality of the online environment. It is also a poor fit with numerous other areas of law with cross-border interaction, such as environmental law. While the territoriality focus – such as focusing on the location of data – has been discredited and abandoned in many legal settings (including areas, such as defamation, closely related to the right of privacy), it appears harder to shake in the data privacy universe. This is partially understandable. Yet we argue that the time has come to reconsider our reliance on territoriality also in the data privacy context. After all, as a filtering mechanism distinguishing between situation in which a state legitimately may claim jurisdiction and situations where a state's jurisdictional claim would lack such legitimacy, the territoriality scores few victories apart from in the most obvious cases.
9. In the case there is an opportunity to reconsider how we approach jurisdiction in the context of data privacy, we must avoid overly broad – and practically unenforceable – jurisdictional claims resulting in a discretionary enforcement. Such an approach might simply undermine the efficiency of protection.
10. Encryption should be protected as an enforceable right. We make this proposition very carefully: a *right* is a very precise concept, at least in European human rights law, whose features make it suitable for the regulation of encryption. A right is rarely absolute and thus it is subjected to some limitation criteria, exhaustive and to be interpreted narrowly. Yet we do not claim here *how* such protection should be afforded or *where* it should be placed in the hierarchy of legal norms. It could be either a new fundamental right or a data subject right within a bundle of her other relevant rights. It could be spelled out by a legal statue (e.g. introduced, in the EU, in the reform of the ePrivacy Directive, as proposed by Buttarelli) or – equally – interpreted by a senior court (as the CJEU did with the right to de-listing).[76] It is then for the technology experts to offer technological solutions, in accordance with the state of the art, for the limitation of the enjoyment of such a right. One thing is yet sure: 'back-doors' and 'key escrows' do not constitute a lawful way to limit the use of encryption. In any

76 Above n. 29.

case, it is a task of central importance and one associated with considerable urgency.

11. A key issue in all this is the tension between the need for transparency on the one hand, and the need for some data collection and use within the national security arena to remain secret. After all, the only way to know that our data is not misused is through complete transparency, and such complete transparency is neither possible nor desirable when it comes to security, equally national or urban. Here we hit a dead end. But perhaps the Snowden *affaire* has brought to the attention a way to cut the Gordian knot. The security agencies' compliance with law is monitored not only by designated bodies but also, at least some of, the very people working in the intelligence community. The key would then seem to be to construct a legal framework that (1) allows us to trust the reports by whistle-blowers, (2) that provides safeguards for whistle-blowers, and (3) that ensures that information revealed by whistle-blowers is used to address violations without jeopardising security and individual lives. To this end, whistle-blowing and other recognised forms of civil disobedience should become a standalone means of protection against the abuse of the requirements of fundamental rights, the rule of law (*Rechtsstaat*) and democracy by global mass surveillance practices.

To use again Saramago, it is true that 'not a day passes' without personal data flowing between both sides of the Atlantic. Data privacy and its protection are therefore entangled in the entirety of political relations between the EU and the US. (This observation is actually valid for political relations between almost any jurisdictions.) Yet the handling and the flows of these data – in Williams' words – remain rather 'unnoticed'. The protection of individuals whose personal data are handled and flown often fall victim to recklessness, indifference or ignorance. Data privacy is a serious matter, it grows and matures rapidly, but nevertheless it is still blurred in the complexity of trans-Atlantic relations. It seems *not* to be the main concern when for example personal data transfers, jurisdictional scope, free trade, encryption or civil disobedience are being regulated. We have therefore made these few modest suggestions for data privacy protection in the trans-Atlantic setting to adhere to requirements of democracy, rule of law (*Rechtsstaat*) and fundamental rights so that data privacy does not share the fate of Icarus. The green cover of this book was chosen to underline this hope.

www.ingramcontent.com/pod-product-compliance
Ingram Content Group UK Ltd.
Pitfield, Milton Keynes, MK11 3LW, UK
UKHW051918100926
8556IPUK00021B/1235

9 781780 684345